Wretched Faces

Famine in Wartime England

1793–1801

Wretched Faces

Famine in Wartime England

1793–1801

Roger Wells

ALAN SUTTON · Gloucester
ST. MARTIN'S PRESS · New York
1988

ALAN SUTTON PUBLISHING
BRUNSWICK ROAD · GLOUCESTER

First published 1988

First published in the United States of America in 1988
All rights reserved. For information write:
    Scholarly and Reference Division,
    St. Martin's Press, Inc.,
    175 Fifth Avenue,
    New York, NY 10010

Library of Congress Cataloging in Publication Data
Wells, Roger A.E.
Wretched faces : famine in wartime England, 1793–1801 / Roger Wells.
p.   cm.   Bibliography: p.
Includes index.
1. Famines — Great Britain — History.
2. Great Britain — Economic conditions
— 1760–1860. I. Title.   HC260.F3W45 1987
363.8'0942—dc19   87–22164
ISBN 0–312–01248–9 : $39.95

First published in Great Britain in 1988 by
    Alan Sutton Publishing
    30 Brunswick Road,
    Gloucester, GL1 1JJ

British Library Cataloguing in Publication Data
Wells, Roger A.E.
Wretched faces.
1. Labor and laboring classes — England
— History — 18th century 2. Famines
— England — History — 18th century
3. England — Social life and customs
— 18th century
I. Title   941.07'3'0880623   HD8389
ISBN 0–86299–333–4

Typesetting and origination by
Alan Sutton Publishing Limited
Printed in Great Britain by
Guernsey Press Company Ltd.
Guernsey, Channel Islands.

For Lily Wells in memory of Len

ACKNOWLEDGEMENTS

Both this book, and its predecessor, *Insurrection; the British Experience 1795–1803*, (Alan Sutton, 1983) derive principally from my D.Phil. thesis, presented to the University of York in 1978. The material published here has been revised, extensively reorganised and augmented, and I have been able, additionally, to draw on a not inconsiderable volume of relevant literature published since 1978.

Many debts were acknowledged in 1983; more have been incurred. However, a fortuitous combination of circumstances, including the passage of time, the long-term failure to invest properly in higher education, serves to sharpen the profile of the achievement of educators in the 1960s. I feel privileged to have studied for a degree in the then newly-created University of York, and I am particularly indebted to the excellence of the history department. That excellence derived directly from the inspiration of the department's first head, Gerald Aylmer, and the commitment of a team of pioneering historians. This view is shared by many graduates, and not simply the handful who went on to become professional historians. I hope that this book, and its predecessor, both reflect something of the superb quality of the courses *and* the tuition at York.

I thank the Controller of HMSO and the Trustees of the British Museum for permission to quote from documents in their possession at the Public Record Office, and the manuscript and newspaper divisions of the British Library, respectively. The Director of Libraries at Sheffield, Earl Fitzwilliam and S.W. Fraser, have given permission for quotation from the Wentworth Woodhouse Muniments and the Spencer Stanhope Collection at Sheffield. I must also thank the staff of these institutions, and all the record repositories and libraries listed in the abbreviations, for the enormous amount of help they cheerfully gave to me, while I spent lengthy visits working in their search and reading rooms.

My colleague, Dr Paddy Maguire read another manuscript on completion and Clive Emsley was equally generous with his time; Malcolm Chase read specific chapters, and together they saved me from mistakes and made invaluable suggestions for improvement. Dr John Chartres and Barrie Stapleton, kindly permitted me to read their contributions to Vol. 5 of the *Cambridge Agrarian History of England and Wales*, and M. Turner (ed), *Malthus and His Time*, (1986), before publication; I regret that my book had gone to press before the editor's essay in the latter was published. Several historians have discussed specific points with me while I composed this book, and in this connection I have benefitted from the comments of Drs Mike Duffy, Douglas Hay, John Rule, John Styles and Professor George

Rudé, and especially Mick Reed, who with his customary generosity also proof read the volume. I must again testify to the magnitude of my debt to my postgraduate supervisor, Professor Gwyn Alfred Williams, and to the value of critical comment received from the thesis' external examiner, Edward Thompson. I have received stirling support from the office staff of the Humanities Department at Brighton Polytechnic, notably Betty Geeves, whose capacity to transform my handwriting into a perfect typescript, reveals palaeographical skills equal to an archivist's. My wife, Hilary, devoted much time and effort to critical evaluation of draft chapters, and saved me from multiple mistakes. She has also sharpened my perceptions of the centrality of the family, which find their echoes here, and Rosie, Zachary and Jasper, have repeatedly proved the point. Errors and mistakes in this work are my own.

ROGER WELLS
Brighton, October 1987

CONTENTS

PART I FAMINE IN WARTIME 1793–1801

1. Introduction: 'to shake the Foundations of the Government of Great Britain'   1
2. The Sociology and Economics of Food: Bread, Cheese, Butter, Meat and Potatoes: the '5 principel Things that poor Pepel want to bye'   13
3. Harvests and Markets in Wartime, 1794–1801: 'called Famine in any other Country than this'   35
4. 'Many an honest man doeth not know how to get one Week or Day over': the Reality of Famine in Wartime   53

PART II FAMINE AND THE PEOPLE

5. 'Extreme Avarice and Rapaciousness': Contemporary Analysis and Popular Prejudices   74
6. 'A more honourable Death than to be starv'd alive': *Taxation Populaire* and the 'Early Phases' of the Famines   90
7. 'Taking Bread out of our Mouths': the Crowd, Food Transportation, and the Midsummer Hypercrisis of 1795   106
8. 'Glorious tho' Awfull Weeks': the Hypercrisis of September 1800   120
9. 'Promoting General Confusion': Popular Political Radicalism and Protest   133
10. Conclusion: Famine, the Defences of the Poor and the Threat to Public Order   161

PART III GOVERNMENT AND FAMINE

11. Intervention versus Free Trade: Securing Imports in Wartime 1794–1801   184
12. Dietary Expedients and Vested Interests: Recommendation versus Compulsion, June 1795 to July 1800   202
13. 'Brown George': Compulsion versus Vested Interests, September 1800 to July 1801   219
14. Public Relations: the State, and Society, and Famine   230

PART IV   SOCIAL CONTROL AND FAMINE

15. Riot Control and the Repressive Agencies: The Role of
    Government   253
16. The Role of the Courts   274
17. 'I Cannot work through this Time of Necessity without
    your Assistance': the Relief of the Working Class   288
18. Paradoxes, Ironies and Contradictions: some Con-
    clusions   315

Notes   340
Appendices   404
Index   458

ABBREVIATIONS

Adm.	Admiralty records, Public Record Office
Ag. His.	*Agricultural History*
Ag.His.Rev.	*Agricultural History Review*
Ass.	Assizes records, Public Record Office
BCRO	Berkshire County Record Office
Beds. CRO.	Bedfordshire County Record Office
BIHR	Borthwick Institute of Historical Research, University of York
BL.Add.Mss.	British Library, Additional Manuscripts
Bod. Lib.	Bodleian Library, University of Oxford
BPP	*British Parliamentary Papers*
BT	Board of Trade records, Public Record Office
BTHR	British Transport Historical Records, British Rail, York
CCRO	Cornwall County Record Office
Chesh. CRO	Cheshire County Record Office
DCRO	Devon County Record Office. FLP. Fortescue Lieutenancy Papers. SP. Sidmouth Papers
Derbys. CRO	Derbyshire County Record Office
DPD	*Debrett's Parliamentary Debates*
Dur. CRO.	Durham County Record Office
Ec.His.Rev.	*Economic History Review*
ECRO.	Essex County Record Office
EHR.	*English Historical Review*
ESCRO	East Sussex County Record Office
Expl.Ec.His.	*Explorations in Economic History*
GCRO	Gloucestershire County Record Office
HCRO	Hampshire County Record Office
HMC	*Historical Manuscript Commission*
HO.	Home Office records, Public Record Office
HPL.	Halifax Public Library
HRO.	Humberside Record Office
HWJ.	*History Workshop Journal*
IESRO.	Ipswich and East Suffolk Record Office
Int.Rev.SH.	*International Review of Social History*
JHC.	*Journal of the House of Commons*
Jnl. Ec. His.	*Journal of Economic History*
Jnl.Int.His.	*Journal of Interdisciplinary History*
Jnl.PS.	*Journal of Peasant Studies*
Lancs. CRO	Lancashire County Record Office

Later Corr.	A. Aspinall (ed), *The Later Correspondence of George III*, 5 vols. (Cambridge 1962–70)
LCA	Leeds City Archives
Lincs. CRO	Lincolnshire County Record Office
LPS	*Local Population Studies*
MAF	Ministry of Agriculture and Fisheries records, Public Record Office
Mid. His.	*Midland History*
Minutes	*Minutes of Evidence taken before the Lords of His Majesty's Most Honourable Privy Council respecting GRAIN and Proceedings thereupon,* (1795)
NCA	Nottingham City Archives
NCRO.	Northumberland County Record Office
NEIMME.	North of England Institute of Mining and Mechanical Engineers, archives department, Newcastle
NNRO.	Norwich and Norfolk Record Office
Notts. CRO	Nottinghamshire County Record Office
NUL.	Nottingham University Library, archives division
NYRO.	North Yorkshire Record Office
OCRO.	Oxfordshire County Record Office
OPL.	Oldham Public Library
PC.	Privy Council records, Public Record Office
PCA.	Plymouth City Archives
PL.	Palatinate of Lancaster records, Public Record Office
P&P	*Past and Present*
PRO.	Private deposits, Public Record Office
RO.	Record Office
SCL.	Sheffield City Library, archives division
	Bag. Coll. Bagshawe Collection
	MD. Montgomery Deposit
	SS. Spencer-Stanhope Collection
	WWM. Wentworth Woodhouse Muniments
SCRO.	Somerset County Record Office
Seventh Report.	*BPP.,* 'Seventh report of the select committee of the House of Commons on the high price of grain' (1801)
SH	*Social History*
SRO.	Scottish Record Office
Staffs. CRO.	Staffordshire County Record Office
T.	Treasury records, Public Record Office
Trans. RHS.	*Transactions of the Royal Historical Society*
TS.	Treasury Solicitor papers, Public Record Office
WCRO.	Warwickshire County Record Office
WO.	War Office records, Public Record Office
Worcs. CRO.	Worcestershire and Herefordshire County Record Office
WSCRO.	West Sussex County Record Office
WYRO.	West Yorkshire Record Office
YCL.	York City Library
YML.	York Minster Library

I

FAMINE IN WARTIME
1793–1801

CHAPTER 1

Introduction

'to shake the Foundations of the Government of Great Britain'

In 1800, inflated food prices reduced the real wages of building workers to their lowest level since 1600, and their third lowest since 1264. More representative and broadly-based real wage calculations covering 1541 to 1871, reveal that during the 1799–1800 agricultural year, they fell to their seventh lowest level, and that during the subsequent season (1800–1) they plummeted further, to their fourth deepest trough. Taking these years together, they represent the second most severe crisis across these three and a half centuries, marginally less devastating than the mid-Tudor crisis of 1555–7. Indeed, although the national picture is complicated by higher earnings in some theatres of industrialisation, living standards for major sectors of the workforce, including the largest, agricultural labourers, and other key groups, notably metropolitan artisans, appear to have experienced a long secular decline from the mid-eighteenth century to 1790. Wages failed to keep pace with an overall slow rise in food prices. Famine-induced traumas in the 1790s thus came on top of the pressures exerted by this long-term phenomenon.[1] That perennial eighteenth-century conflict of interests between producers and consumers of food, threatened to explode into civil war. In October 1800, the Earl of Liverpool, President of the Board of Trade, gravely warned his cabinet colleagues

> that there will be Insurrections of a very serious nature, and that different Bodies of Yeomanry may possibly fight each other . . . . those of the Cities and great manufacturing Towns, who are adverse to the Farmers will fight those of the Country, who will be disposed to defend them.

Current conditions, and responses, threatened to 'shake the Foundations of the Government of Great Britain'.[2]

These were *famine* conditions and responses. That of 1799–1801 was far worse than its slightly shorter, though very recent predecessor of 1794–6.[3] Famine, as we discuss below,[4] is not synonymous with deaths through starvation itself, but enhanced mortality owing to hunger-related disease was common to both famines. The earlier, which endured for eighteen months, and the second which lasted for twenty-two, on any calculation, were characterised by mammoth increases in food prices. They were aggravated variously – nationally, regionally and locally – by interspersed shorter periods in which food stocks, adequate even to price-induced reductions in demand, were unavailable, 'absolute scarcities' in eighteenth-century English parlance. Millions of working-class consumers struggled to exist through these lengthy periods with incomes unequal to even the purchase of a subsistence diet; shorter periods, when no, or little customary foodstuff could be purchased, interposed during these episodes of severe, cumulative pressures. Recourse was had to all types of cereal substitutes, with even nettles commanding market prices. Moreover, recurrent indust-rial recessions, reduced – and at times decimated – demand for labour. Soaring food prices, staggering increases in poor-rates, added to unpre-cedented levels of taxation, struck hard at the middle classes too. These conditions would have been serious for any advanced country at any time, even England with current, vigorous economic expansion through rapid industrialisation. For a country with a powerful government, committed to what many perceived as a *bellum internecinum* against revolutionary France, necessitating unparalleled mobilisation and unprecedented public expend-iture, famine was critical. Nor was that all. England was presided over by an archaic, oligarchic system of aristocratic government, which existed politic-ally independently of at least ninety percent of the male population, in an age of profound ideological challenge to autocratic, unrepresentative gov-ernance. And, that ideological challenge was in the process of evoking, through the democratic movement, a genuinely popular political response, in the form of organised, concerted plebeian agitations – with some bourgeois and even a leaven of aristocratic support – for political reform on democratic principles. In the context of the realities of the political infrastructure, the demand for manhood suffrage had revolutionary im-plications. The conversion of some activists to fifth-columnist plottings in uneven concert with Irish nationalists and the French governments of the nineties, posed a real revolutionary threat. Moreover, if only a small minority would have seriously entertained a revolutionary solution, at least in stable times, the war itself split society at every level; if the most vociferous of the war's opponents found themselves outnumbered, recur-rent crises threatened to galvanise a massive accretion of support for peace. The famines dramatically revealed the fragile equilibrium underpinning national subsistence, and its propensity to collapse. No issue is more powerful than mass hunger; every other facet of life is subordinated to survival. But the quest for survival can take many forms, among them political varieties, which comprised additional options to the people of England in the Age of Revolutions.

British historiography has largely eshewed any detailed examinations of these famines. Historian certainly follows historian in cold statistical representations: 'in the early 1790s wheat hovered about the level of 48s to 58s per quarter. In 1795 it shot up to over 90s (averaging in 1795–6 over 76s) . . . and then in the first year of the new century rose to even greater heights, the average price for 1800 amounting to 113s 10d and for 1801 to

119*s* 6*d*'.[5] Agrarian historians stress the stimulus to rapid investment in agriculture, the resultant impetus to enclose, the intensification of cereal production,[6] and debate whether tenant farmers or their landlords were the principal beneficiaries of inflated wartime food prices.[7] The fact that mass impoverishment, caused by the complete exhaustion of plebeian incomes in purchasing food, also decimated demand for manufactured goods, could seriously, if temporarily, retard the heroic progress of key sectors of the burgeoning industrial revolution, has also been noted.[8] Political historians, including R.R. Palmer, have suggested that material conditions in 1795 'added . . . economic grievances . . . to a general social malaise and a bitter class consciousness as sources of discontent', and E.P. Thompson endorses a nineteenth-century judgement on the same year: '"A new instructor was busy amongst the masses – WANT"'.[9] The *Oxford History* briefly endorses this interpretation, and equally cursorily moulds the key components of the second famine, adverse trade balances, escalating taxes, industrial recession, hunger and rioting, into an explanation of the context of public disillusion with Pitt's apparently unshakeable and unsatisfiable lust for exacting unconditional surrender from France: this required 'someone to rig up a shelter', a bill filled by Addington and his peace negotiations.[10] Piers Mackesy's lacklustre account of the same episode also notes that the urgent need for military reinforcements to police England necessitated withdrawing the army from Portugal, thus exposing the ancient ally to invasion by Spain. The multifarious problems caused by famine on the home front, were perhaps uppermost amongst the devastating array of difficulties which debilitated Pitt, and aggravated fundamental disagreements between ministers and destabilised the cabinet.[11] Asa Briggs is impressed by the effect on 'the poorest and weakest sections of the community', which possessed 'only restricted ways of expressing their discontent with such situations – rioting was the most natural way'.[12] Yet, if the recent spate of fashionable studies of riot has drawn heavily on disturbed episodes during the nineties, their socio-economic context has principally received desultory treatment. Some historians have located various developments firmly in the context of dearth (if not famine); examples include Dr Tann's study of the pronounced move into co-operative corn-milling, Professor Poynter's on the stimulative 'lesson of scarcity' on the burgeoning debate over poverty, and Dr Neuman on the proliferations and contractions of the so-called Speenhamland system.[13] One isolated article on the national situation in 1795–6 ruminates on whether it warrants description 'as a crisis',[14] and though a handful of regional studies has conditioned subsequent textbook treatment of 'crisis upon crisis',[15] a distinguished authority's suggestion that a monographic study of famine was 'badly needed', has gone unanswered for twenty years.[16]

There are some interesting historiographical questions surrounding this omission. Let us commence with the demographers, who exude a naive complacency which appears to originate in a misreading of English agrarian history. Professors Chambers and Mingay, in their agricultural study, correctly state that a combination of 'relatively poor harvests' and 'the unprecedented rise in population, caused demand for agricultural goods to rise faster than the supply' after 1775, thereby necessitating an increasingly crucial importation of grain, meat and dairy produce, despite which 'prices rose to famine heights' in certain war years between 1795 and 1812 following 'harvest failure'.[17] Dr Appleby, in a comparative study of mortality crises in England and France, concluded that England's escape from periodic mass mortality in the later seventeenth and eighteenth centuries, was to be ascribed to 'crop diversification', principally increased barley and oat production. As these spring-sown grains fare differently from autumn-planted wheat (and rye) in the same weather conditions, wheat deficiencies were compensated for by increased yields of alternative cereals; 'the secret in avoiding famine . . . was in balanced agriculture, with wheat and/or rye constituting an important bread grain but with adequate oats and barley to fall back on in times of scarcity'.[18] Appleby's argument has been highjacked by demographers Wrigley and Schofield, and applied to the entire eighteenth century; to England's 'exceptional degree of development in agricultural production', they add 'marketing'. 'What is at issue', declares Schofield,

> is not whether fluctuations in food prices sometimes affected mortality, fertility or nuptuality, for in long and variable series some examples of any relationship are likely to arrive by chance. It is rather a matter of the strength and consistency of the relationship. To address the question by piling up instances, as in so many studies, is clearly a futile exercise; what is required is a rigorous and systematic approach.

Ironically, Schofield himself piles up non-instances to assert confidently that by 'the mid-eighteenth century fluctuations in scarcity and plenty no longer found any echoes in the movement in the death rate'. Moreover, and fundamentally, 'there was a radical break in historical relationships between the food supply and demographic trends at the end of the eighteenth century':

> although population was growing significantly faster than at any earlier period, real wages which had been falling sharply [since c.1731] recovered and began to rise more sharply than ever before. For the first time since the land had been fully settled, swiftly rising numbers proved consonant with rising real wages. An industrial revolution was under way.

This 'rigorous and systematic approach' is in fact an anti-historical sub-sumation of evidence of demographic crises which do not sustain sweeping generalisations about consonance; allegations of 'futile exercises' constitute no more than an ideological device deployed by those dedicated to concepts of the inevitability of progress, a material progress perceived through a *post hoc* identification of inevitability of the over-riding success of industrial and agrarian capitalism. Technically it works; 'only when prices were exceptionally high did mortality rise in the same year; otherwise the upward or downward effect was delayed one or two years'. It all comes out in the wash when 'the population growth rate was measured between each given census date and the census 25 years later'. At worst, we are informed, 'the effect of high prices was primarily to advance by a few years the deaths of the weak, who would in any case have died soon'.[19]

What is really at issue is the failure of later eighteenth-century subsistence crises to engineer a Malthusian positive check with a demographic catastrophe of continental or medieval proportions. In this scheme of things, Malthus himself can be dismissed as an idiosyncratic wart on the intellectual face of England's capitalist progress. 'By an ironic coincidence, Malthus had given pungent expression to an issue that haunted most pre-industrial societies at almost the last time when it could be represented as relevant to the country in which he was born'. Such interpretations confidently enter the litany of historians of industrialisation; 'the Malthusian fear of insufficient food production is one of the most egregious mistakes in the history of economic thought as far as the West is concerned'. Positive checks in the sixteenth and seventeenth centuries can be safely admitted, because nascent Tudor and Stuart capitalism had never been brought to trial before the bar of history in stark contrast to its Georgian successor. We return to Malthus in a moment, but in the *Population History of England* the optimist school has recruited significant support, though the authors prefer covert to overt operations in this *cause célèbre*.[20]

Not so Williamson and Lindert, the optimist authors of several, recent, sophisticated, econometrically-based, contributions to the debate. 'Most of us', they opine, 'care more about people's consumption per lifetime, rather than just per year'. Indeed, even a pessimist, Dr Snell, cautiously dilutes the statistics from famine years by their incorporation in three-year averages, to avoid 'accentuating the appearance of falling wages after about 1790'.[21] Leaving aside those whose lifetime's aggregate consumption was severed through their demise advanced 'by a few years' owing to subsistence crises, the reality of famine conditions on people is reduced to little if these experiences are represented in purely statistical terms, *and then* incorporated into longer-term mathematical calculations. The standard of living controversy is about the experiences of successive generations who actually lived through the classic phase of industrialisation. The fact that millions were affected, from day to day, from week to week, and from month to month, and throughout consecutive years, during two devastating epochs in the 1790s, ought to be of importance for historians. For as Professor Post insisted, with reference to the last great European famine of 1816–7, there is little comparability between weekly incomes and famine food prices, and the means adopted by working people to try to reconcile these major disparities, and survive, require 'systematic exploration'.[22]

The fact that such a reconciliation is 'still awaited' is, of course, one ramification of the greater proposition that the major outlines and features of these famines are simply unknown. The historiographical seriousness of this can be finally illustrated in three different ways. First, a number of investigations into a miscellany of topics, have produced distorted conclusions because key conditioning factors have either been ignored or misunderstood; scholars have been unable to locate their findings within the global context in which developments occurred. Secondly, interpretations of Malthus's population principle have either played down, or largely ignored, the immediate English context in which it was conceived. Finally, the absence of an in-depth study of famine has contributed to a staggering misinterpretation by a distinguished modern historian, Ian Christie, concerned with a key problematic, 'Britain's avoidance of revolution' in the Age of Revolutions.

Examples entering the first category of mistakes and misconceptions include many minor matters, interlaced with others of greater significance for major themes. Dr Stevenson argued that in 1795 the government 'decided to send relief supplies of grain to the coastal districts in an attempt to keep grain in the inland counties'.[23] In fact, the government directed the bulk of its inadequate stocks to London in a desperate bid to preserve order in the capital, selling the residue in the major ports in hopes that free-market mechanisms would distribute it to the most hard-pressed localities. This policy also had the advantage of avoiding the inevitable charges of favouritism (or worse) when government could not meet most of the many urgent requests, powerfully supported by important local grandees. Mr Emsley asserts that the government's tax on hair-powder aimed to conserve the wheat used in its manufacture.[24] In fact, this excise was yet another fiscal device, falling principally on the affluent, and Pitt, secure in the knowledge that only corn unfit for human consumption was used, stoically refused to accept opposition demands for its repeal. Dr McCahill asserts that parliamentary moves to legislate against the feeding of oats to horses were 'undoubtedly frivolous'; in fact, such a statute would have complemented the Act banning the production of white wheaten flour for human consumption.[25] No historian appears to have appreciated that Pitt could not permit statutory sanction to wage increases – as advocated by the Foxites – or the schemes introduced to make poor relief, with allowances in-aid-of wages, equal to the purchase of recipients' normal wheat consumption; these would fatally compromise the prime minister's identification of vital economies to be achieved by reducing wheat consumption, through increasing the use of alternative foods. This policy turned on wheat-price inflation outstripping wages and wage plus relief levels. Poor-law historians are oblivious to several aspects of government policy, which in fact account for changes in local practices, rather than the indigenous, autonomous, local factors claimed, though admittedly few even of the numerous misinterpreters of the origin of Speenhamland are sufficiently crass to conceive it as 'a necessary rescue of the obsolescent sector of the work force'.[26] Recent investigations into popular loyalism in the nineties provide a welcome counterbalance to concentrations on radicalism. A study of anti-French, anti-democratic populist propaganda, contrasts images of English fare – roast beef and plum pudding – with French consumption of 'frogs and soup meagre'. If England was swamped with material explaining that 'the French have been forced to make a paste of bran and cabbage leaves', it may have galvanised some plebeian jingoism in the heady days of war declarations in 1792–3; such tales looked distinctly suspect after the dire experiences of 1794–6, when John Bull's diet was savagely reduced by a combination of market prices and Pitt's retrenchment campaigns. Their repetition in 1799–1801 generated a massive crisis of confidence in Pitt among all classes, which makes nonsense of the claim that 'the whole decade witnessed a surge of popular loyalism, unmatched in the whole of the eighteenth century'.[27] E.P. Thompson seizes on just one element of government policy, the Home Secretary's increasingly strident demand that local authorities used all necessary force to preserve the free market for food against mass mobilisations to regulate it. Thompson uses it to support his notion of an ideologically-motivated state, bent on the final destruction of all statutory embodiment of paternalism. This looks decidedly unlikely, for that same government introduced legislation to alter diet, more to facilitate co-operative flour-milling specifically to challenge the powerful metropolitan cereal-manufacturing trade, and committed hard-pressed financial resources to subsidise corn-importers, to give but three examples.[28]

A modern demographer, Dr Martin, evinces surprise because 'as late as 1796 it could be claimed in parliament that "By the pressure of the times . . . marriage was discouraged, and among the labouring class . . . the birth of a child . . . was considered as a curse"'.[29] This was not pure Foxite rhetoric in support of a minimum wage Act, but a literal truth derived from reality, and it, like Malthus's appearance on the historical stage, can be understood only in its precise historical setting. Most scholars attribute the first edition of the *Essay* to Malthus's entry, behind the conservative cause, in the contemporary philosophical and political debate, unleashed by the French Revolution. The text of the *Essay*, with its repeated and specific attacks on Godwin and Condorcet, certainly supports this argument, though we knew too little about Malthus himself between 1795 and 1798. Barry Stapleton has established that Malthus was a curate, resident in central rural Surrey, responsible for parish register entries, and a contributor to escalating poor rates.[30] The first edition adamantly declared that the poor law

notwithstanding, . . . the state of the lower classes . . . both in the towns and in the country, the distresses which they suffer from the want of proper and sufficient food, from hard labour and unwholesome habitations, must operate as a check to incipient population. . . . Where a country is so populous to the means of subsistence, that the average produce of it is but barely sufficient to support the lives of the inhabitants, any deficiency from the badness of the seasons must be fatal.[31]

Malthus parted company with his key predecessor, Robert Wallace, by rejecting Wallace's notion that the positive check would not be experienced in England until some indeterminate moment in the distant future, with his own perception that it was imminent, and probably already operative.[32]

In 1800, Malthus conceded that many readers of his original offering 'considered . . . it a spurious argument inapplicable to the present state of society'. Now, as a participant in the fierce debate on the causes of current high food prices, he triumphantly declared in a new pamphlet that the 'severe pressure of distress in every deficiency in our crops . . . [is] a very strong exemplification of a principle . . . in the Essay . . . on Population'. And, he continued,

Two years reflection have convinced me of the truth of the principle . . .
and of its being the real cause of the continued depression and poverty of
the lower class of society, of the total inadequacy of all the present
establishments in their favour to relieve them, and of the periodical
returns of such seasons of distress as we have of late experienced.[33]

Although he promised a new edition of the *Essay*, he privately confided that
'the circulation of this pamphlet and the prevailing conversation about the
population of this country', at the moment the legislation permitting the
first census was being debated in parliament,

has caused enquiries to be made about the Essay which is now nowhere to
be bought. This, I hope, will animate me to proceed to another edition,
though, to say truth, I feel at present very idle about it.

Fortified by extensive reading,[34] and his observations on a recent Scandana-
vian tour, and secure in the knowledge that an enlarged, more empirically-
based edition, would command a huge audience in these unique circumstances, Malthus conquered his inertia to publish the 1803 edition with its
masses of detailed evidence.[35]

In stark contrast to the absence of any detailed reference to the 1794–6
food crises in the 1798 edition, its 1803 successor repeatedly referred to the
'scarcities . . . of 1800 and 1801'.[36] This reflected the greater severity of the
second famine, and the confirmation that its predecessor was not a freak.
Moreover, in 1803, Malthus insisted upon 'the change witnessed in the
mortality of late years', which contrasted with the previous absence of
'extraordinary mortality' in English history since 1700. The 1799–1801
famine had activated the positive check.[37] This key element, *and* the origin
of contemporary appetite for such a work, are commonly overlooked.[38]

The rest is well-known. Explanations of Malthus's enduring fame vary.
His 'dogged defence', his 'effective and tough-minded empiricism' in
contrast to the 'woolly-headed Utopianism' of his original targets, and the
fuel injected by his identification of the social security system as a major
cause of poverty, are all advanced. So too is his notion of 'moral restraint',
whether as philosophical and theological dynamite, or an optimistic revi-
sion of the first *Essay* commensurate with concepts of progress.[39] However,
some passages in the second edition tended to refute the relevance of the
principle to England. One exemplar is singled out by Dr Eversley who
expresses wonderment at 'how Malthus could have been such a spectre to
his generation'?

England possesses very great natural and political advantages, in which
the countries that we should in this case compare with her, would be
found to be palpably deficient. The nature of her soil and climate is such,
that those almost universal failures in the crops of grain, which are
known in some countries never occur in England. Her insular situation
and extended commerce are peculiarly favourable for importation. Her
numerous manufactures employ nearly all the hands that are not engaged
in agriculture, and afford the means of a regular distribution of the annual

produce of the land and labour to the whole of her inhabitants.

Of the four deficient harvests which caused these famines, only that of 1795 conformed to Malthus's analysis, and facilitated a partial compensation for a wheat deficiency by barley and oats. The harvests of especially 1799, and to a lesser extent 1800, confuted his optimistic rider. Malthus may have somehow juxtaposed the 1795 experience with the almost unprecedented fecundity of the 1801 harvest, to conclude that English agriculture was capable of rapidly increasing its productive capacity. Experience certainly proved that Britain could secure massive importations even in wartime, and the marked industrial recovery which accompanied the peace of 1801–3 may have been an additional source of this optimism. Conversely, it is difficult to reconcile Malthus's gloomy identification of demographic disturbance with such statements, and they may be no more than an example of his notorious penchant for own goals. We can say with certainty, that the experience of famines generated public awareness of the fragility of national subsistence, which, in turn, provided a fertile socio-political environment for the birth of Malthus's pregnant principle.[40]

Professor Christie's wide-ranging study of the many factors comprising the 'disordered cohesion' which preserved Britain from revolution in the 1790s, nevertheless elevates socio-economic elements to first-rate status. Though he does not directly confront any of the central arguments of protagonists on either side of the standard of living debate, Christie emerges as a fantastic optimist on economic matters. He emphasises that the British nobility was not a 'distinct social caste', and endorses the importance attached by Harold Perkin to upward – and downward – social mobility, which militated powerfully against revolutionary portents; so too did the omnipresent webs of interdependencies between different ranks. A 'buoyant economy created economic opportunities': 'between 1750 and 1800 more people were faring better than before, and the general outlook was of optimism and of reasonable hope for material gain'. If Christie wisely refrains from alleging that economic growth created viable openings for all, he does insist that successful entrepreneurship underpinned a marked expansion of the middle classes, and that the prosperity was shared by a considerable proportion of working people who were able to command far more consumables than consistent with a mere subsistence level of existence. If six out of seven families lived on incomes below those providing 'modest affluence' in 1760, only three out of four did so by about 1800. Great stress is placed on high earnings by skilled men, and in industry, and even more on female and child labour boosting familial incomes. Christie's account largely ignores the devastations of the famines. If he recognises that population growth put increasing pressure on national subsistence after 1760, he also claims that the agrarian sector just about 'kept up with the country's growing requirements'. Occasionally 'slight shortages' were experienced, ephemerally, and locally: 'There never was any crisis of subsistence'. Christie's case turns on an ahistorical juxtaposition of transparently selected evidence from across the entire 1750 to 1810 period. His argument, that 'economic conditions . . . provide a cogent explanation of why, despite occasional fears and alarms, there was no danger of revolution in Britain in the 1790s', is refuted in the following pages. We aim to prove that late eighteenth-century England was a thoroughly appropriate country for the conception of the Malthusian nightmare, despite its internal, detailed contradictions.[41]

The reality of England's predicament lay in the fundamental change in the structure of the country's food supply, as demand for cereals, *the* source of primary subsistence, outstripped indigenous productive capacity. The yield of home harvests from year to year became increasingly vital, while England turned into a net importer of grain in the later eighteenth century. The delicacy of the mechanism governing the ratio between the two sources of supply derived in part from the Corn Laws; these constituted a deliberate exercise in brinkmanship, designed not to preserve a modicum of the national stock as a reserve against a deficient harvest, but to protect the landed interest from low prices. The only statutory changes made in the late eighteenth century comprised minor modifications to the price mechanism, whereby imports were effectively banned while prices remained moderate; this accommodated the upward secular price trend after 1760 in the interests of landlords and farmers. Adjustments to incorporate inflation reduced competition from overseas supplies in home markets. Although the precise figures for bounty payments on exported grain in periods of low prices were also revised upwards, the system was retained,[42] despite the famous economist Sir James Stuart's fears that exports did 'not prove that [all] the inhabitants are full fed', only that a proportion 'can buy no more at the exportation price'.[43] Such reservations notwithstanding, the statistics generated by these arrangements were ambiguous. Nobody could know that 1792 would be the last year witnessing significant exports, but the import figures since 1760 revealed an aggregate, though oscillating deficiency, in home production from year to year. The war, with its inevitable dislocation to shipping, meant that securing the greatly augmented importation necessitated by substandard harvests, *was not an automatic sequel.*[44] From 1793, the ratio of corn stocks to consumption was very low; relatively small surpluses were available, even in the best years, to 'carry over' into the next season. Prices therefore fluctuated in order to equate the supply from each year's harvest, to each season's consumption.[45] The realities of this situation, immeasurably aggravated by the new problems with overseas trade, were experienced for the first time following the deficient harvest of 1794. The country was plunged into a predicament for which it was totally unprepared, either socially, economically, or politically. The eighteenth century state was inadequately equipped to deal with the problems, despite the fact – in Charles Tilley's words – that 'for ordinary people, food, taxes and enclosed fields were the stuff of politics'.[46] Governments eschewed monitoring indigenous cereal production and global grain market conditions; ministers – from 1793 presiding over war on an unprecedented scale – had no solid statistical information even on such basics as population, land use, and agrarian productive capacity – actual or potential. The state's congenital aversion to gathering such intelligence was reflected in the absence of appropriate mechanisms and bureaucracies. Nobody could realistically predict the impact of famine, or the results of measures to combat it, on the economy; hence, for example, the great fears over the huge export of specie in return for foreign grain. These massive problems were critically exacerbated by social factors, notably public ignorance about the fragility of the grain supply, and a robust unwillingness extending to refusals to accept either the reality or the immediate impact of substandard harvests. This – and much more – comprised the situation, and neither it, nor some of the phenomena generated, can be dismissed by attributions to the 'unique circumstances between 1790 and 1815 when . . . wars disrupted the world economy' to spawn contemporary alarm which failed to 'take full account of the open-ness of the British economy'.[47] Only a banal application of retrospection permits such ahistorical complacency, for millions lived through these wartime years of recurrent crises: an entire generation born after 1780 knew nothing else.

*　　*　　*

Therefore, a detailed study of the famines must extend beyond the question of non-revolution which has mesmerised many historians since Halévy. Famine must be examined in the context of the complex economy and society of England. First, the whole subject of the food eaten by the majority of English people, ordinary working consumers, requires exploration in relation to wages, expectations and aspirations – the sociology of food. The nature of harvest deficiencies must then be related to their impact on markets, supplies and consumers. This requires an analysis of the structure of the grain and other food supply systems, market mechanisms, and the relationship of consumers to markets and their commercial operators. This should establish the context to assess the impact of famine on the people. It will also permit the demarcation of the most vulnerable regions, for we cannot assume that the impact on a country of such regional diversities was uniform. Can any relationship be established between the theatres of rapid industrialisation and the incidence of greatest economic dislocation? To what extent did famine exacerbate the social stresses attendant on industrialisation? The remainder of this study will be based on this initial analysis of the impact of famine.

Social reactions are of fundamental significance. They require examination in the context of eighteenth-century expectations and prejudices surrounding living standards, and indeed broader perceptions of the economics of life. They must be studied in the light of traditional reactions to serious deprivation, and a number of questions posed. Protest is central, but did it conform to orthodox forms? Were there changes, and are these to be related to economic transitions or political ideologies, or both? How significant was the new, populist, plebeian, democratic presence? Finally, we must confront one major question, namely, the nature of the threat to order posed by reaction and protest.

In several senses the government's emergency policies to contain famine comprised a counter-reaction to the initial responses of the people. Pitt's ultimate task was to preserve public order and the existing political structure; otherwise, the conservative ideological crusade in the form of war against revolutionary France would have collapsed. The government's policies breached numerous popular prejudices and common aspirations.

Pitt's omega, as we shall show, hinged on the government's relationship with society; the outcome turned on its ability to communicate with people at every level of society. Its eventual failure in its concerted public relations exercises to convince the entire populace that deprivation and the multitudinous additional problems caused by famine were beyond government control, happened during the second famine, in the autumn of 1800. It precipitated a crisis of confidence in Pitt which proved the essential ingredient in his ministry's collapse. It was in these contexts that the organised revolutionaries, the United Britons, the United Scotsmen, and the United Irishmen, launched their insurrectionary confederacy in league with the French in 1796–7, and renewed them with some vigour in 1800–1. I have examined this history in detail elsewhere,[48] but some of the reasons for their failure to command a mass following lay in the performance of Christie's 'disordered cohesion' during the famine years when the potential for a revolutionary tidal wave caused by 'WANT' peaked. Put simply, the ultimate question must be how did a society and its archaic structure of government, threatened politically from without and within, wrenched by the vicissitudes of rapid socio-economic change, experience two lengthy periods of famine, and actually survive intact? The answer lies in a broader analysis than one conditioned solely by the question of the avoidance of revolution. The socio-political mechanisms which we seek to explore, necessitate a penetration to the core of the complex structure of government and society. We must include the state's repressive weaponry, its police, its amateur and professional armies, and its judicial system. The performance of the main agents of public relief, the poor law, charity and paternalism, must also be examined. These objectives ought to reveal many aspects of the very workings of society during a key phase of war, and of economic transformation. And, these essential short-term features need to be related to longer-term considerations, including the standard of living during the industrial and agrarian revolutions, and the development of class consciousness.

CHAPTER 2

The Sociology and Economics of Food
Bread, Cheese, Butter, Meat and Potatoes: the
'5 principel Things that poor Pepel want to bye'

I caught a remarkably large Spider in my Wash Place . . . & put him in a small glass Decanter & fed him some bread and intend keeping him.

A superb exemplar of the eighteenth-century's universal acceptance of bread as *the* staff of life, lies in this casual revelation of arachnidial ignorance of a Fellow of Oxford University.[1] Contemporary working-class budgets[2] demonstrate that cereal-based foods comprised the greatest proportion of plebeian dietaries in wheaten or barley-bread areas, or regions where 'hasty pudding' was prepared by pouring boiling water or milk on oatmeal. In the 1790s the predominant cereal consumed varied regionally, and in some a complex variety prevailed. Very generally, wheaten bread triumphed in the South and the East. Barley was important in western counties from Cornwall to Cheshire, and a mixed barley and wheaten bread was eaten by poorer consumers in counties like Devon, Dorset and Worcestershire, roughly on the borders between wheat and barley regions. Oat consumption, with the exception of certain Midland counties, was principally northern. Rye consumption had largely retreated, and remained central only in North-eastern mining areas. The conventional wisdom of a 'wheaten revolution' by 1800 is overdrawn,[3] and Dr Collins is correct in his insistence that a substantial proportion of the English population subsisted principally on non-wheaten cereals.[4]

However, the eighteenth century did witness a growing preference for wheaten bread among all classes, which necessitates qualification of this crude 'geography of taste'. The encroachments of wheat turned on three major factors. First, improved agricultural methods increased wheat production. Secondly, whatever the parallel increase in barley production, it failed to rise commensurately with population growth, and the escalating demands of the brewing industry fuelled a disproportionate rise in prices relative to wheat. Barley-bread became a less economical proposition for the consumer. Thirdly, wheaten bread, especially the finest, was more palatable than any other variety, especially when eaten hot from the oven.

In plebeian circles, wheat consumption conferred considerable social status. The Londoner's demand for fine white bread was proverbial, despite notorious adulteration, which prompted contemporary satire and rage.[5] Notoriety failed to deter working-class metropolitans; the 'finer Bread' was 'used in the poorer Parts . . . such as Spitalfields' to the exclusion of all others. This distinguished the plebeian Londoner from his country cousins elsewhere in the South, who also ate whole-wheaten breads, but of an inferior variety made from coarser flour. These varieties still conferred status which was fiercely defended. Labourers in the Home Counties resisted mixed breads; they 'rejected the eating . . . not so much because they thought it unwholesome, or did not like it, but because it was not universal. That Idea offended'. Metropolitan tastes were equally entrenched. In 1773, during a relatively minor subsistence crisis, legislation was enacted enabling magistrates to prohibit sales of fine wheaten bread, for renewable periods of three months. The Act established a median quality, bread made from coarse wholewheat flour with the bran only removed, known as Standard Wheaten Bread. The Act's architect aimed to reduce subsistence costs for 'the poor and middling people'; once they appreciated the economy, it was anticipated that Standard Wheaten would become the norm. Hence the Act was framed 'for all events not of a very extraordinary Nature'. However, metropolitan resistence determined parliament against extending the Act to London, and also against further proposals to ban the milling of fine flour. Although the statute was used fitfully thereafter, it testified to the distinction between London, and non-metropolitan southern diet. It is invariably overlooked by historians, but proved of critical importance during the famines.[6]

Elsewhere the encroachments of wheat were in progress in the later eighteenth century, and were closely 'correlated . . . with urbanization'. At Ashton-under-Lyne, once on the 'border' between barley-eating Cheshire and oat-consuming Lancashire, it was said in 1800 that 'Barley and Oat Bread is not in that Estimation that it was some years past among the lower Class'. Commentators in Cheshire, Northamptonshire and Leicestershire, all reported that wheat had taken over in the towns, while barley preserved its dominance among rural workers.[7] Parallel phenomena were present in other locations. Better-paid plebeians at Ripon bought wheaten-bread at the bakers, while their poorer neighbours continued to eat the oaten-mess, as did their equals at Preston, where only forty percent of workers commanded incomes adequate to the fashionable, but more expensive, mixed barley and wheat loaf. Wheaten bread was clearly perceived as a dietary advance. One of Smollett's characters, 'so polemical, that every time he opened his mouth out flew a paradox', said – in the same breath – that 'poverty was a blessing to a nation' and 'oatmeal was preferable to wheat bread'. Plebeian use of wheat proved a further irritant for those upper-class personnel obsessed by proletarian imitation of the consumer patterns of the rich. Only a handful of localities, among them Wharfedale, appear to have remained immune from at least a start of the wheaten revolution; only one report from hundreds analagous to diet thrown up by the famines claimed that workers 'would be very unwilling to live upon Wheaten Bread'. White bread, like printed cotton-clothes, enabled the poor to challenge the wealthy's consumerist monopoly; the sociology of bread is crucial in its own right, and proved a key conditioning factor during the famines.[8]

Dietary economics complicated sociological factors and had a critical effect on plebeian expenditure patterns. In general, the poorer the family, the greater the dependency on bread or cereal. An agricultural labourer with five children in Berkshire, typically spent over two-thirds of his income on flour alone; minute sums were expended on tea, sugar, and a weekly half pound of butter. Only a free supply of potatoes and greens facilitated additional meals from a pound of bacon 'boiled two or three times' weekly. Farmworkers with fewer children bought more bacon and even cheese, but from his 1787 computations the Rev. Davies insisted that agrarian workers in the South and East could 'scarcely with their utmost exertions supply his family with daily bread' alone. Budgeting was so tight, that they 'reckon cheese the dearest article they can use'. Commensurately, between a half and three-quarters of family incomes went on wheaten bread. The economics were simple:

> the same money, that will only purchase one pound of raw meat with its proportion of bone, will purchase about three pounds of wheaten bread. But this quantity of bread will go at least as far as one pound of meat.

Wheaten bread 'could be eaten without . . . butter and cheese', was 'nearer to being a complete food' for those on rock-bottom wages with no alternative in areas 'where every body eats it'. If the original adoption of wheat belongs to the era of lower prices and higher living standards earlier in the eighteenth century, wheat retained its socio-economic supremacy at the end.[9]

The dietary effects of this dependency on wheat are revealed by comparing southern with Cornish agricultural labourers. The latter's greater meat consumption was partly facilitated by its relative cheapness in regions beyond the influence of metropolitan markets, and the considerable consumption of potatoes reflected a local agricultural specialism. But culinary factors reinforced economic ones; 'potatoes require either meat or milk . . . you cannot make hearty meals with them with salt and water only'. Barley remained the Cornish staple, but this more varied diet rarely required the expenditure of more than half of family income on cereals.[10] Parallels can be drawn with diets in oat-regions. A Cumberland farmworker with three children spent thirty-five percent of his income on oats; butter and milk took a further seventeen percent, and potatoes five. Again more meat was consumed. Cheese too achieved a dietary importance in areas like Derbyshire, where it was a significant local product. Many observers favourably contrasted Northern, Midland, and Western diets, with the monotonous wheaten-bread variety entrenched in the South and East. The latter 'In point of expense . . . exceeds, as, in point of nutrition, it falls short of the . . . fare of milk, potatoes, barley bread and hasty pudding'. Modern commentators endorse such views; 'the regional differences in food expenditure were accompanied by a difference of calorific intake', with daily, average, adult intakes ranging from '2823 in the North', to '2109 in the South'. Two major factors emerge. Where poorer quality cereals were consumed – the barley and oat regions – other articles, butter and cheese with barley-bread, and milk with oatmeal, were critical, together with meat and potatoes, because these grains could not provide the complete diet as with wheat. By the 1790s dependency on wheat was greatest among the poorest where wheat was paramount.[11]

There can be no doubt that the agrarian proletariat comprised the most depressed sector of the English workforce by 1790, and their condition deteriorated further during the decade. As early as 1792 a clergyman related the 'pale Famished Faces, the tattered Garments, and the shivering Nakedness of Thousands' in rural Essex, a class whom he believed to constitute the explosive English equivalent of the 'Wretched . . . French Peasantry'. Tradition has it that northern agricultural labourers were, through the effect of higher wages in adjacent industrial centres, better off than their southern counterparts. Similar contemporary claims were made about farmworkers in other part-industrial regions, for example Cornwall.[12] However, this can be exaggerated. Excellent evidence from the mixed industrial and agricultural township of Newbold, near Chesterfield, reveals that farmhands living alongside miners and steelworkers, earned between seven and eight shillings weekly in 1795, roughly equal to their Berkshire counterparts.[13] West Riding landworkers were also in receipt of similar wages. The difference between farmworkers living in industrial regions and those well-removed from urban and industrial theatres, turned on the latter's exposure to the vicissitudes of under- and unemployment. Demand for industrial labour increased the job security for agrarian workers nearby, rather than pushing up wage-rates significantly, though piece rates for agricultural tasks were slightly higher in the North. Pastoral farming outside the nation's premier cornlands helped to preserve the living-in system whereby young landworkers boarded with the farmers; animal management also needed permanently-employed hands, and militated against the seasonal unemployment, increasingly prevalent in arable regions. Nevertheless, there was a rough comparability across the country between regularly-employed farmworkers, not living-in, and nationally they comprised the lowest-paid major sector of the working class. In the winter of 1794–5, when food prices began to soar, these men earned between six and nine shillings a week.[14]

Most regularly-employed workers commanded better wages. Early in 1795, rural craftsmen in the West Riding's eastern agricultural belt, including masons, bricklayers, wheelwrights and carpenters, earned between 1.33 and two shillings per day, up to fifty percent more than their labouring neighbours. Masses of incidental evidences, especially in poor-law records, reveal identical wage rates paid throughout agrarian England. Urban and industrial wages were much more complex. Labourers' incomes at Hull were typically 'so various that it is difficult to enumerate them'. In Leeds, day-labourers earned between nine and twelve shillings, journeymen-weavers between fifteen and sixteen shillings, and self-employed carpenters and masons, eighteen shillings per week. None of the skilled men employed at Nowill's Sheffield spring-knife works earned more than fifteen shillings weekly, and only a tiny elite of skilled men commanded weekly wages in excess of eighteen shillings at the start of 1795. John Atkinson, a tilter at Kirkstall Forge near Leeds earned an average weekly wage of thirty-three shillings during the first half of that year; his colleague, pattern-ring maker Mathew Cook earned twenty-three shillings. Skilled metropolitan artisans were also an important part of this elite; bricklayers and carpenters earned twenty-one shillings per week in 1795, but brick-layers' labourers commanded only fourteen. The disparity between skilled and unskilled urban and industrial workers is also revealed by the weekly 8.25 shillings earned by general labourer George Hay at Kirkstall, and the acidic retort of the notorious governor Aris of London's Cold Bath Fields jail, that 'many people would be glad to be in prison if they could get 13/4 a week for it' – the sum eventually paid to the families of the state's political prisoners.[15]

If this admittedly impressionistic picture is fairly reliable, it is compli-cated by all those statistical problematics bedevilling standard of living calculations. A detailed rehearsal is unnecessary, but it must be remembered that we know little about actual earnings as opposed to wage rates. For the majority we know little, if anything, about the precise effects of overtime payments on the one hand, or the impact of under- and unemployment on the other. We do know that going rates were adjusted for individuals to compensate for ability, industriousness and capacity – the latter commonly conditioned by the worker's age – 'just as their employers think them deserving of'.[16] Subsidiary incomes further complicate the picture; we know that many men, but not how many, earned supplementary cash through undertaking odd jobs, notably in the tertiary sector.[17] Recent historians have emphasised the key importance of family earnings; working women and children added, sometimes substantially, to family incomes. At one end of the spectrum sixteen year old 'boys' earned twelve to fourteen shillings weekly as stokers at Boulton and Watt's Soho establishment, and daily shillings were paid to adolescent sons accompanying their skilled fathers to work at Kirkstall Forge. At the other, a daily threepence was paid to children at work in the Suffolk countryside, and when James Smith's son accompanied him to work on the Cusworth estate in the West Riding, father's derisory six shilling wage was augmented to eight. Demand for female labour was certainly enhanced by industrialism, and not simply in factories. The 'constant business' of proletarian ladies at Wirkworth in the Peak was the 'washing of . . . Lead Ore from the Sand and earth'. Women broke stones in the Vale of Pickering lime-burning industry. Rates of pay in both industry and agriculture varied enormously; women commanded a daily eight pence working on West Yorkshire landed estates, but a knowledgeable observer thought that their Suffolk counterparts could rarely earn more than thirty shillings annually. A clergyman domiciled near York believed that only 'an idle family' did not supplement the head's income by a weekly three shillings throughout 'the whole year'. His own accounts show daily payments of five and sixpence to his casually-employed domestics, and sevenpence to ladies engaged in 'moling for one day'.[18]

Some families, almost those exclusively in urban or industrial locations able to benefit from the increasing moneterisation of women's and chil-dren's labour, commanded incomes on a par with skilled men at Kirkstall Forge. While Atkinson was earning two pounds at Kirkstall (in 1800–1), families of six and seven who all worked in the same Derbyshire mills, collectively earned between 26.7 and 39.7 shillings. Although Dr McKendrick has rightly emphasised such origins of demand for labour within the late eighteenth-century economy, and provided examples of affluent working-class families in London and the Potteries, a feature which would no doubt be reflected by research on other locations, such incomes were 'clearly not typical'. In the majority of proletarian families, the earnings of wives and children were crucial to 'making up the deficit between father's earnings and the cost of subsistence'. As Dr Benson observes, 'few families were dependent simply upon a single, regular, weekly wage', and multitudinous forms of 'penny capitalism' – washing clothes, retailing, odd-jobbing – by wives and children were principally 'defensive . . . one of the strategies adopted by working people to meet immediate financial needs'. High working-class family earnings were rare throughout the agrarian sector, even in the North. Farmer Metcalfe, scouring North Riding hiring fairs in November 1796 for annually contracted workers, recorded intense competition between employers and that 'servants' were 'very dear . . . higher in price than heretofore'. There is no evidence that this shortage was absolute, and it probably reflected farmworkers' discovery that short-term employment on piece-rates was at once more remunerative, and also facilitated an escape from the customary, but oppressive living-in system, which was being eagerly seized by some youngsters. Such distortions did not have a major inflationary impact on wages; on a Cusworth farm, the entire Parkin family, father, mother and two children were earning 13.3 shillings weekly in December 1799, a sum barely equal to the cost of an oaten subsistence diet.[19]

The American historian Gilboy long ago recorded wage increases in the 1790s, and expressed surprise that prices failed to push incomes up 'even more'; her data revealed that northern workers obtained better increases, but other evidence suggests that these were paid in response to post-December 1794 inflation. By late 1799 Atkinson at Kirkstall was earning seven to eight shillings more weekly than in 1795, but colleague Cook won only a ten percent rise. Their labouring workmate Hay augmented his pitiful 8.25 shillings by fifty percent, but this represented transfer to the more arduous task of stoking, and overtime, namely 'looking after the ovens' on Sundays. Wages at Nowill's manufactory also increased, but so too did worker indebtedness to the employer; the two are difficult to disengage, but the evidence suggests that skilled workers here, like their Kirkstall counterparts, were unable to maintain living standards throughout the 1796–9 period. The same feature is encountered in London; bricklayers achieved a rise of fourpence per day, marginally under ten percent, but ironically their hod-carriers with a sixpenny augmentation, won nearly thirty percent. The hod-carriers' experience was not, it seems, representative of the less-skilled and unskilled. Bath roadworkers' living standards fell markedly in the nineties. Wages for rural workers fell even in the most favourable regions like West Yorkshire. Farmworkers soon lost the minor wage improvements obtained in 1795–6, as suggested by threshing piece-rates of 1.7 shillings (January 1795), two shillings (January 1796), and 1.8 shillings (March 1798). Rates for artisans in the same area exhibited a remarkable stability between, and even during the famines. The magnitude of the collapse in living standards during the second crisis provoked many demands for wage rises, among them a petition from Home Office clerks in December 1800, stating that they were 'deprived of the means of support which our situation formerly allowed us'. Intense trade union agitations, most notably in London, certainly won some victories. But masses of evidential snippets suggest that wage rates did not rise significantly between the famines, and that therefore most workers were equally vulnerable, but more badly affected by the much higher prices current in 1799–1801, than in 1794–6.[20]

The statistical problems with wages, earnings, and employment, are aggravated by our ignorance of social structure, including the average size of families, the age distribution of children, and all the possible permutations. But these key components for the establishment of the long-term course of living standards, are not of debilitating significance here. This brief survey of wages and expenditure has revealed the germane characteristics. First, only a small minority of skilled workers in great demand, together with certain large families in a few favourable locations, commanded incomes on a par with the shopocracy, and other lower middle-class sectors whose incomes are unknown but presumably exceeded eighteen shilling a week in 1795. So only a small sector of the working class normally commanded considerable purchasing power, *after* buying a relatively rich diet. Secondly, the vast majority of workers, irrespective of where they lived, and how they ate, spent between sixty and eighty percent of incomes on food. Professor Neale correctly insists that any realistic index of consumption must be 'weighted very much in favour of food'. If families in rural southern and eastern England spent the highest portions of income on food, the most crucial variable everywhere seems to have been the size of the individual family. Thirdly, higher incomes were generally spent on extra and better food, especially on meat, dairy products, and beer. Our dietary evidence suggests that even the more affluent workers ate roughly the same volumes of cereals as their poorer neighbours. The difference lay in the former's *higher percentage* of income spent on meat and cheese for example, and the *smaller percentage* spent on bread corns. This picture was certainly complicated further by the unequal distribution of available food in most families, with men taking a disproportionate share of meat commensurate with both a chauvinist society and logistic support of strenuous physical labour; fluctuations in family fortunes probably affected distributions from week to week, and even from day to day. Some historians express surprise that food rioters commonly intervened over 'foods which were not essential, such as meat and butter'. But to identify this as 'consumer consciousness' is hardly incisive; it even ignores the centrality of such foods to non-wheaten dietaries.[21] Moreover, it should not require much imagination, even from a late twentieth-century academic, to appreciate that butter with bread or potatoes, or cheese with bread, together with regular meat dishes, make a tremendous difference to the quality of life. Even the poorest *aspired* to take something with their bread; what, and how much, depended on income, and also conferred status through the sociology of consumption. 'You who can't afford Butter to your Cabbage

or Bacon to your Sprouts', taunted well-paid Thames watermen. The
working-class housewife not only wanted to buy meat; she wanted to be
seen shopping in the shambles.[22]

The scale and the degree of dependency on the market for food demands
evaluation. If the debate on the impact of enclosure still rages, no present
contributor would now argue that the loss of commons and wastes did not
represent a serious loss for rural workers, and not just labourers. In the light
of very recent, and powerful restatements of the Fabian thesis, Arthur
Young's famous 1800 outburst against the inability of most plebeian
villagers to command 'half an acre of potatoes', and his campaign to ensure
that all future enclosure awards contained provisions for allotment gardens,
can be seen as a very rational culmination of half a century's disquiet.[23]
And, as Dr Mills reminds us, the numbers of common rights remained
stationary even in unenclosed parishes; they did not increase commensurately with population growth, so that even where enclosure was absent, an
ever-dwindling percentage of residents retained proprietoral rights to
produce their own food to supplement wages. However, in some locations,
a proportion of landworkers was enabled to raise some food. Potato patches
were common in Holderness, where labourers also kept cows and pigs.
Public authorities in the Sussex Weald voted poor-law funds to buy 'hog
fattening' for impoverished, plebeian villagers.[24] Mick Reed's reminder that
a significant 'peasant' farming sector survived into the nineteenth century,
should not obscure the fact that such petty agriculturalists were not
subsistence farmers on the continental model. Nor did the famines strike
them in ways found in Europe. English 'peasant proprietors' did not get
locked into the classic vicious circle, consuming corn reserved for seed,
thereby compromising the next season's production.[25] Indeed, opponents
of one Northamptonshire enclosure in 1798 – significantly after the first
famine – argued that many of those craftsmen and domestic outworkers
could convert their petty open-field holdings to cereal production in times
of dearth, not that they normally grew grains. A neat division between
capital and labour may oversimplify rural social structures, but many rural
workers were principally dependent on the market, and vulnerable to price
movements, especially of grains. Contemporary complaints that the larger
farmers, as opposed to smallholders, refused to be bothered with small sales
of produce to plebeian neighbours, are too numerous to ignore. Nothing
'short of compulsion', thundered a Yorkshire cleric, would see 'the Farmers
. . . furnish the poor with milk'. Some farmers continued to supply their
permanently-employed labourers with cheap corn, and the famines were
responsible for a resurgence of this dying tradition, but it still excluded the
seasonally unemployed, and most village craftsmen.[26]

Numerous contemporary observations of the rural retailing establishment comprise one reliable indicator of the intensifying dependency of the
agrarian workforce on the market. 'Bacon, oatmeal, flour, bread . . . are
usually purchased out of the retail shops which scarce a village, consisting of
a dozen houses, is without', asserted a Cheshire taxman. Warwickshire
evidence suggests that in unenclosed, open villages, a proliferation of
craftsmen was accompanied by a marked increase in shopkeeping; in 'the
largest parishes nearly 20 percent of the families were taken up with the

retailing of food alone during the second half of the eighteenth century'. Other reports attribute a rising significance of small, local market towns for plebeian consumers from villages in their hinterlands. Rural bakers, and urban bakers with rounds in the countryside also made an appearance.[27] If we exclude farmers and food-traders from the very detailed list of the inhabitants of Cardington, Bedfordshire, made in 1782, and assume that they all depended to degrees of totality on the market, for bread at least, then we are discussing seventy-two percent of the population.[28]

Estimating the degree of market dependency of town-dwellers on the market is less problematic. Gardens and allotments were under pressure from economic and demographic forces. They were commonly victims of incessant building, a phenomenon which extended to industrial villages, for example in Nottinghamshire, where framework-knitters' garden plots were in retreat. Conversely, some factory-owners attached gardens to new housing, and even an unmarried quarryman was able to rent an allotment in the industrial town of Windle. The poor domiciled in Swindon, a market town, were encouraged to cultivate potatoes on 'waste' ground. But if limited numbers retained garden plots, only potatoes constituted primary subsistence; bread and meal had to be bought. At a conservative estimate, between fifty and sixty percent of the rural population, and up to one hundred percent of urban inhabitants, were dependent on the market. Between twenty-eight and thirty-three percent of the national population lived in towns. If provincial ones remained small in comparison with London, in several regions, urban inhabitants constituted a rapidly expanding proportion of aggregate population. Even allowing for the vulgarity of these impressions, and on a conservative estimate again, between sixty-five and seventy percent of the national population depended on the market for food at the start of the nineteenth century.[29]

Finally, consumers who depended on petty retailers, and their credit facilities, who bought food in small quantities, paid much more (in relative terms) for their subsistence; only the rich bought in bulk, and therefore cheaply.[30] As the Rev. Davies noted, 'the poor man's pocket will seldom allow of him buying a sack' of flour 'at once'. Credit facilities generated an extra inflationary spiral. The *Reading Mercury* granted that 'excessive' retail prices were 'partly occasioned by the extraordinary risk incurred of bad debts', and another observer stressed that petty shopkeepers were at the end of a considerable commercial chain, with merchants' profits at different stages pushing prices up by as much as fifty percent. Small retailers, with plebeian clienteles, also cut costs by purchasing substandard goods, including those condemned as unfit for human use by 'market juries'. In Hertfordshire, 'deemed the first corn county in the kingdom',

> Yorkshire bacon, generally of the worst sort, is retailed to the poor from little chandlers' shops at an advanced price; bread is retailed to them in the same way.

Consumers in places where the Assize of Bread still functioned, like London and York, may have received some protection, though the legal machinery operated principally on only the bigger bakers. Most consumers received little protection, and the Assize did nothing to moderate the costs of short-term credit, nor did it extend to key non-cereal foods.[31]

In conclusion, expenditure patterns and market dependency constitute the paramount criteria here, as opposed to the precise wages earned in different occupations, and the incomes accruing to families of different sizes, child-age structures, and earning opportunities. We have attempted to compile statistical tables to indicate the erosion of living stadards for specific workers based on their recorded earnings, and similar tables founded on current wage rates for other occupations: it is also possible to calculate incomes adequate to the purchase of basic subsistence diets during the famines, by reworking price series. The absence of numerous earnings series is not a severe obstacle. The entire working class, and a not insignificant number of their social superiors, were vulnerable to price increases of these dimensions, which ensured that hardly any workers could get through these devastating crises without drastic alterations to their dietary (and more), and the social vicissitudes that this entailed.[32]

Commercial Systems

The causes and courses of the famines must be seen in the context of the grain and provision trades. One seminal element in British history between the sixteenth and nineteenth centuries, is the development of centres of conspicuous consumption and the parallel growth of regions of equally conspicuous production. London's key role was stressed by contemporaries, and is repeated by historians. Eighteenth-century developments added several new regions of pronounced net consumption, among them the West and East Midlands, West Yorkshire, and southern Lancashire.[33] The problems, which pivoted on freeing populations from the restraints imposed by local and regional agricultural resources, were overcome by a triple revolution, in agriculture, in transportation, and in commercial organisation. Agrarian developments underpinning increased production are too well-known to require rehearsal. It will be remembered that despite these achievements, national subsistence was delicately poised. If overall 'imports of corn rose from 1.4% of gross corn output in 1770 to 7.6% around 1820', thus reflecting the burgeoning longer-term significance of a foreign supply, the key degree of *normal dependency* oscillated inversely with the productivity of each home harvest; any deficiency, small or large, had to be made up by imported corn during the agricultural season immediately following the harvest.[34] This serves to emphasise that *distribution* is the key topic here, and that transportation and commercial organisation are the major components. Only London comprised a region of total consumption. Even the greatest provincial towns remained located in predominantly agricultural regions, and the expanding complexes of industrial villages were within, rather than outside the countryside. The exploding populations of South-east Lancashire, and the West Riding had led furthest towards the situation where the demand for food could not be met from *regional* productive capacity, and required massive augmentation by stocks brought across considerable distances. The same situation was merely embryonic elsewhere; Warwickshire, for example, could still produce an estimated half of its cereal requirement in 1800.[35]

The salient features of regions with a net deficiency can be examined through the examples of the South-west,[36] and the West Riding. The former achieved this status in the 1790s. Each component county contained urban centres. No Cornish town exceeded the five thousand mark, but a buoyant industrial population concentrated in the extensive mining districts ensured that demand for food outstripped the county's cereal growth. In Devon and south-west Somerset, twenty-three towns, ranging in size from Plymouth and Devonport with a joint population of forty-seven thousand, to Northam with just over two thousand, comprised the main consumption centres. All of these centres relied in the first instance on regional agricultural produce. Farmers in the hinterlands of Devon and Somerset towns marketed much of their produce, including butter, in these local centres. Supplies, brought by heavily capitalised millers, were also important in the greater towns. The same situation obtained in several Cornish towns, but others had no corn markets, and, as at Padstow, the townsfolk joined local miners going regularly 'Round to the Farmers Houses in the Country to Purchase their Corn'.[37]

The fragility of south-western grain supplies occasioned some later eighteenth-century comment, but this reflected interdependencies originating in the customary early timing of the regional harvest. Maltsters regularly bought up early barley, which was 'sent out' of the region immediately after one harvest, only to be replaced by stocks shipped from the East later in the subsequent season. These transhipments of barley were the frequent cause of the repetitive and notorious mass mobilisations of miners to prevent cereals leaving Cornwall. In the nineties, the equilibrium of Devon's cereal supply was jeopardised by the rapid expansion of Devonport, wartime naval provisioning, troop concentrations, and POW camps. These also drew off Cornish supplies, further endangering the balance. By the mid-1790s the larger towns and the mining regions depended on a considerable additional supply of cereals from Hampshire, the south-east, and East Anglia. Many south-western farmers appreciated the change, and started to resist the maltsters in preference to holding on to stocks in anticipation of regional price peaks in the summer months immediately preceding the harvest. Regional self-sufficiency went, but localised self-sufficiency was preserved at the small town and rural parish levels.[38]

West Riding dependency on other regions was structured differently. Localised agricultural, marketing mechanisms thrived. For example, Ryedale oat farmers achieved a monopoly 'for several weeks' immediately after the harvest in marts in proximate industrial centres. But the region as a whole depended throughout the year on cereals brought from the East Riding, Lincolnshire, East Anglia, and even London, with more eastwards across the Pennines. The Riding's five greatest corn marts, at Wakefield, Pontefract, Knaresbrough, Leeds and Skipton, all lay on the Aire and Calder complex, or the unfinished Leeds and Liverpool canal. Merchants in these locations purchased at exchanges in the producing regions, either from other dealers or through factors. Markets were interdependent; corn

sold at Ripon and Boroughbridge was subsequently resold at Knaresborough. The key difference between the West Riding and the south-west
went beyond the absolute dependency of the former which relied on an
unremittant supply in contrast the latter's need for a seasonal supply.[39]

By the 1790s these regional marketing systems were subsumed within a
mature national system, in which London played the key role. In 1740, the
Newcastle Journal reported that 'all the [grain] Markets in England have a
natural dependence on each other', and that prices current in London
'governs the Value of all Grain in England'. This governance was increasingly direct. As early as 1726, the *Kentish Post* published a weekly
'London letter' giving metropolitan prices, and later many provincial papers
even at the distance of Stamford and York provided more sophisticated
information on the London market. And, perhaps tellingly, from 1799
Bell's Weekly Messenger had a Monday edition, to disseminate information
about the main market day at the Mark Lane exchange. The eyes of farmers
and provincial merchants were riveted thereon. Winchester bread prices
were 'wholly regulated by the London prices, as all Millers, Bakers, etc.
without regard to the Price he pays for his Corn, wait for the London
returns to fix their Prices' before sale. Grain prices in remoter regions like
Herefordshire, were normally under those in London, but they responded
quickly to metropolitan price movements. In 1801, a parliamentary enquiry
concluded that the London exchange 'cannot but have a very material Effect
on most of the Markets throughout England'.[40]

Any local or regional 'disequilibrium' in the grain supply could 'be
neutralised only by the transportation of goods from one market to
another'. The sole incentive for dealers lay in higher prices current in
deficiently-supplied exchanges. Local provincial prices commonly rose
above those in the capital to attract supplies. On one occasion when
metropolitan prices were surpassed by those in the Midlands, Oxfordshire
millers who 'normally send their Flour to London', insisted that the Oxford
canal be kept open at all costs so that they could exploit the best market at
Birmingham. The greater merchants were able to buy, distribute, and sell
to maximise profits. One major Liverpool merchant house corresponded
with Claude Scott, London's greatest international trader, and big millers as
far away as Hampshire, in addition to maintaining permanent agents in
Chester and Carlisle, important staging posts for cereals en route to
Lancastrian consumers. Earl Fitzwilliam's purchases for his massive South
Yorkshire industrial enterprises, and his extensive Northamptonshire
estate, were so huge that he watched market prices closely. He bought in
bulk when he estimated prices would be at their lowest, in the appropriate
exchange; a regular flow of instructions, including countermands, went to
agents in several Yorkshire, East Anglian and London markets, and he
imported oats from Ireland. If Fitzwilliam thereby saved money, merchants
'made money by operating the market'.[41]

However, merchants and others, did much more than simply respond to
localised deficiencies. They were central to the price mechanism which
rationed supplies throughout the year. Under normal conditions, supplies
peaked in the autumn, when farmers sold stocks to realise the cash for
Michaelmas rent payments. The monthly figures for corn traffic down a

major artery, the East Yorkshire Derwent, prove the point. September and October were invariably peak months, with much lower totals in the May to July period. But wealthy farmers also stored considerable stocks for marketing in the spring and summer when prices normally peaked. Merchants functioned in parallel, and both regularly borrowed from provincial banks to finance these operations. Such loans 'could help to stabilise prices' and the supply throughout the year, according to a financial historian. Some farmers let factors have stocks on credit, so that stored cereals were strategically placed for speedy despatch to the best market.[42] Arthur Young strongly supported this mechanism:

> it is much to be desired, that jobbers, or millers, or monopolizers should take advantage of the [autumn] price and lay in great stocks. . . . They take from the market when there is a plenty, and they bring to market when there is a scarcity; thereby equalizing both prices and consumption.[43]

In an unregulated capitalist economy, the profit motive and the price mechanism were central to the food supply.

The foregoing does not represent the limits of the market's function. In some respects London's demand for best English wheat dominated the trade, and pervaded most regions. Cleveland wheat was shipped to the metropolis, while the locals subsisted on rye. The entire southern and eastern milling trade was geared to supplying the finest flour to London. From any parcel of wheat, millers produced three grades of flour, the finest called 'firsts', a less fine dubbed 'seconds', and 'thirds' which contained the bran. Millers in

> those Counties which have any Communication with London . . . send their fine flour to London; the Whole of the Remainder, Bran excepted, they apply to making a coarser sort of Flour for the Consumption locally.

Metropolitan millers marketed their 'seconds' for southern consumers outside the capital; 'thirds' went for sea-biscuit and for fodder. Parallel developments had occurred in other major consumption centres, including Birmingham and Sheffield. Here a sizeable proportion of urban inhabitants ate the best; the poorer consumed 'seconds', and were joined by others in these towns' hinterlands. The millers, merchants and factors, who organised these distributions, had pronounced vested interests in their survival: 'the Mealman makes more profit by selling the fine and the offal separately than making them together'.[44]

London's wheat came by two main routes. First, metropolitan millers, mealmen, and the greatest bakers, purchased grain in provincial marts. Secondly, wheat passed through the sole wholesale market at Mark Lane. It was financed by the capital's fifty greatest traders and built in 1760. By 1800 the shares were held by a residual, tight coterie of fourteen men, and this monopolistic tendency was reflected in the seventy-two stalls in the possession of a mere fifty-eight individuals and firms. None had more than two stalls, but those who had two used only one; the other was redundant.

It was impossible to sell without a stall, but equally impossible for anybody unconnected with the shareholders or established traders, to take one. Eight stalls were possessed by the hoymen, based in the Kent ports, who bought corn locally, and shipped it in their own boats for sale at Mark Lane. Historically, the remaining stallholders were salesmen, employed on commission. About thirty-five retained this function, acting for East Anglian and South-eastern farmers and dealers, who shipped the cargoes by coaster. Such shipments, which commonly belonged to several owners, were sold by sample, usually within the week of arrival, while still aboard the ships. But the scale of the trade, its concentration in few hands, greatly enriched these factors, many of whom exploited their manifestly favourable position, to deal – and to speculate – on their own account. Stallholders regularly dealt among themselves, often before the exchange formally opened, notably when anticipated price rises fuelled speculation.[45]

Although merchants in several ports, notably Bristol, Hull, Newcastle-upon-Tyne and Liverpool, were responsible for considerable importations, London dominated the overseas trade.[46] Merchant-importers, who had the remaining Mark Lane stalls, were men of immense capitals. In October 1800, two of them alone reputedly had one hundred thousand quarters of wheat, and twenty-five percent of the entire importation through London was said to have been organised by one man, Claude Scott. Some factors also acted as agents for foreign merchants, but they too had a vested interest in the selling price, equal to that of the merchant-importers; it was customary 'for the Factor to have a per Centage' of the price secured 'besides his Commission by the Quarter'. The price of imported wheat was not governed by the volume available, but by prices obtaining for best English wheat. Imported corn was inherently inferior, but normally commanded a constant proportion of the price of best English; sales of imports had no direct effect on English wheat prices, because the former were excluded from the market-inspectors' price calculations. Therefore the profits of all those involved in importation, whether factors or merchants, turned on prices obtained for English wheat.[47]

Ironically metropolitan domination of the import trade was unreflected in London's consumption of foreign wheat, which was used to make the capital's bread only when millers were unable to buy sufficient English. Importers sold their foreign at Mark Lane, but it was used principally in those regions which supplied English to London. Foreign wheat was used covertly, by millers and bakers throughout the Home Counties, and beyond – into Hampshire, Wiltshire and Somerset for example – where its inferior taste gave the game away. The traders responsible disguised it by admixture with English, and sold the product at the price of best English. Considerable profits accrued, and as an Essex tax official noted, the practice 'induces the Miller to give a Sanction to [the] high price of Flour, by paying the greatest Price for best English wheat'.[48]

Evidential problems with provincial markets do not preclude general observations of key characteristics. Prior to their repeal in 1772, Elizabethan statutory restrictions on marketing in general, and wholesaling in particular, did not seriously retard commercial development. Economic considerations, notably the survival of tolls, saw cereal sales withdrawn from pitching markets; the only major one mentioned by the agricultural surveyors in the 1790s, at Reading, was governed by local customs which retained a retail function while its primary concern, sample sales of wholesale volumes, went ahead unimpeded. Sample sales were the norm everywhere. Few, if any market towns had specialist exchanges on the Mark Lane model before the 1820s, and sellers met buyers in the comfort of the larger inns. A part of the recently rebuilt inn at Rhuddlan was known as the 'New Market' as early as 1740; the press referred to the 'market room' at Nicholas Jeffery's Tunbridge Wells inn, where Lord Boyne observed, 'a great many Farmers and Dealers in Corn have . . . a private Market . . . for some Years'. At Chester, 'the pedling Price (as they call it)', was established at similar weekly gatherings. These markets were not exclusive, though monopolistic tendencies are found, for example at Malton where a handful of merchants used their control of transport on the Derwent to keep out interlopers: frustrated Wold farmers transferred to Driffield to exploit competition between Leeds-based factors. Hostile commentators feared the inn-room marts were venues for manipulative, shady, inflationary deals. The directors of the Foss Navigation near York acted 'to prevent a Monopoly' developing on their waterway, by ensuring that company warehouses were let to competitors. Some dealers tried to create local monopolies by taking rural granaries, which eased farmers' transport problems, but removed competition from alternative buyers. Innkeepers themselves were ideally-placed to become dealers, and some, including Mr Pratt, proprietor of the Red Lion at Banbury, traded extensively. The relative importance of semi-closed marts like Malton to the more competitive including Driffield is not known.[49]

The changed role of the miller constitutes another salient feature of the later eighteenth-century grain trade. In 1774, a parliamentary committee confirmed that

> The millers (who till these late years, had no other part from time immemorial in the manufacture of Wheat into Meal for the Bakers) are now for the most part become purchasers of Wheat and dressers of it into Flour for sale on their own account.

Millers, like factors, were well-placed to trade, as opposed to confining operations to grinding. Millers, in stark contrast to bakers subjected to the Assize, were restricted only by the regulation that a sack of flour must weigh two and a half hundredweight. Bakers' profits were controlled by the fixation of bread prices on flour prices, but the latter were not subjected to official control, and this encouraged the growth of the speculative miller. Some of their vested interests have been encountered, and many became very rich. One calculation put the return on grinding a quarter at four shillings, whereas the purchase, manufacture, and sale of this amount, gave a one-pound profit. Among the reflections of the industry's profitability, was the heavy investment in new technology, notably steam power, which greatly reduced costs, and extensive granaries. A York steam mill in 1801 had space for five thousand quarters. Contemporary hostility focussed on this new, speculative function, and a common refusal to be bothered with

miniscule sales to individual consumers.[50] Such attitudes preceded parallel
conservative disgust at the cotton lords, and all their equally-suspect
bourgeois works. In major milling centres like Norwich, it was recognised
that milling required 'much science and great capital', and in some senses
the trade was dominated by extensive concerns with heavy investment in
premises, technology, transport, and working capital. The lowest estimate
for a fully-operational steam mill started at two thousand pounds. Although
the numbers of mills shrank, notably in the Midlands and the North,
through conversions to industrial manufacturing, the commercial success
and importance of the great millers must not eclipse the survival of
thousands of modest, principally traditional millers, revealed for example
by the fines imposed on fifty-six men from forty-two Nottinghamshire
villages in 1797–8, for not displaying a 'Table of the Prices in Money or the
Amount of Toll or Multure'.[51]

The bakers were the millers' primary customers. The Assize of Bread,
with its supposedly strict control of profits, was historically responsible for
a lack of real prosperity in the baking trade. 'Bakers . . . drudge and labour
more for very trifling profits than any other tradesmen . . . . a Baker is very
seldom above a humble mediocrity of circumstances': it required 'little skill
and no capital'. In those towns dominated by a handful of great millers,
bakers also suffered from a lack of competition between their suppliers. A
few great urban millers had retail outlets, among them the owner of the
massive Snow Hill steam-mill at Birmingham, but most withdrew from the
front line between manufacturer and consumer, leaving the humble baker
to face the recurrent 'insult and clamourous behaviour' of plebeian customers. Several 'opulent bakers' traded in London's West End, but their wealth
derived from the sale of pastries and other dainties to the rich. The
metropolitan stipendiary magistrate, Patrick Colquhoun, distinguished
between these entrepreneurs, and the tiny establishments in the 'out streets
of the Town' who supplied the workers. One exception, a man named
Lovell, had a string of East End shops, and made extensive flour purchases
in East Anglian markets. There are suggestions that the bakers' precarious
economic equilibrium put them in the same client relationship which
obtained between petty publicans and prosperous brewers. Millers may
have had to recover bad debts by taking over bakeries – the means by which
brewers came to own so many pubs – but the paucity of examples like
Lovett, suggests that millers quickly sold these unfortunate assets. There
were two and a half thousand bakers in that part of London covered by the
Bills of Mortality, and at least one baker to every thousand inhabitants at
Nottingham. At Epsom the ratio was one to 280. But the supremacy of the
millers is richly illustrated by their total domination of the ancient London
Bakers Company.[52]

The complexity of the bread, as opposed to the flour supply, notably to
large towns, is revealed by the situation in Birmingham: here, bread

> widely different in weight, and which they distinguish by the names of
> ready-money bread, tally or credit bread, and huckster's bread; the latter
> being the smallest, is principally sold by the hucksters, who are credited
> from week to week

by their suppliers. The role of the baker also varied from town to town, and depended on the availability of cheap fuel, the scale of tenement housing with limited or non-existent cooking facilities, the opportunity to purchase small volumes of flour, and regional modes of cereal preparation. Plebeian dependence on the baker was greatest in London, and some large provincial centres; high population density and inadequate tenement quarters forced families to patronise the baker for bread, and for facilities to heat broths, stews and roasts. Half the bread consumed in London was bought the same day, and eaten hot. In the countryside similar factors were at work, and, aggravated by the erosion of fuel collection rights, were responsible for the decline in home baking which so infuriated William Cobbett. Itinerant bakers operated rural rounds, often from an urban base in arable regions. Thomas Smith of Cambridgeshire

> said that on Tuesday . . . he went as he usually does to Hadstock in . . . Essex with a quantity of Bread, about 60 Quartern Loaves & half Quartern Loaves, of which he intended to leave about 20 at a Shop in Hadstock . . . which he serves.

A Knaresborough baker supplied villages throughout the town's hinterland by operating several distinct weekly rounds. On a more modest scale, Mathew Joy of Norwich achieved a reputation as '"the Walking Baker"'; he delivered eight stone of bread on a daily twenty-mile pedestrian slog 'to several villages'.[53]

Home-baking persisted on a greater scale in the North. Newcastle-upon-Tyne remained a low density town, and most working families baked at home with cheap coal. Where 'hasty pudding' survived as the subsistence standard, there was no need for bakers; Lancaster actually had none. But the encroachments of wheat had their effect, and even at Newcastle bakers were attracting plebeian customers as well as middle-class clients. Conversely, many middle-class families baked at home, purchasing meal from chandlers, trading independently of the bakers. The diversity encountered within the local structures of the bread-trade, suggests that while many were little more than proletarian entrepreneurs, there was money to be made.

The commercial structures in the grain trade were unequalled in the other major provision trades. Specialisation in meat production, with distinct breeding regions in the Celtic fringes, the massive peregrinations to English grazing areas, is a well-known element in agrarian history. A number of marketing features require comment. Different types of middlemen played complex roles, notably if not exclusively in the massive metropolitan trade. 'Carcass butchers', who bought fatstock at regional fairs and markets, sold beasts they slaughtered to retail or 'cutting butchers'. Other speculators, termed jobbers, inserted themselves between graziers and butchers. They worked the formal markets, but also patronised unofficial exchanges, like that at the Swan Inn, Knightsbridge; here, beasts nominally en route for Smithfield commonly changed hands under the officious eye of the landlord who recorded 'the Sales in his Yard . . . in a Book'. The scale of intervention by middlemen proved a recurrent source of contemporary disquiet at assumed monopolistic practices. But the sheer size and diversity of the trade, the bypassing of Smithfield – which had neither the exclusive features of Mark Lane, nor a parallel national price-fixing function – guaranteed competition. Similar characteristics were found provincially. Scores of cattle-jobbers lived in villages adjacent to York, whose exchange was but one in a web of interdependent marts, whereby cattle and sheep moved from breeder, to grazier, and on to consumers. A hostile report from 1795, noted an ample supply of beasts 'previously . . . bought in the North by jobbers', at York, where 'instead of being bought by butchers and slaughtered . . . [they] were taken off by another set of jobbers, for . . . Wakefield'. In this way some would reach Manchester. But deals between farmers, dealers and butchers, were not exclusive to formal markets. The Swan Inn had its provincial counterparts, and some publicans engaged in droving and dealing. Many farmers in the Sheffield area relied principally on visiting butchers and dealers to purchase fatstock, as did farmer Ward near Guisborough, who sold much more, normally 'after much wrangling' in his parlour, than he ever did under the auctioneer's hammer.[54]

The butter and cheese trades also developed solid commercial systems, notably again in the supply to London. Metropolitan cheesemongers 'usually employ factors or agents' resident in Cheshire and other specialist production areas. Factors also sent cheese, much of it by canal, to Midland and northern centres of consumption. The major fairs, including Stourbridge and Nottingham, maintained their historic importance as exchanges between dairymen and dealers. The long-distance butter trade also increasingly turned on factoring. The decline in the significance of the public wholesale market is revealed by the continuous fall in the market rent at York. Malton butter merchants emulated the restrictive practices of their counterparts in grain. Butter-producers in Devon, like cheese specialists elsewhere, employed factors in large towns, and even the smallest Devon dairyman supplied London, leaving parcels at wayside inns for the common carrier.[55]

The food supply to major towns observed 'no ruling principle . . . for the reorganisation of local town markets, except the need to meet continuous demand' escalating with population growth. Yet some major characteristics warrant emphasis. With the partial exception of London, all towns and regions of consumption relied on foodstuffs arriving across longer distances, and stocks produced by neighbouring farmers. The key features of the agrarian revolution, especially capital-intensive production, the distinct increase in average farm size in the cornlands, are well known. Eighteenth-century complaints that the greater cereal producers ceased to have any interest in pig, chicken, egg and milk production, were too numerous and too repetitive to ignore. Technical advances were central. Marling transformed the East Yorkshire Wolds into a major corn region during the eighteenth century, and the traditional mixed interests of many farmers, sheep, cattle, oxen, poultry, pigs, and corn, were radically altered, as their production increasingly focused on cereals and sheep. The eclipse of such sources of non-cereal foods, together with the burgeoning demand for vegetables, especially potatoes, for milk and butter, encouraged market-gardening and small dairy concerns in the vicinities of centres of consumption. Many small farmers in Lancashire concentrated on potatoes, and the increasingly ubiquitous production of the root is symbolised by its growth by squatters on cleared forest-land near Nottingham, and by the emergence of small scale, potato-merchants. Lesser farmers near Leeds – as elsewhere – concentrated on milk. 'Market boats' plied many canals, and helped to bring gardeners and their wares to town markets. However, the marked rise in eighteenth-century grain prices and the increase in convertible husbandry practices, helped to ensure the viability of grain production everywhere. So too did the on-going wheaten revolution, as revealed for example by the switch from oats to wheat by small farmers near Sheffield. A combination of sound agrarian techniques, and incisive market perceptions, contributed to ensure that cereal production remained omnipresent; every provincial region of consumption relied to some extent on local grain, and to a greater extent on neighbourhood agriculturalists for non-cereal foodstuffs.[56]

The ancient market places thus retained their functions as direct exchanges between producers and consumers. Indeed, the numbers of market days in many towns increased, especially with the addition of Saturdays. In the 1790s farmers frequented daily markets (except Sundays) in Manchester and Liverpool. The burgeoning demand for food, caused by both rising population and the broadening divisions between the agrarian and industrial sectors of the economy, and further spurred by urbanisation, generated forums in which opportunities existed for countless numbers of people to create an entrepreneurial function. Many artisans, labourers, and their wives, commenced operations with tiny capitals, to tour farms and gardens in urban vicinities, to buy up all types of marketable foodstuffs. These petty dealers were, unlike merchants, factors and jobbers, vulnerable to prosecution by officious authorities under traditional marketing laws. The small fine imposed at Exeter on Mary Samways, a labourer's wife, for engrossing three ducks and a fowl, was typical of the residual, official imposition of the 'moral economy'. Many hawked their wares through the streets; others rented stalls and joined minor agriculturalists in market squares, but ambition commonly pivoted on taking a shop. In Leeds, an eightfold increase in retail establishments accompanied a threefold increase in population between 1800 and 1834. The rapidity of this development, and its ratio to aggregate demand certainly 'caused severe competition and insecurity', and torrents of failures. But for plebeians, if joining the shopocracy did not guarantee either stability or wealth, it opened a door to upward social mobility, and immediate enhancement of social status; the resultant tradition is superbly illustrated by Robert Roberts's account of proletarian shop-owning aspirations in the slums of Edwardian Salford.[57]

The various marketing systems, their differing complexities and structures, certainly generated a situation in which competition theoretically thrived. So many were involved, as producers, merchants, manufacturers and retailers, deploying capitals ranging from pence to hundreds of thousands of pounds, that monopolies seemed impossibly remote. But paradoxes are to be found within these systems. Marketing, in part, still adhered to the customary, open, public function; farmers, gardeners, and their wives did literally come to market with their products. Petty dealers, hucksters and the rest, would sell a gallon of potatoes, a dozen eggs, a solitary fowl, and even half a quartern loaf. Urban streets and squares teemed with retailers who competed with each other, and general and specialist shopkeepers of all grades. The oxen bought in the mart one day, would be in the butcher's pen overnight, and on his stall in joints on the morrow. Conversely, an enveloping veil of secrecy seemed to be falling over the marketing of some commodities, above all cereals. The transparency of the pitching market was disappearing; instead, deals between prosperous farmers, opulent dealers and millers, took place behind the ornate facades of the greater inns. Instead of market squares crammed with carts laden with grain, and resonant with men bargaining, massive consignments arrived and departed by road, barge and coaster; cargoes passed through wharfs, private granaries and company warehouses, disappeared into massive, noisy mills, to temporarily inhabit an unknown, unseen world. Sacks of flour appeared in chandlers' shops, and bread materialised on bakers' shelves. Even the countryside was not immune. The fact that this was all part of a transitional phenomenon, the early stages of a retailing revolution which was to progress to the hypermarket, was no comfort when food prices – ostensibly magically – started to go through the roof.

These paradoxes underlay contemporary confusion. The existence of a national grain market was crucial. Through it, periodic regional shortages were ironed out pretty speedily, *except* when the national stock was deficient. It was the national stock which concerned the classical economists, and those politicians responsible for ensuring national survival in difficult wartime conditions. Both applied macro-economic analysis. But this conflicted violently with traditionally-minded contemporaries who understandably persisted in their perception of the paramountcy of the locality and its subsistence problem. They naturally resorted to micro-economic notions. The resultant juxtaposition of 'micro- and macro-economic analysis reflects the confusion of the eighteenth century itself', writes Mrs Genovese. Professor Coats correctly exonerates the classical economists from charges of malignity, but this does not mean that Coats' parallel exoneration of the traders from contemporary charges of exploitation and profiteering, is invariably justified. Indeed Coats himself subscribes to Adam Smith's cabal theory, namely that whenever 'people of the same trade . . . meet . . . the conversation ends in a conspiracy against the public, or in some contrivance to raise prices'. However, Coats rejects this dictum's applicability to the 'corn producers and traders "as a whole"': they 'were in no position to co-ordinate their forces so as to raise prices', because 'changes in eighteenth-century market procedures' failed to 'bring this eventuality into the bounds of possibility'.[58]

Coats' confidence merits challenge, especially if applied to shortage years, for theory is no substitute for actuality. It must be emphasised that the demand for cereals was inelastic; the relative poverty of most consumers, in as much as they had no savings, meant that they relied – at best – on weekly purchases.[59] Moreover, during the famines, prices accelerated speedily. Farmers, considerable dealers and manufacturers of food, who had access to large capitals, could hoard, and therefore had vested interests in raising market prices. Bakers, and smaller retailers, with much more rapid turnovers, had a less–pronounced identical interest. Bakers' profits rose due to imperfections in the Assize, which permitted more bread to be obtained from the given quantity of flour allowed in the Assize calculations; no doubt the murky role of adulteration was extended too. Chandlers', and other petty retailers' credit services, meant that they too, despite defaulters, made greater profits when prices were high. Moreover, ratios between the price of wheat, and the price of flour, expanded markedly when prices rose; they began to narrow when wheat-prices fell, but disproportionately slowly. In addition, the prices of all foods also rocketed; on occasion percentage rises were greater than cereals.[60]

Inflated profits throughout the food-growing, wholesaling, manufacturing and retailing sectors, were the product of shortages. Market-mechanisms were certainly responsible, but only in part. Coats' confidence reveals an ignorance of certain key features of the grain trade which were exposed by a major parliamentary enquiry in 1801. The purpose of the investigation was not to exonerate grain traders from accusations of profiteering, but to allay fears that commercial machinations were the sole cause of apparent scarcity. The report used guarded language; parliamentary temperance was vital, for if the rumours which had generated universal public execration of the corn trade were powerfully reinforced by a stringent report from MPs, serious disturbances were inevitable, and a bloodbath a possibility. The committee's attentions were confined to Mark Lane; evidence was taken from both dealers and buyers. The latter largely indicted the pronounced monopolistic characteristics of the exchange. One 'considered the City of London to be without a Corn Market'. The salesmen put up such transparent defences, that the report concluded that 'Competition was to a Degree prevented, and the Trade thrown into too few Hands'. Moreover, other practices smacked of manipulation. The salesmen obscured the supply situation: 'a Buyer has no means whatever of judging from the Appearance of the Samples exposed on the Stands, during any Period of the Market, what the Supply is'. Shortages of best English wheat were especially exaggerated because when there were 'few fine Samples the Millers are anxious to purchase at any Price'. This pushed up the prices of home-grown and imported wheat, to the advantage of farmers, dealers, factors, and merchant-importers. It also enhanced milling profits for those who mixed English and foreign in the production of flour fraudulently sold as, and at the price of, best English. Moreover, salesmen were not only able to push prices upwards, but were able to exaggerate the degree of inflation. The market inspectorate was tiny, nepotist, and inefficient; sellers revealed only those sales which suited their purpose. In addition, average prices were calculated solely on sales made on Mondays, when the best corn was sold; sales of poorer wheat, usually reserved for Wednesdays, were excluded. And it was the Monday prices that the new edition of *Bell's Weekly Messenger* (and other papers) disseminated more quickly than the official *London Gazette*. MPs concluded, guardedly to the last, that the Mark Lane operators

> may be tempted to employ their superior Knowledge and Influence they possess in the Market for the undue advancing or maintaining the Prices.[61]

The monopolistic structures of some markets in the producing regions meant that further turns to this national inflationary spiral could derive from this source. In his study of the Corn Laws, D.G. Barnes was impressed by the 'very looseness' of official price-collection and collation, and the manipulative powers of monopolistic middlemen in certain provincial markets is consistently revealed by miscellaneous evidence from across the country between 1700 and 1850. These range from the closure of Liverpool to imports for six months when dealers depressed prices at the key moment by flooding the exchange with low-grade wheat, to the artifice deployed against an Essex farmer, tricked into selling his prime wheat at prices below what later emerged to be the county's average.[62] But these probable, provincial parallels must not be allowed to obscure two fundamental factors. First, when scarcity struck, everybody in the trade appreciated the reality of aggregate deficiency. The degree could only be assessed, as opposed to calculated accurately: as the import trade 'must be a species of monopoly because only a few can be importers', according to one of its defenders, accurate knowledge of certain and potential volumes of imports was the preserve of a tiny élite, who were well-placed to manipulate the market. Secondly, the vice-like grip on London's supply was all the more important, as Mark Lane prices were the most sensitive barometer to the state of the national grain supply, and they governed price movements across the country. At Mark Lane, said a witness, 'the *buying* is a generally a matter of Notoriety, the Advance that it occasions spreads itself through the Kingdom'. MPs agreed that metropolitan influence was perennially power-ful; it became paramount in times of shortages: then the Mark Lane élite could, and did, exploit buyers' nerves and through them, the fears of consumers. Huge profits accrued to commercialists, and greater profitabil-ity was also achieved throughout the entire trade in foodstuffs.[63]

CHAPTER 3

Harvests and Markets in Wartime
1794–1801

'called Famine . . . in any other Country than this'

In an extensive corn country, between all the different parts of which
there is a free commerce and communication, the scarcity occasioned by
the most unfavourable seasons can never be so great as to produce a
famine,

confidently asserted Adam Smith. Many took refuge in his dictum,
including Arthur Young, the influential James Perry of the *Morning
Chronicle*, and the Duke of Portland, Home Secretary 1794–1801. The
emotive word 'famine' was rarely used by Englishmen. The pro-ministerial
press claimed that government policies and the legitimate activities of food
traders would avoid a 'very real famine'. Portland, like most of his ilk, used
the word 'scarcity', except to warn that riots would see 'famine . . .
substituted in place of Scarcity'. Inflated prices denoted 'scarcity'; 'absolute
scarcity' meant that food supplies were physically unequal to demand.
Contemporary officialese's contrived avoidance of 'famine' reflects preference for peculiarly English capitalist terminology to describe clinically
market conditions. Privately, Lord Auckland – the much respected member
of the Board of Trade – had a more realistic perception: 'By famine', he
wrote to Pitt in December 1795, 'I mean the want of Wheat sufficient to
furnish the lower & labouring classes . . . with the species of food which
long usage has made a necessary of Life to them'. As we shall see, there was
a logic to the observation made by that well-travelled Guardsman, Colonel
Clinton, in late 1800, when he insisted that identical conditions 'in any other
Country than this . . . would be called Famine'.[1]
  In chapter 1 we argued that England's grain supply was essentially fragile,
and that the yields of each harvest were critical, as they determined the scale
of imports to meet demand. Prices, and through them, living standards,
were dependent on the maintenance of equilibrium of the supply by
ensuring a sufficiency from indigenous stocks, supplemented to varying
degrees by imports, themselves rendered insecure by wartime conditions.

England's Wartime Harvests

A good farming season traditionally commences with a dry autumn for wheat-sowing, followed by a moderately cold winter, and a relatively dry February and March when spring-corns are planted. Ideally 'showers and sun' characterise April and May. A fine June favours haymaking, but light, regular showers in July are required to complete the growth of both winter and spring corns. Warm sunshine in August and early September ripens cereals, and provides a dry harvesting period. But there is no 'unfailing relationship' between weather, harvest yields, and prices; 'each historical instance of an apparent relationship must be considered in its context, and on its merits'.[2] However apt these analytical guidelines are, the merits prove elusive. The predominant presumption in later eighteenth-century England was that crops would be at least adequate, if not invariably abundant. The last famine, of 1766–7, seemed to be a relic of a bygone age, not least because more recent troubled seasons, 1772–3, 1782–3, and 1792–3, were characterised by ephemeral, and comparatively undramatic price rises. The assumption of plenty is reflected in governmental indifference to annual agricultural progress, which was shared by the press. Even papers serving agrarian regions like the *Kentish Chronicle* and the *Lincoln, Rutland and Stamford Mercury*, published irregular and sparse details of local agricultural conditions.[3] The remarkably rapid, renewed indifference after the terrible experiences of 1795–6 is typified by the solitary report on the 1798 harvest in the *Oxford Journal*. Young's *Annals of Agriculture* provided erratic coverage, and the monthly reports of the adolescent Board of Agriculture were neither detailed nor incisive, though they were fitfully plagiarised by newspapers.[4]

The evidence for the 1794 harvest is particularly poor, despite a belated government survey made in October 1795.[5] Prolonged drought and intense heat over the summer of '94 was the prime cause of deficiencies. 'The ground', in July in Nottinghamshire, 'is so burned and slippery, that you walk in as much danger as upon ice', and in Kent it was 'the driest and hottest season ever known'. Unremittant sun unseasonably ripened immature grains of all varieties; harvesting commenced very early, to be largely complete by mid-August. Wheat was of first-rate quality, but seriously deficient in quantity and 'found to thrash badly'. Whitehall's enquiry revealed expected regional disparities, for example the above-average wheat crops in East Yorkshire, Hertfordshire, and parts of Kent and Lincolnshire. Ten and fifteen percent wheat deficiencies in Bedfordshire, and Buckinghamshire respectively, and a twelve to twenty percent shortfall in barley and oats in both counties, were roughly representative; even where spring cereals were better locally, as in parts of Essex, they were but average. It must be emphasised, however, that solid proof of the degree of short-fall was revealed only as customary winter-time threshing progressed.[6]

Evidence of the progress of the agricultural calendar in the 1794–5 season is much richer; universal interest was stimulated by the recognition that the quality of the 1795 harvest would be critical for national welfare. The winter was the third most severe in the entire eighteenth century, with almost continuous sub-zero temperatures from December to March. In London, 'day after day the iron-grip of the frost continues unbroken. The milk freezes in the milk-maid's pails'. The North, and parts of the Midlands, were struck by recurrent huge falls of snow; arctic conditions were punctuated by temporary thaws and repetitive, extensive, and damaging floods. Winter-wheat was decimated by alternating heavy precipitation and intense cold. A spring drought subsequently affected some regions; a cold spell with frosts in June across the country killed thousands of lambs, even in the South, and retarded the ears filling in such wheat which survived the winter. At the end of June, a late harvest was widely anticipated. Further rain – especially in the south – provoked gloomy observations; Mrs Thrale, for example, recorded that 'no corn can ripen without sun, and here is nothing but inundation', as she watched the lake overflow in the park. If summer rain was not universal, August was abnormally cold across the land. If on balance the summer was poor, the season's effects varied.[7]

Pitt's October enquiry was obstructed by 'the jealousy and miserable policy of . . . farmers' unwilling to reveal productivity to the Bench, who, as landlords and tithe-owners, had their own vested interests, in addition to acting a a channel of communication with government. Nevertheless, it is significant that not one of the sixteen county returns reported even an average wheat crop. Wheat had partly rotted in the ground, and where not ploughed in so that land could be replanted with spring-corns, was thin, whatever the visual impressions on casual observers. However, 'the same cause not operating on the spring sown grain, or rather operating in its favour . . . the latter is superabundant, particularly barley', confirmed an experienced agricultural surveyor. Almost all the returns, both for counties, and the more numerous for hundreds, agreed. If such wheat which was harvested yielded only seventy-five or eight percent of an average, barley was up by about twenty percent, and oats by ten, on normal yields. Moreover, an abnormally large acreage was put down to spring corns. There were also bumper crops of peas and beans.[8]

The first famine was effectively terminated before the 1796 harvest. Massive imports, and considerable sales of government corn in the spring,[9] combined with enhanced consumption of non-wheaten grains, and an unprecedented acreage sown with wheat during the favourable 1795 autumn – conditions which dovetailed with market-perceptions, and advisory propaganda from the Board of Agriculture – accelerated a return to normality. Ironically, the 1796 harvest was 'by no means good', yet thereafter the country was 'as well stocked with Grain as it was some years ago'.[10]

The harvests of 1797 and 1798 were adequate to maintain this equilibrium, but the weather during that 'frightfully devastating year', 1799, was still remembered at Victoria's accession. The spring was dry and cold; vegetation stagnated in June and July, when frosts ravaged backward corns. A late harvest was universally predicted in July, when the weather changed; it remained cold, but rained incessantly. Flooding in mid-August swept off hay which had lain, undried in riverside meadows, for two months. Farmer Metcalfe, who 'never saw . . . Greater floods', recorded 'a man drowned in Thirsk Beck' in Yorkshire. Rain persisted; frantic efforts to cut any corn accompanied brief interludes of sun into September. Then Yorkshire hunters stalked partridges in 'half-ripened corn': in the Midlands, the first hay crop laid rotting, while unripe wheat stood in six inches of water, and where corn was cut and bound 'one may perceive the stocks green at a distance the sheaves grown together'. It was said, even of well-drained districts, that 'It will be November at the soonest before the Harvest be ended'. All corns were badly wind-blown; where unripe, flattened corn was eventually got in, the grains 'must . . . afford far less flour or meal, of a worse quality' than normal. Huge acreages literally wasted. Threshing proved tiresome; grain could not be entirely separated from the ear, and commercial 'straw . . . was full of grain'.[11]

Harvest prospects for 1800 were automatically ominous: Somerset 'farmers complained that they could not sow wheat' as their land was 'so full of water', and in many localities autumn wheat sowing proved impossible. Sheepscombe, Gloucestershire, typically 'had no wheat at all this year'; elsewhere, land was sown, but dangerously late in December, and such wheat was subsequently thin and weak. Reports of spring-sowing condi- tions reveal great diversity, but some regions had ideal weather. Any advantage thus accruing was soon cancelled by prolonged drought through- out June, July, and into August. Among the numerous testimonies to nation-wide aridity and relentless heat, were the lament of a Scottish farmer at this 'killing drought', the complete stop to water-driven machinery at Sheffield, and the temporary retardation of the meteoric career of George Canning as one 'bloody hot day' after another sapped his energies. The heat ruined Norfolk turnips, decimated Kentish hops, and dehydrated potatoes everywhere. If its effects on cereals varied, it augured badly overall. Generally speaking, wheat on heavy lands was either non-existent or ruined, and stunted on lighter soils. Very localised inconsistencies were common; Mary Sturge's own crops of peas and barley were 'very good, but that was far from the case with most of our neighbours'. However, drought dictated an early start to harvesting, and in places, including East Kent and Berkshire, it was over by mid-August.[12]

At that moment, harvesting was interrupted by heavy and continuous precipitation across the country. Certain storms, including the hailstorms in Bedfordshire on 19 August, were remembered for years. The wet con- tinued after the storms, and later reports suggest exaggeration in previous claims of an early completion to cereal-harvesting. It was not finished before the rains, even in normally forward Cornwall. Most regions reported rain damage. Sir Joseph Banks, whose extensive correspondence with scientifically-skilled agriculturalists made him an eminent authority, estimated a wheat deficiency of twenty percent, which he thought could be but partially compensated for by an early harvest of southern spring-corn.[13]

In stark contrast, the 1800–1 season was a farming classic, including a perfect autumn for wheat-sowing. The enormous current price encouraged an unprecedented acreage devoted to wheat, though the clergy's acreage returns doubtlessly inflated it through subconscious comparisons between the abysmal situation in 1799 and its superb successor. Increasing wheat acreages on farms practising convertible husbandry was relatively easy, but some observers were adamant that even here much more land was put down to wheat than was 'consistent with good husbandry'. Permanent pasture was ploughed up in Somerset, and the Kentish Weald, and marginal land was ploughed for spring-corns. In the Pennine parish of Horton-in-Ribblesdale, 'in general ill adapted to the plough . . . more land has been ploughed . . . than in any preceding' season. West Riding clothiers transformed their residual agrarian toehold, according to a Bradford curate, who explained that 'this being a trading neighbourhood, it is foreign to their time to grow corn, but in the present year they have grown considerably more than usual on account of the exorbitant cost'. An early harvest followed; yields were prodigious, with many major arable regions estimating crops double those of 1800. A Somerset clergyman marvelled that a fifth of the wheat produced in his predominantly pastoral village would 'supply all the People in the Parish who need to buy'. Nobody doubted the unparalleled productivity of the 1801 harvest, which finally terminated the 1799–1801 famine.[14]

Market Responses

According to the expert evidence of cornfactor Stonard to a parliamentary committee, a poor harvest would not fuel immediate spectacular price increases if it occurred after a normal year when some cereal stocks remained from the previous season. A key cause of one famine year following another, as 1795–6 followed 1794–5, and 1800–1 followed 1799–1800, was the total exhaustion of the stock in the first famine season; this depleted the supply for the succeeding season. If, as in 1795 and 1800, the following crop was also deficient, the position would be worse. Millers and merchants customarily bought considerable stocks after the harvest, but when there was little 'surplus' from the preceding season, and the current crop was substandard, such purchases were impossible; much new wheat instead of old, would be quickly used for seed, and current consumption would also have to be met from newly-harvested grain.

1799 resembled 1794; in both years the unused remnant of the preceding year's stock (1793 and 1798) helped to stabilise the supply – and prices – in the aftermath of a deficient harvest. In such circumstances, Professor Gould correctly asserts that September 'was too early for the size of the harvest just gathered to be accurately known and reflected in the price level'. Deficiency would be finally confirmed by winter threshing, and as Gould also states, it was then from about March that 'the size of the preceding year's harvest would . . . be virtually the only influence from the supply side at work on the short term level of prices'.[15] This pattern is inapplicable after a year of dearth; then *estimations* of the current crop would immediately govern prices.

In 1794–5 and 1799–1800 the supply and the reflected price followed the first of these two patterns, though prices accelerated faster in 1799 than in 1794 owing to the recent precedent, and, more significantly, the manifestly abysmal harvest weather in 1799. (cf. figures 1, 3, 5, 7, 9, 11) Gradually, in the autumn, supplies to Mark Lane proved unequal to demand, and prices rose relatively slowly from week to week. Parallel shortfalls between supply and demand were experienced in provincial exchanges, and big provincial buyers commonly responded by trying Mark Lane, where 'the appearance . . . of country buyers' was invariably interpreted as another omen foretelling supply problems. Additional signs included the marked tendency of wheat and barley prices in provincial markets in massive centres of consumption like Birmingham, or principally orientated to supplying major regions of consumption like Pontefract, to outpace London prices, to attract supplies, as shown by Figures 1, 3, 5 and 7. Gradually all markets became more sensitive, and affluent farmers restricted sales, and sought alternative buyers, thereby enhancing competition across the entire spectrum of dealers, millers and markets. Big centres of consumption felt the pinch as cereal supplies became more fragile, to be quickly revealed by any extra difficulties, including frozen water communications, and a temporary ban on coastal shipping to accelerate naval recruitment in the winter of 1794–5.[16]

Although prices over the winters of 1794–5 and 1799–1800 were conditioned by the same supply factors, some differences warrant notice. Those with specialist and inside knowledge were clearly aware of England's predicament in 1794–5. In December 1794, the Lord Mayor of London demanded discreet consultations with government to compose measures 'to prevent a possibility of scarcity before next harvest', and in the following February Sir John Sinclair formally addressed the Board of Agriculture on the topic. Miller Howes of Great Yarmouth confided 'Great fears of a famine' to his diary in January, about the same time as a Mancunian advised his brother 'not to sell . . . Wheat . . . at present', despite its 'most enormous price'; the 'very great scarcity' could only intensify with even greater prices.[17] However, when traditional winter charities are examined, organisers were clearly blissfully unaware of the predicament. Virtually none made any provision for an abnormal duration, as typified by the unusual solicitations for further subscriptions at Gloucester and Newcastle-upon-Tyne in February 1795, and the banking of residual funds at Hull in April.[18] Although the press published some gloomy but accurate predictions over the 1794–5 winter,[19] many more exuded greater conviction and urgency in late 1799. In December 1799 government advised local authorities to supply cereal substitutes for poor relief, adding the state's seal of authenticity to such prognostications, and ministers were subsequently criticised for it. All this had an impact on charity administrators, far fewer of whom stipulated terminal dates; the decision taken at Worcester in December to subsidise food and fuel for the duration of high prices was typical.[20] Although ministers soon tried to silence public discussions of the problem, many said that the publication of Arthur Young's famous *The Question of Scarcity Plainly Stated* in March 1800, comprised the final confirmation, and gave a massive upward twist to spiralling prices.[21]

Most observers calculated that in a year of dearth, the highest prices would reflect the shortest supply situation occurring in June, July and August.[22] Rapid price acceleration in the spring comprised an early reflection of market anticipations of shortages intensifying into the summer. This occurred in each year, 1795, 1796, 1800 and 1801, and we have dubbed these crisis months as the 'early phases'. However, a midsummer hypercrisis in conformity with expectations occurred only in 1795. There were no attempts, even at the regional level during the 'early phase' of 1795 to investigate stocks. The Mayor of Coventry conducted a cursory local enquiry in response to riots, but his Newcastle-upon-Tyne counterpart rejected similar suggestions as 'it would alarm the Country'. Predictions of imminent severe shortages in Yorkshire in March '95 were dismissed as 'but local' by an eminent authority, despite mounting evidence to the contrary from elsewhere. In August, complaints that the public had been misled 'with an idea of large stores in the hands of monopolising Farmers, Factors and Millers', peddled by the press, were justified. The midsummer hypercrisis was aggravated by a panic which would have been less intense if the impending exhaustion of stocks had been authenticated by thorough investigations during the spring.[23]

Localised fears of a midsummer hypercrisis in 1800 were articulated, and in view of the 1795 precedent were neither surprising nor fanciful. Big farmers who supplied the important exchange at Devizes responded to public claims of withholding stocks, with a professional surveyor's report confirming that current stocks were half of those usually held in April.[24] But in 1800, authorities even in regions which had suffered grievously in 1795, were confident that they could get by with imports bolstering home supplies.[25] If events confirmed this, the explanation emerges from contrasting 1800 with 1795. In the summer of the latter year, agents from hundreds of towns and even villages, backed by huge funds, joined a nationwide scramble for cereals.[26] Only a handful of towns did the same in 1800, and the superfluity of the move is seen in the expenditure of under half the £600 fund earmarked by York Corporation for cereal purchase.[27] The availability of imported grain prevented the repetition of the scramble in 1800. In the summer, huge volumes of foreign grain were unloaded on to the market, and the same factor also prevented midsummer hypercrises in 1796 and 1801. Market nerves were also soothed by favourable harvest predictions; these proved realistic in these latter two years but not in 1800, and underlaid the dramatic developments in the autumn which we will shortly describe. In addition, high grain prices automatically reduced cereal consumption, and supported government policy to the same end. Paradoxically, prices rose much higher in 1800 (and in 1796 and 1801) than in 1795. But outside the South-west, where recurrent exposure to severe shortages warrants specific analysis, these even higher prices *did not* reflect the critical exhaustion of stocks as they did across the summer of 1795.

These contrasts must not obscure a feature common to all four famine seasons. The significance of non-cereal components of plebeian dietaries has been emphasised, and the supplies of these commodities did not oscillate similarly to grain. Root production was hit by the summer drought of 1800, but the serious potato deficiency of 1800–1 was unique. Dairy and meat supplies are difficult to assess. Provisioning for the armed forces introduced unknown difficulties with the Smithfield statistical series. But there can be little doubt that meat and dairy products on the open market were reduced throughout the second famine, drastically so with bacon, the meat most widely consumed in significant quantities by workers. Price series for bacon – as opposed to evidential snippets – are unavailable, but some factors

indicate the probable collapse in supply. Rising oat and provender prices led
many owners to kill their horses, and even a country clergyman unseasonal-
ly killed his fowls when he had no feed corn, and was unable to buy any at a
'moderate price'. Parallel problems struck small and large pig-rearers, while
the prohibition of distilling, and the steep decline in brewing, must have
decimated the supply of pigs, commonly fattened on a considerable scale as
a lucrative sideline by alcohol manufacturers. The prices of all foodstuffs
rose, and rose greatly. Detailed evidence is fragmentary, but adequate to
inclusion in our cost-of-living indices. These also prove that when grain
prices reached their highest levels, the majority of workers' incomes were
unequal to the costs of cereal dietary components alone. This feature
invokes the authority of the Giffen factor, and while escalating costs of
non-cereals cannot be ignored, their consumption was an immediate victim
of famine-induced plebeian economising. Therefore, the study of the
impact of famine on consumers, must concentrate on cereals.[28]

'Bread is not to be had at any Price': the Midsummer Hypercrisis of 1795

Escalating prices during the spring maintained their upward momentum
through May; in June, the supply to many centres of consumption began to
collapse. Metropolitan bakers had no reserves; the usual stocks at the
wharves had gone, and 'as fast as any Vessels . . . arrived with Flour it was
immediately loaded away in Carts to the Bakers Shops'. This situation
intensified in July. Every centre of consumption experienced the threat, and
many experienced exhaustion, nowhere more acutely than in the Midlands.
Leicester was relatively well-off, but panic occurred when estimates revealed stocks adequate to less than a fortnight's demand. The confusion
generated was typified by conflicting reports from Nottingham; one
claimed that no wheat was available on 18 July, while another stated that
twenty-three quarters were sold, which was nevertheless hopelessly short
of the four hundred quarters normally consumed weekly. On 22 July
Coventry's traders had stocks equal to three weeks' consumption, but no
additional supplies were expected for six weeks. In Birmingham, perhaps
the hardest-hit centre, flour prices doubled during July, and bakers ceased
production. A relief committee was reduced to limit sales of maize to seven
pounds per applicant. Fourteen thousand people were estimated to be at
serious risk, namely the 'great Numbers, who have not a Morcel of Bread'.
On 5 August at Stourbridge, 'Bread is not to be had at any Price'.[29]
   Similar phenomena afflicted the North slightly later. On 20 July,
Newcastle-upon-Tyne had enough for two weeks, but the situation was
complicated by the 'very pressing' competition for stocks for villages in the
coalfields. On 5 August, Hull's greater mealmen declared they would have
to 'stop their mills' irrespective of 'the consequences . . . from the violence
of the populace'. Dealers' stocks at Sheffield had gone, and the bakers were
reduced to a precarious dependence on inadequate supplies from an
emergency committee. Across the Pennines, serious shortages materialised
in all the cotton towns. Wheat was unavailable at Whitehaven at the end of
July, and in the following week Workington had no corn of any descrip-

tion. However, the northern situation was not universally so serious, and the hypercrisis was shorter than in the Midlands. A massive consignment of oats enabled the Mayor of Leeds publicly to dismiss 'a real Scarcity of Wholesome Provision', and oats also proved the saviour at Halifax. In mid-August, the Earl of Lonsdale toured northern marts; serious deficiencies at Carlisle had receded, at Penrith 'Plenty of ev'ry Thing' was available, and if there was still 'very little' corn in big exchanges at Doncaster, Ferrybridge, Wetherby and Richmond, an imminent improvement was predicted.[30]

Nobody could foretell in June that the hypercrisis would strike hardest in the Midlands, the North, and the South-west. No region *felt* immune from starvation. Supplies were universally fragile; delicate equilibriums could vanish overnight. Shropshire farmers who customarily sent stocks through Chester for Lancashire, responded to riots in Cheshire, by diverting supplies to Shrewsbury for shipment to Worcester and Gloucester. Long-distance supply routes closed quickly, and in July short-distance channels followed, leaving even minor consumer centres like Scarborough suddenly exposed to serious shortages. Elsewhere, normal distribution patterns were crash-geared into reverse. At Bristol, for example, customary supplies from the city's north-western hinterland, magically evaporated, and agents from Monmouthshire and Gloucestershire tried to purchase stocks in Bristol to send back up the Severn and the Wye.[31] Another dimension to the hypercrisis revealed itself once victualling contractors, who had the best commercial contacts, and whose stability and capacity were rigorously vetted prior to the award of government contracts, experienced problems.[32] Those who honoured their obligations incurred heavy losses. Others were forced to break their contracts. A Woolwich baker who supplied bread to the naval yards and the Royal Artillery defaulted, and the non-receipt of rations by troops stationed in the North-east finally elicited the contractor's admission that he despaired of securing further stocks and would cease all operations within the week.[33]

The collapse of national, regional and local marketing systems in July[34] precipitated uniform reactions in greater and lesser centres[35] of consumption throughout the country. The affluent subscribed considerable sums, which were augmented by Corporate and poor-law funds, to finance bulk purchases of grain. Agents concentrated their efforts in the major ports. Bristol, Liverpool, Newcastle, Hull, and above all London, were obviously the most appropriate, not least because the bulk of government corn was sold there. Competition intensified; uncertainties increased. 'Proper agents', representing Nottingham, were 'sent to the various Ports', but the borough's *ad hoc* emergency committee was unable to predict success. Buyers from Birmingham at Hull, Bristol and Liverpool, obtained only maize at the latter. Agents from eighty-five towns failed to buy any wheat at Hull on 7 July; some purchased oats, and at Bristol buyers representing Stourbridge tried for a week to secure grain, before settling for salted bacon and pork. The chairman of the town's committee gloomily, but typically, concluded that 'every . . . Exertion appears inadequate'. As these efforts were primarily inspired by the urban bourgeoisie, easy access to professional commercialists was common. But this was not invariable, as represented by the letter of introduction given to the overseer of Windle (Cheshire) to support his quest for 'a little Barley' at Liverpool; 'he is a Stranger to the Business', and needed all the help he could get. And so the scramble started.[36]

Millers and dealers also gravitated to the major exchanges. The four biggest millers at Dover depended almost exclusively on Mark Lane from June, as did many of their Essex counterparts, once their home county was exhausted by supplying London. Other millers, including one from south Hampshire, anxiously applied to metropolitan contacts to enquire if any supplies at Mark Lane were 'for sale coastwise'. Ironically, many London buyers were simultaneously scouring provincial markets. Baker Lovell managed to buy 1544 sacks of flour but only after 'several journeys' across East Anglia. Frustrated agents who failed in the ports, also scoured large and small inland marts, and were soon literally scouring the countryside too, visiting farmers. All available stocks in the Chilterns and Cotswolds were snapped up by itinerant buyers; there was no haggling over prices. Stocks were instantly shipped by canal to Birmingham or by the Thames to London. Desperation is also revealed by approaches made to every conceivable contact, even the implausible. A Warwickshire dealer, pleaded by letter with a Burford surgeon 'to ask the Millers . . . if any of them could supply him with forty-five Sacks of Flour per Week . . . in consequence' of the dealer's wife having been treated by the doctor 'some years ago'.[37]

This exhaustion had been predicted by many farmers, millers and dealers in the producing regions. Indeed, agreements to terminate sales in distant exchanges in favour of reserving stocks for the locality had been taken in April in West Sussex and, in May, in western Somerset.[38] In June, and more especially July, the appearance of itinerant buyers in the countryside extended the panic to the producing regions. 'Smaller farmers' in East Anglia were 'buying Flour' for their own consumption at the end of June, and this clear manifestation of impending exhaustion was repeatedly confirmed by the natural propensity in the early summer to mount semi- and official enquiries in the villages to establish whether stocks were adequate to parochial demand until the harvest. Such investigations exposed a host of local disparities. Only eight of the thirty-two component parishes of the Norfolk Hundreds of Shropham and Guiltcross had a clear sufficiency; thirteen manifestly did not, and the real situation in the remainder was confused. In aggregate, in the first week in July, the residue would suffice only for 'another fortnight . . . which reduces us to great difficulties', the more so as all agreed that the harvest must be late. In Hertfordshire, some hope was generated by a mid-July report that '2 or 3 . . . considerable Farmers' had 'large Quantities of Wheat which they hold back notwith-standing the present enormous price', but realistically, panic could not be averted by rumour. Nobody in the producing regions could be certain of a sufficiency, even at the local level. The reaction, most pronounced in that massive tract of country between the Thames and the Trent, which contained the premier East Anglian cornlands, soon constituted a rural blockade, typified by the Birdchanger (Essex) vestry's decision on 30 June. All stock remaining in farmers' hands was to be bought by the vestry for sale at subsidised prices to working people. The village oligarchs further resolved and unanimously agreed . . . that no Person within the Parish having Wheat in his Possession shall or will send the same or any Part thereof to any Person until it has been offered to

the overseer of the poor. This widespread initiative augured badly for the centres of consumption.[39]

The fact that several other Essex parishes, like scores in Berkshire, calculated simultaneously that cash supplements, as opposed to stock conservation, would enable plebeian villagers to survive the summer, suggests that the agricultural regions were not uniformly exhausted.[40] But the blockade nevertheless had an immediate impact. On 23 July, the Mayor of Leicester reported that his position deteriorated further once 'Many Villages . . . at public Meetings entered into Resolutions not to suffer any more Corn to be removed . . . till after the ensuing Harvest'. Such parochial decisions triggered further moves, notably in market towns and ports in the producing regions, to follow suit once their own supplies were jeopardised. The Great Yarmouth Corporation convened on 15 July to consider 'the alarming prospect of Famine', and 'determined to stop the sending away, any more Wheat or Flour'. Lincoln 'merchants, millers and bakers' autonomously reached an identical decision, whereas their counterparts at Burford were peremptorily ordered by a clerical magistrate to cease secretive despatches to the industrial Midlands, as the local 'Poor are in great Want'.[41]

Nobody knew how drained the country was; reports conflicted, and further confusion accompanied the blockade's extension by populist mobilisations. Birmingham's confidence that a 'sufficient quantity of Wheat and Flour' could be obtained from Oxfordshire and Northamptonshire appeared to be confirmed once 'great Quantities' were released with shipments receiving army escorts. Informed metropolitan opinion insisted that London's problems could be eased by supplies from the Home Counties and East Anglia, but such confidence was shaken when authorities, including the Mayor of Wells in Norfolk, confiscated stocks actually owned by a Londoner and arbitrarily sold them to the town's famished workers.[42] In such conditions panic spread through a multiplicity of often contradictory chain reactions. Some urban authorities paid bounties to suppliers; others stopped non-residents buying. The Mayor of Bristol prevented millers from outside the city resorting to its markets, and his counterparts at Exeter and Cambridge extended the prohibition even to consumers domiciled in adjacent villages. The government secretly intervened to prevent Mark Lane operators from selling to anybody who did not normally supply London.[43] A miscellany of lesser authorities also pitched in with advice, appeals and injunctions. The Berkshire Bench formally encouraged 'all Farmers and Landlords to bring such Wheat as they can spare from the necessary Consumption of their Families, Workmen and Neighbours to some Neighbouring Market'. They were immediately imitated by their Oxfordshire colleagues. Lord Howard inundated his part of Essex with posters enjoining those who 'without prejudice to their own Parishes' could provision Saffron Walden, to do so. Estate-agent Black threatened tenants who refused to obey his parallel injunction with 'a forfeiture of the Landlords good Will and Mine'.[44]

A mass of evidence reveals consumers literally living from hand-to-mouth in many localities, which were devoid of stocks, and uncertain of the source of the morrow's bread. A Maidenhead tradesman who 'baked an extraordinary batch' on a Sunday to serve Saturday's unsatisfied customers, was suddenly inundated by eager clients, and the last loaf was quickly sold to a lady who had travelled several miles. Temporary, but normal, hindrances, assumed a new character. Customary problems with low water levels could terminate flour supplies, because millers had no reserves. When they stopped their mills, customers went without. One miller so circumstanced sent a parcel of grain to be ground at another mill, but the proprietor highjacked the stock and sold it to his own clamourous clients. Dealers received heart-rending appeals 'for what you are pleased to allow' without a mention of price limits. When Saffron Walden ordered two hundred quarters of wheat from Cambridge, they obtained fifty of oats and ten of boiling peas. Rather belatedly, some favourably placed authorities tried to import on their own account; massive funds of five and seven thousand pounds were raised at Hull and Norwich respectively. But the majority restricted their efforts to the home market. Frantic competition served only to intensify and spread the panic, and to drive the prices of available parcels to unheard of levels. The West Riding Bench subsequently advised against repetition as experience proved that 'so many parishes laying in supplies at the same period' served to escalate prices, erode confidence and generate panic. The midsummer hypercrisis of 1795 was dominated by ruthless competition between localities to secure portions of a rapidly vanishing national stock of corn.[45] The contrasts between the summers of 1795 and 1800 are most dramatically revealed by the behaviour of wheat prices, presented in Figures 1 and 3. Wheat more than doubled in price between May and July 1795, but in the same period in 1800 they essentially stabilised at an unprecedented level.

'The Seller is . . . the Master of the Market': the Panic during the Autumn of 1800

Another hypercrisis between late August and November 1800 was caused by market conditions which were operative only to a lesser degree in the autumn of 1795. Despite differences both periods partially conformed to Adam Smith's dictum that supply difficulties in shortage years were commonly at their worst 'immediately after the harvest, when scarce any of the new crop can be sold off'. However, while prices peaked in June and July 1795, these months in 1800 witnessed market falls owing to imports and anticipations of a decent harvest. In June 1795 relief agencies engaged top gear; in June 1800 relief operations closed down. There are, however, greater comparabilities between August 1795 and August 1800. Prices fell, not least because of the release of remaining stocks in expectation of further price declines as some newly-harvested grain reached the markets. In 1800, especially, farmers 'looked forward to a falling Market' and even sold seed corn at the end of July as current prices 'were too alluring to be resisted'. Expectations of a rapid return to normality in August 1800, constituted a national 'happy Prospectus' according to one MP.[46]

This confidence was misplaced in 1795 and 1800, and if it was more exaggerated in the latter, the exhaustion of old stocks was operative on prices in both autumns. This exhaustion was universally confirmed by responses to a government enqury late in 1800.[47] The storms in mid-August eliminated anticipated advantages, and induced a commercial panic. The rain delayed harvesting, and in places damaged thin crops and terminated millers' hopes of replenishing their empty granaries with speedily harvested and threshed grain. In early August, buyers had shown great 'disinclination' to purchase more than was needed for immediate use, in expectation of further price falls. In mid-August some urgency is seen; by the 25th, continued wet weather precipitated a panic as buyers were caught 'entirely out of stock'. By 1 September London was 'bare of Flour almost beyond precedent', and most other large consumer centres were identically circumstanced. On 7 September the twenty-nine greatest Nottingham bakers had under thirty quarters of wheat and twenty-six sacks of flour between them; eight more had none. 'Not an ounce' of flour was to be had in industrial Bilston on 13 September, and ten days later, Birmingham had under a week's consumption. 'Flour was [still] not to be purchased at any price' in the Wolverhampton district at the start of October. Sheffield authorities quickly appreciated that rain negated any chance of an improvement from local sources, and urged public tranquillity to 'encourage a supply from distant parts'. Midland and many northern towns were suddenly and ferociously struck by extreme scarcities.[48]

Sheffield's strategy was compromised as prices rocketed everywhere, even if severe shortages were primarily experienced in the biggest centres. 'The Seller', at every stage in the provision trade, according to the President of the Board of Trade, 'is in fact the Master of the Market'. A flour-factor confirmed that the supply situation would 'not enable the buyers to make a successful resistance'. Scores of big purchasers flocked to Mark Lane from the provinces, but this only served to perpetuate pressures: 'the buyers' were repeatedly 'very numerous, and urgent, especially for wheat' throughout November and December, when there was still 'not that abundance from any quarter that had been expected'. The fine autumnal season also diverted agriculturalists from threshing and marketing, to threshing and sowing unusually great acreages with wheat. Farmers requiring seed competed with millers in marts in the main arable regions, thus aggravating the effect of prolonged supply paucities. Corn merchants at Northampton, an important inland exchange, had a novel experience on 20 October; 'before they could always buy corn at some price . . . but on that day they could not . . . at any price'. Such conditions also encouraged farmers to market little even if withholding necessitated borrowing. Farmers at Devizes maintained prices and liquidity, by regular but small sales of their best wheat. Repeated complaints at denuded markets were made, especially in the cornlands. Farmers swelled with confidence, revealed for example by open assertions in Yorkshire even after the bumper crops of 1801, that '"If our Stocks are untouched till Midsummer [1802] Corn will then advance"' beyond the dizzy heights at which they peaked in the spring of 1801. Ironically, a greater percentage of the 1800 crop was used earlier in the

1800–1 season than usual, owing to exhaustion of stocks prior to the harvest, the huge volumes required for seed, and the deficient yield.[49]

Similar but less pronounced market forces in the autumn of 1795, produced a better supply at less inflated prices. The recurrent failure of the supply to meet Mark Lane demand, complaints at the practices of purchasing standing corn, and withholding by farmers, together with agriculturalists' anticipation of further, severe shortages later in the 1795–6 season, all testify to the delicacy of the supply between September and December 1795.[50] Ephemeral price falls in January 1796 (paralleled in 1801) reflected commercial expectations of supply improvements once the agrarian workforce concentrated on threshing. In the event these were not realised; prices regained their upward momentum in the springs of 1796 and 1801, but severe shortages materialised only in the uniquely circumstanced South-west. Nationally, the situation in the 1795–6 season was eased by ample supplies of barley and oats. In 1801, the operation of a new Parochial Relief Act, which encouraged the public provision of cereal substitutes, also reduced some market pressure on wheat. Although some towns made wholesale purchases of cereals in the autumn of 1800, there was no repetition of the midsummer scramble of 1795, nor was their any recurrence of the blockade. Birmingham raised four thousand pounds in mid-September 1800, and although purchases took a month, organisers were subsequently confident that the desperate situation experienced in September would not recur. Rising spring prices in both 1796 and 1801 ostensibly threatened renewed midsummer hypercrises, but they were avoided by massive imports and good harvest prospects proving accurate. If prices declined more slowly in 1801 than in 1796, few doubted that the dangers passed during both summers. In stark contrast to identical expectations in 1795 and 1800, they were realised.[51]

'"They cannot ship us Wheat on any Terms"': Regions of Consumption and the Incidence of Severe Shortages

The South-west's recurrent exposure to severe shortages warrants analysis in its own right, but the mechanics of the phenomenon were common to every region which experienced the problem, and were also responsible for roughly comparable characteristics. Devastating shortages afflicted the South-west in each spring, in 1795, 1796, 1800 and 1801. Their severity was greatest in 1795 because they persisted into the summer. The region, as we have emphasised, ultimately depended on supplies from the east. Crises were precipitated when these failed to arrive, though the causes of failure varied.

In 1795, the traders who organised these supplies experienced intensifying problems from March. Merchants in the South, notably in Hampshire and Sussex, had their own difficulties, and they responded by abandoning their South-western markets even to the extent of severing contracts. Popular disturbances in the South, which aimed to stop coastal grain traffic, were one cause, but once these were contained by late April, southern suppliers had less remaining inducement to serve the South-west. The local harvest was significantly earlier than most, and any difficulties with shipping might result in cereals from the South competing in south-western marts with new Cornish and Devon grain, or be subjected to falling prices in anticipation of the local harvest. From May, southern entrepreneurs preferred their own local exchanges, and London, and made commensurate new contracts, thus commercially isolating the south-west. This reduced south-western businessmen to frantic *ad hoc* bargaining with anybody, anywhere. Certainly, mineowners could satisfy one major source of Cornish demand, by making wholesale purchases to feed their own employees. Such moves, together with considerable sales of government stocks at Plymouth from March, helped, though the supply became increasingly fragile. In June, in several Cornish markets, 'the last Grain of Barley was delivered out, and Numbers of the Poor went home without any'. Anguished appeals followed; a Penzance merchant, then in London, was told that 'Pease or any thing eatable would be a great relief'.[52] Thereafter, monumental supply problems were overshadowed only by their effect:

> Twenty Bags of Flour were purchased at Truro about a fortnight since. Four of them were distributed immediately. Eight more . . . last week and yesterday we were obliged to give the Poor half allowance only Four Bags that we might reserve the other four till next week . . . not a pennyworth of Bread can be purchased in the Town.

'By cutting loaves and selling it by the pound and half pound', Barnstaple bakers sold bread 'reserved for their own Families to get rid of the sollicitations of the famished multitude'.[53]

Later collapses in the vital long-distance supply routes had different causes. South-western farmers increasingly preferred regional markets to sales of early barley to maltsters at a distance. The best evidence, for 1801, clearly the region's worst year, does not conflict with what is known about 1796 and 1800. In 1801, the long distance trade failed owing to the regional harvest's effect on local prices. There was no autumn crisis in 1800, and south-western centres of consumption drew immediately and exclusively on local produce. Regional prices consistently remained significantly below those current nationally until April 1801. South-western markets failed to attract their customary supply; as one resident put it, 'our Harvest has been abundant . . . & our Market lower than any in the Kingdom in consequence we are left to subsist ourselves'. Even 'the immense consumption of Plymouth' was 'virtually . . . supplied by the Growth of Devon'. Fragile winter-time supplies produced 'most critical situations' with stocks at Plymouth regularly reduced to two days' supply.[54]

The crisis point occurred in March and April. A local observer's point could have applied to any region of consumption: 'the greatest Scarcity has of course taken place in the districts which lie nearest to the centres of Consumption', which in the south-western case, also included the Cornish mining areas. By this point in the season, the producing parishes were also exhausted. An investigation into the Hundred immediately east of Plymouth revealed insufficient barley for the nineteen constituent parishes, and a miniscule wheaten 'overplus' unequal to one week's consumption at Plymouth. The Mayor of Bideford's local enquiry produced similar conclusions; not one in twenty farmers in the hinterland had any marketable surplus of potatoes, and only one in ten had barley surplus to the requirements of their home villages. Thereupon, the situation worsened rapidly in the centres: 'the Goods brought now are really scrambled for and many families go without'.[55]

Regional reactions comprised a microcosm of national responses to the mid-summer hypercrisis of 1795. Scores of local agents scoured first the locality, and then the district, in search of stocks. Many villages imposed blockades, thus throwing long-distance supply routes into sharper perspective. Stocks from afar did not materialise at all in 1795; in 1801 they did, but not until after the widespread imposition of price ceilings by the crowd was belatedly overthrown. Then, and only then, did the unfettered operation of the free market permit South-western prices to rise above those current to the east, in order to attract a supply.[56]

                              *   *   *

If we commence by looking at the second half of the eighteenth century – the long-term perspective – the famines of 1794–6 and 1799–1801 were the most extreme manifestations of the increasingly obvious fact that population growth had outstripped the agrarian productive capacity of the British Isles. However, seasonal factors meant that the equalisation of the supply with the demand for cereals created an inconsistent problematic for the mechanics of the free internal marketing system. In normal circumstances, major shortfalls in the supply could be accommodated by an immeasurable deflation of demand through the price factor, and more importantly, through the importation of stocks adequate to meeting the residual deficiency. Between 1750 and 1790 overseas corn trade statistics reveal considerable importations which coincide with seriously deficient home yields, and were clearly responsible for the relatively rapid restoration and maintenance of equilibrium.[57] The declaration of war in February 1793 undermined the confidence generated by these successful precedents, but this was initially mediated by the impossibility of accurate predictions over indigenous cereal productivity, and the potential disturbance to global grain markets by military operations *and* interventions by governments. Thus responses to harvest deficiencies beginning in 1794 were essentially slow, none more so than the actual behaviour of prices in English markets. The result of these retarded reactions – which include the uncertainties responsible for the crucial delays in securing imports in 1794–5 which we examine in detail in chapter 11 – was the mid-summer hypercrisis of 1795. A combination of stock exhaustion, a deficient wheat harvest, and continuing uncertainties over the availability of imports, served to prolong the crisis. Wheat prices rose, after a temporary fall, throughout the winter before falling significantly in March and April 1796. Barley and oat prices moved broadly in sympathy across 1795–6, but their greater productivity doubtlessly explains their failure to rise proportionately to wheat, a phenomenon common to all markets as shown by comparing Figures 2, 6, and 10.

The prices of all major cereals failed to fall to either their pre-war, or pre-famine levels during the 1796–7 and 1797–8 seasons.[58] Although the successful, indeed record, importation in 1796 restored confidence in the potential of overseas sources for national subsistence even in wartime, the experiences of 1794 were clearly one engine powering the medium term inflation of food prices during the first stage of the war. The second famine fuelled this general inflation and stimulated the increasing dependency on imports. The average annual price of wheat was 64 shillings per quarter between 1791 and 1800, and 84 shillings between 1801 and 1810, while average annual net importations of wheat were 425 thousand quarters during the earlier decade, and 691 thousand during the later. Prices during the second famine show several distinct characteristics. All cereal prices, as shown by Figures 3, 7 and 11, accelerated much earlier and faster in the 1799–1800 season, and from the spring of 1800 retained their unprecedented levels almost throughout, dropping significantly (and ephemerally) only in August. The least proportionate rise was again experienced by oats, though a degree of volatility was periodically experienced in some markets, for example when oats actually cost more than barley. (Compare Figures 7 and 11.) Such price declines as were registered in September 1800, were rapidly reversed; the upward spirals during the autumn were continued across the winter. April 1801 saw a significant fall in all cereal prices, though May witnessed renewed inflation of wheat, before the long-term fall which set in during July and August continued throughout the remainder of the year. Average annual wheat prices in 1800 and 1801 were both just over double their equivalent in 1797; the barley and oat counterparts were even more spectacular, with barley up on 1797 by 222 and 255 percent respectively, and oats by 244 and 231 percent.

Figures 1 to 12 are derived from the statistics returned by the official market inspectorate. We have previously established grounds for treating these with caution. The pronounced relative lowness of Malton prices may with some certainty be attributed to the stranglehold established by the town's cartel of buyers. Birmingham's more pronounced higher prices series probably reflect its inland location and the huge scale of demand, but other, and principally obscure factors probably distort the figures. The mid-summer hypercrisis of 1795 revealed that many dealers derived their supplies through contracting with merchants and millers based in the producing regions and not through the Birmingham market. The volumes of grain entering the inspectorate's accounts are unknown, as is the town's relative importance as a market (as opposed to its consumption) for barley, the price of which appears to be an uneconomic exaggeration. However, despite their detailed imperfections, the statistics represented in these Figures, clearly reveal the integration of markets throughout the country. Price trends are unquestionably uniform, and these would naturally extend through each individual market's hinterland, be it principally urban and/or industrial, or rural. The literary evidence is overwhelmingly categoric that London was the key market, and the most sensitive barometer for the cost of the nation's subsistence. London *demand* was the paramount factor, and this is reflected for example in the generally slightly lower prices current at any one moment in markets closely allied to it, including Colchester and

Chichester in our Figures.

Prices are of course important, but they also tend to conceal significant components of famine conditions. Ironically, prices are not an invariable guide to market conditions. Prices current during the mid-summer hyper-crisis of 1795 are *not* an adequate reflection of the supply situation. Prices were much higher during the spring and summer of 1800 when there were no comparable problems with the volume of grain available. Prices remained below their early summer peak in 1800 throughout September, when many major towns experienced severe difficulties in obtaining volumes remotely adequate to demand. This element serves as a reminder that the famines were punctuated by 'national' physical shortages in the summer of 1795 and the early autumn of 1800, and 'absolute shortages' posed almost perennial problems for the South-west. But the relative rarity of such shortages cannot be mobilised against the identification of famine in the 1790s. For these famine periods exposed consumers to very lengthy periods of sustained very high food prices. Their cumulative impact on consumers is therefore of even greater significance than the incidence of 'absolute scarcity' in contemporary perception and parlance.

CHAPTER 4

'Many an honest man doeth not know how to get one Week or Day over'
The Reality of Famine in Wartime

If upper-class contemporaries principally eschewed the word 'famine', historians, notably those who belong unashamedly or covertly to the 'optimistic school', exude a cavalier attitude to subsistence problems in the age of the industrial revolution. For example, Dr Hayter, studying the deployment of the army as a police force in 'mid-Georgian England', opines that 'the real famine years in the strictest sense of the word had become a thing of the past'; such confidence surely precludes the possibility in later Georgian England.[1] Certain historians have advanced statistical criteria, derived from price-movements, to denote famine conditions. Professor Mitchison decides that 'price rises of 100 percent or more . . . indicate famine, and 75 to 100 per cent indicate severe shortage'. Although Mitchison exhibits some sensitivity with the recognition that famine is an appropriate description when 'the bulk of the population are in danger of starvation and face the certainty of undernourishment', her dependency on prices is another exemplar of that 'crass economic reductionism' which riles social historians.[2] Professor Smout is more wary; food shortages do not invariably generate demographic disturbance in general, or mortality crises in particular.[3] Dr Appleby even challenges orthodox identifications of causal relationships between dearth and disease.[4] Dr Stevenson is also impressed by evidential problems, notably 'the precise contribution of high prices . . . to mortality increases'. While he accepts that subsistence problems caused localised mortality crises in the 1720s, and in many regions in the 1766–7 dearth, he is more impressed by the higher national mortalities of 1795 and 1800 (and 1816) not meeting the demographers' criteria for a *crise de subsistence*. Stevenson, in common with other experts on the 1790s, acknowledges that 'there is ample evidence from contemporary sources that high prices produced distress', but concludes, with special reference to southern England, that food disturbances are 'more plausibly placed within the context of scarcity, high prices, and resentment than of major demographic crises'. 'They were price riots, rather than reactions to famine'.[5]

These opinions partly reflect the absence of an acceptable definition of famine. We are heavily indebted to Dr Oddy for a sensitive appraisal, and a workmanlike typology of famine.[6] Oddy correctly points out that 'famine' and 'starvation' are 'two quite distinct phenomena', and any equation of the two, including the use of 'the terms . . . interchangeably', comprises a cardinal error. Oddy endorses M.W. Flinn's conclusion that 'even in a famine relatively few deaths could be directly attributed to starvation'.[7] Oddy suggests that the 'principal characteristics of a true famine' are 'food shortages' (whether caused by a 'major disruption of earnings' due to serious under- or unemployment, or by defective food supplies), nutritional deficiencies, an epidemical spread of infectious disease, causing widespread illness, and even death. His famine typology has four components. First, restricted diet, principally owing to inadequate incomes, and limited food supplies, can strike both the unskilled and skilled working population. The effects include food cravings, low nutritional status, and physical inertia. The 'at risk' portion of the population comprise children whose physical growth may be retarded, and pregnant and lactating women. The second category, 'psycho-social famine', derives from harvest failure, market disequilibrium and/or recession-induced loss of incomes, which strike entire communities, hitting wage-earners hardest: fear of hunger, social disorder and 'psychogenic morbidity' comprise the main effects. 'Nutritional or true famine' is the third component, caused by a 'failure of market response', and what Oddy describes as a 'lack' or 'breakdown of emergency systems'. Such situations represent an intensification of the second category, and there is considerable variation in the status of those affected, though women, children and the elderly are generally at the greatest risk. Hunger and morbidity, with nutritional deficiency diseases becoming widespread, and aggravated by reduced resistance to infection, are the most notable effects. Oddy's fourth component, 'starvation' strikes the isolated family or individual; fertility is reduced, rapid physical degeneration commences, and death follows. Oddy disclaims that this represents a 'chronology of famine', principally because it excludes 'recovery phases which follow famine'. We might add that many thousands of people in late eighteenth-century England were more or less permanently in the first, 'restricted diet' category; large families, especially where adult male incomes were low, and demand for female and child labour unpronounced, and where family supplements from the rates were not paid (and they were not extensively paid regularly anywhere in England before the 1790s), principally compose this category. In agrarian regions characterised by low pay and pronounced underemployment, especially, if not exclusively, in southern and eastern counties, even men with small families came into this perennial category. It was surely no accident that employers provided food during the harvest. Otherwise employees' common physical inefficiency[8] could have seriously undermined the harvesting operation with its necessity for sustained hard work throughout the hours of daylight. If these groups were thrown into Oddy's second typological category by rising food prices, and the speed and scale of them were severe, a huge sector of the entire working class was soon precipitated into the 'psycho-social famine' category. A combination of factors in both 1794–6 and 1799, propelled some of these into the 'true famine' situation. Food prices alone determined this development, as will be proved in our cost of living calculations.

The similar developments which transpired during both famines exhibit quantifiable differences of degree. *Excessive prices* were common features. So too were the *relentless cumulative pressures imposed by the lengthy durations of high prices*. They attained greater heights and endured longer in 1799–1801, than in 1794–6. In the midst of these lengthy episodes came shorter periods of critical shortages when obtaining any cereal at any price proved difficult. These intervening spasms of hypercrisis reveal dissimilarities. That of the summer of '95 affected, be it unevenly, the entire country. Its September 1800 successor was confined to regions of consumption. The South-west proved exceptional owing to recurrent absolute scarcities. But the impact of high food prices was aggravated by other economic factors, paramount among which was industrial recession, which added the horrors of under- and unemployment to those caused by spiralling prices. Trade recessions were not universal, and their regional impact requires analysis. Moreover, the famines and related phenomena occurred in a period of broad, long-term economic change.

General inflation occurred throughout the nineties; war was the primary cause. In the early years, Pitt raised a disproportionate amount of public finance through loans, which eventually 'strained' the money market. 'Credit inflation associated with heavy war expenditure and government borrowing' initially stimulated 'prices in general', and further inflationary pressures occurred when the unfunded debt peaked. The Bank crisis of 1797, triggered by the panic at the French landing in Wales, exposed the essential fragility of Pitt's financial policies when the many holders rushed to cash the 'huge volume of short-term bills' issued by the government. The immediate suspension of specie payments was no more than an emergency measure. New fiscal measures, the most innovatory, though not the most productive, being the income tax, saw revenue from 'taxation greatly exceed proceeds from loans', which constituted 'a heroic effort to keep the national debt within bounds'. But if the 'drastic fiscal policy' of Pitt and his successors, after 1797, operated to retard further depreciation of the pound, the huge expenditure on foreign corn in 1796, and especially in 1800 and 1801, helped turn foreign exchanges against the pound, thereby adding an additional inflationary ingredient. The contribution of war funding to inflation across the entire 1793 to 1815 period has been exaggerated, but its inflationary effects until 1801 have not. Periodic famine-food prices produced further inflationary twists.[9]

Eighteenth-century historians perceive a close relationship between short-term economic cycles and food prices. High subsistence prices reduced demand for manufactured goods, because working and some middle-class consumers were forced to increase significantly the proportions of income expended on food, thereby reducing expenditure on non-food items. Demand for service industries was also reduced.[10] But general, and food-price induced inflation, escalating indirect and direct taxation, were not the only factors complicating economic performance in the nineties. 'Any increase in the size of the [national] budget . . . increased aggregate demand by an amount approximately equal to the increase in government spending on domestically produced goods', irrespective of changes in the ratio of loans and taxes as revenue sources. The argument that government borrowing reduced investment funds, and when combined with enhanced taxation decreased 'the capacity both to consume and invest by reducing disposable income' is not sustained for the decade. A considerable proportion of loans and taxes came from 'past savings which would otherwise have remained idle'. Thus increased borrowing and taxation enhanced demand because government spending on the artefacts of war injected dormant money into the economy; 'half the military expenditures were for British produced manufactured goods.' Moreover, 'much of the money borrowed was fed into the "circulation of credit" so important for the finance of manufacturing'. Government bonds proved 'a reasonably liquid asset, readily used as collateral for business borrowing'.[11] Buoyant investment in the nineties in key industries, notably iron, engineering, and woollen and cotton textiles, sustains this fundamental thesis.[12]

The erosion of confidence in the Rostovian thesis of 'take-off' into sustained economic growth in the late eighteenth century, has not altered historical perceptions of boom conditions extending into the 1790s from the 1780s. If the massive expansion of cottons alone had neither the power to induce rapid growth throughout the economy, nor fundamentally to break through allegedly restrictive investment levels, the most dynamic sectors of the economy certainly had significant regional effects. Prosperity in the northern textile industries, underpinned by significant investment, symbolised if not typified by Blake's dark satanic mills, galvanised closely integrated industries. For example, Yorkshire iron, provided many tools used in textiles. 'Coal is intimately connected with cheap bleaching', wrote an industrialist, who could have extended the observation to include further textile processes, and additional industries. All industrial growth stimulated the brickmaking and building industries. Marked change was not restricted to textiles. Steel-rolling was revolutionised by Cort, smelting was accelerated by coke, and steam-power made miscellaneous inroads. Moreover, although the reality of technological change and redundancy made repeated appearances in textiles, and the spectre was diffused in fears felt in the many trades in these dynamic regional economies, many technological innovations increased rather than reduced demands for labour. An advertisement for skilled men at a Sheffield metal-works noted that as the forges were worked by steam, not water, employees would not lose time and earnings through dislocations caused by drought and flood. Nevertheless, experiences during the closing years of the eighteenth century proved that industrialisation, even at its most dynamic in the North, rested on a fragile base, at least in the short to medium term. Moreover, the unprecedented wartime mobilisations removed vast numbers from the labour market; the armed forces rose from a peace-time total of 98,000 in 1790 to 437,000 in 1795, and to 482,000 in 1802, the latest figure representing about ten percent of the adult male labour force.[13] If the debate over the precise relationship between population growth and economic expansion through industrialisation is not relevant here, and the precise economic impact of wartime enlistment cannot be established statistically, extrapolation from the dire effects of demobilisation after Waterloo, combined with the termination of demand for the materials of war-mongering, would suggest that Pitt's military crusade had its economically positive dimension.

War stimulated industrial economies across the country, but the loss of markets owing to wartime closures crippled certain specialist industries, for example Devon serge-manufacture. Overall, government demand for manufactured goods peaked in 1797, and then declined slowly. An ephemeral depression in several industries, including textiles, in 1793–4, reflected commercial uncertainties over the reaction of foreign markets to war. Demands for labour fell invariably during the winters, but the exceptional severity of that of 1794–5 precipitated a minor crisis in some industrial theatres, with, for example, concern at the uncharacteristically prolonged and widespread unemployment in Birmingham and Sheffield.[14] Another industrial recession in 1797 was provoked by invasion scares and the financial crisis. But the real vulnerability of the textile industries, most especially in the West Riding and Lancashire, and to a lesser extent in the West Country and the Midlands, was highlighted in 1795, and above all in 1800–1, when subsistence crises caused industrial recession. The second season of the second famine was aggravated when the depth of the recession coincided with the highest food prices in the first half of 1801.

It is no coincidence that East Midland hosiery manufacturers' first experimentation with the infamous cut-ups, which eventually inspired Luddism in that region, belongs to 1795. The practice was sufficiently notorious within twelve months to warrant hostile attention from the local press. Although hosiery exports were complicated by the Directory's ban on imported hose, which stopped English products reaching French consumers through neutral countries, the most important cause of manufacturing innovation lay in the attempt to maintain middle-class home demand by significant price reductions.[15] Although falling home demand certainly affected cottons and woollens at this time, Russian, German and East Indian markets remained buoyant, and together with military contracts prevented a serious collapse. These sources of stability weakened by 1800, and the degree of depression then must be attributed to the effect of famine prices on home demand, namely the diversion of working- and some middle-class purchasing power. In December 1800 the Leeds Corporation, dominated by cloth manufacturers and merchants, petitioned the government; no mention was made of current uncertainty over the Baltic market created by the Armed Neutrality, in favour of emphasising that sales were decimated by 'the general inability of the poor to purchase Cloathing'. A 'ruinous accumulation' of stocks had absorbed most available capital during the previous twelve months. Some West Riding small masters even killed and ate their horses, used to take wares to the cloth halls, and many 'others (heretofore in decent circumstances) have been reduced to poverty' while they struggled to keep their small workforces occupied. These would be laid off imminently, to join the rapidly expanding pool of unemployed created by employers in the more highly-mechanised cotton and worsted industries, who more speedily adjusted labour forces equitably with current demand. Early in 1801, unemployment resulting from factory lay-offs, and the inability of small masters to find further credit, bit hard.[16]

Similar, if less extensive developments occurred elsewhere at this juncture. At Coventry, master ribbon-weavers were in 'the most abject state of distress'; they were unable to meet tax demands, virtually bankrupt, and on the verge of giving up. Most of their counterparts in Devon textiles were also 'gradually sinking the hard earnings of many years' efforts' to survive. However, other industries which might eventually experience falling demands concomitant on flagging living standards and reduced demand from industrial customers and domestic consumers, notably iron and coal, stockpiled during temporary recessions, rather than reduce skilled or scarce manpower. If they were affected, problems came slightly later, and proved more ephemeral.[17]

Tradesmen were severely hit during both famines as working and middle-class consumers were forced to make drastic economies. The evidence, notably respecting service industries, is patchy, but thousands of self-employed skilled men were placed in dilemmas similar to those experienced by George Close of Sheffield, who resorted to frantic touting for custom. Writing to one client in the spring of 1795, Close would be 'very Glad to hear if any of your kitchen furniture wants repairing'; a little later, 'I beg you to Speak to your Gardener to Let me Serve him with Watering pans Or mending them . . . for Trade is very Bad', the worst he had encountered in sixty-two years. Trade worsened; when returning repaired copper pans in the summer, Close's invoice desperately concluded: 'N.B. if you have any Old Pewter Old Cop[per] Or Brass I shall be Glad of it. Tis Scarce And Answers My End Same as Money'. In July 1795, George Boswell, 'Grocer & Mercer' in Dorset, lamented that 'though in the trade I am . . . there is scarce any money to be taken'.[18]

Demand for casual labour especially in urban and industrial locations fell badly; it collapsed most spectacularly, as might be expected, during the second famine in general, and the 1800–1 season in particular, when analysts of the trade cycle record a marked depression throughout the economy. In the latter winter, Earl Fitzwilliam anticipated 'many applications for work' on his massive industrial and agrarian estate in South Yorkshire, but things were little better on his arrival at his Northamptonshire seat early in September 1800. 'Never', he confided,

> was there such a number of industrious persons begging & seeking work in every district. I find it so in this County. I found it so in a still greater degree when I was lately in Yorkshire.

The North was particularly affected because under-employment throughout the labouring sector was aggravated by the collapse in demand for skilled and unskilled labour in textiles. 'Trade' at Huddersfield was 'extremely bad'; at Halifax, 'a great many workmen are out of employment'. However, economic nuances meant that the situation was not uniform. At Oldham, according to weaver Rowbottom's perspective on 1 January 1801,

> weaving of all Sorts is Brisk but wages lowe but Hatting is Extreem bad worse than ever known before for a deal of Hatters are Entirely without work and those that have any are limited to one half but as many as Can

are turning to weaving.

Even here, all the ingredients of a collapsing economy, with too many chasing too few jobs at falling wages, were present. In spite of 'an Exalent fine day' there was 'few Company' at Oldham's Mayday Fair, and 'little Business' transacted. Horses again feature in the evidence, this time from London, where horrifying street scenes of starving animals in a 'frenzy' occurred as 'licensed slaughter houses' were 'not . . . able to Kill fast enough owing to the quantity of horses brought'; even if the 'scarcity of provender' and 'the impossibility of getting old oats' was initially responsible, the phenomenon was another component of recession. The most devastating feature was the shrinkage in the home market. As the Sheffield *Iris* exclaimed in April 1801, buoyant exports in some commodities were a poor guide to national prosperity; how else could 'it happen . . . that the manufacturers should be so depressed when the amount of exports appears greater than ever?'. The sources are unequal to any statistical presentation of under- and unemployment, but there is no doubt that the problem peaked in 1800–1. The forthcoming discussion of the impact of high prices on selected consumers *takes no account of either*.[19]

The staggering impact of famine is revealed by the cost of living calculations.[20] The average weekly cost during the first quarter of the 1794–5 season (6 September to 29 November 1794) for a wheat-based diet for a family with two children in the West Riding was, in shillings, 7.6, and at Birmingham 8.3. In the three subsequent quarters, average weekly costs were, in the West Riding, 8.1, 9.4, and 14.1. At Birmingham, 9.3, 10.3, and 14.2. In the following season, 1795–6, average weekly costs in the West Riding were, 12.0, 13.3, 13.6, and 11.5; at Birmingham, 12.1, 14.3, 13.8, and 12.3. Similar disparities are revealed in the producing regions. If Malton prices represent what people actually paid in the North and East Ridings, costs were consistently marginally below those obtaining in the West Riding. Similarly, Chichester prices were marginally under those current in London. The inflation of non-cereal dietary components, meant that the costs of non-wheaten based diets, namely barley and oats, rose only slightly less severely than wheaten. In the first quarter of the 1794–5 season, average weekly costs of barley and oat-based diets in the West Riding were 8.7 and 7.6 respectively. Oat-based prices then rose to 8.4, and 9.7, and fell only to 9.0 in the three subsequent quarters, with barley rising higher to 9.6, 11.4, and 12.3. During the 1795–6 season, oat-based diets cost a weekly 10.2, 11.2, 11.3 and 8.7, with barley at 12.1, 11.3, 10.4, and 10.8 in West Yorkshire. Again, costs of these alternative diets at Birmingham were slightly more inflated.

Greater inflation during 1799–1801 is vividly reflected by similar calculations. In the 1799–1800 season, average weekly costs of a wheat-based diet in the West Riding rocketed from 11.4 shillings, to 13.7, 15.9, and 16.4. After a slight fall to 15.5 during the first quarter of the 1800–1 season (September to December 1800), they went up to 18.2, and 18.8, before falling to 17.2 during the final quarter, June to August 1801. Costs were higher in other locations, as shown in Appendix 4. The costs of barley and oat-based dietaries in 1799–1801 exhibited similar behavioural tendencies to those experienced in 1794–6, but in the second famine a combination of disproportionate rises in the prices of barley and oats to wheat, and the more vigorous inflation of non-cereal dietary component prices, saw the costs of these alternatives even exceed those for wheaten-based. In the West Riding, an oat-based diet in 1799–1800 cost 11.3, 13.0, 16.3 and 16.9, and barley-based 10.4, 12.4, 14.1, and 16.0. In the 1800–1 season, oaten diets cost weekly averages of 15.6, 17.4, 16.8 and 14.5, while barley cost 17.4, 18.3, 20.4, and 17.2. The disproportionate increases in non-wheaten to wheaten dietaries were even more marked elsewhere, for example at Birmingham, as shown by Appendix 4, which nevertheless reveals that these West Riding price movements were typical, despite regional variations.

It must be emphasised that these figures relate solely to dietary costs. They do not include the cost even of beer, arguably an essential source of sustenance for many workers. The cost of housing, heating and light, and clothing, are excluded. An even greater insight into the scale of inflation, which removes uncertainties caused by evidential problems with non-cereal prices, is provided by an examination of the costs of cereal components alone. The average weekly cost of wheaten bread alone for a London family with two children during the four quarters of the 1794–5 season in shillings was, 5.2, 5.8, 6.5, and 8.8. Their barley-eating counterpart in Devon, calculated on Plymouth prices, would have paid quarterly weekly averages of 4.7, 5.5, 5.9 and 6.5, for cereals. Oat-component costs for a similar West Riding family would have been 4.1, 3.9, 4.5 and 4.9. During the 1795–6 season, the average weekly cost of the London family's bread was 8.1, 10.1, 9.1 and 7.8. The Devonians' barley would have cost quarterly weekly averages of 6.0, 6.0, 5.9 and 6.1, while the West Riding family's oats cost 4.8, 5.0, 5.1 and 4.0.[21]

Once again, a similar statistical exercise emphasises the second famine's greater severity. During the four quarters of the 1799–1800 season, the Londoners' weekly wheaten bread averaged 7.8, 10.5, 12.1, and 12.1. The Devonians' barley cost 6.6, 8.9, 7.3 and 8.0, while oats for their West Riding equivalents cost 6.5, 6.5, 8.2 and 8.2. During the 1800–1 season, average weekly bread costs in London were 11.2, 14.0, 13.9 and 11.8; barley in Devon cost 8.9, 12.1, 17.9 and 18.1, with Yorkshire oats costing 7.2, 9.3, 7.8 and 7.1.

The briefest reference to the wage data discussed in chapter 2 reveals how utterly inadequate most working-class incomes were during most of these extended periods. An approximate chart of the likely course of living standards during the famines for workers engaged in iron-forging near Leeds, in the Sheffield cutlery trade, for rural workers in Yorkshire, and for agricultural labourers in Norfolk and Sussex, has been compiled. Plausible budgets have been constructed for selected workers near Leeds and at Sheffield from the actual wages recorded as paid in their employers' business ledgers. The remaining calculations are less reliable, because necessity dictates the use of wage-rates, and assume that such workers were able to work a six-day week. Full employment was much more likely in rural Yorkshire, than in the agrarian South and East, where the supply of labour exceeded demand, despite wartime mobilisation.[22]

A graphic picture of both famines emerges. The highest-paid workers, the skilled iron-manufacturers and cutlers, weathered both storms; their relatively large incomes sufficed to purchase much more than a subsistence diet at virtually all times, though even they offset inevitable falls in living standards by increasing indebtedness to their employers. Rural craftsmen in Yorkshire, and probably elsewhere, came nearest to emulating this élite of top industrial workers. But these craftsmen's wages were unequal to the cost of a wheat-based diet during three of the eight quarters of the 1794–6 famine (June to August 1975, December 1795 to February 1796, and March to May 1796), though their incomes just sufficed to purchase the oat-based alternative at all times. Their situation was much worse in 1799–1801, with incomes unequal to the cost of a wheaten diet from March 1800 through to May 1801. A 'deficit' of 153.5 shillings accrued in pursuit of a wheaten diet. A smaller 'deficit' of 129.3 shillings was incurred by switching to oats, but a barley-based diet was an uneconomic alternative, incurring a greater deficit of 183.1. So even oat-consumption incurred an average weekly 'deficit' of two shillings, and this figure obscures a peak at 2.25 shillings in the winter months, when such men were vulnerable to weather-induced reductions in earnings. Only the highest paid skilled workers commanded incomes adequate to the cost of food. Overall these comprised a fairly small minority, and that minority shrank further with under- and unemployment advancing during the industrial recession of 1800–1.

The real wages of other workers demonstrate their predicament. Agricultural labourers, whether in the South, the East, or the North, were affected most of all. With three regional exceptions, the wages of this huge sector of the workforce were inadequate to the cost of *any* diet during the great majority of the sixteen quarters of famine conditions. Overall 'deficits' were enormous. Weekly wages on Yorkshire farms were on average almost one shilling below the cost of an oat-based diet for the entire 1794–5 season, and the average weekly 'deficits' of 1.9 and 1.6 shillings, incurred respectively by farmworkers purchasing a wheaten diet in Sussex and Norfolk, emphasise that contemporary concern at the 'uneconomic' wheaten diet was not without reason. Farmworkers' 'deficits' during the second famine achieved incredible levels. The smallest calculated, of 121.5 shillings for the 1799–1800 season, was incurred by a Norfolk family consuming barley. This represents severe weekly 'deficits' of 2.4 shillings, but not as impossible as weekly 'deficits' of 3.5 and 2.75 shillings incurred respectively by Yorkshire and Sussex farmworkers in the purchase of the cheapest possible diets. But these 'deficits' rose to even greater heights during the final season of famine. The purchase of the cheapest diet incurred weekly 'deficits' of 4.25 and 5.5 shillings in Norfolk and Sussex respectively. Yorkshire agricultural labourers averaged weekly 'deficits' of 4.5 shillings between September 1800 and May 1801, before a combination of wage increases and falling prices put all diets within income levels from June 1801.

Unskilled workers in industrial employment fared slightly less harshly. In aggregate, labourer George Hay at Kirkstall Forge earned a little more than the cost of an oaten diet throughout 1794–6, but serious 'deficits' materialised during some quarters. Inevitably, the devastation caused by the 1799–1801 famine emerges from the statistics. Hay's wages, even after transfer to the more arduous task of stoking, proved unequal to the cost of any diet between December 1799 and August 1800, but adequate to oat-costs between September 1800 and May 1801. This adequacy was achieved through working prodigious overtime. The incomplete data for his labouring counterpart at Nowill's suggests a living standard similar to Hay's, at least while he remained a labourer.

These calculations prove that most working-class incomes were unequal to subsistence diet costs; indeed, they were recurrently inadequate to the costs of cereal components alone. Cash, for expenditure on non-food essentials was simply unavailable for very long periods. The second famine was demonstrably far more serious than its predecessor, and its cumulative pressures much more extreme. Obviously, drastic 'economies' became an urgent necessity almost immediately prices began to rise, and continued and greater 'economies' had to be maintained for many consecutive months. For thousands, probably millions, the situation must have appeared to be chronic.

The literary evidence fully substantiates this dreadful statistical picture. As prices rose in the 'early phases', workers found that cereal costs absorbed a relentlessly increasing proportion of income. Eventually, for a considerable majority, cereal costs absorbed entire wages; income levels governed the moment at which this became a reality. Plebeian consumers responded by reducing, and eventually ending, consumption of non-cereal foodstuffs. This point was repeatedly made by corporate authorities replying to Whitehall in the spring of 1796, and by the clergy in their 1800 harvest returns. Lincolnshire workers gradually reduced, and then cut out, the bacon component of diet, which normally absorbed a quarter of subsistence expenditure. Their Hampshire counterparts spent 'their whole earnings & [parochial] allowance in bread only'. In the mining district about St. Austell, Cornwall, the 'People live entirely on Barley, it is the Expense of their Whole Wages to get it alone'. These small selections from the evidence prove that the same phenomenon was present in the low-paid, agrarian South, and the marginally better-paid agricultural regions of the North. It also penetrated higher-paid industrial communities. *Moreover, it was found in all regions, whatever the dominant subsistence cereal.*[23]

Consumers in those districts where wheat had been recently adopted as the standard cereal, reverted to their previous customs. The dictates of the market deserve distinction from government policies from 1795, which advocated the use of wheat-substitutes. This proved more viable in 1795–6 owing to high yields of barley and oats. Yet as early as March 1800 West Country farmers volunteered 'that horses must not eat oats now, they want them for the poor'. But barley was particularly vulnerable to the cold and wet which struck the 1799 harvest, and in many places it was too damaged to be used as cereal. Nevertheless, 'In Nov. 1799', reported the vicar of Winterslow, Wiltshire, 'My poor people took to Barley of their own accord'. Industrial workers in Glamorganshire were likewise 'reduced to the necessity of making bread of barley', and returns from many locations, as widely distributed as the East Riding, Cheshire, Dorset and Cambridgeshire, made the same point. This expedient had a short life during the second famine; it merely delayed inescapable hardships, for barley prices rose disproportionately to wheat. Malt prices also achieved unprecedented levels in 1800–1.[24]

Dietary expedients, equal to continental practices, were reported. The fall in workers' consumption standards during the 1799–1800 season in the rural district about Catterick, was vividly portrayed by a clergyman:

> The poor lived upon Barley Bread as long as there was any, and some few upon Oat Bread; Peas are much used, and also dry'd Herrings with Potatoes, or even Turnips, as a Substitute for Meat.

At East Brent in Somerset, plebeians 'frequently boiled . . . Horse Beans' to 'eat with some Salt', while at nearby Over Stowey a charitable distribution of 'boiling pease' attracted 'a Vast number of the Poor of the Parish'. Nettles, eaten with 'a little salt and pepper' in Eccleshall, Staffordshire, in 1795, were adopted on a greatly extended scale in 1800. In April, weaver Rowbottom began to record their price in Oldham market, and even that arch-optimist Professor Ashton recognised that the twopence a pound fetched, was indicative of 'scores of poor wretches . . . eagerly picking up any sort of vegetable'.[25] No doubt, the numbers of workers resorting to turnips, horse-beans and nettles varied from district to district, and probably within localities, but such expedients were common, and increasingly observed as the cumulative pressures of famine intensified. Famine conditions surely underlay the reversion of the philanthropic to the medieval practice of providing endowments in their wills for bread distributions to the poor.[26]

In spite of such nostrums, many workers were unable to buy sufficient food during the 'early phases' before cumulative factors began to operate. Rowbottom's diary vividly proves the point. On 17 February 1795 he recorded that 'Every Necessary of Life rises Astonishingly So that the poor are in A most lamentable Condition'. The situation deteriorated; in May, 'Every necessary of Life advanced to an uncommon Pitch and Absolutely out of the reach of the lower Class of poor'. He was soon commenting on actual prices, incredulously emphasising that these were 'A fact'. On 8 June, 'An absolute fact, Johnathan Jackson, Badger of Oldham Sells [h]is flower at the price of 2 Shils and 9 pence per peck'. He made similar comments in the spring of 1800. In March he observed

> the poor in a most Shocking Situation a great deal are starving for Bread and verey few can get any thing Better than Barley Bread, Barly Pottages Barley Dumpkins pottatoes Being so Exxcessively dear that the poor cannot by them.

When workers said, that they 'cannot live' at current prices at Buntingford in March 1795, and that they deserved 'a more Honourable Death than to be starv'd alive' in Devon in May 1800, they articulated experiences, and perceptions of their own predicament. These two examples could be multiplied many times from the 'early phases' of the first season of each famine, again long before cumulative pressures peaked.[27]

Thousands, probably millions, tried to alleviate the cumulative effects by

pawning anything that they could. Such desperation was more evident
during 1799–1801. As famine intensified in Staffordshire for example, many
'dragged on a miserable existence by pawning everything about them . . .
even to the very Bed they lay upon, to satisfy their hunger'. Rowbottom
confirmed that 'a Deal of familis have sold their houshold Goods to Exist',
and an East London overseer said that poor-law claimants had invariably
pawned most of their clothes. In September 1800, Derbyshire industrial
workers remonstrated that

> their children were as naked as well themselves, and that they had neither
> money nor credit to purchase them clothing against the winter.

During that winter, enquiries in several northern towns revealed that
thousands dressed in shreds during the day, and went home to equally
'forlorn beds, without linen, and covered only with rags'. Identical
observations were made of workers' plight in industrial villages. Clearly,
clothes, bed-linen and blankets which remained out of pawn, were worn
out and valueless. The fact that the second-hand market was awash with
blankets and clothing extended the 1800–1 textile recession to blankets. The
charitable joined poor-law authorities in massive distributions of bed-linen
and blankets, but found that many recipients simply pawned these to buy
food. When the large employers in the Pennine textile township of
Saddleworth celebrated peace preliminaries in the autumn of 1801, they did
so by an enormous distribution of cloth, which reflected a restoration of
business confidence, crippling stockpiles, and a recognition of a pressing
need for many of their workers two months after famine conditions
retreated on the superabundant harvest of that year.[28]

Begging attained monumental proportions, and was legitimised even in
the most respectable plebeian circles. The arrest of a beggar by the Norwich
police galvanised a 'phrenzy' in the streets, which ended only on his release.
The Birmingham press typically spoke of an 'influx of beggars into the
town'; the hostile reporter was concerned at the ease with which begging
aroused bourgeois consciences and their easy exploitation by imposters. In
fact, it was even more difficult to distinguish those who took 'advantage of
the times' from those reduced to desperation by the times. Desperation,
rather than exploitation, surely underlay the noted increase in belligerent,
aggressive begging. Scavenging was seen on unknown scales with 'children
picking Potatoe pearings on the Dunghill to boil for Food' at Wolverhampton. Mancunian urchins fought off stray dogs competing for bones thrown
from the kitchens of the affluent.[29]

Famine inevitably and invariably struck children particularly hard. The
Morning Chronicle was no doubt scoring political points against Pitt in July
1795, but its observation of the dilemma of metropolitan artisans earning
between sixteen and twenty-one shillings weekly, was accurate. A family
man confronted

> difficulties with which he must struggle . . . painful anxiety that must
> rend the bosom of him whose paternal affections are all awake to the
> demands of children importunate for bread, or to the more distressing

sight of a beloved wife, silent in grief, and pining with hunger.

In the following autumn Cornish miners said that 'their Children are crying for Bread'. 'You Grind Us So Our Children Cant gett bread', exclaimed a doggerel, distributed at Portsmouth. The accuracy of threatening missives, like that stuck to Poole churchdoor demanding 'can you behold your Littell one hanging on there weeping mothers Necks Lamenting and Mourning for Bread', are confirmed by less rhetorical sources. In May 1800, the experienced Birmingham magistrate, Heneage Legge, warned government that 'many Thousands, especially Children, are all but starved'. Ordered off the streets by the Bolton police, labourer William Crook retorted that'"It was very hard that his Children should Claw" (meaning for . . . want of Bread)'.[30]

The two hypercrises, midsummer 1795 and September 1800, with serious shortages of corn, immeasurably aggravated the problems deriving from high prices; they came after the cumulative effects of the latter were manifest. The 1795 example was experienced virtually universally. That of 1800 came after a prolonged period of even greater prices. Then, industrial workers in Warwickshire said it was 'impossible to procure half the bread that their Families have occasion for', and their counterparts elsewhere dramatically spoke of 'dying by Inches'. From about this time, the deterioration in the physical appearance of the working class, forcibly struck observers. The President of the Board of Trade was soon to warn his cabinet colleagues 'that the People are nearly starving for Want of Food, and . . . in the approaching Winter, are likely to starve also for Want of Rainment'.[31]

A journalist reporting the angry crowds on London streets in September 1800, recorded that 'more than one half of them were poor women, without cloaks or bonnets, some with scarcely cloaths to cover them'. The long-serving magistrate and vicar of Leicester presided over unparalleled applications for relief from unprecedented numbers of 'emaciated poor half starved objects of pity'. The new fashionable romanticism, with its devotion to the natural beauties of upland Britain, failed to obscure the human face of destitution for one tourist in Wales in September 1800:

> a more melancholy & at the same time newer picture might be drawn from the consequences of the late dreadfull famine, the visible traces of which are still to be found in the countenance of the poor: in Wales . . . they have most sensibly felt the dimunition in the quality of their food, where the quality was already bad. This . . . appeared to me, to cast a sort of gloom over the country . . . destructive to the antient spirit of the people.

One keynote here was the misplaced confidence in 'late famine', and optimism, premature by almost a year. Steadily worsening conditions were humanly manifested at the following Christmas, the quality of which was an invariable barometer of plebeian welfare. At Oldham Rowbottom recorded,

The Weather is Exalent fine it has been a smal Quantity of Snow with a keen frost but it is now Disolved and the Earth Dry and the Air warm but the Misserys of the poor I am not able to Decribe and it is with very great concern that I state the poor are in a verey weakly Condition . . . . never was the first day of the new year ushered in with such Distressing appearances poor people as may Reasonable be Expected never left off working and not a poor person in this Neighbourhood that had pies Ale or Roast Beef on the Conterary the[y] had Hard work and Light Meals.

William Wyatt concluded his diary for 1800 with an equally telling observation on his Derbyshire industrial village:

a strange Christmas this! I have known every family in this Town have plenty of roast Beef, pies, Cheese & Ale etc very great suppering nights all Christmas, with singing and mirth, great many years when the Water Grove [the main industrial concern] flourished – at this time there is not more than five famileys here that has bread enough. What will be the event of such Distress God knows.[32]

Distress persisted relentlessly throughout the winter and into the spring. In April 1801, in Buckinghamshire, Mrs Fremantle 'visited all the poor in the village' and recorded that 'some are truly starving and look the picture of death'. The situation, at least in terms of scale, was worse in the recession-struck localities. From Lancashire, Thomas Ainsworth assured the first Sir Robert Peel that one encountered 'a deal of thin faces', about the same moment in the spring that William Wilberforce was lobbied by his West Yorkshire constituents. They 'informed me that the sufferings of the poor in Leeds itself were much less than in the surrounding district; yet they spoke of Leeds itself as exhibiting a face of great wretchedness'. Another lobbyist, anonymously penning a letter to the West Riding Bench, insisted that communal 'suffering . . . groweth worse & worse': 'many an honest man doeth not know how to get one Week or Day over'.[33]

   The ultimate expression of the greater intensity of the second famine, and especially its second season, comprised evidence that the distress engulfed most tradesmen and extended to the middle classes. This is not to suggest that those well above the labouring sector escaped the devastations of the first famine, for tradesmen applied for relief, notably during the hypercrisis of 1795. About half of those in receipt of aid at Plympton in Devon were self-employed craftsmen, among them the village blacksmith, tailor, a carpenter, a thatcher, and three shoemakers. East Anglian smallholders were similarly reduced at the same time, and one ramification of distress in such circles was the rapid growth of hostility to the tithe, to be repeated in 1800, as the clergy's exactions were thrown into sharper relief.[34] In 1800, and especially in 1801, tradespeople faced hardships of an unprecedented nature on a scale never encountered before. Shoreditch petitioners empha-sised the 'Miseries of the middle Ranks', and reports from Wakefield and York stressed that their counterparts swallowed their pride and joined the queues at soup-kitchens. The flood of relief applications from such ranks astonished those concerned with both statutory and charitable aid, and angered some including the Rev. Holland in Somerset who repeatedly recorded his encounters with 'persons rather in affluence' and other 'improper' supplicants 'picking the meat out of the mouths of the real objects of charity'. More perceptive fund-raisers at Exeter in March 1801 confronted parallel misunderstandings of the situation with an unequivocal statement that 'the Middle ranks of Tradespeople are considered proper Objects' for aid with subsidised bread. Distress penetrated further up the social pyramid. The fact that the 'middle classes' in parts of the North were reduced to eating barley bread and little else, could possibly be ascribed to the recession; so too could the fact that 'the present complainants' demanding aid at Tiverton 'were of a very different description' from the norm. The recession was less likely to have stimulated the petition to parliament from Holborn householders in November 1800 which insisted

> that not only the lower, but even the middle Classes of Society, who have hitherto lived in Respectability, feel severely the complicated evil, and . . . can scarcely bare the Pressure of the Times.

MPs were assured that these bourgeois had patriotically used cereal substitutes 'from Prudence' in accordance with government policy; now, dietary changes were 'imposed . . . by Necessity'. A miscellany of factors constituted a social revolution to provoke sad, ironic observations, that thousands were 'compelled to solicit that parochial Relief, which they were long accustomed to bestow'.[35]

Wartime taxation and heavy poor-rate demands also impoverished the middle classes. The facts that the residual 110 of the 2144 householders who still paid their rates at Wilton were in difficulties, and Leeds' poor relief was 'wrung in ten thousand instances from the hand of poverty itself', could also be attributed to the recession in textiles. The fact that as early as February 1800, Sheffield rate-collectors were 'forced' to issue a fifth rate-demand before sixty percent of the fourth was paid, could not. Nor could the predicament faced in the Cornish mining village of Gulval the following September; the vestry recognised that 'the Poors Rate is likely to exceed by far, any thing heretofore known', and that many 'obligated in these Rates . . . are unable to support themselves', let alone public funds. The ten richest men in the parish subscribed to a fund to meet the bulk of expenditure, and in many other non-agrarian parishes, public liquidity survived only through massive loans from landowners. The Gloucester-shire Bench publicly ordered overseers 'not to insist too rigorously on Payment', and insisted that middle-class ratepayers should not lose their remaining dignity, the parliamentary franchise. In the end, a major rate crisis was narrowly averted by emergency legislation rushed through in the spring of 1801.[36]

Rating problems and contiguous evidence do not prove that ratepayers suffered from malnutrition; bourgeois pride doubtlessly suffered more than their health even where unprecedented dependence on barley-bread and gruel was experienced. But pride took other forms. It was repeatedly said that those above labouring rank would rather starve than compromise fierce independence and self-esteem in a hierarchical society, and there is little reason to surmise that this was widely abandoned during the famines. For every middle-class supplicant at soup kitchens, and vestry tables, there were many more who went to considerable lengths to ostensibly remain self-sufficient not least because they anticipated difficulties to derive from an ephemeral exigency. Early in January 1801, the vicar of Antony, Cornwall, wrote to Reginald Pole-Carew MP, the local landowner, on behalf of Elizabeth Ellis, who had once run a boarding school in the parish. Might she be permitted to join 'the little band of Pensioners who receive the Meal at Antony house & also to a participation in any other bounty issuing from your or Mrs Carew's goodness'? His reverence explained that the closure of the school, and now prolonged inflation

> must bear particularly hard upon One who had no visible means of earning money, & who had too much pride to solicit charity. Still however I did not suspect how severe her sufferings had been, till, by frequent visits, I extorted the secret. I need not tell you to what hardship an independent mind will submit rather than undergo the humiliation of supplicating a Parish Officer, & I think we cannot too anxiously cherish this sort of honest pride which shrinks from the disgrace of being levell'd with the class of those who are fed by publick bounty.

We do not know how many Mrs Ellis's there were, or how many retired people, living on small annuities purchased in earlier days, tried to adhere to their class ideology. Antony was a small parish, but even here, a vicar with relatively few similar parishioners, needed to exsect the truth. For it is not merely those represented by the 'poor stockinger' who need rescuing from 'the enormous condescension of posterity', because in numerous places, people like Mrs Ellis may have suffered silently and obstinately until they died.[37]

The demographic evidence is, as ever, difficult to interpret. Twentieth-century demographic and nutritional experts are hardly helpful:

> almost any historical pattern of interaction among food supply, food consumption, and the human condition can be identified and studied in some part of the world today, although not necessarily on the same scale *or for the same duration*. What this means, however, is that nutritional mechanisms and consequences that can be discovered only with great difficulty from the usually sparse and inadequate historical data can often be understood with reasonable certainty through access to detailed contemporary information and analysis,

confidently asserts Professor Scrimshaw (my italics). Writing in the same symposium, Drs Catts and van de Walle say,

> because the environment in which people lived and died is considerably different now from what it was then, it is necessary to use extreme caution in transporting the baggage of the present to the past.[38]

We have already encountered the hostility of certain historical demographers to piling up examples of famine-induced demographic disturbance, their commitment to camouflaging these by incorporation in longer-term population movements, and their insufferable arrogance in talking about famine conditions merely killing those who would have naturally died shortly in any case. The human misery behind all this has no place in the *Population History of England*. The likes of Mrs Ellis are not to be found in this schema.[39]

Both our famines were responsible for demographic disturbance, including mortality crises. The numbers of deaths nationally in 1795, were six percent up on those in previous years, and the estimated total of 210,000 was the highest for any year between 1780 and 1818, marginally above the figure of 208,000 for 1800. Historians of London, Devon, and Yorkshire, all note a marked increase in mortality in 1795–6, though the precise role of disease exhibits its customary, elusive character. Moreover, although the striking fall in living standards in 1799–1801 has been used as an exemplar of the demographer's rule that there is no automatic mortality crisis attendant on severe subsistence problems,[40] the national death rate did rise in 1800, and to a lesser extent in 1801.[41] It spiralled upwards in 1802, 1803 and 1804, which conforms to the pattern of delayed enhanced mortality attributed to many famines. Once again, historians of specific localities, including Devon and Yorkshire, have detected increased mortality. In Devon, death rates doubled, while in Yorkshire they rose everywhere by between sixteen and forty-one percent. Figures for marriages and baptisms also exhibit demographic distortions; 'decreases in the "voluntary"rates of marriages and conceptions' are revealed by Devon and Yorkshire statistics, most markedly in 1800–1, and national calculations reflect identical patterns.[42]

Ironically, in view of the more pronounced mortality of 1795–6, contemporaries articulated greater concern at malnutrition, disease and death in the second famine. Such comment is perhaps attributable to the higher prices current, their impact on the middle class, the greater physical emaciation of working people, and the prevalence of epidemic disease, notably in 1800–1. Local authorities began to fear that alimentary diseases, which normally strike hardest in the summer, would occur in populous towns in 1800. In May 1800, Heneage Legge warned that unless the undernourished population of Birmingham got more and better food 'before very hot weather commences, some putrid Epidemic Disease must be the Consequence'. Mancunian doctors confirmed a local epidemic in June which they attributed to the 'wretchedness of poverty and want'. Over the hot summer, many impoverished East Londoners were reputedly 'very sickly', and 'a contagious Fever' broke out. The instant manifestations of fear suggest that many residents, like Legge, anticipated an epidemic. Within days, 'the dread of the Fever was so prevailing that . . . some of the Sick were actually turned out' of their lodgings. Disease certainly struck at those who inhabited the poorest quarters, especially where the itinerant Irish congregated, 'who lodge to the Number of 14 or 15 a House'. The government reacted with speed, as uncommon as it was secretive, and financed emergency, makeshift isolation hospitals for those who had no entitlement to parochial relief. Ironically, more patients died under the auspices of parish authorities than in government centres, not least because the former were swamped by infected, settled residents. 'The wretched poor were lying four or five to a bed' in the fever wards of Spitalfields workhouse, and the death rate in some, but not all, London parishes, shot up.[43]

The 'fever' in London was probably typhus, and it certainly spread to, or occurred in, other regions, especially, but not exclusively, in the first half of 1801, in the industrial Midlands and the North. Nottingham, the Vale of Trent, Sheffield, the textile towns on both sides of the Pennines, and Liverpool were badly affected. There was some recurrence later in the year. An unusually dramatic headline – 'FEVER IN SHEFFIELD' – in the *Iris*, claimed that 'the Poor . . . are perishing in almost every manufacturing town in the kingdom, by a fatal and infectious fever'. In Manchester, overworked doctors attached to the new Infirmary, reported that 'fevers are found to prevail most wherever families have been crowded together in small rooms, and especially where there is not a sufficiency of beds and bed covering'. The medics lambasted many contributory factors, destitute, diseased newcomers, 'thrust into . . . damp and dismal cellars', contagion raging amongst emaciated mill-children who worked nights, and plebeian indifference to domestic hygiene. They suggested, reasonably, that slum landlords must assume some responsibility; improved ventilation, whitewashing subterranean tenements, and the relocation of privies, would help to contain disease. Rowbottom recorded that 'fever is verey prevalent all over the Country' about Oldham, and added that it 'Ended the Misereys of many a poor Creature'; he noted the names of many deceased neighbours whose demise he attributed to the weakening effect of prolonged hunger, as did several West Yorkshire clerics. The Liverpudlian press furiously denied that Yellow Fever had caused 'the late unusual mortality'; ascribing it to 'the exceedingly prevalent . . . Dysentry' was bad enough, but it would not entail further economic dislocation through the immediate imposition of stringent quarantine regulations against the dreaded Caribbean disease. 'Fever' also struck rural communities in the West Country; in Somerset it produced a crop of fatalities, but in Devon a similar type of epidemic rarely killed its victims. Devonian doctors reported that 'it generally goes thro every family where it begins', and once again attributed it to an 'absolute Want' of a proper diet.[44]

Deaths from starvation are not an automatic corollary of famine conditions. There were a handful of authenticated examples, all of which occurred in 1799–1801. In May 1800, the Rev. A.B. Haden relayed medical fears of deaths through starvation in the industrial villages of Staffordshire, but, rumours apart, Haden could report only one case where a doctor confirmed that a 'whole Family was absolutely perishing' from want. Claims that over 140 starved to death in East London in the year ending November 1800, were confounded by an enquiry. The West Riding curate who slyly added the claim that starvation despatched 'several . . . to an untimely sepulchre' to his acreage return, was possibly politically-motivated. Likewise, the anonymous Home Office informant from Bolton who alleged that 'no less than 18 Died from hunger' in the autumn of 1800, was using every device to awaken Whitehall to the very real danger of insurrection in Lancashire. But Rowbottom did record that a stranger 'Died in a stable . . . suposed . . . in Consequence of the want of Bread', and a coroner's jury brought in a starvation verdict on another itinerant who dropped dead in a Birmingham street: an autopsy revealed no food in the deceased's stomach. As Mrs George once exclaimed, 'according to the Poor Law', deaths from starvation 'should have been impossible'. But deaths from starvation were not particularly unusual in eighteenth-century London, and these rumours, together with the concrete examples, may represent a tip of an iceberg. Certainly, many were at risk, especially itinerants and notably the Irish amongst them, the numbers of whom increased dramatically owing to the Rebellion of 1798 and the enormous socio-political tensions both before and after. Those who migrated to the new threatres of industrialism and were already inhabitants of the inexorably growing slums, were far removed from the more integrated communities of rural England, where poor relief and paternalist agencies were more humane, and more effective. It was surely no accident that the lady whom the vicar of Barming in Kent believed to have died of starvation in May 1796, had no settlement in that parish, and was too afraid to return home to claim public assistance, in case investigations revealed her bigamous marriage.[45] In the final analysis, greater emphasis should be put on the horrors of getting through days, weeks and months, somehow, despite the unanswerable protests of emaciated children, and the unsatisfiable entreaties of petrified, loving wives. The experience of hunger, of death, of disease and perceptions of unending crisis, like the *fears* of starving to death, cannot, like the demographers' stock in trade, be quantified. They were none the less real for that.

II
FAMINE AND THE PEOPLE

CHAPTER 5

'Extreme Avarice and Rapaciousness'
Contemporary Analysis and Popular Prejudices

There is something in the effects of hunger and the sight of your family suffering from it which none can judge of but those who have felt it. The equilibrium of temper and judgement is deranged as your child looks up with piteous face and tearful eye, asking with suppressed voice for the bread it knows you have not. I have heard my own child so ask for bread I had not to give, and my prayer is, God help the man so tried. Were it pestilence or famine, plainly sent by our Heavenly Parent, faith in His wisdom and goodness might be summoned up to bear the chastisement. . . . But when you know it is man-made, and therefore to remove it is manhood's duty, then to rest idle contented under it becomes a sin. You turn with disgust from a system of which the Word of God says, 'He that withholdeth corn, the people shall curse him'. Prov. xi 26[1]

Eighteenth-century Britons and foreign visitors were so impressed by the perimeters of deference, inherent in plebeian insubordination in general, and the regularity of collective protest in particular, that the 'mob' became the 'fourth estate' in contemporary parlance. 'You may call the people a mob', thundered Byron in the House of Lords, 'but do not forget that the mob too often speaks the sentiments of the people'.[2] The functional importance of the crowd is revealed by the range of issues on which it articulated a popular consensus, generating 'manifold disorders'. The crowd, with its actual power of numbers, and its inherent threat of violence, was the people's institution, representing an emergent working class, able to forge and enforce unified action to protect plebeian interests. Historians, examining riotous phenomena from national, regional and local perspectives, have relentlessly reiterated the conclusion that 'the most persistent and widespread disturbances in eighteenth-century England were those associated with food'. Volumes of recent research prove 'that one clear consciousness which the eighteenth century did most emphatically have, was a consumer one'. The prices of foodstuffs were paramount; the insistence on a 'fair price', and mass mobilisations to enforce it, guaranteed a pivotal role to price fixing, *taxation populaire* by the crowd.[3]

However, the 1790s proved to be a watershed in English history, and the student enters a 'different . . . territory'. This is not to allege that there was a clean break with eighteenth-century traditions. Certainly, there were challenges to the hegemony of consumerist mentality in popular economic perceptions. As an ever-growing percentage of the population became dependent on the market and money wages for their subsistence, a proportion began to conclude that workers 'would have to command a wage adequate to the buying of bread'. There is evidence of a 'convergence of rising union mentality with declining taxation populaire'.[4] Yet this new, emergent realisation itself derived from developments in eighteenth-century industrial relations, themselves but recently rescued by Dr Rule from the historiographical obscurity bestowed by the Webbs. Labour's pre-industrial traditions and experiences were key, conditioning 'a spectrum of responses' in defence of a variety of traditions, against labour-saving machinery and innovation, against wage cuts, and for wage and piece-rate increases. Reactions included ephemeral dramatic militant episodes, threatening letters, arson, machine-breaking, and the strike. Employee organisations in many trades were advanced; if they failed to bequeath sufficient documentation to attract historians concerned to discover trade unionism through bureaucratic credentials, this must not obscure the regularity of more mundane, almost routine, negotiations between masters and men. Nor should the remarkable incidence of 'collective bargaining by riot'.[5] Numerous strikes, the subject of a statistically-orientated study, reflect failed negotiations.[6] Many London trades were highly organised, and from the 1760s the steady erosion of real wages by the relentless, if slow, upward drift of food prices, found expression in repeated metropolitan combinations and strikes. Provincial parallels include the massive North-eastern turn-out by miners and keelmen in 1765, among hundreds of other episodes.[7] Several historians have noted the distinct upturn in trade unionism in the 1790s, and Professor Christie is impressed by the incidence of successful campaigns.[8] The old, myopic concentration on aspects of the notorious Combination Acts[9], has been replaced by emphasis on the stimulating impact of inflation and oscillating industrial conditions on labour organisations.[10] Such factors can be located within broader, longer-term changes, including the depersonalisation of capital-labour relationships by both rapid urbanisation, and, in certain industries, by the 'inner transformation of capitalist development'.[11]

The watershed of the nineties was multi-dimensional, and if any development represents a fundamental rupture of eighteenth-century populist traditions, it must be the rise of a working-class movement for political reform on democratic principles. While this new ideology drew on an English heritage, its timing owed much to the omnipresent shadow cast by the French Revolution. The 'frequent . . . Jacobin tinge . . . added a new dimension to food disturbances'. If such protest was never 'unpolitical', because it demanded the intervention of authority in support of the crowd's objectives, these themselves increasingly confronted the state's adoption of laissez-faire economic principles in the 1790s. The resultant conflict between populist and governmental ideologies was fuelled by the 'Jacobin consciousness of a minority' on the former side, and the paradoxical posture of the latter's conservative, repressive political stance and its radical, unorthodox economic theory.[12] Government repression extended to tumescent trade unionism, though it was political rather than economic considerations which underpinned ministerial strategy in support of the Combination Acts. Ministerial perceptions were soon reflected in prosecutors' litanies: labour 'associations were easily convertible into every sort of political mischief'.[13]

The catalogue of protest in the decade is not restricted to riots, strikes, and politicisation. For example, moral legitimisation of the poor plundering the affluent was articulated. The use of threatening letters gained a new currency, notably in the countryside.[14] The marked emergence of arson against farmers and millers has evoked historical controversy.[15] Many historians of protest have followed Rudé in identifying 'faces in the crowd',[16] and the key role of women has occupied an entire book.[17] Geographers of riot have deployed spatial analytical techniques enhancing understanding of contrasts between perennially disturbed locations and the apparently equally perennially quiescent places. One conclusion, that the food riot was the primary prerogative of 'town artisans and proto-industrial and industrial, that is non-agricultural, workers', is sustained by the 'list of arrested rioters' comprising 'a role call of the trades and industries of Britain'.[18] Certainly, food rioting in the 1790s was sufficiently fierce and widespread to warrant specific analysis. However, the famines were national, and we must adopt the theoretical appreciation of Professors Hobsbawm and Rudé.

> Human beings do not react to the goad of hunger and oppression by some automatic and standard response of revolt. What they do, or fail to do, depends on their situation among other human beings, on their environment, culture, tradition and experience.

All these components varied significantly across England.[19]

The unique watershed necessitates this holistic approach. Few historians adhere to the conservative methodology of the 'compartmentalist approach', which portrays each phenomenon in a vacuum, despite the tenacity of its current leading exponent, Professor Thomis.[20] With reference to 'corresponding societies, combinations, seditious plots and food disturbances', Dr Walvin concludes that these were 'different areas of the same political spectrum, one merging into and complementing the other'. Dr Booth argues that North-western experiences in the nineties witnessed 'the death rattle of the food riot as a separate entity'; massive, politically-inspired protest meetings presaged Chartist times, and already represented 'the culmination of the separate struggles of trade unionists, political radicals and food rioters'. This is at a remove from Dr Stevenson's confidence that 'the element of "sedition"' in food disturbances 'was smaller than the authorities thought'.[21] Many questions remain. All the traditional defences of the poor were deployed during the famines. New and novel forms were added, and permutations abounded. Their interaction and incidence demand detailed attention, as do the shifts in the nature and structure of popular protests in periods of grave hardship. The multifarious characteristics of protest must be pursued through all their complexities, ultimately to determine whether they reveal anything about the polarisation and politicisation of the class structure, newly emergent in an era of rapid intensification of agrarian and industrial capitalism.

Finally, by way of introduction, historians have noted disparities between food-price series, and the incidence of riot. The most disturbed periods regularly fail to coincide with price peaks. This disjunction is aggravated when annual average prices are correlated with riot statistics. The former obscure critical short-term movements, and the latter's compilation is fraught with methodological and evidential problems. Food prices are central, but they do not exist in a vacuum. Stevenson partly confronts this problem. He demarcates between riotous reactions to pre-harvest price rises, when 'real discontent about prices was most likely to surface', and the 'post harvest months'. The latter comprised 'a classic period for rumour and resentment' caused by 'anticipation and speculation', while assessments of the new crop's yield were incorporated in commercial perceptions, and reflected in market behaviour. A reversal of falling prices at harvest time conflicted with populist logic, and – as in September 1800 – riots could peak, despite the fact that the actual prices were among the lowest monthly ones recorded for the year.[22] The key question turned on whether prices were behaving acceptably and naturally, or whether other illegitimate and artificial factors were at work? Popular responses to high, or even rapidly-rising prices, were not automatic, though popular prejudices, whose deeply-obscured origins testify to the antiquity of the conditioning tradition, invariably manifested themselves. But if prejudices derived from tradition, they were fundamentally qualified at any one time by other aspects, none more centrally than contemporary analysis of the causes of dearth and distress. These analyses were not constant.

The unthinking assumption of adequate harvests by most consumers is evinced by the customary indifference of the press, principally read by townsmen, to seasonal agrarian progress. Famine conditions dispelled the indifference, for urban readerships demanded information on agricultural conditions leading up to the following harvest, which was perceived to end the crisis. Therefore the nature of press information is of key importance during the first famine seasons, 1794–5 and 1799–1800. The characteristics of this journalism reveal little qualitative difference between these two seasons. Reports were constantly confident and optimistic, and invariably predicted good harvest yields, much too early in the season. The press relied on the casual observations of amateurs. The *Stamford Mercury* relied 'on the current testimony of several intelligent travellers', and *The Times* reported the impressions of an MP who made a whistle-stop fifteen-hundred mile tour. Such observers were impressed by 'beautiful looking fields' of corn waving gently in fine weather. But aesthetically endearing rural scenes viewed from the stagecoach were not to be depended upon. Mrs Thrale, ensconced in the Cheshire countryside during the fabulously hot summer of 1800, noted that 'Corn is turning colour apace and a good harvest season is expected': she added, 'Plenty will not very easily be the consequence tho', as the crops are exceedingly thin and light'. Arthur Young's scathing comment on the quality of press reports – that 'the prognostics of the Cockney are not of much consequence' – was incisive, for in June and July 1800 the metropolitan and provincial press rivalled each other in the production of lyrical accounts, to end with a crescendo of harvest serenades in mid-August. *The Times* correlated evidence 'from every part of the finest harvest that has been known'; well might the *Gentleman's Magazine* speak of 'Every provincial paper teeming with joyous tidings'. Cautionary remarks in the *Chelmsford Chronicle*, published in the depths of the cornlands, were abandoned in favour of silence. Many journalists appear to have told readers what they wanted to hear, news commensurate with lower prices in future. Reporting agricultural difficulties could discredit proprietors, and the Norfolk press warned against pessimistic reports, 'inserted no doubt through the means of those pests of society, the monopolizers of grain'. In addition to unreliable sources, many 'newspapers tended to anticipate good crops most frequently out of a conscious or unconscious desire to maintain price stability'. Indeed, this characterised the entire European press, and in dearth years the media wanted to deflate the market, counter the greedy expectations of farmers and dealers, and maintain consumers' confidence.[23]

Adverse weather was deftly accommodated by this optimism, or ignored. The thunderstorms and torrential rain in mid–August 1800 constitute a superb case history. The Kent press merely claimed that rain 'greatly improved' the hops, and if its Sussex rival admitted that the wet delayed harvesting, further commentary was restricted to rain's 'highly favourable' effect on the after-grass. *The Times* excelled even this subjectivity. Daily reports at nationwide successful harvesting ceased abruptly on 20 August, after several days of inundation; a strict silence during the following week was broken by a solitary reference to rain; it extinguished a serious fire in Radnor Forest. Inaccurate reportage was compounded by plagiarism. *The Times'* report of the MP's tour appeared verbatim in the *Newcastle Advertiser*. *Aris's Birmingham Gazette*'s mid-August swansong that even wet weather 'could furnish little pretext to advance the price' of cereals, reappeared three days later in the *Derby Mercury*. Populist self-contradiction wrecked objectivity. On 23 August the *Hull Advertizer*, in the interests of encouraging retrenchment, anticipated a one-third deficiency in all cereal crops; the riotous conflagration in September was inevitable, 'ever attendent on bad harvests'. One week later it complained that prices had not fallen despite 'the plentiful harvest we have had'. Newspapers normally eschewed correction of earlier mistakes.[24]

These predilictions were not compromised by evidence supporting E.P. Thompson's contention that 'every harvest was accompanied by talk of mildew, floods and blighted ears'.[25] Comments about adverse phenomena were made, but there was, for example, nothing inaccurate about reports of devastating flooding in the autumn of 1799. The absence of significant 'scare' reports in the key years, 1795, 1796, 1800 and 1801 is striking. Only one alarm occurred, and this followed identification of blight in Yorkshire wheat late in July 1795. Local press reports were reprinted in the London dailies, whereupon the entire provincial press anxiously covered the story. In fact the government investigated the situation, through experts including Sir Joseph Banks and, once the blight's localised, and undestructive nature was confirmed, newspapers took the lead in announcing minimal damage.

The scare was over within a month.[26] There was neither parallel, nor repetition, even in 1800, when there were ample grounds for pessimism. In 1801, only four of the hundreds of clergymen who volunteered comments on harvest productivity when compiling their acreage returns, claimed any imperfections in the newly-gathered crops.[27]

Misplaced optimism, as opposed to contrived pessimism, for which the press was primarily responsible, misled people from all social ranks over the critical summers of 1795 and 1800. In 1795 Mary Berry was amazed at the contradictions between her own observations and press reports; she found 'corn . . . almost levelled: the papers talk of such prodigious plenty that one would imagine there was a danger of our being devoured by wheat and barley'. Others were neither sceptical, nor able to see for themselves, and took the newspapers at face value. For example, the Rev Bagshaw-Stevens confidently informed a friend in September 1795 that 'Such a Harvest was never known . . . the fields laugh and ring this Autumn'. More important-ly, it was precisely such men who helped disseminate the glad tidings among those at the furthest remove from the press, and who looked to such social leaders for information. The pulpits rang with premature thanks-givings. In mid-August 1800, at White Waltham, Berkshire, 'The Clergy-man, Mr Vansittart son to the member for this county . . . returned thanks for the prospect of plenty'.[28]

Historians are divided on the accuracy of pre-harvest yield projections,[29] but a Hampshire cleric's observation, that 'our most competent judges are ever liable to be deceived, respecting the real state of the wheat crops, until their actual arrival at the barn door', was not wide of the mark.[30] But if press coverage was uniformly, consistently, and irresponsibly, optimistic and misinforming, its impact on the population varied. For people were not blind, but aware of the effects of unfavourable weather on agrarian productivity. Folk-lore identified summertime weather as the vital determi-nant of harvest yields. If the summer of 1795 was relatively dry, it was also abnormally cold, with little August sun. Delayed harvesting coincided with rain. The wet which devastated the 1799 crop, and ruined autumn sowing, was largely forgotten by the summer of 1800; the press definitely ignored this key factor. The blissfully hot summer of 1800 conformed to popular criteria for abundance unlimited. The press emphasised an exceptionally early start to harvesting, long before that visible denominator, rain, struck in mid-August. In 1799, and to a lesser extent in 1794 and 1795, easily observable adverse weather accounted for some crop-deficiency, inducing scepticism at journalistic optimism. In 1800 the weather complemented press reports to generate the greatest expectations of the harvest, and provides a cogent clue to events in the autumn.

Public perceptions of the genuine state of the food supply turned on consensual conceptions of harvest conditions and productivity. These were central to contemporary analyses of the problems caused by the crises, which derived from a popular theoretical model of the food-marketing mechanism. This model, familiar to all eighteenth-century Englishmen, and fiercely defended by an overwhelming proportion of them, was rediscovered by Edward Thompson, who coined the phrase the 'moral economy' to encompass the concepts.[31] 'Moral economy' comprised three basic elements. It demanded pure food, honestly measured, at a fair price. Prices were clearly understood to be dictated by the state of the supply and volumes on the market, an implicit, if conditional popular acceptance of basic, capitalist norms. But theoretically marketing was a publicly-executed, transparent process. The farmer should sell his produce regularly throughout the year in the open market, giving preference to local exchanges. Deviations were considered immoral. The food adulterator was as execrable as the farmer who hoarded to stimulate prices, who used secretive sales procedures to conceal the true level of stocks, or who manipulated prices by any other method, for instance, by fictitious sales. Similarly, the producer who sacrificed the welfare of the local community, by selling in distant markets to obtain higher prices, broke the code. Tradition restricted the legitimate role of the food manufacturers. Custom frowned on dealing by millers; their ancient role confined them to grinding for the bakers, and for individual consumers on a commission basis. Bakers' profits should be strictly controlled in the interests of the consumer. The wholesaler and other types of middlemen were alien to the spirit of the 'moral economy'.

By the end of the eighteenth century this code was partially outmoded. The strictures against adulteration and under-measures remained realistic, but those against wholesalers and engrossing were obviously outdated. The concepts of the 'moral economy' survived in spite of the teachings of the political economists, and the statutory embodiment of *laissez-faire* with the 1772 repeal of the laws againt the traditional marketing offences of forestalling, regrating, and engrossing. Indeed, these statutory changes failed to clarify the law, as the old offences remained proscribed under Common Law, which legally underpinned the 'moral economy'. The code's tenets also survived as the popular guide to the governance of the foodstuffs trades, not least because adulteration, short-measures, and under-weights, together with miscellaneous fraud, kept consumers on guard against everyday market-place malpractices. So too did the formal exposure of the corrupt by 'market juries', and not infrequent prosecution in the criminal courts. But if consumers maintained a logistical suspicion of all food-traders, stable prices in normal times negated the real relevance of those parts of the 'moral economy' in opposition to the operations of middle-men. Dearth subjected all food trades, and the traders, to more profound public scrutiny, to reveal practices radically removed from the ancient ideology. This facilitated beliefs that prices were enhanced, or even caused, by operations which transgressed traditional orthodoxies. Dependency on the market exposed the bulk of the population to market prices. Prices were initially, the crucial issue; were they too high, and if so, why?

Suspicions extended to everybody in the trades, producers, wholesale distributors, manufacturers, and retailers. Initial popular fury was commonly directed at bakers and retail butchers, easy front-line targets, but they were rarely believed to be the authors of unacceptable prices. Demonstrations against them, and even attacks on their premises symbolised mass rage at eroded values, not popular perceptions of basic causal factors, though this is not to deny that on many occasions, specific bakers and butchers had antagonised entire proletarian communities. Protesters may have thought that enforced price reductions at retail outlets would be reversed through the system, back to the middlemen and farmers. Retailers blamed their suppliers. Gloucester bakers passed the buck by levelling accusations of extortion at dealers and farmers.[32] Farmers, especially the rich, were often accused of promoting price rises by withholding corn from market. Sussex farmers allegedly stopped threshing and selling immediately scarcity was reported, and were soon seen as 'the sole cause of the present high prices'. Many rumours had an authentic ring, including that concerning a Cumberland farmer who gave 'directions to his Husbandmen not to thresh . . . expecting the Price still higher' as late as 28 July 1795. Farmers were believed to be too wealthy and too greedy, capable of under-supplying markets when it suited them. A Norfolk customs officer typically complained that autumn high prices in 1800 were not solely attributable to deficiencies; opulent farmers met Michaelmas rent demands from capital, without recourse to sales of the new crop, which they withheld to fuel inflation and their own profits. He added that an 'esprit de corps', fostered by local agricultural clubs, encouraged farmers to ape their landlords, which required enormous profits. Farmers were also accused of avoiding markets in favour of private deals with merchants and millers, a practice odious on three counts. It camouflaged the supply, it facilitated engrossing by wholesalers, and it magically fuelled price rises. Corn was not 'brought to Market where every one may see'. In these circumstances, conspiracies were easily imagined. The vicar of Yarlington reported the erosion of pitching markets at Sherborne and Wincanton; now 'The Dealings are carried on in cautious whispers', with 'bargains' made 'without speaking, by means of papers handed across the table containing the proposals of either party'. Contracts for uncut grain were equally abhorred, especially when substantial ones were settled before grain was 'threshed, and without waiting for the market price at the time of delivery'. The Hampshire Bench identified such practices as 'one means of continuing and increasing the present high price'. Secretive dealing encouraged engrossing, which facilitated monopoly, that bogey of eighteenth-century economic thought. From Oxfordshire Sir Charles Willoughby angrily related his observations to the Home Office: 'Jobbers of every description go round to the Farmers Houses to contract for all their wheat without it's being sent to market . . . . such a Monopoly' was intolerable.[33]

Millers incurred odium over their 'new' role as dealers. The dealing-miller, opined a Cheshire clergyman, 'has numberless opportunities of buying up vast quantities of Corn, and of entering into Combinations with the Farmer'. Millers were also accused of pure speculation, when they made cereal purchases 'not for the purposes of carrying on their Business as Mealmen in manufacturing . . . Flour, but retaining the same . . . untill the Price is enormous and then selling the same again in Gross'. Many townsmen could easily attribute inflated prices to assumed agreements between the two or three big millers who often monopolised flour supplies to lesser conurbations. Identical strictures were laid against other dealers, including Bath potato-merchants, and Salisbury wholesale butchers who 'Scower the Markets', and sent meat elsewhere 'a Carcas' at a time. The smallest purchases of the pettiest hucksters were viewed in the same light.[34]

Engrossing was intimately associated with the despatch of stocks to distant marts, particularly reprehensible in times of shortage. Willoughby linked his itinerant dealers with the vast despatch of grain from Oxfordshire. The 'legal Removal' of corn from the Isle of Wight was objected to owing to fears of stocks inadequate to island demand until the harvest. Nor were these just islanders' prerogatives. Northamptonshire folk viewed overland corn shipments 'as taking Bread out of their Mouths'. Even greater indignation was aroused by jobbers, who had no obvious productive function. The Gloucester bakers knew their audience when they denounced jobbers as 'mere speculators', whose activities had 'a very pernicious Effect on the fair market'. A Hampshire clergyman was typically confused and outraged:

> There are, in this County a sett of Men, commonly called Jobbers who buy any thing merely to sell it again, at an advanced Price; these men speculate in Corn.

Holding markets everywhere on the same day of the week was a much-favoured device to frustrate jobbing. Commentators were rather unsure how jobbers were 'wickedly industrious in keeping up . . . high prices and enhancing them', but were convinced that the root cause lay in 'extreme avarice and rapaciousness'.[35]

The foregoing articulations of the 'moral economy' mostly came from members of the ruling class, emphasising that the concepts were not restricted to those most endangered by famine. Indeed, the 'moral economy' ideal was reinforced by the clergy, magistracy and civic authorities. Church of England clergymen were in a peculiar position. First, religious differences underpinned their dislike of the provision trades' partial domination by Quaker and Dissenting merchants, 'full of malice, ignorant, narrow minded and void of either candour or charity' in the private estimation of one cleric. Secondly, repetitive conflict over the tithe fed clerical suspicion of coveteous farmers. Thirdly, charitably-minded and conscientious incumbents like the Rev. Holland of Over Stowey, Somerset, literally presided over the famine-induced social polarisations in the countryside. On 7 September 1800, as prices suddenly rocketed to confound most expectations, Holland hurriedly threshed new wheat of his own growth and from his tithe, and 'divided it into pecks at a low price' for the poor. One month later he was infuriated at his failure to induce any farmer parishioner to follow suit. In mid-November, his anger at one potato-grower who had sold his entire crop 'before they were taken out of the ground' to a merchant, was enflamed further when another grower, whom Holland had lectured on the immorality of exacting the highest price from local workers, had the temerity to renege on the price agreed for nine bags for sale to his reverence, forcing Holland to pay more; Holland, like many of his colleagues, retaliated from the pulpit. Such experiences reinforced 'moral economy' traditions, and encouraged the intervention of local authorities concerned to protect majority interests against the extortions of a self-interested minority. Many magistrates, especially in the early 1790s, were simply unaware of their legal powers. Earl Fortescue, Lord Lieutenant of Devon, argued when the 1795 crisis broke that the Bench 'should exercise their right of setting the price of the Market'; then 'that provocation to riot would be effectively prevented'. When confronted by disturbances, local authorities repeatedly endorsed the crowd's demand for the implementation of the 'moral economy'. Magistrates could also increase market-place supervision, notably by the vigorous enforcement of weights and measures. In 1795 the Staffordshire Bench decided to police the previously unregulated market at Wolverhampton, with the appointment of a clerk, equipped with standard measures. Increased supervision, the discovery and destruction of false weights and fraudulent measures, enhanced beliefs in rampant profiteering. The same conviction was reinforced when magistrates published their intention to implement the 'laws' against forestallers, regrators and engrossers.[36]

Press stories of profiteering encouraged the Bench to publicly rebuke dealers and farmers. An anonymous letter, threatening both, sent to the Lewes market inspector, was 'read to the farmers in the great room at the Star where the market is held . . . by order of the Magistrates'. Justice Rushworth, summoned from the mainland to a disturbance on the Isle of Wight, discovered that miller Pratt, who was also a merchant and baker, had offered inflated prices for corn, and sold bread at sevenpence more than mainland prices. Enraged, Rushworth privately, but unsuccessfully remonstrated with Pratt; then, in the street with the crowd, Rushworth 'addressed' the miller 'with some warmth, and threatened to send . . . the constables to search his mill for adulterated flour'. The crowd nearly lynched Pratt, he claimed somewhat stupidly 'entirely owing to the inflammatory speeches of the Magistrate'. Such public criticisms exacerbated social tensions, and bestowed official sanction on the tenets of the 'moral economy'.[37]

Many magistrates, once confronted by protests over prices, intervened to order reductions. The relentless adoption of the word 'exorbitant' to describe prices – one journalist even used it when denouncing *taxation populaire*! – reinforced beliefs in artificially contrived price rises. In 1795 the Rev. A.B. Haden ordered West Midland farmers to sell wheat at 84/- at Wolverhampton, only to be rudely shocked 'when the Millers immediately engrossed the Whole and sold the Flour to the Consumer at £8'. This precedent no doubt determined a more arbitrary intervention in 1800 when the Bench 'made the Millers send off to Bilston a load of Flower for which they will not be allowed above 10s. altho' it cost them at Liverpool 17s'. The Bench also supported the crowd's determination to conserve local stocks. In the Forest of Dean, Justice Pyrke negotiated with the farmers, whose grain convoy for Gloucester had been stopped, and secured an agreement that the contents were to be sold in Forest marts at reduced prices. Magistrates also privately imposed remedies consistent with the 'moral economy'. The Mayor of Durham led a boycott of millers; Marquis Townsend evicted mill-tenants who refused to limit themselves to grinding. Worcestershire landowners ordered their tenants to supply the county town, and appointed an inspectorate to record sales, thereby creating an aura of legality.[38]

The Bench, like the crowd, adopted 'moral economy' tenets to deal with what all conceived as essentially a *local* problem. Everybody accepted that higher prices were the corollary of shortages, but the ancient code was relevant when consumers felt imposed upon by the machinations of farmers and traders driving inflated prices to extortionate levels. Distinctions were drawn. The Oxfordshire Bench acknowledged that corn had to flow from producing to consuming regions, but adding magisterial 'opinion that considerable Mischief has arisen from the great Spirit of Jobbing, Forestalling, Engrossing and Regrating, that has too long prevailed'. It was the 'Spirit' that transformed high into excessive prices, and distinctions like that made at Oxford in some senses updated the moral code to accommodate contemporary economic realities. However, logic could ultimately drive the argument that high prices were aggravated by human artifice towards a conviction in what the French called a *pacte de famine*, an 'artificial scarcity' in eighteenth-century English parlance. The logic was bluntly articulated by Wolverhampton petitioners early in 1800; 'the apparent scarcity of Flour' was 'not so much . . . from the late unfavourable Season . . . as from the baneful Effects of Monopoly'. The reasons behind, and the incidence of beliefs in an 'artificial scarcity', are central to the social and political reactions to famine.[39]

Notions of 'artificial scarcity' were *not* classic expressions of the demand for the implementation of 'moral economy' tenets. For example, the near universal panic over famine conditions in the midsummer hypercrisis of 1795, led to a reassertion of one central tenet, namely the retention of stocks for local communities; sheer desperation dictated moves which in aggregate constituted a blockade, imposed by crowds, with or without judicial support. Of course, those farmers and dealers who tried to maintain shipments were held to have transgressed the 'moral economy', and were castigated for their greed. But they were not accused of *causing* the hypercrisis. Their guilt derived from worsening an already intolerable supply problem. Exceptional conditions underlay the development of convictions in an 'artificial scarcity' at all social levels. The belief rarely received its *full* expression following the harvests of 1794, 1795 and 1799, not least because the effect of subjective journalism, for example, was mitigated by visibly adverse weather. At these times it was feared that the crises were *enhanced* as opposed to *caused* by profiteering. The exception, prior to the 1795 harvest, concerned the London meat market, wherein meat prices suddenly rocketed in April, and *The Times* launched a campaign for strict enforcement of 'the laws against forestalling'. This sectoral and transitory episode reveals the distinction between the creation of an 'artificial scarcity' by a conspiratorial *combination* of dealers, and the aggravation of economic difficulties by individual traders whose operations increased prices.[40]

Nevertheless, two factors combined to induce *some* scepticism over the severity of the scarcity in the 1795–96 season. First, several Grand Juries were addressed by judges, including Lord Chief Justice Kenyon, at the Summer Assizes, on the legal position of food traders; the Common Law could be invoked against traditional offences when they unnaturally raised prices. Kenyon, who genuinely perceived himself as a 'guardian' of public morals, was also in receipt of authentic private intelligence detailing the inflationary effect of mercantile operations in big exchanges;[41] he encouraged local judicial vigilance, and in some jurisdictions campaigns resulted, notably in Staffordshire, where the Bench responded fiercely to public pressure for prosecutions 'by way of terrorem'. Prosecutions followed at both the Sessions and the Assizes, and the Rev. Haden even had Margaret Welsh incarcerated 'for Want of Sureties, for regrating . . . Lamb'.[42] Trials took place all over England. Most offences occurred in urban markets,[43] but convictions in the smallest country towns were also recorded,[44] together with indictments for diverting the flow of provisions.[45] In Co. Durham farmers were fined for engrossing wheat.[46] In some regions large numbers of cases were heard,[47] and if many failed,[48] some of those convicted were imprisoned.[49] Public attention was focused on these trials, which served to strengthen popular beliefs in illegitimate practices, and gave some credulity to notions of 'artificial scarcity'.

Secondly, renewed rapid inflation after the harvest automatically fuelled the same suspicions, and also triggered further mobilisations for the local retention of grain. A flood of complaints was also released, notably against millers. At the Treasury, George Rose received 'Letters incessantly respecting the alarming Price of Wheat, as I believe every One' in government 'does now, with Suggestions frequently concerning the Abuses of Millers', implicated principally by the disproportionate increases of flour to wheat prices. The first allegations of monopolistic practices at Mark Lane were heard, and one expert, Governor Pownall investigated the topic in a series of articles in the *Cambridge Journal*. Ministers came under considerable pressure to recognise that 'the Corn Trade is . . . a Trade of Speculation', that 'the Monopolisers of Provisions make an artificial Famine', and that the food trades warranted categorisation as a 'special case'. Interventionist powers were needed 'to regulate Provisions and distinguish them from other Articles of Commerce'. Although ministers successfully eschewed any legislative initiative, these initial identifications of malpractices at Mark Lane had a long-term significance, as well as revealing some conviction in 'artificial scarcity' analyses in the autumn of 1795.[50]

The reality of scarcity was rarely questioned after the dreadful harvest-weather of 1799. Nevertheless, prices achieved unprecedented levels; incredulous churchwardens at Kirkham, Lancashire, committed their astonishment to their account book:

Oatmeal sold this Day in Preston Market at six Guineas pr. Load and Wheat at Three Pounds Ten Shillings p Windle and all other Food very dear.

Even the Home Office, despite its repetitive and resolute emphasis on natural causes when engaged in orchestrating riot-suppression, carefully admitted that 'the deficiency of the last year's Crop may perhaps have been somewhat overrated'. Public opinion revealed a critical paradox; an acceptance of harvest-deficiency was combined with assertions that profiteering had aggravated prices way beyond those consistent with scarcity alone. Braggadocio by food traders accelerated the process. A Somerset potato-merchant 'imprudently boasted of his having purchased 100 Sacks of Potatoes which he was determined to keep up till they should produce 1 Guinea per Sack altho' they cost him only 4s'.[51]

The formation of mass opinion was not conditioned by bombastic assertions of 525 percent profits, or limited to individual's own observations, and rumours of avaricious characters. Beliefs in a general *spirit* of profiteering and extortion, exacerbated by *conspiracies*, were fuelled by several events of national significance before the 1800 harvest. Two trials were crucial. In February proceedings opened against hop-dealer Waddington, who 'had declared that in order to *create a scarcity, and have command of the market*, he would lay out every shilling of the 80.0001 he had by him and borrow more'. Waddington made massive purchases, and contracted for much of the growing Worcestershire crop. Kenyon, presiding in the King's Bench, issued an indictment with the observation that when he arrived on the Oxford circuit in 1795, 'that county was almost in a state of insurrection in consequence of forestalling'. The decision received a rapturous welcome, *The Times* typically exuding satisfaction that marketing malpractices were now the object of judicial investigation which it hoped 'will not be confined to hops'. It was not. Early in July, cornfactor Rusby was convicted for regrating oats at Mark Lane. Kenyon, again in the chair, congratulated the jury on the 'verdict; almost the greatest benefit on your country that was ever conferred by a jury'.[52]

At several summer Assizes, Kenyon and his fellow judges, categorically blamed current high prices on cabals of big capitalist traders. Kenyon sniped at political economists: 'it is cosy for a man to write a Treatise in his closet', but an examination of mercantile practice in the real world revealed 'every avenue of a country town' thronged with forestallers and engrossers whereby 'the country suffers most grievously'. Judges welcomed common-law prosecutions because penalties were stiffer than under the repealed statutes, and stressed that the courts were the forum where 'grievously oppressed' people 'might resort for a remedy'. Judicial intervention against the 'shameless effrontery' of defendants was acclaimed by the press; convictions would 'deter others from following the evil practice'. The *Nottingham Journal* splashed accounts of the Waddington trial across the front page, customarily reserved for advertisements, and also reported in detail on further trials of London butchers accused of forestalling Smithfield. There were many more convictions than in the comparable period in 1795. In the summer of 1800 the courts became the main platform for 'moral economy'. Convictions proved that the scarcity had been exaggerated, and then exploited by profiteers.[53]

Some observers were stunned. In Edinburgh the English 'trials . . . for forestalling and engrossing are talked of . . . as a complete refutation of the speculations of theorists on the . . . corn trade'. The studious James Horner re-read Adam Smith's 'noble chapter' in *The Wealth of Nations*, attended lectures by Dugald Stewart, wherein 'Kenyon did not escape some very pointed allusions', before re-committing himself to *laissez-faire* principles. Few others made such academic enquiry.[54]

Public opinion was conditioned further during June and July by rumours that high prices were maintained by dealers withholding imported corn.

The results of a private Board of Trade enquiry were not published, but they convinced Home Secretary Portland, the minister least impressed by public opinion, that prices were kept up by the 'speculation of the Importers whose Cargoes are actually in the River' Thames. Elizabeth Heber, who had no inside information, confided her conviction of 'an artificial scarcity', based on the incompatability of high bread prices, corn ships choking the Thames, and packed riverside granaries, to her diary. The Rev. Holland made an identical record of his suspicions. Simultaneously the government challenged the hegemony of metropolitan capital, by promoting legislation to establish a massive, milling co-operative. In parliament, ministerial spokesmen asserted that 'artificial causes . . . aggravated the evil'; the President of the Board of Trade announced that 'it was of public notoriety and upon record, that much monopoly existed at present among the dealers in various commodities'. He referred to Waddington, and the Lord Chancellor advanced Rusby's conviction in support.[55]

This represented a major change in government policy; previously, ministers had used the parliamentary forum to publicise their commitment to non-intervention in the home market. Now they admitted that statutory intervention was needed against monopoly. The fact that the cabinet was divided, and that some members were, like the Foxite opposition, too doctrinaire in their support of *laissez-faire* to accept any mediation, hardly detracted from the impact of the change on public opinion. The President of the Board of Trade admitted 'that the Principles of Commerce must to a certain degree be different when they are applied to the Necessaries of Life'; that commercial sphere 'required legislative interference and political regulation'. The Earl of Sheffield, a wide-ranging agrarian and commercial expert, was just one notable convert. In mid-1800, senior ministers confirmed that profiteering had enhanced prices, and that a conspiratorial combination existed among corn importers. A majority of the cabinet had acquiesced in that view. All of these men were steeped in the teachings of the political economists; as practical politicians they were bound to be pragmatists. As administrators they had to find workable remedies. If the grip of Smithian economics was too strong to permit some ministers to support this fracture of free trade, the fact that a cabinet majority was prepared to risk parliamentary defeat in the attempt to disperse the monopolistic nature of London's grain supply, proves that a serious conviction in profiteering had penetrated the highest levels. If such men were so persuaded, there is no cause for surprise that public opinion transformed the tenets of the 'moral economy' into a belief in a *pacte de famine*.[56]

Its fullest expression was modified by the precise timing of the revelation of empirical proof. Rapid price falls at the end of July and the start of August, combined with hot weather, clear skies, and reputedly promising crops on which a start to harvesting had been made, proffered the return of normality. If profiteering combinations had imposed upon the country, the anticipated bumper harvest would prevent recurrence. In mid-August prices rocketed once rain struck. Supplies to the centres of consumption slumped. The populace would take no more; tolerance of commercial artifice was impossible. Fierce rioting engulfed many urban localities, including London, where Mark Lane was closed down for a week. Provincial magistrates, unable and unwilling to control the masses, joined them and forced dealers and farmers to sell at acceptable prices. Suppliers withdrew in terror from town marts, and refused to send supplies to places under price controls. Starvation stared several urban populations in the face. Senior civil servants spoke of 'the state of the contest in this country between the growers, suppliers and consumers'.[57]

Widespread public conviction in 'artificial scarcity' in September 1800 was revealed everywhere. Local authorities demanded the invocation of supposed ministerial powers to impose a maximum price on wheat;[58] such demands were echoed by the press,[59] and more were made for statutory powers to establish a maximum price, notably in petitions calling for an emergency recall of parliament in the autumn.[60] The vicar of Warrington typically insisted on 'immediate Relief'; 'some strong act of Power, as the establishment for instance of a Maximum' would 'be hailed by a starving Public with the loudest acclamations'.[61] The most committed free-traders re-examined their philosophies, seeking and evaluating fresh evidence. Pitt's Treasury colleague, George Rose, interviewed London alderman Shaw, 'who stated the prices of wheat to have been raised from 105s . . . to 122s, by a principal factor, and alluded to Mr. C[laude] S[cott]'. Alderman Garrett 'Stated Mr. Peacock having his warehouses full of flour, and his refusing to sell a sack'. Strange new alliances emerged. Thomas Erskine, the famous Whig lawyer, told the ultra-conservative Kenyon that 'great merchants with great capitals . . . sweep the country before them, in the purchases of the necessaries of life, and they command the markets'; Erskine said that the Chief Justice's legal stance was morally irrefutable too. William Wilberforce mused that while Smithian economics were theoretically sound, 'there was room for abuse'; when 'pushed to an extreme', they 'become mischievous'. Re-evaluation split the cabinet too. Ministers discussed the merits of a maximum. The President of the Board of Trade, the Earl of Liverpool, argued that in 'Times of Distress', the 'Seller . . . can set his own Price, and becomes . . . Master of the Market, especially if every Attempt is not prevented': his defence of classical economics now included suggested new provisions to make the market 'more free'. Commerce, stated Sir Joseph Banks, 'like Fire is a good Servant but a bad Master'. Pitt himself hovered on the verge of conversion; the evidence proved the reality of 'speculations . . . for the purpose of unduly and artificially raising the price'. Only Grenville faithfully adhered to his *laissez-faire* schooling, and thundered at Pitt:

> We in truth formed our opinions on the subject [the price mechanism] together, and I was not more convinced than you were in the soundness of Adam Smith's principles of political economy till Lord Liverpool lured you from our arms into the mazes of the old system.[62]

The fact that some ministers favoured interventionism was public knowledge. The inspector of corn returns at Liverpool, was among those who offered expert advice on this premise. The Earl of Liverpool, and one of his Board of Trade officials, George Chalmers, were attacked by name by the *Morning Chronicle*; the editor, Perry, a capital miller in his own right[63], campaigned against the emergency reconvention of parliament. He repudiated any 'system of checks, regulations and restraints . . . in the sources of the domestic supply' of corn, which he alleged were included in 'the projects . . . floating in the political hemisphere'.[64]

The harvests of 1795 and 1800 were critical because they followed the first seasons of famine; those of 1796 and 1801 were equally crucial, but as they effectively terminated famine conditions, they proved less central to contemporary discussions of causality. Public opinion was misled by the press in both 1795 and 1800, but recognisably adverse weather in the former year, partially defused the impact on popular perceptions. In 1800, the press's impact was reinforced by ostensibly superb weather and other factors. The tenets of 'moral economy' invariably operated in the direction of consensus in 'artificial scarcity'. But this analysis was given its full expression only in the autumn of 1800. Then consumers believed they were the victim of a giant conspiracy, and the contrasts in public opinion account for the dissimilar responses to famine between the autumns of 1795 and 1800.

CHAPTER 6

'A more honourable Death than to be starv'd alive'

Taxation Populaire *and the 'Early Phases' of the Famines*

Introduction: 'Riot Analysis'

Historians unanimously confirm that the food riot comprised the commonest form of eighteenth-century popular disturbance. The evidence suggests that the 1790s was the most disturbed decade of the entire century, though it would be run a close second by the 1760s. Modern historians are greatly addicted to quantification. Edward Thompson is a noted, if inevitable exception, scornfully dismissing assumptions that food riots were simple, automatic plebeian responses to periodic high prices. He also dismissed scholars who computerised data to relate the incidence of riot to short-term price movements. In a study of a related form of protest, the sending of anonymous, threatening letters, Thompson insisted that his own enumeration of extant examples 'may certainly not be allowed to enter the intestines of some computer, as the quantity of premeditated violence in pre-industrial England'.[1] The simplest analysis of this type of phenomena must appreciate that not every riot, and not every threatening letter, will be recorded automatically for the benefit of posterity.

These warnings are repeatedly ignored, with dismal distortions. Drs Walter and Wrightson's positive statement that 'there is evidence of only nine grain riots . . . between 1585 and 1660 in Essex', is central to their 'cumulative impression' that 'the years of dearth' in early modern England 'were not marked by widespread rioting'. This evidence is torpedoed by their identification of a 'flurry of riots' in South-east Essex in January 1629 alone.[2] Dr Stevenson's examination of food rioting 1792 to 1818, speaks relatively cautiously of discovering 'evidence of seventy-four food disturbances' in 1795–6, and 'at least fifty' in 1800–1, before relapsing into an adamant assertion that 'the north-east . . . in spite of its large body of manufactures had only two' during the quarter century. If such shoddiness was isolated, it could be ignored. However, it is central to Stevenson's critique of Thompson's failure to explain 'why some places were almost perennially disturbed while others remained almost completely undisturbed'.[3] This problem has rightly perplexed other historians, including D.E. Williams, and the author of the most sophisticated analysis of rioting during the wars, John Bohstedt. He correctly notes that the 'reconstruction of the crowd's ideology cannot explain why some people acted on that ideology and others did not'. Williams, studying the 1766–7 crisis, uses demographic evidence to suggest that 'hunger rioters were hungry', but that not all hungry people rioted; during these consecutive months of deprivation, Williams identified, to his own satisfaction, 'non-rioting communities' including a number of 'non-rioting market towns'. This process of demarcation, and its possible shortcomings, are not even discussed.[4]

Dr Bohstedt relies on the Home Office papers, the press, and local studies 'which have used many more local sources and so presumably have identified most signficant riots', and also the services of another historian to actually search the key Lancashire Quarter Sessions files.[5] Bohstedt proceeds to conflate sampling with blanket coverage, and while some of his conclusions are probably correct, his confidence cannot be shared. One comparative analysis partially hinges on the 'most riotous' counties, Devon, Cornwall, and Gloucestershire, and those having 'no food riots in 1795', namely Cheshire, Dorset and Rutland. One interpretation turns on the identification of local riotous and non-riotous traditions; Devon towns which rioted in 1795 do so again in 1800–1, while the quiescence of non-disturbed towns in '95 is repeated five years later.[6] Similarly, riots were more common in larger than smaller towns, with seventy-five percent of riots between 1790 and 1810 occurring in towns with more than two thousand inhabitants. Thirty-eight percent took place in London, and the thirteen greatest provincial centres. This apparent precision obscures dubious quantification. The total of thirteen riots in Nottingham across this period, is a hopelessly inaccurate count of disturbances over food prices, and industrial disputes, not to mention riotous expressions of popular loyalism and radicalism, or election disturbances.[7] The 'only significant food riot' in Norwich, we are informed, occurred in April 1796; the exercise of corporate patronage was 'so lavish that the food riot seems almost to have been eliminated from town politics'. But Norwich was engulfed by fierce rioting on at least two occasions in September 1800; arrests followed by prosecutions, accompanied the first. Posses of special constables were enrolled after the second to ensure the corporation's published commitment to 'force' to prevent repetition. This all constitutes a novel form of patronage by any definition. The first riot was reported in the local press, the second to the Home Office.[8] Bolton we are told, 'seems to have been a transitional case; labour organisation seems to have made the food riot obsolete, for Bolton alone among the main cotton towns did not have a food riot at this period'. However, on 5 May 1800, a riotous, stone-throwing crowd, was cleared from the market-place and adjacent streets with considerable difficulty, by special constables, who also made arrests.[9] Some major conclusions, among them 'the emerging picture of massive stability in social relations, not volatility' expressed by repeated riot, Williams believes emerges from his work, and Bohstedt's assertion that 'the social framework for disciplined direct action by crowds could not exist' in

the 'new industrial cities', require careful re-evaluation in the light of more
thorough research.[10] The conclusions of these five historians, all hinge on
the assumption that the majority, if not all riots, from the sixteenth to the
early nineteenth centuries, can be traced in the sources. Initially, evidential
quality demands critical evaluation.

The Home Office papers, including thousands of letters to Secretaries of
State from local authorities respecting disturbances, comprise a major
source. But many historians imply that riots were automatically reported to
Whitehall. The evidence suggests otherwise, even during the 1790s when a
not insignificant number of magistrates believed rioting was manipulated
by political radicals. Provincial Benches were not encouraged to trouble
Secretaries of State with details of every disturbance. One over-
communicative Lord Lieutenant was roundly condemned by a Home
Secretary for creating a regular liaison, thereby establishing a political and
administrative 'principle which would be very injurious and derogatory to
the respectability which now belongs to the Magistracy'. Many justices
prided themselves on controlling their jurisdictions; central government's
involvement embarrassed JPs, and compromised the neighbourhood's
reputation. William Dawson JP, explained to his Lord Lieutenant – not the
Home Secretary – that a Dewsbury disturbance 'was little more than one of
those frays which are perpetually taking place . . . and ought in the first
instance to have been suppress'd by the principal inhabitants'. Heneage
Legge, the experienced Birmingham magistrate opined that 'it is by no
means worth while to harass government with the twopenny squabbles of
every Market Day'; there was simply no point when events were contained
by authority on the spot. 'Principal inhabitants' domiciled in 'almost
perennially disturbed towns', like Witney, Oxfordshire, were familiar with
demonstrations, affrays and riots, and remained calm. Robert Taylor coolly
evaluated the urban situation in September 1800, when the county was
engulfed by disturbances; he recounted, to a friend, that

> Everything is at present quiet and peaceable the Rioters dispersed
> yesterday after parading the Town with loaves upon sticks in good order.
> They are expected to meet this day but no danger is apprehended.[11]

Letters from local administrators to London were rarely mere reports;
they were penned primarily to make requests. This is not to ignore the
frightened or timid justice, though such communicants were in a decided
minority. Temperate magistrates' primary concern was security, especially
the provision of troops. Justices requested military support in anticipation
of trouble, to control disturbances, and to prevent recurrences. They
naturally felt obliged to detail their local predicament. A Leicestershire JP
demanded army support because the populace was 'very riotously inclined',
and the Volunteer Cavalry too dispersed and too weak to contain disturbances. Regulars would 'be the means of keeping . . . the people . . .
peaceable'. Although the army was the last resort for hard-pressed magistrates, and in the absence of a police force, or adequate Volunteer forces, the
sole resort, local authorities had a number of factors to balance before
requesting army aid. The Town Clerk of Oxford refused to request regulars

as that would denigrate the City Volunteers. Ashburton justices wanted troops to prevent further riots, but insisted that their request was kept quiet or they would henceforth 'be marked by the populace'. Many nervous borough authorities may well have considered an occasional market-place eruption preferable to antagonising a considerable proportion of the inhabitants, whether they were urban oligarchs, rate-paying tradesmen, innkeepers on whom troops would be billeted, or frustrated would-be demonstrators. Famine conditions frequently polarised urban societies against rural capitalists and the crowd's attempts to exact redress evoked sympathy from across the urban social spectrum; as a townsman of Weymouth confided, 'the middle sort of people' hoped 'that the mob may be the cat's paw . . . to a reduction in prices'. For many small-town officials a periodic riot was something to be endured in isolation.[12]

Nevertheless, troops were frequently requested, and the army played a key role in containing episodes of fierce disturbances. Historians might be forgiven for supposing that the War Office kept full registers of the deployment of troops against civilians, especially as officers regularly communicated their anxieties that injuries or deaths inflicted by soldiers could end in litigation, despite adherence to Riot Act procedures. War Office papers contain hundreds of demands for army support, and these are important sources. But they do not comprise a complete corpus even of those disturbances which were confronted by troops. A 1795 internal memorandum, appended to a local CO's report on the use of his detachment against a crowd, stated that the GOC – who had not formally reported the matter – 'should have a hint from authority that it is his duty to state to the public departments anything material happening within his District'. The order was not implemented, nor could it be when the army was stretched. In the same year, Richard Whyte commanding the great eastern camp at Lexden reported 'the numberless applications I almost daily receive for Troops, to quell Riots'; 'hardly a Day or Night passes that I'm not obliged to send Parties out to protect and assist the Magistrates'. In such circumstances the War Office could not expect detailed reports, and historians must share Whitehall's frustration at the imprecision surrounding the numbers of riots contained by the military.[13]

Riot enumeration from legal records is impossible. Demonstrators were never, and rioters but rarely, *systematically* subjected to legal retribution, not least owing to the judiciary's sympathy with crowd objectives, and fears that even selective prosecutions could further enflame serious social tensions. Other justices advocated recourse to the courts, and the Home Secretary, the Duke of Portland, increasingly insisted on this policy.[14] Legal records also present technical problems. Records for some courts are non-extant. Indictments, and formal minutes, respecting prosecutions for theft and assault, often do not reveal that offences were committed during a riot.[15]

The press, even at the end of the eighteenth century, is an inconclusive source. Riot made good copy, journalists were addicted to 'blood and fire' sensationalism, and a not inconsiderable proportion of their readership wanted confirmation of their prejudiced views of working people and their supposed Jacobin mentors; but editors were often chary of communicating potentially explosive material. The *Derby Mercury* explained that as 'the accounts published with so much avidity in many papers of riotous proceedings . . . are more likely to extend than suppress the mischief we have cautiously foreborne to do so'. Others agreed, and a minority of newspapers including the *Manchester Mercury* and the *Gloucester Journal* maintained a conspiracy of silence even during the seriously disturbed month of September 1800. Newspapers plagiarised each other's local news; one editor's decision against reportage of a neighbourhood disturbance denied the information to less fastidious counterparts. In addition, reports were frequently imprecise. The *Leicester Journal* reported riots in Hinckley, Coventry, Bedworth and Nuneaton, and merely noted that 'there have been riotous proceedings in several other places' locally. The incidence of riot is not necessarily accurately reflected by the press. No single major source is free from serious limitations.[16]

A further range of problems confronts the analyst. The duration of the crises, the fierce polarisation of conflicting interests, ensured that social tensions remained high for very long periods. Nobody was immune, for the theatre for conflict was universal. Farmer Metcalfe, returning from Thirsk market, recorded that 'A woman insulted me as I went through Sowerby saying I should have a halter provided for me against my return . . . . I told her if every impertinent person was entitled to a halter, she would not escape'. Such confrontations – however minor – were precisely those 'twopenny squabbles' which characterised the market-place. In August 1800, Joe Blamire, a West Riding clothier, escaped prosecution through a public apology, designed to stop others stoning stall-holders in Dewsbury; the apology also revealed 'that the like inhuman Actions have been but too numerous in this Town, and the wicked Perpetrators have generally escaped Detection'. At Ipswich in September 1800, rumours spread that one farmer had demanded excessive prices for his corn:

> some women . . . collected themselves together, and forming a line on each side of the street, thro' which he had to pass, assailed him with such a volley of abuse, that it precipitated his departure . . . . no other weapons were employed than their tongues, so that he quitted the town in safety, and the tumult subsided without any mischief.

The usual sources reveal no West Riding disturbance outside Sheffield and Leeds between January and July 1800; the Ipswich report, from the Cambridge press, is the only incident in Suffolk, traceable for September.[17]

This evidence of omnipresent tensions generating minor incidents suggest that historians should also consider when a riot is not a riot? There was no precise legal definition, and even disparity between statute and common law; the latter required three persons, but the former under the Riot Act, necessitated twelve. Many crowds convened principally to demonstrate. Assemblies 'in St Giles at the Seven Dials', one of London's most notorious districts, 'suspended . . . Loaves of Bread . . . in Crape, with the Motto that "This must fall or we shall rise"'. Saddleworth weavers converged on Oldham 'and gave the Badgers [meal dealers] Notice to lower the price of Flour and Meal or else they would come on Thursday next and Retail it out at a reduced Price'; then 'they went peaceably home'. Authority also made fine distinctions. In May 1800 Legge reported Birmingham's

> alarm at the threats of the Populace, who tho' *not in a state of positive Riot* have for *some days been seizing the stocks* at different potatoe warehouses & retailing them at their own price (my italics)

Similarly, the following September, Earl Fitzwilliam in his capacity as Volunteer commander and Lord Lieutenant of the West Riding, arrived at Sheffield, where

> we found large numbers collected in the principal streets. However no act of Outrage was committed (save hissing, hooting and indeed pelting the Sheffield Volunteers, who were going singly to parade; three of these have been much hurt). Though in such numbers, these people were *not rioting*. The Magistrates . . . listen'd to their complaints: the only grievance was dearness of corn (my italics).

Thus the 'riot' is a complex phenomenon. Progression from demonstration to force was not inevitable; nor was force of numbers and physical force invariably synonymous. The Oldham retailers ignored the weavers' injunction; on the appointed day, 'the mob assembled according to their promise', sold the meal at two-thirds of the asking price, returned the sacks and gave the cash to the owners. A crowd at Carlisle spent all day under magisterial supervision unloading grain from coasters destined for Liverpool. Violence occurred only after remnants of the crowd were fired on by an unpopular merchant while demonstrating in front of his house; then a street bonfire was made of his furniture.[18] Dr Bohstedt's criticism that many historians fail 'to specify how they selected the riots they chose to study, and . . . what they defined as riot' is legitimate. His own criteria, that riots require at least fifty people who proceed to 'physical attack, damage or coercion' to 'distinguish riot from mere "protest"', has its attractions, but too many shortcomings. First, considerable damage was inflicted by far fewer persons. Secondly, the 'fifty rule' fails to distinguish between those perpetrating the violence, and on-lookers, whose support may have been a critical enabling factor for the militant sector. Thirdly, the distinction between riot and protest obscures more than it reveals, and fourthly, many sources do not permit these demarcations with the precision capable of making the resultant statistics mathematically viable, as opposed to impressionistic. Fifthly, it leads historians into the trap described by Charles Tilley, namely reaffirmation of the distorted categorisations emanating from the prejudicial and discriminatory 'perspective of the authorities'. Statistical compilations which convey adumbrations are pointless.[19]

How does one quantify and demarcate between riots and demonstrations when crowds are active for days on end, and/or across an extensive district? At Wells in Norfolk, huge crowds 'had for some days past in the most riotous manner prevented the Shipping of Flour for the Capital'. In August 1795, an apprehensive Mayor of Gloucester related that

The Colliers of the Forest of Dean . . . have for some days been going
round to the Towns in this Neighbourhood, & selling the Flour, Wheat &
Bread, belonging to the Millers & Bakers, at reduced prices; & have
openly avow'd their Intention of coming to Gloucester as soon as the
Soldiers have gone.

Mobilisations on this scale defy meaningful quantification, and aggravate
problems of under-reportage. The major periods of riot are central. As their
intensity assumed insurrectionary proportions, from a local perspective at
least, local authorities normally kept government informed, not least to
secure military support. In September 1800, the Nottingham and Sheffield
authorities wrote immediately disturbances commenced; their Birmingham
counterparts waited three days, and then penned a definitive account.
However, Oxford Corporation did not report the renewal of fierce rioting;
information reached the Home Office from the county jailer after his castle
was attacked. The key aspect remains; serious disturbance was reported in
some way, and major outbreaks in the 1790s did not escape the record,
though details of their component parts commonly did.[20]
    Disturbances, including the relatively minor, which are significant for
any global picture, can be plotted through cross references. A disturbance at
Sheffield on 28 July 1795 is documented by the abandoned prosecution of an
artisan, the Quarter Sessions' subsequent vote of thanks to the Yeomanry,
and the formal letter sent to the CO.[21] Totally unreported outbreaks leave
their mark. Borough authorities regularly published promises to protect
marketeers after disturbances,[22] or arranged for an army presence. Public
apologies, like that by Darlaston folk who set their bull-dogs at millers'
horses,[23] together with scores of incidental references in private letters,
diaries, and even account books, help to fill in the picture. If under-
registration remains, the evidence suffices to reconstruct a survey of
disturbances, and an analysis. Their nature, distribution and effect, their
relationship with other forms of protest, their political content, their threat
to order, their suppression and control, and most of their essential functions
can all be approached.

The 'Early Phases'

The 'early phases', the springs of 1795 and 1800, were characterised by the
start of rapid price increases (repeated to some extent in the springs of 1796
and 1801). The identification of these phases by price behaviour, is
reinforced by comparisons of popular responses at these moments. The
predominant characteristic was demonstrations or riots directed at price
control, and economic conditions were the determinant. Although there are
exceptions which warrant separate treatment, in general, responses accom-
paning the 'early phases' during the second seasons of both famines, 1796
and 1801, clearly echoed those of the first, 1795 and 1800, though the
former witnessed less recorded violence.[24] This methodology has facilitated
spatial analysis elsewhere,[25] and the disturbances are tabulated in Tables 1 to
5.

Taxation Populaire *in the Midlands and the North during the 'Early Phases'*

A chronological list of these disturbances is given in Tables 1 and 2. Midland incidents were more numerous and ugly than those in the North in both 1795 and 1800. Although disturbances were concentrated in March and April of these years, the earlier acceleration of prices across the 1799–1800 winter is reflected in the spate of minor clashes, principally in Lancashire and the West Riding. Chronologically, these fell outside the 'early phase', but as they invariably involved *taxation populaire*, they conform to the overall pattern of those periods.[26] Rioting in the West Midlands also started slightly earlier in 1800, with price-fixing at Birmingham, Wolverhampton, and Leek in February.[27] April experienced the climax in both 1795 and 1800. The first major set of disturbances in 1795 commenced with a massive mobilisation of miners and canal-diggers near Leicester at the end of March. The Volunteers' shortcomings were symbolised by their inability to take prisoners, while markets at Leicester, Ashby-de-la-Zouch and Shackerstone bore the initial brunt of popular fury. More serious troubles developed in mid-April, with repeated descents on market towns, including Bedworth, Nuneaton and Hinckley, by south Warwickshire miners. Simultaneously rioting started to the east at Nottingham. Coventry was engulfed by prolonged disorders when invading colliers were joined by urban workers; arrests served only to galvanise attacks on the town jail, and the restoration of peace necessitated concessions by the Corporation. By this time most of the region was disturbed, with the army, narrowly containing a huge exodus from Warwickshire towns and industrial villages, targetted on the key mart at Burton-on-Trent. Towards the end of April, further riots occurred at Nuneaton, Solihull, Kidderminster, Bewdley, Hinckley and Lichfield. The sole recorded divergence from the imposition of price controls, involved the roughing-up of hucksters attempting to make bulk purchases at Lichfield.[28]

The North-east experienced disturbances in both 1795 and 1800, and although miners were the principal participants in both, a comparison reveals significant changes. In 1795 miners regulated markets at Stockton-on-Tees, Darlington, Durham and Chester-le-Street. These episodes were complicated by strikes of Newcastle tailors and keelmen, over wages and the employment of foreign sailors respectively, but they culminated in an enormous assembly at Gateshead. The army was alerted, but the central role of the miners led the magistracy to insist that coalowners adopted remedial measures. By 1800, most mining employers supplied their men with grain at low and stable prices. This kept one riot-prone occupational group away from the public markets. In 1800 miners struck against such employers who increased the price of their corn, and whilst mobilised, and in passing, intervened in a handful of market-place altercations.[29] Elsewhere, 'early phase' reactions are more strictly comparable. Price-fixing occurred at Thirsk, Ripon and Pontefract in April and May 1795, and at Sheffield, Barnsley and Dewsbury in the same period in 1800. The consistency of 'early phase' rioting is best evinced at Nottingham, with incidents on 18 April 1795, 5 April 1796, and 19 April 1800. The evidence for 1801 is poor, but riots were certainly anticipated at Sheffield and Nottingham in March, and occurred in Lancashire during the 'early phase'.[30]

West Midland comparisons between 1795 and 1800 reveal repetitive popular recourse to *taxation populaire*, and one significant development in 1800. Most riots were confined to their place of origin, but the scale of disturbances increased dramatically once urban and industrial workers set off to tour the countryside principally to inspect producers' stocks. Even towns the size of Birmingham were not divorced from the country, and Midland industrial villages were within, rather than outside rural communities. Workers in both locations heard about nearby farmers' activities, and such information was spread further by rumours. The Oldham weaver-diarist, Rowbottom, graphically records the amalgam of both under the heading of 'Pottatoes':

> not withstanding the verey Great Crop . . . the owners in this neighbour-hood Gave over Sellin before the[y] were all Got up and are reserving them for the Spring when the[y] hope the price will be much raised.

Magisterial announcements leant official sanction to such perceptions. The Salford Bench typically 'directed' in November 1799 'that Hand Bills . . . be distributed to the several Townships within the Manchester Division, encouraging Farmers & others to bring Provisions to Market'. This clearly implied that producers were withholding in anticipation of further inflation, a reason specifically advanced by one Mayor against butchers' proposals to publicly defend their own conduct. Once price behaviour ostensibly confirmed rumours, urban protesters directed their actions against retailers. When confronted by an angry assemblage, retailers regularly tried to shift the blame on to their own suppliers, merchants and farmers. The switch in urban perceptions was revealed by a Birmingham sword-maker's in May 1800 in the midst of disturbances;

> He said, he did feel that Indignation against the Farmers, Millers & others who keep back their Corn to the extreme Distress of the Town, that he thought the Mob were only exercising just Vengeance on those who so richly deserved it.

The culpability of farmers could be ascertained only through the crowd examining their barns. The Birmingham crowd's targets suddenly changed. Violent confrontations with bakers and potato-salesmen on 1 and 2 May, ended, and the crowd went off into the country, to tour mills and farms, notably at Edgebaston, a market-garden centre.[31]

These Birmingham events were anticipated elsewhere in the West Midlands. On 26 April 1800 the crowd fixed prices at Lane End in the Potteries, and then toured farmhouses to insist that farmers marketed significant stocks on the 28th. South Staffordshire colliers did the same. One victim, Edward Willington, farmer of Penn, deposed

> that a Hundred of them or upwards entered his House and said they

wanted what he had that he . . . told them he had neither Wheat nor Malt and that they were welcome to search his Premises.

These protestors discovered at most, small insignificant stocks, not barns bulging with grain, and dairies choked with cheese. In scenes reminiscent of the itinerant assemblage of the popular wake,[32] the crowd demanded contributions to members' 'expences', and in accordance with wake-protocol, farmers bought them off with 'gifts' of bread, cheese, ale and half-crowns. Further permutations of popular objectives at this juncture included the stoppage of corn barges on the canals, as at Lane End, Dudley, Atherstone and Stourbridge. Activists here, like east Shropshire colliers, would not permit cereals being 'sent out of the County & their own families starving'. No doubt, the sheer size of these mobilisations, helped facilitate the broadening of targets, but *taxation populaire* remained central. The evidence for the 'early phase' of 1796 is shadowy, but that for 1801 proves that the crowd reaffirmed its prime objective, setting the price.[33]

Taxation Populaire *in the South and the South-west during the* 'Early Phases', *and the Army Revolts of 1795*

If disturbances in this broad region, listed in Tables 3 and 5, were roughly similar in each of the four 'early phases', sufficient dissimilarities were manifested to warrant separate detailed treatment. Generally, the 'early phase' of 1795 was more disturbed than the others. Four main reasons stand out. First, authority was taken unawares in 1795, until a combination of protests over prices and inadequate poor relief emphasised the intensification of plebeian problems. This ignorance was not repeated after the 1795 harvest, or during the entire 1799–1801 famine. Secondly, with the exception of the South-west, public relief was better organised. Thirdly, if prices were higher in 1799–1801, the food supply was rather better, again with the exception of the South-west. Fourthly, and most crucially, in 1795 the army participated in the riots. In a chronological and geographical sense, Militia involvement commenced in Devon, but its climax came in the South, where they were concentrated. Devon and Cornwall are so peculiar, notably in the 'early phases' of 1796 and 1801, that they are examined elsewhere.[34] Since 1795 was so troubled we will concentrate on it here.

The situation of army units, and rank and file problems, in this region at this time, deserve a brief review. Many regular units, notably those raised in Ireland, were recent creations, badly trained, and poorly disciplined. They contained a significant criminal element, and many other recruits were motivated by poverty, not patriotism. Youthful quests for adventure were regularly fulfilled by altercations with civilians in host communities. Militia regiments had additional problems. Pitt's barrack-building programme had not sufficed to satisfy demand for quarters where troops were concentrated, notably in southern maritime counties. Half-finished barracks were used, as by the soon to be notorious Oxfordshire Militia at Blatchington. A disciplined guard was impossible in the absence of a perimeter wall. There were no beds; men slept in hammocks under leaky roofs in this, the third hardest winter in the entire century. The Oxfordshires were reputedly 'in a very unhealthy state', and some men contracted 'fevers'; their hair fell out. Elsewhere billeting difficulties were severe: 'every Alehouse' in Hastings had at least twenty soldiers accommodated in hopelessly overcrowded, inadequate and uncomfortable conditions. Forced marches, merely to secure accommodation, were commonplace. Militiamen in billets received an 'Allowance . . . for Bread Money', and a similar cash sum for meat. Even where officers organised subsistence, the cost to the men, or the quality of their rations, depended on market prices. The Duke of Richmond was informed by the Herefordshire Militia 'that while the Country People were relieved by their Parishes and Subscriptions, the Soldiers receive no such benefit', and were thus more exposed to the ravages of inflation than civilians. A combination of rank and file discomforts, enhanced by absentee and poor calibre officers, rendered army units particularly volatile at this period.[35]

Minor exceptions apart, rioting commenced in Cornwall in early March, and 'spread' eastwards. These Cornish explosions largely concerned tinners in their descents on the ports to stop coastal shipments of barley, and are examined in the context of this form of disturbance. Across the Devon border, riots which commenced at Bideford on 24 March, conform to the *taxation populaire* pattern dominant in the 'early phase'. So too did riots starting at Exeter on 25 March, but here price controls on grain were extended to butter and potatoes; butter merchants were also stopped from sending stocks to distant markets, and emboldened by these successes, crowds also mobilised to stop grain in transit to a naval contractor's tide-mill at Ide. With the Exeter authorities limiting their intervention to the supervision of negotiated price reductions, price controls were fixed by popular decree in mart after mart during the following week. By 6 April one informant knew of riots in Plymouth, Devonport, Totnes, Ashburton, Dartmouth, Newton Abbot and Crediton; if the tenor of another report, that 'mobs are continually rising in our Market Towns', is correct, no market of any consequence remained unaffected.[36] The climax to the Devon set of riots involved a spectacular attack on another tide-mill, at Kingsteignton. The miller, another naval supplier, was popularly believed to be a main cause of high prices locally, a grievance which could be remedied only through the destruction of his establishment. Accordingly a huge crowd smashed 'every Part of the Interior Machinery of the Mill', and gravely injured the proprietor. This served to animate the magistracy; warrants were issued and three men were subsequently indicted on capital charges at the forthcoming Summer Assize. If this judicial counter-attack militated against recurrent mass action, there is ample evidence of continued unrest in the county during the next three months.[37]

The most portentous events in this sequential chain occurred at Plymouth where the Northamptonshire Militia joined the townsfolk to fix prices. The arrest of a soldier at Devonport by a solitary and intrepid magistrate, for the alleged theft of a loaf, precipitated a turn-out by the unionised dockyard workers to demand the soldier's release. Disagreement between the civil and military authorities was soon public knowledge; the former's capitulation encouraged the army CO, Lord George Lennox, to vent his frustrations in a polemical missive to his superiors. Lennox's uncompromising attitude was soon put to the real test, when a further market-place intervention by his rank and file was terminated only by Lennox's bravery in confronting his mutineers, and ordering an immediate return to barracks.[38] By this time Whitehall was in receipt of information confirming repeated military intervention on the side of the masses. If troops did not assist the riotous forays of the notorious Kingswood colliers in March and April,[39] the 122nd Regiment, stationed in the same region, at Wells in Somerset, intervened decisively at the instigation of 'some of the Town's people'. The 122nd's officers turned a blind eye, and their men, under the direction of locals, regulated the market, and were the vehicle whereby a good many private scores were settled between dissatisfied customers and petty food-dealers.[40] Meanwhile, at Abingdon, the 114th Regiment of Foot, an Irish outfit commanded by Lord Landaff, 'made attempts to spirit up the poorer Part of the Townsmen to attack the Bakers and Butchers'. A series of incidents concluded with a massive riot at the fair on 7 April. The local Yeomanry dared not confront Landaff's warriors, and the War Office was soon in receipt of petitions begging

in the name of God to remove . . . Ld Landaff's regmt. from this place, or else Murder must be the Consequence, for such a sett of Villains never entered

Abingdon before.[41]

In the south-east, local authorities remained almost indifferent to signs of growing social unrest over the winter. Threatening letters received at Petworth in December 1794 were brushed aside; the Kent Bench ignored an attack on a Lamberhurst mill in January, and in February the Lewes press ridiculed women's attempts to stop road shipments of flour with jovial reference to 'petticoat assailants'. Lord Sheffield merely admonished prisoners taken in a fierce *taxation populaire* incident at Worth on 2 March. Thereafter a more grave attitude began to prevail. Fordingbridge justices committed female protesters to the Hampshire Assize, and their Chatham counterparts panicked when striking shipwrights joined forces with Norfolk militiamen and repeatedly set prices late in March. Simultaneously, the *Sussex Weekly Advertiser* speedily changed its tone. The three-month old activities of Petworth pseudonymists were suddenly publicised as proof of 'the dark and malevolent threatenings of gloomy malcontents . . . the violent behaviour of a petulant multitude'; now, any manifestation of social insubordination 'deserved the execrations of all', and breaking the peace warranted 'the severest infliction of the penal statutes'. However, Sir Hugh Dalrymple, the CO at Chatham, refused to share the Bench's apprehensions, and endorsed their request for the Norfolk's removal with a

NB. I think we have hitherto had tumults of a very gentle & mitigated Nature. I hope it will continue so.[42]

If Dalrymple's complacency was not shattered almost as he put pen to paper by another Militia-led imposition of price controls at Canterbury, it

certainly was by the next fortnight's events. No sooner had the press widely
reported army participation in Devonian riots, than Militia units participated in parallel events across the South. The Gloucestershires were
culpable at Portsmouth and Portsea, and the Herefordshires at Arundel and
Chichester. A West Sussex clergyman rushed directly, and significantly, to
the regulars at Brighton to inform Lt. Col. Bishopp of the Lancashire Light
Dragoons that militiamen 'from Plymouth all along the Coast to Chichester
had been in a State of Commotion on Account of the high price of Bread
and Provisions'. Moreover, their officers were powerless, and their men in
cahoots with locals. Order was restored at Chichester only through a total
capitulation with the release of military and civilian prisoners, and a
mayoral promise to enforce price reductions. The Mayor of Portsmouth

> published a manifesto to the people conceived in such soothing terms as
> . . . collaterally admits the power of the mob to be uncontroulable.[43]

Order was collapsing; its restoration appeared increasingly unobtainable
as the main agent was instigator and participant in its breakdown. Even
Bishopp, who kept a cool and calculating head throughout this series of
disturbances, anticipated that the contagion would spread to the regulars
from 'the Example of these other Regiments'; he paraded his own men
whom he invited to state grievances, a move he concealed from the War
Office. At Chichester, GOC Richmond took vigorous measures, ordering
officers to mount piquets to arrest soldiers out of quarters at night, and
hastily arranging a field day to get the Herefordshires out of town. While
Richmond then admonished the men, he nonetheless felt compelled to
'promise . . . them speedy redress'. Privately he conceded 'that the safest
way to preserve quiet will be to move this Regiment to some Barrack that
can contain the whole'. Whatever happened, troops and people must be
separated.[44]
    The worst event in this chain of military-inspired revolts was still to
come, and involved the Oxfordshire Militia, ironically in a barrack, but the
unfinished one near Seaford. Awful living conditions were aggravated by
provisioning problems, and on 14 April matters came to a head when beef
bought in Seaford proved to be bad. Lt. Col. Langton returned the beef, but
the compromise reached involved costlier meat, and pay deductions. The
men claimed that prices were extortionate and that 'they should have
nothing left for washing'. A parade-ground confrontation preceded two
hundred men decamping for 'Seaford, saying that they would go and be
revenged on the butchers'. Officers who made arrests were assaulted. A
return to quarters was negotiated, but the men insisted that 'we will have no
prisoners, if any, one and all'. Secretive plotting overnight was followed by
mutiny in the morning; four hundred men with fixed bayonets, and in
regular order, entered Seaford to be met by Thomas Harben, JP and
Volunteer CO. He offered free wheat to the troops, who cheered, promised
no violence, but insisted on visiting the butchers. Their meat went on sale in
the churchyard; cheese, butter, 'and every other article' were added after
visits to the grocers, and all comers invited to purchase at reduced prices.
The pubs were then invaded, and beer prices similarly deflated. At this

point Langton arrived, and he got some men to return, symbolically carrying 'their Meat upon the points of their Bayonets'. The remaining men went off to investigate local complaints of coastal shipments of flour from a tide-mill in nearby Newhaven Creek. Horses and carts were commandered, and 168 sacks of flour were carted off to Newhaven under an escort with some lusty, triumphant horn-blowing. Millworkers also informed the militiamen that the sloop Lucy, recently loaded with flour, was still in the Creek. A detachment boarded the ship, and hauled her down to Newhaven quay, where 325 bags of flour were neatly warehoused bar a score sold 'to those who chose to purchase'.[45]

By midday on 15 April Newhaven was overrun by more than three-hundred soldiers, who strutted about with bayonets, and unsuccessfully scoured the town for ammunition. Most were soon installed in the pubs, and too drunk, so their officers later said, to be approached. More grandiose plans flowed with the drink. Brewers were to be forced to reduce their prices, and farmers to modify their demands, clear indications that local retailers were blaming their suppliers. Meanwhile a monumental binge was partly financed by compulsory sales of captured flour. But if the Militia controlled Newhaven, other plans were afoot to oust them. The County Sessions was actually sitting when the distraught constable arrived at Lewes, though it was symptomatic of the terror prevailing that only the chairman, Sheffield, and one colleague dared to accompany General Ainslie to Newhaven, even though they were escorted by the Royal Horse Artillery. This formidable force was met outside the town by Langton. His men beat to arms, fixed bayonets, and faced the Artillery. A slanging match between the opposing rank and file commenced, but brave words from the Militia hardly disguised their fears. A parley was agreed, which commenced in the comfort of the Ship Inn. The militiamen agreed to withdraw with their officers, '"but not with the Dragoons"', and at 5 p.m. they set off 'peaceably and willingly Singing God save the King'. But at the bridge a minority, vociferously reminded their colleagues of oaths taken never to evacuate Newhaven before accomplishing their mission, fell out, and reoccupied the town. Sixty mounted an overnight 'guard' while more than two-hundred others returned to barracks. Unapprised, the Artillery re-turned to Lewes.

Before the evening civilian participation was minimal. The Militia was encouraged by knots of women at Seaford, and Harben was hard-pressed to stop more positive involvement by locals. Greater fraternisation occurred between the guard and Newhaven folk over the night; everything edible in the pubs vanished, and liquor supplies were maintained only by ninety-seven gallons of beer taken from a brewery. In the quest for food, civilians identified grocer Greathead, unpopular as a 'barge Master', concerned in flour transhipments. His cellars were looted, and in the melée his watch and other items disappeared. Eventually the soldiers went to sleep, more or less where they drank or collapsed; they were in beds and stables all over the place when the regulars, with Artillery and Yeomanry support, took the town in the morning. Some fighting occurred, but few injuries were inflicted while these men were arrested. At this moment 160 Oxfordshires reappeared from the barracks to 'bring home the Guard'. This party was fired upon by the Artillery, but it took Bishopp's Lancashire cavalry over an hour to round them up, during which fierce fighting produced a crop of serious injuries, mostly sustained by militiamen. Over two hundred were now under formal arrest: the entire regiment was disarmed, and nineteen prime suspects incarcerated in Lewes jail, together with two civilians concerned in the raid on Greathead's establishment.

The district remained very tense, with ominous manifestations in the aftermath of the mutiny. At Brighton disputes arose

> between some Regiments of Militia and the Lancashire Fencibles, who are called by the Militiamen, SHORT-LOAF, – BLOODY BACK etc. for the part they took in quelling the mutiny.

The Duke of Richmond worried over the inevitable security problems caused by keeping so many men under lock and key, while he received reports of repeated threats, made in anonymous bills, to rescue the prisoners. Witnesses to the mutiny went in fear for their lives 'as they are pointed out as objects of revenge'. A major scare occurred almost immediately when a bizarre, nocturnal incident near Lewes generated rumours that

> six or eight hundred men had gained possession of the Artillery's cannon and that it was the intention . . . first to seize the arms taken from . . . the Oxford Militia . . . deposited in the old House of Correction.

Volunteer and regular troops rushed to the town and 'the whole day exhibited a scene of military parade and public confusion'. Richmond got the Oxfordshire moved. The mutiny received prodigious press coverage; it formed one of the very few items of distant home news entered by the Oldham weaver-diarist Rowbottom. And, militiamen participated in further riots, including those at Guildford and Petersfield, and were encouraged by civilians to do so elsewhere, as at Exeter and Reading. Militiamen on Portchester POW camp duty threatened to release their charges if prices were not abated. The Mayor of Hastings testified to the 'exemplary loyalty of the Warwickshire', but on the flimsiest evidence and in the same breath, anticipated their leadership of disturbances, and demanded their removal. Richmond had ample grounds for his uncertainty on 21 April, 'whether we can or cannot in future depend on the Militia'.[46]

Pitt personally took charge of the government's speedy response to the collapse of military discipline. He had already, on 14 April, adopted Richmond's advocacy of replacing cash allowances by rations, because in prime ministerial estimations, May 'would be the most likely month to produce Disturbances' and then Militia loyalties would be critical. Orders to provide bread rations were issued on 18 April, and the Oxfordshire's concern with meat was reflected by a further order, made one week later, to introduce meat rations. The troops were informed hastily. Those in the South-east also received a homily from Richmond who insisted that mutinous soldiers would be severely punished, and promised that 'every attention is paid to . . . real wants when properly and regularly represented through their officers'. The ration orders were issued in the deliberate absence of the responsible minister. As the opposition later complained in the Commons, additional rations were

> given to the soldiers as a mere gratuitous donation of the King himself, and it was evidently intended thereby to impress on the . . . soldiers that it was the King alone, and not the representatives of the people who . . . were to pay the whole.

This was not simple Foxite constitutional oratory. The costly remedy of the militiamen's grievances was cunningly contrived to encourage patriotism.[47]

Concessions, rather than the harsh and much-publicised retribution meeted out to the Oxfordshires, won the Militias over.[48] Private Cook, later pleading for his life, told the Court Martial that his comrades' grievances over food prices had 'been since relieved by his Majesty's most gracious interposition with Regard to Bread which allowance to a Common Soldier is a material alteration'. Meanwhile, the press strenuously contrived to restore public confidence in the army. Stories of further military involvement in riots were vigorously and repeatedly denied. Kentish disturbances at the start of May received no publicity. By contrast, field days and army alacrity received copious coverage. The Mayor of Hastings withdrew his demand for the Warwickshire's removal. Newspaper editors who erroneously claimed army participation in June riots were prosecuted by the Treasury Solicitor following high level military investigations into the facts. Pitt even reprimanded opposition MPs in the May debates on the new allowances, for referring to past incidents. Foxite jibes that Pitt had capitulated to 'the demands of soldiers with arms in their hands', stuck nonetheless.[49]

*   *   *

Taxation populaire dominated 'early phase' protest over much of the country. Crowd objectives reveal some variation, notably when price-fixing proved ineffectual, and where the sheer scale of mobilisations permitted crowds to implement further facets of the 'moral economy'. The mutinous Oxfordshires verged on being an exemplar with their threats to brewers and farmers. Other permutations are reserved for later detailed analysis. The 'early phase' of 1795 was the most violent of any of the four parallel periods, not least because of the army's role. Moreover, this riotous phase was quickly followed by the midsummer hypercrisis, which Pitt correctly forecast as likely to be more disturbed. During that summer a panic induced crowds in numerous localities to adopt an alternative primary tactic to *taxation populaire*. In the face of famine local stocks had to be conserved; those actually in transit on roads, rivers and canals, or stored in market towns in the producing regions, were seized for the consumption of locals in the vicinities of these towns and the lines of communication.

CHAPTER 7

'Taking Bread out of our Mouths'
the Crowd, Food Transportation, and the Midsummer Hypercrisis of 1795

Demands for the conservation of stocks were made throughout rural areas, in market towns, in river and coastal ports, and even in farming villages, to form the strongest motivating force behind crowd actions in the major productive regions. A huge tract of country, extending from the East Anglian coast to the Severn, bounded in the south by the Thames and Kennet, and to the north by a line drawn west from the Wash south of the industrial Midlands was affected. A superficial look might suggest that these widespread disturbances comprised a mere extension of the fierce *taxation populaire* episodes in the 'early phase', but this is partly disproved by the extension of the midsummer troubles to previously undisturbed districts. Case studies help to reveal the development of the dominant stock–conservation motive. This facet of the 'moral economy' is also emphasised in regions where it perennially dominated popular objectives, and where shifts in this dominance occurred in response to changing marketing practices. Contrasts between riotous activities in the producing regions and the centres of consumption in the summer of 1795 strengthen this point. The virtual cessation of the internal circulation of grain posed massive problems for the latter, and the intensity of rioting across the entire country deserves detailed investigation in its own right. Indeed, if Pitt had not restored Militia loyalties, the devastating impact of these developments could have proved to be cataclysmic.

Popular Demands and Case Histories

The historical peculiarity of English provincial administration and parliamentary representation helped to preserve the concept of the locality as a distinct entity, still described in contemporary parlance as one's 'country'. In normal times with stable prices, the 'export' of provisions from a district was unremarkable, but escalating prices triggered fears of total exhaustion through commercial activities, and these spread speedily in May and June

1795. In every producing region, hundreds of workers were involved in moving stocks from farms to the centres of communication, and away to the centres of consumption. Corn is a bulky commodity, and these operations were unconcealable. Only fear and price rises could guide consumers in anticipations of total exhaustion. A definitive conclusion was beyond the ruling class. In Oxfordshire, where corn shipments were brought to a standstill, no two magistrates could agree over the degree of deficiency. If the Bench could not estimate how much provision could be safely spared, workers could not be expected to. For the masses, the despatch of any food meant graver depletion and higher prices.[1]

Fear of starvation riveted popular attention on dealers and communication systems. Fears were aggravated by hundreds of agents for urban authorities scouring the countryside in the desperate scramble for stocks over the summer; then 'the Poor . . . begin to be very discontented and talk loudly'. A chain reaction set in, with magisterial concern over the security of roads, rivers and wharfs. 'Many false bad things' were said about Shardlow Wharf on the Trent, where cargoes were shifted from coasters to barges; the local JP ordered merchants to expedite operations. Dealers adopted secretive methods. At Towcester grain 'to be taken to Birmingham in the night' was hidden in lofts. Home Counties millers abandoned the waterways in favour of nocturnal road shipments. But such practices provoked more sinister rumours, notably that such grain was clandestinely, and illegally shipped to France. Millers, even in Buckinghamshire, Berkshire and Oxfordshire, had to combat such accusations. In East Anglia, where identical rumours were more plausible, one MP concluded that whatever the truth, 'It makes a good deal of noise'.[2]

Two case histories, both from East Anglia, which virtually escaped 'early-phase' violence,[3] reveal the relationship between the different though complementary crowd objectives, *taxation populaire* and stock-conservation. At Cambridge in mid-July, popular claims 'that no bread could be got at any price' on some days, determined deputy-mayor Martook – the 'undisputed dictator of the town' – to examine stocks. In mid-enquiry, a crowd seized and 'very methodically' unloaded a flour barge destined for Ely. Their action proved a godsend to Martook, who had discovered dangerously depleted supplies; brushing aside the protests of Lord Lieutenant Hardwicke, whose broader responsibilities led him to try to get the crowd to desist, Martook bought the flour. Bread went on sale at subsidised prices on the morrow. But early that morning the crowd regrouped in response to wholesale deals between the town and 'country' butchers; the populace stopped the despatch of meat, and sold it at reduced prices. Martook intervened again, but only to use Corporate funds to subsidise workers' meat as well.[4]

The well-documented riot at Saffron Walden on 27 July also reveals a crowd which assembled originally to stop grain shipments, going on to implement other parts of the 'moral economy'. The workers' predicament here was representative of those in many market towns. A relief fund was extended only by a recently-imposed emergency poor-rate. Orders for considerable supplies of oats and wheat had secured a derisory volume of boiling peas. The decision to exclude those not formally settled in the town from relief inflamed a sector of the population, and the remainder were infuriated by what was on offer. On 18 July the Mayor approached all known holders of stocks, after dealer Hall reneged on a deal to supply Saffron, in favour of more lucrative prices obtainable elsewhere. Other local merchants were also engaged in shipments to distant marts, and on 27 July tempers finally exploded. Wheat destined for Cambridge, and lodged at two inns, was seized; Charles White, a baker and cornfactor, and Hall, were interrogated 'whether they had got Wheat in any other Place', and subsequently transport was requisitioned to bring a consignment from a granary at Sampford, eight miles away. All this wheat was pitched at the Market Cross for sale at reduced prices; butchers' and grocers' commodities were then also subjected to *taxation populaire*. Unable to obtain immediate military aid, the Mayor acquiesced in enforced prices, and organised rationing to which those previously excluded were readmitted. The initiative temporarily lay with the crowd; one activist warned a butcher against breaking the price code, saying that if the masses reconvened 'they should not be without Arms and he then flourished his Spade in Imitation of the Exercising a Firelock'. Arguments ended on the arrival of troops two days later.[5]

Disturbances in this region exhibit complex interconnections. The failure of Saffron to acquire customary grains at Cambridge may be partly attributed to disturbances there. Higher Cambridge prices encouraged Essex grain holders to market there, at Saffron Walden's expense, which in turn underlay Saffron stock-conservation on 27 July. *Taxation populaire* was clearly a secondary objective in both towns, but both these incidents stimulated price-fixing in their localities. The Chatteris crowd desired a JP to 'superintend' the sale of meat at stipulated prices 'as the Mayor had done for Cambridge'. Two days after the Saffron riot, a crowd at neighbouring Great Chesterford, insisted that an itinerant baker reduced his loaves to prices imposed at Saffron.[6] Similar interconnections, including the 'knock-on' effect of riot, were visible throughout the summer, and underlay conflagratious developments.

The Creation of the Blockade in the Producing Regions

The fiercest riots in these regions occurred in the larger market towns, especially milling centres like Bedford and Norwich, together with communication centres, represented by Oxford and Tewkesbury. Such towns also had hundreds, and some thousands, of urban workers in a variety of industries, who were dependent on the open market, and were thus consumption centres in their own right. Workers here also reeled under the impact of high prices, which they reasoned would escalate further if stocks accumulated by merchants were despatched elsewhere. At Bedford, a Mr Harrold, 'a very considerable factor & miller', sent 'several hundred loads of Wheat' from his Olney Mills, and was held responsible for the 'excessive scarcity of Bread-corn' confronting exasperated townsfolk. After a prolonged struggle between 9 and 21 July, the County Yeomanry appear to have abandoned escorting Harrold's carts, and no more left Bedford. A rigid embargo was also imposed at Norwich, where the 'populace are assembled and will not suffer a sack to go'. At Oxford, complaint at the continuous shipment of corn by canal for Birmingham was aggravated by rumoured sitings of miller Bolase's sacks in France. Bolase's enforced self-defence admitted that he dealt 'with Persons who resided within the Distance of Coventry, Birmingham' and other Midland centres. The canal became 'that Damned Cut' in popular parlance, and despite the 'concilatory' publications of the Town Clerk, Oxford remained 'in a tumult' with 'strong symptoms of rioting' between 10 July and 6 August. Eventually, it was said that the protestors 'appeased themselves with an Idea that Parliament, when it meets will order' the canal 'to be filled up'.[7]

Flour barges in transit were detained in scores of places in this broad sweep of country, including Bath, Newark-on-Trent and Tewkesbury. Many incidents exhibit symptoms of panic, including the gladiatorial ladies of Tewkesbury, who somehow berthed barges moored in mid-river, and carted the flour off in their aprons. Sir George Onesipherous Paul, the long-serving Gloucester magistrate, reacted to the scale of this phenomenon with the assertion

> that this is but the Beginning of an Evil that will turn to desperate consequences; the Cry of Want of Bread which is real forms a Body of Insurgents . . . . things wear a very unpleasant Appearance, the more so as the popular Cry . . . has gained allmost the whole people to the side of Plunder, they think it justifiable to seize this Vessell & sell the Corn.

The roads proved no safer. Thomas Higgens, a dealer passing through Witney with seventy sacks of flour for Birmingham, was pursued by a crowd for over five miles to Long Hanborough, where his horses collapsed. Here, outside the Bell Inn, the crowd swelled, 'swore the Wheat and Flour should go no further and they would have it there': the whole was 'pitched . . . on the roadside' and sold under the supervision of the constable. Higgens was seriously assaulted. Martha Pritchard, leader of vigilantes policing a Herefordshire turnpike, told the driver of a miller's cart that 'we will not hurt you because you are a Servant but if your Master was here we would kill him'.[8]

Popular positive policing of the lines of communication became widespread, and was commonly started after incidents like that at Witney. 'The mob dispersed' after stopping shipments of corn at Towcester, but 'part staid on the high road to stop any more corn being sent away'. The Privy Council learned that in Northamptonshire 'People were stationed on the roads to alarm the Country when attempts were made' to shift consignments. At 4 a.m. farmer Kay of Yarpole encountered a ladies 'Council of War' at a turnpike gate 'waiting for Lovett's Cart'. In Sir George Paul's jurisdiction problems intensified daily; 'from the disposition' of the people

> I see We must come to blows before we are quiet – the Corn is seized in every direction & they have an Idea they were to live by plunder, & indeed by plunder they must live unless we can restore protection to the Canals & Roads as no Grain can be safely carried on either.

Only a massive reinforcement of the army could 'stem the Torrent that is running in the Country'.[9]

The torrent flowed backwards into the heart of the countryside, often with minimal violence in the villages, which accounts for scanty evidence. R.J. Buxton MP reported a July stoppage at Barham, Norfolk, where 'the people rose'; he was unconcerned because 'they were very peaceable their only object was to prevent the Wheat being carried out of the parish', and he laconically concluded, 'that is the case in many places'. Farmers in some Norfolk parishes who withheld wheat in hopes of catching even higher prices in distant marts just before the harvest, were the victims of 'frequent mobs' who inspected barns, and insisted on sales of stocks to parishioners only throughout the summer. Short-distance transfers of corn in the North Riding were also interrupted. One participant, Miss Mary Atkinson of Bridforth later sadly

> saith that . . . she was unhappily concerned in obstructing (with several others) Mr Cleaver's waggon & committing a misdemeanour on the high road . . . which she is sorry for.[10]

Magistrates repeatedly capitulated to this populist policing and frequently revealed their own sympathies by supporting the crowd with formal injunctions. Norwich Corporation issued instructions 'compelling' city 'Millers . . . to send their Goods to Norwich only'. A chain reaction commenced. Great Yarmouth, deprived of supplies from Norwich, imposed its own embargo on grain shipments. By mid-July most eastern sea and river ports were shut. Metropolitan baker Lovell had flour detained at Lynwade Bride, Great Yarmouth, King's Lynn, Wells and Fakenham on the coast, and other consignments in inland Norfolk and Cambridgeshire. His flour at Wells, together with 274 quarters of wheat belonging to a Nottingham relief organisation, was sold off by the Mayor early in August. The Mayor told the Privy Council that his arbitrary conduct prevented riot and a 'total Want of Bread Corn'. Where corporate powers were non-existent, individual magistrates filled the void. Flour shipments were detained in the streets of Burford and Witney on the orders of clerical JPs. Village vestries, themselves commonly under popular pressure, filled power vacuums with decisions to conserve all corn for parishioners, which cut off supplies to Peterborough among scores of other towns. The Bench threatened obdurate merchants rather than riotous workers. Miller Harrold was told not to expect the Mayor of Bedford's protection, and pointedly informed that the town's relief committee was the most appropriate customer. Miller Dodson of Godmanchester, Huntingdonshire, eventually abandoned his attempts to honour contracts to supply Coventry; crowds detained every cartload, his drivers soon refused to face the populace, and the County Bench 'consulted Counsel to prosecute him'.[11]

The scale of the blockade, where imposed by reported disturbances, can be gauged from Tables 6 and 7. But as in mid-July 'the women have assembled in considerable bodies, and prevented any waggons passing through with corn . . . in most of the market towns of Suffolk, Norfolk', this tabulation of specifically recorded incidents seriously underestimates the magnitude of popular mobilisations. No region escaped similar occurrences, as indicated in columns 3 of Tables 8 and 9. Yorkshire rioters effectively closed the Aire and Calder, vital for supplies going from the coast, the East Riding, and Lincolnshire, to the industrial heartlands of the West Riding.[12] But these particular disturbances did not occur in the *producing* regions. They were extensions of the *taxation populaire* which predominated over the summer in the centres of consumption. Here, the desperate situations developing during the midsummer hypercrisis were partly due to the blockades effectively imposed by popular action in the producing regions.

The Midsummer Hypercrisis of 1795 in the Centres of Consumption

Authorities in the centres were keenly aware of the ramifications of the blockades for them. The industrial Midlands, Lancashire and the West Riding, were hit worst. The closure of East Anglian ports jeopardised London's supply, though the government's preoccupation with the capital softened the impact.[13] In the centres, supplies were so fragile that even temporary stoppages made the difference between days with scanty stocks in the shops, and days when there were none. Complaints from big centres against the blockades reached a crescendo. The Mayor of Chester knew that supplies from Shropshire were stopped on the roads, and that more were being diverted down the Severn. It is a measure of the strength of the blockade that these diverted supplies did not reach Bristol, whose Mayor simultaneously complained furiously at the blockade. Both men insisted that only 'immediate steps . . . to restore the Trade to its usual and natural Channel' could avert 'very serious Consequences'. Frustrated magistrates at Birmingham tried to explain that flour seized at Burford 'was actually purchased to make Bread for the Inhabitants' of their populous town. In utter desperation the Birmingham Bench contacted their Oxfordshire counterparts,

> thinking that a Letter from one Magistrate to another . . . will have the effect of prevailing on that Gentl. to put the Laws in full force & see that the Property of an Individual is safely restored.

They appended a distinctly ominous threat to this plea for legal propriety:

> if Corn & Flour are not permitted to be brought from Oxfordshire & the neighbouring Counties to this Town there is great reason to fear that the Workmen of this Place & its neighbourhood who all of them know that there is an Abundance in the Counties will sally forth and make great confusion in the Kingdom.

The recipient of this missive, the Rev. Knollis of Burford, cunningly used it to divert the Home Secretary's attention from his own arbitrary conduct, and to demand troops 'in case of a threatened Attack from Birmingham'. The deliberate fostering of rumours that the frustrated populace of Birm-

ingham would sack country places like Burford, illustrates urban desperation. But bakers and millers in the centres lobbied Volunteer officers to
mount escorts for their shipments. The lethal potential of this interaction of
pressures was articulated by the Mayor of Leicester. Convinced that 'the
Volunteer Corps of our own County will do everything for us', he
approached the War Office for permission 'for a Detachment of our own
Cavalry to proceed into' Northamptonshire to guarantee 'a very secure
Escort'. He ominously concluded that 'we sho'd think it very hard to want
Bread through the Etiquette of our own Corps interfering with that of
another County'. Given the pressures on rural local authorities, which of
course included many members of rural-based Volunteer regiments, this
type of proposal could terminate in civil war, as evinced by the pregnant
events at Barrow-on-Soar near Leicester. Villagers there had decreed that
no 'grain, grown in their Parish' should be despatched; the crowd frustrated
a nocturnal attempt to send two waggon-loads to the county town, and –
under the auspices of the local clerical JP – such of this corn not sent to the
mill for immediate manufacture, was left in the church. Several hours later,
a tired detachment of the Leicester Yeomanry, led by another magistrate,
arrived in expectation of a riot and in no mood for negotiation. A
confrontation with the crowd served only to fortify the Volunteers'
determination to get this wheat to Leicester, and they replied in kind when
shots were fired at them from nearby houses. Two villagers were killed;
another was mortally wounded, and at least six others were injured. The
Yeomanry then escorted one waggon away. In fact the government had
already acted to forestall armed descents by Volunteers on the producing
regions by instructing the regulars to police all communication networks:
market-town garrisons were also reinforced.[14]

   The desperation of the authors of these letters reflected that of their
plebeian constituents, who were reduced to traditional responses. No
particular protest pattern emerges. Demonstrations and riots against all
types of food suppliers, including relief organisations, occurred repeatedly.
Countless descents on farmers happened where the countryside was not far
removed from urban markets. Grain shipments were commonly seized by
the inhabitants in the industrial hinterlands of great centres.

   The West Midlands were engulfed by intense disturbances throughout
the summer. On 2 and 3 June, colliers invaded several market towns,
including Wolverhampton, Dudley, Walsall, Tipton, Wednesbury and
Darlaston. Although they were contained by the army, concessions were
won, including the compliance of local farmers with a maximum established by two JPs at Wolverhampton. Abrogation of this agreement three
weeks later coincided with the intensification of the blockade. On 22 June,
two thousand colliers and nailers from the Dudley district searched mills,
attacked army detachments, and then embarked on a lengthy tour to
inspect farmers' premises. A combination of concessions by farmers and the
arrival of military reinforcements brought some respite, and the main
scenes of disorder shifted further west. The same occupational categories
were involved in identical actions in Shropshire, which the Earl of
Warwick designated 'an Insurrection' at the end of July. Major businesses
ground to a halt as employers joined the military and the magistracy in a

prolonged campaign to preserve a semblance of order. Many incidents must have gone unrecorded in the ensuing melée. One which made the press had a satisfactory ending and a moral content. Justice Sparrow persuaded those responsible for the seizure of a barge near Stafford that its contents were for the poor of Wellington in Shropshire, and it was permitted to proceed.[15]

These West Midland disturbances took on an even greater aspect with a massive social explosion in Birmingham in late June. The town's milling and baking trade was dominated by miller Pickard; his huge Snow Hill steam mill was one of Birmingham's industrial showpieces.[16] June featured numerous altercations between his staff and customers; rumours abounded, including one claiming that massive stocks were 'buried under the mill'. However, a strong military presence maintained public order, until a detachment left speedily to confront rioters elsewhere on 22 June. The crowd which quickly assembled outside, and then stoned Pickard's mill, believed all the troops had gone. After four hours of protest, and an ineffectual recital of the Riot Act, Snow Hill was cleared by the remaining regulars with Volunteer support. The Bench, in the belief that military patrols 'served only to draw crowds of idle people . . . to look at them', dismissed the army at 8 p.m., leaving a precautionary guard at the mill. Crowds reassembled on the troops' withdrawal. The guard made arrests, and then fired, killing one teenager and wounding another. The guard was extracted from their predicament only by reinforcements rushing to the scene, though the final dispersal of the crowd necessitated a bayonet charge and further arrests. The prisoners were immediately despatched to the county jail at Warwick, and cavalry patrolled the streets overnight. They failed to prevent the posting of 'written papers of the most criminal nature' demanding vengeance and calling the people to arms, allegedly of Jacobin origin.[17] Official leaflets stressing the impolicy of attacking 'armed men' did not deter a gang beating up a member of the mill-guard who was recognised at his billet on the morrow, and the town remained tense for days. The death of the other casualty on the 27th was not the occasion for renewed violence, owing to massive military reinforcements arriving from as far off as Carlisle. Subsequent threats of revenge led one JP to retire from active service, and judicial directions devolved on Heneage Legge, the Volunteer Cavalry's CO.[18]

In July, a pattern of disturbances reminiscent of that in the West Midlands, engulfed Derbyshire and Nottinghamshire. Striking miners joined framework-knitters on 'getting a notion that some particular persons had stored up corn'; grain seized at various farms was taken to Trent-side mills for grinding. The army was too stretched to contain the mobile forays by different crowds. JPs and Volunteer Corps were subjected to repeated, nocturnal call-ups. It was impossible for any gentleman 'to pass thro' any Village . . . without being insulted', reported one resident. Fears that all law and order forces would be 'overpowered by the rioters, who keep us in perpetual alarm' were entertained well into August.[19] Conversely, northern mining districts escaped rioting on this scale; disturbances at Bishop Auckland and Berwick-upon-Tweed convinced authority that troubles would spread, but Pennine lead-miners never made their anticipated descent on Richmond, and outside specific major towns, protests were relatively muted.[20]

There were serious and bloody scenes in Sheffield and some Lancashire cotton towns. Sheffield's working population's almost unique reputation for insubordination, riotousness, devotion to democratic ideology, and participation in organised radicalism, was reflected in the facts that no magistrate actually lived in the town, and one of those domiciled nearby, Colonel Athorpe, always carried a card inscribed with the salient clauses of the Riot Act. Rioting commenced in the 'early phase', and arrests were made during further incidents on 2 and 13 June; in the event, fears that the 'Birmingham contagion' would take root proved premature, and the next reported incident, the stoning of a flour-mill was contained by the Rotherham Volunteers under Earl Fitzwilliam. His temperate troop deployment restored order, if not calm, and earned the formal thanks of the Bench in Quarter Session.[21] Fitzwilliam's pragmatism was not the forte of Colonel Athorpe, the next Volunteer commander to face crowds on Sheffield streets. During June, a subsidiary source of tension derived from the non-payment of bounties to a new regiment raised by Colonel Cameron, and unwisely still quartered in the town barracks. Solidarity between the recruits, relatives, friends and neighbours, was further cemented when the town's relief organisation upped the price of their subsidised flour. Handbills linked military and civilian grievances. Cameron's troops were popularly expected to mutiny and lead the crowd to seize the relief committee's warehouse. Some recruits certainly loaded their muskets and others filled their pockets with stones. The vicar, the elderly Rev. Wilkinson genuinely believed in an extensive conspiracy, to be launched from the barrack parade-ground, and an expectant crowd turned up to watch. Athorpe, summoned from dinner at Wentworth Woodhouse, killed his horse in a furious twelve-mile gallop, and he then forgot to transfer his Riot Act card when donning his uniform. While this was retrieved, he and his Infantry faced the crowd for three-quarters of an hour. His card restored, Athorpe recited the Riot Act; the crowd responded by encouraging Cameron's warriors to attack Athorpe's. In a desperate attempt personally to arrest an inciter, Athorpe was hemmed in, and with his replacement steed rearing out of control, he unsheathed his sword, and lashed out 'on every side'. Several people were hurt; Mary Needham later exhibited her scarred face to a jury which was also told of a man kept off work by injuries to his 'private parts'. Athorpe also later claimed that 'He was alarmed, being among such a crew; his life was not worth a moment's purchase'. Extricating himself, he rejoined his men, and confronted the now stone-throwing assemblage for an hour; the troops then opened fire, killing two men, wounding others, 'and the rest fled on every side in consternation'. That night, surgeons were stretched to treat all the victims.[22]

Minor disturbances continued through the night, and a huge demonstration greeted Athorpe's emergence from his hotel in the morning. Authority imposed a curfew, and blamed the casualties on 'the Wickedness of a Few designing Persons' rather than 'the wants of many'. Athorpe, who was popularly, and soon formally, accused of offences ranging from assault to murder, concentrated on amassing evidence of 'Jacobin' participation. But the funerals of the dead failed to produce the anticipated riots. The *Sheffield*

Courant attacked the account given in James Montgomery's radical *Iris*, and soon half the county's press was partisan. The incident generated a major stir. When the tourist MacRitchie arrived he went straight to 'get Captain Stewart's account'. Once a coroner's jury supported him, Athorpe prosecuted Montgomery. Athorpe's success with a jury of conservative farmers at the Doncaster Sessions was virtually assured. The jury had no time for Montgomery's impassioned defence based on the testimony of 'poor persons', which counsel insisted was of no 'less weight than the evidence of the rich', and was equally unimpressed by scarred faces, and the little girl who had had to explain to her parents why she came home covered in blood. Montgomery went to prison for six months for criminal libel, sentenced by Athorpe's colleagues on the West Riding Bench.

Disturbances in the cotton towns, which posed severe logistical problems for the army, were equally serious. A series of *taxation populaire* riots at Manchester terminated in injuries inflicted by soldiers and recourse to curfews. Stockport was saturated with regulars in support of the Volunteers, and the containment of several affairs without much bloodshed pleasantly amazed a professional officer.[23] At Oldham, where 'those Swailers that Caused meal to be so dear' provoked price-fixing, prisoners were almost rescued after a furious fight with an army escort taking them to prison in Manchester. Rochdale proved the setting for the worst violence. After several days' *taxation populaire*, the Bench resorted to the Infantry Volunteers whose arrival was greeted by taunts that they 'dared not fire, as they were loaded only with saw–dust'. Bayonet charges produced running battles, as the crowd dispersed in one street, and regrouped in another. In a final confrontation

> orders were given for the front line of eight to fire, afterwards for the second rank of the same number. The latter fired into the air; but by the former two unfortunate old men were wounded, and died in a few hours; a boy also received a ball in his arm . . . and it is reported another person was slightly hurt.

Of the eight shots fired at the crowd, only one missed; one of the dead was hit by three bullets, the other two. If the shootings cowed the Rochdale proletariat, the news failed to deter their Oldham counterparts, the participants in another violent riot on 5 August.[24]

Elsewhere, disturbances were not punctuated by equally serious incidents, but few, if any populous places were entirely free from demonstrations. At Bristol, meat prices were fixed, and fish–supplies to Bath stopped. The local press ignored most incidents, but corporate expenditure of £500 on army reinforcements 'to suppress riots' speaks for itself. GOC Rooke clearly still distrusted the Militia unless accompanied by regulars. At Hull, as at Sheffield, street demonstrations greeted the relief committee's decision to raise their prices, and at Nottingham, like Birmingham, rioting started after an army detachment left the town.[25] London did not escape, though popular protests over food were complicated by radical hostility to the government, and by other issues including residual grievances over the crimping activities responsible for fierce rioting in 1794. July 1795 was a tense and disturbed month, but major incidents did not develop before the huge demonstrations against the war and the attack on the royal coach in the autumn.[26]

Blockade Imposition and the Famines

The devastating national potential of blockade imposition in the producing regions was realised only during the midsummer hypercrisis of 1795. With the exception of some recurrence in East Anglia in the following autumn,[27] no major blockades were imposed in the 1795–6 season, or during the entire 1799–1801 famine. There were exceptions with crowds stopping consignments in both periods, but such behaviour was either isolated,[28] or subsidiary to the implementation of other facets of the 'moral economy'. Non-repetition must be ascribed to problems deriving from high prices as opposed to 'absolute scarcities' in contemporary analyses. These recurred, but were confined to major consumer centres in the September 1800 hypercrisis; then a peculiar combination of factors meant that there were few grain shipments traversing communication networks; blockading was unrealistic. However, in two regions, the Forest of Dean and Cornwall, blockading proved the principal popular response during both famines. This statement is more true of West Gloucestershire and East Monmouthshire, reflecting shifts in Cornish farmers' marketing habits between 1795 and 1800.[29] These similarities, and the changing emphasis in Cornwall, both illustrate the key conditioning effect of local and regional socio-economic structures on precise forms of popular protest.

Forest of Dean farmers, like their Cornish equivalents before 1796, were more interested in larger urban markets than in meeting local demand. Complaints over supply difficulties experienced by small Dean towns like Ross-on-Wye were a recurrent feature of eighteenth-century dearths,[30] and in 1795 the Chepstow Bench tried to force Forest farmers to sell locally. However, satisfaction of Bristol's huge demand depended in part on constant supplies arriving down the Wye and the Severn, and Foresters were infuriated by such shipments continually sailing through riverport market towns. Dean miners would have seen eye to eye with their Cornish counterparts' announcement that

> they will not bear Starving when they see Grain carried out of the County without any brought to Market where every-one may see there is Corn & may Purchase at a Price Demanded.[31]

Other similarities included miners' proverbial riot-proneness, and juridical problems. Cornishmen were usually 'in a transitory State going from one Mine to another & not belonging to the Parish where they work cannot obtain Relief' under the Poor Law. Great parts of the Forest of Dean were extra-parochial altogether. A 1788 report estimated that over four-hundred cottages lay outside parish boundaries, themselves so inconclusively mapped that agreement over demarcation and hence responsibilities was impossible. Moreover, the extra-parochial parts became a dumping ground for unmarried mothers, harried off to these spots for delivery. Population grew rapidly, and in 1801 it was estimated that a definitive survey of boundaries, people and habitations would take months. Many Foresters had no access to poor relief.[32]

The Foresters' first offensive, in June and July 1795, saw corn-barges stopped, and their contents forcibly sold. Dean millers who supplied Bristol and Gloucester were attacked. Disturbances were uncontrollable by the local judiciary, even with army support, and a shipment of government flour for Hereford only got through with a powerful escort. As late as mid-August the Mayor of Gloucester plausibly claimed that his town would be exposed to a literal invasion by miners if the garrison was reduced. But the Foresters' campaign secured sufficient sustenance for the summer. Repetition was stimulated by price rises in the autumn, with millers' carts turned back, and barges stopped; the men of Ruardean policed traffic on the Severn. The arrest of some of these vigilantes, and an enhanced military presence freed the waterways, but not the district, from tensions over the winter. Renewed attacks on river transport in March 1796 brought swift military retaliation, which combined with the imposition of capital sentences on the Ruardean men at the Lent Assize, to drive further protesters to adopt secretive, intimidatory tactics. The main targets were those justices held responsible for orchestrating repression. Mr Pyrke of Little Dean narrowly escaped assassination, a colleague's mansion was sacked, and pot shots were fired at guests attending a fashionable garden-party.[33]

Disturbances commenced in 1800 in the same month as they were contained in 1796. Flour waggons were stopped, but Pyrke, mindful of his previous experiences, adopted a more circumspectful profile, and negoti-ated sales at reduced prices. His conciliatory conduct probably encouraged an escalation of the Foresters' militancy, and flour barges on the Wye were stopped. The Foresters' determination withstood vollies from the army, and even then 'It was with much difficulty that the barges were . . . allowed to proceed . . . and the mob only dispersed under a threat of intercepting them further down the river'. Barges were seized at Monmouth on the morrow; some were rescued by the army, others were unloaded by the protesters. Disturbances then petered out; Dean farmers were certainly intimidated, and the arrival of imported flour at Bristol was an undoubted additional factor favouring localised marketing. Inaction during September 1800 reflected the exhaustion of old stocks, and the inability of farmers to thresh wet corn. Once farmers were able to take advantage of high prices in distant marts in the spring of 1801, a further crop of riots commenced with barges stopped, riverside granaries inspected, and seized flour sold off. The publication of recriminatory complaints at the inactivity of sections of the magistracy by Hereford merchants, suggests that the flow of cereals down the Wye was seriously impeded by widespread, but under-reported disturbances.[34]

Cornwall was disturbed equally frequently, and in 1795 was the first region in the country to sustain serious riot. The miners' first invasion of Penzance on 10 March took the authorities completely by surprise. The invaders 'had absolutely entered the Town before the intention was known', namely to investigate reports of barley shipments from the port. Miners' fears were confirmed, and the offending parcels were seized and sold. A second invasion some days later was easily beaten off by a strategically placed Volunteer regiment, but authority in every port thereafter anticipated identical attacks. Helston officials were relieved when a threatened inspection failed to materialise, and the Rev. Giddy was almost pleased that he had to confer with only 'an insolent deputation . . . from the miners of Wendren'. Port Isaac and Padstow were less lucky. Coastal shipments were violently prevented at both, in a series of incidents which confirmed official intelligence of considerable organisation among miners across a broad district. Crowds came from a huge triangle formed by St. Agnes, Redruth and Truro, up to thirty miles away. Men from Rosemundy left on the morning of 21 March, reached St. Columb at 4 p.m., where they were feasted by sympathetic residents, and arrived at Padstow at 9 p.m. still 'in the greatest good order'. An aborted inspection of St. Austle terminated this series of raids aimed at deterring corn 'exports', and with the exception of minor, apparently isolated *taxation populaire* at Callington, Fowey and Helston, comparative tranquillity returned over the next six months. The cessation of 'exports' and the arrival of considerable stocks of government flour were responsible.[35]

The anti-export riots at St. Agnes and Helston immediately after the 1795 harvest, clearly represent a transitory stage in popular action.[36] Cornish farmers' new concentration on local markets was quickly reflected by changed popular perceptions of responsibilities for subsistence problems; withholding farmers were now identified as opposed to merchants. Miners were the principal participants in crowds which toured the countryside in November 1795, and again in the spring of 1796. Farmers were ordered to market their corn at stipulated prices. When these arrangements collapsed, as. at Truro and Redruth, they were reimposed through *taxation populaire*, and maintained by intimidatory attacks and anonymous warnings. The evidence of riot, but not of scarcity, is poor for 1800, and in 1801 miners went on the offensive, again in the countryside, somewhat earlier in January. The County Bench quickly appreciated these changes in the form of protest, and in March 1796 acted to shield the agrarian from the mining communities. They argued, with some success, that mine-owners must assume the responsibility for securing their employees' subsistence, 'to prevent that Time and Expense to which' miners 'must otherwise be necessarily put in looking after it'. The Bench also advised farmers against withholding.[37]

*   *   *

The 1795 hypercrisis was one of the two most violent periods during the famines. The scale of violence reflects the imposition of the blockade, and the resultant severity of the problems caused thereby in consumption centres. Stock-conservation remained an important facet of the 'moral economy' as shown by events in the Forest of Dean, and its appearance periodically elsewhere, but protest was capable of rapid adaptation to changing economic realities as revealed by Cornish experiences. The absence of army participation in *taxation populaire* episodes during the 'early phase' of 1800, is one reason for that period's less violent record than its 1795 equivalent, but the scale and nature of protest in both periods is roughly comparable. Different economic conditions were responsible for the non-recurrence of the problems of the summer of 1795 during the summer of 1800; the severe shortages of the former contrast with the huge volumes of imported grain reaching England in the latter.[38] The second most violent epoch in September 1800 exhibits a number of conditioning features. No blockading developed in the producing regions, because relatively little grain was ready for marketing, and rural fears of imminent exhaustion were unlikely. Demand from urban centres could not be met from residual imports; absolute scarcity combined with public convictions in artificial causation of critical shortages in the biggest towns. Commercial machination was universally suspected, and this triggered urban rioting on a scale and intensity probably greater than their predecessors in identical locations in the 1795 summer.

CHAPTER 8

'Glorious tho' Awfull Weeks'
the Hypercrisis of September 1800

Chronologically, rioting commenced at Sheffield at the very end of August after a 'sudden advance of flour'; it spread to Nottinghamshire, attaining considerable ferocity in both the borough and the county, before catching on across a broader tract of country. Derby was affected on 4 September, Leicester on the 5th, and during the following week, rioting was experienced throughout the West Midlands. By the 15th disturbances had begun in London on a scale not seen since the Gordon Riots of 1780. Other areas, especially Oxfordshire were badly affected by this date, and elsewhere disturbances were common, if more isolated, and not the centres of conflagrations like that engulfing the Midlands. The nature and the intensity of the riots originated in the economics of shortages, popular causal theories, and the dominant popular remedy, namely the subjection of corn to a maximum price.[1]

The Borough and County of Nottingham

The first disturbance comprised an aggravated Saturday night demonstration against Mansfield millers on 30 August. Late on Sunday evening a sequence of much more serious events began at Nottingham. Authority was caught unguarded; Town Clerk Coldham claimed that the initial riot was a reaction to high prices and flour shortages. However, a plebeian resident, J. Golby alleged that

> the Bakers and flour Sellers had . . . a private Meeting on Sunday and had agreed to Raise the price of flour up to Six Shillings A Stone on Monday, and there having been But a very Scanty Supply all the Week before [this] Exasperated the Inhabitants to that degree that they Begun with them on the Sunday night.

The Blues enforced a partial dispersal after the stoning of millers' and bakers' premises. Crowds reassembled in the morning to search Trent-side warehouses, and flour belonging to Arnold spinning-mill proprietors Davidson and Hartley was seized with 'famine-impelled eagerness'. Even reinforcement of the Blues by the borough Infantry and Cavalry Volunteers failed to contain the desperate scramble for flour, and the Blues had been on continuous duty for twenty-four hours when they were ordered to mount street patrols throughout the night of 1 September.[2]

There was no respite for the weary troops on the 2nd. On dispersal, crowds joined others, regrouped elsewhere, or split into large mobile bands. The Mayor arranged for assistance from local Corps of County Yeomanry who rushed to the town, summoned by flags flown from the steeples, as exhaustion debilitated the original armed forces. At 3 p.m. *The Times*' correspondent posted his report: 'there is not even a prospect of the riot subsiding', due to the non-arrest of 'the women . . . the principal aggressors'. The arrival of another party of County Yeomanry escorting prisoners taken in adjacent industrial villages, provoked a determined rescue attempt; a volley wounded two people in the crowd, which responded by stoning the Volunteers so relentlessly 'That they Cou'd Load Their pices no more', and had to be rescued by the Blues. This violent finale concluded events on 2 September.[3]

Massive crowds reappeared on the 3rd. Ferocious 'fighting . . . in the Meadow plats', was followed by the ambush of a Volunteer Cavalry patrol near the Leather Bottle, 'the most vicious part of the Town'. An unhorsed soldier was 'plundered of all his military accoutrements' and savagely beaten until he begged for his life. In the midst of this pandemonium, a stupendous thunder storm struck, damaging buildings, but ending what Golby described as 'one of the most Glorious tho' awfull Weeks that was everr seen'. The crowd was indeed victorious. The Riot Act was never implemented despite mayoral threats to the populace, tempered somewhat by his promises to the middle class, whom he wanted to enrol as special constables, to suppress disorder 'without the effusion of blood'. His appeals for civilian assistance went unheeded, despite a second specific request to twenty-two named 'respectable Gentlemen'. All food shops were shut; official warnings that continued rioting would end all supplies to the town were ignored. Authority capitulated. *The Times*' reporter talked of a 'real panic' gripping 'all the opulent'. The crowd had not only withstood fire from the army but had shown an alarming unity; the old divisions between royalists and radicals evaporated. On the 3rd William Watson received a letter about Nottingham events, while he fought to contain disorders in the industrial villages. It said

> That the Troops are almost wearied out; and that they still show every disposition to rise again, and which I fear is the case, when the messenger came. . . . And I fear that Doctor Wylde is no longer able to Act, being quite worn out with being constantly out Night and day.

Moreover, the Infantry Volunteers, largely drawn from the artisanry, had started to desert, unable to stomach the 'Implacable hatred' of their friends and neighbours in the crowd.[4]

Disturbances spread to the surrounding district on 1 September with 'considerable Damage' to mills in at least four villages. On the 2nd sectors of the Nottingham crowd scoured the adjacent countryside, and returned with confiscated corn. In several industrial villages they 'were joined by some of the manufacturers'. The prisoners sent to Nottingham came from these parties, but arrests failed to deter the notorious framework-knitters of Calverton among others. On the 3rd the town crier was forced to 'publicly declare' an assemblage making for Caythrop Mill, and a large crowd moved off setting prices here, and at every other place through which they passed.[5]

In some senses these rural disturbances proved invaluable to the beleaguered borough authorities. On 1 September they circularised local landowners who were asked to put pressure on their farming tenants to supply the town; this implied that the onus for the restoration of order now lay on the farmers. Farmer Volunteers on duty in Nottingham were cajoled into selling wheat at £4 per quarter, and were joined by others in a transparent attempt to avoid unpleasant confrontations. The Corporation also secured 130 quarters elsewhere. Although the Mayor seized the opportunity when announcing these facts to publicly refute popular beliefs in his legal power to set corn prices, these stocks were disposed of at subsidised prices. The idea of a maximum price between local agriculturalists and the town quickly began to catch on; it was followed within days at Mansfield. Landowners led by Sir Gervase Clifton, tried to extend these leads towards a county-wide agreement. On 7 September a County Meeting, constitutionally called by the Sheriff convened, but was poorly attended. Those present would concur only in recommending farmers to thresh quickly and notify Nottingham authorities of sales to prevent profiteering by millers and bakers. Nevertheless, the populace registered a great triumph. As Golby put it, with pardonable exaggeration, the

> Gentlemen Begun to be frightened and A Metting of the Sheriff and Country Gentlemen has been held . . . and they have agreed to Compel their Tenants to bring the Corn to Market and to sell it in small quantities to the poor Thus has the price been Lowered almost 4 pound a Quarter by nothing but the Courage of the People in Declaring against Oppression . . . . the Gentlemen said if the Farmer Cou'd not Live when it was Lowered they wou'd sink his Rent . . . . Dismay has been the Consequence to the Farmers and the Gentlemen Otherwise, their Avarice wou'd never have suffered them to have come down.[6]

It proved a hollow and ephemeral victory. Lord Middleton did agree to deduct the difference between £4 and the market price from his tenants' rents, and other landowners rode round visiting farmers, but the whole operation was straitened because agriculturalists had little saleable corn, and they were still struggling to complete the harvest in adverse weather. There was much private hostility, and indeed venom. J.W. Emmerton bluntly confided to his absent brother that the maximum was imposed by 'some wrong headed people in order to procure quiet'; the 'neighbourhood' could not 'furnish' enough corn, and if the merchants were unable to supply Nottingham, the populace 'must . . . experience want'. Other problems included the £5 maximum at Leicester, and farmers who marketed there, as opposed to Nottingham, were 'equally considered . . . philantrophic'. A mere twenty-five quarters of wheat had been sold by local farmers to borough bakers by 9 September, and the volume sent to Mansfield was unequal to two days' demand.[7]

In Nottingham large crowds milled about quietly now that cheap flour was on sale. But authority shared the oft-stated popular view that continued order hinged on the maintenance of supplies at agreed rates. On 7 September a closure of the bakeries was narrowly averted by the arrival of corporate stocks, bought at £7 the quarter; considerable sums would be lost, the Mayor was under mercantile pressure to end the maximum, and was also reputedly worried at its effect on the supply. On 11 September he received a lengthy missive from the Home Office, ordering the maximum's immediate abolition.[8] He seized the chance to shift responsibility on to Whitehall. Handbills announced the town's dependency on distant supplies, themselves conditional on civil order, which would now be enforced at any cost, and in spite of inevitable price rises. In a further display of opportunism, authority suggested that the populace should trust that 'the wisdom of the Legislature will devise some effectual way of relieving the consequent distress of the poor'. The Mansfield Bench simultaneously removed their maximum, ominously stating that if they had exceeded their authority, they had severe powers under the Riot Act.[9]

Reactions were more violent in the county. Mansfield experienced fresh disturbances, and in the villages riotous sorties against those who had promoted the maximum, and were thus held to have reneged, led to nasty clashes. Volunteer detachments guarded likely targets. They deterred an attack on Clifton's mansion, but at the home of a colleague 'the Mob met with a warm reception', with one man hit in the leg and 'another had a piece of his skull shot off'. The Blues drove another band into the swollen Trent. Thereafter, protest adopted a secretive guise, with nocturnal meetings convened 'by the signal of a Gun firing'. Emmerton weighed up the defences of his home as residents related the 'terror that prevails in the . . . Villages'. Army reinforcements were rushed to Nottingham, 'to keep the Mob quiet', according to a diarist, and an uneasy stalemate obtained, punctuated by inflammatory posters, threatening letters and graffiti, and a concerted, covert campaign to induce desertions in the remaining loyal Infantry Volunteers. Nightly curfews, enforced by army street patrols, the early closure of stipulated pubs, and some arrests produced a 'tolerable quietness' by 23 September, in the Town Clerk's estimation. But authority refused to publish the texts of anonymous missives 'from a fear that they might inflame'; the conspiracy was joined by the press, whose reports – or lack of them – Emmerton informed his brother, meant he would have 'little knowledge of what is passing'. The rest of September was spent in assessing damage to properties, and arguing with the county authorities over relative payments to the Blues who had served in both jurisdictions. The total cost came to £733, and argument still raged in January. If they declined to pay the Blues, the Corporation did bestow the freedom of the borough on the regiment's officers, an honour extended to all Volunteer officers, and to one farmer who continued to supply 'the Poor with Corn at a very low Price' ever since the riots. It was the sole wreath laid on the grave of the 'moral economy'.[10]

Birmingham and the West Midlands

Rioting radiated south and west from Nottingham during the first week of September. On the 4th some disturbance at Derby occurred the very day a plagiarised account of a Sheffield riot appeared in the local press, together with news of Nottingham events. On the 5th serious, but under-reported riots commenced at Leicester with the imposition of a maximum, and 'almost every village' was in turmoil within days. Rioting struck Chesterfield and parts of Derbyshire on the 6th, and between the 8th and 10th crowds composed principally of miners invaded the market towns of Coventry, Nuneaton and Ashby-de-la-Zouch, in a series of disturbances which appear to have originated at Bedworth. They spread rapidly into Worcestershire and Herefordshire, but Warwickshire remained at the heart. Every mart was soon guarded by Volunteer Cavalry, who also pursued itinerant bands across the county. After a week the Volunteers were exhausted, and perhaps protesters too. Regulars replaced the Volunteers.[11]

In the midst of this conflagration, a series of major incidents erupted in Birmingham. They had similarly inauspicious beginnings to those at Nottingham, and initially centred on rumours, current at the end of August, that Crockett, farmer and great grain merchant of Handsworth, had claimed that he 'and nine more of his Associates corndealers coud advance the Marketts all over the kingdom when they pleased'. On 8 September Crockett was spotted in Birmingham and hooted through the streets by a pack of small boys. He left under police protection, but the crowd swelled and meeted out customary justice with half-bricks to other suspect traders before the army intervened. The next morning, crowds, again composed principally of adolescents, demonstrated at Pickard's Snow Hill mill, as they had in 1795. After those experiences Pickard had provided blunderbusses; now he prepared to use them. Immediately cobbles were thrown, his men opened fire, wounding two lads, one fatally, the other dangerously. Regulars and Volunteers dispersed the crowd after a recital of the Riot Act. The streets were deserted by 1 p.m., but rumours spread with astonishing rapidity. By the morning of the 10th the entire town believed that 'a Child had been . . . shot in its Mothers Arms'. Strong army patrols prevented huge assemblies, but frustrated demonstrators stoned the troops from the safety of the alleyways. At the end of the working day, crowds milled about, excited by a workshop blaze, the arrest of a would-be incendiary of Pickard's mill, and in anticipation of the coroner's enquiry to deliberate on the 11th. On that day, further expectant crowds were disappointed by an overnight adjournment, but vented their anger by fixing butter and vegetable prices.[12]

The 12th, the day the verdict was confidently predicted, began with a huge military presence on the streets, and sales of a particularly grotesque cartoon, best described by the graphic indictment against the printer. The print depicted a figure representing Pickard with the firing off of a Gun or Blunderbuss from the upper part of the . . . House and a Woman before . . . with a wounded Boy bleeding in her Arms and a Label containing the Words . . . 'My Murdered Child – Shot!!' and a Man (i.e. Pickard having an Ear of Barley upon his Hat . . . and . . . hanging by the Neck from a Gibbet erected at the same House with his Face towards the Figure of the Devil . . . [saying] 'A proud Look, a lying tongue, and hands that shed innocent Blood'.

Crockett appeared too, on the gallows' steps, cursing his greed. Printer Pearsall's arrest failed to stop massive sales. Meanwhile the inquest went badly for Pickard. In the event no verdict emerged on that day, but the miller announced his intention to sell up, and gave the first option on his entire business to the newly-constituted relief committee.[13]

The worst disturbances so far threatened to erupt on the 13th, a Saturday. However, the crowd achieved two critical victories. First, the relief committee announced its immediate take-over of Snow Hill mill. Secondly, the inquest jury returned a murder verdict. To the people this meant that the law would take care of Pickard, and authority the conduct of the bread supply. One ugly scene was narrowly averted when the other casualty's death was wrongly reported, and a handful of provision dealers were attacked. A sector of the crowd moved off to Edgebaston and Handsworth to visit market-gardeners, farmers, and perhaps Crockett. These sorties were contained by the army, but not before some agriculturalists, not including Crockett, had some scarring experiences. The latter possibly account for the marked subsequent improvement in the town's vegetable supply. Tensions eased gradually; when the other lad did die on 4 October, the coroner's jury brought in a justifiable homicide verdict, which implies a more settled atmosphere.[14]

Birmingham acted as another central theatre fuelling the conflagration sweeping westwards. Colliers, metal-workers, and locksmiths, were the primary participants in numerous descents on market towns; Wolverhampton, Walsall, Stafford and Kidderminster bore the brunt of them, though their hinterlands were disturbed for days on end. Initial objectives hinged on *taxation populaire*, with bakers and millers the prime targets, but once again crowds subsequently visited farmers to whom some of the blame was shifted. This stretched the regulars and Volunteers, and a range of evidence relating to 'great & numerous Alarms' across extensive tracts of semi-industrialised country, suggests that a mere catalogue of reported disturbances would seriously underrate the scale of disorder. Civil unrest subsided by 20 September, except in the Potteries and northern Derbyshire where the last ten days of the month proved critical. Ironically, the last recorded riot involved the stopping and looting of corn barges near Wolverhampton, also at the end of the month, and the sole recorded example of this form of protest, which reflects the comparative absence of long distance supplies. A combination of military containment, agreements between some farmers and millers to honour local maximums, backed in places by the Bench, and some restoration of steady supplies, saw the end of overt disturbance. Covert forms, similar to those in Nottinghamshire, continued.[15]

The City and County of Oxford

Three key factors conditioned disturbances in this region. First, the traditional conflict between Oxford University and Corporate authorities, impinged. Secondly, the closer proximity of urban inhabitants to considerable corn country ensured a greater relevance to the third factor, the addiction of some farmers to imprudent boasting about withholding stocks while prices climbed even higher. One rodomontader was seized and bound, and narrowly escaped a ducking across the border at Abingdon on 1 September. The Mayor of Oxford's failure to suppress anonymous posters advocating *taxation populaire*, deterred farmers from 'stirring from home' according to the Vice-Chancellor, who also believed that the City Volunteer Infantry would not repress price-fixing. He successfully approached the Home Office for a detachment of regulars. Their arrival incensed the Mayor, a Volunteer officer. When cereals, butter and meat, were all subjected to *taxation populaire*, the Mayor distinguished himelf by sanctioning the action, and refused to summon regulars or the Volunteers; he then appointed a committee to prosecute people detected committing traditional marketing offences. That committee's publications served to confirm the current

> general notion . . . that the Farmers, relying on the protection of the armed Association, keep the Corn in the Barns & sell it at their own Price.

Oxford mealmen retaliated by threatening to sue the Mayor, whom local farmers tried to bankrupt by blacking his promissory notes, but this conflict did nothing for plebeian consumers who found food difficult to come by, and tensions soared after 10 September.[16]

By this time other towns were disturbed, notably Banbury on the 11th, where an invading posse of weavers from neighbouring textile villages fixed prices. The weavers left with the promise of a townsmeeting to adopt remedial measures, fixed for the 15th, whereupon the indigenous population turned over the farming, corndealing proprietor of the Red Lion, and others. Intelligence that the weavers intended to return to exert pressure on the 15th, determined the Mayor to resist. Volunteer discipline was stiffened by regular troops, rushed from Oxford. This force was used immediately on the weavers' appearance. Prisoners included Whitmore, the leader, taken in possession of a letter, graphically describing in Jacobinical language, the crowd's early triumphs at Nottingham. Whitmore and two others were committed to Oxford jail, but the escort had to fight its way out of Banbury.[17]

It also had to fight its way into Oxford Castle. Oxford had been in turmoil all day too, with repeated attacks on merchants rumoured to have sent corn to Birmingham, and a mass inspection of canal wharfs under mayoral supervision. When this crowd encountered the escort, Whitmore 'thrust his head through the window' of the chaise, 'shewed his hand cuffs and called out "a large loaf for a shilling"', 'the general watchword'. A furious battle commenced outside the Castle; eventually, and only after the jailer

> found . . . two Prisrs. & the Constables under the Wall when he took hold of one of them desiring the[y] wod hold by each other and dragged them within the Prison Wall,

the three were incarcerated. The crowd spent two and a half hours stoning the jail and tried to stave in the main gate; the magistracy were conspicuously absent in spite of being contacted by a turnkey, who slipped out of the Castle at grave personal risk.[18]

The Oxford crowd reconvened on the morrow to spend the entire day touring farmers to insist that they marketed wheat at stipulated prices on the following Saturday. Impressive discipline, which preserved the Castle from another siege, was maintained over the next three days. Each evening about 250 assembled with 'a complete appearance of system, under some Person or Leader, who gave the word of Command to March & Disperse', to 'sally out as soon as dusk and return home before light'. Participants claimed that while they abstained from violence their activities remained legal. The Corporate authorities, already under Home Office investigation for magisterial inactivity on the night the jail was attacked, did nothing to oppose these nocturnal excursions. Saturday 20 September, the day stipulated for farmers to attend the market, proved critical. By then, coincidentally, a new Mayor had been sworn in, who adopted a more vigorous policy with the appointment of special constables. The farmers however 'confessed in the Market' to the new Mayor

> tho not without some hesitation (as was natural when the Multitude were so close at hand) 'that they were called upon to make this promise' that they conceived themselves bound by it, and 'that they should not go from it'

but only on 20 September. Protection was now promised, and a subsequent mayoral announcement dismantled the maximum. If there were no reports of popular resistance, the people remained in an ugly temper, directed notably at the meddlesome University authorities. Threats of further disturbances if the three Banbury rioters were severely punished were appeased by their release on bail, though the Vice-Chancellor was stoned in the streets the day preceding the Sessions.

Events at Witney, where workers were additionally troubled by the recession in the blanket trade, took a similar turn to those at Oxford. The imposition of a maximum on 11 September drove farmers elsewhere, and the crowd retaliated by visits to farmers between the 19th and 21st. The local Bench capitulated after members were 'grossly insulted', and instructed farmers to obey crowd dictates. It was confidently asserted that the Lord Lieutenant, the Duke of Marlborough, would order his tenants to observe the maximum. He was soon in receipt of another of the Home Secretary's missives, and if Marlborough issued no order to his tenantry he refused to show the letter to his subordinate justices. The tenor of further communications from other JPs suggests that once they had adequate army support, they overturned maximums, though farmers here and there still honoured agreements with the crowd. Meanwhile at Oxford magisterial pronouncements taught the populace to look for parliamentary redress, and the Corporation's petition for an emergency session early in October probably eased tensions in conjunction with the release of Whitmore and friends.[19]

London, the South and South-east

The first disturbances in this vast region commenced independently in direct response to price rises at the end of August. Those in the first week of September were relatively minor, tough probably seriously under-reported. Reports of attacks on millers and bakers, with *taxation populaire* concern Portsmouth, Poole, Blandford, Romsey and Overton, and suggest a localised conflagration starting in Hampshire and spilling over into Dorset. Fears of a chain reaction were articulated, notably by the Mayor of Southampton, but not realised, until after week-long metropolitan riots. The latter clearly evoked a provincial response,[20] and identical observations apply to the two subsidiary series of riots in East Anglia.[21]

London was reputedly almost drained of flour at the start of September, but fears of a spontaneous insurrection passed while soaring prices directed popular hostility to the major merchants. The explosive situation was exploited by opportunist factions among the revolutionary underground.[22] On Sunday 14th, posters produced by the Jacobin printer, Merryweather, circulated; the timing was crucial:

> Sunday being a leisure day with the poor, was artfully chosen as the best for circulating the poison among them, for on that day they communicate more with each other, and, no doubt, the high price of provisions gave rise to general condolance and irritation.

The posters, stuck-up on London Bridge, the Monument and elsewhere, called for demonstrations on the morrow, a Monday and the main exchange day at Mark Lane. The authors of 'Famine' were identified as those with 'extensive monopolies', though the message also stressed the sovereignty of the people. Lord Mayor Combe organised large posses of constables, with Militia and Volunteer Cavalry concealed in reserve. By 9 a.m. London was beset by a number of crowds. The largest, two thousand strong, thronged Mark Lane. Here, Combe's address was greeted by cries of 'bread, bread, give us bread, don't starve us': '"Cheap Bread Birmingham and Notting-ham for ever"'. The police cleared the market hall, and violence was restricted to 'Hooting . . . Hissing', and elbowing dealers. Prudency dictated the closure of the exchange, but Combe felt able to leave by 1 p.m. Recalled, he read the Riot Act in the afternoon, and most people drifted away; those remaining 'seemed more like a Crowd of Curiosity than a Mob for Violence', and were left under police surveillance at 5.30 p.m.[23]

That evening once 'the working classes were at leisure', crowds roamed through Westminster and into the East End, 'Mobs . . . in every Street in thousands'. Several houses in Mark Lane were damaged, and the police assaulted; driven off by the Volunteers, this contingent rampaged through Shoreditch and Whitechapel, smashing the 'doors and windows' of every baker en route. Such activists were watched by thousands of spectators, whose numbers contributed to the confusion. Parading Volunteers were derided and stoned to chants of 'Bread! Bread!'. Several notorious provision merchants were visited, including cheesemonger Wood of Southwark, accused of throwing overkept rotton cheese into the Thames, and the infamous cornfactor Rusby, recently fined in the celebrated show-trial. Rusby escaped over his back wall, while his house was sacked until the crowd was driven off by the Guards, sent poste-haste on War Office orders. The streets were not quiet until 1 a.m., when an exhausted Combe returned to the Mansion House to pen a short account for Home Office consumption. The crowds had been lightly opposed; there were some arrests, but no serious injury to soldiers or civilians.[24]

Crowd discipline and organisation, especially the systematic street-light smashing to prevent identification of individuals while rioters paused to attack specific premises, was sufficient to convince the Tory press of a Jacobin plot. Combe, a Foxite Whig, was unconvinced, unable to 'discover any Concert or System in the Tumult'. The 'numerous seditious little papers . . . scattered about', represented printmakers' customary exploitation of current affairs, for cartoons depicting forestallers had been on sale throughout the summer, and which now competed with politically-inspired, printed 'inflammatory Ballads'. But the immediate targets and slogans of the crowds prove that popular hostility was principally directed at the most infamous of the greater merchants. Quakers were especially vulnerable. A Saffron Walden Quakeress put it succinctly:

> Many of our Society being in the Corn Trade . . . have been supposed to have considerable Influence on the Market, and some ill-designing Persons have industriously circulated an Idea that they occasion the present high price of Bread Corn; this has so enflamed the minds of the People against friends that it seems as if no abuse either of the Person or Character would be too great, inasmuch that it is hardly safe for men Friends to be seen in the Streets,

notably in London, where 'Things look very serious'.[25]

Recurrent mobilisations were anticipated on the evening of the 16th, though there was no obvious central assembly point. The day was spent in examining fifteen prisoners, only four of whom were committed for trial, which aggravated rising tensions between Combe and the Home Office. The latter pressed for more arrests and less tolerance of street demonstrations. The City did adopt the Secretary of State's suggestion that the £100 reward already on offer for information leading to the identification of those responsible for the initial poster campaign, be increased to £500. Greater precautionary measures included the embodiment of all Volunteer Corps by 4 p.m., and extra regulars put on stand-by. Unpopular traders published exculpatory statements and lobbied for permanent guards. Numerous crowds assembled, but were opposed more vigorously by the regulars, whose deployment was primarily responsible for the lack of serious incidents, and greater Home Office satisfaction at the evening's outcome.[26]

Intelligence reports of a premeditated attack on Mark Lane during the less important business hours of Wednesday, were responsible for strong contingents of regulars and Volunteers on duty by 8 a.m. Previous targets were now protected by Guards detachments, and the owners of retailing establishments ordered to remain open. All police leave was cancelled. Mark Lane remained quiet, but women from the East End poured into Bishopsgate in what seems to have been a preconcerted design to attack Wood's shop. They were foiled by the police, who preserved order without effecting a dispersal. In the evening 'the mob got bolder', and even when ruthlessly chased by the Cavalry, inflicted damage on selected commercial premises, as well as stoning the army. Again, serious injuries were avoided and 'the Populace dispersed . . . about their Bed Time'.[27]

The experienced London stipendiary magistracy were pleasantly surprised that during three days of continuous activity, incidents were restricted to expressions of 'particular resentment' against the more notorious traders, to be distinguished from any 'general disposition to riot and disturbance'. Others reacted equally coolly. The Rev. Smith of Westminster School praised Combe's 'alertness & energy of conduct', and Henry Grimston, from the comparative safety of Pall Mall, assured a provincial correspondent that the Lord Mayor had 'quelled the mob'. Nevertheless Combe incurred criticism, to which he responded on the 18th with the announcement that the Riot Act would be henceforth rigorously enforced. His statement was responsible for a remarkable change in crowd tactics that same evening. Instead of remaining 'stationary where they first assembled', crowds now followed a disciplined and extensive itineracy, chosen to facilitate quick stoning attacks on selected targets. Moreover, the lamps in lighted streets were systematically smashed. Both developments posed serious security problems:

> The rapidity of movement gave . . . rise to a thousand reports, and great alarms; no one could tell where the mob was, but every one knew where they had been.

Unable to catch the crowds, Combe could not enforce the Riot Act. The Cavalry arrested but two people. Moreover, such discipline reinvoked fears of political motivation, and press reports spoke of 'rather well dressed . . . leaders . . . to the number of about a dozen'.[28]

Suddenly, Combe was attacked from all quarters. The Lord Chancellor vituperatively exclaimed that 'the Lord Mayor is proceeding like his Predecessor in 1780 & will produce similar excesses'. In response to Home Office pressure, which included equipping every stipendiary with detachments of regulars, Combe proposed on the 19th 'to cover the City . . . with Troops'. Every available Volunteer was on duty. These precautions worked; although crowds assembled, they were clearly intimidated, and only one act of violence was catalogued. Nevertheless, authority considered that Saturday 20 September was 'more than any other best calculated for the

Assemblage of People about the Markets', and reactivated the precautions of Friday. Shopkeepers who wanted to close early were ordered to remain open. A number of fleeting attacks were mounted on previous targets, minor affairs erupted in several markets, and the infamous inhabitants of St. Giles mobilised in the Seven Dials. But the populace was obviously overawed again. The Home Secretary summarised the

> opinion of all the Magistrates [that] the mob was of the meanest description, & so easily intimidated that Mr. Ford, with the assistance of one constable only, took three out of the midst of them without any molestation or the smallest risk.

Many more arrests were made. Despite previous fears of a Saturday night explosion the army withdrew at 1 a.m. with 'scarcely a creature remaining in the streets'. The maintenance of heavy policing over the following three days saw the situation cool remarkably quickly. The Volunteers were all dismissed by 24 September; Combe discontinued his daily reports to the Home Office, and mutual congratulations were bandied about between London's defenders.[29]

The London riots triggered others across the South-east. On 18 September bakers' shops were stoned at Windsor, and attempts were made to start a riot at Kingston-upon-Thames. Rioting in towns to the south of the Thames estuary commenced with a massive demonstration at Rochester on the 19th, followed by Saturday night *taxation populaire* in Sheerness, Woolwich and Deal. These, and other relatively mild disturbances across the South-east revealed several characteristics. Marketing methods and related abuses were perceived to be at the root of inflated prices. The Tunbridge Wells populace at last mobilised to remedy a long-standing grievance, secretive dealing in the 'market room' of one of the Spa's inns. Margate millers were attacked for mixing low-grade imported flour with Kent's famed product, and selling it at top-class prices. Riots in one town commonly had repercussions elsewhere. Authors of inflammatory bills at Rochester and Portsmouth referred to riots in other places, in the latter case stressing the protesting precedent even in 'that Aristocratic Place Southampton'. Market-town riots began to penetrate the countryside. Midhurst disturbances were speedily echoed by *taxation populaire* in the tiny West Sussex village of Easebourne. Many rural residents feared that London's example would be emulated in the heart of the countryside. An inhabitant of Swanbourne, deep in Buckinghamshire, anticipated 'some disturbance in this neighbourhood', while the lack of documentary proof may conceal the scale of minor eruptions, like the 'trifling . . . disturbance' recorded at Hinton Ampner in Hampshire by the itinerant diarist Captain Hervey. However, these disturbances followed those which had provoked the strongest refutation of maximums by the government, and rioters here received little if any magisterial support for the tenets of the 'moral economy'.[30]

No region was entirely unaffected by the September mobilisations. In the North, disturbances at Sheffield on 27 August, 2 and 8 September, were echoed at Leeds on the 16th and 25th, and at Hull and Darlington on the

19th and 22nd respectively. Rioting in the North-west gripped Blackburn, Wigan, Lancaster and Bunbury.[31] Even the West Country, with better crops largely harvested before the rains, had a series of *taxation populaire* incidents at Montacute (Somerset 13th), Devizes (14th), Milborne Port (16th) and Bristol (19th). In Gloucestershire striking clothiers turned to protest against allegedly withholding farmers.[32] But even where crowds such as these 'switched' their actions, the urban character of protest was relatively rarely eclipsed. The greater merchants remained the villains of popular perceptions, though of course mobilised crowds vented anger on lesser commercialists. Both these elements are vividly reflected by the fact that September witnessed the only fierce metropolitan food-rioting during the entire eighteenth century. Food riots were to swamp the South-west during the winter of 1800–1 and the following spring. Nevertheless, the September 1800 disturbances were in many senses a climax to a tradition, inherited by Georgian England, in which popular responses to subsistence problems were dominated almost exclusively by the ideology of the 'moral economy'. After September, democratic politics began to dominate plebeian reactions to continued famine conditions. Several regions, including those which had been major theatres of orthodox protest, the Midlands and the industrial North, were centres of a marked recrudescence of the plebeian democratic movement. The seminal nature of that movement in the 1790s necessitates an examination of its relationship to older forms of protest occurring throughout that unique decade. Otherwise those 'new' or evolving dimensions to protest generated by famine, which has led one historian to speak of the 'death rattle' of the food riot by 1801, are inexplicable.[33]

CHAPTER 9

'Promoting General Confusion'
Popular Political Radicalism and Protest

In the context of England's socio-economic and political structures in the 1790s, democratic ideology pivoting on manhood suffrage had revolutionary implications. How could a society which so ostentatiously hinged on the very unequal distribution of wealth, bolstered by a political system excluding all but the very rich, survive the implementation or imposition of democracy? The first genuinely working-class movement for political reform on democratic principles was the most salient development of the decade. The increasing severity of Pitt's repression reflected the devastating implications of the ideology, its penetration of an ever-broadening sector of the proletariat, as represented by the burgeoning geographical extent of the organised movement during 1792–4. These factors were aggravated in government perceptions by the anti-parliamentary strategy behind the democratic Conventions, superb vehicles for further rapid politicisation of the masses, which might ultimately eclipse parliament itself. Historians continue to debate the geography of the movement, and the degree of penetration achieved in plebeian circles. The latter is a key problematic, notably because the nineties witnessed only a part of a longer politicisation process, the making of the English working class, and no test can be devised to measure the impact in the initial stages. We are on firmer ground with respect to geography. The evidence of corresponding and other radical societies contained in parliamentary reports, the seized documents of activists, the residual remnants of covert government intelligence systems, and the open reports to the Home Office from magisterial sources, when added to a critical evaluation of other sources, reveal an almost universal working-class radical presence.[1] Many societies adopted self-protective fronts against officialdom and officious neighbours. The 'Book Club' at Helston was just one. Lazy or disinterested authorities eschewed addition to government intelligence, and some regions were beyond the pale of active authority. The president of the 'Book Club' contrasted his predicament with the complete autonomy enjoyed by radical proletarians in the adjacent mining districts of Cornwall. Edward Thompson's interpretation, that during the 'war years there were Thomas Hardys in every town and many villages throughout England . . . biding their time, putting in a word . . . waiting for the movement to revive' accurately reflects this omnipresence. It encouraged conservative fears of the movement's potential, but in the last months of 1794, several factors combined to allay apprehensions. The state strengthened its legal powers. In the Volunteers Pitt created a massive force of armed amateurs, who disseminated and reinforced patriotic, loyalist political principles. Wartime mobilisation of regular and Militia soldiery, whose loyalty was largely and uncritically attributed to the severity of military discipline, comprised an equally omnipresent police force. And if the notorious Treason Trials produced 'acquitted felons' instead of convicted traitors, they served to dampen the spirits of popular democrats.[2]

In August 1794, Joseph Ritson opined

> With respect to a revolution, though I think it at no great distance, it seems to defy all calculations for the present. If the increase of taxes, the decline of manufactures, the high price of provisions and the like, have no effect upon the apathy of sans culottes here, one can expect little from the reasoning of philosophers or politicians. When the pot boils violently, however, it is not always in the cook's power to prevent the fat from falling into the fire.[3]

The 1794–5 season of the earlier famine generated the first real *national* crisis with manifestations of the fat landing in the fire. Two remarkable characteristics of the 'early phase' and to a lesser extent of the midsummer hypercrisis emerge. First, relatively few attempts were made by popular radicals to exploit civil disorder. Secondly, considering the alleged 'reds under the bed' mentality of many magistrates and other establishment stalwarts, few identifications of a populist democratic presence, let alone offensive, were claimed for the riotous episodes prior to the midsummer hypercrisis.

Crowd personnel were naturally given to revolutionary panegyrics, notably when confronting authority. During an early Norfolk disturbance in December 1794, R.J. Buxton was blandly told by a participant 'that they should soon be like the French, & as to the Military they were nothing in their hands'. Michael Sidebottom seized a West Riding Yeomanry Cavalryman's bridle and announced that none of the soldiers 'should return alive for that they should have pikes and other instruments that would do for them'. The Cornish miners' call to arms, which appears to have meant bludgeons, provoked a prodigious alarm in the spring of '95, as did their strictures on inflated rents causing high prices, and their boasts 'that they should have Estates etc. in less than a Fortnight'. The Bailiff of Penryn panicked when he was unable to get his horse reshod, surmising that all the blacksmiths were absorbed in pike-production.[4] Rioting over bread automatically evoked the spectre of the ostensibly humble origins of the French Revolution. The early participation of the army in food riots, notably the April Militia mutinies, checked thoughtless assumptions of military loyalties. The traumatic shock was revealed by those able to advance only Jacobin subversion in explanation. A Chichester clergyman assured Lt. Col. Bishopp that 'there are Seditious People of the lower Class . . . going about from Place to Place to excite the Soldiers to these Proceedings'. Neither he, nor the Chatham Bench who suddenly asserted that the West Middlesex Militia had been 'tampered with', offered any concrete evidence, which also eluded the hardnosed military enquirers at the Court Martials of the Oxfordshire militiamen.[5]

Public concern over army involvement in the enhanced scale of rioting evoked different perceptions of what could transpire. One well-informed and temperate contributor to the *Blackburn Mail* on the Militia mutinies, noted that

> the cap of liberty was not exhibited on pikes at Chichester, but the French trick of inflaming the populace in exposing the things cried against was practised; by holding up beef and loaves on sticks . . . conducted by similar worthy characters to those who had first the honour to lead the revolutionists in France – a raw indisciplined militia and a rabble of women.

French experiences achieved a fresh relevancy, and assumed a new currency. Estate-agent Black enjoined tenant-farmer Lincoln to contribute to relief collections in Huntingdonshire, and warned that

> without such attention we shall soon be in the same wretched State that the unfortunate People of France are brought by a Set of designing Knaves who have nothing to lose themselves, and are now living on the plunder of those who were the Protectors of their Country, and upon what every honest man had got by his Industry.

The riotous 'early phase' eruptions of ninety-five formed the backdrop to the intensely disturbed summer; in such circumstances, a loss of nerve, with paranoid identifications of a mysterious Jacobin plot, by some, including magistrates, was to be expected. Buxton was 'afraid that the dearness of provisions is only a cover for something worse . . . . Where this will end God knows', an opinion conditioned not by riotous plebeians, but by the receipt of an anonymous letter, which 'though badly spelt bears the Marks of something above the Vulgar'. However, it is the paucity of such perceptions which impresses. The balanced appraisal of Sir George Onesipherous Paul when combating fierce and widespread riots in Gloucestershire, typified the majority view of active magistrates in most regions:

> Paines doctrines had only been inhaled by a few in 1793, when they were industriously circulated . . . . the Cry of a Want of Bread . . . forms a Body of Insurgents, & amongst these are mixed a Number of Seditious Persons whose Business it is to excite the Number to Mischief, & make them Deaf to Reason . . . . on the other Hand, if Corn is so dear that they cannot purchase sufficient to satisfy their want, Sedition will take the advantage of acting on an empty Stomach[6]

The duration of the crisis, its intensification, and violence, finally permitted exploitation by democrats, which exhibited contradictions and no overall strategy. In Liverpool, a group of pilots, a unionised trade, who patronised a radical pub known as 'Ned's' in Fenwick Street, deliberately engineered a riot. Leaving work after collecting their wages, they started a noisy demonstration, which attracted its principal support from children. They then headed for a working-class district, where the noise induced 'a great number of People' to emerge from 'the Cellars and Houses'. A large crowd toured bakers and provision dealers to enforce price reductions, and to confront the police, while the pilots slipped away to regale themselves at 'Ned's'.[7] At Reading, in the immediate aftermath of the Militia mutinies, democracts, including 'one Mackall, a dissolute and notorious character', tried to subvert the Sussex Militia by exploiting the non-announcement of their pay rise. Thomas Goss, wheelwright of Exeter, harangued soldiers 'about Equality and the Proceedings in France', thereby inciting 'them to Mutiny, Insurrection and Rebellion' according to the prosecution. The tension guaranteed such responses by both excited plebeians and nervous local authorities. The death sentences imposed on Oxfordshire militiamen galvanised crude handwritten attempts to politicise the troops; papers distributed at Lewes and Chichester invited the 'Soldiers to arm, arise and revenge your Cause' against the 'Aristocratic Foe' in general, and 'those bloody Numskulls Pitt and George' in particular. Similar posters went up in the aftermath of the Birmingham shootings:

> To arms, fellow Townsmen, and resist the cruel oppressions of your wicked rulers, whose intentions are to starve you all to death.

The authors, sarcastically noted a JP, 'were not instigated by Dearness of Corn, but had Intentions far different for the relief of the Poor'. The most successful political stimulant to riot occurred, almost inevitably, in the radical stronghold of Sheffield. A Jacobin was certainly responsible for the ferocious but neat encapsulation of the grievances of the masses and those of fresh army recruits, which underlay the riot terminating in the shootings on 4 August:

> Treason, Treason, Treason, The People's humbugg'd. A Plot is disco-vered, Pitt and the Committee for Bread[8] are combined together to starve the Poor into the Army and starve your Widows and Orphans . . . . And may every wearer of a Bayonet be struck with Heaven's loudest thunder that refuses to help you[9] . . . . Sharpen your Weapons and spare not.[10]

Repression enabled radicals to pinpoint ironies, none more potent than that which emerged at Birmingham. The local Bench 'gave us plenty of Ale & spirits to urge us on . . . when we were rioting for Church & King' in 1791, but 'Now we are rioting for a big Loaf we must be shot & cut up like Bacon Pigs'. This failed to solve the radicals' dilemma. Norwich democrats grasped the nettle by ruling that they would not only expel any member joining disturbances, but would pass the evidence to the judiciary. As disorder increased over the summer, the authorities could plausibly blame it on the radicals, and thereby justify ruthless suppression too. Historians concur in the considerable accretion of support to the London Corresponding Society [LCS] during the second quarter of 1795, and their provincial counterparts fared similarly. But this renewed populist enthusiasm threatened to backfire. At Portsmouth, one radical club attracted rising nightly audiences principally of 'Journeymen shoemakers' and sailors: 'at times they allude to the high prices and scarcity of provisions – then it is time to assert the rights of Men to secure themselves from being starved & hint Kings are not quite necessary'. Militant talk of procuring gunpowder followed. Firm direction, discipline and co-ordinated politicisation were desperately needed. Popular democrats had to go on the offensive, but there were considerable dangers unless actions accorded with the non-secretive, non-violent model postulated by the original LCS leadership.[11]

The signs, even in London, were a curious combination of the optimistic and the ominous. A mammoth meeting convened by the LCS, allegedly of over 100,000, went off peaceably on 29 June. Demands for manhood suffrage and annual parliaments automatically headed the list of resolutions, but supportive ones lambasted the government's unremitting international aggression, and unconditionally attributed high food prices to war. Public interest in proceedings was prodigious. *The Telegraph* sold three thousand copies on 30 June, principally owing to its report, and another edition was run off on 1 July. An excited LCS secretary Ashley told his Executive Committee that over one thousand non-members had applied for an official account. The LCS published a 'Narrative of Proceedings', together with an 'Address to the Nation and to the King'. The Home Secretary blocked the latter, and refused to confer with LCS spokesmen. Meanwhile recruits flocked in, and a flurry of communications arrived from exhilarated provincial supporters, including those at Birmingham, Coventry, Bradford, Leominster and Tewkesbury. Delegate 'Citizen Buck from Sheffield' conferred personally with LCS committees. A major offensive was in the making.[12]

If order was preserved in London on 29 June, it rapidly evaporated thereafter. The capital's subterranean presses released a flood of ephemera after St. George's Fields.[13] One JP reported hundreds of addresses, some specifically to soldiers, of a 'seditious tendency' littering the streets. Others were no more than political doggerels. 'A SPECIFIC CURE FOR SEDITION AND FAMINE', concluded rhetorically, 'Mr Pitt calls a pinch of Snuff a Luxury: What will he call a Morcel of Bread after a while?'.[14] Large crowds assembled nightly. Multifarious targets were attacked, perhaps best illustrated by one perambulating group shouting, '"Damn the King, Damn Pitt, we will have bread at 6d. the Loaf"', which concluded operations by sacking a crimp house. Some incidents were clearly unpremeditated, like the riotous release of a deserter. Others were not, notably the 'many' outrages 'committed by a set of persons, not very numerous, either hired or lovers of riot', who formed the nucleus of a crowd before escaping to the rapturous applause of assembled hundreds, 'the instant they have done mischief'. Experienced observers spoke of visits from people 'whose principal object appears to keep the Metropolis in a state of harassment'. Food prices remained a central issue. Demonstrations included a ritual 'performed before every Baker and Butcher's Shop' by a motley band of off-duty soldiers and youths: 'a Most dreadful Moaning (as the Mob call it)'. A crowd which assembled in Charing Cross market, mainly comprising boys according to the prime minister, went off to smash Pitt's Downing Street windows. Fears that a group would investigate rumours of huge flour stocks at Kingston-upon-Thames, and intelligence reports that radical elements were bent on burning the monarch's own corn stacks in Berkshire, were not realised, though secret-service agents converged to mingle with the populace at Windsor. The Home Office was absorbed with the daily despatch of orders to the Bow Street Runners, the stipendiary magistrates, and the military. Regular and Volunteer troops patrolled the capital throughout July, to continuous harassment. Army reinforcements moved up from southern and eastern counties, and contingency plans were laid to release the Guards from duty at Hampton Court. If these precautions preserved the metropolis from cataclysmic disorder, they did not terminate populist political developments. One observer noted that 'the democrats are taking every pain to persuade . . . the lower class . . . that the scarcity is occasioned by the bad management of ministers'. 'What has Billy done', exclaimed a female admirer, 'He can't send rain or sunshine'. Even a prison riot inside Newgate was ascribed to malign LCS influence. These London disorders, like their provincial equivalents, placed an unpleasant onus on democratic leaders. They had to grapple for control, and direct protesters' attentions to major political solutions. It constituted a monumental task.[15]

The Sheffield Constitutional Society was the speediest and most successful reactor to this type of predicament. On 11 August, just one week after the riots, a monster meeting convened on Crook's Moor, under the chairmanship of Barrow from the London-based Friends of Liberty. The hard-hitting speeches and resolutions filled an eleven-page pamphlet. Every topic, the unnecessary, immoral war, enhanced taxation, the inflated national debt, economic depression, crippling poor-rates, and the abrogation of the constitution by the suspension of Habeas Corpus, were all marshalled in support of customary democratic proposals for parliamentary reform as the key prerequisite for acceptable government. The subsistence issue was central to these arguments. British and foreign armies were 'fed with that bread which our famished Peasantry have long cried for in vain'. Soldiers were forced 'for the sake of . . . decorum to throw that flour upon their heads which . . . eager appetites would gladly convert into food', a fact compounded by Pitt's refusal, for fiscal reasons, to ban hair powder manufactured from wheat. Ministerial pronouncements of abundant cereal imports were ridiculed: 'our Families are starving'; 'Give us Peace, and Plenty will follow'. However, the meeting recorded its implacable opposition to 'all riots and disorderly assemblies on any occasion'. Leaders were adamant 'that the legal and constitutional method of Petitioning the Throne is the proper resource of the suffering people at this alarming season'. They added, ominously, that 'when we ask for Bread let not the Father of his People give us a Stone'. The message was soon spread energetically throughout industrial Yorkshire. One major activist, Dennis Shaw, convened a series of meetings during September and October, 'haranging great numbers of people . . . in language greatly defamatory of the King, the Government, and the Legislature'. Shaw's principal purpose was the creation of 'Primary Assemblies who are to hold a correspondence' in places like Bingley where no societies existed. The precise contents of Shaw's speeches are not revealed, but two magistrates, who had their first taste of popular political agitation at this juncture, took alarm at proposals 'to proceed to the Election of Delegates to a National Convention' and rumours of arming.[16]

Norwich radicals adopted a parallel role in East Anglia. The Norwich Patriotic Society, a federation, had branches and contacts in many small towns and textile villages, including miller Watson of Saxlingham and weaver Tooke of Saxmundham. Norwich democrats seized on subsistence issues in July, and circulated literature:

> were you determined legally to correct the errors of state delinquents, you would not be reduced to the dire necessity of eating bran: your tables would be furnished with the bounties of Providence, and the guilty authors of your distress would be sent to Germany to eat straw.

Membership of the Norwich societies increased so dramatically during August and September that excited discussions were held over the feasibility of running a candidate at the next general election. Tooke campaigned vigorously over the summer; on every June Sunday, in the villages, he lectured substantial assemblies 'of the lowest Class' on democratic principles. October witnessed a further flurry of meetings, commonly addressed by 'a man with a . . . cockade in his Hat'. One speaker, James Breezer, was eventually arrested for selling printed propaganda urging the formation of 'popular societies' because 'concentrated force will avail more than individual exertions'. Any enquiry into 'the Cause of your Distress' would reveal that 'the present unjust and unnecessary war has hastened that Crisis of Misery which a defective representation must necessarily produce'. 'An adequate representation' was the sole cure. The region was still disturbed by food rioting at this time, and propaganda also warned against Pittite chicanery:

> The Minister's Object is to hold up to popular odium the farmers, millers, bakers etc. A few there may be foolish enough to withhold their goods from market . . . . But why condemn the whole for a part?

Pitt would 'gladly instigate you to riot and plunder' so that 'His devoted volunteer corps' could shoot 'two or three dozen misled Citizens' and the judges 'hang as many more — this would accelerate his darling object of governing us by a *military aristocracy*'.[17]

The democratic movement rejuvenated across the country. Meetings on Uley Common in Gloucestershire were reported to the Home Office by a worried JP, and to the LCS executive by delegate C. Jeffery who came away with printed propaganda. Reinvigorated members of the Chichester Society opportunistically maximised plebeian interest by discussing means to combat profiteering, and their liaisons with the LCS made the county press. LCS papers prove the formation of new societies in many places, including Truro, Whitchurch, Tewkesbury, Spilsby, Bradford and Carlisle, and more in the Home Counties. Hundreds of provincial democrats looked to

London in the early autumn, not just for pamphlets to advance local politicisation, but for concerted leadership in a national campaign. The political momentum had to be channelled into an offensive. Otherwise populist energies might, as feared in East Anglia, degenerate into renewed food rioting and expose citizens to Pitt's 'military aristocracy'.[18]

The metropolitan campaign intensified in October, with lectures and debates heating the political climate. Unprecedented recruitment strained the LCS's organisational powers, and fierce argument erupted over infidel membership. Unity, even over famine proved elusive; the question at the London Forum on 22 October was 'Ought the present high price of bread be attributed to a scarcity of grain – a secret monopoly – or the unavoidable consequence of war?'. The main attack, mounted notably by Thelwall, relentlessly emphasised poverty, but the war and the political system which facilitated it was the permanent target: 'all the Miseries to which the Poor are Subject . . . proceed from unnatural and Impolitic Wars and War proceeds from Corrupt and vicious Parliaments'. Thelwall inevitably returned to this theme at the huge public meeting which eventually convened on 26 October in Copenhagen Fields: he insisted that

> It is not the crimp, it is not a baker, a miller or a maltster no nor even a few dispirate and avaricious monopolisers – those are not the authors of your sufferings . . . . It is the system that you must reform.

The Whig *Morning Chronicle* seized on this part of Thelwall's speech, in which he also projected the futility of rioting, to denounce current opinion

> that the late harvest was an abundant one, and that the dearth arises from monopoly etc. Such assertions tend to shut the ears and understandings of those who suffer most from scarcity against truth and reason, and to make them resort to mistaken means of relief, which were they to succeed in, would convert scarcity into famine.

Despite an unprecedented attendance, the meeting was well-disciplined, and the dispersal orderly. But the overall effect was similar to that of its predecessor, St George's Fields, which was followed by multifarious disturbances. On 27 and 28 October tension gripped London, 'an intolerable state of affairs' according to a surgeon, who purchased a cane-sword because the 'streets are grown so dangerous'.[19] In these circumstances, the sequel, a massive demonstration against war, famine and government was unavoidable. The royal procession to open parliament on 29 October was a natural focus, and the well-known assault on the king's coach the result. Riotous conduct, so immediately after Copenhagen Fields, suited Pittite opportunism, and the notorious Gagging Acts were the logical response of a government intent on proving that plebeian politics provoked civil disorder from which even the person of the monarch was not immune. The fundamental constitutional dimensions inherent in the proposed legislation, transformed the whole nature of the political struggle, and with the new issue the democratic movement retreated from the offensive to the defensive.

The centrality of famine to the democrats' cause was an immediate casualty. Debaters at 'the Temple of Reason' and other political forums often mentioned 'approaching famine', the impossibility of securing adequate cereal imports, and recurrent food rioting in passing. John Gale Jones cunningly politicised one notion peripheral to the 'moral economy', the engrossing of farms, which the king encouraged as a landlord. But much greater energies were expended in self-defence. Speakers insisted that there was no proof that the monarch's attackers on 29 October 'either belonged to the LCS or any other rational society whatever'. Jones theatrically refrained from even the insinuation 'that the Stone thrown at the King was thrown by a Spy'. Could an explanation be found in the fury of 'starving individuals'? Then there was the hoary problem of the Foxites; was 'not the only means left to oppose . . . Despotism . . . a junction of the Whig Interest' and the LCS? Was Fox just another place-seeker: had 'the System corrupted the Man'? Did he deserve the 'confidence and support of the real Friends of Liberty'? Tempers were lost and ominous references were made:

> Forty thousand men associated together, will not very easily be separated. Men who have been Delegates, who have been used to the discussion of political Subjects, to attend Committees, and to transact other official Business, will not easily return to insignificance.

Repressed reformers might become revolutionaries, even assassins; Charles I and James II were mentioned. 'Soldiers would remember that they were Citizens, and . . . nobly refuse to become the Executioners of their Countrymen'. Street-fighting tactics were discussed, arming advised, and violent revolution predicted.[20]

The LCS threw every resource and strained every nerve in the campaign against the Bills during their parliamentary progress. Forty thousand tabloids were ordered on 24 November, together with a thousand 'posting Bills' and 'Men . . . employ'd to stand with poles in the Streets with posting Bills on them'. Every contact was used, including the powerful metropolitan trade unions who were warned that the proposed laws would encompass their activities. One 'Executive Committee' elected after a delegate meeting of 'the Journeymen of the respective Branches of Cordwainers, Taylors, Hatters, Curriers, Weavers, Carpenters, Staymakers, Smiths, Bookbinders, Printers Etc', organised petitions against the Bills at eleven pubs, and invited their members' signatures. The LCS was clearly staggered as recruitment maintained its heady momentum; 'the degree of Patriotism brought into action by this stretch of arbitrary power is much greater than the most sanguine Patriot could have expected'. The LCS campaign had a series of climaxes in the three monster meetings, addressed by Foxite MPs, on 12 November, 2 and 7 December.[21]

The enactment of the Two Acts proved an equally massive anti-climax. The magnitude of defeat was emphasised by Foxite participation, both inside and outside parliament, the orchestration of opposition from the enfranchised in county after county, and in borough after borough, a classless *casus belli* of 'Old and Young Rich and Poor' in LCS parlance. Defeat was debilitating, its ramifications immediate; psychological exhaustion was as potent as the fear of the state's new powers. The LCS leadership nonetheless found the energy to restructure the organisation, and to alter the rules respecting divisions to circumvent the Seditious Meetings Act. New recruits came in during the 1795–6 winter, though not to compensate for 'the vast numbers who . . . left'. Some new societies formed, as at Gravesend, Selby, Worcester, and Melbourne in Derbyshire. If fewer Birmingham citizens met, growth was achieved in other West Midland towns. In Manchester, a major regional centre, the struggle over the Gagging Acts galvanised fresh socio-political polarisations, with renewed riotous clashes between opposing plebeian factions. The Manchester Corresponding Society survived repeated attacks from Church and King enthusiasts. Chichester citizens were victimised by a local 'tyrant', but their club survived after pep-talks from Portsmouth-based speakers.[22] Harassment damaged. The seizures of Binns and Jones, liaising with Birmingham, proved problematic for the London leadership. Frequent provincial prosecutions, minor in themselves like the arrest of a speechifying pamphlet-seller at Dewsbury, and the twelvemonth imprisonment imposed on Lincolnshire blacksmith Tye of Bourne for denouncing the 'rascally despotic government', opeated *in terrorem*.[23] The LCS coined the emotive phrase 'a reign of terror' in 1796.[24] High food prices and lower winter-time demand for labour, reduced plebeian political funding; lack of cash for subscriptions as opposed to lack of interest, was primarily responsible for the collapse of the LCS's 1796 publishing venture with *The Moral and Political Magazine*.[25]

Populist political activities in some major provincial centres continued almost unimpeded; the turmoil of the 1796 general election facilitated expressions of strengths in places including Norwich and Nottingham. Occasionally, anger over government subsistence policies was heard at the hustings, as with cries of 'No Barley Bread' screamed at Ipswich candidates.[26] In London, and the North, serious talk of arming commenced. In December 1795, the LCS formally admitted that

> You are told that civil Liberty is annihilated, and that your only hope is in Arms – we pretend not to say at what degree of depravity on the part of Government actual insurrection becomes the duty of the People.

In January 1796 discussants at the Green Dragon in the capital included Irishmen who claimed association with both the United Irishmen and the Defenders. One of the Binns brothers made his first recorded visit to Dublin in the following November; the subsequent shadowy emergence of indigenous physical-force metropolitan groupings was reinforced by the evolving alliance with the increasingly insurrectionary United Irishmen and their new Defender partners. But these developments were essentially one medium-term product of the repression, and above all the failures of 1795–6.[27] The London-based informer James Powell neatly contrasted 1796 with 1795; in the latter year

> new divisions [were] branching out ev'ry week. I was no sooner out of office in one Division when I had only to branch to a new one & I was

sure to be elected. It was not so this year instead of branching off, two or three divisions were joining again into one.

Shrinkage clearly compromised Powell's penetrative prowess, but it also illustrated the magnitude of the democrats' defeat. As 1796 progressed, falling food prices had their effect, stimulating LCS recognition that the 'Patriotism of many ebbs & flows in proportion as the Price of Provisions – the Obstacles to Reform & other temporary Circumstances vary'.[28] Plebeian democrats were fully aware that famine was the universal topic; it was *the one* which could be exploited with maximum effect. No other issue could provide such a forceful vehicle for politicisation. In 1795, the democratic leadership made but a start. They had pronounced decisively against riot, possibly as at Sheffield with considerable success. But their politics of famine eschewed the 'moral economy', in favour of emphasising the war and its perpetration through a corrupt, unacceptable system of government, which facilitated Pittite negations of the popular will. The ministry's counter-offensive, which pivoted on the Gagging Acts, quite fortuitously from Pitt's perspective, not only wrenched the democratic movement away from the attack to the defensive, but in so doing compromised the maximum exploitation of famine, the key issue.

The virtual collapse of the movement as an open, publicity-seeking political force, and the failure of the LCS's own publishing venture, increased the importance of the radical press as an agent of politicisation. The London *Courier*, before a change of ownership at the end of the nineties dramatically transformed its political calibre, achieved a national profile. In Manchester, Cowdroy's *Gazette* maintained a radical commentary, as did Flower's *Cambridge Intelligencer*. Repeated prosecution eventually forced Montgomery to moderate the views of *The Iris* at Sheffield. The political impact of such journalism must not be underestimated, and it was reinforced by what appears to have been a growth industry after 1795, the mixed productions of the metropolitan and provincial subterranean press, political cartoons, song-sheets and parodies. The police periodically hounded street vendors of these broadsheets, particularly in London, but authority rarely conducted protracted, systematic actions against such enterprise. The Mayor of Portsmouth, for example, sent two such productions to the Home Office in July 1800, with a rider that he would not normally have bothered Whitehall with such ephemera, except that one, an 'Epigram' had the London printer's name, and the other, a parody on a promissory note of 1798 vintage, was supposed to originate in moves to rejuvenate the local Corresponding Society.[29] Given the context in which these circulated, even those devoid of democratic content were political in their tone, as exemplified by the gruesome cartoon distributed at Birmingham during the September 1800 riots.[30] Radical printers, like Crome of Sheffield, a member of the revolutionary United Englishmen, produced extremist and neo-political material. His 'Good News for Poor People', belonged to the latter category, and comprised a spoof farmer's letter admitting traditional marketing offences, and predicting the ruin of agriculturalists and grain merchants from over-speculation. It also claimed a bumper 1800 crop, which thus fuelled popular prejudices of artificial famine. Countless cartoons had identical functions. The ability of plebeian democracts to use the subterranean press is nicely revealed by the members of a political club which convened in a Liverpool pub. In 1797, a proposal to print a 'Republican Song' – '"Injured Freedom or Brethren unite"' – in broadsheet form was adopted. Each member subscribed twopence, and received a dozen copies from a print run of two hundred. 'Citizen Saxton', who was not a printer, 'could get at the use of a Press at an Acquaintance', and the song-sheets were subsequently encountered 'in different places'. Many lowly democrats could 'get at' printing presses, and regularly resorted to this mode to politicise. Several reports of 'Hand bills . . . of the most inflammatory and treasonable kind' were received during the earlier famine, for example from Bristol in November 1795; during the first six months of 1800 such production flooded the streets, notably during disturbances.[31]

In March 1800 the *Leicester Journal* typically referred to the circulation of 'vicious political publications'. One exemplar was an infidel broadsheet, parodying the dying confessions of capital convicts, which attacked avaricious farmers and demanded a new king and constitution, 'a new Contrivance' according to one JP. Such devices were believed to have contributed to Midland riots which followed, during which some magistrates were terrified into inaction, and the Volunteers 'divided' over orders to confront crowds. Handwritten bills advocating *taxation populaire* were a recurrent feature of eighteenth-century protest over subsistence issues; they commonly evoked a popular response, and this was maintained in the unique circumstances of 1800. The difference was the regularity of political content:

> Will Ye English fools have Billy Pitt for a God, & Starve you in the midst of Plenty cant you smell the Fustey Bread[32] Blood for supper, Damnation seize Pitt and george & all in the name of such varmin, down with them.

If such inflammatory addresses were inevitable in places like Birmingham, a striking feature of protest at this time was the appearance of political overtones in such appeals all over the country. The Guillotine was symbolically added to bills advocating *taxation populaire* at Malden, and another suggesting a strike at Hitchen by 'all poor treadsmen and labourers . . . & see whats to be done', also claimed that 'vile Oppressors' enslaved the poor with a 'yoke of bondage' whereby 'your Libberty and freedom is intirely lost'. Similar sentiments respecting 'the most shameful encroachments on . . . Liberties and Rights' were added to a traditional threatening letter sent to a Sussex farmer. In May, posters distributed through industrial and rural Wiltshire had the insurrectionary tone of the United Englishmen; the contents juxtaposed soaring food prices, notions of the 'moral economy', and a revolutionary solution. Graffiti was deployed to similar ends, for example the '"Cheap Bread or No King"' chalked on Banbury church door.[33]

If the LCS and several provincial societies had publicly eschewed riotous modes of achieving redress, changed circumstances at the end of the century, epecially the 1799 legislation outlawing the LCS by name, proved the futility of residual hopes of new campaigns on the open-handed model adopted against the Gagging Acts. The use of anonymous bills to enflame the situation during the first months of the second famine may reflect little more than frustration, for it is certainly difficult to penetrate the strategic objective of those responsible. That they were clearly *products of politicisation at the local level* is suggested by events at Bath. During the multi-dimensional political crisis of 1797, an exasperated Town Clerk finally confronted a group of 'six Journeymen Shoemakers & a Journeyman Smith, who are much addicted to inflame & promote sedition', notably by 'Alehouse' speeches and political broadsheets. Arrests were made, but the Town Clerk's legal offensive was the victim of the Crown Lawyers' marked reluctance to become embroiled in the prosecution of lowly, local, provincial democrats.[34] The Bath contact, one of a long list of names and addresses seized on a Londoner involved with physical-force radicals, was a journeyman shoemaker. In March 1800 a terrorist campaign commenced in the city. Several arson attacks against brewers and provision dealers produced one spectacular fire which gutted a huge granary. The campaign was underpinned by dozens of handbills, some headed 'Peace and a Large bread or a King without a Head'; a reward notice referred to the 'many Seditious and Treasonable Papers . . . stuck up . . . in different Parts of this City, exciting the Populace to Violence and Insurrection'. A salvo of 'anonymous threatening letters' sent to local luminaries formed another ingredient of this blitz. One recipient, the deputy-mayor, insisted that the authors 'will not intimidate me', and if authority failed to capture any terrorist, they announced intentions to resort immediately to the army in the event of disturbances. The uneasy peace over the summer was shattered when Somerset colliers invaded in October. Then the 'ill-disposed Inhabitants . . . of the lower Class' chided the miners for parleying with the Bench, and for not having 'come in a different Manner and bring pikes, instead of sticks . . . to keep off the Dragoons'. One prisoner 'interrogated . . . about the Meaning of these Words . . . acknowledg'd he had used them in Allusion to the Proceedings of the Irish Rebels'.[35] Such evidence suggests that the interpretation of democrats' strategy by one experienced Birmingham JP may be accurate; in May 1800

> there are certainly many very active & ill disposed Persons, who instigate the Boys & Women to be riotous, in hopes of promoting general Confusion.

What might materialise from 'general Confusion' was anybody's guess. Jacobin perceptions are revealed by key parts of J. Golby's account of events at Nottingham in September 1800, penned during the maximum's enforcement, and while landowners discussed rent reductions for farmers:

> Thus has two Species of Vilains been Brought to Reason by the Courage of the . . . Inhabitants and Convinced I am that the People United may and Can Shake off any Species of Oppression at any time they may think proper . . . . other Counties will Catch the same disorder when they hear of this.

Quite simply, successful mass mobilisations would teach the proletariat where power ultimately resided.[36]

Since 1797, the United Englishmen [UE] had comprised a residual, revolutionary vanguard. Neither their shadowy existence, nor their survival into 1800 can be charted in detail, but several reliable facts can be established. First, a minority 'who had differed . . . on the propriety of persevering in the LCS', created the UE, thus emphasising their emergence as a direct and indigenous response to the 'operation' of the repressive legislation, 'that consummation of all Tyranny' in United parlance. The UE intended to implement constitutional rights to forcibly resist tyranny and their insurrectionary strategy led to co-operative planning with the United Irishmen [UI] and their French allies. The UE's military tactics hinged on risings in London and the provinces, in conjunctioin with the UI, in the event of a French invasion of Britain and/or Ireland, moves which would imperil British defensive capacities. In this context, insurrectionary options devised included the assassination of the king, Pitt and other cabinet members, and the firing of royal dockyards, all aimed to generate maximum confusion. These plans were initially thwarted by the defeat of the Irish Rebels in 1798, the simultaneous seizures of the UE leadership in London and Manchester, and the French failure to invade with adequate force. The Irish alliance survived; so too did expectations of the French. UE penetration of the army, especially the Guards and the London Militias, was never rooted out. The UE sought to capitalize on any national crisis which promised massed populist mobilisations, and to maximise popular hostility to the establishment. The meridian moment of alienation could be exploited. The Green Dragon, run by Morgan in Fore Street, was a regular venue for these insurrectionary cadres, known as 'the Mountain Party' by metropolitan radicals. The London leadership split early in 1800, and a new or reorganised 'Committee of Assassination' was formed in response to pressure from impatient revolutionaries in the army who pressed 'offers . . . to assassinate the person known by the title of king'. Another group, 'The New Union of United Societies of England, Scotland Wales & Ireland', who were more aware of the realities of the turgid negotiations between British and Irish revolutionaries, and Buonoparte, recognised the danger of any pre-emptive strike at this precise juncture. They tried to ditch their impatient brethren but made it clear that they reserved the right to concur with 'whatever may be done by the People in their Sovereign Revolutionary character'.[37]

In March 1800 soldiers' beer allowances were replaced, in the interests of 'Public Oeconomy' according to C-in-C the Duke of York, by cash payments. These speedily proved unequal to the rise in beer prices, doubly so for billeted troops whose beer payments were incorporated in inadequate lodging allowances. The Guards, 'unavoidably dispersed in public houses throughout London', except when on specific non-metropolitan duties, were soon seething with anger, which extended to most regiments stationed in the capital.[38] Rising food prices provoked anticipations of public disturbances, and rank and file soldiers openly stated their determination to mutiny if ordered to repress riotous crowds. Outraged militiamen 'talking about their Penny being taken away' in East End alehouses, 'added that

Government will repent of it', and one observed that '"they can only send the Volunteers against us and I should have no Scruple of thrusting my Bayonet into the first"'. The resultant conjunction of disgruntled troopers and alienated metropolitan proletarians, convinced soldiers involved in revolutionary plottings that their time was ripe. The First and Third Battalions of Guards were notoriously suspect among soldiers themselves, and contained revolutionary cells who were in cahoots with disaffected members of the other regiments.[39] It was said that an attempt was to be made on the king's life; this rumour was current by mid-May among some London radicals, including known United Englishmen.[40] It was passed down UI networks to surface in Dublin, elsewhere in Ireland, and on the continent in exiled Irish circles, before 15 May.[41] On that day George III survived *two* assassination attempts. At a major military review in Hyde Park, he was shot at from a barrack window by an unknown soldier, under cover of a *feu de joie*.[42] The bullet wounded an official twenty feet from the king. Government intelligence immediately covered up the truth,[43] and it was implausibly ascribed to the accidental use of a live round in an official item published in *The Times* on the 16th, a statement which the editor found neither 'conclusive nor satisfactory'.[44] Fears of a recurrence were assuaged by new regulations for firing parties at festivities and the introduction of uniform packaging for blanks; these were accorded maximum publicity. Nobody, including the head of the ordnance who conducted an official enquiry for the C-in-C, appears to have confronted the difficulty of explaining how a member of a firing squad at a ceremonial could have aimed horizontally, instead of into the air, and escaped detection.[45] Soldiers themselves unanimously ascribed events to an assassin. Some clearly disapproved, while others were ecstatic: '"By God he deserves to be Shot"'. Several predicted imminent repetition; '"The King will be done for yet before the Birth Day"' celebrations on 4 June.[46]

That afternoon, the Rev. W. Harper distinctly overheard cobbler Lappard

> say . . . that though . . . the King had been popped at that morning he was going to the Play where he would meet with a peal that Evening.

At the same moment, conversations among artisans, including shoemaker Smith, known 'to be a violent Democrat', in the Hope pub, John Street, near Tottenham Court Road, also centred on the morning's events in Hyde Park; one discussant, Whitcombe

> added that the King had a great deal of Corn which he refused to sell at a moderate price to people who were starving – that he was going to juggle his Arse in Drury Lane Theatre that Evening, but that he would have another shot before he came back.

That evening, silversmith James Hadfield, veteran of the Flanders campaign where he was severely wounded in the head and subsequently a French POW, fired a pistol at the king in the threatre. The slugs only peppered the royal box, and the audience overpowered Hadfield. He was interrogated at length, first by magistrates attending the play assisted by the Duke of York, and then at an emergency session of the Privy Council at 10 p.m. Only subsequently did Hadfield manifest symptoms of insanity, of a religious character, and he spent the period awaiting trial in a strait-jacket.[47] The extant secret-service intelligence and other official evidence is inconclusive on Hadfield's mental state.[48] Some senior government supporters stressed that while legal precedents were ambiguous, the most recent tended to facilitate defences on the grounds of insanity. Examining the 'legal and *political* propriety of admitting the plea of lunacy', the Marquis of Buckingham insisted that if Hadfield escaped on such grounds, it 'will . . . inevitably encourage Jacobinical treason to avail itself of a means so obvious as this which is put into their hands'. The degree of 'acuteness in the examination of Hadfield' was intensely debated at a private dinner attended by the Prince of Wales.[49] The prosecution, led by the attorney-general, may have been unnerved by the prospect that Hadfield's defence was led by Erskine, hero of the Treason Trials of 1794, and the most formidable lawyer of the day. The prosecution contrived to present a lame case, and claimed ignorance of the key defence evidence, which induced Lord Chief Justice Kenyon to intervene decisively in Hadfield's favour. If the attorney-general was ignorant, it must be ascribed to Home Secretary Portland, an unlikely subterfuge. The facts were incontrovertible, but only the court could rule on Hadfield's sanity.[50] Ministers could no more make political capital from proving that Hadfield was an associate of metropolitan insurrectionaries, than they could from admitting that the Guards were riddled with regicides. *The Times*, probably prompted by the government into adopting a less critical approach in the interests of smothering public fears of revolutionary portents, insisted that there was no 'just reason for connecting his crime with the extraordinary occurrence . . . in Hyde Park'. Its report added, revealingly, that the French should not take heart from either event: even George III's death would not produce 'any change . . . with regard to peace or war, in . . . internal or foreign policy . . . unless it were an increase of vigour and resolution'. A modicum of evidence respecting Hadfield's friend and mentor, and supposed instigator, Bannister Truelock, made the press, but he too subsequent to his arrest, manifested religious frenzy and insanity, and was never brought to trial.[51] Truelock, who in Professor Harrison's cautious judgement was a 'more sinister' character than Hadfield, was in fact a well-known and at times outspoken democrat; if the extant evidence does not connect him with any revolutionary organisation, it reveals that he talked politics with militiamen, and predicted the formation of a republic following George's assassination. Several of Truelock's fellow shoemakers were involved with the UE, but his possible political motivations were merely obscurely hinted at publicly.[52] Information that Hadfield 'was a man of Democratic principles', frequented radical pubs including the Red Lion, Clerkenwell, and the Baptist's Head, St John's Lane, and had recently taken to drinking at the notorious Green Dragon, was technically irrelevant to the prosecution's case. That concentrated exclusively on the uncontrovertible fact that Hadfield had fired a gun at the king. Allegations of political motivation would have undermined the defence of insanity, but it would have required the unthinkable, exposing a handful of key government spies by putting them into the witness box.[53]

If Hadfield's attempt produced a flood of loyalist addresses, it also stimulated a tide of anti-monarchial demonstrations. The failed assassination bid was 'generally known about the streets' adjacent to the theatre within minutes, but when the king's coach left it was assailed by a crowd 'running alongside . . . hissing and hooting' derisively, and one of the escort was unhorsed. At Portsmouth, a street-vendor of a printed 'form of thanksgiving for his Majesty's escape' was denounced by Richard Morgan shouting '"Damn and bougre the King and Constitution . . . I wish his bloody Block was off"'. Even rural England was not spared pro-regicide utterances.[54] In London, thereafter the secret service maintained a much closer surveillance over army personnel, and prodigious precautions were taken over the royal birthday celebrations on 4 June, when further assassination attempts were confidently predicted in plebeian circles.[55] United Englishmen feared arrest in the aftermath of the Hadfield episode, and while many adopted a lower profile, the Guards remained a topic of serious UE conversations. Authority never rooted out disaffected soldiers, as revealed by their involvement in the international conspiracy of which the celebrated prosecution of Colonel Despard and his associates in 1802–3 was but a semi-tangible component.[56] There were further rumours of metropolitan risings over the summer of 1800, and in the autumn secret agents reconnoitering in Birmingham learned that radicals there entertained 'great expectations' that a revolution would commence in the capital following an armed initiative by guardsmen.[57]

This tension, which was not confined to London, had only begun to subside when the September hypercrisis broke. That crisis's potential for politicisation was immeasurably enhanced by the Home Secretary's autocratic declarations of harvest failure, eulogies on free trade, and insistence on public order at any cost. The issue of a Royal Proclamation irretrievably identified the king with this round of repressive negation of populist policy. An unprecedented but unco-ordinated politicisation campaign was launched in every democratic centre, and soon engulfed most urban and industrial regions. In some places democrats resorted to the subterranean press; elsewhere only handwritten bills circulated, but the contents of these addresses were remarkably uniform. This proletariat of North Shields was informed

> No more ye Britons vainly boast your freedom of a Nation
> When Laws are only made for those Miscreants of Creation
> a Proclamation from the King for Men to cease complaining
> such Vengeful threats will surely bring an end to unjust reigning
> When King's neglect the peoples good with reason we complain
> Ower Allegiance then is understood to be absolved again

In Birmingham bills percolated 'the Public Houses where the Societies of Work men are held'; entitled '"Vive La Republic"' they asserted 'the necessity of dethroning the monarch as the only mode of relieving the peoples distresses'. All of this was accompanied by torrents of revolutionary graffiti; 'the walls of the manufacturing towns throughout the kingdom', according to one witness, 'were too small to contain the quantity of sedition that was written'. Thomas Butterworth Bayley, the senior Mancunian justice confirmed that

> The Public Eye is dayly saluted with Sedition in Chalk Characters on our Walls. And Whether the subject regards Bread or Peace NO KING introduces it. This is a shocking Idea to be thus familiarised.[58]

No region completely escaped these campaigns, which comprised the opening stages in a developing revolutionary situation, in precisely the vogue postulated by Bayley. The Home Office's reaction reveals an unusual combination of nervousness and firmness. Contingency military plans to preserve order in London were repeatedly updated to accommodate events over the autumn, and Home Office officials repetitously ordered metropolitan stipendiaries to cleanse the capital's buildings and streets of 'seditious and treasonable' ephemera.[59] The police were issued with sponges to wash off graffiti. The distribution of 'inflammatory' materials in Birmingham, not only stimulated Portland to insist on the immediate employment of 'twenty Agents to Watch during the Night', but also to meet the cost – an unprecedented use of central funds. Other local authorities received identical instructions, if not the money, including those in minor towns like Luton. Special undercover agents were despatched from London to infiltrate radical circles, notably in the Midlands. Portland categorically stressed 'the utmost importance that a stop should be put to' democratic exploitation, and where local authorities – in co-operation with Home Office agents, or not – could identify the individuals responsible, Portland promised warrants, and royal 'messengers assisted by proper Officers of the Police' to effect arrests.[60]

The king's refusal to receive a petition from the London Common Council demanding an emergency parliamentary session, served to aggravate and extend the period of popular hostility; it formed the subject of yet more inflammatory appeals castigating the monarchy and offering republican solutions.[61] Remnants of democratic organisations, including the LCS and the Sheffield Constitutional Society, were initially wrong-footed by the speed at which the *political* crisis broke; it took time for activists to concur on an attempted relaunching of an old-style movement hinging on public meetings. The metropolitan UE eschewed participation in the September riots, deciding on the 18th to 'take no Part' though they 'Wish Success to the riots'. Plebeian democrats of all persuasions were originally incapable of more than anonymous sloganising; the initiative passed to the London Council, and to the other establishment bodies which petitioned for parliament's recall in October. This challenge was politically more dangerous to Pitt at this moment than anything either sector of the democratic movement was capable of mounting immediately. Pitt aimed to stop petitioning by Corporations and the like, and any recrudescence of the democratic movement, by recalling parliament. The announcement served to weaken the impetus behind the democrats, who agonised over decisions to try to mobilise the masses through public meetings in defiance of the law. Where revivals on orthodox lines occurred, they were easily suppressed. A meeting summoned in South Yorkshire was abruptly terminated by the intervention of the Bench and Yeomanry Cavalry. The LCS tried to convene an assembly on Kennington Common shortly before parliament met, but this too was crushed by a display of force. The UE fulminated and discussed tactics for 'another Meeting in three Places – to harass troops as in France', but within days decided to 'postpone' a decision to 'Wait for What Parlt does'. A spasm of terrorist activity in the West and East Midlands occurred, but most democrats decided to await the outcome of parliamentary proceedings.[62]

Popular dissatisfaction with parliament's policies, which amounted to little more than a re-enactment of previous measures and endorsement – however diplomatically engineered –· of the Home Office's original identification of causal forces, was immediately exploited in a renewed wave of Jacobin sloganising which saw out 1800. Again, a remarkable concurrence of sentiment is evinced across the country from rural Kent to industrial Yorkshire. Bread, monopolists, and the eradication of 'blood-thirsty Tyrants' were juxtaposed in hundreds of bills, like those sent in from Kidderminster and Windsor.[63] Parliament's reaction enriched the soil cultivated by democrats since September. The period over the 1800–1 winter is *very confused*. The most likely explanation is that activists who rigidly adhered to LCS orthodoxy were encouraged by the accidental, and short-lived, expiry of the Seditious Meetings Act, to try to relaunch their movement, within which a hard-core of revolutionary converts struggled to expand their own organisation. This picture emerges where the evidence is clearest, in the industrial North. In London, Thomas Spence published his advanced theoretical pamphlet, *The Restorer of Society to its Natural State*, and loosely organised some of his closer disciples to propagate his revolutionary message. Some of these men, but not Spence himself, were currently involved in physical force plottings, and permutations of Spence's plans for land reform quickly entered the lexicon of revolutionary politics.[64] All these democratic offensives drew heavily on subsistence issues, the government's actions, and parliamentary negations of the popular will.

One convenor of a planned mass meeting in the West Riding opined that 'speculating, ingrossing & extortioning of every Article of Life' explained current prices; he added, 'men encouraged it – part of the Statesmen has and is dubbling their Rents'. In Leeds, also in March 1801, Christopher Bennett joined operatives discussing corn prices and observed that 'it was a Pity Parliament had ever interfer'd about allowing coarse Meal to be made'. John Whittles 'immediately clapp'd him . . . on the shoulder and said . . . what are you turning', and advised Bennett to join a secret, oath-bound, political organisation to which Whittles and thousands more belonged. Whittles was one of an organisational caucus behind recent nocturnal mass meetings on Hartshead Moor. The centrality of subsistence issues was vividly revealed to secret policemen penetrating radical groupings in Nottingham. These spies 'frequently heard them say they wished things were ten times dearer than they are, as then all the people would be of one mind'. In November 1800, 'It was an universal opinion that there will be a general Disturbance & rising in February and March unless things are cheaper'. The view that only radical political change could restore customary and acceptable plebeian

living-standards achieved a broad proletarian currency. In Lancashire it was
said that the populace were

> told in Jacobinical prints of the cheapness of necessaries in France, &
> unfortunately the comparison seems to make them indifferent to every
> Tie of social or rational Attachment. . . . The severity of the times has
> made too many proselytes.

Across the Pennines, even a sceptical Lord Lieutenant, Fitzwilliam, admitted that 'the People' of the West Riding 'talk'd of revolution, as a remedy
for famine'. The threat of imminent revolution, spearheaded by disaffected
troops, was appended to an anonymous letter sent to a Midlands landowner, demanding intervention against speculating farming tenants. No region
was free from such juxtapositions, whereby popular prejudices and radical
politics ascribed total responsibility for famine to the state. In December
1800, North Kent labourers conspired, not to attack farmers and millers,
but to 'take up Arms against the Government'. Posters distributed at Rye
identified the Volunteers as the immediate agents of the state who were
'kept under Arms to keep people in Rouguery and Slavery all the Days of
our Lives', and ominously added that the people outnumbered amateur
soldiers whose 'opretion' was 'the same as in France . . . before the war
began'. Spence advised Volunteer soldiers to lay down their arms, and his
followers in the UE adopted his land plan to promise regular soldiers in
their revolutionary vanguard, plots of ten acres as a reward for their
successful participation. Popular political disaffection peaked in the spring
and early summer of 1801; it was probably more intense than its predecessor
in the autumn of 1795. Thomas Hardy acutely tuned to the temper of
metropolitan workers, reported that 'the people when speaking of an
invasion . . . say what is it to us who come down', a view shared by many
pillars of the establishment, including Arthur Young.[65]
    The tangible manifestations of universal mass alienation exhibit major
regional differences. In the West Midlands, a Jacobin-inspired panic,
undermined the collective nerve of the Bench, and a huge area was saturated
by troops for the duration of the famine. In the East Midlands, severe
tension generated an inadvertant conspiracy of silence, engulfing the
regional press and most magistrates. Fierce political agitations absorbed
Nottingham and most industrial villages. While many democrats sought to
express their alienation and advance their cause through public meetings,
other entered the UE's insurrectionary plots. Similar divergences transpired
in Yorkshire and Lancashire, and events in the latter were complicated
further by the industrial agitations of the cotton unions. Renewed repression of open meetings, held legally during the brief expiry of the Seditious
Meetings Act, drove the more determined activists into revolutionary
ranks. The government orchestrated unremitting repression in London
from September 1800. One victim was Spence, who was arrested, tried and
imprisoned in mid-1801, a telling testimony to ministerial fears at this
moment, as it was Spence's only court appearance during his twenty years
of radical activity in the capital. Metropolitan radicals had fewer options
than those available to at least some of their provincial counterparts.

Londoners were faced with the stark alternatives of inaction or revolutionary conspiracy throughout the entire remaining eight months of famine.
The Despard conspiracy testifies to the fact that a not insignificant number
took, and adhered to, the insurrectionary alternative. By 1800, revolutionary democrats were effectively constrained by French foreign and war
policies. Mass alienation caused by famine could be exploited to strengthen
a revolutionary vanguard through recruitment, and might operate crucially
in the event of an insurrection synchronised with an invasion. The
experiences of the second crisis proved that famine-induced alienation could
not be simply channelled into an open, indigenous, mass movement, with
power to dictate radical political change.[66]

Further questions concerning the role and potential of the democratic
presence can be asked of the remarkable events in South-western England in
the spring of 1801. In March GOC Simcoe asserted that 'the law of the
country was totally overthrown from the Paret to the Teign', and the fact
that some of his letters were erroneously filed by the Home Office with the
Irish correspondence speaks for itself. The region was swamped with
riotous mass mobilisations, which eclipsed the machinery of law and order.
Dozens of Volunteer companies mutinied; the magistracy demitted. The
government concluded that 'the possession of an adequate and commanding
Military Force is unquestionably the first step to be taken to enable the Civil
Power to resume its authority'. Simcoe's contingency plans mirrored
strategies appropriate to an invasion. Infantry were stationed in the towns
with Cavalry support to 'pursue . . . the Mob into the Country', creating a
'Cordon for the protection of the Farmers' and to 'segregate the Peasantry
from the Inhabitants or the Town'. The Lord Lieutenants of Devon and
Somerset were ordered by the Home Secretary to return home immediately
to reinstate the magistracy once the army suppressed the populace.[67] These
unique circumstances permit two key questions. First, what role can be
ascribed to democrats and trade unionists in the collapse of the region's legal
and administrative systems? Secondly, what influences did they exert on the
course of events subsequent to that collapse?

The economics of the south-west's sudden exposure to one of the worst
'absolute scarcities' during both famines have been established.[68] But the
real situation was alien to the consensus of opinion on causal factors as
prices rose over the 1800–1 winter. Public opinion was typified by the
'resolutions . . . produced read and approved' at a meeting of 'lower class'
Exonians on 23 March; depleted marts and soaring prices were attributed
'to the Farmers not bring their Corn to Market, & not from Scarcity'. This
analysis was not merely a plebeian prerogative; 'the Tradesmen immediately above them . . . have imbibed these ideas', together with many members
of the Bench and most Mayors. Simcoe reported that 'the language of all
Classes' uniformly condemned the farmers. From 'The general Conversation of the Country Towns', he concluded, 'more industry was used to
disseminate opinions of their Avarice, than to meet the Scarcity with the
economy and patience . . . recommended by the Legislature'.[69]

Major south-western towns like Plymouth and Exeter had a radical
presence; democratic political ideology was also popular property in many
lesser textile towns, and groups in the Cornish mining districts had liaised

with the LCS. But problems and reactions were not uniform across the region. If Cornish miners' employment prospects were sound and wages high, and demand for labour in the ports, notably Plymouth, buoyant from wartime stimulation, the textile industry hovered on collapse.[70] Although the textile trades were among the most unionised in the nation, economic realities reduced them to virtual impotency. Cornish miners had a notorious reputation for collective action, especially over subsistence matters, but many of them, like agricultural labourers, were protected by their employers with supplies of subsidised food.[71] At this juncture, only the Royal Dockyard workers had the industrial muscle for militant trade unionism. At Devonport, each of the several trades elected a committee, from which delegates were appointed to a Central Committee. Representatives from this body liaised with their counterparts in the other naval yards, and through the systematic 'communication of Events' had created a power base so that 'the whole navee works in all the yards are liable to be Protracted by what may be done in the Case of an Individual in either of them'. Power bred independence, and a vigorous interest in current affairs. The Devonport men stopped every morning for breakfast, 'and under the working Sheds have Bread and Butter Clubs, here the seditious talk politics and disseminate their Sentiments'. In March, the unions were locked in negotiations with the Navy Board. On 1 April, that Board in London pronounced against permanent wage increases to union representatives; instead payment of temporary supplements to counter inflated living costs were to be paid on scales governed by individuals' family size. The Board manifested relief when delegates 'appeared satisfied' with this offer.[72]

Parliamentary policies and ministerial actions since September 1800, notably the drives to cut cereal consumption, evoked a hostile regional response. When the 'common men' of the Dartmouth Volunteers mutinied, they told their officers

> that Govert had been applied to long enough & nothing done for them, therefore it was high time they should do something for themselves to prevent their Families from starving.

Bills posted at Stratton had democratic overtones:

> My fellow Sufferers and Country Men, now is the time to exert yourselves and shew yourselves Men and true born English Men, not to be inslaved by any Nation or Power of men on Earth: now is the time to come forward and take Vengeance on your Oppressors.

Bills distributed in Somerset textile towns confronted Pittite policies with revolutionary panygerics;

> On Cursed Statesmen & their Crew
> Let Bolts of Vengeance Fly;
> Let Farmers and Engrossers too,
> Like Brutes be doom'd to die,

Then shall we Live as Heav'n design'd
On finest flour of Wheat
When all the Knaves are put to Death,
Our Joys will be Complete
Then Rouse your drooping Spirits up
Not Starve by Pitt's Decree,
Fix up the Sacred Guillotine
Proclaim French Liberty.

Although similar literature circulating Cornish mining areas animaverted on French examples as 'a lesson to England', 'firm . . . Language' was advocated in petitions for Pitt's dismissal and peace. Local officials were impressed by floods of such 'jacobin' prints, spread by 'Vagrant . . . carriers of sedition' which encouraged indigenous 'disaffected Rascalls' to adopt enlarged profiles; concern at the demise of the Seditious Meetings Act was also registered. But the Stratton bill's notion of 'redress or Vengeance' was essentially limited;

Assemble all emediately and march in Dreadful Array to the Habitations of the Griping Farmer and Compell them to sell their Corn in the Market at a fair and reasonable Price.

This evidence clearly reveals that democrats adhered largely to orthodox notions of 'moral economy', and insisted that it be imposed by traditional means. Unionised textile and dockyard workers were to be central to that policy's implementation. The most advanced democrats were at most in hopes that the lessons learned through successful mobilisation over one issue, might be extended to others. 'Moral economy' received the stamp of democratic idealists' authority.[73]

Avaricious farmers were nearer to hand than royal despots and ministerial tyrants. Towards the end of March the populace of South-western town after town descended on rural hinterlands to force farmers to agree to market their remaining stocks at stipulated prices. The scale of these actions, and their duration, were impressive; the official corn returns from over half the region's market towns reveal the imposition of price controls for weeks. Simcoe's lament at 'the System of Compromise all around me' neatly summarised the collapse of many official agencies. No Corporate authority acted against riotous sorties from their towns, and hardly a county magistrate stirred, except to supervise agreements between crowds and farmers. It is no exaggeration to speak of the abdication of the Bench. Moreover, the initiative was commonly taken by Volunteer soldiers, who were joined by their officers.[74]

The considerable organisation and discipline shown by these mass mobilisations did not derive exclusively from the participation of Volunteer soldiers. The two thousand people who left Exeter 'filed off in divisions' in three distinct directions. Effective collusion between crowds followed: from Exeter

> Men stiling themselves Delegates 'selected and appointed' by the Mob,
> constantly communicate from Town to Town and by this Means carry
> Intelligence from Place to Place,

instructing people at Exmouth, among them, on acceptable prices. Delega-
tions between rebellious textile towns were facilitated by 'the numerous
associations of Wool-combers', union branches masquerading as Friendly
Societies, which were particularly numerous in Devon and Somerset.
Wellington woolcombers drafted a series of resolutions which they sent for
the endorsement of Cullompton and Tiverton colleagues. Modbury crowd
leaders, all textile workers, 'correspond by private messengers . . . with
other societies'. Uffculm weavers convened formally, and then formed the
nucleus of a crowd; they subsequently issued a handbill to deny riotous
intentions, and to legitimise decisive policing of markets. The Sheepwash
crowd agreed to regroup on 2 April after a scheduled meeting of a Friendly
Society.[75]

Devonport dockyard workers were drawn into disturbances. On 31
March townswomen set market prices; violence commenced, and the arrest
of two women and a dockyard artisan, precipitated a lengthy confrontation
with 'the Dockyard Gentry'. They downed tools on learning of the arrests,
and approached the Bench, who were supported by soldiers, including 'the
Artillery with four field pieces, loaded with Grape and Canister'. Undeterred, the Central Committee negotiated the prisoners' release with magistrates anxious to avoid a bloody finale. The Committee proceeded to open
talks with butchers and bakers; the unionists rushed into print to pressurise
both, and to enjoin civil order. The bakers agreed to impose price ceilings,
and although this initiative finally collapsed after more violence and another
strike, this owed much to the Pittite MP and Devon Militia commander,
Colonel Bastard, who was determined to crush displays of proletarian
power.[76] Elsewhere, magistrates were conspicuous by their absence, and
the power vacuum was filled by genuinely populist creations. At Totnes a
'Committee of the People' was elected, served by a 'clerk', to administer the
market and to discipline obdurate farmers and food traders. The committee
completely usurped the Corporation, and promised to 'protect Persons and
Property from the least outrage' so long as their regulations were observed.
Their orderliness was also emphasised by their decree – 'N.B. The better to
prevent Confusion Women are required not to attend the Corn Market'.
Durable populist administrations also emerged at Newton Abbot and
Modbury. 'The Newton Regulators' ordered the town crier to announce
fixed prices each market day, and the constables to arrest recalcitrant
farmers. Nicholas Wakeman, 'the leader of the People' at Modbury, chaired
a four-man committee which met daily to regulate the town. On one
occasion Wakeman granted a 'free passage' to flour desperately required in
hard-pressed Plymouth. Wakeman earned his nickname, 'Buonoparte'.[77]

Trade unionists were no strangers to democratic ideology; indeed the
unions, like Friendly Societies were democratic organisations. The leading
role of unionists in many orthodox crowd formations, their regular
emergence as spokesmen in negotiations to implement the 'moral economy', and their acceptance of popular office when the traditional arms of

governance collapsed, emphasise key factors respecting mass mobilisations. First, there was no simple replacement of popular analyses of economic realities based on the 'moral economy' by an alternative 'unionist mentality' with a central tenet that *wages* must be adequate to enable the purchase of a proper diet whatever the price.[78] Secondly, South-western experiences in 1801 confirm the key relevance of the 'moral economy' to the problems arising from severe food shortages. It provided the only rational ideology appropriate to an imposed restoration of normality in these desperate times, when starvation stared – or appeared to stare – thousands in the face. Populist policing of the local economy to force farmers to supply neighbourhood markets, and millers to abandon sales in distant locations, and make both supply their own district at stipulated prices, comprised the sole *apparently realistic* solutions to the perceived predicament. If the forcible imposition galvanised a power vacuum, then the populace elected their own leaders, including the 'idolised' Wakeman of Modbury, and 'Master Chigley . . . made . . . a King' during the 'kind of insurrection' by the poor of Over Stowey in Somerset. No historian, and no contemporary, radical or conservative, could foretell where such power usurpations might lead, let alone end, in the event of a massive conflagration. The reimposition of the state's law and order in the South-west took many months, perhaps a year, after rioting ceased. It was achieved only in conjunction with remedial measures, including a huge augmentation of poor relief, and such a temperate *de facto* use of the army and the courts that the Home Secretary was astounded at the disregard displayed for the strict enforcement of the law by all but a tiny minority who did respond positively to Whitehall goading.[79] These phenomena speak volumes about the internal mechanisms of English society, and none more forcibly than the testimony to the sheer impossibility of containing mass action by brute force alone. English society was too complicated, its organs of governance too diverse and liable to confront, rather than simply complement each other, to permit the rule of the unsheathed sword. The fact that the Home Secretary's fiat was insufficient, in spite of ample military support for South-western Benches, conveys a measure of the very real limits to the power of the state at this time. It was these limits that the democrats would have to exploit, if they were ever to achieve their desired reforms through mobilising the masses to impose a political solution.

Who can fault Lancastrian Thomas Ainsworth's 1801 assertion that

there is nothing to fear from Jacobinism further than availing themselves of the distracted state of the country and the common saying of the poor it is better to die in a battle than to be starved in our powers.

The conservative pamphleteer Bland, writing in 1800 of the potential of plebeian mobilisations, was equally incisive;

the seeds of commotion are widely sown; and the eruption of a single riot may be the commencement of a formidable insurrection and that a signal for more.

One witness to the south-western conflagration identified 'the machinations and designs of the ill disposed' rousing the masses 'to tumult and riot,
to acts of violence and plunder'. He added, shrewdly, that if the crowd
mobilised initially to

> satisfy the demands of hunger, yet when people had adopted the
> sovereignty and taken redress into their own hands, the most penetrating
> eye can not foresee what the result may be; more especially in these times
> when the principle of revolution has infected all of Europe more or less,
> and has deluged part of it in blood.[80]

Some democrats, including insurrectionary converts, did anticipate success through this precise strategy. But their great problem turned on getting
the masses to make the political transmutation whereby the 'moral economy' was jettisoned in favour of perceiving the ultimate solution in
parliamentary reform on democratic principles. This problem was examined by Benjamin Flower in two major articles in his radical *Cambridge
Intelligencer*, published during the September 1800 hypercrisis. Spence also
approached the problem, from a different angle, early in 1801. In his first
article, Flower castigated the 'most lethargic indifference' of the populace to
the repeated failures of Pittite war and foreign policy: Flower studiously
avoided the issue of the food supply. In the second, he insisted that the
'primary cause' of scarcity was the war, 'the scourge of this country and of
Europe, that source of crime and misery'. While not denying commercial
malpractices – 'the evil stands recorded in our courts' – he relegated them to
a subordinate status. Flower accused 'the ministerial prints in particular' of
heaping abuse on corndealers, millers and farmers, 'to turn public attention
to secondary causes only', thereby diverting criticism from the war. He
implied that the resultant rioting suited Pitt, and warned against participation which risked 'Ruin'. But Flower did

> not wish to inculcate, even in the lowest members of society, mean and
> servile submission under oppression. No. Let the poor think and speak as
> FREEMEN, and as BRITONS. Let their voice be loud for PEACE.

The 'people' must 'make use of every means the law still allows them for
associating' to engineer a mammoth, petitioning peace movement, until it
achieved an unstoppable momentum.[81]
    Spence acknowledged that the 'unprecedented dearness of Provisions sets
every head on devising . . . a remedy', and his visionary advocacy skilfully
played on current notions of monopoly, oppressive state powers, war and
famine, to dispose of the popular solution hinging on the redivision of large
farms into smaller units. The landed elite would never willingly compromise their immense wealth by radical restructuring of agrarian capitalism, nor
jettison their political supremacy; the two were inseparable and both had to
be destroyed before 'anything else than the utmost screwing and grinding of
the Poor' could be achieved. This must be done at once on pure Spencean
principles as explained in his publications:

For the public mind being suitably prepared by reading my little tracts, and conversing on the subject, a few contiguous Parishes have only to declare the Land to be theirs, and form a Convention of parochial Delegates. Other adjacent Parishes would immediately on being invited follow the example and send also their Delegates, and thus would a beautiful and powerful new Republic instantly arise in full vigour. The power and resources of War, passing in this moment into the hands of people from the hands of their Tyrants, they, like shorne Samsons would become weak and harmless as other Men. And being thus as it were scalped of their Revenues, and the lands that produced them, their Power would never grow, to enable them to overturn our Temple of Liberty.

This was not impracticable; the precedents were the American and French Revolutions, and the great British naval mutinies of 1797. The latter contained the essential blueprint. The sailors had expelled their officers in a bloodless revolt. As the ratio of landowners to workers was a mere fraction of the ratio of naval officers to sailors, 'such a Mutiny on Land' could easily overthrow the landlords. 'So the people' in their conventions 'have only to say the Land will be ours and it will be so'.[82]

In Flower's scheme of things, peace, with its assumed precursor, Pitt's replacement by Fox, would be the first stage in a political transformation climaxed by parliamentary reform. But the situations producing food riots were too intense and the problems too immediate for such strategic philosophising, let alone Spence's quixotics. The established tenets of the 'moral economy' were much more relevant than novel Painite principles. Suspect farmers and millers were part of the local community, and therefore targetable; monarchs and cabinet ministers were neither in the immediate context. Landowners, even when domiciled in their country mansions were hardly vulnerable to small village populations; nor were landlords primary targets when urban crowds descended on the countryside. Moreover, during the biggest mobilisations, the landed gentry either turned a blind eye, or adopted an intermediary role and earned kudos through negotiating with the populace and their victims, or arrived at the head of a military force.

Populist dependency on the 'moral economy' emerged as a potent enemy for radicals, which they never successfully confronted, let alone confuted. Indeed some democrats, though clearly not all, supported both orthodox ideology and the traditional means of enforcement. Whitmore, a leader of the radical and unionised stocking weavers in north-west Northampton-shire, with a letter from a brother Jacobin in Nottingham advocating *taxation populaire*, mobilised his supporters to regulate Banbury market in a thoroughly traditional fashion.[83] Much 'general confusion' accompanied the implementation of the 'moral economy', but it operated to detract attention from more global political considerations. It directed popular antipathy to the iniquities of the local capitalist economy and its function-aries, rather than to the political structure which supported them. The autumnal crisis of confidence in Pitt in 1800 precipitated a popular, political response, but it was upstaged by the petitioning movement from constitu-tional bodies, and was partly suppressed by the state's repressive agencies.

The democratic offensive was always semi-secret even in its metropolitan, Midland and northern epicentres. The significance of the famines lies in the longer term; they were among the more portentous experiences which provided empirical evidence of the iniquitous workings of the unreformed political system, which penalised and impoverished working people, and enriched the wealthy. This was of restricted consequence to the distressed manufacturers of Modbury faced with an empty market-place; the solution then lay in the well-tried, limited and essentially 'conservative' tenets of the 'moral economy'. Once enforced, most of the enforcers had achieved their aims; direct action exposed them to considerable risks, both at the time, and subsequently, if a legal counter-offensive was launched. If the food riot was a terrifying weapon of the urban and industrial proletariat, the riot was inherently heavily circumscribed by tradition; it could not be transformed into a political movement, nor be made a vehicle for instant politicisation. If famine mobilised the masses, it did so principally within a customary framework. In some senses the crisis were too short for radicals to effectively exploit riotous explosions, or even mass deprivation. In 1802 a Yorkshireman considered that

> with plenty of Trade, and the great improvement in the condition of the lower orders of society which has now taken place, pernicious doctrines will not be disseminated with much effect.[84]

CHAPTER 10

Conclusion

Famine, the Defences of the Poor and the Threat to Public Order

Riot was not an automatic response to intolerably high prices. Its incidence reveals varying stimulants, and alternating crowd objectives, notably the 'moral-economy' tenet deemed appropriate. Riot patterns reflected changed economic factors, and alterations to popular perceptions of famine's causal forces. The latter holds clues to riotous intensity at any one time. Paramount here is the September 1800 explosion. Riot was never universal, or the only form of protest. Seminal ideological developments account for the 'Jacobin tinge' to many riots, but there were other changes which warrant analysis. Trade unionism clearly accelerated in the 1790s. Arson assumed serious proportions in some rural regions. Such phenomena need to be related to riot. Ultimately we must concentrate on the problem of public order, and the crux of the matter for society, and therefore for central and local government. How did popular responses to famine, the interacting defences of the poor, imperil law and order and the socio-political equilibrium?

Rural Protest

The dependency of rural workers on the market, and their exposure to price movements, was not in aggregate radically altered by either the development of truck systems by farmers in some regions,[1] or the marked increase in poor-relief payments throughout the countryside.[2] The evidence for rural food riots is sparse. The record is probably hopelessly defective owing to the small numbers involved, the commensurate lack of serious violence, too minor to warrant attention from the press or the courts. The blockade of 1795 was not imposed without demonstrations and threats in rural communities, and its enforcement produced handfulls of arrests, though not invariably prosecutions, as revealed by the case of two West Sussex labourers released after being locked up for seizing butter, a basket and linen cloths, from a petty dealer. The four Hampshire labourers who were prosecuted for stopping a cart going to Romsey in April 1800 may represent the tip of an iceberg. So too might those Lincolnshire labourers prosecuted for a violent demonstration against the shopkeeper of tiny Brank Broughton.[3] Other rural disturbances derive from 'moral-economy' tenets, but are not food riots as such. They include the detention of seed potatoes and cabbages in Somerset villages, where 'peasant' proprietors survived in strength; the same features were probably responsible for the sole recorded anti-tithe riot, at Lifton in Devon. However, itinerant bakers in rural areas were subjected to *taxation populaire* in Cambridgeshire, Essex, Dorset, and Somerset – in the 'closed' parish of Montacute. Village shopkeepers and bakers' roundsmen regularly blamed their own suppliers in market towns. Baker Smith told enraged customers at Hadstock that 'he had no Orders to fall from the Millers'. Rural workers' attentions were thus directed to local market-towns, where the real villains were to be found, together with the anonymity that the countryman lacked at home.[4]

The rural poor commonly participated in market-town disturbances, and authority regularly distinguished between their townsfolk and 'country people'. Posters summoning demonstrators to Chichester percolated through adjacent villages. Villagers domiciled near Kenninghall 'established . . . a Communication' before 'parties of 20 or 30' came into the market from different directions. The Mayor of Cambridge's decision to subsidise townsmen's bread led to 'a battle between the Country People and those of the Town' after the former's participation in the preceding riot went unrewarded with their exclusion from relief. At New Alresford 'disorder began by groups of people coming in from the adjoining parishes, and assembling together'; then 'some Farmers were very positively charg'd by the Labourers . . . with possessing much unthresh'd wheat'.[5] The detailed evidence of a riot at Saffron Walden reveals the leading role of urban artisans and labourers; once assembled they went to nearby villages 'to force away the labourers' whose interest in stock conservation and reduced prices ought to be identical. The Mayor launched a wave of prosecutions, but the name of only one countryman was known by witnesses, and the case against him was dropped; defendants were all townsmen, well-known by the crowd's urban victims, and easily identified for legal purposes.[6] This suggests that country folk, as opposed to the inhabitants of smaller towns, enjoyed a degree of protection in such circumstances, as does the case at New Alresford where the four labourers charged were town dwellers, not from the ranks of the villagers who started the riot. However, this argument must not be pushed too far; three rioters indicted at Romsey were all from the village of Chilworth.[7] New Alresford events also reveal how predominantly urban crowds obtained the information necessary for selective strikes at farms in rural hinterlands.

The bulk of recorded market-town food riots belong to the 'early phase' of 1795.[8] These reveal some juxtaposition of issues, food prices, wage rates, and poor relief levels, especially in the South and the East where wages were lowest, employment least secure, and market-dependency greatest. There were precedents for such juxtapositions,[9] which became more common during the famines. In Sussex, Cocking overseers were beset by riotous claimants in December 1794, and on 2 March 1795 twenty-five married farmworkers with 104 children between them, marched in regular order from Hurstpierpoint to Lewes to present their case for additional benefits to the Bench. However at Funtingdon, their counterparts struck for daily wages to be increased to two shillings, and strike calls were also made in rural Berkshire. Another strike at Edenbridge, Kent, in February 1795 ended in the Assize dock. Hoddesdon agricultural labourers withdrew their Friendly Society deposits in the following July to finance strike action. But the juxtaposition remained, to be neatly symbolised by another demonstration at Lewes in February 1801. The Buxted contingent 'had set out with the Determination of lowering the price of Provisions', but others, from Chiddlingly, East Hoathly and Framfield, were there to lobby the Bench for increases in weekly relief rates.[10]

Nevertheless, the famines witnessed some extension of trade unionist actions in the countryside, notably in the South, the Home Counties and East Anglia. In Sussex, unionist principles may have been more broadly disseminated after the building unions penetrated the rural districts. Representatives from 'all' construction trades in ten parishes convened at Storrington on 27 February 1796 and a further meeting in March facilitated the participation of a 'larger company' from previously unrepresented villages. In May the Chequers Inn at Maresfield hosted a convention of 'Working men' in the blacksmith and wheelwright trades. East Anglian farmworkers may have owed something to traditions sown by textile workers in the more prosperous times, earlier in the eighteenth century. Friendly societies were numerous in all these regions. Moreover, there were precedents for collective action by agricultural labourers, including that set in 1793, the year Isaac Seer, 'the first known farmworkers' leader' was arrested during an Essex dispute.[11] East Anglia saw the beginnings of a determined movement forged by farmworkers in the autumn of 1795. The men of Norfolk argued that 'The Labourer is worthy of his Hire', and complained

> that the mode of lessening his distresses, as hath lately been the fashion, by selling him flour under the market price, and thereby rendering him an object of a parish rate, is not only an indecent insult on his lowly and humble situation (in itself sufficiently mortifying from his degrading dependence on the caprice of his employer) but a fallacious mode of relief, and every way inadequate to a radical redress of the manifold distresses of his calamitous state.

Wages should be governed by the price of wheat. A Heacham labourer was elected 'Clerk' to a proposed 'general Meeting': delegated messages of support were invited from every village to launch parliamentary lobbying. Nothing further is recorded. The language of the statement suggests radical involvement, and open-air democratic meetings were held at the same time in the region. Some activists may also have supported Samuel Whitbread's minimum wage campaign. His exertions were said to have encouraged strike preparations by 'Farmers Servants & other work-people in Hertfordshire', where the MP maintained relationships with lowly democrats.[12]

Some farmers did increase wages under pressure from their men in

1795–6, and again in 1799,[13] and the resultant disparities may account for
the numbers of local wage campaigns during the 1799–1801 famine. The
same regions were affected as in 1795. Again, ideological commitment was
often weakened by similar juxtapositions.[14] The success rate is elusive, but
notable defeats followed recourse to violence. In June 1800, two or possibly
three separate movements were vigorously repressed. Workers from the
Essex marshes under 'Captain' Wakelin forced other employees in the
Steeple district to strike, only to be confronted by the notorious and bullish
Rev. Henry Bate Dudley, who organised a full-scale 'hue and cry'. One
hundred more men, 'privy to the intended insurrection' melted away from
Southminster. After making arrests, Dudley prevailed upon the Bench to
use county funds to prosecute the leadership at the Assize, where Lord
Chief Justice Kenyon subscribed to magisterial rigour by informing the
three convicted that their offence 'bordered on High Treason'. While he
refrained from enlarging on the relevant precise legal niceties, he found a
willing ally in *The Times* which advocated the greatest publicity to the
prison sentences to show farmworkers 'the consequences of combining to
distress their employers'. In Berkshire, a riotous sortie from Thatcham was
surrounded by the Volunteer Cavalry, largely comprising farmers, and
crushed. In Kent, more farmworkers were prosecuted, and other rural
employees, including Kentish biscuit-makers, and Hampshire journeymen-
millers, came before the courts.[15] These were all serious defeats. Whitbread's 1795 statement was equally true of 1801:

> artisans and other working people contrive at times of public scarcity,
> and at periods when they deem it fit, to make demand of advance in their
> wages, and compel their employers to make such advances; such
> proceedings were . . . out of the power of the husbandman.[16]

These defeats, the apparent decline of food rioting in these regions, and
the enhanced importance of poor relief are reflected in two emergent
phenomena. First, arguments over, and dissatisfaction with, parochial
payments and relief-schemes were responsible for an increasing number of
violent – if minor – altercations in the countryside. At Winkleigh six people
compelled the overseer to sell subsidised barley to them despite a vestry
ruling that 'they were Men of Ability had no Head Money and did not want
it'. At Poughill, a similar row terminated in the looting of a parish potato
store.[17] The suppression of riot and trade unionism proved that the forces of
law and order were equal to overt protest in the countryside. This fact was
responsible for the second development, namely the rise of covert rural
protest, notably the sending of anonymous threatening letters and arson.
The Berkshire bill calling for a strike, also threatened incendiarism on the
premises of farmers who refused to raise wages. The sense of frustration felt
by protesters frustrated by overwhelming repressive force was revealed by a
doggerel:

> As we cant have Riot
> We'll do Things more quiet
> As provisions get higher

The greater the Fire

Arson, and anonymous letters which usually threatened incendiarism, played a new and significant role in rural protest in the South and the East, especially where attempts to win increased wages failed. Typical recipients of threatening letters included the agriculturalist who 'ran' Brent; he was told 'by the poor of this Parish' that if 'some provision . . . is not made . . . your House & barns & Wheat Mows & Potatoes' would be 'set on fire': the same penalty would be paid by Suffolk farmers who refused to market their stocks.[18]

The distinct rise in arson cases in the second famine over the first is charted in Table 13. Arson had a long history as a mode of exacting private vengeance, and this tradition was maintained in the 1790s with the burnings of the stacks of those responsible for the prosecution of petty thieves.[19] But incendiarism was resorted to by those exacting *public* as opposed to private vengeance, with victims selected from the locally infamous, including tight-fisted overseers of the poor. A Sussex farmer who 'stupidly said he would not thrash until wheat was £40 pr. load' lost £500 worth in flames. Some JPs hoped that arsonists would limit their activities to the notorious, only to be disappointed like Sir St. John Mildmay in Essex, when threats were extended to all 'the most opulent & most considerable Farmers'. Identical blanket threats were made elsewhere, but incendiarism never reached such proportions, owing to the perpetrators' discrimination. Odiham labourers announced that

> *we know* Every Stack of Corn about this Country and Every Barn that have Corn concealed . . . . the poore in Every place is willing to tell us the Farmers that ask the most Money and Likewise the Millers that Bid the most.

Edward Augur, the 'Ruler of the Parish' of Eastbourne, was told that incendiaries 'shall begin first with sonthing to be Longing to you'.[20]

Threatening letters in rural regions usually insisted on the retention of stocks for sale at reduced prices in the locality. With the exception of as yet marginal anti-tithe protests, there was no significant difference between the grievances of urban and rural workers. The 'moral economy' was equally relevant, though the nature of protest did begin to change, dramatically in the case of rural arson. If Odiham farmers meant to starve the workers, the poor were 'Determind if thare is to be Starvation it shall be a General thing not a parcial one for Both Gentle, and Simple shall Starve if any Do'. This extension of populist conceptions of morality was at once peculiarly rural, and a chilling class response to those who denigrated the destruction of food in times of death.[21]

Fourteen separate cases of arson have been found in 1794–6. Berkshire fared worse with four, Sussex second with three, and Suffolk and Norfolk jointly third with two each. East Anglia probably had more, because reports in the autumn of 1795 suggest that incendiarism achieved some intensity as an adjunct to orthodox food rioting. Three of the Berkshire cases possibly correlate with other forms of protest, namely the suppression of riotously-made wage demands, and *taxation populaire*.[22] All other cases of incendiarism appear to be isolated, but the three counties affected, Somerset,[23] Wiltshire, and Hertfordshire,[24] were to experience more numerous incidents in the second famine, as were Suffolk, Norfolk, and Berkshire. Other counties, including Shropshire, Derbyshire, and above all Essex, the scenes of fires in 1799–1801, appear to have escaped precedents in 1794–6. Conversely West Riding incidents in 1794–6 were not repeated later.[25] The incidence of arson in 1799–1801 falls roughly into two main periods, the spring and the autumn of 1800, and these coincide with the maximum disturbance in non-rural locations. Distinct outbreaks of incendiarism can be traced. The south-east experienced a wave of arson attacks accompanied by threatening letters in the 'early phase' of 1799–1800. A more concentrated campaign occurred in East Anglia in April 1800. In these regions, protest reveals sharp contrasts between the famines. In 1795 both regions experienced considerable *taxation populaire* but little arson in the 'early phase'. The reversal in 1800 was perhaps symbolised by the extension of arson threats to corporate authorities in Hampshire. In some regions, incendiarism began to replace the riot as the dominant form of protest.[26]

Prior to 1800 incendiarism elsewhere was scattered. Somerset and Shropshire had three attacks each, but only one incident was recorded in each of five other counties. Arson and threatening letters were used extensively in East Anglia, and more surprisingly Derbyshire after the harvest. East Anglia suffered at least eighteen arson attacks on barns and ricks. The intensity of the outbreaks stimulated a joint public announcement from three insurance companies that they and not the farmers incurred the losses; to injure 'Persons who cannot have offended' was immoral. Farmers mounted vigilante patrols in Suffolk villages. Testimonies to sudden public awareness of a new threat included newspapers which publicised ancient punishment for incendiaries – death by burning – and the rapid incarceration of proletarians like Mrs Jane Bungy of Middle Bockhampton, Hampshire, who merely referred to the new defence of the rural poor.[27]

All bar one of the 1800 fires were started under the cover of darkness, very often in the evening. The Marquis of Buckingham explained that they commenced

> at the same hour in the evening, viz. at eight o'clock [which] sufficiently shows that they have been produced by the labouring poor who at that hour are going home.

In this context, Buckingham's speculative idea that arsonists came from 'very hard pressed parishes' hints that East Anglian incendiaries belonged to 'open' rather than 'close' villages, and fired properties when returning from work in the latter to their homes in the former.[28] Conversely, Mr Charlesworth's belief that East Anglian incendiaries were rural textile workers experiencing the traumas of the final collapse of their industry, is feasible, though it cannot assign responsibility for Sussex fires, where there was little manufacturing.[29] Virtually no culprits were caught, but whomsoever they were, they could take satisfaction in the registration of their protest. The mere threat of arson caused prodigious alarm amongst landowners, justices and farmers, as their letters on the subject prove.[30] The threatening letter and arson played a similar role to the riot; it forced the ruling classes to examine the complaints of the poor, and it stimulated greater relief measures. For repression was not the sole answer; the rulers of the countryside responded by digging deeper into their pockets.[31]

If the famines witnessed Captain Swing's emergence from the ranks, theft, the most potent of the rural poor's defences, remained their bulwark. A statistical survey is not possible here, and while contemporary claims of a crime wave warrant scepticism, there is little doubt that both famines, notably the second, saw aggravated criminal activity in the countryside. The Duke of Bedford was not contradicted when he made political capital from 'the miserable wretches, whose poverty left them no other resource but depredation', and continued to suggest that his fellow peers would find the empirical evidence 'If they repaired to the fields or the woods'. Privately Bedford told the Home Secretary that

> the farmers and the inhabitants of every village suffer so much from the constant depredations of those who really do not have the means of boiling their pot without stealing from somebody.

Whether Bedford himself skulked in Woburn ditches is an interesting speculation, but Lord Lansdowne was just one colleague who complained in late 1800 of the 'manifest . . . disposition of the common people to commit Burglarys and other crime'. Another, Viscount Middleton advanced the unprecedented number of felony charges to be heard at an 1801 Sessions, as a more important commitment than supporting government in the House. Commenting on a recent spate of 'robberies', Reginald Heber noted that 'food alone was stolen' during house-breaks-ins. A journalist wryly opined over Lincolnshire thieves, that 'Hunger will . . . "make its way through stone walls" and why not through quick-sett hedges'.[32]

This was not just political rhetoric, party hyperbole, or class invective. The staid minute of the Stockland vestry represents countless others:

> Whereas several Gardens cultivated Lands and orchards within this Parish have been frequently robbed and plundered of Cabbages Carrots Potatoes Turnips . . . and many Sheep . . . lately stolen from the Commons . . . the Principal Inhabitants

contributed to a prosecution fund.[33] Rutland and Nottinghamshire were just two counties in which thefts of one or two lambs, sheep, and cattle at a time reached epidemic proportions, sure signs of rustling for personal consumption.[34] The massive increase in poaching, especially nocturnal, found one expression in the 1800 Night Poaching Act, with the introduction of mandatory prison sentences, a savage restatement of privilege attached to property by the notorious Game Laws.[35] Farmworkers had perhaps always believed in some right to purloin food from their employers; James Smith called his son 'a rascal for taking too much' at once, not for stealing any.[36] Sir Charles Willoughby, chairman of the Oxfordshire Bench, was just one JP who believed that such crime achieved unacceptable proportions in 1800; it comprised a 'breach of trust' the more reprehensible as by its nature it 'frequently escaped attention'. Willoughby urged 'exemplary punishment', and with farmers increasingly spying on their workforces,[37] several Benches embarked on crusades. A special Sessions convened in Northumberland to sentence one unfortunate

> to stand in the pillory on Jedburgh fair day . . . his head uncovered, his neck on the jugs (an iron collar) and a label on his breast, containing these words . . . 'For Stealing Corn from his Master'.

Transportation followed.[38] Of course the rural poor continued to steal; and they stole from each other. Sneak thieves who did not practice class-conditioned discrimination include spinster Hannah Moore of Petworth who filched 'part of a Loaf' from labourer Frances Gosden, and John Muggeridge of Fittleworth who raided the home of fellow labourer Thomas Hawkins to loot bits of white and brown loaves, one and a half pounds of butter, and an 'Earthen Pot', together valued at elevenpence. The inhabitants of Over Stowey, Somerset, were appalled at their experience of a new criminal phenomenon – pilfering from the vegetable patches of the poor. More discriminatory rural thieves increasingly felt God to be on their side, and stealing from the rich achieved a new standing in populist mentality. Was not 'the Great Fat Bellied Farmer . . . riding about' while his workers 'hungered'? 'Tom Nottage', exclaimed an Essex worker,

> is a damn Rouge . . . you sink [lower prices] for we have rob your Mill seavel Times and we will rob it again.[39]

The Role of Industrial Action

Recent historiography has penetrated the cloud obscuring eighteenth-century worker combination, and established the virility of trade unionist tactics. The 1790s were clearly a watershed; more and more trades, in an ever-increasing number of places, took their first steps, or consolidated their emergent unionist tradition. Novel features include the perfection of the rolling strike by paper-makers in the South. The famines were central to all these developments. Dr Rule writes that

> Masters were not always insensitive to the pressures of rising food prices and often compromised on wage demands based on cost of living grounds. This was especially evident during the highly inflationary years of the French Wars . . . but in some cases employers expected their journeymen to take a cut in wages when food prices came down again.

Some of those at the top of the social hierarchy, including the Foreign Secretary, advised landowners to increase their workers' wages, as models to be imitated by all other employers. Conversely resistance to 'a rise of wages by those who knew the difficulty of lowering them again' was common.[40] Moreover, notably in textiles, oscillating demand caused by changes in the military requirements of British and allied governments, wartime interruptions to overseas markets, and the devastating impact of famine on the home market, threw the adverse effects of the march of machinery into sharper relief, to generate Luddite-style protest. These juxtapositions add to the historian's difficulties in evaluating the role of industrial action. That taken by smaller occupational groups, including strikes, often went unrecorded. We do learn of victories, among them those scored by tailors at Newcastle-upon-Tyne and Hull; Reading master ribbon-weavers agreed to 'such addition' to piece rates 'as fully satisfied the hands', and in the small Lincolnshire town of Burgh Le Marsh, twenty-seven labourers achieved their demands after they 'entered into and signed a league under pretence of wages'.[41]

The first advent of inflationary pressure over the 1794–5 winter stimulated waves of wage demands, threats of industrial action and strikes. In January William Devaynes MP solicited subscription funds to subsidise bread, coal and clothing to head off anticipated strikes by metropolitan artisans; this he argued would 'get their good Will, as well as their Work, and keep them quiet'. Devaynes was an ardent Reevite, and it is ironic that Thomas Hardy was an early victim of a strike from which he tried to extricate himself with an appeal to the 'Society of Journeyman Boot and Shoemakers'. Negotiations elsewhere also broke down. Journeymen fullers at Exeter rejected a proposed increase to nine shillings per week, and struck for twelve. When other Exeter textile workers struck in March they stated that 'the Wages of almost every Class of Mechanics throughout the Kingdom hath been considerably augmented'. Apparently inexorable inflation galvanised action by more and more workers in the summer. Coal miners in Cumberland, Lancashire, Derbyshire and Nottinghamshire launched vigorous campaigns which included strikes. Nottinghamshire also witnessed protracted negotiations in the hosiery industry. Manchester spinners forced wage increases, but only after their first month-long strike. Metropolitan trades striking at this juncture included journeymen bakers, millwrights and coal-heavers; ugly scenes in the latter dispute were narrowly avoided through the Lord Mayor's intervention. The highly-praised 1773 legislation providing magisterial arbitration in the Spitalfields silk-weaving industry was invoked, thereby keeping 'numerous inferior workmen' off East London streets, and away from the riotous crowds infesting London over the summer of 1795.[42]

Parallel wage offensives were mounted during the 1795–6 season and both those seasons comprising the 1799–1801 famine. A number of features warrant emphasis. Some major groups' adoption of militant action became increasingly regular. In January 1796 the Leeds press complained

that the inhabitants of this town should so frequently, in the winter season, experience a want of supply of coals at the coal-staiths, by the colliers at Middleton collieries refusing to work without an advance of wages.

Undeterred the men won additional binding fees and subsidised coal from

Lord Middleton. Earl Fitzwilliam's South Yorkshire miners fought an identical campaign in 1796–7. Miners increasingly exploited the fact that wage and conditions varied between coalowners. Strikes at other Yorkshire pits in late 1799 commenced when the owner, a Mr Thorpe, tried to reduce wages to levels paid by neighbouring employers. This episode stimulated attempts by owners to agree on wages, though this initial essay failed.[43] By 1800, many north-eastern coalowners had introduced subsidised flour schemes for their men. Attempts by one of the greatest, Lord Delaval, to alter prices and rations, provoked a massive confrontation in April. A major victory followed the Bench's intervention, with Delaval ordered to honour his contracts and legal proceedings against miners' leaders dropped. All this militancy served principally to prove the utility of industrial action to major occupational groups. In 1795 the Kingswood colliers fought off the demands of the tithe-owner, and in 1801 they rejected *taxation populaire*, which they knew had been implemented elsewhere in the West,[44] in favour of a strike:

> a Body . . . of between 4 and 500 determined not to work to deprive this city [Bristol] and the Manufacturers in the Neighbourhood of their usual & necessary supply of Coal, blindly fancying that they should by these means compass their wishes . . . viz: a Reduction in the price of Provisions.

Protracted negotiations with the Bench produced greater poor relief. An ideologically unsound result perhaps, but the Kingswood men's experiences certainly proved that they could win strikes, despite ample army support for the Bench.[45]

Conflict over wages stimulated by inflation in the 1790s was juxtaposed with other industrial disputes in the textile industries, many of which were undergoing rapid change. Units of production inexorably increased in size; if Lancastrian cottons had more factories than any other textile sector, symbolic new erections were found in woollens, including Gott's Bean Ing Mill in Leeds, and John Jones' Staverton Superfine Woollen Manufactory in Wiltshire. Worsted spinning was following cotton on the path to mechanisation. Machine-scribbling in woollens, virtually universal in Yorkshire, was rapidly expanding in Wiltshire. It helped to undermine the socio-economic viability of the family in the classic domestic system. The élite shearmen of the Yorkshire and Wiltshire woollen industries were threatened with extinction by gig-mills and shearing frames. This challenge epitomised technology's potential. Power-loom experimentations were well-known and current initiatives served to aggravate innate fears. The emergence of great capitalists, Arkwright, Peel, Greg, Gott, Jones and their ilk, challenged the customary roles of small-masters and their journeymen, notably through the attack on the key, labour-restrictive, apprenticeship system. These menaces to employment, status, and earnings, were immeasurably aggravated by inflated food prices. In 1795, unionised woolcombers in Nottinghamshire and Yorkshire began to co-ordinate opposition to those who threatened traditional skills and apprenticeships. One inter-branch communication insisted that unless every technological innovation was resisted, successful implementation would simply encourage further labour-saving devices. Lancashire cotton spinners selectively struck against employers who jettisoned apprenticeship agreements in order to train as many new workers as dictated by demand rather than observe the limits imposed by employees. Blacklists were circulated by both sides. In August, Somerset and Wiltshire clothworkers rebelled against scribbling machines, and then extended their campaign to all new technology. The campaign plus 'the disposition of the People . . . from the high price of provision renders the aid of the Military particularly necessary' said the millowners. Wincanton, Wells and Shepton Mallet all had

> New Machinery erected lately . . . by some of the principal Manufactur-
> ers [which] requires some regular force constantly . . . at least 'till the
> price of provisions shall be reduced to the accustom'd average, & the
> working manufacturer, a little reconciled to the modern necessary
> improvements.

Disputes over technologies in textiles, and high prices could well see a riotous conjunction between cloth-workers and the notorious Somerset miners who 'may again refuse to work' while they visited farmers and forced food-price reductions.[46]

These textile campaigns' climax was retarded by the second famine. In the North, in both cotton and woollens, they overlapped with the constitutional and revolutionary sectors of the democratic movement. Democrats used every issue, including industrial ones, to win converts. One group 'meeting to consider what were the first steps they should take . . . concluded that they should pull down all the Machinery which would restore the Manufacturing business to its old Channel'. Others advocated putting 'a stop to spinning by machinery'. But if famine conditions enhanced the relevances of both the industrial and political movements, poverty militated against the former. The end of the famine, and peace, restored demand for most – but not all – textile goods. Greater prosperity released new energies and produced new funds for industrial action. John Beckett, a Leeds industrialist, explained in May 1802 that the 'universal clamour for higher wages' was facilitated 'now that provisions are lower': workers said that '"we can live on our grease"'. Certainly, 1802 witnessed the appliction of the cotton unions to parliament for statutory regulation of their industry, and the most violent episode of the fight against gig-mills and shearing frames in Wiltshire, before violence was eclipsed when the men of Wiltshire joined their Yorkshire brethren in the parliamentary lobbying of 1802–3.[47]

The Combination Acts made little apparent difference to these or many other unionist offensives. Many judges were indifferent to eighteenth-century anti-unionist legislation. In 1793, the Recorder of Lancaster 'recom-mended a Compromise between' journeymen shoemakers and their em-ployers, and promptly celebrated his success by exacting extortionate fees from the latter. The Anglican aldermen of Leicester took a special delight in intervening on behalf of workers in dispute with their Dissenter employers. This tradition of non-compliance with laws relating to industrial relations was maintained in spite of their reiteration in the Combination Acts. The Mayor of Newcastle responded to Home Office enquiries about a Keelmen's strike which threatened to deprive London of essential winter fuel in January 1800, with laconic claims that he had

> not been able to trace any Combinations, or any Detention of the local Vessels, beyond what arises from the Owners and their Seamen differing as to . . . Wages . . . . The Demands of Sailors are generally governed by the Price of Coals at Market, and they are in Consequence pretty uniform with each other in their Amount, and perhaps it is to be lamented that the late high Prices have induced a too frequent Compliance of the Owners, as well as incited unreasonable claims from the Sailors.

No formal charges had been laid against the Keelman, and the Mayor proposed no action in spite of, or probably because of, the sailors' lengthy and awesome tradition of protracted riotous disputes. The Home Office had to goad Lancastrian justices into the use of the Combination Acts against the cotton-spinners, and their Wiltshire counterparts had never believed industrial law was a viable weapon against the shearmen until instructed on the spot by a London stipendiary magistrate sent down on Home Office orders. Metropolitan unions, more immediately under the eyes of the Home Office and its stipendiary agents, were equally undeterred by the new powers, other than to circumvent them. Journeymen bakers burned their minute books, but kept membership lists, and promptly printed their wage demands and agreement to strike in order to win them. Attempts to use the summary powers under the Acts produced troublesome appeals to the Sessions. 1801 witnessed much strike action in London; information is scarce, probably because the metropolitan press shied off creating new alarms shortly after the September riots. *The Times* spoke of wage demands from 'conspiracies of . . . various Trades', and James Montgomery of the Sheffield *Iris* – who was becoming more virulently anti-unionist – reported that over the 1800–1 winter

> Great numbers of Journeymen in London, particularly Printers, Cabinet-makers and Taylors, notwithstanding the strong laws to the contrary have . . . entered into combinations for an advance of wages.

The irrelevance of the Combination Acts was reflected in the wage rates of compositors and tailors. The formers' increased from 24/- to 27/- in 1796, and to 30/- weekly in late 1800; the latter secured rises from 21/- to 25/- in 1795, and to 27/- in 1801 despite 'a more determined resistance' by employers which included strike-breaking by women. In spite of rumours that Pitt intended further legislation against 'benefit clubs and societies' in order to smash the unionism of 'restless mechanics', the Home Office remained aloof where industrial action undermined neither the economy nor law and order.[48]

Navy Board negotiations with its employers, mentioned above, led to concessions, and it was only the Devonport men's participation in riots, the release of prisoners and heavy confrontations with civil and dockyard authorities which finally determined the Home Office on intervention. Trade unionism revealed new dimensions in some regions during the nineties. Inter-union solidarity emerged in the prolonged strike of most branches of the Sheffield cutlery trade in July 1796. When the journeymen silversmiths struck in 1797, they learned

> that a Number of Persons belonging to the different Manufactories of this Place (provided we should make proper application) have proposed to render us some relief.

The silversmiths had replenished their funds in the year since the previous strike, and politely declined the offer, while adding that they would be 'equally willing' to give aid to other Sheffield unions in future disputes. In 1799, West Country woollen workers joined the Brief Institution, which originated in Yorkshire, and thereafter that trade had a national organisation. William Cookson, industrialist and Mayor of Leeds in 1802, complained that unionist principles 'would soon extend beyond computation':

> Perequisites, priveleges, time mode of labour, rate, who shall be employed etc. etc. are all now dependent on the fiats of our workmen, beyond all appeal; and all branches are struggling for their share of these powers. It is now confirmed that a bricklayer, mason, carpenter, wheelwright, etc. shall have 3s. per week higher in Leeds, or in Manchester than at Wakefield, York, Hull, Rochdale or any adjacent towns.

The cloth-workers positively encouraged other trades to unionise. They shortly came to the financial rescue of Sheffield cutlers. And it paid off; in the strike over the summer of 1802,

> Every class of workmen make a common cause with that of the clothworkers and every turnout for advance of wages is supported by general contributions from almost every class.[49]

However, this impressive catalogue of evidence does not imply that unionists invariably won disputes, and never suffered defeats in the courts. Sheffield trade unionists were vulnerable to prosecution before and after the Combination Acts. A strike by three hundred weavers and labourers of Glemsford collapsed on the arrival of the army. A second strike by Newcastle tailors terminated on a mere magisterial admonition. Strikers were imprisoned. Among the victims were five Norwich 'hotpressers', two Stockport hatters incarcerated for picketing, and Durham paper-makers. Violent tactics against strike-breaking Hertford bargees, landed twenty in the dock.[50]

Nevertheless, unionist organisation, negotiation, and reversion to strike tactics, certainly ameliorated the position of some workers during the famines, and reduced such workers' participation in food riots. This might be inferred from events subsequent to the defeat of industrial action, as at Glemsford where 'several are still refractory, & have hope, on a future day of joining a Sudbury Mob'. But this conclusion must not be pushed far. Riot participation by Devonport and other West Country unionists has already been encountered, and on other occasions powerful industrial groups played a major role in food riots after they achieved victories over their employers. In the summer of 1795 Nottinghamshire miners celebrated success in a short strike by seizing corn remaining at farms and forcing millers to grind it. Victories did not seriously detract from certain groups of workers' customary leadership of the eighteenth-century crowd. And, ironically, neither industrial muscle nor riot participation, prevented increased resort to thieving. Embezzlement by West Midland nailers was endemic, but it is not insignificant that it achieved such an unprecedented level in 1800 that employers initiated an investigation at their annual meeting, and decided on a counter-offensive. The nailers were among the most riot-prone inhabitants of that region.[51]

The Threat to Order

What then of the threat to order posed by these inter-related facets of popular protest and reactions to famine? Trade unionism and industrial action were not major short-term challenges to constituted authority. Contemporaries who foresaw and feared the cumulative effect of hundreds of campaigns resulting in labour perennially challenging the hegemony of unrestrained capitalism, had a point. However, in the immediate context, combination reinforced rather than undermined public order. Violence was a recurrent element of eighteenth-century industrial disputes. The relative paucity of major, protracted, violent strikes during the famines, reflects employers' willingness to grant wage-increases, and this removed to some extent a traditional source of violence. Indeed, there was only one exemplar of a major industrial, violent dispute during these years; and this strike, in the North-eastern coalfield in 1800 ended once miners throughout the coalfield achieved parity amongst themselves. This episode reinforces the view that combinations, and the discipline generated by disputes, militated against disorder. Devonport unionists imposed their authority in negotiations with bakers, butchers and magistrates, to preserve the peace. Their objective is of greater significance than their violent reaction to failed negotiations. The other major cause of industrial violence at this time, technological and organisational innovations which threatened skilled workers with savage wage cuts and redundancy, was an issue essentially tangential to the famines, *except* where a close correlation existed between falling demand for manufactured goods and the impact of high food prices on consumers' purchasing powers. Famine and wartime market difficulties threw the machinery question into sharper relief in Lancashire cottons and Yorkshire and West Country woollens. However here, the workers' protective campaigns predated famine, and their main thrusts took place later, notably with the parliamentary investigations of late 1801, 1802 and 1803. Rapid inflation proved a principal cause of burgeoning unionism in the nineties, yet the deployment of most labour tactics did not produce serious challenges to order, and on balance, probably had the opposite effect.

The impact of threatening letters is difficult to assess. Many recipients obviously ignored them. Others, like Lord Braybrooke in Essex reasoned that publicity would 'inform . . . more mischievous men . . . of the contents . . . which they might otherwise not have seen'. In the event the scale of these protests in Essex made the county press, but Braybrooke would have endorsed the editor's view that they deserved 'manly contempt'. A Somerset JP informed the Home Secretary only after he and several parochial officials had all received anonymous missives.[52] Arson could not be dismissed with contempt, manly or otherwise; a fearsome weapon, it terrified propertied members of local communities. However, with the exception of a handful of localities, incendiarism did not achieve serious proportions. Its real impact was localised, and if the press gave its incidence a grander currency, arson achieved but secondary status as a threat to order. Its arrival as protest was portentous of later developments, especially in those regions later to be the main theatres of Captain Swing. The universal upsurge in theft, even where there is evidence of a Robin Hood mentality legitimising larceny from the affluent, was no real threat to order. There was sufficient robbery of the poor, by the poor, to facilitate propagandist shorings up of the sanctity of private property. Whomsoever stole a pig 'from the widow of the late Mr Charles Lee' in Sheffield was easily castigated; however 'trivial . . . such losses may seem . . . they are bitterly felt in a poor family'.[53] The famines did not see any marked resort to banditry, perhaps on an Irish model, though of course criminal gangs operated in both urban and rural Georgian England. The propertied's perception of theft's threat to the social equilibrium tended to exaggeration, and if larceny was a severe blow to poor victims, it was not a challenge to order, but the exacerbation of an existing problem. On their own, neither theft, threatening letters nor incendiarism challenged the ascendancy of authority. Together, an *in the context* of the challenge represented by riot, they were emblematic of an embryonic collapse of order. The impact of riot had a national significance and effect, and indeed certain ramifications were felt internationally.

The riot was the most common, the most universal, the most violent, and therefore the most frightening form of social protest. Historians correctly insist that the 'English crowd . . . killed no-one deliberately in the food disturbances'; the crowd's violence was not its greatest threat.[54] There are innumerable examples of smashed windows and other property damaged, and countless occasions on which farmers, millers, merchants, bakers, carters and bargees were roughed up, but excessive violence by any definition was not a primary feature of mass mobilisations. This is true even of the south-west in 1801 when magisterial abdication and the torpor of the Volunteers permitted the creation of crowd hegemony. Recurrent reports testified that the crowd

> went round to the farmers with a rope in one hand, and a paper in the other, by which the farmers were to engage to sell their corn at reduced prices.

Invariably, the primary object was the cementation of agreement between producer and consumer. Hence the paper and the signature with their legally-binding connotations. As the Totnes 'People's Committee' insisted, they went 'to claim Humanity of the Farmers', to obtain 'promises to prevent an approaching Famine . . . by bringing regularly to the Market Bread Corn & in the proportion to the Quantity they possess'. The latter rider exudes reasonableness. The halter symbolised the crowd's numerical supremacy, its ethical justification and moral paramountcy. Violence occurred only when targets prevaricated or refused. Thomas Hookaway's experiences were typical when the multitude surrounded his farmhouse;

> on his hesitating to sign a person came up . . . & pulled out a Rope saying 'if you do not sign here's your Trussel and I'll truss you up' on which many present said 'well done . . . hang him up' & particularly one John Jones Jnr said aloud 'hang him up hang him up'.

Hookaway signed. A 'farmer of Kingston was suspended' by his feet at Modbury, and although it was said that only the intervention by the 'gentlemen' prevented a lynching at Chard, the virtual garrotting of farmer Coneybear in an Ashburton street was the 'most vicious' in scores of incidents detailed to Devon's Clerk of the Peace. Given the crowd's desperation and power, its self discipline is remarkable. And neither famine produced a fatality at the hands of the crowd. Indeed, participants were relatively easily intimidated, at least on occasion. The men of Crediton withdrew with a volley of stones when a farmer recognised a leader and threatened to 'apply to a magistrate'. Heroic, and successful self defence by crowd victims include the Plymouth baker, a Volunteer, who put his antagonists to flight with an unsheathed sword, and a sixty-year old Oxford butcher, who 'with his Cleaver in his Hand, most resolutely & effectually resisted'. But the intrepid comprised a minority; if help was not at hand, most targets acquiesced and complied, be it perhaps like farmer Savery at Modbury who 'considered' his signature in the circumstances 'not to be binding'.[55] Opposition from the police, magistrates and the army was the cause of popular violence, much more so than even obdurate victims.[56]

The crowd's ability to create populist administrative organs from its own membership, complements its marked insistence on honourable behaviour, notably its well-known refusal to countenance looting or pure theft, and its intolerance of gratuitous or grievous violence to the person.[57] But if cleaver-wielding butchers were able sometimes to deter, and brave constables, intrepid magistrates and respected 'principal inhabitants', could effect dispersals at times, nothing should obscure the fact that mass mobilisations comprised a fearsome, awe-inspiring prodigy, seemingly endowed with limitless, unstoppable power. Rumours that Cornish miners, invariably among the toughest and most militant crowd personnel, had threatened farmers with murder, lynched several millers, waylaid and cut off the ears of a soldier, swamped one plebeian's mind when he penned a vivid account of a tinners' invasion of Truro:

> it appears as if men are worked up to a fit of desperation. I walked by

some of them with a few other Citizens, tho' we declared we where their fr[ien]ds, yet their jealousy & hatred run to such a heigth, that the[y] threatened us with instant death (with many *other expressions which I shall forbear to say*) Justices obliged to fly with their riot act many knocked down. I suppose their muster was about three thousand but *mark only three parishes* of men. . . . The[y] are gone to arm themselves, and . . . we expect them to return to morrow, a much larger number, God knows the event, as the[y] are belching out such threats, that every man will expire in the place, indeed, it must astonish every thinking man to see their determined resolution.

If the miners could intimidate a working-class radical, no wonder those from more elevated social ranks confirmed that they 'struck terror wherever they went', by appearing as 'an eruption of barbarians invading some more civilised country than their own'. Farmer Owen of Shropshire was not exaggerating when he

saith that being terrified by such an Assembly of persons about his Dwelling House and by the Threats that they used . . . and out of Fear that they may proceed to Acts of Violence against his person or property,

he did as he was bid. In tension-torn Nottinghamshire, the impossibility of 'reconciling Mrs Bettison to my leaving home', put a stop to husband John's normal business for weeks after rioting ceased. Establishment claims that the crowd overthrew all order were neither paranoid, invective, nor hyperbole; there was ample justification for the view, expressed for example by the Gloucestershire magistrate Sir G.O. Paul, that if mobilisations were not contained, thousands would be reduced to 'plunder' in order to survive.[58]

Moreover, crowds were not invariably or solely composed of God-fearing but hungry folk. There was commonly an element present *ad captandum vulgas*, and evidence abounds of the immorality of the mob to balance the morality of the crowd so favoured by sympathetic historians. Repeated reports of crowds disciplining members who tried to steal, and who did thieve articles unconnected with subsistence matters, suggests that theft was common and probably rampant. Industrial workers who scoured West Midland farms in 1800 may have been infuriated by rumours of huge hoards not being substantiated on their inspection of barns. Their extortion by menaces of cash may derive from the protocol of the wake, and be legitimised as payment for people who took time off from work to impose popular justice. Their insistence on being fed with bread, cheese, beef and beer drew on identical ethics. They may have needed pick-axes, pitch-forks and other improvised weaponry to defend themselves, but it is impossible to ascribe the removal of shoes, boots and 'divers wearing Apparel' to anything other than looting.[59] Crowds protesting over food contained their petty deviants, including pickpockets, like assemblies at fairs, boxing matches, and the scaffold. Grander criminals were also present as revealed by the arrest of the celebrated highwayman Zachariah Hughes at a riot in Leek.[60] Disturbances, and the destructive impact on order, were vulgarised, for example by the Plymouth burglars who recruited seamen to form an armed gang, whose itinerant exploits, culminating in a ferocious attack on Honey's farmhouse, terrorised an entire neighbourhood.[61] Protesters did not invariably stimulate glowing accounts from admiring observers; denigrators of the mob had solid empirical evidence.

The cosmic characteristics of riot seriously challenged the hegemony of law during the famines. The crowd clearly revelled in erosions of magisterial authority, but ironically, the ruling class commonly legitimised itself through endorsement of crowd objectives at the local level. These appeared to be viable solutions where riot remained 'a kind of informal give-and-take that shared several characteristics of institutional politics' in smaller urban centres; here riot was a manifestation of 'direct contests of co-ercion' between those who suffered deprivation and those who ruled. Where social equilibrium was still underpinned by 'horizontal' *and* 'vertical' socio-political relationships, riot 'mobilised networks of people and relationships that already existed', and in Dr Bohstedt's words, was containable by 'community politics'. Where that vital cohesion had been destroyed or was under pressure, notably from rapid urbanisation, greater violence came from the actions of both protesters and authority. Mancunian riots in the nineties were no longer 'intelligible politics' because the 'optimum framework for bargaining by riot' had dissolved; 'impersonal police measures' replaced the traditional machinery for 'communal bargaining'. The same might be said of towns with a markedly different socio-industrial structure from Manchester, especially Birmingham, and possibly Sheffield. But whatever the value of comparative analyses at the *micro* level, especially Bohstedt's work on Devonian and Lancastrian towns, historians regularly fail to perceive that the greatest threat posed by the crowd, irrespective of location or authority's attitude, lay in its success.[62]

The 'moral economy' was implemented in the context of threatened or actual violence. The threat had an immediate, and medium-term detrimental effect on market supplies, especially on goods brought by local producers. A fall in Birmingham potato prices was owing 'only . . . to a temporary alarm at the threats of the Populace', and Bath authorities were pleasantly surprised that their 'Market was supplied as usual' with potatoes under imposed price ceilings. For as Charles Rashleigh reasoned, 'those who have supplied the Markets will not carry their Goods there to be insulted' or worse, and more often than not supplies declined or even collapsed after disturbances. Violence at Plymouth 'obliged . . . vendors . . . to make a precipitate retreat' and thereafter 'a much greater Scarcity' materialised; 'the Goods brought are now really scrambled for, & many families go without'.[63] Urban authorities commonly reacted by publicising their determination to protect salesmen 'and their Property'.[64] Edward Thompson's assertion that the 'expectation of riot' kept prices down cannot be tested; there is considerable evidence that the anticipation of riot in large marts like Blackburn and Sheerness, medium ones like High Wycombe, and even tiny Hinton Ampner, deterred many marketeers from attending. Actual disturbances decimated future supplies and then accelerated inflation. Poole market was typically 'very sparingly supplied with butcher's meat and vegetables' following disturbances, and the prices of 'every commodity' were 'greatly enhanced'.[65]

Price controls aggravated the impact of violence. Havoc followed where the Assize of Bread operated. The Oxfordshire Assize was governed by that set in the county town; *taxation populaire* in Oxford saw the Assize set on artificially reduced flour prices, but county bakers could not obtain flour at such prices and therefore they could either invite prosecution for ignoring the Assize, or cease basking, or incur huge losses. The first two options would galvanise 'tumults in every Village'. The crippling effect of riot on short distance supplies was vividly revealed throughout the South-west after farmers were visited on their doorsteps in 1801. Kingsbridge was adequately served by neighbouring farmers on the first market day following mass action, but in subsequent weeks 'no corn . . . of any consideration' was available. The imposition of fixed prices at Bideford created a 'want of a proper supply', and such corn on sale 'was with much difficulty delivered out to the poorer sort . . . by the Peck to each person, and not nearly sufficient'. Emotive scenes followed:

> The General Cry of the Poor is that we are Starving, we are Starving alive, many of them with Money in their hands saying that they could not get a Potato . . . Nor a Penny Loaf . . . to save their lives.

But, in the majority of cases, farmers had to sell in nearby markets, even if sales were to dealers. While there are exceptions, concrete evidence of large stocks in the hands of local agriculturalists in periods of maximum scarcity is rare.[66]

Absolute scarcity normally struck consumption centres, themselves invariably and ultimately dependent on supplies despatched over considerable distances by commercialists. Violence threatened their profits rather than their persons; so too did imposed prices and goods seized in transit. Potential losses were huge; a Reading cheesefactor normally had £6000 to £10,000 worth of cheese en route from Gloucestershire to London. Evasive action was taken by all who could. At Totnes, miller Pulling reacted to *taxation populaire* by immediately assessing 'how we are to make the most out of the Flour in hand, which for us is a serious quantity'; he decided 'to ship 50 or 60 sacks for London'. At Plymouth, 'all the Corn Factors, Agents Merchants etc . . . countermanded their orders', and corn ships sailed for the East; a temporary respite was achieved only by Colonel Bastard's arbitrary intervention ordering naval victuallers to buy all corn 'which was not unshipped, as well as that which was actually reshipping'. Parallels can be found wherever maximums were imposed. Provision 'Factors sent word' to Nottingham 'that they would bring no more Corn till the rioting was over'. Experience soon convinced the Corporation that attempts to supply the town through public purchases under the maximum were unrealistic, and the Mayor was forced into public admission of his 'error in taking the Corn Trade out of the Millers and Bakers hands'. Wholesalers' attitudes wrecked the price agreements between Plymouth retailers and the dockyard workers after a mere four days.[67]

The cumulative impact of riot, maximums, and agreements to conserve local stocks with their aggregate blockading effect, crippled the national grain supply. The worst experience certainly belongs to the summer hypercrisis of 1795, but parallel potential devastation accompanied every peak in popular protest. Riots spread. It is immaterial whether the cause was imitation, or a uniform reaction along lines of communication.[68] The chronological and geographical conflagrations of rioting during the 1800 harvest are clear. Riots commenced at Sheffield on 27 August, spread to Mansfield (30th), to Nottingham (1 September), via the industrial East Midland villages to Derby and Leicester (4th and 5th), to Birmingham and the West Midlands (8th to the 13th), to Coventry and Banbury (9th and 11th). Rioting in London started on 15 September, and was echoed in each Home County by the 22nd. In Kent a line can be plotted along which protest spread to Rochester (19th), Sheerness, Canterbury and Deal (20th), and finally to Margate, Sandwich and Tunbridge Wells on the 22nd. Similar conflagrations include those in Hampshire and Dorset, namely Romsey, 1 September, Poole (4th), Portsmouth (8th), Blandford and Southampton (9th). A westward thrust commenced at Abingdon (1 September) to pass through Oxford (8th), Witney (11th), Cirencester (13th), Stroud (15th), and finally Bristol on the 18th.

Several regions were notoriously riot-prone, notably the mining districts of Cornwall, Somerset, Gloucestershire and the Forest of Dean, and all industrial ones, none more so than both the East and West Midlands. Here serious mass mobilistions could erupt at any time, not least because authority was weak; a few resident and active magistrates and respected 'principal inhabitants' at most, confronted considerable plebeian communities. A similar situation obtained in many populous towns, including Manchester and Sheffield. The anciently constituted authorities in others, like Coventry and Bath, may have managed to retain their grip in spite of population growth, extended urbanisation and proletarianisation, but they were vulnerable to incursions from the insubordinate populations domiciled in their hinterlands. In September 1800 the Coventry crowd passively awaited the arrival of Warwickshire miners whom they 'proceeded to welcome . . . with shouts and acclamations', whereupon serious disturbances commenced. Popular intervention could be maintained for days in considerable centres hosting numerous food traders. The obvious case history is London in September 1800, but at Nottingham posters urging recurrent resort to the streets appended 'A List of Corn Factors', to argue that 'These men have not yet been visited'. Identical literature at Cambridge 'pointed out many respectable Dealers in Corn, Flour'. Imposing popular demands directly on all the villains identified took time; backsliding marketeers regularly stimulated repetitive onslaughts.[69]

Riot generated genuine and mammoth problems for commercialists, who were, it must be emphasised, essential for the functioning of the national grain market so critical to the subsistence of consumption centres. Claude Scott, the greatest importer, pertinently told the Board of Trade that he would continue to import irrespective of bounties 'If I did not feel personal Danger in having anything more to do with the Corn Trade'. Scott referred to an untypical moment, when metropolitan rioters singled out merchants for attack, and he was also addicted to special pleading. But the recurrent target of Birmingham protesters, the town's biggest merchant-miller,

Pickard, did cease trading on 12 September 1800. More lethally, riots jeopardised the international trade on which England's survival increasingly depended. While Scott addressed an anxious Board of Trade, a Danzig merchant informed his London correspondent that all available wheat would be directed to British markets which 'had a decided preference, but a general alarm prevails on Account of Disturbances' convulsing the country. It was seriously suggested that unless the British government 'openly declare to the World, that it will without Delay, make good all Depredations on Private Property arising from such a Cause', the foreign merchants, so crucial in the import trade, would divert supplies to other countries. Major British importers could simply invest their capital in other commodities or in public funds. Here lay a very real danger. Lesser commercialists, who limited their activities to the home market, could not pull out so easily as international merchants who organised shipments in hired vessels and through rented warehouse accommodation. Men like the Pullings of Totnes, with considerable fixed capital in milling and haulage capacities could not abandon business so easily. The most intrepid might insist on army protection, but others could start to wind down operations, and take evasive actions. They could avoid trading with actually disturbed and riot-prone districts. Most major consumption centres were very vulnerable to self-protective mercantile measures. Their implementation would accelerate a vicious encirclement, with riot deterring supplies, empty markets stimulating renewed violence, and further disturbances annihilating commercial confidence. Ultimately, from a global perspective, the entire country would be affected. In this context the 'positive' aspects of popular intervention, discouraging mercantile malpractice, militating against maximum exploitation, rivetting public attention on the poor's plight and galvanising greater relief measures, pale in significance. For these latter characteristics of protest, however important, were essentially localised. The historian's assessment of riot must also adopt governmental criteria. Macro, as opposed to micro economic examination of the grain trade reveals the dangers of protest to national subsistence in general, and the consumption centres in particular. Staving off starvation in the most vulnerable locations necessitated the speediest suppression of riot. As Arthur Young among many others insisted, machinery existed to protect those endangered, but little could be achieved if grain was unavailable. The ultimate anarchy could be exploited only by the revolutionaries, not Pitt's conservative front.[70]

III

GOVERNMENT AND FAMINE

CHAPTER 11

Intervention versus Free Trade
Securing Imports in Wartime 1794–1801

There was no official machinery for monitoring the agricultural sector of the economy. Therefore the government took time to appreciate the reality and the potential of the crisis dawning in the 1794–5 season. Investigation commenced in late November 1794 through the Board of Trade, a sub-committee of the Privy Council. The Board's president, and cabinet member, Lord Hawkesbury, was a career politician; assiduous, and hard-working, he was soon to pride himself as an expert on the grain trade. However, his dogmatism, his dictatorial manner, and his old-fashioned 'neo-mercantalist' ideology which at times produced an idiosyncratic approach to the problems deriving from famine, created dissensions among his colleagues.[1] On 27 November Hawkesbury implemented prerogative powers to ban cereal exports and permit imports at the lowest and nominal duties. The Board interviewed Claude Scott, the greatest international grain merchant in London, who had acted as a government agent on the outbreak of war to buy up grain which otherwise would have gone to the French. These stocks, and more, had been clandestinely if timely disposed of by Scott in the English market to avert serious problems shortly before the 1793 harvest. His 1794 analysis was gloomy. Home-grown grains were seriously deficient. Wheat crops in southern Europe and the United States were also poor in 1794. Most of the Canadian surplus was already purchased for Iberian markets, where some would be taken off by French agents. The French would also drain the produce of the Elbe region. Baltic wheat was excellent, but exports were banned; English merchants would not speculate in these conditions, because it would require ships sent in ballast, and an indefinite wait without any guarantee of export permission. By 10 December ministers were convinced that serious wheat shortages would develop before the 1795 harvest, and that mercantile caution left government no option but to import directly on its own account. Scott was to oversee the entire operation 'with the greatest Secrecy', as 'any Disclosure of the intended Purchase of so great a Quantity' would enhance prices, and possibly 'delay the taking off the Prohibition'.[2]

Publicly the government remained mute. Pitt even refused privately to admit 'the danger of a scarcity' to a supporter, R.J. Buxton MP who purposefully dined at Downing Street to warn the prime minister. Early in January ministers made no official response to the London Corporation's warning that only 'decisive and vigorous measures to procure a very considerable importation of wheat' by government could ward off 'serious . . . Scarcity'. The Home Secretary also rejected the Lord Mayor's demand for legislation to expedite the capital's cereal supply, 'which might . . . create an immediate alarm'. Nor did the cabinet invite parliamentary comment. Two minor Bills, extending duty-free importation of all food-stuffs in neutral ships, and prohibiting Scottish provision exports, were quietly slipped through. The January and February debates on the proposed hair-powder tax provoked Foxite demands for statistical representation of its use by the army, and the inevitable articulation of fears of impending wheat shortages. Pitt dismissed such 'discussion as very disorderly, and calculated to do no good'; it might promote unspecified 'mischief'. Ministers probably privately informed leading Foxites that the matter was in hand, and that publicity would accelerate prices and endanger diplomatic endeavours to get Baltic prohibitions lifted. Fox ignored subsistence matters when demanding a debate on the state of the nation, and when his irrepressible colleague Jeckyll advocated official enquiries into commercial malpractices in the grain trade, another Whig successfully steered proceedings into a consideration of the Prince of Wales' debts.[3]

Monitoring during January and February dashed any ministerial hopes of securing a sufficiency through Scott's purchases in the Baltic region. By the end of January he had secured small volumes at Danzig, Elbing and Konisberg; much larger stocks could be obtained through Prussian ports if the embargo was lifted in Britain's favour. The Foreign Office opened negotiations, while the Board of Trade, with senior ministers including Home Secretary Portland in regular attendance, concentrated on Canadian wheat. Considerable volumes were in the hands of merchants, including English ones at London, Liverpool and Bristol. But these were ear-marked for Spain because the availability of return cargoes minimised shipping costs; if ships now in Canadian ports came to Britain, they would have to return in ballast, thereby increasing the price of the wheat. Merchants might reconsider destinations in the spring in the light of current prices, and transatlantic vessels called at Cadiz for final orders; some owners might redirect stocks to Britain. If the government in February wanted to obtain these supplies it would have to intervene 'either by restriction, or inducement'. After the experience of the American War of Independence no British government would impose legal restrictions on Canadian commercial operations with countries at peace with the imperial power. Bounties and the use of naval ships were among the ideas floated, but merchants interviewed by the Board were adamant that, if government wanted 'every Bushel to be shipped to Britain', ministers must guarantee to purchase 'all Merchantable wheat and Flour' at prices adequate to 'indemnify' the owners. On 20 February, the Board, attended by Pitt, acted decisively. Canada merchant John Brickwood, principal source of the Board's North Atlantic intelligence, was instructed 'to Purchase all the wheat he can obtain from Canada' and to arrange transhipment.[4]

By the end of February government agents were purchasing all available wheat in northern Europe and Canada. Little is known of Brickwood's activities, except that his convoy's departure was delayed while the ports filled their naval recruitment quotas. The Prussian embargo was still operative in April. While Prussian merchants would take no further commissions from Scott for fear of offending their own government, other holders of wheat were not selling in anticipation of price rises across northern Europe. Serious competition was met from French agents. By 2 April Scott had procured a mere 47,000 quarters and no export licence; if this were granted another 80,000 quarters should be obtained. Scott feared his inability to meet 'the Wants of the Country', not least through anticipation of a 'general scramble' in markets under Prussian control, unless only Britain was exempted from export restrictions. All these uncertainties increased ministers' concern; so too did authoritative predict- ions, privately made by Arthur Young, that the next British harvest would be late and deficient. On 8 April the government concluded that the nation's problems 'may continue even beyond the ensuing harvest'. The Foreign Office ordered ambassadors throughout Europe, 'in all the Countries bordering on the Mediterranean', and in the United States, to foreward full details of harvest prospects 'of the different sorts of Corn' in their postings. Ministers now perceived shortages extending into 1796, and were no longer solely concerned with wheat; any and every type of cereal was now required from every possible source.[5]

The transformation in ministerial perceptions was variously evinced. Proposals from a London-based Canada merchant on 7 January were not even acknowledged, and more from a firm with American interests were endorsed 'consideration postponed' in February. In April serious discus- sions commenced with the Turkey Company over possible supplies from the Levant. Securing stocks in Egypt would require unorthodox diplomatic initiatives. North African grain was threshed 'by trampling' underfoot and was consequently 'very dirty'; as supplies could not arrive before Decem- ber, a specific proposal 'was not attended to'. Meanwhile some successes accrued to Scott and Brickwood. Brickwood's fifty-six ship convoy would return in the early autumn with 60,000 quarters from Quebec. Scott despatched forty-six ships on 21 April, correctly anticipating that their departure would pressurise the Prussians into granting the licenses. Scott expected their return in mid-June with 80,000 quarters. As the Prussian harvest was promising, he hoped to obtain 80,000 quarters more. In the event, by 10 July he had secured only a further 23,000 quarters of wheat, 11,000 of oats, and 6,700 of rye. Export licences remained problematic, but on 8 August another convoy was sent.[6]

The English situation deteriorated rapidly in June and July. The bulk of imports had not arrived, and ministers were convinced that the importation programme would have to be maintained for a further year. Canadian wheat was rarely threshed until November, and exports usually com- menced only on the thawing of the St Lawrence in the spring. Therefore 'great Exertion' was needed to secure supplies from the Canadian 1795 crop for use in Britain during the 1795–6 season; a special buyer was sent to circumvent the current 'necessity for purchasing from the Second Hand'. In America, French agents were buying 'every Species of Provisions, particularly Grain and Flour' and even contracting for unharvested wheat. On 24 July the government decided to compete through secret purchases. A trial consignment of 5000 quarters of North African hard brown wheat was also ordered, together with special Portuguese millstones to facilitate the experiment. By midsummer the government was buying oats in Ireland, and leaving no possible source unexplored in stark contrast to intentions in December 1794.[7]

During 1795, government corn derived from three main sources. From January grain cargoes aboard neutral ships putting in to British ports were purchased, and subsequently the navy forced neutral ships encountered with grain for France into Britain. In April cargoes on detained Dutch vessels were bought, and immediately sold at Plymouth for the hard-pressed South-west. Remaining stocks were put at Scott's disposal; he was 'to reship . . . to any Port where there may be a demand' taking care not to overstock any one. By the end of June, 13,500 quarters of wheat had been sold at Plymouth, Gosport, Great Yarmouth, Hull and London. The most important supplies, from the Baltic and Canada, the second and third sources, had not arrived; although the former were expected over the summer, precise predictions were impossible. On 26 June government decided that internal distribution was too sensitive to be left to an agent, and the Privy Council assumed directions at its weekly crisis meetings. On 5 July the first of many requests for stocks, which principally arrived through the Home Office, was considered, and a directive issued to under-secretary John King on the wording of the answers. The Home Office assumed responsibility for announcing Privy Council decisions; Portland became increasingly alarmed at the possible political repercussions of this essential but unpleasant role. Hawkesbury was invariably present at Council meetings during the next two months, with Portland and other ministers in regular attendance. Hawkesbury once ordered a consignment without consultations, but during a weekend and only of one hundred quarters to calm fears of an 'insurrection' at Rochester, uncomfortably close to London.[8]

The government was unable to meet many demands before 20 August. Supply arrivals were erratic, and actions on predictions so potentially disastrous that distibutive directions could be made only weekly. Ministers aimed to ship stocks to regions in greatest need, but London's demand was paramount. Only half the capital's normal supply came through the usual channels in the first three weeks of June, and as this deficiency worsened Mark Lane was beseiged by 'Deputations' from as far away as Yorkshire, commissioned 'to purchase Wheat at any Price'. On 1 July Scott was instructed to sell 7,000 quarters weekly , and on the 3rd he was secretly ordered to restrict those sales to millers who confined their operations to meeting London demand alone. Where possible Portland was to discourage provincial authorities from despatching agents to Mark Lane, and to disguise sales policy. But metropolitan supplies remained critical. By 20 June Scott was virtually the sole salesman; he sold to 164 millers, leaving seventy more 'disappointed'. On 23 July his limit was increased to 9,000 quarters weekly, and to 15,000 on 19 August when the numbers of provincial requests had fallen, the bulk of Scott's first purchases had arrived, and he had negotiated further contracts. The greatest proportion of available wheat was committed to London, permitting Hawkesbury's claim that government had preserved the capital 'from the utmost Distress, if not Famine, and . . . secured . . . the Peace of it'.[9]

Similar claims could not be made over the provinces. The distribution of severely limited stocks proved extremely problematic. The Council decided to sell at current rather than low prices, to prevent speculation, and to encourage farmers to market residual stocks. Ministers said that unsurmountable practical difficulties prohibited attempts to send supplies to designated inland consumption centres; instead corn was sold on the open market in the larger ports on the assumption that some 'may pass into the interior counties'. Applicants from these districts were informed of supplies despatched and invited to employ their own agents. Manchester authorities were directed to Liverpool, and their Bodmin counterparts to Plymouth. Rigid adherence to this policy generated friction, jealousy and competition, all aggravated by misunderstandings, themselves partially ascribable to the government's refusal to invite requests or even to broadly publicise its programme. The chairman of a relief committee at Hull relayed his fury at Scott's agents asking £7 per quarter. Acrimonious exchanges between civil and military authorities followed the latter's refusal to detain three of Scott's ships weathering a storm at South Shields. Nottingham Corporation applied for a specific consignment on the erroneous intelligence that an identical petition from Sheffield had succeeded. Henry Hobart, MP for Norwich lobbied for a direct supply from the Baltic convoy whose imminent arrival at Great Yarmouth was predicted; the confidence exuded by the city's press was rudely shattered days later when the Council's refusal was known. Many agents in the ports were outbid, and secured none or inadequate volumes.; ninety-five failed to get any from the first consignment on sale at Hull. The Council received fifty-five applications in July, and, excluding appeals from military contractors, twenty-eight during August. Over fifty of these were refused outright, or the applicants told to send to ports over twenty-five miles distant. Twenty-two supplicants were merely informed of stocks already despatched to nearby ports. A mere nine applications were successful. Government stocks of oats, rye, maize, maize–meal and rice were also sold off in provincial ports, and some applicants were informed accordingly. The Council also rejected appeals made in person, one from the Earl of Stamford, another from Hobart, and two from Heneage Legge on behalf of Birmingham, perhaps the most critically-placed consumption centre. Despite Birmingham's qualification as a "special case", and further political lobbying from that famous practioner of the art, Samuel Garbett, ministers were determined to avoid charges of partiality.[10]

The political and social structure was manipulated in this intense lobbying. At Gloucester, a public meeting mandated the Mayor to approach London. The Rev. Giddy attended a 'Justices Meeting' at Penzance and added his signature to 'a letter to . . . Portland . . . stating the distress of the County and praying for relief'. MPs were under no illusions when involved as to the political ramifications of success and failure. E.J. Stuart was told if his almost prescribed intervention with Pitt succeeded 'You will fix the Attachment of this Country to You for ever'. Several Lord Lieutenants applied after pressure from subordinate magistrates or meetings of 'principal inhabitants'. Most applications came directly from those at the apex of local society. The most tortuously routed came from Scarborough, via the local army CO, his regional superior, the Minister at War, and the Treasury, to take six days. No other request took so long to arrive, and only one from men constrained to explain that 'Nothing but dire Necessity would induce us to trouble you [Pitt] with our Correspondence who fear that not only our Persons but even our Characters are unknown to You'.[11] After the July Quarter Sessions MPs were inundated with enquiries. In Hertfordshire William Baker 'made it my Business in every Conversation . . . to do justice to the unremitted Exertions of Government' and to explain distribution policy. In Sussex, Lord Sheffield addressed the Grand Jury on the same subject, stressing that 'as the large towns were in greater want, and had not the resources we had', his county must not expect assistance. Such tasks were arduous in the face of anxious local authorities, and also threatened to politically compromise ministerial supporters.[12]

The government partially hid behind the non-party Privy Council when taking these disagreeable decisions, but this camouflage provided little political protection. Some applications were addressed to individual ministers by politically significant individuals or groups; they also privately lobbied senior politicians in support of requests sent through public, official channels. Unsuccessful MPs, frustrated Lord Lieutenants, Mayors and aldermen, and country squires, were all central to that interdependent web of clientage and patronage through which pumped the lifeblood of the political system. The crisis inevitably challenged the political equilibrium, so recently shored-up by the juncture of the Portland Whigs with Pitt, and argument immediately developed within the cabinet over subsistence policies. That debate was coloured by the most delicate specific conflict of interests experienced. On 5 August the Privy Council sent wheat and rye flour to Whitehaven in response to Cumberland's Lord Lieutenant Lonsdale's request. Within days of the decision, Lonsdale's proverbial enemy, J.C. Curwen MP demanded a consignment for Workington, Whitehaven's rival. A protracted legal battle between the two families meant that Portland was Lonsdale's embittered enemy, whereas Portland was Curwen's 'old patron'. Hawkesbury and Lonsdale were long-standing Tories. Government stocks were too low to permit another shipment to the north-west Hawkesbury was the minister most closely involved with the importation and distribution programmes, but Portland's department communicated the decisions. Portland's rejection of Curwen's application would coincide with the arrival of stocks at Whitehaven. Hawkesbury left it to Portland's discretion whether 'to mention the Quantity sent last week to Whitehaven tho' This Supply . . . must be of Service also to Workington'. Portland's letter to Curwen was masterfully tactful but the message was Hawkesbury's. After this episode, Portland was the most vigorous opponent, and Hawkesbury the strongest advocate of continuing the current policy into the next season. Portland was also the last minister to concede the deficiency of the 1795 harvest.[13]

Hawkesbury predetermined this last issue in an expert 'Memorandum on Corn' penned on 4 August. He argued for further imports; whatever the excellence of spring-sown barley and oats, wheats would be poor, and the country unusually drained of all cereals. The demand for seed wheat would reduce market supplies in the autumn, and Hawkesbury anticipated shortages and renewed inflation 'particularly . . . before Christmas'. The greatest problem turned on whether government or free-market forces were to secure imports. He acknowledged the 'Commercial and Political' objections to present policy. The Foxites were determined free-traders and had to be faced in the next parliamentary session. Merchants would not compete with government in international markets; some might be bankrupted. The government 'must provide for the whole of the deficiency' at 'enormous' costs. The 'distribution . . . will be very difficult, and embarrassing'; ministers risked accusations from hard-pressed regions of 'Partiality', and ultimately exposure to the claim 'that to oblige the People to trust to' government 'for their subsistence, is a Contrivance to make them dependent'. On the other hand, mercantile 'Confidence . . . is already much shaken', and if free trade failed ministers would encounter charges of negligence. Hawkesbury perceived a compromise. If government bought wheat stocks marginally larger than the greatest volume ever imported in one year, it could be used to offset expected autumnal shortages, and the residue used as a reserve to unload on the critical London market to deflate national prices if these threatened to reach unacceptable levels at any time during the remainder of the 1795–6 season.[14]

Hawkesbury approached two experts, Sir Joseph Banks and Lord Sheffield for opinions for cabinet consumption. Banks opined that government could never secure sufficient to affect wheat prices in home markets; if any supplies were obtained, the facts should be released to facilitate commercial calculations and maintain business confidence. Banks also believed the evidence of a poor wheat crop was inconclusive, and advocated caution. Meanwhile Portland jettisoned Whig principles further, and took to secretly lobbying the king, forwarding optimistic harvest estimates to Windsor, together with reports of markets suddenly glutted with home-grown wheat. By the end of August George was convinced that crisis conditions were retreating, discontinued his insistence on weekly reports, and subscribed to Banks' position over government purchases. Further 'directions for the purchase of bread corn' by government were withheld. The semi-official Board of Agriculture advocated the planting of extra wheat to pre-empt further harvest shortfalls, while the government did nothing until 30 September. Then, alarmed at renewed price rises, the Privy Council re-opened its enquiries and interviewed Scott, Brickwood and the Lord Mayor of London. These experts, wrote a minister, unanimously expected an ephemeral short-term fall in prices 'immediately after the harvest', preceding further rises before finding their 'true level' in November. Such precautionary investigations should have been made earlier; as yet the cabinet had agreed only to try to hold prices by a reduction in wheat consumption and the reform of the Assize of Bread. Now it was forced to try to hold prices immediately with further sales at Mark Lane.[15] By 10

October the cabinet was despondent. Portland was 'utterly unable' to identify means of 'substantial and effectual relief'. The price of wheat in America was prohibitive, Flanders and Holland over-run by the French, and the Portuguese harvest unproductive. No Baltic corn was available before the spring, and no Canadian before the summer of 1796. Now, Brickwood and Scott were ordered to procure wheat anywhere and at any price; another firm, Turnbull Forbes was commissioned to purchase in any Mediterranean port. The government approached the Sicilian Court with offers to despatch 'a Frigate . . . with Bullion' to pay for wheat. Costs now were inconsequential, as 'the preservation of the internal tranquillity of the country' was at stake. Defeated, Portland gloomily concluded that even the positive facets of previous and now recurrent policy had 'in no way reconciled it to me'.[16]

Parliament was scheduled to convene at the end of October and ministers expected a hostile grilling by the opposition over subsistence policies, past, present and future. September and October evoked only studied government silence. 'Government is so secret in its affairs, so mysterious' that even the Speaker of the Irish Commons who was in London was unable to glean anything. Silence provoked rumour, debate and anxiety. Bristol merchants formally complained that they could not compete in overseas markets for grain with government, though as Sheffield sagely pointed out they had to contend with French agents who commanded 'the whole capital of the Nation'. Conversely, the Cornish bench conveyed its decided opinion that government intervention was the sole security against commercial short-comings. Their Gloucestershire counterparts lobbied for a full-blown parliamentary enquiry into national subsistence. Ministers concentrated on their parliamentary defence. Scott and Brickwood were asked for the names of reliable great traders to give evidence to proposed parliamentary committees. Hawkesbury ordered his officials to compile a detailed account of past policies 'in one View': it was now 'very important to ascertain all the Facts . . . which induced the Privy Council to take this Business into their own Hands'.[17]

The decision to abandon interventionism is shrouded in secrecy too. Pitt certainly spent parts of the second half of October juggling with schemes for importation bounties. If the decision was taken in order to dilute the range of issues on which fierce Foxite opposition was expected *after* Pitt determined on the almost anti-constitutional measures to flatten the newly resurgent democratic movement once it had proved its mettle, at least in ministerial estimations, by the attack on the king's coach, then it was decided in an almost frenzied hurry. The cabinet was equally certainly equipped with a new policy to take to parliament, though this was pragmatically obscured by statements made to parliament in the early days of the session. Fox instantly committed himself to the view that the country's past subsistence problems would have been mitigated better if the importation had been left to free enterprise, as opposed to governmental intervention. Pitt weakly advanced the problems posed by the French government's commitment of massive state funding to intervention in international markets; he equally transparently protested that ministers had no finite policy, but sought parliamentary consideration prior to tackling the problem. Pitt's contrived innocence at least had the advantage of securing agreement for reversion to select committee procedures, which meant that the government would be shielded, with eventual decisions ostensibly emerging from parliamentary deliberations, as opposed to the exercise of ministerial fiats. Parliamentary machinery was also activated to investigate the equally sensitive issue of the 1795 harvest's productivity. The inclusion of all merchant MPs and all knights of shires gave the committee a broad political base while guaranteeing an inbuilt ministerial majority.[18]

Evidence of the select committee's work is scarce, and the truth difficult to disentangle from the self-interested assertions of merchant witnesses anxiously seeking government contracts, and the equally self-indulgent manoeuverings of the cabinet disguising the ditching of awkward policies. The state of the international grain market was ominous. Global prices were rising with shortages developing. Merchants in the Baltic regions anticipated greater profits through supplies to the Dutch under their new French protectors. Some British ships, chartered by English merchants who were presumably privy to ministers' new strategy, were unable to secure cargoes on arrival. Some merchants alleged to the committee that if imports were left to 'the Casual and very uncertain Speculations of Individuals' the country would 'be left almost destitute of foreign supplies'. In retrospect Sheffield castigated ministers for decisions taken on political as opposed to economic grounds; he complained that 'Pitt sometimes forms a secure little junta and reposes on' Dudley Ryder, the select committee's chairman, and 'the young Jenky', Hawkesbury's son and the future prime minister. The father was not responsible in Sheffield's estimation. He concluded that ministers abandoned interventionism and 'afterwards promote[d] a report from the corn committee in favour of relinquishing the trade . . . directly in the teeth of evidence and common sense'.[19]

The committee's first report identified imports as the primary, but not the sole remedy. Differential bounties were advocated, payable on defined volumes from various regions of origin. In debate Pitt conceded the case against unequal bounties but adhered to the limits. The first 30,000 quarters of wheat to arrive from Mediterranean (including North African) ports, and the first 500,000 quarters from other European or North American ports, would qualify for a pound a quarter bounty, together with five shillings on the first half million quarters of maize, and ten shillings on the first 100,000 quarters of rye. Bounties on oats and barley were not advised as home-grown crops were adequate. All bounties were to cease on 1 September 1796.[20] Although the announcement that government would stop cereal purchases was made in the Commons on 13 November, the formal order to all agents was delayed until the 21st. Ministers had certainly refused offers of stocks while parliament deliberated, but it was months before agents' foreign correspondents received countermanded instructions, and it took even longer for the agents to ascertain the volumes actually secured on governmental account. Scott resorted to rhetorical analogy when pressed by Pitt for accuracy in June 1796. This 'would almost be impossible as for a Commander of an Army to make a return of his Troops during a Battle'. For months governmental buyers bought incalculable volumes; simultaneously merchants bought almost every grain they could secure in foreign exchanges, convinced that bounties would accrue. They were aided by a diplomatic offensive to secure advantages for British merchants in overseas markets. Moreover, the French harvest was much better than expected, and demand from that quarter slumped, effectively diverting more cereals to Britain.[21]

Few provincial requests for government stocks arrived in the autumn. The south-west was still poorly placed, and limited amounts were sold there, but other demands were rejected with reference to parliament's decision.[22] Stocks were clandestinely unloaded on the London market when prices accelerated in the autumn, but neither Scott nor Brickwood sold more than a thousand quarters on any one market day. Brickwood's total sales in London totalled a mere 13,200 quarters up to March 1796, and these small secretive sales did nothing to curtail inflation during the November to February period; indeed, in London 'the general complaint is that Bread is rising while Government keep good Wheat lock'd up'. Moreover, the bulk of commercial imports were not expected before the spring. Trouble was to derive from the government's failure to monitor commercial progress effectively during the winter. Neither ministers nor merchants had finite ideas of the scale of purchases for the British market. Meanwhile governmental stocks went on rising, though this was concealed by reiterations that the state was no longer engaged in buying; instead, a misleading assurance was given to the commercial world that government would 'sell what might have been procured in limited quantities . . . at the Market price'. Rising prices across the winter simply encouraged merchants to extend their limits and buy more, convinced that cereals would maintain their upward momentum until the late summer. Ministers concurred, and held on to stocks to prevent any recurrence of the 1795 midsummer hypercrisis. With prices steadily rising in the absence of significant imports, a repetition looked likely, if not inevitable. In March the government panicked; Scott alone sold 20,000 quarters in the first three weeks of that month. His intervention was widely reported, and it initiated a downward spiral of prices.[23]

Thereafter the government was cornered. It possessed considerable stocks for which vast sums had been advanced; Scott received over £1,250,000. Further supplies were still arriving. In mid-April government gave 'public Intimation' that original estimates had exaggerated aggregate deficiencies, but this came too late and merely confirmed transformed mercantile perceptions. Official announcements served to warn farmers, not importers; with the provincial press prophesying 'glutted' markets, home producers tried to catch the tail of peak prices, thereby flooding the national market. The government persistently aggravated the situation with continuous sales at Mark Lane; from 6 April Scott and Brickwood were jointly to sell 6000 quarters weekly, and the order 'to try' to dispose of these quantities was repeated as late as July. Government sales across the country may have mitigated the price collapse in London. Ministers were unnerved by the omnipresent political implications of broader intervention. It took no action in response to specific requests, like that from the Isle of Wight advocating government sales locally to deter farmers from withholding. No stocks were released in the provinces, until in desperation and secure in Scott's specific assurance that objections would not arise, 8000 quarters of wheat just arrived from Sicily were sent to Bristol in August. Government wheat was increasingly unsaleable; Scott sold only a weekly average of 1500 from his 4000 quarter quota in the twenty-one weeks from the end of March. On 16 August he was unable to shift a bushel from the 41,000 quarters warehoused, and some consignments were still in transit on the high seas.[24]

Scott's problems were shared by commercial importers. Millers' preference for English wheat propped up prices for indigenous produce to a degree, and forced a disproportionate fall in demand, and prices, for the foreign commodity. Wheat imports totalled 879,000 quarters, nearly double the quantity in 1793, and thrice that of 1795. While Scott had his 41,000 quarters, merchants had another 100,000 quarters in granaries and more stored aboard ship, which reflected acute storage shortages. Buyers in recognition of continued price erosion bought only the smallest practical volumes at a time. Desperation set in; on 26 August 'the pressing desire of the Sellers . . . to quit of as much as possible' depressed the price of imported wheat to £2 per quarter. Experiences in Hull, Liverpool and Bristol, were identical.[25] Although the cost of bounties was huge, they failed to cover mercantile losses, calculated at £205,458 by a Commons committee. Clearly, both government and parliament gave the greatest possible encouragement to importers. Ministers had not acted decisively till the London wheat price topped 126/–, and thus compounded distorted perceptions of market movements. Price rises in Britain over the winter of 1795–6 were reflected in overseas exchanges, and were fuelled further by the provision of a 'positive bounty', which operated incrementally. This type of bounty was 'really a gift to the Foreigner . . . because he will immediately raise his Prices to a level with it'. The government resisted, and then capitulated to demands for a parliamentary enquiry in 1797. The report was not incisive, and ignored several fundamental questions, including consideration of whether the scale of mercantile importation would have depressed prices irrespective of governmental intervention after April 1796. The report emphasised the inducement of bounties, and the private 'Recommendations of the Executive Government'. But ministers succeeded in turning a deaf ear to demands for indemnifactions, in spite of superficial claims that 'Mercantile Calculation' was jettisoned in favour of patriotic considerations, and much more sinister prophecies that the mercantile community might be fatally cautious in a recurrent crisis.[26]

In 1796, imports certainly prevented a recurrence of the severe pre-harvest problems of 1795. But the experience of the role of imports across the entire 1794–6 famine had manifold effects. First, the essential vulnerability of the nation to harvest failure, and all that entailed, was proved. If no formal machinery was erected to monitor agrarian progress across the season, ministers now welcomed authoritative information on the subject, and Hawkesbury at the Board of Trade regularly surveyed world grain markets. Secondly, interventionism had exposed ministers to political dangers and administrative strains. Implicit parliamentary rejection of this strategy effectively removed it from the list of options. Thirdly, the problematic inter-relationship between government expenditure, global grain markets, and stimulating the commercial sector had been encountered over bounties, but the real issues remained unsolved. The government needed to re-examine the market impact of bounty schemes, implementation costs, and means to guarantee mercantile security. Fourthly, commercialists had proved their ability to extract the country from severe difficulties. The successful aspects of the importation also conditioned future responses to dearth of those outside government circles. As early as November 1799 the press asserted that imports 'cannot fail to reduce' grain prices, and monotonously reiterated the assumption in spite of the market's stubborn refusal to comply. As we have seen, the contradictions between market behaviour and the scale of the importation, was crucial to developments in public opinion during the summer of 1800.[27]

* * *

Ministers were cognizant of potential subsistence problems, and international market conditions much earlier in 1799 than in 1794. In August 1799, Hawkesbury, now Liverpool but still at the Board of Trade, advocated the invocation of a recent Act,[28] extending prerogative powers to ban exports and permit duty-free imports. Liverpool confirmed poor harvest yield prospects, and anticipated little succour from Europe where harvests were expected to be equally poor; imports would derive principally from North America. But the government was caught in a dilemma. The decision to invade Holland put a premium on available shipping. The short parliamentary session from 24 September to 12 October was primarily summoned for legislation enabling the Militia to serve overseas. Only minor Acts, one to stop Scottish distilleries until March 1800, and another extending the implementation of new prerogative powers from three to twelve months, concerned national subsistence. Pitt, anxious to cement commercial confidence, categorically confirmed cabinet decisions eschewing interventionism, and hinted that bounties might be introduced in the new year. Ministers' commitment to the ill-fated Dutch expedition certainly gave priority to military rather than commercial deployment of shipping, but subsequent Foxite claims of negligence on the food issue were more broadly based. The truth remains elusive; ministers asserted that the provision of new bounties in the autumn was commercially superfluous, and would have encouraged inflationary speculation in the home market. Nevertheless, Fox's later and private interpretation of the evidence suggests that his supporters had a strong case.[29]

During the interval between parliamentary sessions, Pitt received Arthur Young's extremely pessimistic appraisal of the 1799 crops, and the abysmal autumn sowing conditions which auguered so badly for the 1800 wheat harvest. Current yields of all cereals were 'worse than ever known', and the total situation comprised 'the most alarming prospect of scarcity I have witnessed in forty years'. Prerogative powers were invoked banning the English distillation of wheat, and ministers later regretted their miscalculation in not obtaining new powers to ban the use of barley by the same industry. Conversely, promising intelligence emerged from a comprehensive ministerial enquiry into commercial activities. In stark contrast to 1795, the French harvest was excellent, whatever Young said; no French competition was anticipated, but on the contrary there were hopes of securing grain from France and her controlled territories. Ministers grasped this nettle with the issue of special licenses to circumvent trading restrictions, including the ban on the re-export of 'colonial Produce to France', and to facilitate financial exchanges. By December Scott had bought 30,000 quarters of Baltic wheat, and other merchants had secured 50,000; strenuous efforts to beat the ice were underway, and 60,000 quarters were imported between 25 September and 20 December, to a chorus of optimistic press reports. No publicity accrued to the irony of England's consumption of Napoleon's staff of life. Now the government also took steps to keep abreast of the situation; weekly accounts of imports arriving at all ports were ordered, together with regular intelligence of overseas prices from all ambassadors. Here, the only cause for anxiety came from universal price rises, partly ascribed to the currency of exaggerated reports of the British deficiency, which had already stimulated an export ban in Prussia, uncertainties in North American exchanges, and nervousness over imports causing a price collapse in England in the spring. A handful of merchants panicked and cancelled overseas orders.[30]

The scale of such orders had to be balanced with these signs of mercantile jitters. Treasury ministers were divided over the issue of bounties. Pitt juggled with different schemes. He was 'inclined' towards guaranteeing prices on imported cereals within a clearly defined time-scale. There is no evidence that Pitt or the Board of Trade consulted commercial spokesmen on this issue, though after 8 February all information received by government departments on the topic was sent to Lord Liverpool; he was to select items for parliamentary scrutiny. The new session commenced on 21 January and was dominated by the momentous questions of the Dutch debacle and the first Consul's peace overture. The select committee elected to investigate national subsistence worked relatively slowly, and confined itself to reviewing the Assize of Bread laws and proposals to reduce wheat consumption with a ban on the sale of fresh bread. Its brief was extended to include bounties on 7 February after Foxite pressure; its report, advocating 'bounties', was published on 6 March. The details suggest that the inspiration was Pitt's. Baltic wheat was excluded; wheat coming from Mediterranean and North American ports was to have a price of 90/– per quarter guaranteed. Payment was to be regulated by the average price of British wheat; if that fell beneath 90/– the difference was to be made up by a 'bounty'. The opposition's insistence on the inclusion of Baltic wheat was reluctantly conceded after lengthy debates, and a guaranteed price of 80/– was fixed. All indemnities were to operate until 1 October 1800, and the Bill became law on 4 April. Ministerial spokesmen insisted that the subject be 'discussed as little as possible'; two further Acts extending similar provisions to oats and rye were hardly discussed in either House. The question did not concern government again until the end of May.[31]

The Earl of Liverpool, writing privately later in the year, asserted

that a few of the principal Corn-Factors in Mark Lane have it . . . in their

Power to set the Price of Wheat, as it may answer their Interests . . . they have augmented the Evils arising from real Scarcity, by producing an artificial Scaricity. . . . The Fortunes made by Corn Factors . . . have of late been very great.

Liverpool concluded wearily that 'It has been my Lot to deal more with Corn-Factors and People of that Description' than Home Secretary Portland. Liverpool's convictions were partly formed by his experiences over the summer of 1800. "Bounty" provisions and astronomical British prices conditioned world markets to facilitate a greater cereal importation in 1800 than even in 1796. But English prices did not collapse, and Liverpool attributed it to Mark Lane mercantile machinations. Metropolitan merchants subsequently alleged that the indemnity malfunctioned and demanded changes. Once again, the truth is difficult to extricate from the conflicting statements of the President of the Board of Trade and the merchants. At the end of May over three hundred grain ships choked the Thames; every granary was full. Rumour claimed that this reflected a conspiracy to maintain astronomical prices. Stories that much imported wheat was musty and unfit for Londoners' notoriously delicate palates circulated; the 'Practice . . . of crying down the Foreign Wheat', maintained the demand for English at Mark Lane, and thus the key metropolitan price. Importers exploited both London's demand for the finest wheat and the willingness of provincial consumers to eat poorer quality stuff.[32] More rumours said that bottlenecks developed, slowing down the turning and airing of grain aboard ship, prior to sales; no sooner had one jam cleared than more followed. In June and July, Liverpool's officials made three separate detailed investigations. The first two were inconclusive owing to the obstructions to overworked customs staff by all and sundry. The third produced documented evidence of virtually every granary packed to its limits, with ordinary warehouses temporarily converted to house grain as well. There was no real shortage in June while prices rose steadily until late July.[33]

The exclusion of foreign wheat from the official price calculations, and the paramount demand for fine English for metropolitan consumption, kept English wheat prices high in London and throughout the country. Paradoxically, prices for imported wheat were pulled upwards by those obtaining for English, as opposed to the latter being pushed downwards by the considerable volumes of available foreign. The most plausible explanation is that the very best imported wheat was consumed in London, with insufficient sales to deflate prices for English wheat. This maintained prices in provincial markets where considerable volumes of imports were sold. The penetration of the cereal-producing South and East by imports was proved by the clergy, customs officers and taxmen, who were asked to comment when making their harvest returns. The vicar of Stevenage typically reported large shipments sent up the Lea to Ware and Hertford from London. Sussex ports, including Hastings, Rye, Shoreham and Chichester, all received coastal shipments which were dispersed into their hinterlands. Dependence on imports increased during the summer; East Sussex 'would actually have been in want of Bread, but for the supply of

Foreign Wheat'. Millers mixed it with English at Ongar in Essex in proportion of nine to one: consumers commonly complained of the 'very indifferent sort of Bread produced', notably its musty taste.[34]

Provincial merchants in all major, and some lesser ports, imported just over half of the aggregate volume of foreign corn; imports went principally, but not exclusively to industrial and urban centres in their hinterlands. Here, consumers' dependency on foreign cereals was greater and of longer duration than in London and the south-east. The Manchester magistrate, Thomas Bayley, was asked to publicise imports arriving at Liverpool as early as February 1800. This source was emphasised in all the thirty-five Lancashire parochial reports, and in twenty-six of the thirty-seven from Cheshire. The vicar of Blackburn typically estimated that three quarters of local demand was met by imports. Liverpool also supplied the industrial Midlands. The Stone Navigation Office recorded the passage of 301 tons for the Potteries, and another 2169 tons for Birmingham, Dudley and Wolverhampton; a further 705 tons were cleared for Stourport and Tewkesbury, and 701 more tons for Derby and Leicester. Similar observations were made of large shipments reaching the West Riding and the East Midlands from Hull. Rural communities also benefited. In a remarkable reversal of normal trade, over 2300 quarters of wheat went up the Derwent to Malton; half the corn consumed in the Vale of Pickering over the summer was imported. An identical pattern was reported from parts of Lincolnshire.[35]

Ultimately, even if indirectly, every consumer in the country depended on the unprecedented importation. During August, expectations of a bumper harvest coincided with farmers unloading residual stocks on the market at the time of traditional price peaks, and prices fell, but not to the level where the indemnities became operative. The London importers, whose ships were continuously arriving, had difficulty in selling this wheat. In August the importers hung on to their wheat in anticipation of a fall in English wheat prices to trigger the "bounty" mechanism. They miscalculated; English wheat prices remained in excess of 90/–, though imported wheat could not command the 80/– and 90/– levels the legislation superficially guaranteed. Merchants who marketed during August lost money, or claimed to; others who withheld were preserved by the rapid acceleration of prices in late August and September, which pulled up prices for foreign grain, but prevented the operation of the indemnity.[36] This entire episode proved crucial. First, it established the successful dependency on imports. But, secondly, that very success did not have the anticipated impact on prices, and public suspicions of artifice appeared confirmed by common observation, including the choking of the Thames with grain ships. Thirdly, the merchants subsequently demanded changes to the indemnification system on the grounds of losses – real or narrowly-avoided.

One is again confronted with a conflict between the statements of self-interested metropolitan merchants and the Earl of Liverpool. Provincial customs officers reported a handful of mercantile losses, all made during the ephemeral price decline in August; otherwise customs intelligence confirmed the Liverpool inspector of corn return's conclusion that the importation was 'very profitable' with merchants 'materially increasing their capitals'. North-eastern calculations claimed a four shilling profit per quarter on rye, and private accounts reveal that this could be bettered by some. Claude Scott privately told the Treasury minister, George Rose, that he had sold twenty-five percent of the foreign wheat which passed through Mark Lane; no figure was mentioned, but it could not be less than 150,000 quarters. Scott slyly informed the Board of Trade that he had imported.

> three times as much as any other Individual . . . which paid me a profit of 15 per cent, although at the Period of the great fall in July . . . I should have been very glad to have closed the Account without loss.

One suspects that he did not 'close the Account' in July: Liverpool's cynicism is entirely understandable.[37]

Pitt was forced by the crisis of confidence in his government into an unplanned autumnal parliamentary session.[38] Ironically, political rather than economic considerations facilitated parliamentary interventions over the renewed national subsistence problem which was universally conceded in government circles. Grenville ruminated on 'how we are to struggle through another winter'; Addington speculated on the impact of high prices on the war effort. Liverpool, who was plagued by ill-health, and tetchy over the reluctance of Privy Councillors to attend the Board of Trade's investigations into market practices during the summer, was convinced that national self-sufficiency in corn was a thing of the past. Disagreements were unfolding in the cabinet. Grenville argued against legislation to encourage further imports because he feared the political ramifications from claims that such policies generated an unfair competition between merchants and farmers, and produced 'an artificial supply poured in at the expense of I know not how many millions to the state'. Pitt and Liverpool recognised the necessity to legislate to stimulate imports, but disputed the mode best calculated to reconcile mercantile security and public expenditure. Pitt, who was also periodically ill, was more sympathetic to importers' complaints; it was 'very important to remove these objections'. He advocated indemnity payments calculated on 'the actual Price at which' parcels of imported 'corn may sell', and minimum prices guaranteed on cereals varied according to their place of origin. Pitt instructed the Board of Trade to ascertain price levels which would ensure profit margins on 'Corn of a reasonable good quality from different parts of the world respectively'. Indemnities for poorer grades should be fixed proportionately. The Board was also to establish the normal relative price of foreign to English wheat; Pitt thought four-fifths. Indemnity payments would be calculated on the average price of foreign corn, itself expressed as a percentage of the market price of English, and the price *actually obtained*; this was to be confirmed by certificates issued by corn-market inspectors. Time limits between the date of import and sale, and regulations relating to weights should be 'settled with the trade' in discussions between representatives and the Board. Pitt refused to take chances by ignoring objections to the previous year's scheme.[39]

In contrast, Liverpool was satisfied that the scale of the importation proved the utility of the 1800 legislation, and argued for its re-enactment with additional payments on the first cargoes to arrive to expedite the exercise. London importers were duplicitous; they now claimed that they would not repeat the previous trade under past legislation. They demanded changes which Liverpool believed were a camouflage for a means of making even greater profits. Moreover, only London merchants collectively complained; those in the outports had not mounted a campaign. Pitt's price guarantees removed any incentive to achieve the best price because the difference would be made up by the Treasury. With assured profits there was no danger of inadequate imports, but Liverpool angled for Grenville's support by arguing that the very success of a huge importation would depress prices, and 'operate as a Discouragement to Agriculture. The Country Gentlemen and Farmers . . . would cry out'. Liverpool's health kept him away from the key cabinet meeting where his analysis was presented by an official; it was heard 'with the greatest attention', and though it had 'a very considerable effect', Liverpool lost the argument.[40]

Liverpool's position was sustained, be it inadvertantly, by the merchants themselves. Claude Scott distinguished himself by hinting that he would quit trading unless ministers committed themselves even more forcibly to resist *taxation populaire* and provided merchants with armed guards to protect them from 'personal danger'. He advocated guaranteed prices for wheat and rye. Scott had the temerity to state a higher price for imported wheat than any of his London colleagues in spite of his conviction that 'the price itself will be sufficient inducement to the merchant to import, independent of any prospect of bounty'.[41] The latter point was echoed by William Morely because massive orders had already been sent. Merchant Breese reiterated the point made in 1795 that bounties only operated to inflate prices in foreign exchanges. And it was revealed that the British market was the best in Europe, notably for Baltic merchants, who collated 'minute information' on it; 'they regulate their purchases and sales thereto'. Moreover payments for cereals sent to the other major European centre of demand, the Iberian Peninsula, were delayed for between eight and twelve months. British merchants advanced deposits and paid balances 'immediately on receiving the Account Sales'. As Baltic prices were 'entirely governed by those in Britain', the diversity in the levels of price guarantees suggested by merchants to the Board, was curious. The Board eventually compromised on £5 per quarter for wheat from any source until 1 October 1801.[42] Ministers, armed with the information and the decisions, took concrete proposals to parliament. The select committee procedure was activated, but importation regulations were not a source of contention. Pitt's initial plans, as refined by the Board of Trade, were adopted and rapidly passed into law. Subsequent Acts encompassed imported rye, barley, oats, maize, beans and peas. Committee spokesmen emphasised that changes in the "bounty" system were needed to guarantee commercial security without incurring prohibitive public expenditure. Admissions that "bounties" increased prices abroad failed to provoke the furore expected by Grenville. MPs were satisfied that 'a bounty on importation becomes in times of scarcity, wise and expedient'.[43]

Once again the importation succeeded. Nearly one and a half million quarters of wheat and flour arrived, though oats were up by only seven percent on the previous year, and barley imports declined by nearly sixteen.[44] However, prices rose until the spring of 1801. One cause was the

Brown Bread Act, discussed below, which during the critical January to February period, put a premium on the best wheat, at the expense of poorer qualities, including much foreign which could hardly find an outlet. This was the primary reason behind the Act's speedy repeal. During April 1801 buyers satisfied only short-term demands, and in May Mark Lane was 'effectually clogged with wheat'. In marked contrast to 1796 the importers avoided completely flooding the market by holding on as provincial demand rose. Prices were also maintained by the scanty supply of English wheat. Experts predicted only slight indemnity payments. Rapid price falls occurred only in late July, when a superb harvest looked assured and confident rumours of peace negotiations circulated.[45] Interestingly, only one plausible claim of continued mercantile machination at Mark Lane was sent to ministers, in January when prices continued inexorably upwards despite '700 Corn Ships in the River' Thames.[46] Perhaps this represents a major shift in public perceptions with imports being seen, not as the source of restored living standards, but national survival. In some senses this also reflects acceptance in the permanance of the inflation of the nineties.

In December 1800 the 'corn committee' calculated an aggregate wheat deficiency of two million quarters inclusive of the anticipated importation. During the autumn session, Bills were rushed through adding rice and maize to imported commodities enjoying price guarantees, and to indemnify customs officers who had illegally prevented the re-export of rice on Treasury orders. Pitt assumed that wheat imports would 'abate' prices, but leave them 'high enough to check the consumption'. One third of the wheat deficiency was deemed to be compensated for by rice and maize consumption, and the rest by 'economy' and the use of non-wheaten foodstuffs. The importation programme was to operate in tandem with wheat-substitution policies which were equally important to the government's strategy for repelling famine in wartime. We must now turn to the evolution of these latter elements.[47]

CHAPTER 12

Dietary Expedients and Vested Interests

Recommendation Versus Compulsion, June 1795 to July 1800

The advocacy of any dietary change, be it reductions in the quality of wheaten-bread, the substitution of other cereals, or the introduction of gruels, would encounter stiff resistance from working-class consumers, and confront long-established vested commercial, manufacturing and indeed political interests. The Board of Trade at Hawkesbury's instigation launched investigations into the possibilities of reducing wheat-consumption in January and February 1795. These proved inconclusive. Experts, including agriculturalists, and spokesmen from the milling and baking trades, gave conflicting testimonies, but the Board was satisfied that under the current Assize of Bread laws, bakers could not profitably supply coarser bread. Legislation was needed, but this would endanger millers' profits, and produce a confrontation between them and their powerful allies on the London Corporation, and the government. Moreover, the impact of coarser bread on nutritional standards, and the degree of reduced demand for wheat, were both hotly disputed. The Board accepted that plebeian Londoners would resent and possibly resist any challenge to sociologically-determined popular prejudices. The subject was dropped. Hawkesbury refused to entertain the Board of Agriculture's argument for £37,500 worth of government bounties to stimulate potato-production, though not the case for the importance of the root as an additional source of food during the harvest season of 1795.[1]

During April 1795, metropolitan concern at rocketing prices was reflected by an enquiry in the operation of the Assize by an aldermanic committee. Defects were found in the price-determining mechanism. The committee, impressed by the escalating differential between the prices of flour and wheat, argued that bread prices could be better contained if the base for the Assize was extended from flour alone, to a combination of flour and wheat prices. The Privy Council, significantly attended by Pitt, Portland and Dundas, as well as Hawkesbury, briefly delayed consideration of the report, so that the latter 'may procure professional Gentlemen to hear the Evidence'. Experts included Claude Scott, the King's Baker, and the Mark Lane Inspector. The Council rejected the report, and told the Lord Mayor that it was too late to seek legislation, too risky for experimentation, and too much uncertainty existed over the benefits calculated for consumers. The meeting released a flood of rumours that the government 'intended to make Bread at a reduced price for the poor'. Nothing was further from the truth. At this stage ministers were adamantly opposed to 'any kind of compulsion' to force consumption of 'coarser or different' types of bread. They took refuge in the argument that smaller quantities of the best wheaten were more nutritious than larger amounts of less-fine, and that a switch to the latter would not reduce aggregate wheat consumption. This camouflaged ministerial aversions to gambles with coercion.[2]

Within six weeks the government, faced by sudden and serious shortages, compromised this decision. Some non-metropolitan authorities had implemented the 1773 Act limiting the quality of wheaten bread; the lead given by Bideford Borough was followed by the Devon County Bench at Easter. Lord Sheffield 'prevailed on' Sussex millers to limit flour production to Standard Wheaten, and claimed that consumers 'will be well satisfied with it'; his opinion carried weight with ministers. On 1 July Pitt circulated a scheme to reduce wheat consumption, and hurriedly invited the Lord Mayor and London MPs to a Privy Council meeting on the 2nd. The Councillors were to publicise their 'Engagement' to personally abstain from finer bread than Standard Wheaten, and from best flour in 'luxurious . . . other Articles'; they would 'recommend to all their Fellow Subjects to enter into a like Engagement'. The Lord Mayor immediately objected; the bakers would not comply unless the legislation he had advised 'as a necessary Measure some Months ago' was enacted. Ministers reiterated their refusal and insisted that the Council's current objective was

> to induce the People, by setting them Example, to prefer a coarser sort of Bread during the present Emergency, and . . . to save for the Relief of the People some Part of the Quantity of Flour now consumed in their own Families.

By the same token, the greater the engagement's adoption, the greater the saving.[3]

Ministers eschewed provoking the inevitable populist backlash when cabinet nerves were raw over the political ramifications of the importation and distribution programme. London aldermen were now in a quandary. First, they were expected to publicise their personal adoption of the engagement, and secondly, they had that very morning commenced discussion of a Common Council plan to subsidise the poor's bread; this had adjourned solely to permit the Lord Mayor's attendance on the Privy Council. Alarmed, ministers insisted that the Londoners' plan would increase wheat consumption. Ministers now expected the Lord Mayor to return to his Common Councillors, get their plan abandoned, and also act as ministerial spokesman in the capital to obtain voluntary reductions in metropolitan wheat consumption. The Lord Mayor naturally preferred legislation, outside his control, to effect cuts; all the odium would then fall on government. If ministers persisted in their disbelief of the milling and baking trades' obduracy, it was cynically suggested that Privy Councillors could 'derive more satisfactory Information from' trade representatives than the Lord Mayor had passed on at 'several' meetings. He left with ministerial instructions to expend all funds on 'a Substitute for Wheat' ringing in his ears. The issue of the engagement was deferred for him to forewarn his Common Councillors.[4]

The imminent arrival of 60,000 quarters of wheat enabled the Londoners to defer their decision too. The Privy Council pressed ahead, and interviewed Bakers' Company officials on 5 August; disagreements between them did not obscure the fact that the milling trade would not alter production patterns unless legally compelled. The Council officially approved Sheffield's arbitrary actions in his county, and ordered the Home Office to advise all provincial correspondents accordingly. The Council optimistically contemplated a switch to coarser bread in the capital too, once problems with the Assize were surmounted. Ministers commended the charitable disposition in the country, and if they eschewed a 'general plan' for their direction, they advised the expenditure of all funds on wheat substitutes. On 6 August the Council failed to find ways round the existing Assize laws in consultation with the judges to universally introduce coarser bread. Meanwhile, Hawkesbury busied himself with experiments and calculations with coarser grades, only to be confronted by figures purportedly showing that compliance with the 1773 Act would incur milling losses. The Lord Mayor was primarily concerned to avoid unpopularity, notably over the expenditure of relief funds. If ministers ruled out direct subsidies on fine bread, he demanded written instructions on substitutes from the Council which he would reveal 'at a private Meeting of the Aldermen' before their adjourned conference with the Common Council on the 7th. This strategy would ease the revocation of the original plan. The Council obliged with a variant of suggestions being distributed by the Home Office, with a rider that 'One of the best Substitutes' was 'the Distribution of . . . Meat, together with such Vegetables as can be procured'.[5]

The Engagement was then issued; Privy Councillors would confine themselves to the Standard Wheaten until 1 October 1795 and urged adoption by 'all Our fellow Subjects'. The king characteristically seized the opportunity to demand a decimation of upper-class gluttony by restricting all meals to one course, but ministers had more urgent and even less tasteful tasks. On 10 July the Common Council cunningly deflected ministerial advice with an engagement not to use hair powder made from wheat. Hair powder was a recent victim of Pitt's fiscal innovations, and the Common Council's opportunism was deftly calculated to cause maximum political embarrassment. Ministers reacted nervously and defensively; the Council summoned a starch-maker who proved that only 20,000 quarters of inedible wheat was used in annual manufacture, and the government then insisted that the tax was 'extremely productive' and irrelevant for 'the lower Class of People'. The Londoners were instructed to implement the government's contingency plans which turned on wheat-substitutes.[6]

Ministers now desperately re-examined the Assize laws respecting the production of wheat loaves coarser than Standard Wheaten and mixed breads. These served only to baffle the Crown's Law Officers; three Acts were relevant but 'The Language . . . appears obscure . . . too loose to authorize . . . a positive Opinion'. The 1773 Act, which could be extended to London voluntarily by the Court of Aldermen, permitted the sale of wheaten bread coarser than Standard independently of the Assize. Assize tables for a variety of mixed breads were included in the 1758 Act, and these were unaffected by subsequent statutes of 1763 and 1773. The 1758 Act controlled the prices of mixed breads but only the qualities specifically demarcated could be sold. The Bench when fixing the price of Standard Wheaten under the 1773 Act was unable to alter the prescribed ratio between flour and bread prices, and this theoretical circumvention of the trades' objections was legally inadmissable. New legislation was required; without it the problem of London was insoluble. The struggle between ministers and the London authorities developed over the next fortnight. On 15 July a 'Committee of Merchants, Bankers and Trades' administering a relief fund, and supported by the Common Council, advocated an indemnity for bakers who sold Standard Wheaten at prices higher than those fixed by the Assize. This was rejected. The Privy Council seized on weight regulations to suggest another way round the problem, but its hopeless tone at this juncture can be assessed from the alternative suggestion – could 'Sea Biscuit . . . be brought into Use'? The Londoners were instructed to confer with 'those Persons of the Profession, whom they usually Consult on such Occasions'; if neither proved possible, relief funds should be spent on compensating bakers for selling Standard Wheaten at a loss. Ministers insisted that the Lord Mayor set Assize prices on Standard Wheaten 'and that it should be publicly known'. The government argued 'that an Example set at this Time by the Magistracy of . . . London would produce great Effect'; metropolitan demand for wheat would fall, and even more importantly, if this economy was adopted in the capital, ministers were confident that it would be imitated in the provinces.[7]

The state of play on 18 July was nicely revealed by the Lord Mayor's claim that he was unable to convince his aldermanic colleagues that the implementation of the 1773 Act 'was perfectly consonant to law'; in fact they perceived 'a struggle between the [Privy] Council and the Court of Aldermen, which should do the unpopular act, as they call it, the breaking of the law'. Meanwhile the city's milling establishment was grinding to a halt in anticipation of orders to limit production to Standard Wheaten. In a last-ditch attempt to engineer a ministerial retreat, the Lord Mayor suggested that the entire scheme could be counterproductive. If Standard Wheaten went on sale 'may the people think they are at liberty to use it profusely and so spoil the plan counterbalance all the difference'?[8]

Ministerial stubbornness paid off, but the Act's implementation was immediately challenged, and Soho baker McEwen, hauled before a stipendiary magistrate. A furious altercation exploded between McEwen who produced flour samples to an unresponsive JP; on the imposition of a two pound fine, McEwen's companion retorted '"Is this justice?"'. The magistrate 'put himself in a violent passion', had the interrupter arrested and released only on giving sureties to appear at the Sessions. McEwen and the other bakers petitioned the Privy Council who they claimed 'were perfectly aware' of the impossibility of profitably producing Standard Wheaten under the Assize. Unmoved, the Council dryly ordered McEwen to seek legal redress if he felt wronged; 'their Lordships cannot interfere in a Business of this Nature'.[9]

In July, another dimension to the government's changed policy involved the embargo suddenly imposed on the re-export of rice, in stark contrast to earlier ministerial indifference to rice's potential in March. The Board of Agriculture was also producing exigency proposals. Its advocacy of charitable and parochial funds to subsidise the cost of the poor's 'necessaries of life' was deleted at government insistence; instead specific suggestions for the use of wheat substitutes were inserted. The Board's revised plans included a receipe for soup, made from meat, turnips, potatoes and carrots, to be supplied by parochial authorities. The public soup-kitchen was now conceived, although its immediate impact was slight.[10]

The Home Office seized every opportunity to recommend wheat substitutes, notably when conveying official regrets at the inability to comply with requests for government corn. Precise responses were tailored to the information received. The Mayor of Newcastle-upon-Tyne had banned fine flour production, engineered a city resolution in favour of coarse flour, and now proposed to subsidise the poor's bread; he was told to spend the money on substitutes. Meat and vegetables were usually recommended, though government thought that north-eastern customary consumption of rye made it a legitimate region for trials with maize. The War Office cut embodied militiamen's bread allowance, and made up the deficiency with substitutes.[11] The Privy Council engagement was hurriedly printed for distribution at midsummer Quarter Sessions. Superficially the response was excellent. The engagement was adopted all over the country; county, corporate and village authorities formally voted their support. County Benches, including Berkshire, Somerset and Devon, printed and distributed additional copies of the engagement. Other Benches, including the Surrey County and the Nottingham Borough, implemented the 1773 Act. Parochial decisions, recorded in vestry minutes prove that the principles of retrenchment permeated society at every level. In Somerset Tom Poole experimented with cereal mixtures, and even turnips in bread. The poor of Battle had had subsidised flour since February; on 21 July the vestry transferred the subsidy to Standard Wheaten and neatly avoided conflict with suppliers by listing the recipients and paying subsidies direct to millers and bakers. Dagenham vestrymen typically resolved to 'prohibit in our Families all superfluous modes of using either Bread, flour or meat', and 'strongly recommended others to Practice the same Necessary Economy'. Some enthusiastically experimented with more ambitious schemes, including one to create soup kitchens in every County Durham parish. The press teemed with reports, and helped to generate considerable optimism that self-denial 'by the higher and middle classes' was the insurance against starvation.[12]

It is impossible to gauge the policy's economic impact. Some savings must have accrued through the abstentions promised by the affluent, and more from its enforcement on the poor by vestrymen and charity organisers. Poor law recipients at Battle were not the only victims. Sheffield charity leaders publicised their personal adoption of the engagement, supplied only Standard Wheaten and offered cutprice oatmeal, rye, peas, and rice, in addition to potatoes at prime cost and soup at a penny a gallon. The example was followed in part by their Leeds counterparts who urged people 'in every situation of life' to eat some oats. Sir Joseph Banks' inability to purchase pastries at wayside inns in Northamptonshire convinced the itinerant baronet that the engagement was effective. But market-place realities had already forced drastic economies in working families. Further, officially-inspired dietary expedients generated stubborn proletarian resistance, and the hostility of the milling and baking trades. Supporters of government strategies went to ridiculous lengths. The Tory *Manchester Mercury* reported the use of oats and 'coarse mixed bread' by the opulent, and asserted that

> if the working class would generally adopt the use of it, they would find their account both in health and expence. Nothing can be more unwholesome than the fine white bread they are in the habit of eating hot from the oven. It is, in short, not less hurtful to the constitution, than to the pocket.

Statements by various bodies suggest that Standard Wheaten enforcement was fairly hopeless. The Berkshire Sessions would only 'particularly request' the trade to bake the bread, and pessimistically stressed that 'all Ranks' were 'equally bound to Submit to . . . the unhappy consequences of the present Scarcity'. There is no evidence of prosecutions even in Devon where the 1773 Act was nominally operative longest. The Oxfordshire Bench complained that bakers ignored the order. Their Birmingham counterparts, presiding over the worst hit major centre, believed that only 'compulsion' would see millers abandon their normal gradings.[13]

Hampshire workers were 'discontented with the idea of Household Bread' and abetted by their employers, resisted grandee-inspired attempts to implement government policy. Lord Carnarvon explained that

> the farmers here absurdly prefer the rise of Wages which does not relieve in proportion to the number of a family, & reject the plan of delivering provisions at a reduced price, imagining that they shall not give satisfaction to the Poor, but become, by the Interference Objects of their ill-will. They say that the Poor will not be put out of their usual course of provision even if it is given to them.

The Londoners were not alone in seeking to escape the responsibility for taking unpopular steps. In the heart of Lord Sheffield's country, Sussex, farmers reported their employees' complaints at subsidised 'brown bread'. The county press blamed the millers who continued to manufacture fine as well as Standard Wheaten flour, thus pandering to the 'extravagance, perverseness, or prejudice' of some workers, which 'makes others discontented'. The 'poor as well the rich should consider that a BROWN LOAF is better than NO loaf'. A disgruntled observer in Hampshire said that 'Our

Labourers have refused to eat any bread but the finest . . . & throw the
Standard Wheaten into Riot'. Similar protests were made by customary
wheat-eaters outside the South. The Stockport relief committee sold
cutprice oatmeal, but it gave

> little Satisfaction to the common people who are still clamarous and insist
> on having wheaten bread, altho' every assurance has been given them that
> it cannot be obtained.[14]

The last two informants also reported disturbances; substitutes and coarse
bread provoked unrest, and many local authorities turned against energetic
advocacy. Fine bread at Bedford was subsidised, but as the Mayor tactfully
told the Home Office, in quantities insufficient to prevent recipients
supplementing it 'in a great measure with potatoes & other vegetables'.
Even in Devon, Grand Jurors were too nervous to risk public recommendation of mixed breads. Immediately the Sheffield charity's wheat supply
improved, fine flour was added to its commodities to answer complaints
against the rough article. Many local social leaders did what they could; in
Wiltshire J.J. Butt had 'been trying to do some little good by quieting the
common people, & inducing a frugal use of our present stock until the next
Harvest'. Few were prepared to emulate the Lancastrian gentleman who
sacked all his domestic servants for refusing to eat brown bread. But
ministerial insistence on this policy threatened a further conflict between
government and local authorities. Ministers may have studiously and
technically avoided legal compulsion, and as the parliamentary session
closed on 27 June, before the full extent of the emergency presented itself,
ministers had few options. The implementation of unpopular policies was
left to local administrations who also had to confront any immediate
repercussions. The summer hypercrisis revealed a host of problems,
emanating from a complex mixture of popular prejudice, commercial
practices, and untidy legislation, which certainly compromised government
endeavours to keep the ship of state afloat without famine in wartime.
Ministers recognised that the problem would recur; Hawkesbury for one,
was adamant that

> the Inhabitants of this Kingdom should be gradually taught not to rely
> wholly on a Supply of Bread made of Wheat, and particularly of the finer
> Sort of it, for their ordinary Subsistence.

But this form of public education, which meant penetrating a political
minefield, lay outside the legitimate scope of executive direction; it was a
task for the unreformed parliament.[15]
    Initially, Hawkesbury was confident that the engagement had operated
fruitfully as 'an example . . . the Rich had already set' to the poor, and that
legislation could be limited to tinkering with the Assize to restore profitabil-
ity to Standard Wheaten production. While recognising the value of barley,
maize, rice, potatoes and other vegetables, and 'the coarser sorts of meat' as
wheat substitutes, he saw little need for state intervention: 'the Pressure of
the times will probably induce the more indigent Inhabitants to look out

for' wheat alternatives. Lord Sheffield, chagrined at rebuffs from the milling trade, advocated new 'restrictions' on it, and insisted that ministers must devise changes to the Assize to take to parliament. Once the cabinet belatedly accepted the deficiency of the 1795 wheat crop, preparations were made.[16]

The engagement was renewed on its 1 October expiry to run until 1 December 1795. The Privy Council made extensive investigations and the emergent picture painted by the expert witnesses conditioned ministerial objectives. Wheat was in short supply, but barley and oats were plentiful. Nobody denied proletarian preference for the finest wheaten bread, and substitutions would be 'irksome' administratively. But mixed breads were consumed in parts of the provinces, and market pressures were also dictating increased non-metropolitan recourse to barley. Several experts argued that 'the poorer Orders' would consume coarser and mixed breads if everybody ate them. The evidence suggested that even Londoners' objections could be overcome if means were devised to tackle the sociological determinants of dietary patterns. With superb stocks of barley looking the potential saviour, and with the knowledge that the consumption of breads other than the finest wheaten was commoner than supposed, the government's original ideas retained credibility. Problems hinged on the identification of policies to expedite dietary innovations.[17]

Dearth conditions customarily directed public hostility towards the millers, and the summer of 1795 was no exception, but the increasing disparity between wheat and flour prices encouraged fierce accusations of profiteering. In late October wheat cost the same as in June, but flour was seven shillings a sack dearer. The Lord Mayor reiterated his earlier demands to set the Assize on a base of wheat and flour prices. Ministerial post-bags proved considerable public pressure for legislative action against the milling trade. One communication analysing the behaviour of the wheat and flour price ratio was pragmatically inserted in the Privy Council's public relations exercise, namely its detailed published minutes. A consensus emerged, stimulated by what an expert described as the milling establishment's 'daring conduct since the harvest', insistent on extending statutory control from baking to milling. The big metropolitan millers fought back, claiming that normal oscillations in the ratio had been misrepresented to generate 'an unjust Stigma'. The exclusion of corn-manufacture from price controls comprised 'encouragement, and by that encouragement . . . [London] has been supplied cheaper than it would have been' because good supplies were dependent on healthy profits. The real meaning of this defence was that the London millers engaged in a highly speculative business, and that their considerable profits would evaporate if their activities were legally controlled with the bakers'.[18]

Another battle between ministers and the London authorities loomed on the latter's obduracy in the face of government insistence that they calculated suitable changes to the Assize mechanism. Delaying tactics and petulant comments on the destruction of the metropolitan milling trade, induced a change of tack by ministers. If the switch to Standard Wheaten was difficult to engineer, the use of mixed breads would conserve wheat stocks; as the existing Assize tables were inadequate to the balance of

interests, price economies for consumers and viable profits for traders, the
Lord Mayor was instructed to devise tables 'to extend . . . to Bread made of
White or Household Wheaten Flour, with $\frac{1}{3}$rd, $\frac{1}{4}$th and $\frac{1}{5}$th of the Flour of
Rye, Barley, Oats, and Indian Corn, and with $\frac{1}{3}$rd of Potatoes'.[19] By the
time parliament convened the government had adopted Hawkesbury's
strategy of weaning consumers away from fine wheaten bread. Pitt almost
immediately informed the Commons that national subsistence hinged on
imports, and the reduction of demand for wheat through maximising
mixed-bread consumption. Changes to the Assize would permit the latter.
His announcement was instantly challenged in some well-chosen cautionary
remarks from Fox. It was all very well for 'the more opulent' to experiment
with mixed breads, but their perceptions were essentially unreal; bread
formed an inconsequential proportion of their diet and MPs must remember when 'talking of bread for the people . . . that . . . to the poor it
constitutes the chief, if not the sole article . . . of subsistence'. There was no
guarantee that the proposed breads were nutritionally adequate, and
plebeian consumers may require commensurately greater quantities, which
would nullify the aims of the exercise. Fox, who had already extracted an
admittance from Pitt that war was a cause of the present crisis, intimated
that the opposition would maximise political capital from ministerial resort
to statutorily-induced dietary change. Pitt cannot have welcomed another
emotive issue in the uniquely tense political climate generated by cabinet
proposals to neutralise the popular democratic movement. Moreover,
divisions emerged in the government. Hawkesbury's strengthened central
strategy, the introduction of some legal measures to implement the
retrenchment ideal, was challenged. On 8 November Lord Auckland
penned his complaint at Hawkesbury's dogmatic control of the Board of
Trade; 'it is painful for one to hear in silence that the measures proposed are
wise & efficient, when I am not convinced', especially when the 'Evil
involves the tranquility & perhaps the existence of the Country'.[20]

Auckland rejected retrenchment through legislation because it would
'prescribe what is to be substituted' for wheat; it could even lead to
malnutrition and disease. To compel 'the labouring Classes to eat the
Mixtures . . . would be more dangerous to the Peace of the Country than
all the Jacobinism of the Times'. Auckland advanced a much more subtle
and sophisticated strategy, 'honest, manly and intelligible', namely 'a
solemn Engagement' to cut consumption by 'a proportion to be ascertained'
by the most affluent 'three or four Hundred Thousand Families'. Upper-
class self-denial might launch the dietary revolution required; 'All the lower
Classes will comprehend it. They will admire & venerate it . . . and many
of them will gradually imitate it'. The lead should be taken by MPs once the
select committee had deliberated: 'the effect would be beyond all description, both on the feelings and gratitude of the Country'. That committee's
first report, published on 16 November, concentrated on imports, but in
passing noted the equal necessity for substitution. Forthcoming shifts in
policy were leaked to the press. On 14 November *The Times* reported that
the rich were to abstain from wheat 'to leave a larger share of the stock . . .
to those whose subsistence it is more immediately essential'.[21]

Pitt accepted Auckland's proposals and integrated them into the crucial role assigned to the select committee. Its further reports would argue the case for wheat-substitutes 'but without exhibiting more alarm and Dismay than is necessary to produce the salutary End in View'. Both houses of parliament would produce resolutions of members to be then 'recommended by the King to every part of the Kingdom'. Essentially, options which were bound to be unpopular, were decided by the executive, which then shielded itself behind proposals ostensibly emanating from the select committee, endorsed by parliament, and urged on the country with the king's prestige and authority. Privately Pitt hoped for a broader consumption of mixed breads through their distribution by charities and under the poor law. Publicly Pitt emphasised that savings were 'to be confined to the opulent and middle Classes . . . to whom Wheat is not an essential article of food'. Over 900,000 homes were liable to the window tax; if half that number of families cut wheat consumption by a third, a million quarters would be saved. He hoped that the other half would comply too, reducing demand and prices so that 'the requisite supply would be secured to the poor and labouring classes at a reasonable rate'. The committee's third report, produced on 9 December, tactfully emphasised that non-wheaten and mixed breads were staple dietary fare in some regions 'where Labour and Industry are carried to as great an Extent as in any other'; it admitted the necessity to 'sacrifice . . . some Degree of Indulgence, or . . . Prejudice' while firmly rejecting statutory intervention. The upper and much more numerous middle classes would 'unite voluntarily' to cut their wheat consumption by a third; this was the first immediate step, but the report pandered to those perceiving long-term advantage in eroding dependence on fine wheat, with the claim that the setting of the proposed example would eventually 'extend . . . to all Classes of the People'. These points were reiterated in the debates over the formal parliamentary engagements. A few MPs including Sir Joseph Banks staunchly maintained their conviction that only statutory prohibition of fine wheaten-flour production would answer. Fox, whose original objections were largely accommodated, said little; his supporters invoked constitutional quibbles over the legitimacy of parliamentary engagements. Opposition peers ridiculed the inadequacy of the measure; the Duke of Bedford distinguished himself by advocating legislation compelling all bread to contain one-third potato-flour, but if this comprised another attempt to bait ministers it was evaded by a restatement of cabinet conviction that compulsion was unnecessary. A handful of Whig peers, including Earl Fitzwilliam, refused to sign the Lords' engagement on constitutional grounds.[22]

While this parliamentary victory transpired ministers maintained their quest to change the Assize of Bread so that retrenchment was not jeopardised by existing law. The Privy Council eventually tired of repeated confrontations with the consistently obdurate London authorities, and capitulated by passing the entire problem to the select committee. Parliament essentially evaded it. A new Bill simply repealed legislative clauses covering the Assize on mixed breads and wheaten coarser than the Standard; those clauses governing Standard and finer wheaten varieties remained on the statute book. Breads freed from the Assize were controlled only by a new stipulation that their contents must be marked on the loaves;

mixtures and prices were lamely left 'as the Maker and Seller thereof shall deem proper and reasonable'. The Act constituted a charter for food adulteration and represented a complete capitulation to the commercial forces opposing ministers. No rationale was even advanced; the government presumably anticipated that bakers' profits would rise on mixed and coarse breads, and would therefore make them, thereby effecting retrenchment. But if the government had technically removed bakers' objections there was no certainty that their customers would tamely accept the product.[23]

Copies of the parliamentary engagements were distributed for consideration at all Epiphany Quarter Sessions. Numerous and diverse bodies from Grand Juries to village vestries, and even the attenders at a South Yorkshire Court of Sewers, formally adopted the resolutions. This facilitated publicity; St Nicholas vestry in Newcastle-upon-Tyne argued in handbills that mixed bread consumption 'by the Poor' following the example of 'the Rich', was the means 'to have bread . . . from this time to the next harvest'. The Home Office urged all local authorities to impose substitution in public institutions. The Lancastrian Bench responded with a draconian cut in prisoners' diets,[24] and some poor law administrators made relief conditional on accepting mixed breads.[25] The Board of Agriculture publicised the results of experimentation with differing mixtures.[26] But the key strategy of encouraging workers to imitate the affluent proved problematic. Nottinghamshire workers mixed in barley when wheat was short but when supplies improved they 'left off mixing'. The Probus vestry in Cornwall adopted economy resolutions and wearily agreed 'as far as in us to induce our Labourers to follow the same Examples'. An impressive miscellany of difficulty is encountered. The Devon Bench reimposed the 1773 Act which they simultaneously admitted was 'not competent'. Gloucester bakers denounced mixed bread as insufficiently nutritious. In Sussex, Lord Sheffield was denounced as a 'overbearing superior' and entrapped into a slanging match with millers in the columns of the county press. St Giles vestry in Reading agreed to co-operate with all corporate suggestions for economising on wheat except admixing barley. In Norfolk the engagement was 'much misunderstood'; reassurances over the absence of compulsion must have especially confused those forced to consume mixed bread by overseers of the poor. The Stowmarket Bench received an eighty-strong demonstration against the wheat-barley mixture available at Wetherden, and a dispersal needed the intervention of the Queen's Bays. Flamboyant resistance rarely came from the more elevated; one 'very violent' Hertfordshire clergyman not only 'has nothing but fine bread in his house', but also the temerity to announce from the pulpit that 'the poor have nothing else to live on and they are right to insist on having it'.[27]

The government preferred to combat rapidly rising springtime prices in 1796 with large clandestine sales of its own grain at Mark Lane, to seeking legislation to enforce retrenchment, which Pitt simultaneously ruled out. Pitt believed that the programme had essentially failed; obstinacy from 'the labouring classes . . . to make the experiment for themselves' after the example, derived from inaccurate 'objections . . . so successfully addressed' to plebeian 'ignorance or . . . prejudice'. In March urban authorities were formally contacted by the Home Office to determine if the upward spiral in food prices was in spite of widespread compliance with policy, or through its neglect.[28] Over 180 returns were made. Many were blatantly evasive. Several boroughs had implemented, though not necessarily enforced, the 1773 Act. A high percentage claimed that bakers and millers obstructed their enquiries. But in many places customary dietaries meant that government policy of wheat retrenchment was either superfluous or inappropriate for significant proportions of consumers. The reply from Malmesbury encapsulated the permutations of responses to prices, supplies and official recommendations in such areas:

> the better sort of people [normally] used bread in their famileys of a mixture of two thirds wheat flower and one third of barley, the poorer Treads men etc, mixt somewhat more barley meal, and the poor people mixed very little wheat with their barley, and the very poor people eat nothing but Barley.

Market prices during the dearth no doubt caused most consumers here to alter their cereal ratios. Replies from about 130 towns claimed successes, though some reported proletarian resistance, and the gist of others was that achieved economies were dictated by the market, charity organisers and poor law officials, rather than anything approximate to patriotism. Any reader of these reports is forced to admit, as were ministers, serious doubts over their integrity. Many officials confronted by a governmental enquiry opted for the easy way out with unsubstantiated claims of the one-third wheat consumption cut. Few were as tactless as the Mayor of Winchester whose conviction in the required saving was based on the mixed bread supplied to the College, and significantly to Assize judges.

Respondents who were able to blame millers and bakers, and/or the workers, were more honest. Bakers at Bath and Newcastle-upon-Tyne ignored the Standard Wheaten order. Millers at St Albans and Gravesend were among the many who 'proved refractory'. Appropriate resolutions proposed at Berwick-on-Tweed, Salisbury and Chichester, were not adopted, at the latter 'on Account of a very strong Opposition principally from the middling and lower Ranks of People who attended [the formal meeting] on that Occasion'. The Mayor of Wootten Bassett vituperatively exclaimed that 'the lower order (or indolent labourers and paupers) would . . . prefer half a pound of the fine Wheaten Bread, to a pound of mixed'. Very few respondents were as candid as the Bailiff of Reigate, who tempered his cognizance of mixed-bread consumption elsewhere, with pragmatism dictated by his observation of its debilitating effect on the handful of Surrey labourers who tried the stuff: 'amongst . . . the poor Labourers, who have scarce any Sustenance but Bread . . . I have neither urged nor wished a Mixture of Bread'.

A critical evaluation of the survey revealed a marked hostility shared by all social groups to both parliamentary advocacies and dietary expedients. It was aggravated, as at Cambridge, when the affluent's example was ignored; 'the rich think it a great hardship, that they should abstain from their usual food, when all their indigent neighbours refuse to make any sacrifice'.

Others complained that a combination of the policy and the license allowed to the trade by the 1795 Act enabled adulteration and exploitation on a unprecedented scale; why else were price differentials between mixed breads and fine wheaten so small asked several authorities? In the autumn of 1799 ministers recalled earlier experiences, programmes which were 'so little attended . . . productive of so little good'. The history of failure was admitted in the 1800 corn committee's first report in February; compulsion was ruled out from the start. But Liverpool adhered to his view that population increase had outpaced agrarian productive capacity, and that short and long-term security dictated reductions in current degrees of dependency on wheat.[29] The seriousness of ministerial appraisal of the developing crisis in the autumn of 1799 is reflected in their immediate determination to find means of diversifying the nation's diet, in spite of earlier attempts foundering on the complex interaction of economical, financial, commercial, nutritional and sociological factors, which remained to be overcome.

These 1799 evaluations should not obscure the fact that once the problem receded in 1796, Pitt eschewed confronting the factors responsible for famine in wartime. Proposals by Dr Buchan, the very successful author of the populist *Domestic Medecine*, to turn his propagandist expertise to combatting sociological dietary determinants, were entertained and then dropped by the Board of Trade in June 1796.[30] Minor modifications to the Assize of Bread in London from 1797 fixed bakers' profits on the amount of flour used by the sack.[31] The Board of Trade did intervene in a dispute between the metropolitan grain trade and the former proprietors of the co-operative Albion Flour Mills, who in 1798 wanted to restore the venture, dormant since a destructive fire in 1791. The Mills' history, and the Board's role in 1798, were to be of importance to government policy in 1800. Albion Mill supporters claimed that when their enterprize flourished, the oscillations in the ratio between wheat and flour prices were not experienced. Moreover, the co-operative did not send flour to provincial marts, in marked contrast to commercial traders. The private sector objected to the monopolistic potential of the co-operative, and said that its lower prices were achieved at the expense of quality. But the Mills' opponents' real objections hinged on the exposure of milling profit margins. This aspect of the conflict was to be remembered by Liverpool, though in 1798 the co-operators were outmanoeuvred by the traders and their allies on the Corporation.[32]

The retrenchment ideal was kept alive during the inter-famine years largely through the campaign of Count Rumford and the Society for Bettering the Condition of the Poor, to publicise the soup-kitchen as a cheap and beneficial urban charity. Kitchens were established in London and some big provincial towns, including Manchester, Birmingham and Newcastle-upon-Tyne, over the winter of 1797-8. Supporters said that they reduced the poor rates and taught workers 'to feed themselves in a more frugal manner'. The movement was stimulated by the coincidence of the worsening subsistence situation and the opening of the model kitchens for the 1799-1800 winter. More were established in most substantial towns, and extended to numerous estate-villages by landowners. The press extolled their virtues at ridiculous length; 'the art of communicating relief to the Poor, in times of scarcity is only beginning to be understood', boomed one journalist. The Lewes press claimed that soup retailed 'at a very low price' at Brighton, was 'rendered much more palatable' if bones were stripped, crushed and boiled in. Anything remotely edible could be used.[33]

Retrenchment was resurrected independently of government by the press, including the *Blackburn Mail*, the *Bath Chronicle*, and the *Norfolk Chronicle*, in late 1799. Individual enthusiasts, among them inevitably Lord Sheffield, renewed past efforts in recognition of the aggravated seriousness of the unfolding situation. Sheffield used the Sussex press: it was incumbent 'to save bread corn as much as possible', but switching to coarser wheaten and mixed breads was inadequate; potatoes, rice and meat hashes should be provided by charity and poor-law officials. This flood of propaganda had a national effect. At Berkhampstead the intinerant Captain Hervey encountered publicity announcing sales of low-price soup, rice puddings, potatoes and 'household bread'.[34] The cabinet's conviction in the deficiency of all cereals[35] led ministers to personally experiment with, and exchange soup recipes. The expanding soup-kitchen movement helped to overcome government reluctance to formally relaunch retrenchment programmes. George Rose speculated on the advantages of 'some general plan' for soup to be advanced by ministers. 'Your acquaintance Count Rumford has his merits', wrote Lord Wycombe to his regular correspondent, Lord Holland, but 'I do not think the invention of bad Soup by the union of Ox Heads with Potatoes the noblest flight of human genius'. Wycombe's sarcasm eloquently symbolised upper-class faith in the plan.[36]

After prolonged internal discussions the government announced more extensive plans on 20 December. Lord Lieutenants were to ask all Epiphany Quarter Sessions to assess implementation of the 1773 Act, though the rider admitting its irrelevance in some regions, and 'particular' inapplicability for London, reflected greater ministerial wisdom. The idea that metropolitan example would pave the way for provincial imitation was exploded, and the Act's adoption should occur where the Bench saw 'no Objection'. The government adopted Sheffield's perceptions of the great role for soups. A new engagement in support of Standard Wheaten was drafted but dropped.[37] The Home Office received few letters on the subject before March 1800, but replies invariably suggested the expenditure of relief funds on soup, not cereals of any denomination, unless the local supply collapsed completely.[38]

The government's campaign evoked a broad and many-sided response from local authorities. The Norfolk Bench instructed all parishes to implement 'the Plan of Soup Establishments', which were also created in many villages in wheat-producing counties. Earls Fitzwilliam and Fortescue left the respective burghers of Malton and South Molton in no doubt as to their patrons' wishes. Many County Benches opted for the 1773 Act, sometimes with additional instructions. In Gloucestershire attentions were drawn to the 1795 Act permitting mixed breads, together with dire warnings against 'secret Adulteration'. The Cheshire Bench ordered Petty Sessions to regularly set the Assize, and the West Riding judiciary advocated mixed breads and greater use of oatmeal. Elsewhere, there were problems and obstruction. The 1773 Act was useless in Cornwall because wheaten flour derived from other counties. The Berkshire Bench abandoned the attempt on the representations of Reading bakers. Only one Devon baker attended a conference with the County Bench, which retaliated by reminding overseers that they were not compelled to give aid in cash and could supply foodstuffs directly if they wished.[39]

Government concern that the scale of the crisis had been underestimated, and increasing evidence that it would extend beyond the 1800 harvest, produced major policy changes. Identical concern permeated other important circles. A shift within London aldermanic ranks saw a new majority favouring legislative intervention to stiffen retrenchment so long as it contained commercial safeguards. The Kent Bench had already implemented the 1773 Act, and its Surrey and Middlesex counterparts were strongly rumoured to be about to follow; all three counties contained big metropolitan districts. In this more hospitable climate ministers steeled themselves to amend the Assize and extend the principles of Standard Wheaten regulations to London itself. The Foxite *Morning Chronicle*, a staunch supporter of metropolitan milling interests, accepted defeat; it now attributed the statutory introduction of coarse flour to ministerial neglect and incompetence in not seeking import 'bounties' much earlier. The Board of Trade drafted a Bill to prohibit the manufacture of flour superior to Standard Wheaten, and also to give supervisory powers over mills and their equipment to the judiciary. It was sent to the select committee. The available evidence is not clear about subsequent events. Lord Sheffield later attributed a ministerial retreat to pandering 'to the supposed daintiness of the Metropolis'. The Lord Mayor, also a committee member, certainly leaked highly sensitive information about its proceedings, which strongly implies a panicky retreat on the part of members of London's governing bodies, fearful at an holistic confrontation with the entire metropolitan proletariat. Aldermen were definitively told that the committee was not going to recommend compulsory measures after all, thirteen days before its report was ready. The Lord Mayor's explanation, that the committee had accepted the well-rehearsed argument that the consumption of coarse flour would not reduce aggregate demand for wheat, was the one eventually formally advanced by the committee. The effect of the leak can be seen in the Kent Bench's speedy revocation of the order implementing the 1773 Act well before the committee officially pronounced. There is a strong suspicion that whomsoever was responsible, adopted this strategy to galvanise an anti-ministerial majority in order to engineer a last minute government defeat. Other county Benches responded quickly with revocations too. Sheffield rightly said that the committee's report was 'a declaration against those . . . Magistrates . . . who have with Alacrity obeyed the instructions' from the government in December. Other magistrates were outraged, including Staffordshire's Rev. A.B. Haden who anticipated 'the Miller's restraining Bill' would have equipped him with powers to teach local millers some long-overdue lessons. Some MPs, including Addington and Wilberforce, adhered to their conviction that retrenchment could be achieved only through statutory instruments. Three Acts reflect this concern. The first was merely a cosmetic measure forcing millers to take out licences. The second which tinkered with the Assize price-calculation mechanism irritated the trade and little else. The third, rushed through within days of the select committee's report banned the sale of hot bread; in future bread sold by bakers had to be twenty-four hours old; it was estimated that this would reduce metropolitan bread consumption by a tenth.[41]

Thereafter some ministers planned secretly a much more subtle thrust in what was now perceived as a straight fight between the cabinet and the metropolitan milling trade. The Board of Trade re-examined its records relating to the Albion Mills and enquired closely into the operations of a Birmingham co-operative founded in 1796. Certain facts interested Liverpool. First, the Birmingham concern had cornered a significant sector of the market, and had successfully sold coarse flour and bread. Secondly, the co-operative undercut the private sector and still emerged with a ten percent profit. The detailed accounts proved that healthy profits accrued in the production of coarse flour and bread, thereby powerfully supporting the conviction that the complexities of the metropolitan trade were fiercely upheld solely to maintain massive profits.[42] The Board did not supply these details to the Commons committee commensurately with established procedures. Liverpool's investigation into the importers' manoeuvres in June confirmed his strong suspicions of commercial machination, and encouraged him to reject the trade's claim that Londoners would not eat coarse bread. He ingeniously argued that the high proportion of migrants domiciled in the capital meant that many residents were born in regions where poorer breads and non-wheaten cereals were standard fare. He indicted the entire London milling trade. The real cause of the 'Evil' of metropolitan obstinacy over wheat was 'the Millers . . . themselves'; they 'make an unreasonable Profit, particularly in Times of Scarcity'. When he first took over the Presidency in 1786, millers' profits were two shillings per sack; now, and particularly since the Albion Mills' demise, they had climbed 'to the enormous Amount' of fourteen shillings, despite considerable technological investment, 'the only instance in which the improvement of machinery has not diminished the price of an Article made by it', he wrily concluded. In addition the greatest millers were in effect a cartel, able arbitrarily to set prices to which lesser competitors and bakers had to comply. The London authorities were hoodwinked by the great dealers of the Bakers' Company on whom they relied for information; no wonder that the principal traders were 'certainly very rich'.[43]

On 9 June the government sprung a Bill in favour of the newly-formed London Flour Company on the Commons; devised by past proprietors of the Albion Mills, with Board of Trade support, it hoped to capture a tenth of the metropolitan market. The Company would confine operations to Standard Wheaten production and reveal its accounts for parliamentary scrutiny; although a cabinet minority opposed the idea, the wily Liverpool calculated that Company profits would dispel the trade's claims respecting coarser flour manufacture. Ministerial supporters made no secret of their convictions in the current crisis's aggravation by mercantile machinations, or that the nation's increasing inability to feed itself reflected a long-term, recurrent problem which could resolved in part by dietary change. The

Morning Chronicle spearheaded the opposition, emphasising the critical role of the commercial and milling establishments in a free trade economy; it denied unfair practices, denounced the Birmingham scheme, and defended metropolitan dietary preferences. The paper's cause was inevitably backed by the Foxites in parliament, where dissident government members, including Spencer Perceval, voted with them; a Commons majority of twenty-eight on the first reading, slumped to four on the second. The Bill was badly mauled in the Lords with a two thirds reduction in the Company's proposed productive capacity. Liverpool dragged himself from his sick-bed to attend; with the Duke of Clarence adding royal dignity to the opposition, the Bill passed by a single vote, and then only through the 'Decency of some Members of the real Opposition' who abstained.[44]

With total attentions riveted on this herculean parliamentary battle, the government took a very crafty step, with the almost surreptitious introduction of a Bill permitting the Lord Mayor to fix bread prices on either flour *or* wheat prices. This could obviate current difficulty with the Assize's precise price-determining mechanism, and more importantly neatly confronted the issue of the escalating divergence between wheat and flour prices. The onus of deciding whether Mark Lane wheat or millers' flour prices were to determine the cost of bread, was deftly deposited with the Lord Mayor. The Bill, piloted through the Commons by George Rose and Liverpool's son, attracted no attention and was on the statute book by 30 June, while debates still raged round the London Flour Company Bill.[45]

During the first season of the 1799–1801 famine, government tentatively started to legislate to curb wheat consumption in moves which began to confront the deeply entrenched vested interests of the metropolitan trade. The ban on fresh bread sales was said to have reduced metropolitan consumption by a sixth; infringers were fined, and a Bill indemnifying bakers forced to supply fresh bread to troops on the march was needed.[46] If other savings derived principally from the soup-kitchens, retrenchment policies had had a qualified success. Ministers remained divided over the issue of compulsion; some thought that the government had already gone too far. Others thought a proper balance had already been achieved; Portland held that all practical measures 'for obviating the consumption . . . have been resorted to under the sanction of the Legislature', and that 'all resources . . . in the power of Government are wholly exhausted'. A handful, led by Liverpool, were convinced that further statutory initiatives must not be ruled out. Several MPs agreed at least with interventionist programmes; Addington wanted the tithe lifted on potatoes, and Wilberforce advanced statutory proposals to expand arable cultivation. Indeed ministers had had to resist backbench pressure for legislation to force poor-law authorities to relieve in cereal substitutes. If Lord Sheffield bitterly resented 'the refusal of the Legislature to inforce any management' in the interests of retrenchment, he was assured of some parliamentary and ministerial support which might increase dramatically when famine reappeared after the 1800 harvest.[47]

CHAPTER 13

'Brown George'

Compulsion Versus Vested Interests, September 1800 to July 1801

Immediate recourse to retrenchment programmes after the 1800 harvest was bedevilled by several major factors. First, a very uneven response to the policy during the 1799–1800 season was revealed by the survey, conducted at government behest by the clergy and local officials when making their harvest returns. It was once again very difficult to disentangle the closely inter-related effects of market pressures, the policies of charity and poor-law administrators, and the combinations of arbitrary enforcement and exemplary approaches of the grandees and their subordinate close associates. The former was possibly the main source of a marked adoption and recourse to barley in the North, which was so pronounced as to be remembered by Samuel Bamford as 'Barley Days'. Rice too encroached on customary northern dietaries. It was ascribed to upper and middle-class example, but it is probable that its successes in oat-regions owed much to the similarity of preparation; however, complications arose as 'the poor after eating rice are soon very hungry'. Rice was a major ingredient of the poor's soup, but grandee panegyrics never overcame popular prejudices against rice in wheat-eating districts. The survey may have given ministers qualified support in the relevance of retrenchment, but the historian able to examine the administrative records of poor-law officials is more impressed by experimentation with Speenhamland-type scales, and much more commonly, the extention of static wage/family cash supplements. All bar three of the thirty-three returns from Sussex parishes at the heart of Lord Sheffield's country revealed regular supplementary cash payments, and more to cover the cost of fuel, clothes and rent; these all facilitated recipients' expenditure on finer grades of wheat. Seven parishes sold subsidised fine flour, but only six coarser varieties. Certainly, the measures taken during the 1799–1800 season had been unequal to launch the desired dietary revolution.[1]

Nevertheless, the imposition of retrenchment ideology was sufficiently powerful to have galvanised fierce popular reactions in hundreds of localities. The poetic rejection of soup and coarse bread, coupled with demands for subsidised fine wheaten, addressed 'To the Broth Makers and flower Risers' of Maldon, Essex, encompasses many plebeian feelings on the subject:

> On Swill and Grains you wish the Poor to be fed. . .
> The Hogs rise up in judgment for eating of their food
> While you Puffed up Gentry eat the Best of what is good
> But we will make your Windows fly likewise your Doors Indeed
> Unless half a crown a peck the flour our poor Children for to feed
> Here's a hint upon many you all know very well
> I mean your Broth [sub]scribers for you'l all surley go to hell
> Had you but Consented to let us had the flour
> We should [have] all a Reasons to have blessed you every hour
> So now to conclude we shant at this time say anymore
> For our Determination is that we will have the flour
> Our children cry for Whitebread there Belleys for to feed. . . .

At Romsey soup provoked popular demands for 'what they call their natural food'. Parliamentary support for retrenchment may have been woefully inadequate in Lord Sheffield's view, but it served, notably through the 'Stale Bread Act' to indict the edifice of the state in more politically-advanced plebeian eyes: a Birmingham poster protested,

> Will ye English fools have Billy Pitt for a God, & starve you in the midst of Plenty cant You smell the fustey Bread Blood for supper, Damnation serve Pitt & George, & all the name of such varmin, down with them.

Hostility was aggravated by unpragmatic utterances by local retrenchment enthusiasts, including the Devon farmer who had the temerity to say 'that Barley Bread & Tatoes was good enough for the poor'. He was dubbed 'Mr. Great Carcass' and death threats followed: 'God sent Meat into the World for us Poor as well as Rich'. Soup, stale and coarser breads, were unacceptable; they threatened the social fabric. The Essex doggerel clearly indicates that whereas orthodox charitable aid reinforced deference, the new modes reversed the process: the social hierarchy could not be legitimised by gruel.[2]

Recipients' reactions were one cause of growing disenchantment among the philantrophic. The revealing struggle which engulfed Malton, Earl Fitzwilliam's pocket borough, when he tried to relaunch the soup kitchen in December, derived from the previous season's experiences. Most recipients reputedly gave their soup to their pigs, but hostility was extended to the borough shopkeepers and merchants who had subscribed to the charity; they flatly refused to repeat the exercise at a stormy public meeting, where they were only just persuaded by the Earl's resident agent to subsidise coarse as opposed to fine wheaten bread. This failed to head off the Earl who exploded: 'I cannot subscribe my Money to get for the People of Malton, as full a Meal of Bread as they are accustom'd to in plentiful years'. Here lay the rub for subscribers in fact looked to Fitzwilliam for a substantial contribution; if he wanted soup, he could have both the privilege of paying for it and the odium for supplying the stuff. The poor eventually had soup and fish, and most of the cost fell on Fitzwilliam with previous subscribers paying nothing or derisory sums. Those beyond the pale of Fitzwilliam's proprietoral grasp magnanimously supplied their employees with subsidised fine wheat. What proved to be the chaotic shifts and turns, reversals and sudden advances in government policy also helped to create situations like this. Lord Sheffield had some justification for his view that the lack of ministerial and parliamentary consistency before July 1800 had discouraged 'those who indeavoured to establish economy', and that they 'will not make further exertions'.[3]

The nature of the September 1800 hypercrisis militated strongly against the economy ideal. Consumption centres bore the brunt of very real shortages, and if some survived by increasing poor-law payments and charitable endeavours, others, including Worcester, Doncaster and Sheffield, hurriedly funded community purchases of bulk grain supplies.[4] The immediate reaction in towns of all sizes, and even in some country villages, was to facilitate workers' purchases of normal dietaries. Retrenchment was not forgotten completely; it was advocated by some press correspondents,[5] reiterated by some Benches,[6] and implemented by some charities and poor-law authorities.[7] It surfaced in renewed campaigns for soup-kitchen subscriptions.[8] But this comprised but a superficial resumption of retrenchment, not least because a powerful consensus of public opinion held that the scarcity was wholly artificial, and this operated strongly against suggestions that relief could, and more importantly should be obtained through substitute foods. The broad-based crisis of confidence in Pitt's government which grew directly and speedily, alienated many thousands of locally influential people from all past ministerial programmes. The government itself was partially paralysed. The Home Secretary retained the energy to privately make an 'indispensable condition' of his personal gift of £300 to a fund raised in his home county of Nottinghamshire, that it must be spent on obtaining corn for sale at prime, not subsidised, costs to impoverished consumers. But publicly he retreated, typically informing the Birmingham Bench

that when an Evil of this Nature is treated as one that is subject to our Control . . . it is arrogating that to ourselves which does not belong to the limited means possessed by human Individuals.

Even after Pitt capitulated to public opinion with an emergency recall of parliament, sources close to the government affirmed privately that 'Recommendation to be economical is all that could be expected' from the legislature; ministers 'mean to appoint an open committee, but have nothing to propose in it, and look to no measure from it'.[9]

This torpor was reflected in the three weeks which elapsed before the committee reported, and in its simplistic advocacy of reduced cereal consumption by the wealthy. Ministerial insecurity and loss of credibility extended to many MPs: to ensure 'the greatest weight and solemnity to such a recommendation' requests were formally orchestrated from both houses to invoke the king's personal authority through the issue of a Royal

Proclamation 'for this purpose'. Its broadest circulation, 'from the most populous city, to the smallest village' would 'engage the serious Attention of the various Classes'. The Foxite opposition acquiesced; members were joining ministers in parliamentary panegyrics on the virtues of free trade, and unusual unity was unbroken at this nervous stage. Formal protocol by contrast was shattered inadvertantly in the hurry, leaving Portland to deluge the monarch with sycophantic apologies, while the king's printer was ordered to print thousands of Proclamation copies for instant metropolitan circulation before George had even seen the text. Speed also generated ambiguity. The Proclamation's categoric appeal to people 'who have the means of procuring' cereal substitutes was compromised by that to 'all Masters of Families' who were equally urged to cut bread consumption by a third 'and in no Case to suffer' levels 'to exceed one Quartern Loaf for each Person in each Week'. In contrast to the committee's statement, the king appeared to be extending that limit to every subject. The Proclamation was immediately derided. The *Hull Advertizer* was soon campaigning against plebeian claims that the royal statement was irrelevant because the price of a Quartern per person was beyond workers' means, to stress that this injunction was addressed solely to the affluent. The *Norwich Chronicle* detected Jacobin opportunism behind rumours designed 'to distress the feelings of the poor'. Nevertheless, in many circles the Proclamation was 'treated . . . with the utmost levity and ridicule'.[10]

Parliamentary unity and the containment of the feared insurrection in the Midlands by saturating the region with troops,[11] restored some confidence, and ministers began to plan more stringent measures. Pitt personally toyed with a ban on wheaten flour production, in favour of enforced mixture of two thirds wheat and one third barley. Subsequent reports from both houses added propaganda to substitute advocacy; the normal currency of non-wheaten breads had been greatly extended by the crisis. Maize formed 'a considerable part of the food of all classes . . . in America'. The Lords published 'Minute detail' in the form of recipes for various uses of potatoes, peas, rice and maize, as the relevant 'knowledge . . . is not yet universally diffused'. Soups using 'the cheaper parts of beef and mutton' with rice produced a good pottage for 'labourers'. Other interests were pandered to, including poor-rate payers': poor relief in the form of soup could reduce costs by over sixty percent. The Lords also claimed in passing that the monarch's 'solemn call' was addressed 'to all classes'; moreover, in their second report the Lords advanced a ban on wheat flour finer than something rougher than Standard Wheaten.[12]

The Commons committee's first report had urged poor relief in wheat substitutes as cash payments permitted recipients to 'purchase . . . bread to the usual amount'. Pitt wanted legal enforcement, and early on delivered a pre-emptive strike against probable criticism by alleging that many JPs had already achieved it. In fact he was concerned at the lack of magisterial powers. If the Commons committee subsequently eschewed 'a peremptory rule', it advocated giving magistrates compulsory powers for use where possible. Petty Sessions were to evaluate local situations to see if relief in cereal substitutes was possible, and then report their findings to special Quarter Sessions, where unfavourable analyses would be re-evaluated. The

order for the Bill immediately threatened parliamentary harmony. Privately, Fox in secession argued that the way to 'teach . . . the poor . . .
economy' was to aid in cash;

> when they find that by buying rice etc instead of wheat, they can put a
> penny in their pockets, they will of course do it. That is if it is really as
> good for them as supposed.

Fox supported 'voluntary economy', not the 'abominable . . . compulsive
adoption of a new sort of food' which would provoke disturbances. The
opposition represented these proposals as a full-frontal assault on plebeian
John Bull; it removed the poor's legitimate 'discretional power' to spend as
they wished; it forced 'inferior food' down unwilling throats, nullifying
prejudices, preferences and rights. Ministerial spokesmen accordingly
emphasised that the proposed statute was an enabling Act, not a compulsory one, and fancifully imagined that it 'allowed the magistrates to consult
the feelings and prejudices of the people in each parish'. The proposal was
weakened to permit the Bench to force overseers to pay up to one third of
relief per claimant in cereal substitutes. It became law as the 'Act for the
Better Provision for the Poor and for Diminishing the Consumption of
Bread Corn' on 22 December 1800, and represented a step in the direction
of compulsory enforcement of retrenchment policy.[13]
Simultaneously, fish supplies and consumption were increased by new
legislation. Acts permitting the duty-free importation of Newfoundland
fish, exempting salt used in fish-curing from tax, bestowing immunity for
fishermen from the press-gang, and suspending export bounties on whiting
and pilchards, followed. If exaggerated calculations of the resultant increase
in the nation's aggregate food supply also followed, parliament confronted
the financial restraints with the provision of £50,000 to fund the creation of
fish depots at the major ports. Volunteer administrations were to publicise
the scheme and to distribute stocks throughout their hinterlands, especially
to poor-law authorities, eager to secure cheap provisions. The Hull
committee was advertising economical dried fish, and stressing that they
made good meal when ground with dried potatoes or rice, as early as 22
December.[14]
The Act prohibiting the sale of fresh wheaten bread was re-enacted on 15
December. Ministers then took one more, but ill-fated step, the most
aggressive to date. The Commons committee's fourth report, available for
MPs on 17 December, confirmed categorically that retrenchment through
'measures of permission and recommendation' had failed. A massive saving
of 450,000 quarters of wheat was calculated if wheaten flour finer than a
type containing the bran, and therefore greatly inferior to Standard
Wheaten, was banned. New Assize tables were promised, but the ban came
into operation before these were established, so the new product went on
sale without price control. Fox warned his partisans against supporting the
measure, confident that it would be repealed. In the event the opposition
remained largely mute, and the Bill was rushed through in five days before
the short Christmas recess. Ministerial supporters congratulated themselves
on the classless nature of the Act. Pitt stated that this was the ultimate

measure in the retrenchment programme; in the absence of compulsion 'no good could result'. The Brown Bread Act was to operate between 1 February and 6 November 1801.[15]

It proved an immediate and abysmal failure on its implementation throughout the country. It was attacked, most fiercely in the Whig press: in the *Manchester Gazette's* satirical estimation it was

> likely to work WONDER throughout the Kingdom. By some it is whimsically term'd PITTS PURGING PILLS – by others BROWN GEORGE – and it has been cried through the streets of this town by the name of the SCOURING BILL.

Millers instantly took advantage. A Somerset miller actually sold bean flour as wheaten made according to the new law. In Hertfordshire farmer Carrington recorded that the millers 'mix much bad wheat with it'; no wonder 'it is not liked of'. In Sussex 'unadulterated' coarse brown flour was unobtainable, and 'the dissatisfaction which prevails . . . from the compulsory use . . . is greatly aggravated by its admixture, adulteration and extreme high price'. The colour clearly facilitated adulteration. Sir Thomas Turton who confronted rebellious consumers, confirmed that the bread samples produced by the protesters 'were extremely indifferent . . . disagreeable to the taste'; he had no intention of personally testing allegations that eating it produced 'bowelly complaints'. If London millers secretly adulterated this flour, they succeeded. They certainly used only the very best wheat, probably through fear of the metropolitan proletariat; poorer grades of wheat, including most imports, found outlets only elsewhere in the south-east where London surpluses were customarily sent in the form of poorer quality flour. Use of inferior wheat may explain the cause of greater, more militant popular reactions in the south-east, which were principally confined to Surrey, Sussex and Kent, and mixed with complaints over the price and inadequate relief levels. At Icklesham the Act led to a six-week break in the assiduous vestry's mixed-meal supply, at the expense of considerable additional friction, revealed principally by a battery of new and draconian rules against poor-law claimants who refused to 'Eat and make use of the' flour 'as it comes from the Mill', and the necessity for the installation of new anti-theft devices to the parish stores.[16] The Act was certainly repealed speedily, with formalities allegedly forced on the monarch during his February 1801 bout of madness. Ministers, most of whom were in the process of resigning, were gravely embarrassed; they said that foreign grain could not be milled in this way, and reverted to the old claim that coarser flour simply increased the amount of bread eaten. Lord Sheffield said that the Act's sole defect was non-provision against adulteration.[17]

Voluntary retrenchment, the aim of both parliamentary reports and the Royal Proclamation, had its by now customary response, ostensibly favourable but with shortcomings in practice. The usual range of bodies came to favourable resolutions, especially endorsement of the weekly quartern loaf per head limit. Patriots promised abstention from pies and pastries, and at Halifax from dinner parties too.[18] Recipes for soups were swopped between relatives, and even among stage-coach passengers. Some vestries reversed earlier decisions to subsidise workers' bread on receipt of the Proclamation, and the Faringdon vestry publicly waded through one parliamentary report and promptly ordered consignments of herrings from Bristol and London.[19] Big urban soup-kitchens achieved impressive distributions, in part reflecting the scale of poverty, but also developing administrative expertise where 1800–1 was their third or fourth season. The Leeds institution distributed 33,572 quarters of 'creed rice' and 270 barrels of herrings, in addition to 20,000 quarts of soup. Other towns including Oxford and Maidstone had their first experience of lengthy queues of pot-carrying supplicants. In Yorkshire Sir George Cook added two-thousand pounds of rice to his traditional Christmas gifts of an ox and bread to the poor of Bentley. Loyal churchwardens in the Cornish parish of St. Stephen-in-Branwell piously spent four shillings on 'different prayers for to desire people to live with economy in their families to prevent a famine'. Public refusals among the rich to adhere to community engagements were rare though the Moreton vestry in Essex added a rider to members' minuted agreement to cut their wheat consumption by a third, recording that 'George White of the Wood Farmer refused to adopt any measure of Oeconomy either to himself or family'. On the vicar's recital of the Proclamation from the pulpit at Bramfield the parish clerk cried out 'Burn the Paper', and when rebuked, retorted that the document originated not with George III but his ministers, '"a set of fellows & pickpockets"': the entire village joined in the joke, none more fervently than the churchwardens, much to his reverence's chagrin.[20]

The revival of voluntary retrenchment in late 1800 revealed the uneven real commitment to the ideal soon to be reflected in the reception of the Parochial Relief Act of December 1800. Ministers were again in retreat, and most were soon embroiled in the confusion generated by Pitt's resignation and the king's illness. Portland who survived, as yet, at the Home Office, abrogated responsibility for the Act's implementation, which was decidedly left to local administrations. Portland explained to the senior Mancunian magistrate Bayley on 6 April 1801:

> I need not remind you of the manner in which both Houses of Parliament have occupied themselves for the purposes of alleviating the Distresses of the lower orders . . . or refer you to the constant exertions of their Endeavours to the same Effect, as you may be assured that no means will be left untried by them to afford Relief, but by the Members of Administration no such Expectations can be held out, nor will their situation allow them to interfere in this respect but in their Capacity as Members of the Legislature.[21]

Portland promulgated the ideal privately,[22] but publicly the Home Office was occupied with public order, and the revitalised democratic movement. Even after the spectacular revolt of the South-west in the spring of 1801, ministers left implementation of the Act to authority on the spot, with the exception of the odd hint respecting the availability of fish. In the case of Devon this meant that Lord Lieutenant Earl Fortescue was left to orchestrate its tardy adoption.[23]

The Parochial Relief Act was anticipated in certain parishes,[24] but the special Quarter Sessions arrangements were the key determinant across the country. Some Benches did consult widely; in Hertfordshire farmer Carrington treked to St. Albans for 'a meeting of the justices and all overseers to consider what substitute instead of wheat bread for the poor, or to save Wheat as much as possible'.[25] This wording implies an informed debate, and where such procedures permitted those who would form the implementatory vanguard to voice their nervous apprehensions, even autocratically-inclined magisterial enthusiasts may have had second thoughts. There are interpretative problems with the evidence,[26] and the press almost religiously eschewed comment on procedures in the districts served, irrespective of the Act's implementation or not. The difficulties confronting favourable and vigorous Sessions' chairmen, can be seen in the response by thirty-three parishes to Lord Sheffield's Sussex Bench; only one proposed any alteration to deeply-entrenched relief programmes, and very few others intended to pay even lip-service to the Act. Only grandee-dominated Petworth really entered into the required spirit, where

> they think an improved handmill to grind wheat at a public soop establishment and Oven to bake coarse bread a Shop for the Sale of rice Herrings or other articles . . . may be established with Success at the Expense of the Parish so as to relieve the necessatious poor.

In Nottinghamshire the Thurgarton Petty Sessions ambitiously ordered all parishes to publicly fund cattle fattening; the meat with rice and potatoes, were to be retailed to poor-law claimants. In stark contrast, JPs for the Williton Division of Somerset, represented hostile administrations; idiosyncratic only in their bluntness, they reported

> the general dislike we found with the Poor to entertain against being compelled to take any part of their Relief in any other than the usual way. And we have found it much better to leave the Poor . . . to their own choice of food concluding that they would be well disposed to lay out the Parish relief & their own earnings to the best advantage.[27]

The implementation of the Act mirrors these extremes. It was easier to administer in villages than in towns, and it was seized on by some parishes in the so-called 'Speenhamland' counties, where structured wage supplements proved exceedingly expensive, to cut costs. One Oxfordshire division ordered relief paid in 'shop goods'; a family of eight in previous receipt of 11/6 per week, now received fifteen pounds of rice, four of cheese, two of bacon, and some 'coarse sugar . . . for rice', which cost ratepayers less than seven shillings. The Berkshire Bench maintained pressure on defaulting parishes for returns, and eventually a majority in most divisions claimed to be supplying wheat-substitutes, coarse beef, rice, herrings, barley and peas; where claims can be checked with parochial accounts they prove to be accurate. But parochial compliance often turned on unremittant judicial vigilance. On 15 January 1801 the Norfolk Sessions ordered parochial returns, and adjourned until 11 February. The seventeen justices attending then instructed parishes not enforcing the Act to reconsider, and re-adjourned for a month. Then but seven magistrates convened, and restricted their orders to insist on returns from such parishes as had made none. Only one did so to the two JPs present at that adjournment, and the full Bench at the Easter General Sessions concluded that the Act had 'been Executed . . . as far as Circumstances will admit'.[28]

Oxfordshire, Berkshire and Norfolk were primarily rural counties. The Act's implementation in towns posed mammoth problems, some of which proved insoluble even by herculean efforts. Retrenchment in the larger already proceeded through the soup-kitchens. Such was Birmingham's case; the overseers protested that they had nearly ten-thousand weekly claimants, for whom 'Substitutes . . . in Lieu of Money' were administratively 'impracticable'. Massive purchases of the County Bench's suggested substitutes, rice and potatoes, would drive local prices to prohibitive heights. The measure's unpopularity could easily turn current high social tensions into a fierce revolt. Similar points were made at Newcastle-upon-Tyne and Norwich, though the Court of Guardians at the latter had not shrunk from forcing substitutes down that minority of their charges residing in the workhouse.[29]

Elsewhere a combination of genuine difficulties, notably over the availability of substitutes, and various obstructive tactics, compromised the Act's effectiveness. The latter includes justices in Lower Bramber, West Sussex, who advanced 'the plainess of our understandings' as an excuse for inaction, and some Warwickshire overseers who 'had rather pay the money than give themselves any trouble about the Poor'. The Staffordshire Bench even resorted to newspaper adverts to pressurise recalcitrant colleagues into attendance on the Bench, a device used by one Petty Sessions to intimidate obdurate absentee overseers. Stafford Borough Sessions recorded 'many unsuccessful and abortive attempts' to implement the Act, and relief payments in cash clearly predominated throughout the county. Relief schemes reported by the Warwickshire press did not conform to the Act, and flatly contradicted the confident formal minutes of the County Bench. Perhaps pride of place ought to go to Clitheroe vestrymen who decreed on 5 April 1801 'that the Overseer shall . . . give the preference to Paupers whether they shall have Relief in Money or Rye Bread'.[30]

The government likewise scored a qualified success with fish distribution schemes. Committees at Plymouth and Exeter invited applications from the parishes, but if the latter was accredited publicly for having 'furnished comfortable meals to thousands of poor families', its records prove that they were principally domiciled in the county town. A handful of rural authorities made token purchases, but the most favourable had already contracted for experimental consignments of Cornish pilchards. Large quantities supplied through Hull and Liverpool were eaten across the North. Earl Fitzwilliam encouraged trials in West Riding centres, and ordered client authorities at Malton and Wentworth Woodhouse to do so. Many soup-kitchens, including the mammoth Soho establishment, supplied herrings, and new subscriptions to finance supplies were collected at Stockport as late as May 1801. Disappointments with rotten consignments occurred, including one of 50,000 which reached mountainous Saddle-worth, high up in the Pennines. Elsewhere local authorities commonly capitulated to popular prejudices against fish, especially in non-coastal regions. The scheme had cost the Treasury over £9000 by May, and the extra demand stimulated a three hundred percent rise in Scottish prices; fishermen were said to have made fortunes.[31]

Finally, renewed fierce resistance from plebeian consumers was not restricted to the 'Brown George' fiasco, but extended to every facet of retrenchment and its enforcers. The contents of the vicar of Bideford's Christmas sermonising, and the conflict generated by the distortions to traditional charities and orthodox relief under the poor law, were vividly reflected in the appropriately Christian-inspired Yuletide response, anonymously written by a dissident member of his flock:

> Mr Parson this is to let you know you had better read no more about pinching our Bellis on shoe Lowrance of Bread, you had better open your heart and shew more Generosity about the Poor and preach Charity instead of pinchin Bellis or else you wish some more sutch Starve poor Pinch Gut fellows have your House down about your Ears. . . . This is the first Notice.

Another attempted to divide the local oligarchy with praise of the Mayor's past generosity, coupled with a warning against conspiring with 'that ungenerous Clergyman that wants to starve the poor'. The political origins of retrenchment, and its attempted implementation through the state's hierarchial governmental machine, was another vehicle for Jacobin politicisation and terrorist threats. The constable of Wakefield was just one local official who experienced both with the receipt of a note damning

> King George the third and Billy Pitt may hell be their portion for ever and ever down your Red herrins Potatoes and you all that have anything to do with it . . . damn your eyes the devil if you stint us to a quartern loaf.

The idea of fighting the Earl Fitzwilliams, Lord Sheffields, *and* the ancestors of Ned Ludd and Captain Swing, to confront eventually perhaps an English Robespierre, was too daunting for thousands represented by the Williton JPs, Bramfield parish officials, and farmer 'White of the Wood'. Clitheroe workers had probably never seen, let alone subsisted, on rye bread; these were dangerous expedients. But they were in their way highly appropriate for a nation locked in a war not just for global economic supremacy, but for the survival of traditional society, orthodoxly unequal distributions of wealth, and the political oligarchy which constituted the English ancien régime. In the context of stated French war aims, international and internal revolutionary plottings, and intense social unrest, the fact that ultimately so many who had so much to lose from the implementation of the type of Jacobin philosophy readily available in editions of the *Rights of Man* and *Agrarian Justice*, were unconvinced that national survival hinged on Pitt's perception of national subsistence, is remarkable. For many were opting, especially in 1800–1, for neutrality in what was increasingly seen as a burgeoning showdown between the English proletariat and the 'Farmers and Engrossers' allied to the 'Cursed Statesmen & their Crew' of 'pick-pockets'. This suggests that there were serious inadequacies in communications between government, the state, and society. It is to this last facet of Pitt's performance in times of famine to which we must now turn.[32]

CHAPTER 14

Public Relations

the State and Society, and Famine

The government's experiences with importation, substitution and retrenchment, proved that if pragmatism conditioned the evolution of ministerial
policies, major problems revolved round the state's relationship with
society; *communication* was central. Debate on famine's origins was continuous, but at key moments, notably the summer of 1795, the spring of
1800, and above all the autumn which commenced with the following
September hypercrisis, 'public opinion' principally subscribed to notions of
'moral economy'. This popular analysis generated serious economic, social
and ultimately political problems for Pitt. The 'moral economy's' remedies
were imposed by the crowd and threatened public order. Secondly,
whether backed or not by local authorities, these measures comprised a
recipe for economic disaster. Thirdly, the ultimate extension of the
arguments inherent in the populist code, *in certain circumstances*, was that the
crises were produced by human artifice, which inevitably spawned the
claim of 'artificial scarcity'. Fourthly, the adoption of such views by those
on whom law and order depended, eroded their will to function as
governors of local communities. The Rev. A.B. Haden, a Staffordshire
magistrate, was idiosyncratic only in unequivocal statements made to the
Home Secretary. 'As a Conservator of the Peace', Haden wrote in 1800,

> I shall always stand forward to protect it, but I can never attempt it, at the
> hazard of my Life, for enriching one part of the Community and
> supporting them in the most glaring Acts of Oppression at the Expense
> of the Comforts, Happiness and even the Existence of the other.

Volunteer officers were similarly inclined: they too 'never intended to give
Security to the inhuman Oppressor, whilst the Poor are Starving'.[1]
  The 'moral economy' directly stimulated violent populist intervention
while simultaneously weakening community resolve to contain disorder.
Pitt's prescriptions for national survival, food distribution through free-
market mechanisms, and retrenchment, turned on acceptance of the reality

of scarcity by those who governed locally. In this quest the government utilised laissez faire ideology, bolstered by constitutional considerations pivoting on the sanctity of private property, to construct a theoretical legitimisation of its remedial measures. If local authorities could be persuaded to accept this logic behind increasingly unpopular policies, their influence could be deployed in the interests of implementation and recognition of necessity across the broadest social spectrum. If not, famine conditions were unreal, and untraditional remedies were superfluous.

The blockade of midsummer 1795 comprised the first major challenge to free trade and seriously jeopardised distribution of government corn. If government departments consistently refused to bow to local pressures for intervention in the grain trade,[2] the Privy Council declined to formally restate official policy when it first discussed food rioting in March 1795. Before June, Home Office instructions merely demanded the immediate and effective suppression of disturbances.[3] However, on 26 June the Privy Council rejected Sussex petitions demanding an end to coastal corn shipments in order to conserve local stocks; petitioners were told that 'even if such a power did reside' with government, 'it would not be prudent to exercise it'. A rationale on free-trade principles was appended. It was reiterated in most subsequent Home Office letters on the topic as the blockade intensified. Authorities like those in Birmingham who suffered the worst effects were also informed that the blockade illegally prevented 'an equal Distribution of the present stock for the relief of those Counties which are most in want'.[4]

Eventually, on 22 July, army escorts were provided for corn shipments passing through the worst affected districts. Because JPs were supporting some stoppages, the Lord Lieutenants were circularised and instructed to impress the illegality of such action on their judicial subordinates, and that such action merely exacerbated problems elsewhere to further jeopardise social stability. Ministers appreciated that demands in support of public order would evoke greater sympathy than insistence on self-denial by those in better-stocked regions in the interests of the severely pressed. Some JPs whose illegal actions came to specific Home Office notice were written to directly, including the Mayor of Bristol and the Rev. Knollis of Burford. However, the army was more instrumental than these communications in putting grain in motion for the hard-pressed Midlands. Every form of Whitehall intervention generated serious friction between central and local authorities. The appearance of unsolicited troops in Oxfordshire, sent to overthrow popular embargoes, suggested that *government* was forcibly moving stocks, an interpretation shared by the Bench. The Lord Lieutenant of Northamptonshire, the Duke of Grafton, was also infuriated and frustrated: 'In many parishes', he fumed, 'poor families have not been able to procure bread for their Money'. The Bench was

> indeavoring to relieve them by every means . . . but . . . all our Efforts
> will prove ineffectual; if it should be true, what is circulated here, but
> which I will not believe, that some wealthy farmers are to be supported
> by a military force, in conveying from hence the Corn, we would be
> happy to pay for, Even at the unconscienable Price, at which . . . some of

our shamefully interested Farmers have sold it for at a Distance.

If true Grafton expected Home Secretary Portland to countermand the orders for military intervention. Ministers were unmoved, though not unapprehensive; Hawkesbury advised an immediate response, to include categoric 'support' for the 'principles' government 'has hitherto avowed'.[5]

Such reactions convinced ministers that tolerance of Home Office intervention had its limits, be they ill-defined. If the army's role preserved the populations of Birmingham and Leicester from famine in the summer of 1795, the improved national position in the autumn meant that stocks detained in a further outbreak of blockading, in East Anglia, were not so desperately needed, and army escorts were not sent in. Where possible, Portland reacted cautiously even over the summer. He refused to sanction an Oxfordshire justice's request for intervention against farmers who agreed not to sell stocks out of their parish. The Woodstock baker who claimed that he lost a valuable contract through the Rev. Knollis's arbitrary actions was told to seek redress in the civil courts. The Home Office eschewed greater responsibility; 'the notice given by Government' to the Lord Lieutenants, 'was by way of caution only'. The government was walking a tightrope, but however warily ministers trod, they emerged from the summer of 1795 fully committed to free trade in the home market.[6]

Recurrent blockading was but one of the government's problems once the crisis extended into the autumn. Price rises served principally to generate considerable public scepticism at the reality of deficiencies, and ministers came under pressure to adopt remedies enshrined in the 'moral economy'. September however saw ministers concede inadequate yields, and the necessity for imports and retrenchment. Public opinion had to be manipulated to accept deficiency, and hence the need. But reactions to past substitution and free-trade policies proved that ministerial perceptions of remedial imperatives were socially and therefore politically explosive. Every facet of policy initially depended on establishing proof of a substandard wheat harvest; ministers could then demonstrate that this caused inflation. Much unsolicited information reached Whitehall, but for every informant who identified agrarian origins, two more saw machinations by farmers, millers and merchants. No consensus was possible from such evidence, yet the government's case required consensus based on substantive facts. Between 20 and 24 October major merchants and millers from London and the Home Counties were formally examined. Agreement that deficient wheat crops were partially compensated for by abundant barley and oats was achieved, but the testimony of such interested parties was open to scepticism. On 24 October ministers belatedly decided to channel local information through the Lord Lieutenants. Through County Benches they were

> to procure an account of the produce of the several articles of grain comparing the same with the produce of a fair crop of every such article of grain in common years and with the produce of the crop of 1794.

A less scientific or statistical method cannot be imagined, nor one so open to ambiguity, but the extraction of more precise evidence erected the hoary problem of compulsion. This was adamantly rejected by Pitt; it would infuriate and alarm. He naively imagined that 'such general information as magistrates can furnish from their observation and inquiry' would suffice. There was no time to seek inquisitorial powers, which might further inflate prices, and would certainly be represented as a further infringement of liberty, inconceivable when ministers were on the threshold of defending past and advocating further subsistence policies, and drafting the notorious Gagging Bills.[7]

The magistracy's survey took too much time to be incorporated in the Commons select committee's first report on 16 November. While admitting the insufficiency of replies received, the committee concluded from members' private sources of information and that coming from the corn trade, that the 1795 wheat crop was lighter than that of 1794 (itself ten to twenty percent deficient), and no more than seventy-five to eighty percent of an average crop. Barley and oats were up to twenty percent above average. By 9 December, the date of the committee's third and final report, the bulk of the returns were in, but they were incomplete; compiled 'upon so many different principles', they prohibited any meaningful comparisons and aggregations, so the committee resorted to reiterating the first report's estimations. If parliament effectively confirmed ministerial perceptions of deficiencies, it all rested on inconclusive, inauspicious evidence.[8]

Parliamentary endorsement of ministers' past and continuing commitment to free-trade principles was also sought, together with support to politically strengthen the cabinet's determination to resist public pressures for interventionist policies commensurate with 'moral-economy' tenets. Ministers had concluded that current economic conditions alone dictated caution when evaluating rumours of commercial 'combinations', to which 'too many' people were 'always ready' to impute rising prices. However political expediency required a specific investigation, and grain traders were summoned to be asked the single question, 'Have you any Idea of the Supply of Wheat being withheld from the Market in Consequence of Combination?'. Although these witnesses were interviewed individually in the interests of 'candid' responses, they were hardly pressed. Cornfactor Breeze typically opined that 'I have no such Idea: I believe the Thing to be impossible'. These men agreed that 'rich Farmers will of course keep up their Wheat in Expectation of high Prices', but there was no suggestion of malpractices here; indeed this was commensurate with free-market economics, and of importance in ministerial eyes in spreading the release and sale of the available stock throughout the season. Hawkesbury did follow up complaints of fraudulent practices made by correspondents; and these were diplomatically inserted in the Privy Council's published *Minutes* covering all aspects of subsistence policies since January 1795. But this was primarily an exercise in political and public relations.[9]

The question of MPs' satisfaction remained. The Foxite opposition was pre-occupied with resisting the Treason and Seditious Meetings Bills. The Whigs' prime contribution to solving subsistence problems lay in Whitbread's agricultural wages Bill. Its failure is customarily attributed to Pitt's promise to introduce a similarly motivated, but much more ambitious scheme to reform the poor relief system. The fact that Whitbread's proposal would have militated decisively against the government's retrenchment policy is invariably overlooked. Empowering magistrates to fix wages according to the price of bread would have stabilised the purchasing power of agrarian wages and their principal expenditure on wheat. If the Whigs hoped to force Pitt to admit that his policies also eroded sturdy plebeian independence through increased reliance on the poor rate, and reduced the quality of workers' diets, they failed.[10] The Foxite leadership had no interest in exploiting popular empathy to grain producers and merchants. They were concerned to portray famine conditions as another price paid for Pitt's ideologically-motivated war. In this they did succeed, and not merely through rhetorical flourishes over 'famine clings to war as plenty does to peace', or by emphasising the scale of destitution with but one head in ten able to feed his household. They wrung an admission of war's contributory role from the prime minister. But whatever the magnitude of differences between the parliamentary sides, both agreed that the scarcity was real and not the product of artifice.[11]

Interventionist populist proposals were entertained by some of Fox's backbenchers, and he implied that it took all his authority to prevent their expression in the House. His failure to discipline the irascible member for Ipswich, Edmund Lechmere, played straight into Pitt's hands on 3 November, the day ministers revealed the full range of contingency plans. Lechmere's contribution facilitated unanimity between the leaders of both sides in support of laissez-faire economics. Lechmere subscribed to a popular notion that rising average sizes of farms encouraged the ascent of highly-capitalised farmers, who used their wealth to conspire to withhold grain. His remedy, a favourite with several pamphleteers, lay in compulsory sales to publicly-owned granaries. Fox seized on the issue, and devoted his superb oratorical powers to a full-blown defence of Smithian economics in land, agriculture, and trade. Pitt concurred, be it more circumspectfully because all his proposed remedies, including the defence of the free-market, required government intervention of sorts. Government had a positive role to play and Pitt admitted it, while acknowledging that it conflicted with his personal economic theory. But this unanimity came at a key stage, with the respective leadership of Pitt and Fox laying to rest the bogey of the artificial scarcity analysis, implicit in any attack on middlemen and farmers. The episode also opened the way for the exoneration of the corn trade by the select committee. In their third report, an analysis was appended in defence of the itinerant corn-jobber; they organised supplies through different markets to consumption centres. Conspiracies between them were simply denied; sheer numbers precluded combinations between farmers. Withholding by big farmers was praised: 'it is well they did, we should otherwise have been quite starved in August'. Many MPs spoke in support of these contentions. The entire parliamentary operation served to venerate the free market and its operators. The producers, distributors and manufacturers, were not only acquitted of populist accusations, but sanctified by this political exercise.[12]

Dismantling the blockade had revealed dangerously imprecise limits to the exercise of executive powers; governmental restatements of the law through the Lord Lieutenants had not established the illegality of populist actions to conserve local stocks, even amongst the judiciary. The reinstatements of local blockades in East Anglia and the Forest of Dean in the autumn were ominous signs that an escalation of this type of action remained a distinct probability at any time over the 1795–6 season. Portland referred some of the letters respecting autumnal blockading to the crown's Law Officers, requesting a definite statement of existing law, and if necessary, codification proposals. In the Officers' estimation, magisterial 'Exertions' were wanting to enforce the law, not new legal provisions. They added a rider, that it could

> perhaps be deemed expedient to pass a new Law with suitable provisions *professedly* for the purpose of protecting the Circulation of Grain . . . and which perhaps it might be prudent to extend to other kinds of Victual.

The government decided that it was; Pitt informed MPs that the illegalities of such obstructions 'had not been understood', and proposed a Bill 'to explain and enforce them'. One MP reported Grand Jurors approaching an Assize judge for a legal opinion 'because some doubts were entertained upon even the right of internal transportation'. The government got its Act but the real reason did not lay in Pitt's parliamentary claim of the inadequacy of existing 'specific penalties'. The actions of food rioters exposed them to many capital charges. The new Act's lesser penalties were designed to encourage prosecutions under it. First offenders on summary conviction could be jailed for one to three months. Recidivism invoked jury trial and transportation penalties. The Act did not repeal any other relevant statute. If the Act facilitated subsequent Home Office communications on the subject, its limitations can be inferred from the Home Secretary's specific orders to Pembroke JPs in March 1796, to remove their prohibition of coastal shipments of corn.[13]

In the highly emotive onslaught on the government on 1 March 1796, Fox failed to prevent some of his more senior supporters from supporting Lechmere's resurrection of the 'artificial scarcity' analysis; shortages were 'mere bugbear', no longer caused by unacceptably affluent farmers, but by monopolistic, conspiratorial millers and dealers. Lechmere advocated the appointment of two corn inspectors for each parish to record every farm's productivity. This was hardly orthodox Whiggery, and perhaps supporting Foxites like Tarleton and General Smith were over-reacting to the recent upsurge in London wholesale prices, shortly before the government flooded the market. Pitt, who was genuinely angry, appealed to MPs' conception of their elevated social status and commensurate economic enlightenment; would they 'lend themselves to confirm vulgar prejudices, to mislead ignorance, and inflame discontent'? Further attempts to reintroduce the subject by Lechmere in April were stifled by the inquoracy of the house, perhaps a ministerial tactic; in May Lechmere conjured the support of ten Whigs, but the imminent end of the session nullified their legislative proposals. Lechmere's crusade served to keep the issue open, and perhaps gave the analysis a veneer of respectability, which reinforced the suspicions of men like Haden. But Lechmere's Commons rump could not reverse the process of parliamentary legitimisation of government policy.[14]

The ministry's commitment to free trade was consistent with the legislation passed over twenty years earlier repealing the sixteenth-century statutory embodiment of the 'moral economy'. It is of course realistic to interpret the overall transition as the 'triumph of the new ideology of political economy', but the government's insistence on free trade was pragmatic rather than doctrinaire. Ministers did not stress the ineptitude of 'moral economy' until its implementation threatened to starve several populous centres, and wreck the government's critical strategy of distributing stocks bought on the world market through the unfettered home market. Moreover, interventionist policies were resorted to, and with 'bounties' indeed extended. If Smithian economics were invoked to support elements of the government's total programme, this was hardly Edward Thompson's 'celestial triumph'; nor was the Duke of Portland a willing 'Temporal Deputy'. He and his cabinet colleagues were precipitated into a crisis of unprecedented magnitude, which presented a severe test for Pitt's government. As Home Secretary, Portland was responsible for communicating ministerial decisions and later policies to those on whom the government depended for the implementation of essentially unpopular measures. No sane politician would welcome such a crisis, however 'wedded to Abstract Notions' as Hawkesbury denoted classical economic ideology. In fact the government deserves some praise for not taking what in the first view might have seemed the easy way out, acquiescing in the implementation of the 'moral economy' and somehow blundering along.[15] The debate occasioned by the 1794–6 famine partly repeated its predecessor following the 1766–7 crisis which ended with the repeal of the statutes against traditional marketing offences. In 1796 the parliamentary leadership committed itself to free trade, but that commitment was neither absolute nor unconditional; the precedents for legislative intervention in 1795–6 were amended and extended significantly in 1800–1, and this proves that Pitt was capable of economic management when it was calculated that effective dividends would accrue. Legislation could increase the supply of food, and by facilitating substitutions wring more sustenance from available stocks. The internal distribution could not be centrally directed and minutely supervised by the tiny administrative departmental staffs of the day. This was the crux of the matter, and indeed is the crux of the whole subject of laissez faire and the state in modern times.

Nevertheless, the 1794–6 crisis recast the problematics of commercial exploitation. Experiences fortified some local authorities' belief that unfair practices were a contributory cause, and the crowd rediscovered artifice with greater conviction. The crisis demonstrated the paramountcy of persuading local officialdom that substandard yields underlay the problems; everything else turned in this acceptance. The procedures developed by the ministry for the necessary exercise in public and political relations was an equally significant legacy of the first crisis. Experiences, some of which were bitter, proved that the parliamentary approach was more effective, and less explosive than statements and directives from executive departments or even the 'non-party' Privy Council. This option was non-existent during the summer of 1795 for parliament was in recess. The so-called

'Temporal Deputy' and his colleagues were anxious to abandon their exclusive policy formation, and opposed to the naked use of executive powers. They sought parliamentary endorsement of their policies, an essential strategy clearly revealed by the reasons behind new legislation to protect the internal food distribution systems. For England's social, administrative and political structure did not readily accommodate positive and autocratic handling by Whitehall, even in the cause of celestial triumphs; politicians were pragmatic animals, and, where possible, they avoided upsetting the delicate equilibrium of state and society.

The government readopted the policies and the strategy used after the 1795 harvest on the recurrence of famine conditions in 1799–1800. The appalling weather in the summer and autumn of 1799 militated powerfully against the 'artificial scarcity' analysis, and the Commons corn committee's reports merely endorsed the established fact of harvest failure. Together with the reiteration of free-trade principles, they provided the government with sound arguments to insist on the speedy suppression of disturbances. Once these became serious in March 1800, Portland primarily feared that popular blockades would aggravate market-place shortages; the Home Office alerted the Volunteers and issued general orders to the army to assist the civil authorities to maintain the flow of provisions. Provincial authorities who questioned the reality of scarcity, or more commonly who believed that prices rose out of all proportion to deficiencies, were lectured by the Home Office on the free-market economics of the supply system, and the unconstitutional aspects in forcing owners to sell their property at imposed prices. Such communications invariably invoked parliamentary authority, enabling the Home Office to portray itself as the custodian of constitutionally-determined policy. Portland's missives were often strongly worded; the Rev. Haden was told that

It would . . . be absurd in the extreme to suppose that what is stated in your letter . . . namely 'that the Poor are Starving in the midst of Plenty' is a matter of fact.[16]

Many remained unconvinced that scarcity was *solely* responsible for price levels prior to the 1800 harvest; their scepticism was reinforced by the apparent imperviousness of the market to the massive importation. Pyrrhonism before the harvest posed relatively few problems for ministers, but the phenomenon of soaring prices and intensified dearth after the harvest transformed public attitudes. Mere cynicism evaporated, to be rapidly replaced by a universal belief in malpractice, a 'pacte de famine'. Parliament was in recess and the executive had to wrestle unaided with what essentially was a redefined version of a long-standing problem. In fact the Home Office was non-plussed too: 'I feel myself at a loss on a subject which eludes investigation and appears at least to submit to no rule', repined under-secretary John King. But these admissions were not made publicly; instead Portland fiercely and fatally adhered to the government's consistent position in spite of the changed calibre of the problem. Indeed, Portland's temper is revealed best by his intended prosecution of one of the king's chaplains, and a nephew of the Bishop of Durham, for publishing an

anti–monopolist tract in October. Portland's tenacity was matched only by
the vigour of his intervention.[17]

In September 1800 magistrates who temporized with rioters were
publicly castigated by Portland. Numerous missives were based on the text
of a letter sent to the town clerk of Nottingham, where the Corporation had
endorsed the crowd's imposition of price controls, and deliberately shifted
the onus of maintaining law and order on to local farmers who were
pressurised into supplying the regulated market. Portland asserted that

> whenever any reduction in the price of a Commodity has been effected by
> intimidation it has never been of any duration, and besides, by having
> things out of their natural and orderly courses, it almost necessarily
> happens that the evil, instead of being remedied returns with increased
> violence.

Popular remedies drawn from the 'moral economy' were counter-
productive; a deficient supply could be rectified only through the mechanisms of the unfettered free market.

> I am satisfied that whenever a scarcity of Provisions exists . . . the only
> means which can lead effectually to obviate it, and to prevent the Grain
> from rising to an excessive price, consist in holding out full security and
> indemnity to all Farmers and other lawful Dealers, who shall bring their
> Corn, or other commodities regularly to market and in giving early
> notice of a determined resolution to suppress at once, and by force, if . . .
> necessary every attempt to impede by open acts of violence, or by
> intimidation, the regular business of the Markets.

Nottingham Corporation was ordered to stop price-fixing and to publicise
their 'determined resolution' to forcibly protect market suppliers.[18]

Portland resorted to unprecedented managerial directives with obdurate
or deeply prejudiced local authorities. Troops were sent to Oxford when
the University authorities reported the capitulation of the city magistracy to
rioters. The army's unannounced arrival infuriated the City Volunteers.
Town clerk Taunton registered a formal complaint, adding that the
enforced reduction in butter prices could not 'be reckoned' a riot. The
Home Office told him that it comprised 'a violent and unjustifiable attack
on property, pregnant with the most fatal consequences to the City'; the
Bench should act accordingly. The troops would be removed only on the
University's request. After mid-September Portland increasingly emphasised the property ideal, demanding a 'religious observance of the respect
. . . due to private property', to deactivate the propertied classes' current
support for popular objectives. Once rioting commenced in London,
Portland resorted to the ultimate instrument, a Royal Proclamation against
riots and significantly 'for the protecting and encouraging the free supply of
the Markets'. The text was also closely based on Portland's letter to
Nottingham.[19]

If Portland calculated that the Proclamation's prestige would rectify the
glaringly obvious inadequacies of ministerial formulations, he was speedily

undeceived. Oxford Corporation launched a legal offensive against traditional marketing offences; Taunton became secretary to the prosecution
committee. Farmers responded by boycotting the market, and Portland
angrily exclaimed that 'if the Corporation . . . was to be deprived of all
manner of food, they could not be put on harder fare than they are'. The
City Bench studiously eschewed intervention against crowds which
stormed the County Jail to liberate prisoners from Banbury and toured
farms in the adjacent countryside.[20] More reports of riots reached the Home
Office, including incidents in South Wales where the magistracy also
acquiesced in crowd-imposed prices. Portland's faith in the Proclamation
evaporated; at the end of September he advised a renewed appeal to the
nation's JPs through 'another circular letter' to the Lord Lieutenants. It was
never sent.[21]

Announcing the cabinet's revocation of a second letter, Portland claimed
that

> The outrages which have been committed have been confined compara-
> tively to so small a proportion of the Kingdom that it appears unneces-
> sary to make an extraordinary call upon the vigilance of the Magistrates
> in those counties where good order has suffered no interruption; and in
> those where disturbances have taken place the accounts which are daily
> received prove that the people are universally returning to a sense of their
> duty.

Portland told the king that published official correspondence had played a
part in 'the restoration of good order'; further formal restatements of
government policy were unnecessary, and counter-productive. 'It may be
most prudent in the present state of things to avoid any step which may
tend to create alarm'. In fact the cabinet had embarked on a campaign to
limit the political damage caused by Portland's heavy-handed intrusions. It
was too late to head off an embarrassingly public confrontation between the
Home Secretary and the Lord Lieutenant of Oxfordshire, the Duke of
Marlborough. The Duke had been ordered to direct military operations
against crowds leaving the jurisdiction of the City of Oxford, and new
mobilisations at Witney. Marlborough had dutifully published the Royal
Proclamation in the local press, but had added an ambiguous rider claiming
that the Oxfordshire disturbances occurred 'at the instigation of mischievous and disloyal Men'. It was also so confidently rumoured that
Marlborough intended to instruct his own farming tenants to market their
corn and observe popular maximums, that he received unsolicited encouragement from the Mayor of Oxford; such a directive would not only
'endear his Grace to everyone', but 'will answer every person', doubtless a
reference to the University Vice-Chancellor, the Secretary of State, and, in
the aftermath of the Royal Proclamation, the king himself. Marlborough's
reply to Portland's letter of 22 September is unfortunately non-extant, but
the tenor of the riposte drafted by the Home Secretary on the 29th, suggests
that Marlborough believed the scarcity to be artificial, and supported the
imposition of price-ceilings. Marlborough's response convinced Portland
that further government action was necessary, not just to reimpose public

order, but to counteract claims emanating from the most prestigious social ranks of agrarian and commercial exploitation. The final version of Portland's rejoinder, sent on the 30th, is of critical significance. To the reiteration of the remedial qualities of the free market, Portland added a categoric justification of the wholesale dealer, and an equally categoric assertion that the current hypercrisis derived directly from a deficient 1800 harvest. According to the minister, a twenty-five percent deficiency was 'the most sanguine estimation' of that crop; 'many . . . thought' it forty percent short. Marlborough was ordered to use all his 'great Influence and Authority' to reverse public 'Prejudices' against farmers and merchants, and to uphold the sanctity of private property, which included the right to 'withhold' stocks from the market; otherwise 'the whole Order of things must be overturned and destroyed'. Portland decided to publish the text 'as soon as possible in some of the public prints'. Although he prided himself on a judicious use of words to 'set' Marlborough's 'mind at ease at the same time that I intreat better judgement', Portland was unable to resist concluding with a scathing rider that publication through the press was 'perhaps unfortunately the only way there is of it being communicated to the public'.[22]

All these points were repeated to magistrates who subsequently intimated their support of maximums.[23] Portland's intrusions certainly encouraged Benches to suppress riot, but popular disturbances on the scale of those in September were sufficient to convince JPs of the danger from the masses; moreover, the dire effect of riots on the food supply to many urban centres convinced most authorities that order must be reimposed despite the strengths of ruling-class prejudices. This is not to claim that ministerial statements succeeded in converting public opinion to accept the alleged benefits of withholding and engrossing, or the reality of the autumn scarcity. Indeed the opposite was true. If ministerial desperation led Portland to publicise arguments with obdurate grandees, the latter did not emerge as chastened victims of governental wrath; Portland's own reaction back-fired, and served to discredit the ministry throughout the social spectrum.

The press played a central role. Few newspapers supported Portland.[24] Pamphlets supporting free trade, including Arthur Young's celebrated *The Question of Scarcity Plainly Stated*, received hostile reviews.[25] *The Times* typically noted that observations by Lord Chief Justice Kenyon and other judges at the trials of several merchants over the summer flatly confuted Portland. *The Times* also attacked, though it refused to publish, the letter to Marlborough: whatever the nature of the scarcity 'we submit whether it is prudent . . . to insist on the fact. It will do more to raise the price of corn, than the largest bounties will contribute to diminish it'. *The Anti-Jacobin Review* lambasted Portland's letter which

> certainly put a sudden stop to the markets. In many instances . . . corn already ordered to the market, was returned to the barn, to wait that advancement of price which the Secretary of State's letter encouraged the farmer to expect.

Identical opinions were expressed long afterwards. In December 1801, a Leicester vicar opined that

> Portland's Proclamation . . . [was] a hasty measure, [which] operated as a kind of watch-word to establish amongst the Farmers and Graziers, Corn Factors, Corn Jobbers, Millers, Mealmen, Bakers etc., a most nefarious system of monopoly and peculation.

Another clergyman commented 'that we have paid dear for his opinion'. Nottingham's historian, Blackner, writing in 1815, asserted that ministerial pronouncements raised 'the price of grain to a pitch unparalleled in the history of the worst times'.[26]

The reaction against Portland intensified. The Rev. Haden characteristically communicated his disgust to the minister himself. 'Ever since', noted another correspondent, 'the Farmer tells you the[y] have a Right to sell their Corn at such Extravagant prices the[y] have the Proclamation for it'. An Oxford pamphleteer pleaded,

> let it not be recorded in the annals of history, that in the year 1800 the Farmer, the Dealer, the Miller, and the Baker were protected in their properties, and that the poor had nothing done to redress their grievances!

In Cornwall, the perceptive Charles Rashleigh made the most incisive comment on the situation, with his 'private Opinion' that

> Lord Kenyon by too much Violence on one Side, and . . . Portland, by his foolish Letter, in the other, has done more Mischief than all the Wisdom of Parliament can make amends for I know the Discontent is very general.[27]

In Oxfordshire, where Portland's interference was particularly resented, an anonymous protester threatened an arson campaign

> in Consiquence of a Letter that the Dork of partland Sent to the Vice Chancelor . . . Directing him to send Round to the farmers to Assure them he would percure them Every purtcion [protection] and would justify them in Selled Thier Corn for wat the plead to ask.

Wheat now cost £50 instead of the crowd's £20 maximum. Portland received an unsigned vitriolic epistle addressed 'To the most Excrable Wretch & Damned Villain generally called the Duke of Portland'. The author could not

> help taking notice of your dareing and impudent address to the Lord Lieutenant of Oxford, wherein you have the dareing effrentery to support that falacious Lye – a real scarcity . . . . Monsters in human shape as you should . . . experience a real good horsewhipping.

Identical sentiments graced Ipswich graffiti: 'Damn the Duke of Portland as a Fool for having written of the Scarcity of Corn'.[28]

Portland's heavy-handed rejection of the 'moral economy', his blunt and public criticism of the magistracy, and above all his single-handed arbitrary declaration of another massively deficient havest, precipitated a crisis of confidence in Pitt's administration. Initially, this crisis was aggravated by the ministry's refusal to recall parliament for an emergency session. A powerful movement for parliamentary intervention was launched in London. At an emotive meeting on 3 October the Common Hall decided to petition the king on the throne; aldermanic objections were over-ruled, and in the charged atmosphere the new Sheriffs 'had not the courage to refuse' and prepared to leave for Weymouth at 5 a.m. on the morrow. Ministers had planned for parliament to sit in the new year, and now sought time by invoking constitutional quibbles over the London petition. Portland portrayed it as a politically motivated move to embarrass the government. There was no precedent for the receipt of Common Hall petitions on the throne, and it was couched in irreverent language. Its receipt should be delayed until the first Levee after the monarch's return to St James's. The Sheriffs were refused an audience. On 9 October tempers reached fever pitch at a Common Hall called to discuss the rebuff. The City Remembrancer was summoned, and on the 12th the aldermen endorsed the Common Hall, thereby invoking the Corporation, and circumventing the crown's ostensible objections.[29]

This stalling was completely counter-productive. From the Midlands Sir John Wrottesley reported that

> The people in general appear very much disaffected towards Government they blame Ministers for persuading his Majesty not to receive the Petition of the Livery of London on the Throne,

which appeared to confirm everybody's worst fears that ministers were 'determined not to redress any of the Grievances which exist'. Many local authorities came under pressure to use their constitutional weight. A rowdy crowd at Kidderminster insisted that authority represented the 'distressed situation . . . to his Majesty's ministers as they are sure that nothing short of legislative interference can give them effectual and permanent relief'. Kingswood colliers said the same to the Mayor of Bath. Demand for an emergency session rapidly became universal. Pro-government newspapers advocated petitions from across the country. Oxford followed London on 5 October, Worcester on the 9th, Nottingham on the 10th, and Abingdon on the 14th among many others. Pittites like the Rev. James Wilkinson, the experienced Sheffield magistrate, were forced to participate; Wilkinson chaired a townsmeeting and 'as there appeared a perfectly peaceable & orderley Disposition in the Assembly, I consented' to a remarkably disrespectful petition: as 'the Executive Government is engaged on other Objects of the highest National importance', parliamentary intervention over food was paramount. Disillusion with the arbitrary exercise of ministerial power was very widespread. Abingdon petitioners typically asserted that there was 'no possible Remedy for our Grievances, but in the

Wisdom of Parliament'. Many supporters saw an emergency session as the sole remaining mode of controlling seething discontent. The Oxford Corporation's petition was advanced in an attempt to dissuade the crowd from stoning the Vice-Chancellor who unwisely strayed on to the streets. In the vicar of Burnley's view only a recall would 'satisfy the Minds of the lower Classes that all imagineable Care is taken'. 'Let the Parliament . . . fairly fight the poor man's battle', pleaded a northern journalist.[30]

Many petitioners, and their supporters, automatically assumed that parliamentary intervention would secure the statutory embodiment of the central tenets of the 'moral economy'. For example, a Cheshire clergyman was confident that the abuses of dealing-millers 'will soon become an object of attention in Parliament'. Moreover, the fact that certain ministers were convinced of commercial malpractice was public property.[31] Formal pro-roguation of parliament expired on 11 November. On 8 October, the very day that Portland informed the Birmingham Bench that the crisis had already been 'obviated as far as Legislative Efforts are available',[32] George Rose was lobbying Pitt and Loughborough in favour of an emergency session. Rose argued that even if 'no effectual measure can be taken for the relief of the country', people 'may at least see the subject has not been neglected'. The cabinet provisionally anticipated a thorough enquiry 'into the real State of the Crop' under Privy Council auspices, but on 9 October Pitt's concern at reports of insurrectionary developments in the Midlands,[33] coincided with nervousness over the political ramifications of antagonising public opinion by inaction over the burgeoning petitioning movement. On 9 October Pitt decided to recall parliament, and secured the cabinet's unanimous consent on the 10th. Pitt projected his strategy in an interesting note to speaker Addington:

> I see nothing so likely to prevent the progress of discontent and internal mischief as what we have more than once found effectual, and cannot too much accustom the public to look up to – a speedy meeting of Parliament. Even if no important legislative measure could be taken, the result of Parliamentary enquiry and discussion would go further than anything towards quieting men's minds, and checking erroneous opin-ions, while on the other hand if petitions for Parliament were to spread generally (as I have little doubt they will) and were to be disregarded, a ground would be given for clamour, of which the disaffected would easily avail themselves for the worst purpose.[34]

Cabinet unity over this strategy camouflaged disagreements over what could be achieved. Grenville perceived the entire operation as a mere exercise in public relations. Ministers were also divided over the issue of harvest productivity. It was William Fawkener's estimation, from the Board of Trade, that Pitt, Windham and Portland, were 'clearly . . . high scarcity men'. Liverpool, side-swiping at Portland, believed that parliamen-tary investigation would prove that the harvest was 'not so defective as Some Persons have of late represented'. Portland insisted that the 'fact' of deficiency was the 'first point we have to make' through parliament. Liverpool cautioned against dependence on the testimonies of a handful of metropolitan corn merchants, and by 25 October the cabinet had decided on the broadest possible survey, through the clergy, the tax inspectorate, the customs, and Petty Sessions. The debate in cabinet also turned on the issue of free trade. Portland bluntly argued that the population must be schooled 'that with[ou]t the aid of Monopolists & Engrossers they must starve', and looked to parliamentary correction of 'the lamented doctrines which were promulgated from the Bench in the course of the Assizes'. Grenville concurred that only parliament could 'effectually stop this torrent of ignorance and mischief' which had dissolved law and order. Liverpool sniped at Portland with criticism of the Royal Proclamation, which promised protection to farmers, but had not inspired 'the least Hope of Relief or Consolation for the Poor'. As President of the Board of Trade, Liverpool was convinced of mercantile malpractices, and certain that parliamentary peddling of free trade principles would fail 'to operate on vulgar Understandings'. 'People feel that they suffer, and observe that other Persons grow rich from their Distress'. Liverpool was unable to resist irony, targetted at Dundas's mentality:

If . . . Insurrections should unfortunately happen, it will indeed be very singular, that the French Philosophers, by their wild Principles in favour of Political Liberty should have destroyed the Government of their own Country; and that the French Oeconomists (from whom Dr. Adam Smith, has borrowed all his Doctrines) should, by Principles in favour of the Liberty of Trade, carried to as great an Extravagance, shake the Foundations of the Government of Great Britain.

In Liverpool's estimation, ministerial tenacity over free trade would probably end in 'civil war, town versus country'. If Liverpool lost the debate in cabinet, his position emphasised the delicacy of the government's predicament.[35]

The decision to recall parliament was well received; crowds 'clapping and huzzaing' accompanied the London Sheriffs to St James's. But expectations of radical remedies grew. The poor, according to one Devonian, 'look to Parliament for relief, and have been taught by mischievous or ignorant people that Corn will soon be reduced to 7/6 the . . . Bushel, by a Maximum being fixed'. Tensions increased as the session approached, with everybody 'agitated and anxiously waiting the Result of Parliamentary Deliberation'. Once the session commenced on 11 November attentions were riveted on proceedings; 'We Country Folks are gaping after what passes in Parliament'. Many believed that Pitt had bought but limited time. Remedial measures must 'relieve . . . distresses . . . and . . . conciliate minds': otherwise 'no exertions of the Magistrates, or disposition of the military . . . will prevent the most serious disturbances'.[36]

Ministers were uncertain over their normal parliamentary support, and so nervous over the appropriate tone, that Pitt and Grenville deliberated at length over the text of the king's speech. Pitt wanted to destroy the 'moral economy's' credibility while recognising the need 'to soothe rather than irritate': 'calm discussion and patient investigation' was more harmonious than 'a dry and peremptory tone for which . . . men's minds are ill-prepared'. It was 'essential to show a disposition to enquire' into suspicions of commercial malpractices. Great care was prerequisite. Was the phrase '"injurious to the community" too vague to answer the purpose?'. Theoretical contradictions attended interventionism with bounties, and non-intervention in the internal trade; care was needed 'not to blend the foreign with the domestic trade in provisions, as what is said about the latter will not apply to the former'. The speech recommended an enquiry into allegations that malpractices enhanced prices above those attributable to deficient yields alone; care should be exercised so that remedial measures were addressed to specific abuses identified by MPs, as opposed to statutory embodiment of the entire 'moral economy' edifice. MPs must distinguish between abuses, and the 'regular and long established course of Trade . . . indispensable to the present state of Society, for the supply of the Markets'.[37]

The Foxites demonstrated a remarkable forbearance; in Lord Holland's words, opposition leaders 'disdained to derive popularity from exposing opinions which they thought unsound though generally held by the people, and sanctioned by the greatest legal authorities'. Holland, who privately accused Kenyon of an 'admiration of a mistaken and pernicious system', publicly praised both Portland's exoneration of the merchants from charges of monopoly, and his letter to Marlborough. If Holland was unable to resist reiteration of the opposition's claim that scarcity derived from the war, in the Commons Grey refused even to move an amendment to the king's speech, 'rather too formal a declaration of an active opposition' on a delicate subject, and Richard Brinsley Sheridan determined 'to avoid anything which could prevent unanimity' between Commons' front benches.[38]

If the Whig leadership stressed the principles of their old mentor Burke, opportunist supporters wanted to exploit the 'clamour for bread and peace', and incorporated populist ideology into their speeches. Theophilus Jones used the emotive issue of war contractors engrossing stocks. R.B. Robson implicated Arthur Young's pamphlet, published under Board of Agriculture auspices, lambasted the Royal Proclamation and Portland's epistles as causes of unrest, and criticised bank loans which financed withholding. However, the opposition's main thrust attributed inflation to wartime fiscal innovations. Very little was said on the reality of scarcity until it was confirmed by the Commons select committee's first report on 26 November. W.W. Bird, the Whig MP for Coventry, erupted; he and his constituents were convinced that scarcity was illusory; 'the great evils to which it alone could be attributed, monopoly and extortion were still without a remedy' even being proposed. Bird was decried on all sides. Pitt seized the opportunity for an all-embracing defence of ministerial policy, and to denounce price ceilings, the subject of noisy advocacy by the Earl of Warwick in the Lords. According to Pitt the concoction of artificial cheapness would destroy the retrenchment programme, and he concluded with a psychological appeal for MPs to 'guard against the influence of popular prejudices'. Grey and Wilberforce among others rose in support. Sir William Pulteney contrasted the select committee's temperate and analytical approach, with populist fanaticism on the streets. Sheridan advocated the impeachment of selected judges. Bird must have felt humiliated, friendless and isolated, before relief came in the form of a slanging match between Grey, Wilberforce and Burdett on matters marginal to the report. Bird's isolation proves MPs' satisfaction, or acquiescence in Pitt and the committee's strategy; remedies through importation and substitution must come first, and the economic causation of famine conditions, including the issues of monopoly and profiteering, should be dealt with later. Bird's embarrassment, the promise of future investigations, and the commitment of the parliamentary leaderships, combined to stifle any further articulation of the 'moral economy' on the floor of the Commons.[39]

In the Lords, ministers had to contain the 'vivacious and voluble' Warwick, the recent author of two tracts condemning monopolistic merchants, private marketing, and withholding farmers. He gave all his farming tenants notice to quit, and remained unrepentant after an interchange of letters with Portland. On the fourth day of the session, Warwick denounced 'exorbitant profits' in the provision trades, 'productive of so much injury to the rest of the community', to argue for a £4 wheat-price ceiling. Undeterred by haughty attacks from Grenville, sarcasm from Loughborough, and kept off the Lords' select committee, Warwick greeted their confirmation of deficient yields with proposals to license cornfactors, who were to be prevented from dealing other than on commission, and for powers for County Benches to fix wages and prices until June 1801. These were negated without a division. Isolated like Bird, and frustrated at his parliamentary impotence, Warwick retired to his Castle, where he consoled himself by taking 'on all the men who want employment to work in and about his Park'. He was the one painful thorn in the government's side, for 'Warwick and Bread are common all thro' the country'.[40]

Within parliament, cabinet strategy worked. Select committees in both Houses confirmed serious harvest deficiencies. The second report from the Lords, published in early December, briefly examined the vexed question of the grain trade, and inevitably reaffirmed the advantages of the free internal market and the untrammelled activities of its operators. Rumours of monopolistic 'combinations' were the unrealistic and inaccurate products of 'suspicious and vague reports as usually prevail in times of scarcity'.

> What have been represented as deep schemes and fraudulent practices to raise the market, have only been the common and usual proceedings of dealers in all articles of commerce, where there is a great demand, and where great capitals and great activity are employed.

Categoric assertions of the market's purity, and the 'highly useful' role of the great merchants, prove that objectivity was sacrificed to politically-motivated whitewash. The aristocratic autocracy of Grenville, who had hand-picked the committee, shines through here. The Commons were more circumspect. Some MPs at least had urban electorates to worry about. Pitt had diplomatically promised a rigorous examination of the mechanics of the grain market, once the Commons committee had finalised proposals for national subsistence. When it reviewed its activities in the sixth report published on the last day of the session (31 December) it claimed that its enquiries into the trade were in hand, but incomplete. Their tactics were clear; the subject required 'peculiar caution, from the danger which might attend an erroneous judgement, misled on one hand by popular prejudice, or on the other by plausible theories'. Although such reservations had not characterised proceedings in the Lords, the Commons would renew its investigations in the new year; at this stage the Commons committeemen refused to 'hazard any hasty suggestions or statements'.[41]

In a parliamentary sense the cabinet scored a resounding victory in spite of ministers' original differences. With two exceptions, parliamentarians did not use their key platforms to advance claims of monopoly, malpractice and fraud. Some MPs clearly quietly wished success to Warwick. Grey talked of the 'inclination to a maximum' among MPs, and Wilberforce privately 'made no secret' that statutory price controls 'would be a perfectly just measure' if not 'impracticable'. There is shadowy evidence of dissidents being disciplined by party leaders. Lord Chief Justice Kenyon, undeterred in the face of moves by a handful of madcap Pittites to bring his 'conduct before the House of Lords', was eventually silenced by a blatantly unconstitutional royal summons, and an equally unconstitutional letter from an un-named Secretary of State. Warwick was threatened with the loss of his Lord Lieutenancy, as he had 'mistaken the true Interests of the Country'.[42]

Although the Commons committee's investigation into the trade was concluded over the winter months, it was no accident that its conclusions were withheld until the last report (the thirteenth across the two sessions), published in June 1801, when public and political attentions were riveted on the threatened invasion and superb harvest prospects. The proposals to put Mark Lane under the control of the London Corporation and to impose restrictions on dealing by factors other than on commission, were quite radical, but the committee advised legislation reserved to a future session. The reasons advanced for these proposals flatly contradicted the committee's claims that the unfair practices identified had not 'contributed materially to enhance the Price of Bread Corn'. The report went undebated; its proposals were shelved by Addington, with the sole exception of the General Enclosure Act to increase agricultural productivity, itself the object of prolonged lobbying by the Board of Agriculture. That Bill was 'emasculated' by lawyers' and clerics' concern with fees and tithes. The final report was an integral part of Pitt's cunning strategy; it was a final sop to public opinion and undisciplined MPs who had to be kept quiet during the remaining term of famine.[43]

The government shielded itself behind parliament in order to reject 'moral economy' as an answer to subsistence problems. Political conflict over ministerial policies to combat famine had no direct bearing on Pitt's resignation. The extra work sapped his stamina, injured his health, and widened differences between members of the cabinet, and in these ways contributed to the near-debility which underlay Pitt's refusal to precipitate a major constitutional crisis with the monarch over Catholic Emancipation.[44] The most significant aspect of the government's tactics from September 1800, the use of parliamentary as opposed to ministerial authority to declare harvest deficiency, to support laissez-faire economics, and to enforce retrenchment, all of which involved specific negations of the popular will by a carefully orchestrated, and indeed elaborate exercise in public relations

by the state, was its essential failure. The local ruling class was the first
target; if the squires, clergymen and aldermen could be persuaded, there
were hopes that their influence would prevail and engineer changed
perceptions of causal forces among a broader social spectrum. But public
opinion remained obdurately traditional. In this it ironically reflected the
real opinions of many grandees, who could be heard castigating ministers,
notably Grenville and Portland, their executive and parliamentary
strategies, and the members of the select committees of both Houses,
during private dinner parties in London in the spring of 1801. They also
fulminated against the millions expended abroad on corn, and in the same
breath, accused the farmers of having got 'the whole markets . . . now in
their power'. But, when they returned to their country mansions, they
recognised the futility of articulating their support for 'moral-economy'
tenets to hostile and ostensibly unrepentant cabinet ministers. The persistent strength of that ideology in provincial ruling-class circles was vividly
proved by developments during the cataclysmic revolt of the South-west in
1801. Identical persistence is revealed throughout the country by the
clergy's acreage returns, made in the following autumn, which teemed with
complaints of malpractices by farmers, millers and merchants, although
observations on these topics were not invited. Nor did these comments
comprise a mere restatement of the legitimacy of the 'moral economy' for
the clergy repeatedly insisted on the necessity for governmental and
parliamentary intervention. Malpractices would continue unabated 'if not
checked by Parliament'. Clergymen still

> devoutly and earnestly wished that the Wisdom of Parliament may devise
> some Method whereby to shackle the Hands of the Covetous among
> Corn Dealers and the wealthy Farmers.

The Rev. Henry Davis of Faldingworth wearily concluded with his sincere

> wish that speculation in Bread was finally abolished.[45]

IV

SOCIAL CONTROL
AND FAMINE

Introduction

Famine conditions seriously aggravated the scale and changed the nature of the unprecedented challenge to the British ancien regime in the 1790s. Socio-economic devastations were explored in Part I; the contents of the chapters comprising Parts II and III, repeatedly suggested the key role of the English Justice of the Peace. The unpaid, amateur magistracy were critical in many spheres. The government's propaganda campaigns were principally, if not exclusively, directed at them. The Bench formed the government's primary mouthpiece in the localities; JPs were important moulders of public opinion in general, and of opinion among less elevated officials on whom the Bench depended to a degree. The Bench had ultimate control over the statutory social security system, the old poor law, whose precise functioning assumed an increasingly significant role in the government's plans for national survival. The famines provoked considerable and very widespread violent protest; the dangers represented by violence were even overshadowed by its debilitating threat to the effective distribution of available food, as revealed for example during the midsummer hypercrisis of 1795, and the revolt of the South-west in 1801. Again, the Bench was central; as conservators of the peace on the spot, they had ultimately to devise and direct the means of upholding law and order by containing their rebellious subordinates. Magisterial options included asserting their own local prestige to command crowds to disperse. They could summon the aid of the predominantly amateur police, and augment them by swearing-in special constables. They could invoke the aid of the Volunteer and regular armies. The use of all these agencies, however conditioned by other factors, largely depended on the Bench. It is therefore necessary to examine the effectiveness of the magistracy and these other agencies in their policing roles. What were their methods, and how successful were they in containing protest? What were the social effects of their deployment, and did repeated recourse to them lead to any changes, or significant developments?

The magistracy also largely controlled the legal system. They had absolute control over Petty and Quarter Sessions, and a vital part in the legal process whereby people became defendants in the Assize courts. All courts were a major executant of social control, but they were not used invariably or automatically in response to riots. However, sufficient rioters were prosecuted to warrant an analysis of the courts' function. In what senses were the courts' theoretical roles as the *ultimate* upholder of order in the hierarchy of agencies engineering social control, put into practice? And, what relevance has their use to any discussion of the reality of the democrats' denomination of Pitt's 'Reign of Terror'?

A less obvious, and certainly less dramatic element behind social control, is encountered in the unique and virtually universal system of poor relief; the statutory system's hallmark was its *fluidity*, which facilitated numerous options open to on-the-spot administrators to tailor aid programmes to combat local conditions. But the statutory system virtually collapsed in some regions in 1800–1. Other, non-statutory forms of relief were widely introduced. How did they complement the legal relief system? How effective were they? Our earlier analysis of living standards proved that a massive sector of the population was unable, unaided, to command the most basic of subsistence levels; wretched faces became a reality; destitution stalked the land; families were unable to clothe themselves; children literally cried for bread; begging assumed unheard of levels. The famines caused serious malnutrition, disease, and ultimately demograhic distortions with increased death rates, decreased birth rates, and delayed marriages. Amelioration certainly came through the relief agencies, but to what degree and are regional variations visible? Did the mode of implementation constitute a significant agent of social control in itself? What was the relationship between relief and repressive agencies? Did the statutory system, bolstered by its voluntary partners, play a major role in averting the revolutionary potential of the overall challenge to aristocratic political hegemony?

CHAPTER 15

Riot Control and the Repressive Agencies

The Role of Government

No government can tolerate riots. Pitt's government stressed their threat to food-distribution mechanisms, and also resorted increasingly to strong reminders of the sanctity of private property. The Home Office rarely entered into details over riot control in its communications with provincial magistrates, and official demands for the prosecution of protesters were not consistent. Most letters from Whitehall were replies; relatively few were sent in other circumstances. The executive genuinely believed that precise tactics were best left to those on-the-spot. Ministerial reluctance to intrude into local administration was fostered by tradition, cemented by pragmatism, and strongly reinforced by the unparalleled delicacy of the state's relationship with society during the famines. Nevertheless, an analysis of those instructions which were despatched forms an appropriate introduction to late eighteenth-century riot control, not least because it reveals that Portland, and his principal assistant in this work, under-secretary John King, had very definite ideas on the subject. Moreover, government adopted an increasingly intrusive presence.

A major problem lay with magistrates who temporized with rioters, thereby confronting the Secretary of State with a *fait accompli*; subsequent ministerial insistence on stringent measures against offenders implied criticism of the Bench, and could be interpreted as unwarranted intervention. Some JPs who admitted temporizing were even praised by the Home Office, notably before the midsummer hypercrisis of 1795. The release of prisoners from Wisbeach jail by the Rev. Oswin was dictated by their threatened liberation by an overwhelming force, but his diplomatic claim that his prisoners had expressed contrition, permitted John King to endorse Oswin's conduct. On occasions, Portland looked to magisterial displays of social leadership to disperse crowds; he even told the Cornish Bench to engineer dispersals of miners with explanations of parliamentary policy in the autumn of 1795.[1] A conciliatory, but containing role was also assigned to 'principal inhabitants', and in some respects the use of special constables drawn from the affluent extended it. Portland considered them as important adjuncts to the army as well. The specials could form a front line of defence, remonstrate with crowd personnel, perhaps prior to the army's arrival on the scene. If such persuasion failed, rioters were informed of the impending resort to troops. Portland advocated special constables in his lengthy instructions to South-western Lord Lieutenants during the serious disturbances in 1801; they could help police broad areas when the army was severely stretched.[2] But judicial advocacy of the virtually obsolescent *posse comitatus* was not reiterated by Whitehall.[3]

The redundancy of traditional emergency forces was principally achieved through the staggering success of the Volunteer movement. The government's appeal to the propertied, and in the early days to working people too, to form armed associations to guard against foreign invasion and internal upheaval, equipped the state with an unprecedented, tailor-made opponent of riot in almost every locality. The Home Office's commensurate reaction to scores of disturbances was to place almost unconditional confidence in this agency's prowess. With the significant exception of recalcitrant Volunteers, with whom we deal below, ministerial concern centred on praising militaristic alacrity. Volunteer Corps required little external manipulation, for domestic disturbances provided the sole opportunity for exhibiting their mettle; the chance was eagerly seized. Nathaniel Winchcombe, who commanded a Corps in the oft-disturbed Gloucestershire textile belt, greatly exceeded his cartridge allowance in training his men hard, believing it 'right to be prepared in case of riot'.[4] Portland repeatedly extended formal thanks to Volunteers for riot control. The CO of the Worksop Volunteer Cavalry was typically left in no doubt of ministerial perceptions of his Corps' value.

> The disposition they manifested for the protection of Property and the preservation of good order is meritous, and I hope you will do me the justice to take the first favourable opportunity of assuring them of the gratefull sense I entertain of their zeal.

With successful operations invariably evoking unqualified praise from high authority and in the king's name, the effect was encouraging to say the least, even if it principally reinforced the enthusiasms of often frustrated amateur soldiers.[5]

However, there is one significant difference between the famines. In 1794–6 the government left Volunteer deployment to COs and JPs on-the-spot; they must act at once to preserve 'the peace of the County . . . without waiting for orders from a distance'. In March 1800 Home Office fears of a recurrence of blockading dictated a general alert transmitted to all Corps through the Lord Lieutenants; COs should use their own authority to assemble their men in anticipation of disturbances, and were also to respond immediately to magisterial summonses. The circular also conveyed the government's satisfaction at the Volunteers' past and expected future conduct.[6] The regulars also received similar instructions now. This was an innovation, for although a general order for the regulars to assist the Bench was issued in the summer of 1795, it was principally designed finally to end the long-standing eighteenth-century confusion over the legalities surrounding the use of troops against civilians.[7] It signally failed; in 1795–6 cumbersome administrative procedures, with requests duplicated to both the Home and War Offices, and further confusion deriving from the constant communications between these departments, led to misunderstandings, notably when troops were sent to assist JPs who had only reported riot, as opposed to demanding military aid. Bureaucratic uncertainties jeopardised the magistracy's invariable ability to take speedy repressive measures.[8] The March 1800 initiative was designed to save time, to prevent chaos generated by legal ambiguities and administrative complexity, and to restate and facilitate the government's insistence on instant riot suppression.[9]

Thereafter the Home Office increasingly advocated the deployment of the regulars to forestall potential disturbances and against actual riot, and expected its faith in the professionals to be shared by the Bench. Nottingham Corporation was typically ordered to arrange army street patrols when tensions increased, 'as there can be but one opinion that prevention is better than punishment'. The show of military strength – as opposed to force –

> will convince those who are disposed to commit riots that they cannot escape punishment and thereby bring them without exposing them to the danger of a conflict with the Military to a sense of their duty and of the implicit obedience which it behoves them to pay to the Civil authority and to the established laws of the land.

Home Office demands for the full use of the army achieved a commensurate climax in September 1800; the Royal Proclamation adopted the same policy by instructing 'all Our Officers both Civil and Military' to use the Riot Act. The Proclamation's legitimisation of all necessary military force was repeated in scores of letters to provincial authorities; 'the moment . . . the authority of the Civil Power is disregarded . . . resort cannot be had too soon to . . . the Military'. The sole ground for temporizing with rioters was a strategic feint until the army's arrival permitted the Bench acting 'against them with a certainty of success'. The Mayor of Banbury who failed to deploy the force of regulars and Volunteers he assembled, received a typically unequivocal reprimand:

> when you found that the power of the Magistrates and the reading of the Riot Act were alike disregarded, it became your duty, how painful soever it might be, to enforce your Authority and to compel an obedience to the Laws, by the Military Force under your direction.

In future he was 'to have the earliest recourse' to the troops. Various authorities were instructed to publicise such intentions.[10]

Thereafter Portland's orders were even firmer, and his actions innovatory. In September 1800 few provincial magistrates invoked the Riot Act with the celerity required by the Home Secretary, who was irritated further by the total indifference of several JPs. Once rioting commenced in

London, Portland attempted, without any subtlety, to pressurise Lord Mayor Combe into using the troops; when Combe exhibited his Whiggish disinclination, Portland intervened directly, initially alerting all metropolitan Volunteers, who were ordered to liaise with the chief London stipendiary, Sir Richard Ford, at his office in the Home Department. Ford, John King and Portland, were jointly responsible for subsequent deployments of the troops, who received instructions to arrest 'Rioters in their progress'. The Home Office, as opposed to the City Authority, decided when to release the Volunteers from daily duties, and send the regulars back to barracks.[11] Unsolicited troops were distributed through Oxfordshire on Portland's orders, and reinforcements sent to Nottingham 'in consequence of information received' in Whitehall of continued disturbances, and not at the Corporation's desire.[12] The order to saturate Birmingham and the West Midlands with regulars to prevent the massive insurrection anticipated by Home Office intelligence in November 1800, formed one climax to this development.[13]

Government dependency on the army was thus transparently increased. In some senses, only a completely fortuitous coincidence of external factors permitted it. The scale of wartime mobilisation was of course unparalleled. But the famines occurred when British troops were not extensively deployed in continental campaigns, and after the Irish crisis, which necessitated unprecedented legislation to permit the Militia to serve overseas, had passed its peak, and drained England of available troops. Nonetheless, in periods of maximum disturbance, notably the summer of 1795, some local and regional COs were unable to respond to every magisterial request.[14] The army was again stretched in September 1800, not least owing to the Duke of York's refusal to 'diminish the cavalry round the Metropolis'. Further complications derived from the simultaneous necessity to augment South-western forces when Napoleon ostensibly began assembling a new invasion flotilla; greater strains were imposed by the Home Office's military policy in the West Midlands, but this was in November when riots elsewhere had subsided. Rioting was less likely once the emergency parliamentary session got underway, and some populist energies were rechannelled into the resurgent democratic movement.[15] When the next round of extensive riots erupted, in the South-west in the spring of 1801, Portland was assured of adequate military forces; he ordered GOC Simcoe to calculate 'the Force that will be necessary to restore and maintain good order', and respond 'by the Return of the Messenger who will wait'. Simcoe got his reinforcements, and Portland was enabled to opine that

the possession of an adequate and commanding Military Force is unquestionably the first step to be taken to enable the Civil Power to resume its authority and give that energy to the Law by which alone private Property can be protected.

It is true that widespread difficulties with the Volunteers in general, and those in the South-west in particular, qualified Portland's past confidence in that agency, and thereby enhanced his dependency on the regulars. But in this case Portland was not referring to a town the size of Banbury, or even a city, but a vast area of several hundred square miles.[16]

Abrogation of the traditional understanding that army deployment against civilians occurred only under magisterial superintendance, was a logical extension of this increased dependency. The Riot Act technically permitted military intervention only against crowds which refused to disperse in the hour following a JPs recital of the key clause. Portland increasingly insisted that 'Acts of Violence . . . supersedes the necessity of acting under the Riot Act'. He specified damage to buildings, searching them, and the seizure of food, but the gist of these instructions eroded the relevance of the Riot Act for most elements of 'moral-economy's' imposition. The constitutional obligation to maintain the peace, and to oppose force by force, applied equally to civilians and soldiers; this view was endorsed by the Lord Chief Justice, and enshrined in the Royal Proclamation. Portland accordingly encouraged commanders to act on their own initiative against rioters, and even break up passive assemblies where authority had 'previously directed the Military to keep the King's Peace in that Quarter'. Categoric assurances from the Home Office were passed to Colonel Bastard, the fiery commander of the East Devon Militia, that

> whatever Acts of Power he may have found it necessary to have recourse to in the course of the . . . Contest [riot suppression in the South-west] will be most readily sanctioned and confirmed and that no time will be lost in taking whatever Steps may be necessary for that purpose.

Ironically, the Riot Act itself was the major casualty of this Whig Home Secretary's policy.[17]

This advocacy of speedier recourse to force was supported by rising Home Office emphasis on criminal proceedings against rioters. Magistrates who decided on prosecutions during the first famine were invariably praised; selection of the 'most guilty' constituted 'necessary severity' in the interests of 'salutary example' to 'prevent . . . similar outrages'. But ministerial endorsement of decisions already taken, and intimation that recourse to the courts reinforced executive policy, was very different from either ordering prosecutions, or by directing committal and subsequent legal proceedings. The administration of justice was the unqualified preserve of local authorities; magisterial autonomy was paramount, not least because it preserved vital options, ranging from simply binding people over to keep the peace, to arraignment on non-capital or capital charges. Outside interference in these processes caused considerable friction. Lord Rolle's self-proclaimed autocracy extended to the exclusion of his Lord Lieutenant; Rolle 'is to have no one interfere where he acts as Justice'. Clerk of the Peace, Richard Eales, 'seemed much hurt' the moment the Treasury Solicitor took 'Prosecutions out of his Hands'.[18]

In the main, government very wisely refrained from intruding. The Home Office repeatedly stressed that local circumstances should dictate judicial tactics. But if government rarely involved itself in the processes, its support for 'exemplary punishment' peaked in the autumn of 1800, and was emphasised by the Royal Proclamation and numerous Home Office communications. The capitulation of so many authorities in the face of the

September riots posed a complex problem, as did the virtual abdication of the South-western Bench in 1801. The removal of popular impositions threatened fresh trouble, and its negation in Portland's estimation turned on existing prosecutions operating *in terrorem*. Magisterial counter-offensives must be underpinned by prosecutions proceeding. But here, if the government was applying pressure, detailed decisions were reserved for those on-the-spot, not least because as Portland told Lord Mayor Combe, *his* legal initiative 'cannot come from any [other] quarter from whence it will be attended with a better effect on the public mind'. Fuelling the crisis of confidence sapping the strength of the government in the autumn of 1800, by a rigid insistence on prosecutions, would have been extremely perilous.[19]

With one fundamental exception, the government resisted temptations, and several magisterial demands, to issue Special Commissions of Assize to try rioters. Some JPs genuinely conceived Special Commissions to be appropriate, and not just because they would tend to absolve the local Bench, and transfer the inevitable popular hostility to the state. Ministerial strategies are difficult to establish in this context. One clue may lay in the relative paucity of arrests during the September riots, but then the political ramifications of Special Commissions and their clear object of 'exemplary punishment', were potentially lethal. Ministers possibly believed, and certainly acted on the premise, that Special Commissions must be reserved for the most exceptional circumstances. Only one was issued, to deal with some soldiers and civilians active in the 1795 mutiny of the Oxfordshire Militia. Army participation in subsistence disturbances seriously jeopardised national security, and the maximum publicity accorded to capital sentences and executions comprised an identical warning to soldiers and civilians. The fact that Pitt was not embroiled in a major political crisis at this precise juncture may also be of significance.[20]

Special Commissions proved that the government sought death sentences. The infancy of the movement to purge many capital crimes from the statute book does not mean that many factors which compromised the strict enforcement of the law were inoperative in the 1790s. Food rioters were very vulnerable to capital charges, but at the most critical periods, the weight of public opinion clearly supported rioters' objectives, if not their means. Few could condone the execution of people intent on enforcing public morality, even if they placed themselves outside the strict letter of draconian laws. Ministers wisely refrained from public suggestions that the ultimate penalty ought to be imposed. But this did not propel Portland to extend mercy *after* death sentences were passed. Two luckless men, arrested and tried while disturbances raged in Somerset in 1801, were left to their fate; Portland's tactful lamentation at the necessity for execution did not obscure his pleasure at the demonstration 'of certain and capital punishment' of rioters.[21] He rejected clemency appeals for two Dean Foresters in spite of well-supported petitions, embellished by favourable observations from the trial judge.[22] On other occasions Portland recommended mercy for certain jointly-sentenced convicts, leaving a token execution to proceed. Lesser sentences were more regularly mitigated when appeals from neighbourhood notables were supported by trial judges. This feature supports

Douglas Hay's analysis of the patronage system's importance in mitigating criminal sentencing, but Home Office resistance to several appeals indicates that if ministers were opposed to multiple hangings, they certainly wanted some.[23]

Magisterial approaches to the Home Office to share the costs of prosecution were almost invariably refused.[24] However, the government was prepared to tender legal advice to local administrators, who were sometimes invited to forward documentation for an official legal opinion. This occasionally produced the return of detailed instructions, but the Home Office normally restricted involvement to legal advice on difficult cases, including the Bedford town crier who whipped up a crowd to seize a miller's cart, and an Oxfordshire mason who threatened to incinerate the homes of plebeians who refused to join a crowd. Provincial JPs often submitted inadequate details, and had to rest content with a general statement of the law as conditioned by precedents. Portland eschewed seizing on these liaisons to engineer capital charges. Indeed ministerial caution, identical to that displayed over directions in cases against political offenders, characterised the Law Officers' responses, and the Home Office issued some warnings that a failure to convict was worse than ignoring incidents.[25]

The government was in a peculiarly weak position with JPs who refused to use the army, or who declined to prosecute. A handful received strongly-worded letters from Portland, who on one occasion went behind recalcitrant magistrates' backs, by encouraging others, with whom he had a personal connection, to use the military.[26] This tactic had its dangers, and others militated against the prosecution of justices for neglect of duty. It was considered once, against the Mayor of Oxford who ignored a violent siege of the County Jail; a lengthy and vituperative investigation amassed a documentary mountain, and even elicited the acquiescence of a reluctant Attorney-General, but the prosecution was abandoned on receipt of an unconvincing explanation from the Mayor. Portland's subsidiary campaign against the town clerk was also dropped.[27] The Home Secretary was infuriated by magisterial conduct in September 1800, and he was soured further by the hostile reaction to his firm line. The improvement of the political situation once Addington replaced Pitt, leaving Portland as yet undisturbed at the Home Office, failed to produce firm measures from Portland, even against blatantly unco-operative justices in the South-west. Lord Lieutenant Fortescue's litigious crusade was frustrated in one case by the obstructive Mayor of Totnes; Fortescue threatened to lay the case before the Home Secretary for a decision 'as to the means it may be necessary to have recourse to for supplying the want of a Jurisdiction in . . . Totnes'; GOC Simcoe wanted the jurisdiction of Deputy Lord Lieutenants extended to Boroughs to deal with such obduracy, but Portland would not even consider challenging the traditional structure of local power, 'having once in my life experienced the effect of what was called an attack on the chartered Rights of Man'. It was too dangerous, even when circumstances seemed to warrant it most.[28]

Direct ministerial involvement was almost exclusively reserved to situations where government had a special responsibility. Royal dockyard workers and members of Volunteer Corps who actively supported South-western rioters in 1801 were two examples. Volunteer participation was seen as a species of mutiny, and viewed seriously:

> Nothing can afford a more dangerous and destructive example, than that those who are entrusted with Arms for the maintenance and security of the publick tranquillity, should be left at liberty to use them for its destruction.

Several COs were ordered to initiate punitive measures, and if necessary call on the regulars for support; the futures of several Volunteer regiments were the subject of subsequent Home Office recommendations to the king. The Treasury Solicitor prosecuted officers from Brixham who had accompanied their own rank and file and the crowd on descents into the countryside.[29] The Devonport dockyard workers had just won pay concessions from the Navy Board when they participated in riots, and negotiations with local JPs and food suppliers, which eclipsed the powers of the authorities; they advanced their cause by strike action. Although Fortescue oversaw the state's retributive campaign, the decisions to sack and prosecute leading trade unionists and rioters among the government's own employees, were taken in Whitehall. Trade unionism received a heavy blow with the dismissal of over fifty men, some of whom were also prosecuted by the Treasury Solicitor. If the local justices succeeded in shielding some potential defendants from Fortescue, the belligerent Colonel Bastard and the Treasury Solicitor, Fortescue prevailed upon the latter to extend his activity to the prosecution of other Devonians involved in disturbances outside the Plymouth district. The exceptional nature of these South-western proceedings must be emphasised; normally, the local Bench retained absolute control, and magisterial attitudes and their activities against riots and their perpetrators remain central to the analysis of the use of the repressive agencies to maintain social control.[30]

The Role of the Magistracy

The magistracy directed operations against the riot at every stage; they are encountered addressing demonstrators, reading the Riot Act, seizing prisoners, and supervising military deployments. The magistrate decided for or against prosecution, recorded witnesses' statements, issued warrants, and selected judicial victims. JPs' judgements were a key factor, and this theatre for individuality militated against a uniform response. Many justices were as deeply steeped in 'moral-economy' traditions as those against whom they were supposed to act. If some were too old or infirm for the strenuous actions required, others, for example the notorious Rev. Henry Bate Dudley – in a minority to be sure – positively enjoyed orchestrating vigorous repression. The problems presented by riot varied across time and from place-to-place. Confronting several hundred famished miners was very different from combatting handfuls of angry shoppers in a small market town. These multifarious circumstances do not permit justices' responses to be quantified; the use of the Riot Act, the call up of the troops, and other tactics, were not conditioned by average crowd sizes. Patterns can be established. How did magistrates perceive their personal powers, and how were they used? What attitudes are revealed by decisions to make arrests, and to mount prosecutions? How speedily did the Bench resort to the army? Was the Home Secretary's clearly increasing faith in the army reflected in magisterial practice and attitudes?

Many justices initially adopted a low-key response to riot, even in populous centres, and at times of maximum mobilisations. The Rev Dr. Cobb, vicar of Charlbury, eschewed military aid, and set off with a few constables, 'without Staves or any Weapons of Offence or defence', to confront crowds several hundred strong, rampaging through the Oxford-shire countryside. Cobb stated his

> hope . . . that having been conversant without Offence for ten Years as a Magistrate amongst many even of the Rioters, my influence might serve if not to Stop the illegal proceedings, or to divide the Councils of the disturbers of the Peace, to produce a Relaxation of their mischievous Exertions.

Cobb clearly preferred to try his prestige, 'a fond hope perhaps', to effect a dispersal; hundreds of 'two penny squabbles' were stopped by JPs acting alone, with a few constables, or a more numerous posse of speedily-sworn specials – 'mob Constables' in popular parlance. An eye-witness to riotous scenes in Lower Broad Street, Plymouth, related how a squad of specials confronted the crowd, and 'used round sticks to disperse the people, and particularly the Mayor, who laid about him in every direction, sparing none'. Such strategies necessitated strong nerves, as the numbers of assaults and superficial injuries to magistrates reveal. Nevertheless, big assemblies, even in militant places like Leeds and Sheffield, were dispersed in this way. A clerical magistrate, his curate, 'a very slinging young Clergyman', and an attorney, 'a very stout man', even had the temerity to brawl with miners armed with bludgeons in the streets.[31]

Dr. Cobb anticipated that he would personally know some of the rioters, and such familiarity comprised a pivotal facet of control. The police who confronted and dispersed a crowd stoning a market inn at Tunbridge Wells, did so without reference to the local JP, Lord Boyne. He was subsequently informed that

> the persons hereunder mentioned appeared to be very Active: viz–
> 1) William Mercer of the parish of Tunbridge Carpenter.
> 2) George Divall of Tunbridge Wells Fishmonger.
> 3) Thomas Wells the Younger of the same place Fishmonger.
> 4) William Haiter, Coachman to Mrs. Brown a visitor at Tunbridge Wells.
> 5) William – Footman to Mrs Grovesnor of the same place a Widow lady.
> 6) William Newham of the same place Jorneyman Shoemaker.
> 7) William Sawyers, a lad of about 16 years of age the Son of William Sawyer of the same place.

Boyne 'sent for' a selection of these characters, which induced a minor panic, and others came voluntarily; warrants were issued against two more, but Boyne then restricted himself to 'severe reprimands'. Reginald De la Pole ordered three ladies from Colyton, Devon,

> to appear before me at my Hous at Eleven o'Clock Friday Morning next to answer the complaint of James Spurway for saying they are resolved to take and carry away forcibly all the Tabs of Butter belonging to him.

Witnesses were also summoned, but the matter was resolved in his worship's kitchen; no other legal proceedings followed. Such procedures, which were rarely documented, were nevertheless common, and occasionally elicited favourable, if slight, press coverage. But if a 'seasonable Exhortation' or 'severe reprimand' in the 'big house' was an ordeal for humble folk, it also comprised a temperate response while reserving more ominous options.[32]

Magisterial prestige, commonly combined with robustness, could maintain the peace, notably in less populous places. Justices responsible for the greater centres often had fewer options; they were less likely to command respect or to know any rioters whom they encountered. Indeed some Benches acquired a reputation for timidity and even cowardice; Norwich justices, it was said, were adequate only to ceremonial swaggerings on official Corporate occasions: 'when activity is required and courage is wanted' to impose order in the streets, 'they are as bad as a parcell of old women'. Other JPs acted resolutely in the belief that challenges to their authority were best met by immediate, if token arrests. But this did not invariably lead to the prosecution of prisoners. Earl Fitzwilliam, who was not the man to tolerate social insubordination, revealed a common magisterial mental process, when with army support, he encountered a massive crowd in South Yorkshire:

> Those who could be spoken to, were directed to lay down their Bludgeons, which order was complied with, almost universally: but one young man being refractory . . . I order'd him to be seized; more in terrorem, than for anything he had done: in truth neither He, nor any other had committed any act of outrage: but being there assembled together in considerable numbers with Bludgeons, in their hands, I trusted that I should stand justified by Law, for directing a Man, so circumstanc'd to be seiz'd, though the Riot Act had not been read. He was committed for examination . . . when he will be bail'd: indeed the ground of the charge against him seems very weak.

Magisterial leniency, indeed their 'soft-peddalling', rather than severity was the norm, even where prisoners were taken. Chepstow JPs committed one man for theft, remanded another 'for further examination', and released eight more whom they considered 'misled by false rumours'. Sureties to maintain the peace, and to stand trial if summoned, were regular ploys, adopted by the Rev. James Wilkinson, the dominant judicial figure responsible for Sheffield, a notoriously unbridled town. The bulk of prisoners seized in the fierce rioting at Nottingham and Birmingham, like their counterparts responsible for the less dramatic events at Norwich in September 1800, were simply bailed on providing sureties for good behaviour.[33]

Such relatively mild proceedings dispersed rioters in scores of places, and nothing could be more inaccurate than Dr. Hayter's assertion that 'the use of the army appeared to most contemporaries to be inevitable' to restore order.[34] Portland's claim that leniency encouraged crowds is not without empirical support, but it should be emphasised that the seizure of morally-motivated activists, and the threat of prosecution, served to infuriate the populace, and lead to aggravated actions, including the attacks on jails which we have encountered. It was popular insistence on the release of prisoners which first sparked dockyard workers' involvement in Plymouth disturbances; they struck work on at least two occasions, confronted the army, negotiated with the justices, and forcibly released prisoners, one of whom they secreted in the yard. This provoked a debilitating conflict *within* authority, with fierce internecine arguments developing between naval and army officers, JPs, the clerk of the peace, the Lord Lieutenant, and the Home Office.[35] Making arrests was a gamble; if it worked on occasions, it enflamed others. No doubt, JPs on-the-spot could evaluate the populace's mood, and temper their responses accordingly. Mistakes were made, and realities made a mockery of the blanket injunctions for arrests and arraignments increasingly issued by Whitehall.

Decisions to summon troops, and more critically, their use, were taken neither lightly nor automatically. Magistrates were customarily cautious. Even a militaristic moron like Colonel Athorpe, the man principally responsible for one fatal incident at Sheffield, did not use his firepower until after he had narrowly escaped serious assault, and seen his men stoned for most of an hour. Even in London, where disturbances evoked awesome memories of Gordon, and more terrifying predictions of Jacobin-inspired insurrection, Lord Mayor Combe's aversion to army intervention was overcome only by ministerial directions. In September 1800, Earl Fitzwilliam made a fine distinction when policing Sheffield streets: 'though in such numbers, the people were not rioting', and the Bench preferred inviting 'complaints', to driving the crowd off with the army. The Mayor of Plymouth did not send for the troops until he was nearly taken prisoner himself by the crowd. The troops cleared the streets and were immediately ordered back to barracks. There they were confined when fresh violence was anticipated, save for cavalry patrols sent to patrol the main roads into the town 'to preserve the farmers and others coming to market from being molested'. The Mayor could not personally supervise the numerous potential flash points, but he clearly did not want to assert his authority at the head of the army.[36]

Suggestions of immediate magisterial recourse to the army are unhistorical exaggerations. Troops were often not available in the first instance, and even when they were actually backing up JPs, they were not necessarily sent into action. The Devonport Bench blandly told Portland that 'many hundreds would have fallen' if they had used the troops actually under their direction, in an incident which a hostile witness described as a judicial capitulation 'in the face of an insulted soldiery who were ready and willing to act if called upon'. Indeed, the Mayor of Bath's remark, that it 'was found impracticable to disperse the Mob by fair Means', namely expostulation, suggests that he entertained moral objections to the use of the army. Justice and Volunteer officer Holland Watson of Stockport noted that the populace's 'distressed', condition meant that 'every one feels an unwillingness to proceed hastily to extremities, even against rioters'. Mayor Walford of Banbury opted for five hours of largely futile negotiations with rioters who took over the town, to the use of the adequate troops at his disposal; after a critical Home Office response, Walford ordered a cavalry charge on a subsequent occasion, but then reverted to verbal persuasion with an obdurate rump of protesters.[37]

Magisterial dependency on the troops is difficult to assess owing to incomplete data, notably the War Office's failure to record the details of the army's policing function. Magisterial reluctance did not extend to ultimate refusals to use the troops, especially after the Bench was repeatedly challenged by rioters. In some regions, and during certain critical periods, justices admitted that security depended on the army. The West Midland Bench acquiesced in the Home Office's decision to saturate the region with troops against feared insurrection in November 1800; magisterial dependency was elicited only through repeated investigation by a special Home Office envoy, and this episode reveals that a combination of pride and apprehension of possible constitutional connotations underlay JPs' aversion to admitting the fact.[38] Such dependency tended towards self-perpetuation. In July 1801 the Bilston justice, the Rev. A.B. Haden, made a significant appeal, long after fears of insurrection had subsided, and months after the last food riots:

> This part of the County is by far the most populous; and as nine-tenths of the Inhabitants are of the lowest Class and naturally given to idleness, riot, and excess, of course a Military Force adequate to their numbers should be kept upon the spot.

Experience dictated this perception; the troops' planned removal meant that replacement 'for Assistance in case of Emergency' would have to come from Walsall or Wolverhampton. But

> in case a Riot should suddenly break out in the dead of Night . . . how am I to send to either of those places, surrounded perhaps by a riotous Assembly, and what is to become of me, my Family and property during the long interval that must take place before the Soldiers can arrive? I only asked for a Serjeants guard, which would answer every purpose: because being stationed on the spot they would prevent almost the possibility of mischief.

Haden was not the proverbial, and largely mythical, alarmist; he was the most conscientious member of the Staffordshire Bench, and repeatedly confronted rioters in the 1790s.[39] However, Haden lived in a heavily populated, non-nuclear industrial zone. Barrack-building in most major towns, including the notoriously unruly like Birmingham, Manchester,

Nottingham and Sheffield, endowed them with a permanent military presence. Local authority opposition to barracks petered out in 1795; its non-recurrence might be attributed to the silent dependency of officials on this military ubiquity, with its obscure manifestations, including the surprise registered at the 'old women' of Norwich's preference for special constables rather than soldiers to patrol riot-torn streets in 1796. Urban authorities in places without barracks lobbied hard to preserve a military presence at times. Elsewhere, frequent recourse to the Volunteers generated a similar dependency on that force.[40]

Local authorities' experiences during the 1794–6 famine encouraged dependency on regular and Volunteer forces as the most efficacious repressive agency. Identical convictions permeated parliamentarians' perceptions; representing the urgent need to remove maximums in September 1800, Sir Samuel Romilly appreciated that it would stimulate

> fresh riots . . . if the number of armed volunteers that are spread throughout . . . the country . . . did not make it impossible that any commotions, in which only the lowest part of the community takes part, should be carried to any formidable height.

This confidence was partially exploded by the numbers of incidents in which amateur soldiers became unreliable, or actually mutinied, during the September 1800 crisis and thereafter in the second famine. Troubles with the Volunteers are examined in detail below, but they can have operated only to increase magisterial dependence on the regular army.[41]

The Troops and the People

The regulars, both cavalry and infantry, emerged as the most effective anti-riot force. This efficiency was not compromised by the facts that the regulars were subjected to brutal discipline, and were recruited from poverty-stricken and criminal elements. Nor were the British army's deficiencies, as exposed in continental and colonial theatres against the French, reflected in its policing role. The same could be said of the Militia once their living standards were reformed in 1795 in direct response to their participation in *taxation populaire* incidents. These mutinies were exceptional, as were the politically-inspired rumblings among the Guards and elements of other regiments in 1800. Despite these, no evidence exists of refusals by the regulars to oppose the crowd in the manner determined by their officers; the establishment had good cause for its satisfaction with the performance of the regulars on the home front.

Their arrival, notably the cavalry's, frightened the crowd. The LCS stalwart, John Gale Jones, appreciated the 'terror which is generally exhibited by an unarmed multitude upon the first appearance of a military force'; he ruminated on the 'most formidable appearance' of troops engaged in bayonet practice. 'The very Sight of the military Dispersed' a huge crowd rioting at Birmingham. Earl Fitzwilliam reported that

> The party of the Blues, and the mob on its return to Sheffield, met suddenly and unexpectedly at an angle in the road; instantly the mob dispers'd in every direction, climbing over walls, getting into the windows of Houses, some fording the river, all makeing the best of the way back to Sheffield.

The element of surprise was critical here, for the Sheffield crowd's hallmark was not timidity; a total dispersal did not obtain here, nor did all crowds melt away on the army's arrival.[42] Many personnel took evasive action by regrouping elsewhere. Soldiers were commonly stoned, and particularly ugly scenes occurred when crowds, especially those composed of industrial workers, resisted. Cornish tinners invading Truro on 6 April 1796 were immediately driven out 'at the point of the bayonet' by the Worcestershire Militia. The miners regrouped to confront the Mayor at the head of the troops. His recourse to the Riot Act 'rather encouraged' his assailants who responded with vollies of stones, and then in the words of a plebeian witness,

> made their attack on *the Soldiers and stood the charge*, broke many bayonets and also the fire from a Six pounder, many wounded and some taken prisoner.

A second bayonet charge and a further cannonade over miners' heads cleared the field. The Rev. E. Giddy recorded the incident in military terms: 'Truro attack'd but the insurgents repulsed'. Nor was this an isolated example; Penzance had to be defended similarly in 1795.[43]

The magistracy commonly put the troops in an offensive posture, but took care to preserve regular formations. Isolated soldiers could inflict unnecessary injury, as nearly occurred in one street melee when a militiaman 'ran at a Collier with his bayonet and wd. have killed him' but for a clergyman's physical intervention. Magistrates strove to avoid injuries. The Mayor of Bath typically ordered 'the Troops to act firmly but without Violence'; his Truro counterpart insisted that the cannonade was aimed above the crowd's heads. Cavalry drew up with swords symbolically unsheathed, and 'rode gently through' assemblies, or alternatively 'charged firmly, without the sword'. More drastic tactics were reserved for particularly stubborn crowds, including Mancunians 'obliged to save themselves' by flight in every direction when charged 'at full gallop'. The cavalry normally used the flats of their swords, vigorously at times; Haden supervised a detachment 'riding about among' the crowd 'striking such of them as were refractory with the flat part'. 'Many' New Alresford 'rioters were very severely beaten on the back and head' in a similar manoeuvre. Surprisingly perhaps, few deaths were recorded. A child was trampled to death at Banbury, but rumours of people killed by cavalry charges usually proved incorrect once the dust settled. Nevertheless, witnesses were repeatedly surprised at the absence of fatalities. *The Times* incredulously reported that nobody was 'mortally wounded' at New Alresford.[44]

The cavalry's 'superior utility' over the infantry was repeatedly confirmed by experiences. Infantry deployment incurred several disadvantages.

They had none of the *imperium* of soldiers on horseback, and their relative immobility, when armed with bayonet and rifle, made them more lethal in some respects than cavalry. A bayonet charge was one option; Newark rioters were 'defeated . . . without bloodshed, excepting a few slight wounds with the point of the bayonet'.[45] Infantry could usefully guard buildings and installations, thereby remaining stationary. But these duties exposed them to injury from missiles, and the safest defensive tactic was to fire. Where fatalities occurred at the hands of regulars or Volunteers, as they did at Rochdale, Birmingham and Sheffield, this situation prevailed. Infantry deployment was minimised wherever possible, and the sole example of regulars inflicting death happened at Birmingham where a huge crowd surrounded a small picquet and attempted to rescue its prisoners. On balance, the restraint of the regulars deserves greater emphasis than most aspects of their policing function.

Several reasons must be advanced in explanation. First, the magistracy's reluctance to use troops, and their temperate orders to COs have already been encountered. Most army officers shared these prejudices. Secondly, class allegiances between the rank and file may have encouraged moderation. The evidence is rarely specific, but troopers at Wolverhampton 'bid' riotous miners to 'get out of the way, telling them at the same time that they liked a large loaf as well as they did'. It was said that the Seventh Dragoon Guards, stationed at Gloucester, had a 'thorough good understanding' with the 'common people', whom the soldiers advised '"not to put up with the small bread"'.[46] Thirdly, this source of temperance may have been reinforced by chauvinistic factors, as women predominated in so many crowds. On the other hand scores of witnesses testified that troopers were exposed to 'insult and injury'. But the fourth, and most important reason derives from the strength of the army's presence, and its operation on community consciousness. The government speedily reinforced the army in regions where disturbances assumed insurrectionary proportions, and the arrivals of dozens of detachments by forced marches had a quick debilitating impact on protesters, as revealed by events in the South-west in 1801.

In March, before serious rioting commenced, GOC Simcoe had 1600 militiamen, 650 infantry, and nearly three hundred cavalry at Plymouth and Exeter. Cornwall contained fewer troops, with small cavalry and militia detachments stationed in six towns. Existing forces were adequate to the despatch of parties to all riotous Devon towns. Simcoe's total force was rapidly increased from under three to over eight thousand men, of whom nearly two thousand were cavalry or artillery. Seven hundred mounted soldiers were incorporated into a highly mobile force under Simcoe's personal command. The Duke of York as C-in-C refused further augmentation on the sufficiency of this provision 'if the Magistrates will only make use of them and allow them to act'. Simcoe sent infantry to every urban centre, with cavalry support to 'pursue . . . Rioters issuing out . . . and to follow the Mob into the Country'. This strategy aimed to 'form a Cordon for the Protection of the Farmer', and to 'segregate' rural and town populations. These tactics were not appropriate in every region's case, but the significant fact emerging is Simcoe's ability to plan and execute a realistic military campaign.[47] Elsewhere, on exceptional occasions, the army was unable to respond to every requisition, but the monthly returns of troop dispersals throughout the famines indicate that district COs were able to send detachments to most trouble spots for at least a short stay. These facts cannot have been lost on protesters.

The depressant effect of the army's presence can be inferred from the fact that the populations of even notoriously riot-prone Nottingham and Birmingham waited for rapid exoduses of troops to other trouble spots, before taking to the streets. John Gale Jones' perception of plebeian awe at the army is regularly evinced. The failure of the Oldham crowd to rescue arrested rioters from an army escort evoked a pathetic account from weaver Rowbottom, depressed by the wounds inflicted on his militant neighbours by troopers 'firing their pistols and Slashing away with their Swords'. The Oldham crowd thereafter had no stomach for physical clashes with the army.[48] No doubt this explains the limitation of resistance to stone throwing. Rumours of grandiose attacks on army patrols percolated in riotous episodes, but like that claiming that West Midland miners killed four cavalrymen and their horses, proved to be incorrect. A Surrey Fencible was unhorsed 'and dangerously wounded with a pitch-fork' in a murderous melee at Halstead in Essex, but even here the district CO reported that his men were universally 'terminating riot'. Cornish miners ambushed a solitary dispatch rider, and reputedly cut off his nose, but this singular, opportunist guerilla action, followed the tinners' defeat at Truro. Events do not seriously qualify the effectiveness of the regulars as a police force.[49]

The same cannot be said of the Volunteers. Their policing capacity was established by events during the first famine, and largely lost through those involving urban-based infantry regiments in the second. Rural cavalry corps, recruited from the farmers and landowners, remained reliable, but experience proved that even they had their shortcomings. A Pontefract inhabitant contrasted the efficiency of cavalry and infantry regiments after their deployment against West Riding riots in 1795, when

> the decided Advantage that the Infantry possess'd over the Volunteer Cavalry was clearly proved. For though they had to March from Wakefield, yet they were here in a few Hours, when the Cavalry were scarcely collected from the surrounding Country, in Force sufficient to command Respect.[50]

But infantry regiments drew on all ranks of urban society; labourers and artisans filled the ranks, and lower-ranking officers were drawn from the bourgeoisie. Unlike their cavalry counterparts, infantrymen did not have to command resources adequate to horse maintenance, and plebeian enthusiasts were often accoutred by their more affluent neighbours. Some COs enthused about the resultant social mix. William Spencer-Stanhope MP's typical pride, that the West Riding Volunteer establishment boasted 'an Epitome of the Island itself . . . We have Weavers of Wool of Cotton of Linen we have Colliers and . . . Smiths', was rudely shattered. For the enthusiasm of urban infantry comprising working men was destroyed by a number of factors. First, they were drawn from precisely those strata who were hardest hit by the famines, especially the second, which afflicted those well above the labourer. As Charles Rashleigh, among many others noted, if urban Volunteers 'get no Bread, their Ardour will rapidly abate'. Second, they were also affected by public opinion on the causes of dearth. Third, loyalties were strained by the autocratic and arbitary conduct of some commanders; Colonel Athorpe even had the unthinking temerity to railroad through an address supporting the Gagging Acts purportedly from, of all regiments, the Sheffield Volunteer Infantry. Dimensions to embryonic class-based conflicts included the resignations from one Bolton corps after the CO gave evidence against the weavers' campaign for statutory wage-regulation to a parliamentary committee, and the erosion of good will amongst those who stayed. Fourth, and most importantly, they were adversely affected by their experiences of active service against the crowd.[51]

The Rochdale Infantry 'behaved with the greatest coolness & propriety' when on duty during which two rioters were shot dead. The CO subsequently related that

> the Devil in the Shape of Women is now using all his influence to induce the Privates to brake their attachments to their Officers, and I am sorry to add has already debauched three from their duty, by delivering up their Arms and Accoutrements.

Identical reactions were reported from Sheffield in the wake of the parallel incident there; 'the poison spread', not least because rank-and-filers were castigated by their neighbours and workmates. But if these were ominous portents, disillusion achieved serious proportions in 1800, long before the September hypercrisis. Portland's March circular stressing great governmental dependence on the Volunteers as a riot-control agency was badly received. William Lorraine, who captained Northumberland Volunteers, read Portland's circular on the parade ground and

> endeavoured to persuade them of the Propriety but I much doubt of my success as they volunteered their services only in case of Invasion or the Appearance of the Enemy on the Coast . . . . I fear that they will by no means relish the Idea of leaving their homes to do that duty, which they conceive belongs to the regulars. I must own that I can't help thinking this an impolitic measure: it appears to be spurring a willing Horse & I am apprehensive that it will probably occasion a greater Disturbance than that which it is intended to quell.

Metropolitan volunteer officers warned after Portland's circular that Londoners were quitting their regiments in droves; the explanation advanced, the absence of both invasion threats and 'internal Commotions . . . to subvert the Constitution', was less than a half truth.[52]

Candid appraisals were rarely passed to Whitehall; Lorraine's disengaging honesty got no further than his Lord Lieutenant. Widespread deployment of the Volunteers as police during the 'early phase' of 1800 completed the erosion of the urban infantry's reputations, especially as their operations served only 'to protect the worst of villenly & oppression'. Some associations responded with public declamations against 'the Idea of being . . . instruments of protecting any Description of Men in their sordid views of Avarice and Oppression' as a Midland regiment put it. Patriotic appeals fell on increasingly deaf Volunteer infantrymen's ears as the struggle developed between urban consumers and rural producers. Devon Volunteers became 'the Farmers Bull Dogs' in 'vulgar' everyday speech, a view eventually endorsed by many officers too. The cancerous development of disloyalty was variously evinced. Volunteers in the Potteries were openly 'divided' over the issue of riot-control. In Staffordshire doggerels addressed to the men insisted that plebeian soldiers were hapless pawns of the rich, enrolled merely 'to protect their lives and their ill gained property'. Elsewhere, mutinous missives circulated through the ranks on pain of 'a good thumping' for any member who informed the officers. Infantrymen dared not enter West Bromwich pubs, and at Sheffield, public censure in working-class circles was capped by vicious beatings-up in the streets.[53]

Some COs responded by demanding formal renewed declarations of willingness to oppose riot; a trickle of favourable ones was forwarded to government, but pride, ignorance and arrogance amongst the officers shielded ministers from an accurate picture of the degree of disaffection in the ranks. An early climax occurred, inevitably enough at Sheffield, where the Junior Corps dissolved itself in June after some disturbances; the published explanation, that 'no . . . Symptoms of Riot' had appeared in spite of soaring food prices, was a blatant lie. A subsequent climax came with the September crisis. On 2 September, a day designated for demonstrations against living costs, 'many of the privates . . . secretly left the town early' to avoid the bugle-call. Of the remainder, only a handful went 'singly to parade' and braved the crowd. Three were 'much hurt' in the turmoil. Thereafter, 'the very great inveteracy of the People against' the loyal rump was best illustrated, according to Lord Lieutenant Fitzwilliam, by the reception of one of them at work: 'the other workmen immediately beset him, took him by the heels and held his head in a tub of water, till he was almost drown'd'. The officers later interviewed every man at his home, only to conclude that rankers 'have had Meetings among themselves, and have entered into formal Resolutions' not to obey their officers. Fitzwilliam, who emerged from the first famine with a high and unqualified regard for all Volunteers, now modified his views; events demonstrated the continued utility only of the yeomanry.[54]

Sheffield's experiences were far from unique. Birmingham Volunteers, 'formerly so popular . . . now find themselves as unpopular and perpetually exposed to insult'. The middle-class London Light Horse Volunteers, whose key metropolitan role was reflected in the unique arrangement whereby they could be called out only by the Home Secretary himself, virtually collapsed as an effective force. Seventy-eight men resigned between February and November 1800; two more were expelled, and only twenty-one replacements recruited. The regiment was fifteen percent under strength. Although 467 of the 540 soldiers attended the massive military carnival in Hyde Park on 4 June, a mere 281 turned up for formal review by the king one month later. When ordered on duty against the September rioters, many members 'either paid no attention to the summons, or chose to judge for themselves the urgency of the service' despite urgent written appeals sent to absentees. If this 'maxim' was 'subversive of all discipline', worse was to follow when they were again ordered on duty against the mass meetings called by the LCS on 9 November. Then 'the LVH never mustered so few upon duty'. Remedial measures eluded a committee of enquiry, which provoked only further resignations, including officers. Attempts to deploy infantry regiments foundered in degrees of disaster in town after town in September. But COs, often with the connivance of the Bench, concealed these realities from Whitehall. The Mayor of Banbury ignored problems with the Volunteers in his correspondence with the Home Office, but it later transpired, through the advertisements page of the local press, that six men had aggravated their original offence of 'withhold-[ing] their services during the Riots . . . by offering such Excuses as were unbecoming Soldiers'. Insubordination, and even mutiny, was commonly overlooked by commanders after the receipt of apologies. Even Earl Fortescue who conducted a vigorous campaign against Devon Volunteers who joined the revolt of the south-west, accepted a 'hearty contrition' on occasions; otherwise, 'the spirit of Volunteering' would have been irrevocably crushed. But in September a conspiracy of silence emerged. Nottingham Corporation forwarded copies of all handbills published by them during the riots to the Home Office, except the one threatening legal action against people who induced desertions from the Volunteers by persuasion or threats. The Mayor of Poole admitted his reservations over the Volunteers, but only in support of his demand for regulars. Colonel Palmer conveyed his surprise at his dutiful Hampshire men 'of the lower order' who were 'experiencing difficulties' in feeding themselves. The press gave an equally distorted picture. The *Kent Chronicle* proved exceptional in its report of the Margate Infantry Volunteers' support for rioters, but a plagiarised account in *E. Johnson's . . . Sunday Gazette*, omitted all references to the Volunteers' conduct. Only the *Morning Chronicle* drew attention to the insubordination rampant among the Volunteers, but this inclusion on 15 September, was central to a major article defending the grain trade and attacking the government.[55]

If ministerial perceptions of Volunteer loyalties in September are problematic, the final riotous phase left no room for doubt. Ominous portents of South-western developments occurred in December 1800 when urban corps publicly declared against protecting 'the Roags of Farmers', against whom they promised an offensive while they 'have a drop of blood in our bodies'. Mutinous murmers were heard on parade; clergymen read threatening letters from Volunteers to their startled congregations. GOC Simcoe reacted by extracting fresh oaths of allegiance from corps after corps, and the county press soon teemed with suitable declarations, but in the medium term these proved less significant than the resignations by those who refused to subscribe. Moreover, those who did comply were not to be trusted, and their officers knew it. One who was uncharacteristically scrupulous admitted that

the Volunteers in general have an Opinion that they cannot be punished and whilst they hang together Government will be afraid to punish them.

The Officers have lost much Power over them through not having been able to enforce, in a summary Manner, the payment of those Fines which almost every Company agreed to, when first formed.

Simcoe's optimism that his 'proper precautions' would disperse 'our little Cloud' was not shared by many townsmen who recognised that their Volunteer neighbours would not indefinitely bear arms on behalf of rural communities. The Chairman of the Cornish Bench opined that the services of the Volunteers from the towns and mining districts 'must be purchased on Condition of fixing a Maximum and other terms which we abhor'. Indeed the Sidmouth Company had already distinguished themselves in December by forcing magistrates to fix food prices.[56]

Who were these mutinous Volunteers? The Brixham officers represented that class of townsmen, somewhat above the rank of artisan, whose encouragement of South-western crowds was considered to be of special significance. Lieutenant Pridham kept an unspecified shop; Lieutenant Collier was a schoolmaster, and Captain Saunders was, perhaps surprisingly, a butcher. The Dartmouth crowd was led by 'Tradesmen' Volunteers; so too were their counterparts who refused to suppress a Honiton riot. Shenstone Flood was described as a 'Master Tailor', three others as cordwainers, and the remainder as a wheelwright, a sadler, a mason, a 'Woolcoomber' and a 'Victualler'. Delinquent Banbury Volunteers belonged to the same strata; here we find a grocer, a druggist, a coal-merchant, a 'salesman', and perhaps surprisingly again, a baker.[57]

From 1798 the government 'discouraged the arming of the urban poor', a decision anticipated in 1795 by Fitzwilliam, whose surprise at plebeian Volunteer loyalty did not remove his suspicions of 'the Mass of the People'; he refused proposals for new infantry regiments. However, as Spencer-Stanhope's address revealed, in 1799 many workers remained enrolled, and as late as 1803 several 'labourers' were still members of corps at Exeter which had also participated in earlier riots. Northern Volunteer regiments contained an even higher proportion of workers, and this was reflected in several mutinies outside Sheffield.[58] In 1800–1 there were few recorded food riots, as protest took political forms with mass meetings and a recrudescence of the insurrectionary United Englishmen's organisation,[59] which denied a theatre for Volunteer mutinies when ordered against the crowd. Nevertheless, these regiments were suspect; political 'corruption' was widely 'supposed', and 'great doubts . . . entertained as to the Volunteers acting', reasons which one JP used to refuse to sanction the execution of arrest warrants by a company.[60] Other parallels between the contrasting riotous and political protests in the South-west and the industrial North in 1800–1, include middle-class sympathy for plebeian movements. The defection of the northern urban Volunteer establishment is inherent in this sympathy. The phenomenon emphasises that the famines, especially the second, hit those well above the 'lower classes'; poverty engulfed skilled workers and tradesmen, and inflicted severe cuts on middle-class living standards, and alienated them from the government and its policies. Volunteer desertion symbolises the extent of that alienation; Pitt lost the effective service of the infantry, both as policing agents and as the patriotic party. South-western events proved it to ministers, in spite of the impressive conspiracy of silence over many examples of mutinous companies.

George III himself testified to government unease with the Volunteers with his insistence that the invasion scare over the summer of 1801 be exploited;

> for the not having had any attempt at invasion has certainly . . . cooled the ardour and diligence of the Volunteer Corps and perhaps of the embodied militia.

The inauguration of inspecting Field Officers to maintain a professional eye on the Volunteers in close liaison with the Commander-in-Chief when volunteering revived with the recurrence of war in 1803, reflects the disillusion with the movement at the highest levels; this owed much more to what the Volunteers were used for during the famines than it did to Napoleon's failure repeatedly to flush the English body politic with adrenalin.[61]

CHAPTER 16

The Role of the Courts

We have established that there was no automatic recourse to the courts, and that local judicial autonomy was not over-ridden by central government. A crude guide to the use of the courts against rioters is provided by column 8 in tables 1 to 12. As their compilation is in part based on legal muniments, they exaggerate recourse to prosecution, at the expense of hundreds of unrecorded 'twopenny squabbles'. The role of the courts cannot be established with statistical clarity, and the tables prove that resort to formal legal proceedings bore no relationship to either the occurrence or the intensity of disturbances. None of those arrested in fierce rioting in the Borough of Nottingham were prosecuted, nor were the courts used to restrain potentially dangerous developments at Sheffield in September 1800; lesser riots, for example at Overton, New Alresford and Romsey at this time, produced a crop of indictments at the Hampshire Michaelmas Sessions.[1]

Most magistrates believed, theoretically at least, in the efficacy of the courts as agents of social control. Phillip Rashleigh's reaction to springtime rioting in Cornwall in 1795 was typical:

> I don't think we have had any serious disposition in the People to disturb the Government, but when Riots begin on one Account they proceed to others before they are corrected, and therefore I think where the Offence begins Punishment should ensue, and the first sacrifice will be the least evil.

Many magistrates, at least on occasions, acted on such principles. Nottingham Corporation launched prosecutions after the first serious riot in the 'early phase' of 1800, and a spokesman insisted that sentences of imprisonment and transportation were 'peculiarly calculated to stop the course of lawless violence . . . at a Crisis'.[2]

Prosecution of rioters presented problems; overall it seems that the process was easier against people arrested on-the-spot, than against participants who had dispersed. Certainly arrests multiplied judicial options. Thirty rioters were seized by troops in Nottinghamshire on 3 September

1800. The JP in charge, Bingham, on his 'way home'

> committed 16 to the Southwell House of Correction and dismissed the
> remainder. I examined them every week till the Nottm Sessions and
> generally dismissed two or three upon their procuring Sureties for their
> good Behaviour; the whole were thus dismissed excepting four, two of
> which are committed to Nottingham Gaol for the Assizes,

and the other two bailed to appear at the same court. Bingham's strategy
was tantamount, as he hinted, to holding hostages for the restoration and
maintenance of order; it also permitted the identification of 'the principal
instigators'. The four committed had taken leading parts, and were jointly
responsible for forcing a town crier to summon the crowd. Nearly fifty
rioters were arrested by troops directed by Sir John Wrottesley and the Rev.
A.B. Haden; all the prisoners were incarcerated in Wolverhampton jail, to
be confronted and identified by their victims, during a two-day investigation. Specific charges were laid against twenty-six, and recognizances to
prosecute exacted from the relevant witnesses; the remaining prisoners were
largely spared. Two named offenders, who were not in custody, and never
came to court, emphasise the significance of arrests in the judicial process,
especially in districts in which industrial workers had a huge numerical
dominance, but considerable anonymity. The indictment of four, let alone
twenty-six, after one incident, was uncharacteristic.[3] Prosecution was
commonly reserved for a selected prisoner or two, arrested with others. Of
the many forces operative in a post-riot context, the strongest militated
against rather than for legal proceedings, especially where activists initially
remained at large. The well-documented Devon disturbances of 1801
permit a detailed case study.

   After over a week's uninterrupted and virtually unopposed rioting, Lord
Lieutenant Fortescue arrived in Devon with Home Office orders in his
pocket. The army's presence was necessary to restore magisterial security,
and to reactivate the Bench, Fortescue's first task. His second hinged on
identifying and indicting the most culpable crowd activists. Fortescue's
campaign was frustrated by a number of forces, in spite of formal support
voted by the unprecedented attendance of JPs at the Quarter Sessions. On
his arrival, only two people were in custody; his suggestion that they
warranted prosecution for High Treason was ill-calculated to sustain the
sympathies of his subordinates, and compounded the effect of the immediate trial and execution of two rioters over the Somerset border, while
disturbances still raged. These well-publicised hangings, with full military
guards, and fears of savage popular resistance and reprisals, had a major
impact on subsequent legal administration across the south-west. In
Somerset another rioter was transported, not hanged; the Grand Jury
reduced another capital charge to a non-capital alternative, and threw out
several other indictments altogether. Juries acquitted the remaining prisoners tried at the Assize, and all other cases went to the Sessions. So too did all
Cornish cases, despite the decision to finance prosecutions from the county
rate by JPs who were doubtlessly also forcibly reminded of their own recent
experiences of the adverse effects of hanging food rioters.[4] In Devon

Fortescue's determination was diluted by a speedy return of magisterial indifference. Totnes JPs were typically 'glad to let off the offenders upon the Idea that there is plenty of Corn and that they were incited by Hunger', without even recourse to justice Carpenter's semi-escapist advocacy of dropping cases on the offenders' issue of a public apology. The recurrence of threats, which had initially helped to deter magistrates from actions against the riots, now persuaded them against prosecutions. Several received 'repeated threats of assassination', and the courageous rump who remained committed to Fortescue's line still had to confront intimidated witnesses: 'no man likes . . . to bear the Odium of Informer', or face the 'danger that may follow'.[5]

The inter-action of forces can be examined minutely at Totnes where Fortescue had an ally in miller Welsford, who advocated 'establishing the point' of the sanctity of private property by the criminal conviction of those responsible for imposing 'a maximum on my property'. Fortescue directed a county justice, the Rev. Kitson, to investigate offences committed by Totnes rioters outside the Borough, and the Mayor those within. Kitson was warned 'not . . . to expect much . . . co-operation' from the latter. Initially, farmer Palk agreed 'to prosecute if he could be protected', and named three assailants; he subsequently withdrew his powerful verbal evidence when Kitson returned with a colleague to formally take depositions; Palk's 'Door not broken open . . . no halter ever heard of . . . no threatenings to do . . . personal injury'. Kitson's attempts to imprison Totnes rioters identified by more stalwart witnesses dissolved in farcical incidents. One of the accused produced no less than eight alibis; the escape of another was transparently engineered by a Borough constable, leaving Kitson to wearily acknowledge his 'failed . . . endeavours to send those to a Court of Justice who were properly pointed out to be made Examples in it'. Proceedings now devolved on the willing Welsford and the obstructive Corporation. The town clerk airily denied all knowledge of indictable acts. Meanwhile Welsford received anonymous threats of reprisals, and a visit from the vicar, himself implicated in the abdication of authority during the riots, who insisted that Welsford's future in the town was conditional on his acceptance of a token apology from a leading crowd activist. Welsford capitulated; Fortescue exploded with rage, but an interview with Welsford failed to rekindle his enthusiasm, and the Lord Lieutenant was mortified further by the refusal of the Treasury Solicitor to take the case further. On realisation of Fortescue's predicament, Totnes suspects suddenly 'became visible again'; 'the sort of Triumph manifested' publicly by the relieved populace induced the despatch of Kitson's clerk to reconnoitre to establish if these comprised 'indecent exultations'. Fortescue did manage to get indictments against twenty-three Devonians; more than half were prosecuted through extending the operations of the Treasury Solicitor's local agents, initially employed against delinquent Devonport dockyard workers and the Brixham Volunteer officers who had led one crowd. Thus the bulk of these cases were *not* the product of the normal legal process.[6]

The forces unleashed against Fortescue were not exceptional in similar circumstances, and the fact that they could largely defeat a determined Lord Lieutenant in close liaison with the Home Office and the Attorney-General, speaks for itself. Some JPs pre-empted most problems by permitting prisoners to enlist; one JP secretly arranged for a rioter, against whom there were evidential problems, to be press-ganged. Determined magistrates, their subordinate officials, and witnesses, were all at risk, and regularly subjected to threats of further overt protest, with or without covert acts of 'private' vengeance. Wrottesley and Haden's mass arrests in Staffordshire, the effect of which was admittedly aggravated by their uncharacteristic search for capital charges, promised to provoke an uglier series of events. From the Potteries Heathcote received what he considered to be authentic intelligence

> that there is a regular Plan formed to release the Prisoners in Gaol . . . as soon as the Militia leaves Stafford, the Correspondence . . . is carried on between People here and from thence by persons that meet at Stafford under a pretence of going to visit the Prisoners, and in order to prepare the Minds of the Multitude for the Event when it is ripe for execution they bring acct. of the hardships of the Prisoners and Subscriptions for their Relief are carried on secretly in all the different [industrial] Works.

The prisoners' moral innocence was proclaimed by anonymous letters – 'the cause . . . is only Bread' – to demand that the Bench desisted, as 'we are either for War or peace'. These two JPs were frightened, but unmoved, their resolve stiffened by an intensified military presence. But the Bench's bravery did not necessarily extend to all those involved, who were only too aware of their isolation in a unanimously hostile community, and of the army's inability to provide permanent protection. The town clerk of Winchester, who took depositions, was told that 'he must take his chance', and his main witness instructed to 'Prepare your self for the next World'. Bingham's Nottinghamshire crusade was finally undermined by offers to pay for damage caused by rioters, backed by threats to the obdurate; Bingham later lamented that

> the Evidence has either been intimidated or bribed, and they will not speak out so plainly at the Assizes as in their depositions taken upon oath – in Short Both Farmers and Evidence seem afraid of more disturbances and that in that case they will be particularly pointed at, and indeed such is the general timidity that few seem willing to prosecute on this occasion.

Magisterial indifference to prosecution is more understandable if their strenuous activity – and all it involved – foundered in pusillanimous testimony from the witness box.[7]

Systematic use of the courts was therefore impossible against rioters, and the same went for other creators of unrest. Cases deriving from the tensions generated by famine conditions heard by the Hampshire Sessions in 1800–1, included two persons who independently and openly threatened arson, strikers, seditious speech-makers, and more who challenged the rulings of poor-law officials, one group of whom smashed Abbotsam workhouse windows on consecutive days. But this does not reflect the systematic use of the law; offences and alleged offenders were assessed independently, and decisions taken individually.[8] The famines saw no novel uniformity in the law's usage, with the partial exception of a move towards a more rigorous use of the law in the industrial North-west in 1800–1. In December 1799 the Lancashire Bench announced its determination to use anti-trade union legislation, and a number of men were imprisoned. Rioters from Stockport and Ashton-under-Lyne in February, from Bolton in May, and from Manchester in July, August and October 1800 were all prosecuted. The legal offensive was subsequently maintained with cases mounted against rioters from Eccles, Chorley and Ashton, and extended to political activists; indictments for 'making, reading, hearing and listening to divers seditious speeches' and 'riotous assembly' at open air meetings were brought, together with more serious charges for administering illegal oaths, and the attempted seduction of the troops. But the apparent severity as represented by one execution and several transportations should not obscure the partial undermining of this more determined official offensive by social tensions and unrest. The JP who decided against Volunteer assistance to execute warrants, dropped four of the cases on the spurious grounds that 'we had got the worst' three offenders. The fact that the Lancashire Bench suddenly asked for formal advice on the legal necessity for magisterial supervision of regulars opposing 'actual Riot', also suggests that some JPs were near the point of abdicating their responsibilities like their South-western counterparts.[9]

However, the numbers of rioters who did appear in the courts in spite of factors militating against, warrants a brief analysis of the judicial mechanisms, though aspects are shrouded in mystery. Grand Jurors did not record their decision making process, and jury-room proceedings are the best-kept secret in English legal history. Few trials, except of traitors and murderers, received extended press coverage, and little is known about court-room events, except where trial judges reported information to facilitate the Home Secretary's decision over well-supported appeals for clemency. But there are few problems with sentences; judges had a limited prerogative to commute death to transportation sentences. Fines or short-term imprisonment, with or without whippings, could be imposed on minor offenders. The percentage of indictments returned ignoramus by Grand Juries, the nature of the precise charge determined upon, and the acquittal rate are all of significance.[10]

Case histories offer an incisive approach. In May 1800, Wrottesley and Haden ended up with over sixty prisoners; their request for a Special Commission was rejected, but the Bench pressed ahead and substantiated the capital charges they clearly sought against twenty-five people, fifteen of whom faced two or more capital counts. The Grand Jury promptly reduced these to indictments for petty larceny on all but seven individuals. Six of these seven were subsequently acquitted; Emma Birks was convicted on well-supported counts of leading participation in successive riots and sentenced to death. Of the remaining twenty-one tried, twelve were found guilty, and mostly sentenced to three months in prison, though their release depended on providing acceptable sureties for good behaviour. Birks was respited by the judge, presumably at the Grand Jury's desire; she did not hang. The Grand Jury clearly drastically modified the intentions of the committing justices; trial jurors opted for leniency in six out of the seven cases where the JPs were supported by Grand Jurors. On the trial jurors' one capital conviction, the Grand Jury again interposed to undermine the strict application of the law.[11]

Evidence from other proceedings supports the basic findings of this analysis of the history of rioters arraigned before the Staffordshire Midsummer Assize of 1800, in spite of the fact that that court heard more riot cases than any other court at a single sitting during the famines. The fifty percent acquittal rate is similar to those at the Devon Assizes in 1801–2, which dealt with those offenders whom Fortescue and the Treasury Solicitor managed to indict, and the Lancashire Sessions where four of the nine defendants from Ashton-under-Lyne were found not guilty. Higher conviction rates where several prisoners were tried did occur. Thirteen of the fifteen tried at the Cornish Midsummer Sessions in 1801 were sentenced, but the rate reflects guilty pleas on non-capital charges, probably following 'deals' struck between defendants and the county prosecutor. Therefore a veritable plethora of factors ensured that most courts had relatively few cases, rarely more than ten, even after intense disturbances. Most defendants appeared on non-capital charges, in spite of the technical ease with which food rioters could be capitally arraigned. Thus there were few chances of mass hangings or impressive convoys of transported convicts. Indeed, most punishments were mild. Typically inconsequential fines of sixpence and a shilling were imposed on a dozen rioters convicted at Easter 1796 sittings of the Northumberland and City of Newcastle Sessions. The Bench at the Surrey Michaelmas Sessions in 1800 were

> unanimously of opinion that under all the Circumstances Lenity was the measure most likely to occasion the affair to be buried in Oblivion [and] discharged the Men, on giving Security for their good and peaceable behaviour for two years, and we trust we shall be quiet.

Many Grand Jurors and Quarter Sessions chairmen concurred and scores of people benefited from the resultant leniency. Five Durham miners appeared at the Easter 1796 Sessions, gave formal sureties to answer any summons to attend at a future sitting, and that was the end of the matter.[12]

However the numbers of acquittals across the country reflected sympathetic trial jurors, notably at Borough Sessions; authority, it was said, could 'hardly suppose that the little Tradesmen and Householders' who comprised juries 'of a Country Town who certainly feel the Pressure of the times . . . can be free from Prejudice' in defendants' favour, even when evaluating evidence adequate to convictions by 'an unbias'd petty Jury'. This factor was weaker in Assize courts, where juries were commonly dominated by farmers; if some were intimidated, others were not, including one who volunteered his view that the execution of two Dean miners should proceed, because 'so much mischief has been done by these People that an example is highly necessary'. However, this vindictive fellow declined to entrust his name to the Secretary of State.[13]

Some judges had similar views. Mr Justice Hardinge harangued Glamorganshire Grand Jurors, whom, he insisted, should ignore common compassionate claims 'that in such times the Poor can scarcely be considered as moral and free agents', and were the innocent victims of 'ringleaders and powerful incendiaries'. Hardinge's conception of mercy turned upon 'determining what examples of capital punishment are necessary, and where the line should be drawn', which he wished to reserve to himself; his audience largely ignored his injunction to apply the law strictly when indicting. Other judges refused appeals for clemency, determinedly leaving such decisions to the Home Secretary. Others commuted death sentences, leaving one of the capitally convicted rioters to pay the supreme penalty symbolically, on the grounds that a token hanging 'was absolutely necessary to the peace . . . where the offence was committed'. Likewise transportation sentences did not invariably proceed to exile. At Nottingham, judge Rooke commuted two of his four transportation sentences at the behest of Grand Jurors. Chief Justice Mansfield, who presided over the trial of a Stockport rioter charged with larceny, commented that

> It was thought necessary by Mr Justice Burton and myself to order him to be transported for the sake of example. . . . It appears probable that without any very wicked intentions he might be deluded into . . . this offence, under a mistaken Notion that as he . . . professed a willingness to pay for what they took, At a price which they . . . fixed, they could not be guilty of stealing, and [as] his Conviction makes it improbable that any such Delusion should again take place,

Mansfield recommended the remittance of the punishment. Professional judges were neither united, nor consistent, in either their imposition of severe sentences, or their attitudes to commutation. Some were obviously prepared to use the scaffold, on occasion at least; others were clearly unhappy at the imposition of even transportation. If the attitudes of some affected their conduct in the court-room, many rioters owed their acquittals to judge *and* jury.[14]

These additional factors ensured that few rioters went to the gallows. In many ways this was fortunate, for hangings were not unvaried occasions for popular holiday debauchery, depicted in so much contemporary comment, and uncritically regurgitated by many historians. The hanging crowd had its own morality, and its own powers of discrimination. To expect acquiescence in the execution of people for the enforcement of populist perceptions of marketing morality, was demanding the impossible. Death sentences were imposed by at least six tribunals. The Court Martial on the mutinous Oxfordshire Militia sentenced two soldiers to be shot; two more, and two civilians, were sentenced to hang by the Special Commission. One rioter was executed in Devon in 1795, another in Cornwall in 1796, the same year as two more were hanged at Gloucester. Two others suffered in Somerset in 1801. The inadequate evidence suffices to prove very hostile reactions, including violence or its threat, in every single case.

Only Thomas Campion, of the three rioters sentenced to death at the Devon Summer Assize in 1795, was executed. The magistracy brushed off numerous threats, 'should the Culprits Suffer', and implemented their decision to hang Campion near the scene of the attack on Kingsteignton Tide-mill. Thereafter, intense unease was evinced by officials; the execution was advanced by a week to try to pre-empt the build-up of hostile public opinion, but the High Sheriff's intelligence suggested

> that a general spirit of disatisfaction . . . has manifested itself amongst the lower Class of People in . . . Bovey Tracy and that district at the sentence . . . and there being great Reason to fear an attempt will be made to rescue the Prisoner either on the Road to, or at the Place of Execution, unless proper precautions, are taken to prevent such an Outrage.

The decision to proceed miles from Exeter posed a massive security problem, which was aggravated by residual disorder. The Sheriff summoned regulars from Exeter and Plymouth, and Volunteers from across south and east Devon. De la Pole's yeomanry were away from home for three days on duty. There are no details of the hanging, but in 1841 a local historian recorded the event as a 'military execution'.[15] Similar manifestations accompanied the execution of a Cornish miner in 1796. His employer, Vivian Trevethick, tried to mollify public opinion by lobbying to have the body buried in the victim's parish. Here the corpse was accorded a solemn version of a hero's reception by a vast assembly. Subsequently 'vengeance was openly threatened against all who were supposed to have had any share in causing this man's death'. A strong military presence was essential. Identical military precautions were taken over hangings in 1801 at Taunton, 'instead of Ilminster by way of example'. Authority exuded relief and surprise when the 'populace showed no signs of commotion' on the day.[16]

Alienation clearly increased in equal proportion to the severity of the examples made. However, these executions affected the subsequent administration of justice in the region. In Devon, seven capital cases were held over from 1795 to the Lent 1796 Assize; three indictments were then dropped, three more ended in acquittals, and the seventh defendant had died. In Cornwall, Lord De Dunstanville, who had vigorously opposed moves to commute both death sentences in 1795, later interposed for a transportee's reprieve. No rioters were tried after disturbances in 1800, and every 1801 trial was confined to the Sessions. The failure of clemency petitions for the two Dean miners in 1796 had a less dramatic effect on the course of justice in Gloucestershire. After the 1801 riots, Sessions chairman, the Rev. Foley, argued that Grand Jurors 'reserved' the most culpable offenders 'for a more solemn tribunal armed with higher powers of life and death', but only three of the twenty prisoners were tried at the Assize. Here, one was transported, another imprisoned for a year, and the third acquitted. Foley imposed fines of a shilling on such of the seventeen who pleaded guilty at the Sessions, but those found guilty after having the temerity to protest their innocence, went to prison.[17]

The executions which followed the Militia mutinies however, belong to a class of their own. The Militia's concentration in the South mirrored their key role in the event of an invasion. Orders for strategic discussions between the C-in-C and the Home Office, reflected the serious degree of ministerial alarm, which was fully shared by the GOC responsible, the

Duke of Richmond. He believed that the reimposition of control on the entire Militia turned on the outcome of 'this Business'; he demanded 'speedy example', and 'real punishment . . . on all the Men . . . taken resisting in Arms'. As these exceeded two hundred, death sentences on all were impractical, but Richmond advocated specific penal legislation to enable them to be sent 'to the West Indies, or on Board the Fleet'. If ministers warily rejected this option, they certainly wanted severe retribution. Richmond immediately launched a thorough investigation; he had selected twenty-two soldiers for trial within three days of the effective collapse of the mutiny. Only two were to appear before a Regimental Court Martial. The remainder faced capital charges; fourteen were to be tried by a General Court Martial, and such who were cleared by that tribunal, were then to join the other six, selected for criminal trials with two civilians. The Court Martial was restricted to Militia officers; the presidential appointment of Colonel Sloane reflected his experience, and membership of the Commons, where he could be the government's spokesman. The Court Martial sat from 5 to 22 May, and appears from its own detailed record to have proceeded with scrupulous fairness. Of the fourteen, one was not tried, four acquitted, and six sentenced to floggings of between five and fifteen hundred lashes. Three men, all of whom had clearly planned the descent on Seaford, were sentenced to be shot. None of those acquitted were retried, and one of the capital convicts was spared on condition of military servitude for life in Australia. Of those sentenced to the lash, one was pardoned, and the numbers on the rest reduced, but not sufficiently to negate the minor mitigation that only three hundred lashes were to be inflicted at once. The executions and first instalments of the floggings were scheduled for 13 June, nearly two calendar months after the mutiny.[18]

The announcement of these sentences aggravated existing tensions in southern England; rumours, fuelled by threatening letters, that the populace would join three regiments pledged to prevent the executions, were universally current. The Special Commission, which convened at Lewes immediately after the Court Martial, proceeded in this atmosphere. The inaudibility of the Assize sermon was ascribed to the clergyman's nerves. The local police were augmented from across the county. Fears were entertained over the quoracy of the Grand Jury, which promptly distinguished itself with a transparently contrived reduction of the values involved on one count to non-capital sums. In the event their 'merciful intention' was circumvented by Henry Brook and John Etherington's conviction on counts of riot. The trials of privates Midwinter and Avery had to be postponed until the normal Summer Assize, as the key witnesses from the sloop *Lucy* could not be contacted in time. This compromised the strategic planning behind the issue of a Special Commission. Privates Sykes and Sansom were convicted for the larceny of huge amounts of flour, and Mr Justice Buller left no uncertainty of the imminence of execution. His observation that their offence was aggravated by 'the AMPLE PROVISION made for Militiamen' was ridiculous, for these men died for the cause of better rations. The hanging of all four was also fixed for 13 June, at Horsham. Order here, and at the elaborate military execution planned at Brighton, would be guaranteed by a massive influx of troops into Sussex, including recently-arrived veterans from continental campaigns.[19]

Clemency petitions for the soldiers were brushed away. The king familiarised himself with procedures adopted for executions under the Mutiny Act, and penned detailed instructions pertaining to maximum publicity and 'utmost solemnity'. Richmond was to assemble 'all the Troops, Regulars, Fencibles, and Militia . . . encamped at' Brighton to witness the executions and floggings. This was not mere retribution against the Oxfordshires, but a fierce warning to every soldier in the country. '"I am to die for what the Redgement done"', wrote Edward Cooke on the eve of facing the firing squad, '"I have done no harm to no person . . . I am going to suffer innocently Dear Brother"'. Each regional GOC received orders with 'Copies of the . . . Sentences', which were

> to be circulated among all the Corps without exception in that District under your Command which having been distinctly read to their Men assembled together, under arms, for that express purpose, are to be enter'd in their Orderly Books, to the end that their Comg. Officers may from them be better enabled to support a Uniform Course of Regularity, a sound Discipline amongst them by holding up to them, if necessary, so striking an Example, of the fatal Consequences, that must attend their suffering themselves as Soldiers, to be led astray from their Duty, or to be governed by any other principles, than those of a strict obedience to their Officers.[20]

On 13 June, infantry regiments, with cavalry and artillery marshalled in their rear, lined both sides of the valley near Brighton Camp; 'a number of loaded cannon' were aimed at the firing ground. The High Sheriff reported that 'The scene was the most awful and impressive I ever beheld', and added the significant rider that 'not the smallest symptoms of opposition, resistance or revenge appeared'. The floggings came first:

> The men capitally convicted were then marched up between the two lines of the army accompanied by a clergyman, and escorted by pickets from the different regiments of horse and foot; at the upper end of the line, after a short time spent with the clergyman, they were shot by a party of the Oxfordshire militia who had been very active in the . . . riots, but had been pardoned . . . . the awful ceremony was concluded by the marching of all the regiments round the bodies . . . laid upon the ground. If this did not satisfy Richmond's insistence on 'real punishment' for all the guilty Oxfordshires, the blood which 'oozed out' from the coffins over the pall-bearers who had just shot their mates, while on their way to burial, perhaps sufficed. Decency devolved upon a local shepherd, 'who cut the turf' round the unmarked graves outside Hove churchyard 'into the form of coffins, bearing the initials of the sufferers', which he maintained for decades.[21]

The Sheriff then proceeded to Horsham. There were no reports of disturbances. The press related emotive scenes between Sansom and his wife, who had travelled from Oxfordshire to be with her husband. Readers

were further treated to a full account of the 'bungling job' on Sansom
performed by two experienced Old Bailey hangmen, and a heart-tearing
account of a subscription collected 'by the gentlemen' to defray Mrs
Sansom's 'expenses . . . and to comfort her under duress': one wonders if
she ever told her children of their father's 'becoming . . . behaviour' with
the other three on the scaffold. The Home Secretary was manifestly relieved
at 'the good order and behaviour of the troops' at Brighton, and echoed the
Sheriff's suitably pious hopes that 'An example so unusual and so terrible
will . . . have the desired effect'. But this obvious satisfaction did not
extend to the reprieve of both soldiers sentenced to die by the Summer
Assize, in spite of the Grand Jury's view that 'the example already made' in
June was enough. Private Avery was thought 'half a fool' by the trial judge
and reprieved 'on pretence . . . of a weak understanding'. The Lord
Lieutenant thought that this sufficed to establish authority's merciful bent,
and as he had 'heard of no circumstance in favour of' private Midwinter,
concluded

> that if . . . better discipline is not established in the Militia they will
> become the curse of the Country. As the Officers are not too apt to
> enforce it I cannot recommend relaxation in such a case to the Civil
> Power.

This 'candid opinion' sealed Midwinter's fate.

In conclusion, two questions warrant answers. First, did the role of
government in the use of the repressive agencies provide further support for
contemporary categorisations of Pitt's 'Reign of Terror'? Secondly, did the
ministry's part in the maintenance of law and order during the famines
provide that 'ample evidence of the growing involvement of the state in
local affairs', which Dr. Calhoun ascribes to 'the numerous exchanges of
letters between the local magistrates in "disturbed areas" and the Home
Office regarding disturbances'? Did these comprise 'one of the most
significant manifestations of the tendency towards centralization which was
strong during the industrial revolution'? To what degree were the traditions
of local autonomy transgressed?[22]

The 'Reign of Terror' traditionally turns on government action against
popular political radicals. Seditious speech and publications were the
concern of 'most overtly political trials'; the 'less than two hundred
prosecutions for treason and sedition over a decade, hardly constitutes, in
itself, a reign of terror', writes Mr Emsley. We may also accept that the
Crown Lawyers entertained a distinct bias against the prosecution of minor
figures and minor infringements of the sedition and related laws. On the
other hand, the quasi-legal harassment of plebeian politicians, and the
severe problems incurred by those prosecuted, even if found not guilty,
together with the use of *ex-officio* informations and special juries, were
greatly feared weapons.[23] The passing of yet more legislation against trade
unions, and executive decisions to prosecute constitutional reformers like
Thomas Hardy for treason, as well as revolutionary conspirators like
Arthur O'Connor and Colonel Despard, all added to the fiercely repressive
tone. So too did the conscious creation of an ultra-conservative military

establishment with the Volunteers. At the Home Office, Portland moved in the direction of creating standard anti-riot procedure, as revealed by the Royal Proclamation and his supporting statements on the full use of the repressive agencies in September 1800. The government certainly created the instruments of terror, and in its clandestine formation of a centralised, secret intelligence bureau under the auspices of the Alien Act, began to construct some of the machinery of an authoritarian state. The use of spies as opposed to *agent provocateurs*, doubtlessly intimidated radicals from formal organisations after the experiences of 1795.[24] But with the exception of the arrests ordered under the re-suspensions of Habeas Corpus, the government did not arm *itself* with special new arbitrary powers. This contrasts vividly with Pitt's innovatory statutory enactments and bloody militaristic repression in Ireland, Professor Williams' theatre for 'England's real reign of terror'.[25] If the government obtained the legal instruments for repression, in England these were largely delegated in practice to the local authorities. This aspect of social control is vital.

Harassment of politically-motivated individuals principally turn on the attitude of local authorities outside London; considerable regional and local variation resulted which encouraged some to argue for a more uniform application of repression. Aaron Graham, the experienced stipendiary magistrate, sent to the West Midlands as a Home Office special envoy to assess the insurrectionary threat in the autumn of 1800, recommended that loud-mouthed democrats at Wolverhampton be given 'a hint of the suspension of Habeas Corpus Act'. But Graham neither insisted on this, nor supervised its implementation; the ultimate decision rested with the local Bench. Where, but only where, magistrates adopted this policy, democrats could feel that they were 'ruled by a rod of iron' in their subjection to ruling-class dictates. However, the democrats were in a minority; in most places, and at most times, they comprised but a fraction of the population. When popular protests are considered we are no longer examining a deviant minority. Cornish justices asserted that 'Almost every individual in the Mining parts of the Country where the Riots happened, was more or less concerned in them; so that each Man feels it his own Cause'. In many cases, large numbers took to the streets, and if elsewhere the numbers of participants in one disturbance were less than a tithe of the population, they represented the majority. Thus during the famines authority was not confronted by an unrepresentative minority; in this sense the majority were brought under the Pittite repressive umbrella, and directly exposed to the power of the state. Do these factors warrant any reinterpretation of the applicability of the alleged 'Reign of Terror'?[26]

This question turns on the degree of social control achieved through the use of the repressive agencies, which is bedevilled by contradictions. Resistance to riots and the steps taken against rioters, repeatedly provoked further if not greater disorders. Arrests did not invariably produce humble dispersals, but commonly stimulated renewed action to remedy fresh grievances. The decision to prosecute was frequently productive of threats to justices and witnesses, which often did thwart the functions of the normal legal machinery. The famines terminated in a crisis of control with the Volunteer movement. These are features of disorder, not social control.

Nor does order characterise the situation where one form of protest is
supplanted by another, be it when riots are replaced by politically-inspired
and orientated movements, or incendiary campaigns. The same interpretation applies where massive outbreaks of larceny obtained. For disorder was
manifestly rife throughout the famines.

Apparent contradictions in the localised effects of the use of the repressive
agencies serve to emphasise that in the final analysis, the maintenance of
order remained a local affair. In one town the troops effectively crush riot;
heads are broken and the populace remains cowed. In another the start of
criminal proceedings had a similar effect; at Totnes, Fortescue's offensive
'completely frightened and humbled' the riotous elements, and even if none
appeared in court, the perpetrators denied the Lord Lieutenant a further
chance to arraign them.[27] Elsewhere the restoration of order was conditional on the capitulation of authority to mass demands, be they the release of
prisoners, or the implementation of the 'moral economy'. The variety of
responses is bewildering, the more so when the local authorities adopted a
proverbially English mixture of 'hard' and 'soft' tactics, with almost
simultaneous shows of force and concessionary moves. But this is the
picture which emerges, both regionally and nationally.

The reasons lie in the essential preservation of local autonomy. Portland's
strongest injunctions for the prosecution of rioters, issued in September
1800, and then formally supported by the king, coincided with a marked
decline in the use of the courts in the most disturbed regions. Perhaps this is
best symbolised by the fact that but two of the twelve people executed for
offences connected with riots during the famines, were hanged in the
second. Decisions to prosecute were largely left in local hands, and attempts
by Whitehall to apply pressure on the customary custodians of law and
order, were rare, and in the principal example, in response to the revolt of
the South-west, proved largely counter-productive. The huge military
reinforcements despatched to the Midlands in the autumn of 1800, and the
South-west in the spring of 1801 were exceptional, though they were
commensurate with Whitehall emphasis on the civil obligations of soldiers
to maintain the peace, over-riding the traditional necessity for magisterial
supervision of the army's policing function. But these were portentous,
developments, and support Calhoun's thesis of the enhanced role of the
state, though this dimension escapes him. On the other hand, these Home
Office initiatives were both responses to the torpor of the Bench, and the
virtual abdication of the magistracy. And, even when the generals took
effective command, the army was used with the same habitual moderation
as when directed by the Bench. Moderation *is* the key description; its
accuracy is confirmed by the fact that policing by soldiers was a normal
feature of eighteenth-century life. In many situations the magistracy had no
alternative option, though this did not invariably entail supplicating a
Secretary of State. The key consideration is the precise use of the regular
and Volunteer armies. Although we have encountered some ugly incidents,
several of which (but incredibly few relatively) produced fatalities, the
magistracy *and* commanding officers strove to keep these to the minimum.
Indeed, the experiences of primarily Volunteer infantry regiments, suggest
that their tolerance level respecting the infliction of serious injury or death,

was remarkably low. In addition, the Militia mutinies and the spread of disaffection in especially the Guards, suggest that the tolerance of professional soldiers was not markedly higher. In this context the comparative paucity of very bloody clashes between the troops and the people, may have proved critical to the continued reliability of the army.[28] However, these qualifications do not permit the militaristic and legal dimensions of the state's repressive policies to be interpreted, as they customarily are, in isolation. The state's calibre, the justification for contemporary notions of a 'Reign of Terror', requires an analysis of these key dimensions operative in tamden. The isolation of the legal factor, when qualified by emphasis on the precedents for some of the legislation passed in the nineties, and qualified further by stress on the relatively restrained use of the laws permitting prosecutions, generates a myopic picture. The regular, Militia, and Volunteer armies, were widely deployed against protesting crowds; the threat of their use, in accordance with *government* policies, was universal. These militaristic considerations in the context of the state's adoption of additional and fierce legal powers, contribute greatly towards an identification of the state's repressive stance; the government's resort to multifarious intimidation and terror – military *and* legal – then becomes crystal clear.[29]

The riot, the most common and the most dangerous form of protest, was a calamity. It signalled a breakdown in communications between that vast sector of the population experiencing intense deprivation, and the affluent ruling minority, who were statutorily compelled to prevent starvation. The extent of hardship made some violence inevitable. The comparative temperance of the magistracy modified the government's clear call for more violent deployment of the repressive agencies. The army and the courts played a role in the maintenance and restoration of order, though these processes were neither automatic, nor simple; they exude complex contradictions. Key questions still remain. Why did order not collapse more often, more dramatically, and less ephemerally when it did? Why did these collapses fail to engulf the entire country? The answers do not lie simply in the operations of the repressive agencies; after all, these were *extraordinary* measures. We must analyse the much less obtrusive but more important role of provision made by public and private charity, and above all, under the unique English poor-law system.

CHAPTER 17

'I Cannot work through this Time of Necessity without your Assistance'
the Relief of the Working Class

The laws have made wise and humane provision, by the poor rates, for the relief of all great distress. The parish officers are bound to provide against such; and if they do not do their duty, there is an appeal to the justices, who will force them to its performance. No person whose honest industry cannot provide for them, are in this kingdom in danger of starving. To prevent such a horrible evil, exertions such as never were yet heard of, would be made by all ranks of people that have property, to assist the suffering poor that remain quiet . . . . such are our poor laws, that they are made to pay . . . they must feed such as cannot feed themselves. The wealth, therefore of the higher classes ought to be considered as a fund upon which the lowest may draw with confidence and security, while they do it legally.

Arthur Young's confidence was echoed by scores of magistrates and others during the famines.[1] His emphasis on the 'quiet' poor, and 'legal' relief applications, were central to his argument against riot, and in the 1790s the system adhered to the ideals of its Elizabethan authors, the best social security and control apparatus that man could devise. Whigs, radicals and utilitarians might fulminate against various aspects of the statutory system, but they avoided openly questioning its role as the fundamental progenitor of order; indeed, their recurrent castigations of the 'servile dependence' generated by the edifice was tantamount to a recognition of this role. One historian, reviewing the system's verbose and polemical early nineteenth-century opponents, noted that they 'constantly underestimated . . . the contribution of the English poor law to communal stability and cohesion', but of course, they had no interest in emphasising telling arguments for its retention. The abolition of payments to able-bodied claimants in the 1830s galvanised fears of universal insurrection. However, the analysis of the function of poor relief necessitates an escape from the contemporary debate over the costs, demographic effects and morality of the system; its actual operation is crucial.[2]

Flexibility was the system's vital characteristic. In essence the law insisted only on public provision for those unable to support themselves. In practice, this was left to the administrators, over whom the magistracy retained ultimate supervisory powers. Most eighteenth-century statutory amendments were permissory, not obligatory. With the exception of Pitt's 1795 Act, which prevented recourse to the Settlement Laws to effect removals until a resident actually claimed relief, statutory responses to famine in the nineties adhered to the permissory tradition. The absence of detailed compulsory clauses provided almost unlimited administrative scope; autonomy gave parochial authorities considerable discrete powers, and these militated against a uniform response across the country to famine, which as we have established produced different problems in diverse districts. Moreover, the food-supply situation was subject to very rapid change, notably in the hypercrises. Administrative autarchy, and the absence of restrictive enactments permitted speedy responses tailored to meet rapidly changing local circumstances.

However, the poor law was not all-embracing. Charity was a significant adjunct to statutory provisions; the two regularly worked in tandem, and created such diversity in the preservation of working people from starvation, that any scientific, statistical analysis of the effectiveness of relief is out of the question. The complexity of the situation obtaining in many localities is typified by a detailed account of relief provided at Hayes in Kent in 1800–1. 'Some Bread' purchased from communion funds 'was given to the poorest every Sunday after Church'. Each autumn 'Every Family' received a stock of potatoes at half price. 'Most of the poor' had skimmed milk, some free, others at a penny per quart. Free clothes went to 'large families and very poor persons', and extra provision was made for pregnant working–class wives. 'Additional Relief when Bread is very dear' included soup, low-price coal, and cheap meats. Higher summertime agricultural wages were maintained throughout the year and the parish provided work for women and children 'as are not in the school'. These benefits were funded from the rates, by subscriptions and by affluent parishioners; free medicine came courtesy of the vicar, and fuel at wholesale prices from the coal merchant. This complementation of statutory by charitable relief produced endless permutations almost everywhere. Mancunian charity administrators demanded detailed accounts of individuals' exact circumstances, earnings, rents, number of dependents, amounts of poor relief, and a precise calculation of the 'further relief . . . requisite'. At Charlton Adam in Somerset the rates were used only to clear a deficit incurred by a subscription to subsidise bread costs, and the Blything Union in Suffolk actually achieved a rate reduction in 1795–6 through farmers supplying their labourers with cheap corn. In Lancashire, Cartmel overseers minimised expenditure on provision of cheap oatmeal by excluding workers who secured wage increases to combat inflation. Their Cornish counterparts at Ludgvan similarly excluded employees who received subsidised barley from 'any Mine, Stamping Mill, Smelting House, Rolling Mill or otherwise'. In villages, observed Colonel Bastard, soup could be supplied to the poor 'Gratis, by any Individual', and many workers benefited from soups from the kitchens of the big house. Soup supplies at Ford in Northumberland were restricted to 'indigent Labourers and paupers' at the expense of permanently-employed 'Labourers'.[3]

The reduction of all this to statistical clarity is obviously impossible. Statistical compilations can be used as a rough guide to the material value of relief in certain circumstances, and have been compiled where this is possible,[4] but they are such blunt and crude tools that they cannot do justice to such an amorphous subject. Relief provision was a *social process*, and the calculation of for example, *per capita* costs, obscures vital functions. The timing, nature and relevance of relief to the precise problem, are clearly central. So too are the relief mechanisms, for famine conditions put a huge sector of the population in immediate debt to the establishment. How did the ruling class utilize this feature to control the bulk of the population affected by severe deprivation?

Relief During the 'Early Phase' of 1795, and the Question of 'Speenhamland'

Lower agricultural wages, marked decreases in demand for labour in rural, industrial and urban locations, were winter-time norms in the eighteenth century; living costs always peaked, and the exceptional severity of the 1794–5 winter immeasurably aggravated seasonal problems. Poor-law administrators anticipated a steep rise in relief claims over the winters, and charitable endeavours also increased. 'At this season of the year', observed a newspaper correspondent in February 1795, 'I have noted in the daily prints a profusion of paragraphs as stimulants to charity'. Miller Howes of Hunstanton was a typical philanthropist; 'every Year' at Christmas he 'distributed Bread Tickets, a Shilling each amongst the Poor People . . . in order to sell Meal cheap'. However, winter charities assumed a greater importance in the 1790s; they became increasingly institutionalised, and ran for up to three months. The famines clearly sealed this development. A fund started at Henley-upon-Thames in 1791–2, was repeated each year and expended on bread subsidies for thirteen weeks which was 'much more beneficial to the poor, than a liberal donation at Christmas only'. Although Birmingham charity organisers disclaimed any intention 'to introduce regular annual Subscriptions' in December 1794, and a Hull fund was launched in 1795 with the residue and accrued interest from a predecessor of 1789 vintage, continued inflation and economic imbalances ensured that a significant sector of the populations of the bigger centres needed support over the winters. The typical reaction of poor-law authorities, commonly supported by formal magisterial pronouncements from Epiphany Sessions, and charity officials, was to guarantee a bare minimum of the poor's 'absolute necessities'. Incredible diversity is encountered. At Wigan, the customary Lancashire fare of oatmeal, potatoes and bacon, was distributed through a fund to four hundred families from January to March. At Sherborne and Stamford the workers' ability to buy other necessities was facilitated by weekly allocations of free loaves. The poor of South Molton and Barnstaple had cheap wheat from Earl Fortescue, the local magnate.[5]

The rates were widely used in the wheat-eating South and East for the same purpose, and in the Midlands primary cereals derived from the same source.[6] Thousands of parishes throughout the country paid out cash to people 'in need', tailoring the amounts to fine calculations of claimants' necessities. Private philanthropists paid cash too, on the same principle. Charity and poor-law officials provided food, fuel and clothes; the latter also commonly assisted workers to honour rent demands. As one commentator exclaimed, workers must have their basic requirements at 'regular and reasonable prices' or be enabled to meet inflated costs.[7]

The introduction of a multiplicity of different schemes threatened to produce antagonistic anomalies. The Speenhamland decision of 6 May 1795 has through fortuitous factors, notably historians' endorsement of its condemnation by the Poor Law Commissioners in the 1830s, become the most notorious attempt to standardise relief in one administrative division, but the complexity of the total context of its origins has escaped recognition.[8] Sir Charles Willoughby, the experienced Oxfordshire magistrate, worried over 'every Justice exercising his discretion' generating in 'some few instances too much' relief, 'but in many more, too little'. The problem was increased by non-formally settled workers, and this inducement to establish 'a general Remedy' was enhanced by the realisation that extraordinary aid measures had to continue. Recent impositions of uniform relief levels proved ephemeral and inadequate in precisely those regions where the agrarian labour force was most exposed. Oxfordshire epitomised these; many parishes had made 'all the Labourers Roundsmen . . . as soon as the Harvest . . . finished', and paid four shillings to married men with an additional sixpence for each of the first two children, and a shilling for the third and above. By November 1794 workers were 'absolutely in a state of starvation', and the Bench at the Epiphany Sessions raised the basic rate from four to six shillings, and preserved existing child supplements. They decreed that 'when the utmost exertions of a family cannot produce' these incomes, the wages actually received 'must be made up by the Overseers exclusive of rent'. Buckinghamshire Sessions simultaneously made an identical order. The JPs thus established that parishes guaranteed these incomes, but made no provision to offset further inflation. There were *no scales basing relief* on alternating living costs, and they were not the strictest antecedents of Speenhamland.[9]

The Berkshire and Hampshire Sessions both convened on 14 January. The former acknowledged escalating prices, and hoped that those in receipt of subscription funds in-aid-of wages would be kept off the rates; if not, workers were to receive an 'additional allowance from the rates, in proportion to the difference between the usual and present price of bread'. Their Hampshire counterparts issued no parallel directive, but invited information on the calculation of relief payments, and the food required by a labourer 'to do Justice to his Employer'. These decisions provoked debate in the region; the entry of two Berkshire residents into the fray was no accident. The Rev. Davies published his evidence on the condition of the agrarian workforce, collected some time previously, and Sir F.M. Eden launched his broader investigation into poverty. The *Reading Mercury* printed a number of articles on the subject, including one advocating wages based on wheat prices, probably penned by Charles Dundas, the Whig MP who also chaired the Berkshire Bench. It was Dundas who argued at the Easter Sessions for 'permanent' wage increases, because incomes had not increased 'in proportion to the very high price of provisions' which showed no sign of falling. Meanwhile, he asked his colleagues to use their local knowledge to consider the case for implementing the 1563 Act which enabled the Bench to fix agricultural wages; the famous Speenhamland adjournment on 6 May would discuss these and 'other circumstances', and 'if approved of . . . limit, direct and appoint the wages of the day labourer'.[10]

Confusion over their rejection derives from an ignorance of the overall context of Dundas's proposals; Mark Neuman correctly dismissed the claim that they were torpedoed by a doctrinaire disciple of Adam Smith,[11] for as we have seen, the Whigs were greater devotees of laissez-faire ideology than their Tory rivals. The Foxites advocated wage increases, and were shortly to throw their weight behind Samuel Whitbread's legislative proposals for a minimum agricultural wage. Dundas's scheme thus had heavy political overtones, and it is significant that both the Oxfordshire and Buckinghamshire Benches were chaired by Tories. Whitbread's campaign to persuade the Hertfordshire Sessions to act to augment wages generated a bitter wrangle, and the MP emerged from the heated debate in a minority of one. Many trembled at the suggestion that wages were too low; Sir Christopher Sykes put Davies' book on an inflammatory par with Tom Paine's writings. In Berkshire, there were other critical factors. Prices rose rapidly between the Easter Sessions on 14 April and the Speenhamland adjournment; while further inflation was anticipated before the harvest, few prophesised that prices would not then fall to customary levels. Wage rates fixed on early May prices would not meet those expected in June and July, but they would invoke the old maxim that anything was superior to temporary wage increases, which were difficult to revise downwards later. Wages fixed under the 1563 Act could not be tailored to individuals' commitments; if wages were calculated on cereal prices, what size of family was to be the norm? Were single men and childless couples to receive wages commensurate with the support of three or four children? Moreover the Act permitted only the fixing of maximum, not minimum wages. Anomalies were inevitable. The Bench could not use it to reconcile employees' and employers' interests. The Speenhamland announcement categorically confirmed the inexpediency of magisterial 'assistance by regulating the Wages of Day Labourers', under the Tudor legislation.[12]

The Bench under Dundas's leadership equally categorically insisted that workers ought to live off their own; all employers were directed to raise wages 'in proportion to the present Price of Provisions', which would allow employers to adjust wages to individuals' commitments. The Bench published the famous scale to facilitate differentiation, whether prices rose, stabilised or fell. This, as the county press correctly informed rural readers, would permit

labourers in husbandry to increase *their pay* so as to enable them to *provide sufficiently for themselves and families*, in proportion to the present unavoidable high price of bread and other provisions (my italics).

The same scale was also adopted for poor-law payments to the 'impotent and infirm Poor' with whom the Bench was additionally concerned: the scale was to be observed by overseers in payment to permanent 'Pensioners' as well. The scale thus represented minimum incomes for *all* poor, whether employed, unemployed, unemployable, disabled or ill. The Bench phrased the announcement clumsily in a typically telescopic fashion. Rates based on the 'price of Wheat' for wage and poor – relief assessments were necessary 'whether produced by his own or his family's labour, *or* an allowance from the poor rates'. The press correctly demarcated between the instructions given to employers and overseers; the report cited above, as opposed to the formal announcement, continued by stating that the magistrates 'unanimously agreed to adopt a rule or allowance to poor people applying for relief'.[13]

The Hampshire Bench adopted a similar but less well thought through plan at the same time. Similar because weekly wages were governed by the current price of a bushel of wheat plus one shilling, but creative of anomalies by containing no provision for the needs of large families. However, it contained no reference to relief levels, and thus none of the fruitful ambiguities foisted on Berkshire. It was rescinded on 14 July; the magistracy was ostensibly satisfied that 'wages are already in an improving state' through 'local advancement' which precluded a county-wide directive. However, they now tacitly admitted that if the entire burden of meeting the living costs devolved on employers, labourers with large families would lose their jobs. The Sessions now decreed

That the proper subsistence of labourers with their families . . . should be ascertained; and their income rendered adequate to their necessary expenditure – first by the wages from their employers; or where from infirmity[14] or the number in the family that is impossible . . . the difference between the highest income from the best employment, and their lowest outgoing under the best management should be made up in relief granted by the parish officers.

If the Bench failed to place the entire onus on the employers, the justices insisted that farmers should do as much as possible by usurping the 'shopkeeper's' function, and supply their men with food 'at prime cost'. The Sessions also issued the Standard Wheaten Bread order at the same time, perhaps hoping that farmers would seize on this cost-containment mode.[15]

The inadequacy of static relief payments underlay the introduction of sliding scales based on the price of Standard Wheaten Bread in Oxfordshire. Some resistance was encountered, probably as in Hampshire where farmers upped wages slightly rather than incur the poor's 'ill will' through supplying lower quality food. Popular odium thus fell on authority, and Standard Wheaten orders compounded failures to enforce tolerable wage rates. The farmers' notorious exploitation of relief scales by forcing parishes to foot part of the wages bill followed. Elsewhere, the Sessions may have discussed variants on the Berkshire scale, as in Gloucestershire, but orders were restricted to general directives to increase relief, which preserved parochial autonomy over the details.[16] Diversity characterised responses, even under the ostensibly uniform system imposed on Berkshire. At Tilehurst, the vestry took over retailing; five other parishes combined to subscribe to a fund to pay wage supplements. Direct subsidies to bakers were paid by subscription charities at Taplow and Wallingford, but by parish officials at Brimpton and Uffington.[17] The latter system was particularly popular in East Anglia.[18] Static relief payments on diverse restrictive principles, notably to designated families, or with respect only to children, were common.[19] In other areas, especially where vestries decided that sufficient provision was obtainable through the market, regular schemes were avoided in favour of individualised payments on precise calculations of claimants' needs. Relief governed by the sliding scale overcame the problem of rapidly rising prices almost perfectly, and most importantly contained expenditure by falling with prices. But costs were nevertheless phenomenal, notably owing to the size of payments to families. The introduction of the Oxfordshire scale immediately doubled the previous static supplements paid to a father of five earning seven shillings, from four to eight shillings; crude quantifications of relative costs are given in Appendix 10. Mammoth increases in expenditure led some Berkshire parishes to resort to inadequate static payments before the 1795 harvest.

Another major development during the nineties, the escalation of truck payments, was accelerated by action to maintain basic living standards before the 1795 harvest. This was unimpeded by the numerous eighteenth-century statutes against truck, not least because employers came under pressure from both employees and public authorities. Truck, especially in remoter rural regions, whereby farmers sold cheap corn to their men, had maintained a precarious existence; its advocacy by several leading agricultural experts may have speeded its growth in response to earlier inflation in the 1790s, especially in the West Country, in some Midland counties and in parts of East Anglia. The system spread during the 1794–5 winter, and again during the summer.[20] Similar existing schemes run by industrial employers received favourable press attention. The idea was rapidly adopted by Pennine lead-mining concerns, and by North-eastern coal-owners following disturbances. During the annual binding season in August, the miners seized on the opportunities created by pressing demand for their labour, to negotiate more generous retail contracts, and a universal application of the scheme.[21] Some Cornish mine-owners, under pressure from parochial authorities, responded to the central role of their men in the spring riots, by undertaking to supply their corn. The idea was subsequently formally adopted by the County Bench, which insisted that here lay the solution to the complex problems attendant on high and volatile prices, the fragility of the county's cereal supply, and the high proportion of non-settled men working in the mines.[22]

If a plethora of relief schemes were extended and launched once it was appreciated that necessity would not be confined to the customary winter period of common hardship, additional relief was neither universal nor adequate. The absence of many patriarchs in London for the political season retarded relief in some locations, and several were, like Lord Carnarvon, genuinely horrified at the conditions they encountered on their return to their fiefdoms. Widespread rioting was also a testimony to inadequacies of relief. It oiled the wheels of charity, and galvanised local authority responses. The public meeting convened in response to riot and to discuss 'the security of the city' by the Mayor of Chichester, decided that security required only a subscription to fund 'general' relief. At Honiton, in parallel circumstances, the vicar personally lobbied rich parishioners to create a fund to subsidise workers' cereals, and an Ashburton JP paid a fourpenny subsidy 'out of my Pocket' on each bushel of potatoes sold. And where extra relief was not the product of direct experience of riot, it was often visibly organised to pre-empt disturbances.[23]

Several aspects of relief operations at this period assumed a key contemporary *and* historical significance. First, the full burden of financing that relief was largely evaded by employers, *at least through the medium of increased wages*; costs were principally met by charity and from the rates. Secondly, the workers were taught that authority had the ultimate obligation to provide against severe material deprivation, even if pressure through riot had to be brought to bear. Thirdly, difficulties with precise quantification do not obscure the receipt of relief by a considerable proportion of the populations. Subscription charities aided at least ten, fifteen and twenty percent of the respective populations of Reading, Hull and Nottingham. Forty percent of the population of York applied for assistance through the parochial clergy. Authority in the mining hamlet of Newbold near Chesterfield rejected claims from about ten percent of applicants, but still ended up supporting thirty-seven percent of residents, including some childless couples. Similar ranges are encountered in country parishes. In Essex, twenty-three, twenty-five, and thirty-eight percent of the respective populations of Great Parndon, Romford and Copford, were assisted from the rates, and at Bardfield in Berkshire, twenty-four percent. On these figures between fifteen and forty percent of the national population were aided by charities or poor-law officials between January and June 1795.[24]

Fourthly, relief was invariably conditioned by desires to preserve established consumption patterns; Standard Wheaten rules were indifferently and fleetingly applied. In some ways, bread subsidies or relief in-aid-of wages, conformed to notions of 'moral economy'. So too did local official endorsement of the preservation of stocks for local consumption. The two commonly went in tandem as exemplified by the Birdchanger vestry in Essex, which decreed against any movement of cereals across parish boundaries in favour of sale to workers at controlled prices.[25] But in either, or both ways, these illumine the fifth characteristic, that authority acted to guarantee a supply, if necessary through the despatch of agents to distant markets. The last consideration also emphasised that Speenhamland or other varieties of relief in-aid-of wages was not universally applicable, especially in regions perennially afflicted by supply problems, and more widely during the midsummer hypercrisis. There was little point in obtaining cereals *and* paying cash to counter inflated prices; administrative simplicity here dictated the sale of subsidised corn, not payment of money supplements. The supply situation, and very recent experiences with modes of aid, were factors when officials considered post-harvest relief measures.

Poor Relief after the 1795 Harvest

The persistence of high food prices after the 1795 harvest encouraged advocacy in some quarters of wage increases adequate to current market-place realities. Sectors of the press, including the *Blackburn Mail*, argued that employers should be 'squaring . . . the price of labour with that of provisions', and the Suffolk Sessions formally demanded that the county MPs seek appropriate legislation. The Whigs certainly had quite widespread local support, but Whitbread's parliamentary failure, and the government's retrenchment programme, together with the experience of many difficulties, as in Berkshire, effectively ended the debate over wages. The Hampshire Bench soldiered on in this cause at a number of autumn adjournments under the chairmanship of the Whig, Lord John Russell. The Bench initially suggested that all farmworkers needed a weekly nine shillings, and promised further guidelines for family incomes on completion of a detailed survey of conditions and aid-schemes throughout the county. This revealed so many variants of augmented wages, family supplements and cheap bread schemes, that the Bench abandoned all attempts to impose some uniformity, except with the stipulation that parishes should provide work for claimants' wives and children. This reflected one member, the Rev. Edmund Poulter's, utilitarian obsession with indiscriminate aid provisions inducing idleness. The Bench did suggest that the rates could be contained if middlemen's profits were squeezed through parishes accepting the function of shopkeeper to the poor, but otherwise the magistracy confined themselves to emphasising the need for 'unremitting attention' to public welfare. It is worth reiterating the increasing disparity between wages and prices detected in the mid-nineties by the wages historian Gilboy; with the dubious exception of the extensions of truck, future famine relief derived not from employers, but from charitable and poor-law sources.[26]

Very few parishes felt compelled to guarantee supplies after the harvest; the only exceptions to the speedy demise of those established in villages like Fillongly and Kenilworth (Warwickshire), occurred in East Anglia where fresh disturbances to conserve stocks erupted in the autumn.[27] Winter-time flour doles were common in most years, and that of 1795–6 saw their use on an abnormally extensive scale, which suggests that parishes made bulk purchases so that costs of payments to pensioners could be contained by cutting out retailers' profits.[28] Excluding middlemen's profits certainly underpinned the marked entry into the potato wholesale market by public authorities in the autumn.[29] The exceptional tiny minority of parishes who organised food supplies on any scale throughout the 1795–6 season include some outside the south-west[30] where markets proved most erratic;[31] the numbers of West Country exceptions to the national trend rose significantly after springtime rioting in 1796.[32]

The fact that cash payments dominated relief under the poor law during the 1795–6 season must not be interpreted as a massive spread of Speenhamland scales. Indeed, payments under these retreated, even in Berkshire, where vastly inflated costs dictated economies which normally meant jettisoning the scale altogether. The Oxfordshire variant, introduced in the summer of 1795, was subsequently replaced by the Sessions' reintroduction of the manifestly inadequate static incomes, first calculated in January 1795.[33] Gloucestershire was one of the few counties, if not the only one, to introduce a new sliding scale in 1795–6, but it was quietly ignored by most parishes.[34] Speenhamland maintained a precarious toehold, but where relief was systemised, static payments were the norm;[35] elsewhere overseers calculated relief for each claimant on an individual basis. But cash payments, irrespective of systemisation, except where made to the aged, infirm and unemployed, were *de facto* wage and/or family supplements: these help to explain the disparities which impressed Gilboy. Truck, which expanded still further among industrial and rural employers,[36] completes the equation, but not necessarily in isolation. At Mark Sherborne near Basingstoke, agrarian wages were raised to nine shillings; farmers sold cheap corn in quantities sufficient to support a family with one child; cash supplements were paid by the overseers with respect to each additional child.[37]

Statistical problems to not prevent some analysis of the value of these various modes of relief. Ironically, truck, especially at the hands of industrialists, proved to be the best safeguard against famine; workers were protected against depleted stocks and empty market places. Industrial employers were not so miserly as many of their agrarian counterparts,[38] some of whom restricted the availability of cheap corn to volumes woefully inadequate to the support of families, in addition to the exclusion of the unmarried and the childless. Workers were of course still exposed to market forces with respect to non-cereal dietary components, and the impact of price movements was also felt where truck arrangements did not extend to the supply of all a family's corn requirement; such families experienced falls in their living standards.[39]

Payments under sliding scales proved the second most protective form of relief. Assessments of cereal requirements varied. The Berkshire allowance, calculated on forty pounds of bread for a two-child family, was the most generous. The Gloucestershire scale at the same point 'guaranteed' only thirty-two pounds, but differences in the assessment of sums needed for other necessities, roughly equalized the value of aid under both scales. The bread component of the Oxfordshire scale was identical to Gloucestershire's, but the former contained no allowance for other items. This parsimonious scale was savagedly reduced in one Oxfordshire division; similar cuts on the Berkshire scale were also imposed, by fifteen percent in Aldermaston. The generosity of the Old Windsor vestry, which increased the bread allowance, was very untypical. Most recipients of aid under the scales obtained little more than a basic subsistence diet, heavily dependent on bread; their entire income was unequal to the purchase of anything other than food.[40]

The value of subsidised cereals varied widely. Most recipients were thereby enabled to command from three-quarters to slightly more than a basic subsistence diet. Chelmsford overseers supplied farmworkers with wheat at six shillings per bushel, but severely restricted volumes buyable by 'mechanics' earning twelve shillings per week. Ironically, the figures suggest that the labourers achieved a higher standard of living in 1795–6 than in any other season during the entire decade, whereas artisans were rudely exposed to life on the breadline: and Chelmsford was among the more generous parishes. At Tolleshurst D'Arcy, also in Essex, authority sold wheat at nine shillings per bushel, which merely maintained the customary inability of farmworkers to command a wage adequate to the purchase of a basic subsistence diet. The experiences of individual workers who were permitted to buy half their weekly requirements of oatmeal from a Newbold (Derbyshire) charity from February to August 1795, are given in Appendix 6. Only one example, the better-paid collier Fryer, was enabled to buy a subsistence diet every week (bar two) throughout this period; weekly 'deficits' incurred by others after the nominal purchase of such a diet, increased as the summer hypercrisis intensified, labourer Spooner's climbing from 1/6 to over 5/–. If the Newbold charity ameliorated the impact of inflation, it failed to guarantee subsistence diets to the lower paid at any time.[41]

These deficits from Essex and Derbyshire were serious, but not so grave as those incurred by the recipients of static supplements. Examples from the East Anglian parishes of Great Bardfield, Great Sampford and Terrington appear in Appendix 7; these reveal that such payments did not constantly enable workers to command incomes adequate to the purchase of even the cereal component of diets, and that recipients incurred 'deficits' for a considerable period, *without* any consideration of other dietary items, or necessities, including clothes, fuel and rent. The Great Sampford vestry occasionally reviewed static supplements; those paid at Terrington were among the more liberal, which puts the greater misery experienced at Great Bardfield in perspective.[42]

Evidential problems preclude evaluation of urban relief schemes, but nothing suggests that they were better than their rural equivalents. In London, the authoritative Patrick Colquhoun monitored the performance of bread charities, which he claimed were 'generally monopolized by the Clamarous, gin drinking poor to the exclusion of the Sober and industrious'. There is no need to accept his Hogarthian perceptions to the letter, but his observations do suggest that the respectable working class were placed in a cruel sociological predicament. Their living standards collapsed whether they queued with mendicants, prostitutes and the permanently pauperised, *or not*. All of this material points to three main conclusions. First, no relief scheme guaranteed claimants any more than a bare subsistence diet, and many thousands received much less. Secondly, the start of many programmes was delayed until long after inflation had seriously eroded plebeian purchasing powers. Great Bardfield workers, for example, did not receive their three penny *per capita* supplement until mid-June 1795, when wages were almost totally expended in the purchase of cereal components alone.[43] Thirdly, and in some ways most importantly, relief costs, irrespective of the mode, placed an unprecedented burden on the rates, as shown by expenditures in specimen parishes tabulated in Appendix 9. The costs of famine relief in 1794–6 were enormous; a determination to contain them during the second famine, combined with the higher prices current in 1799–1801, increased the inadequacies of relief measures already experienced in the mid-nineties.

Poor Relief 1799–1801

The relief measures adopted inevitably resembled those initiated earlier. In some parishes farmers or landowners sold cheap corn to all workers; elsewhere their bounty was distributed by committees. Truck advanced tremendously; in the rural sector, it is encountered for the first time in Yorkshire and Shropshire. More significantly for the longer-term, it achieved increasing institutionalisation in industrial locations. Its existence was reinforced and its currency was extended in Cornwall. It took off in Glamorganshire. Its intensification in the north-east was reflected in mineowners' creation of contacts and contracts with major cereal importers, and investment in corn-milling machinery. Some industrialists turned pragmatism into philanthropy; mineowners at Callington, and the London Lead Company at Hexham, supplied cheap grain to all the poor in their communities. But benevolence was not universal; farmers at Werlingworth withdrew sales of cheap corn to all parishioners, and those at Saxtead unceremoniously decided that the relief of workers with large families was a public responsibility, not their's.[44]

The 1799–1800 winter witnessed numerous attempts by poor-law and charity officials to stabilise the costs of the poor's bread in rural communities,[45] and in urban centres in the north[46] and south,[47] though charity funds were principally expended on soup kitchens. Epiphany Sessions ordered Standard Wheaten Bread, advocated retrenchment, and recommended soup.[48] The wages issue was dropped after Whitbread's aborted efforts in the Commons in February 1800. In January, the Berkshire Sessions refused to implement Standard Wheaten, but demanded economy, and specifically

> recommended to Overseers and to all Persons giving Assistance to the Poor during the present Scarcity, to give such Assistance in other Articles of Food as Potatoes Pease Soup Meat Herrings Rice etc rather than in Bread, or *an Increase of Pay* (my italics).

This total rejection of the earlier Speenhamland policy is lost on the county's most recent historian of poor relief, in spite of its typicality of other decisions in the region, represented by the Oxfordshire Bench's categoric avowal of the 'impropriety of . . . a fixed rule of allowance for relief'. Their Buckinghamshire counterparts ordered that all parochial aid 'beyond the usual Relief' must be given in soup 'in Lieu of any extra allowance in Money'.[49] Speenhamland retreated; if that system persisted in a few Berkshire, and a handful of Gloucestershire parishes, and the calculation of relief on meal prices made an appearance elsewhere, for example at Hethersett in Norfolk and Brede in Sussex, the most common form of systemised aid was static supplementation of wages and pensions, and static child allowances.[50] These schemes spread even further in regions like East Anglia where they had been used extensively before,[51] and achieved a greater currency in those which had not, including Somerset, Warwickshire and Yorkshire.[52]

Few parishes reviewed the level of static supplementation in the context of further, rapid inflation in 1800, and relief values plummeted. The dozen adjustments made at Wingfield, and the seven in the Loes and Wilford Gilbert Union, were unusual; the single one made at Wrabness in the first eight months of 1800 was representative. The fact that Petty Sessions repeatedly convened to consider relief matters, which magistrates regularly and fondly advanced in their own defence against criticisms, should not obscure the evaporating values of relief tabulated for typical parishes in Appendix 8. An Essex pseudnonymist quite rightly linked deprivation with deficient relief levels; families were 'all most starved', yet 'tha low me 4 and 6 a week' for six children. The claims of the Essex press, when reporting the 'crime of anonymity', that in 'no county, are the wants of the poor more strictly and liberally attended to', were both ridiculous, and symbolic of assumptions that escalating rate demands reflected the payment of adequate aid. Inflation also eroded the value of charitable distributions. At Lambeth

some old women who had partaken of the charity distributed weekly . . . were observed to go away dissatisfied and grumbling, because their loaves were not so large as they used to be.

In real terms, the value of a sixpenny loaf fell visibly and monotonously.[53]

Heavy costs, as opposed to concern over diminishing values, underlay changes to relief schemes before September 1800; this dovetailed with the increasing hostility to merchants, to provoke many parishes into direct provisioning to eliminate commercial profits. This contrasted with identical moves in 1795 where parochial purchasing was a response to fears of total scarcity. In 1800 this fear was absent except in the south-west which was the sole region to resort to public provisioning on those grounds.[54] Queen Camel in Somerset responded typically to escalating monthly rate demands with a June decision to levy a special rate to finance 'a village Shop to supply the Poor . . . with the necessaries of life on reasonable terms'. In this context further cost-containing exercises were tried. Queen Camel vetted relief applications to decide exactly what beneficiaries could purchase weekly. Elsewhere the price of flour was varied according to family size, or fixed as a percentage of the market price. Quantification of this evidence presents the normal problems, but where parochial shopkeeping replaced static supplements, authority was forced to consider the amount of food supplied, rather than take refuge in arbitrary, and generally stingy cash calculations. If generosity was not the rule, this aid system did more to arrest the erosion of living standards, though the cost of so doing was significant. Costs were reflected by the speedy reversion to cash supplements after premature anticipations by many vestries of an imminent return to normality in the summer of 1800.[55]

Poor-law authority economies took many forms. Speenhamland was compromised further, for example by the Kingston Lisle decision to regulate calculations by 'what the industrious family might earn . . . not

. . . what the idle and negligent do earn'. Parochial shopkeeping facilitated some savings; at Terling in Essex, the numbers of villagers deemed eligible for cheap fine flour in August 1799 were increased in February 1800, but coarse flour replaced it at the same price in March; the price was increased for non-settled and childless claimants. The similar provision of cheap oatmeal in many Lancashire parishes over the winter, was abandoned in response to unprecedented oat prices in the spring, and messes of barley and herrings substituted. Some charities, including the massive Manchester subscription, survived into April and May only through parallel substitutions. The reverse process, the replacement of cheap provisions by static cash supplements, was very rare at this junction.[56]

The substitution and contiguous changes as at Terling represented a decline in rural relief values roughly equivalent to those imposed by urban soup kitchens. If kitchens made an appearance, often relatively fleetingly, in scores of villages, their administrative shortcomings in country locations were generally quickly recognised.[57] Urban kitchens advanced tremendously over the 1799–1800 winter; if the government's economy ideals were trotted out in support, the main stimulus derived from the appreciation that the pockets of neither philanthropists nor recipients could meet the costs of orthodox bread charities on the grossly extended scale now requisite. Soup ingredients more than doubled in price, but it was commonly hoped that long-term economies would materialise; once recipients accepted soup, relief costs would be permanently reduced. Evidential problems preclude precise quantification once again. The Canterbury establishment was exceptional in operating a six day week. The thrice weekly distributions at Sheffield were more typical, and as at Manchester, Leeds and Hull, the statistics suggest that between ten and twenty percent of their total populations received a weekly quart of soup, plus some rice, herrings and potatoes. Percentages were even higher in smaller centres, thirty-three and thirty-five at Oxford and Reading respectively. If urban schemes experienced any uniformity, it was with demand continually outstripping and exhausting resources; the problem rose in proportion to the size of the supplicant sector of the population.[58]

Count Rumford, the successful European advocate of soup charities, was initially concerned with aid to the most indigent poor, and beggars comprised the bulk of clients at the experimental establishment at Bath in the earliest days in 1796. The famines, principally the second, vastly extended relief from this source up the social scale. The common assumption, relentlessly articulated, was that soup was very nutritious and particularly apposite for assisting families burdened with many children. The press teemed with the most unscientific and ludicrous claims of soup's value, and a multitude of fashionable upper-class exponents, like Lord Sheffield, did great violence to the sociology of diet. Much soup, or rather gruel, was of poor quality, and frequently inedible. Where experimentation enhanced quality, costs escalated, and further trials hinged on improvements to appearances and taste, not the calorific value. Most kitchens were in apparently chronic financial straits, and quality and the scale of operations were regular victims as charities economised to struggle along into the spring of 1800. Recipients suffered quality collapses while bread and other food prices soared to even more extravagant heights.[59]

The autumn hypercrisis in 1800 witnessed aberrational urban efforts to obtain cereal stocks.[60] Once the panic receded, the relentless erosion of relief values recommenced. Soup kitchens started earlier as the winter approached, and funds originally raised to guarantee cereal supplies were soon channelled into the kitchens, and expended on other substitutes, like the despised salted herrings. The chorus of demands for further economies by relief schemes was swelled by the prognostics of Epiphany Benches; many parishes returned to static cash supplements. The Parochial Relief Act was not an unqualified success and where it was implemented the chief casualty was relief value. Moreover, the effects of all these sources of further serious decline were aggravated by the fact that more and more people came to rely to various extents on parochial and charitable relief over the 1800–1 winter, while grain prices peaked in March and April. Almost every overseer's account testifies to the mammoth extension of their roles. At Modbury in Devon, the 126 relieved weekly in February 1800 grew to 181 in one year; at Gnosall in Staffordshire a parallel proportional rise from fifty-six to seventy-six is recorded, and these figures indicate at least fifteen percent of the population receiving assistance. Only our ignorance of family size prevents categoric proof that these figures represent half the population in receipt of relief.[61] Fifty percent of the population of Exeter was receiving aid in March 1801. Soup distributions increased dramatically; at Birmingham 7500 quarts were sold weekly over the 1799–1800 winter, and 16,000 in November 1800; it rocketed to 20,000 in February 1801. At Manchester and Leeds soup sales merely doubled between the two winters, but the prodigious quantities of rice and fish distributed in 1800–1 speak for themselves. In villages, for example at Shinfield in Berkshire, decisions to permit 'industrious people, as do not receive relief' to purchase cereal substitutes from the overseers, a move facilitated by the Parochial Relief Act, represented further, if incalculable, extensions to the proportion of the population supplicating public aid.[62]

Social Control through Poor Relief

The ruling establishment's regular response to all forms of protest was to increase relief from both charities and under the poor law. Indeed, some anonymous letters were penned primarily to insist on greater assistance, and where arson threats were appended, strenuous remedial efforts almost invariably followed. Incendiarism in Shropshire galvanised a county meeting at which members of the Bench led urgent appeals to reassess all facets of relief. More localised responses were probably typified by the reaction of the West Pennard vestry in Somerset to an outbreak of petty thieving: legal fees for prosecuting offenders came to ten pounds, but the food bill topped two hundred. But these immediate and often successful responses must not obscure the less spectacular omnipresence of poor relief, and the social processes so pervasively central to the function of social control, which were fulfilled throughout these extended periods of mass deprivation.[63]

Contemporary awareness of these functions was frequently, if partially evinced. The Norfolk Agricultural Society's competitive awards for independent and industrious workers customarily excluded recipients of parochial relief; in July 1800 they added the rider, 'that termed Bread-money in times of Scarcity excepted'. A boom in East Anglian off-shore fishing pushed up wages, and a report noted that poor relief to those engaged became 'almost unnecessary'. The famines, and the intensification of poor relief, rapidly advanced utilitarian consciousness. Sir George Onesiphorus Paul could conceive of 'no . . . worse . . . State of Society' than when workers were 'living on the Fund of Benevolence': already, he exclaimed in August 1795, 'Gratitude' had gone and 'the claim of poverty on Riches . . . is taken as a right'. T.B. Bernard, a leading light of the soup-kitchen supporting 'Society for Bettering the Condition of the Poor', among others, was soon publicising his view that indiscriminate relief 'superinduced . . . an indolent habit' in all, and undermined 'the distinction between independence and poverty'. But few immediately examined the full ramifications of the social process. The Foxites attacked pauperisation, and workers' dependencies on 'the bounty of their master', 'the charity of the rich', and the poor law, but Fox's principal emphasis was on disenfranchisement through the receipt of parish relief. Relatively few county voters came into this category, and if Fox was confining his remarks to his numerous and unique Westminster constituents, his rhetorical flourish, 'what was the state of a country which first compelled every man to dependence and then reduced him to servitude?', deserves a broader interpretative answer than he advanced from the floor of the Commons.[64]

The employing and affluent classes administered both the poor law and the charities; the process, which according to Fox indebted 'every poor man' to his richer neighbours, is so similar that they can be treated together. The first characteristic was the subjection of claims, and claimants, to a searching investigation of individuals' personal means. This aimed to establish not just 'want', but its 'cause . . . ascertained', and the relief calculated 'proportioned to . . . merit and distress'. In the Sandford Union in Suffolk, the ages of applicants' siblings were recorded to facilitate the payment of differential relief rates. But such 'minute enquiry' was not restricted to handfuls of claimants in small country communities. Manchester charity officials visited every appellant in their homes, and made 'a daily report' on each family in a remarkable bureaucratic exercise for the eighteenth century. Permutations are encountered in other populous places, including Durham and Halifax. If the prevention of fraud was commonly, and no doubt legitimately, advanced in justification, the information was increasingly used to implement growing convictions in punitive demarcations over relief administration between the 'idle' and the 'industrious poor'. The treatment of those falling into the former category varied. Barton charity governors merely 'reprimanded' the 'negligent'. Elsewhere sanctions were imposed. Oxfordshire 'Gentlemen and Yeomen' were invited to name claimants whom 'they observe to be idle, disorderly, or frequent public houses'. Such people at Bingfield, Berkshire, were stopped from purchasing at the vestry's new shop. At Old Windsor it was categorically stated that the 'industrious, orderly and frugal ought to be better taken care of than those who are of an opposite Character . . . even with respect to subsistence'.[65]

Scrutiny and discrimination were obviously easier in rural locations; the smaller relative numbers of poor to the affluent enabled the latter's use of personal knowledge of the former. In urban situations, notably the greater industrial centres, more numerous claimants increasingly lived at a geographical remove from charity subscribers. The much deployed device of giving tickets to philanthropists to distribute to claimants partially overcame these problems, though Sheffield subscribers had to be urged 'to take the Trouble of visiting . . . Paupers . . . in the Park, the Crofts' and elsewhere, and the Birmingham charity committee acknowledged subscribers' difficulty 'to determine what Objects are the most proper'. The services of overseers and churchwardens were enrolled, but even where a bureaucracy was created as in Manchester, it must remain doubtful whether either all the deserving received legitimate hand-outs, or that serious frauds were avoided. Considerable efforts were made, and would-be claimants in quite substantial places including Stroud and King's Lynn were literally spied upon, and identification facilitated by the publication of lists of recipients' names. Other modes of enhanced supervision included the partial or complete removal of overseers' autonomous powers to aid, in favour of vestry authorisation, and the appointment of full-time relieving officers. But urban poor-law authorities, ratepayers and charity subscribers, could not rival the supervisory options available to their rural counterparts. Another common expedient adopted in the countryside, as at Great Parndon in Essex, was to relieve 'each Sunday *at* Church in provisions'; presumably non-churchgoers were placed in a dilemma. They certainly were at Greenford in rural Middlesex where tickets to purchase from the new shop were distributed after church; the vicar categorically stated that non-ticket holders were turned away if they had no acceptable excuse for 'absence from church'. The vicar brazenly boasted that 'the congregation is greatly increased'. But such stratagems were simply not available in places like Sheffield, if only because there were insufficient pews.[66]

An integral part of this increased surveillance, and possibly the most significant product of the overall extension of public authority over great sectors of the working population, occurred with the enforcement of the traditionally indifferently applied dictum of statute law, that able-bodied relief-recipients be put to work. Horror at rising costs coalesced with fears over the social impact of relief, notably on children. Many vestries assumed that children of ten or twelve could earn their own keep, and applied pressure on parents by omitting adolescents from relief calculations. But concern in the later nineties extended to children eligible for aid; rural oligarchs at Hethersett in Norfolk exclaimed in support of parish work for children, 'or else they must have been relieved without doing any Thing'. Their South Weald counterparts in Essex, while busying themselves with work schemes, voiced a more sophisticated concern over 'bringing up the Children in some habits of Work thereby preparing them for service'. In July 1795 the Hertfordshire Bench directed that every parish 'set to work . . . the Children of all Parents . . . not thought able to . . . maintain' their offspring. Other Benches moved in the same direction in 1795, and this was reflected in inter-famine developments: the bulk of decisions belong to the second famine, especially during the 1800–1 season, when relief costs peaked together with alarm at the pernicious side effects. The Warwickshire Bench typically insisted that parochial authorities put the poor to work 'particularly . . . at this time' to ensure that

> what is done for the relief of the industrious Labourer be not converted into the encouragement of the Idle and Profligate.[67]

The work most commonly organised by parishes, spinning, was most appropriate for the wives and children of working men in receipt of allowances. Considerable capital requirements and additional administrative effort militated against such schemes in populous places, though Newcastle-upon-Tyne proved an exception where 'the Out and In-poor' were placed together in extra buildings specifically hired for 'Spinning and Knitting of all Kinds'. Rural dwellers were more vulnerable to the traumatic removal of all vestiges of independence by the intrusion of public authority into the home. At South Weald the vicar supervised raw wool distribution on the familiar basis of 'the number in their families under 10 years of age'; wool was collected on Mondays from the vicarage, and the previous week's work handed over to 'be weighed and reeled again to detect waste or false reeling'. Payment 'varied with the price of bread', but 'To encourage good spinning' *poorer* work was penalised. Other expedients included the payment of 'full earnings' to increase spinners' hours at Moreton. The children of all claimants at South Molton and Ludgvan were bound out as 'Parish Apprentices'. Another variant, admittedly uncommon, was to increase allowances for children who went to school.[68]

This major extension of public authority over claimant families was consolidated by many more minor regulations to govern behaviour. If most were irksome, they symbolised enhanced control over daily lives. One of the most common, the adoption of which amounted to a craze, was to terminate relief to those who persisted in keeping a dog. Although there were precedents, including the demise of 128 dogs in a week at Thatcham in 1791, its widely reported adoption in 1795, and repetition in 1800, was particularly apposite when food traditionally reserved for the pigs was declared fit for human consumption. Gleaning too came under widespread scrutiny, farmer Metcalfe in the North Riding even recording precise biblical references to the practice in his diary. The Terling vestry advanced their crusade on behalf of 'the goodness of the industrious and orderly poor', by preventing gleaning by single people 'except widows'; those still eligible had to give farmers advance notice; failure to do so, or to report illicit gleaners, was penalised by having 'the weekly allowance of flour . . . taken from them'. The Burtonwood vestry in Lancashire turned its collective benevolent eye to the public provision of 'Gunpowder, Coals or Ale' to celebrate Guy Fawkes' Day, and instantly discontinued this 'very needless expense'. Such attacks on recreation, comforts and customs represent further deteriorations in living standards.[69]

If these examples do not suffice to ridicule the confident assertion by a recent historian that 'punitive notices . . . are markedly absent from the vestry minutes during the critical years of shortages and the supposed threat of revolutionary disturbances',[70] a cursory trawl with a leaky teaspoon reveals hundreds. The history of poor-law administration is, of course, peppered with examples of the harsh treatment of claimants, long before utilitarian enthusiasts invented the horrors of less eligibility. The famines were no exceptions; we might mention the Suffolk day labourer who was forced by his vestry to pay for a replacement spade from his meal allowance, and the draconian cut in flour dole imposed by the Ludgvan vestry on a character who opposed these oligarch's opportunistic seizure on the issue to force him into the workhouse. Fears of revolutionaries, supposed or real, did not deter the Salford Bench from threatening to withdraw statutory and charitable relief from those who resisted magisterial injunctions against trade union activity, or the Oxford authorities who excluded riot participants from a corporate charity. Relief was conditional on subservience even in populous places. The degree of subordination *imposed* can be gauged from the Hampshire autocrats who threw a claimant out for 'stepping into the vestry without being sent for', and the JP who imprisoned him for his refusal to apologise. A letter from an estate steward to his employer is too eloquent for comment:

> you will have a very serious loss and disappointment in your Bacon this year . . . the largest Hogs . . . mostly bad . . . and . . . a very small part of them is now eatable; but none of those parts fit to eat in your Home . . . the Poor People would . . . pick and Eat part of it . . . would you have me . . . give it Away to the Poor?

The poor were to remain subservient, take what was offered, and acquiesce in the arbitrary administration of their affluent neighbours. Where this control was strongest, in the countryside, substitute foods were literally rammed down claimants' throats. Sir Christopher Sykes of Sledmere in the wheat-eating East Riding, 'had such persons who will live on Barley Bread alone . . . supplied by the Overseer . . . at 4/– a Bus[hel] but those who will not must buy as they can'. Chigwell vestrymen likewise turned their backs on workers who refused to eat mixed breads. Nor were claimants automatically protected by urban status. Press accounts of charities were not objective, and doubtlessly obscure all varieties of abuse, and one is at a loss to decide whether the privately communicated intelligence of the Malton poor's refusal to *buy* fish heads is more remarkable than the decision by charity officials to offer them for sale.[71]

The new control, affecting that unprecedented proportion of the population forced to solicit assistance, was at its most effective in the rural South and East, and is probably reflected in the decline of riot and its partial replacement by covert protest. The charitable certainly saw their donations as a means of purchasing respect and influence among the workers, and hopefully exemption from protest; this was repeatedly implied by the press. John Drowas, a Cornish mine-owner, who extended sales of cheap corn to his miners to all in his host community, insisted that it 'not only tended to quiet the Minds of the People but gave me an Influence over the Neighbouring Tinners that hardly any other Circumstance would have raised'. Drowas perceived that his 'liberality' was 'honoured' immediately, and calculated on having acquired a power which might be critical in the medium and long term. In one sense he anticipated achieving the same type of status, as a pillar of the community, that others inherited through generations of paternalistic landownership. In this fashion the *nouveau riche*, the employers in the new theatres of industrialism, could hope to struggle towards the social position of those at the top of the hierarchy in more slowly changing traditional communities. Of course, many factors, from the ruthlessness of industrial capitalism to the neo-egalitarianism of late eighteenth century radicalism, militated in opposition. Only one Shropshire iron-master, John Wilkinson, was commemorated in a folk song, and actually achieved a rough and ready parity with landed proprietors like Earl Ashburnham, whose 'virtuous ways' reinforced a long lineage of benevolence, to find its reward in the lyrical compositions of an estate blacksmith. Poor relief and philanthropy were vehicles of social control, even in the short-term as recognised by Arthur Young among scores of others. But there were limits governing these vital agents behind the maintenance of law and order, and indeed the status quo; they were critically exposed by the contrasting developments across the regions during the seemingly inevitable crisis in relief, which struck the country over the winter of 1800–1.[72]

The Crisis in Poor Relief 1800–1

Social control through the rates and charities turned both operations into theatres of increasing fierce conflict. Protesting recipients sometimes appeared in court. But famine relief also generated conflict between ratepayers. The 'best Regulations for supporting the Poor' adopted at Wells in Norfolk provoked a strong reaction from 'the lower Trades people' who were 'dissatisfied at what they are to contribute'. The sources, notably the press, considering the magnitude of such struggles, are remarkably silent; editors generally eschewed comment, probably through fear of the consequences. The *Cambridge Intelligencer* proved a partial exception, by reporting the decisions of poor-law authorities, emphasising the increasingly 'heavy . . . burden' imposed by rate demands, and insisting that the unprecedented scale of relief operations did 'not keep pace with the daily increasing distresses of the poor' in the autumn of 1800.[73] The poor law crisis was particularly potent between November 1800 and April 1801. It was caused by a complex mixture of financial and administrative problems, recipients' reactions to all aspects, especially the retrenchment campaign, and partially promoted by the socio-political responses to the government's attitude, policy and strategy after September 1800. But the crisis was neither universal nor total because the major causes were not simultaneously present in every locality. The non-implementation of the Parochial Relief Act in many places precluded the full development of popular hatred of substitute foods. Some districts avoided the heaviest financial pressures because the poor were neither so numerous nor so concentrated as they were elsewhere. The effects of the interaction of all these factors varied very considerably. Few regions experienced all, and fewer still endured the full cumulative impact of all at full strength.

The position of the non-settled poor was a perennial eighteenth-century problem, though not of the magnitude alleged by the poor law's most hostile laissez-faire and utilitarian critics. Many industrial centres could never have developed without migrant labour. Tolerance is well illustrated by the simple and representative decision taken in Staffordshire by the Brewood vestry in February 1800 to 'allow Wm Mason of Dudley 2s p Week till Provisions are cheaper & Wm Rea 1s per week till the like'. Some local magnates adopted a self-proclaimed 'liberal line of Conduct', exemplified by the Marquis of Salisbury's railroading through a Hatfield decision to relieve all resident claimants indiscriminately. Salisbury significantly publicised the move through handbills, and added the rider that harmony was best preserved if all parishes followed suit. However, the majority of poor-law authorities decided, sooner or later, to restrict aid to the formally settled. This was a well-tried expedient enshrined in the legislation, and resorted to in places on the immediate onset of crisis. Handsworth, one of the Birmingham parishes most thickly populated by migrants, was quickly off the mark in December 1794, about the same time as the autocratic and parsimonious vestry at Midhurst in Sussex ordered the arrest and expulsion of all newcomers not in possession of a settlement certificate. Pitt's 1795 Act illegalised this brand of severity, but it still permitted the removal of non-settled residents on application for assistance, and was therefore of minimal protection to migrant workers during the famines. In January 1795 Norwich Corporation rejected the entreaties of their own overseers 'to extend' cash payments to resident 'Aliens' in difficulty, and this policy made further strides after the summer hypercrisis, with for example, determined attempts by Hull authorities to 'rid themselves' of non-settled poor. The policy was re-invoked more widely in 1799–1801, with vestry following vestry in listing 'the real Parishioners' in the parlance of Wansted Essex rulers. At Ludgvan all claimants were forced 'before the Justices to swear to their Settlement', and the recalcitrant punished by the withdrawal of their flour allowances. The timing of these decisions regularly coincided with innovatory relief measures, and were clearly designed to minimise the inevitable extra costs. Adoption of the Parochial Relief Act proved a common stimulant, and among the casualties was the more altruistic tradition at Brewood.[74]

The Brewood minute recording the withdrawal of the 'allowances of flour from all the non-settled resident poor belonging to other Parishes', also instructed officials 'to inform the overseers' of such residents' parishes of the fact. The precise predicament of such migrant workers varied. Dr. Neuman noted that 'the device of one parish billing another for the relief of the latter's settled paupers was widely employed in an extra legal fashion during the first part of the nineteenth century'. The famines were central to this development, as inferred by the Brewood minute, which initially put the onus on the other parishes to make some arrangement, either with the Brewood overseers, or the individual claimant. Some parishes accepted the settlement certificate of such migrants who had them as security for repayment of relief costs. This was specifically stated at King's Lynn in November 1795; luckless non-certificate holders were sent packing. Norwich adopted the same policy, which became common in Norfolk from that year. Where co-operation achieved this degree of institutionalisation, recipients may have experienced fewer problems, but bureaucracy created its own hurdles; for example, the value of the eight-shilling static payment paid through the Cambridge overseers to a city resident by the Barton vestry was quickly eroded in November 1800, and only the charitable 'assistance of a few individuals' permitted the recipient to get by while his case was referred back for reassessment to Barton.[75]

Migrants were commonly left to their own devices. J. Gray walked to Henfield from Brighton and negotiated a fourteen-shilling payment for his family of five boys. Further supplication proved necessary once rent arrears were compounded by the redundancy of one son. This time Gray wrote, promising 'If it lay in my Power to get a long I will not trouble the Parish any More': a one-off payment of two guineas in March 1796 sufficed. Those unable to write generated huge demands on their literate neighbours; in Bristol, David Lowe kept off the parish through income gained by writing letters. Applicants so circumstanced, regularly used this device to exert pressure on their home parishes. Blacksmith Nathaniel Snelling, domiciled at Colchester, reminded the 'Gentlemen' of Medfield Suffolk, in January 1801, that 'all parishes allow some thing to famileys at this time'; could Medfield 'Send me Some Money to help Me in this time of Necessity And to pay my Rent as I Can not work through it without your kind Assistance'. If refused, Snelling would 'be obliged To bring the family home'. Another permutation is revealed by a letter from W. Ashby of Gravesend, on behalf of his employee, W. Burgis, to his place of settlement, Burwash in Sussex. Ashby admitted that Burgis's wages were inadequate; workers with Gravesend settlements were entitled to subsidised flour, and Ashby offered to supply Burgis on the same terms if Burwash reimbursed the cost: if Burwash offered no 'Allowance I am Cirtain he must sell his goods and Come home'. Faced with this threat many parishes paid up; everybody hoped that the crisis would pass, and absolutely nothing would be gained when the alternative to denials of relief to parishioners in work elsewhere was probable unemployment on their return home. This process of relief was eased where vestries specifically left such aid to the overseers' discretion; agonising delays doubtlessly occurred where claimants had to wait for a formal vestry meeting.[76]

Additional difficulties could occur where non-resident claimants' parishes relieved in kind, and these were aggravated by the Parochial Relief Act. Some vestries might have hoped that making potential claimants collect aid in kind would deter applications. Nonetheless, the list of parishioners who collected provisions and coal at Thirsk names people resident in over forty locations, some over twenty miles distant. When Ludgvan stopped flour allowances to the non-settled, they extended them to non-residents, including Francis Jennings who had to come eight miles from Redruth to collect. Two people were reported to have died on such missions during the dreadful winter of 1794–5. A nineteen year-old lass died on the road, travelling from Brighton to Melling in Kent to collect relief. A sixteen year-old youth died overnight on losing his way back to Conisbrough in the snow after collecting, with his ten year-old sister who miraculously survived, two stone of meal from a Tickhill charity. These reports were not contradicted, evidence that such journeys were commonplace.[77]

The question of aid to the non-settled was a further source of particularly savage treatment. The unsettled were excluded from aid at Scruton and Saffron Walden even during the summer hypercrisis of 1795; such decisions contributed to at least one riot in Essex, though pragmatism usually seems to have deterred repetition in more populous places. But if claiming relief from nearby parishes did not erect insuperable problems for migrants, many who lived in the larger industrial centres and above all in London, were to all intents and purposes on a par with the Irish, who were of course generally ineligible for statutory assistance. The members of the fourteen-thousand Catholic Irish households in London at this time were proverbially neglected by the philanthropic, except in St. Giles which had a good charitable record. One of the few specifically Irish charities launched in 1796, significantly and primarily aimed to 'clothe the ragged'. Subscription charities were the major source of aid for many migrant and Irish workers; their aggravated destitution owed more to their legal status than the gin-addiction alleged by Colquhoun. In any event, the operation of the settlement laws exposed claimants to greater stress; the number of removals soared, and the Handsworth campaign finally provoked an angry crowd, reputedly eleven-thousand strong threatening the mansion of one of its architects, Matthew Boulton.[78]

The relative importance of statutory and charitable relief in densely populated locations cannot be quantified. The tremendous boom in subscription charities is attributable to four main factors. First, in the hyper-crises of the summer of 1795 and the autumn of 1800, they financed the massive exertions to procure stocks. They secondly minimised rate increases, and thus the difficulties caused for poorer ratepayers. Nevertheless, only a handful of small rural parishes escaped significant rate rises.[79] Thirdly, as was emphasised, they preserved claimants from ignominious applications to parish officers. Fourthly, and most importantly, they were, with a handful of distinctly uncharitable exceptions, a means of assisting the non-settled without legally qualifying recipients for subsequent statutory relief. Sir Frederick Morton Eden, commenting on the massive West Street, Soho soup shop, in the centre of one of London's poorest and partly Irish quarters, insisted that 'many thousand persons, who had no other means of [extra] support, received occasional relief' in soup, salted pork, potatoes and rice over the 1800–1 winter.[80]

During that period charity administrators correctly anticipated unparalleled claims for aid, and the need for unprecedented funding; the latter materialised, only to be repeatedly outstripped by demand. The affluent paid through their banks, but the operations were underpinned by thousands of small contributions from the middle and tradesmen classes, collected in 'house-to-house' canvasses in big towns like Manchester. Contributors of between one and three shillings to one rural fund included joiners, shopkeepers, small-holders and the workhouse farmer. It was precisely these classes who felt the severity of the pinch in 1800–1. A comparison between subscribers to charities during both famines at Newbold, Derbyshire, shows that receipts doubled in the second, but the numbers of donors declined dramatically, notably to a second appeal floated within two months of the first. The fund's replenishment depended on vastly increased contributions from the vicar, the major employers, and finally by appeals to local grandees, none of whom had donated before or had a personal stake in the township. Parallel progressions are encountered in the cities. Small donors provided about a quarter of the initial fund at York in the autumn of 1800, but it remained operational throughout the winter almost entirely on cash from major commercialists, aldermen, the banks, and the resident clergy and gentry.[81]

The collapse of support from the 'middling people' was partially a reflection of the crisis's impact on their family finances, and partially a reflection of the belief in 'artificial scarcity', compounded by the hostile reaction in precisely these social classes to executive statements and parliamentary proceedings in the autumn of 1800. 'Those who have the Management of the poor in the Towns have never done their duty by making proper provision for them', commented a JP; others agreed that 'the Tradesmen' and the 'middle sort of people' believed that their responsibility, as ratepayers and philanthropists, for the poor, was absolved by the apparent conspiracy amongst farmers and merchants which produced empty market-places. A more sophisticated variant of this analysis was articulated at Tewkesbury; subscriptions 'only tended to keep up the price of Provisions and enrich the monopolisers'. In those regions where the impact of famine on the economy was intensified by industrial recession, especially in Lancashire and Yorkshire, anti-government feelings engulfed the middle classes, and undermined aid operations. In December 1800, in Lancashire, canvassers were told on the doorsteps

> that these Charities only abetted the mischiefs and miseries of the Country, that they would not give one Farthing, that the Poor must speak out and act for themselves that their Distresses would bring it about at last, and that this compulsion was necessary to effect a Peace. This was the language of some very respectable but disaffected persons.

In the West Riding, where the staggering scale of increased rate demands can be extrapolated from the figures tabulated in Appendix 9, a ratepayers' strike began to escalate. With their trade on the brink of ruin, many were either literally unable to pay their bills, or no longer willing to prop up the local community seemingly on behalf of a government which they despised. The 'amazing increase' in relief applications made no difference. Justice Dawson 'threatened the Principal inhabitants' of Dewsbury with his arrival 'at the head of the Military' to enforce payment of 'weekly Paupers' and the rates.[82]

Aversion to repetitive rate and charity demands was further fuelled by the retrenchment policy's many-sided implementation, and the hostile response of recipients to it. Details of these disincentives to charity rarely appeared in the press. At Sheffield, perhaps the town most thoroughly opposed to the government, we cannot penetrate the inter-action of political and personal financial motives which created difficulties for the soup organisers. But problems there were. 'Frequent appeals' for further donations through personal canvasses galvanised resistance as early as February 1800; in April subscription books were opened at the banks and the Cutlers' Hall to circumvent doorstep confrontations; the strategy was repeated in December. Unprecedented sums were raised, but the numbers of donors declined dramatically; the void had to be filled by big subscriptions from commercial and industrial houses, and appeals to grandees like Earl Fitzwilliam and the Duke of Norfolk. In London relief administration collapsed; officials abandoned the policy of restricting aid to those nominated by subscribers. One committee made an inspection of conditions at the homes of a token one-hundred claimants, and extended relief to fourteen-thousand all-comers, 'not merely to persons recommended'. Identical changes were made at Sheffield where the relative paucity of contributors aggravated the problems caused by ten-thousand weekly applicants; 'it became utterly impracticable to make out Tickets apportioned to the exact number in the respective Families'. These urban problems certainly meant that recipients were no longer 'dependants with assigned places in a network of patronage', but this surrender occurred only after a struggle, and the resort to treating 'the poor as a faceless mass' was not the product of policy, as sometimes alleged, but of necessity.[83] Order at outlets evaporated; a free-for-all developed. In Manchester a nine year-old girl was 'trampled' to death and a pregnant lady 'much injured' in a stampede to buy cheap potatoes. In Hull, some pot-carrying supplicants walked over two miles, and in Lancashire many complaints were made at the time wasted in queuing and fetching gruel. In London Bernard apprehensively watched the vast queues, and mused over the impact on 'the morals of the lower classes' when experiencing frustrating delays while herded together. Soup and other commodities frequently ran out, infuriating unsatisfied customers; serious rioting at the Nottingham Soup Kitchen on Christmas Day 1800 necessitated army reinforcements being rushed from Birmingham. Newspaper editors ignored these incidents, preferring transparently unreal eulogies on the supposed benefits of soup, rice and herrings, for deprived urban workers.[84]

A plethora of other administrative problems savaged efficiency. The strain, emotional and physical, on overseers was immense. In Somerset Tom Poole was 'so much occupied by the poor people' that he hardly salvaged the time for personal business, and certainly not to maintain his regular correspondence with S.T. Coleridge. Overwork was aggravated by ratepayer resistance to repeated demands; some overseers were fined for neglect of duty, but the relative rarity of such prosecutions reflects magisterial awareness of the sheer scale of the problem. Many overseers had inadequate social standing; those in North Devon were too parochial and inexperienced to negotiate wholesale transactions at Plymouth. Their desperate counterparts in Hertfordshire resorted to appeals for pecuniary and administrative assistance to absentee landlords, in hopes that such solicitation did not comprise 'unwarrantable intrusion'. Some places tried to contain their difficulties by appointing more parochial officers, but this also served to expand the numbers who faced the debilitations generated by a multiplicity of problems, the nature of which militated against full documentation.[85]

Relief administrations first began to collapse totally, almost inevitably in London's East End, notably in Bethnal Green, Mile End and Spitalfields. It proved too severe and too close to the seat of government to ignore. Secret-service funds were clandestinely pumped into parochial coffers before the summer of 1800, but once these were exhausted, the problem recurred with redoubled severity. Of the 630 assessed premises in Mile End, 529 contributed £1455, and another seventy-nine a paltry £329. Most ratepayers were in hopeless arrears; 'every advancement in the rates caused an almost proportionate deficiency in receipts'. By November all three parishes were bankrupt; relief could not be extended to a tenth of legitimate claimants, and it was eventually unilaterally withdrawn from all except the aged and unemployed. Even then no more than a fifth of what the workless received in more affluent metropolitan quarters was paid. This left between sixteen and seventeen-thousand people, comprising 'a large portion of the poorer labourers and manufacturers of various descriptions' without any relief-in-aid-of wages. The select committee confronted the problem in December. MPs recommended a government loan to be repaid under future legislation. Pitt concurred, and countered parliamentary opposition with the claim that the East End's poverty problem was uniquely intense, even in London. Eventually twenty-thousand pounds were paid, twelve of which went to Bethnal Green, or as George Rose stressed on behalf of the Treasury, 'the poor . . . would starve'. The grant forestalled impending disaster, though some lined the pockets of corrupt local officials, and argument still raged in 1816 in spite of an inconclusive report soon after the event.[86]

Pitt's optimism was belied by the conjunction of further price rises, economic recession and disequilibrium. The London situation was paralleled across the northern textile belt, and in old textile towns in Essex, Wiltshire, and the Midlands. The East End precedent guaranteed pressure for similar aid to the provinces. The rebellious ratepayers of Dewsbury quickly petitioned Whitehall, and Wilberforce was soon being furiously lobbied by his West Riding constituents. Petitions were referred to the select committee over the winter. Investigation suggested no recourse except to central funds; ministers, including Pitt and subsequently Addington, were aghast. But even Sheffield was not Spitalfields, and if the committee advised prompt payments, each application required magisterial endorsement and was subjected to close Treasury evaluation. The inevitable delays resulted in vivid contrasts between the immediacy of payments to the East End and those made to the provinces, and are comparable to the earlier favouritism accorded to London at the expense of the provinces, over government grain distribution in 1795.[87]

Nevertheless, more applications threatened to swamp the Treasury, notably from places which could advance unique problems or claim special status. The extra-parochial Forest of Dean had a good case. Few residents had any right to statutory relief. Charities were inoperative owing to subscriber inpecuniousness. The corollary of the monarch's personal stake in the Forest ought to be a massive royal donation, argued the Chairman of the Gloucestershire Sessions. If the Forest was not typical, any involvement of the king posited problematic ramifications galore; exhausted charities and potentially bankrupt poor-law authorities had a much broader currency, and in the probable event of their rapid spread, cataclysmic implications were all too obvious. In April 1801, the select committee made further recommendations. Loans were made available to parishes when the rate currently levied 'exceeded greatly' the sum raised in 1799–1800. Details of the decrease in the numbers of ratepayers, and annual sums collected over the past five years, were to accompany applications. Repayment of Treasury loans, in half-yearly instalments, were to commence no later than 1804. Although there is little evidence of advances made under these arrangements, principally because the technical availability of monies coincided with what proved to be the end of the crisis, these unprecedented, and some said unconstitutional measures, indicate critical factors. The government accepted the committee's anticipation of a massive impending collapse of the poor-rate system, which might engulf many densely populated locations; loans could stave-off this collapse, which would be even more dangerous once philanthropy crumbled. The stabilisation of the resultant situation required repayments to be spread across thirteen years.[88] The dilemma galvanising this unique response by the state comprised a further major ingredient concentrating Addington's mind on the paramountcy of peace.

CHAPTER 18

Paradoxes, Ironies and Contradictions
Some Conclusions

This book has a two-dimensional rationale. First, the empirical history of wartime famine was unwritten. Secondly, national survival during these episodes requires explanations beyond the problematic of Britain's avoidance of revolution. Famine impinged on most facets of life, and is therefore relevant to the many debates between historians of England in the classic phase of industrialisation, notably that generated by Edward Thompson's seminal *The Making of the English Working Class*. But every topic examined exudes paradoxes, ironies and contradictions. This was not simply an age in which government eschewed economic management on the theoretical principles expounded by the likes of Adam Smith and consumed by leading politicians including the Younger Pitt. It was not a period in which central government simply and firmly exerted a new, powerful directorship over the organs of provincial and local administration. It proved not to be an epoch in which the bonds of traditional paternalism were severely loosened and replaced by the untrammelled mechanics of the free market; famine provided a forum for the reinforcement of orthodox paternalism in the more stable communities, and a major opportunity for its vigorous extension through the urban bourgeoisie to the emergent industrial theatres. There was no simple and fundamental weakening of the old ties of the statutory social security system in some intensifying utilitarian climate dissolving outmoded socio-political values; there are elements of both. But this is not to deny the uniqueness of the 1790s. Its unusual calibre derived from repeated socio-economic crises alone. The war, and all it represented, together with the birth of an alternative challenging democratic political philosophy among working people, combined with the famines to make the nineties unique, and one of the most traumatic decades in modern English history. Developments will not submit to any simple analysis, nor should they permit another example of historians' penchant for taking refuge in notions of an age of transition. Professor Christie's 'disordered cohesion' was more disordered and less cohesive than his picture allows.

316   WRETCHED FACES

We suggested that the complacency of the historical demographers was subtlely manipulated by the apologists for the historical development of English capitalism. To what extent has the empirical study of the famines exposed their confidence, what revisions can be suggested, and how can the less clear-cut findings here be incorporated into the demographers' long-term analysis? The demographic evidence presented here is not exhaustive but it is suggestive; the ostensibly authoritative study by the Cambridge Group is itself based on only a statistically small sample of parishes. Recently discovered regional disparities include the 1792 peak of the birth-rate, and speedy decline to pre-1780 levels in part of the Wiltshire-Somerset cloth belt, which coincided with the rapid introduction of labour-saving technology. Further population studies may expose disturbances similar to those revealed by the Norwich Bills of Mortality. A twenty-five percent increase in the death-rate in 1800 is principally attributed to child mortality. Demographers studying twentieth-century famines insist that 'the deaths of infants and children . . . account for most of the deaths when death rates are high', and the marked vulnerability of children is also emphasised in each of the 'at risk' components in the first three of Dr Oddy's four-stage typology of famine. Our literary evidence reflected the particular precariousness of children. Age specific mortality analysis, like that available for Norwich, plus the identification of significant falls in the birth rate – of ten percent in 1800 at Norwich – when equated with the baby-boom following on in 1803, helps explain the absorption of short-term dislocations by medium-term demographic trends: 'within five years the compensation is complete'. The typically optimistic utilitarian coldness in the Cambridge *History of Population*, that food 'price variations merely advance or retard the timings of death for those with a foot already in the grave' is unhistorical. Children perennially had one foot in the grave, and the 'compensation' did not extend to the parents of a famine-imperilled generation, who had to confront scenes like that described by Lowery which we cited at the start of Chapter 5. In 1801, three Hertfordshire families were prosecuted for 'nearly starving' children 'to death'; it is significant that every case involved daughters. The evidence of famine-induced demographic disturbance in the 1790s is irrefutable yet demographers' addiction to moving averages continues to conceal it. Barrie Stapleton's very recent analysis of the parish registers which Malthus himself helped to compile, religiously reduces the statistics to nine year moving averages. Yet even this method fails to eliminate burial rates exceeding baptism rates in one parish in Malthus's part of central rural Surrey; the full scale of suffering can be established only through more fundamental research, as recently argued in a comparative analysis of 'life under pressure' in England and France between 1670 and 1870. Historians of this period cannot uncritically subscribe to the confidence of the Cambridge Group.[1] Nor ought they – in stark contrast to Professor Mokyr – tolerate econometricians like Lindert and Williamson whose sophisticated methodology apparently cannot remove the need to use poor-relief figures from 1801 of all years, in order to manipulate a base line of 19.9 percent of the population receiving assistance at the very start of the nineteenth century, falling to a mere 6.2 percent in 1867, in support of their optimists' case in the standard of living debate.[2]

J.D. Post acknowledged the difficulty of reconciling 'famine food prices with weekly wage rates'; he cautioned that 'Sources of income or food that existed have probably since become concealed', but advised that 'the way in which labouring persons bridged the gap between income and outlay in times of dearth still awaits systematic explanation'.[3] Such an analysis is unfortunately beset by evidential problems; we do not have any plebeian's diary which systematically records the achievement of day-to-day survival. Suggestions can, however, be made, and a start is possible from the premis established by a recent expert on contemporary problems: 'Even in famine . . . food is available; people starve because of inability to command food. They do not have the money to buy it or the socially or politically sanctioned right to receive it free'.[4] Dr. Appleby asserts that 'the crucial variable in the elimination of famine was not the weather but the ability to adopt to the weather . . . in the temperate regions of England and France human responses to climate were more important than the climate itself in both causing famine and eliminating it'. The Cambridge Group also detect a partial explanation of the English experience in this train of thought;

> the institutionalisation of communal responsibility for individual survival through the poor law may have secured a more equitable distribution of food in times of crisis than would have occurred if allocation had been left to market forces tempered by individual charity

Comparisons between England and continental Europe in the last great European famine of 1816–7 reveal the 'inadequacy of public relief' across the latter and the 'unwillingness of the propertied classes to accept the concept of state responsibility for relief'. In England, by contrast, 'Poor relief was well established', and the mendicancy problem was no rival to its continental counterpart which made 1817 the 'year of the beggars'. Comparisons also reveal differential death-rates across Europe, which can be ascribed to the varying degrees of state involvement with the problem, the relative success of governments, and the levels of philanthropy.[5]

In the nineties the unique English poor law, assisted by charities, achieved a much more equitable distribution of food than was remotely possible through the free market. However, our desired reconciliation of wage and price rates will not materialise through mollifications accruing from relief measures. Indeed the gap widened as relief values fell, particularly in the second famine. Reconciliation and explanation require other factors. Those in work might hope to increase wages, either through appeals to employers' humanity or through industrial muscle; alternatively, and/or additionally, increasing indebtedness to employers, had its attractions. Overtime might be worked where available, and supplementary jobs taken where possible. Wives and children could work, perhaps when in happier circumstances they would not. But such options were curtailed during the famines owing to falling demands for goods and services. Moreover, it is clear that employers, including the largest single group, the farmers, tried to shift responsibilities on to public authority; employers also eschewed responsibility by encouraging their workers to seek charity. Sir Frederick Eden calculated that if women and children were included as beneficiaries, 'nearly a fourth part of the population of England and Wales . . . receive occasional relief' from Friendly Society membership. A proportion received aid from these sources, notably where specific initiatives were launched to combat the exigencies, especially with wholesale purchases of primary foodstuffs.[6]

All bar a tiny elite of workers were forced to economise, and economise drastically whatever aid derived from self-help organisations, the poor law and charities. Amongst the immediate casualties were those consumer goods identified by Professor Christie as the common, if not universal, attributes of relative proletarian affluence in normal times. Many were forced, with varying rapidity, to reserve all funds for food alone; replacement clothes and footwear, adequate heating and light, were also fairly immediate objects of economy for many too. Rents were partly or unpaid; arrears mounted. Market prices dictated dietary economies, though options varied with individuals' circumstances, regionally, and from time to time. Consumers could switch to cheaper cereals, notably wheat-eaters in 1795–6. Regional variations include the significant northern switch to barley in response to prohibitively-priced oats in 1799–1801. Many wheat-eaters reduced and eventually excluded all non-cereal items of diet; this expedient was adopted even by those who were customarily dependent on foods like milk, bacon, potatoes and cheese with non-wheaten cereals. Some were reduced to cutting out cereals altogether, to rely on potatoes and anything else commandable including beans, peas, turnips and even nettles. There are reports of men, including miners, collapsing at work through lack of food; beggars exploited this scenario; feigned fainting in the street proved remunerative. There is a distinct possibility that further economies were achieved by reserving more of the shrunken volume of available food for adult men, and stinting further the consumption of women and children to ensure that the main wage-earner maintained strength sufficient to continue working. Such were the literal causes of wretched faces. Further expedients, including the pawning of clothes, bedding and household goods, underlay ragged appearances too. This made only one further resort, to begging, possibly easier. Pilfering and thieving were clearly another resort for hundreds of thousands. Ultimately, for men and youths, only the armed services offered a final refuge. At Oldham, Rowbottom regularly recorded the names of his neighbours driven to enlist by aggravated poverty. If wages were poor, and invariably irregularly and tardily paid, the recruit himself could expect adequate food, while their families had a special claim on poor-law authorities, even if the more niggardly were the repeated subjects of magisterial orders.[7]

If the foregoing falls short of 'systematic explanation', wretched faces themselves form the final part of the equation; the visible realities of serious deprivation were manifest in spite of the tremendous exercise of political will to mobilise resources against famine. In his 1803 edition Malthus recognised the reality whereby Britain's industrially-generated wealth overcame agrarian deficiency by funding cereal importation. By 1800, the big grain importers were confident that global markets had geared themselves to meet indigenous British shortfalls; no other nation's resources could compete, with the exception of France's. That was never fully tested by competition in global exchanges, with the partial exception of 1794–5. Britain's mature commercial arrangements underpinned the supremacy deriving from wealth. The exception was the first famine season, 1794–5; then a combination of factors, including a failure to anticipate British market realities, rather rigid English international commercial practices, fear of competition with government contractors (including British) in overseas marts, and sheer inexperience, generated the lethal situation developing which was just contained by the ministry's eleventh-hour intervention. These experiences encouraged a realignment of the international grain trade, and Britain emerged as the premier market. Thereafter, intervention in the form of price-guarantees and 'bounties' was economically strictly unnecessary. Pitt refused to risk abandoning national subsistence to free-trade economics, globally applied. A miscalculation would have fatally compromised the war effort, and, given the internal threat, the future of the British ancien regime. But Pittite survival, initially turning on huge importations of foodstuffs, involved another political risk, namely antagonising the backbone of the British political system, agrarian capital. Ministers instantly appreciated that imports automatically competed with indigenous produce; the willingness to commit vast sums of public money to enhance that competition could have conjured a devastating political backlash. This spectre haunted politicians' perceptions; unnerved further by the confrontations with agrarian capital's commercial and manufacturing allies, governments had no stomach for sustained experiments with national subsistence once the exigencies passed.

But the emergencies stretched Pitt's political will beyond offending the nation's farmers to offending the proletariat through retrenchment. The state's actions guaranteed that there were very real connections between high prices, dietary deprivation and hunger, and government policies; these were increasingly recognised throughout society. The government calculated a significant amelioration accruing through the extraction of more subsistence from a given volume of primary foodstuffs, and further relief by increasing the supply of uncustomary foods, like maize, rice and soup; both necessitated radical dietary change. Pitt progressed, or rather lurched, towards compulsory measures. A range of circumstances, including the socio-political situation at its most dangerous in London, the opposition of very powerful economic interest groups, and the fortuitous compensatory factor of successful yields of barley and oats, enabled ministers to assess and reject compulsory measures in 1795. They were forced on to the agenda again by the more serious shortages obtaining in 1800. The Parochial Relief Act represented a step towards compulsion, though no British government had the power equal to making that type of measure obligatory. The Brown Bread Act was, given the options, the ultimate in compulsory measures. The government had prepared some of the ground; discussions with experts, the trade and the metropolitan authorities, had exposed many of the very real difficulties attendant on achieving retrenchment by such means. The London Flour Company legislation had contradictory achievements. On the negative side it revealed the strength of opposition which split the cabinet, and wrecked every ministry's supposed automatic majority in the House of Lords. The latter form of desertion was epitomised by the vote of the king's son against his father's ministers. On the other hand, despite the compromises, the Company's operations would expose the enormous profits in the milling trade. If the Company managed to meet a portion of London demand with coarser bread, the argument that this form of retrenchment risked a revolt by the metropolitan proletariat was weakened. Together, consumer satisfaction, and the exposure of the real causes of commercial obstruction, the preservation of exploitively-achieved huge profits, should have equipped ministers with key arguments for compulsory measures. This strategy was weakened by the enforced reduction in the scale of the Company's operations, and the inevitable delay before publication of its accounts. Pitt nevertheless pressed on and obtained the Brown Bread Act. Its failure must be attributed to the unsuitability notably of foreign wheat and the health problems attendant on its use. However, the milling establishment preserved Londoners' health, and itself from a fierce backlash, by using the best grades for metropolitan consumption. Elsewhere adulteration attained unprecedented levels, and therefore the trade was culpable in the legislation's complete failure. The apparent absence of political recoil upon that failure must be ascribed to its coincidence with the major constitutional crisis caused by the monarch's recurrent insanity, and further aggravation of the political confusion by Pitt's protracted resignation.

The inward collapse of the ultimate compulsory measure does not obscure the limited success accruing to other modes of retrenchment despite the difficulty of distinguishing the play of market from other germane forces. But all forms of retrenchment galvanised conflict at every level. The fact that the issue was not consistently exploited by the Foxite opposition was a source of relief for Pitt. The hostility of plebeian consumers had a broad effect; it was responsible for the distinct lack of commitment to the ideal evinced at the bottom of the hierarchy of governance, amongst the overseers of the poor, churchwardens and vestrymen in the villages, and their urban equivalents including bailiffs and common councilmen. In its mildest, least formal implementation, retrenchment required the support of such local leaders who were in the front line when it came to exposition of policy and principle to consumers. The roles of vestrymen and freemen were more direct when formal decisions to subscribe to voluntary retrenchment were taken in 1795, and crucial when example-setting was supplanted by local implementation as policy, as instanced by translation into poor-relief procedures. But people of this rank were commonly caught in the middle. On the one hand they confronted dissatisfied and angry workers; on the other they faced intense pressure from their own social superiors, aldermen, landowners and magistrates. We have encountered the likes of Sir Christopher Sykes ordering overseers to implement retrenchment, and Earl Fitzwilliam's equally arbitrary conduct in dictating the form of aid provided by a charity funded by the affluent in a thriving market town. A significant proportion of apparently 'democratic' decisions at vestry level to subscribe to engagements, and to tailor relief measures accordingly, were railroaded through by Pittite landowners and clergymen. On the other hand, for one reason or another, some men with equally autocratic authority decided against its use to enforce economy. Whether they acted alone, or collectively with like-minded colleagues, notably on Benches, they literally led resistance to the government, and were responsible for friction between local and central authorities.

The very structure of authority created arenas for struggle which threatened local social equilibrium. At times, and in places, disequilibrium assumed serious proportions and the governmental edifice began to collapse. There were, of course, many additional factors at work. Growing disenchantment with the government in general, and its commitment to war in particular, ensured that the issues of war and famine became increasingly inseparable. Savage cuts in living standards were not solely experienced by workers, for they extended rapidly to the capitalist classes, and not just to minor representatives. For the latter, war and famine pushed poor rates and taxes to unprecedented levels, and induced economic recession too; economic imbalances and difficulties began to wreck some regional economies. Reactions were equally varied; examples of the extent to which they could go, and were going, included the beginnings of a ratepayers' strike in Yorkshire, the refusal on political grounds to repeat charitable subscriptions in Lancashire, and the dangerous rejection by urban authorities of adequate extra poor-relief provision in favour of blaming the agrarian sector, which was experienced most fiercely in West Country towns. Such phenomena were all forms of desertion causing the structure of governance to come apart at the seams. The deserters included representatives of institutions and organisations central to the functions of the constituted state, men in authority at every level from parish clerk to the JP, who in turn depended for support on 'principal inhabitants', together with people specifically entrusted with the enforcement of order, amateur constables and amateur soldiers. These desertions were one aspect of a broader development, the cancerous growth of war-weariness, which threatened to unite millions from all social classes to demand an end to the war whose objectives appeared unobtainable and outdated, and whose costs were simply prohibitive.

All these factors reveal the limits to the power of government in late eighteenth-century England. Others include the size of the state's bureaucracy which prevented more interventionist measures. Although there were important political considerations, and the cynic would not add ideological ones, the paramount reason behind the government's decision to leave the internal distribution of its own grain to the free market was the absence of an appropriate bureaucracy. Ministers certainly took the political decisions, but a large cabinet majority emerged against extending the policy of purchasing corn unless of absolute necessity after the 1794–5 experiment. The government's overseas deals were principally executed by private merchants employed as agents; the government's direct role was limited to diplomatic advances to foreign powers for economic favours. Once ministers calculated that tinkering with British purchasing power on the international market through price guarantees would suffice, they were imprisoned by their reliance on the self-interested opinions of commercialists. The President of the Board of Trade was politically experienced and incisive, but neither he nor his 'department' initially had a profound knowledge of the international grain trade. The President was a quick learner, but his eventual cynicism, deriving in part from repeated exposure to the special pleadings of creatures like Claude Scott, did not extend to the construction of a case adequate to release the cabinet from its bondage. Pitt himself proved over-cautious in his determination to avoid future political quagmires by pandering to the complaints of international grain merchants when faced with the certainty of national subsistence problems. He was more ruthless when the problem receded, and refused to consider reimbursement of the merchants who claimed to have lost considerable sums due to faulty or ambiguous legislation governing the 1796 importation. Further limits to the government's power were revealed in the confrontations with the milling trade. Again, ministers had no other source of information than the manufacturers themselves; they defeated the government in 1795, and if they lost the argument respecting the London Flour Company in 1800, the failure of the Brown Bread Act in 1801 represented their victory. In some senses retrenchment represented a defeat for the trade, but it created countless opportunities for profiteering through adulteration. Patriotic appeals for retrenchment repeatedly failed to evoke a deep patriotic response; permissory legislation failed to unleash universal energies in Pitt's professed national cause. Government advocacy of Rumford soup kitchens was a less effective vehicle for their spread than the scale of the problem and the prohibitive costs faced by the philanthropic when administering their charity. Even meaningful surveys of agrarian productivity and monitoring of policy effects were beyond governmental resources. The early dependency on magistrates and clergymen for the former symbolised ministerial impotence, and this was hardly redressed when ministers were reduced to seeking remedial intelligence through putting additional burdens on their own hard-pressed tax and customs officials.

Similar impotence was exposed by the government's failure to achieve the demanded degree of law and order. The eventual direct support of the king, through the Royal Proclamation of September 1800, failed to produced the required military repression and its underpinning by legal prosecutions. Those responsible in the localities did not push things to the extremes enjoined by ministers. The army did not adopt the role to which it was increasingly accustomed in Ireland, though many regiments policing England in 1800 had cut their spurs on Irish soil. The army, with the possible fleeting exception of a handful of Irish regiments, exhibited no blood lust at home at any level. The Volunteers' performance in 1800 and 1801 proved that ultimately they could not be repeatedly used for crowd control and remain uniformly loyal. The famines did not witness the unleashing of the full barbarities of the legal code. The land was not covered in gibbets; rioters went to neither the scaffold nor the colonies in droves. Public disturbances were not turned into major agencies for enforced recruitment as they were in Ireland. Time after time the magistracy acquiesced in the crowd's impositions, and many JPs preferred acquiescence to resistance, especially if the latter enhanced the violence. Magistrates clearly sought negotiation rather than military or judicial force; this increased friction between the Bench and the Home Office. With exceptions, which are too few to alter the picture, the magistracy adopted remarkably soft tactics in increasing opposition to the demands of the king's ministers.

This evidence all sustains the fundamental point that the ruling class was not united. The range of additional examples is impressive. At the top perhaps, the role of Assize judges could be crucial. While the Duke of Portland thundered away at the unconstitutional elements of the 'moral economy', Lord Chief Justice Kenyon and his colleagues thundered against working-class oppressors, the speculating merchants and manufacturers whom the people held primarily responsible for their miseries. Assize judges ensured that some real popular retribution against the alleged projenitors of wretched faces was meted out, ironically in the king's courts. Their lordships received stirling support for judicial retribution from the JPs in their Quarter Sessions. Their, and their class's support of 'moral-economy' tenets, and adoption of notions of a *pacte de famine*, never far from the surface in times of dearth, gave both greater currency. Malthus was inevitably appalled at the 'extreme ignorance and folly of many of the higher classes . . . particularly the clergy', whom he accused of encouraging riot; he estimated that their role exposed 'half the gentlemen and clergy in the kingdom' to prosecution 'for sedition'.[8]

Malthus's remedy turned on the rapid creation of departments of political economy in the English universities. However, there are other possible interpretations of ruling-class divisions. Excessive zeal in maintaining order and the strict letter of the law, and in enforcing retrenchment, was relatively rare. Temperance in these matters operated as a palliative; it contained the deteriorating relationship between the Bench and the people, and enabled the magistracy and the courts to retain some popular credibility. The poor law and the charitable agencies did succeed in preserving some cohesive social bonds, though this should not obscure the regularity of very harsh usage of claimants on occasion. The structures of these systems provided the ruling class with the opportunities to act in the interests of the populace in a very public manner. If there were exceptions, and repeated crises attributable to inward collapses and over-enthusiastic backing for Pitt's many causes, these functions indebted a large sector of the population to the local establishment. The urban bourgeoisie were also given a forum to emulate traditional rural paternalism. *In toto* the effect of all this was enormous. The rulers of local society, whether orthodox and stable, or newly emergent and pioneering, performed as tradition dictated. On occasions, of course, such responses had to be forced; all forms of protest were instrumental in prising out greater and more generous provisions. The famines permitted the ruling class to relegitimise itself.

But relegitimisation was not complete, and paradoxes derive from the complexities. Paternalist and charitable aid veered from the traditional subsidies on bread to the distribution of unorthodox foods; soups and gruels were very poor substitutes in both nutritional and social terms. Soup certainly emerged as a last ditch mode of averting widespread starvation, but the greatest dependants were itinerants, migrants and the Irish. In some senses these groups *did not have* the same right to aid as the indigenous, stable populations, who had substitutes, including soup, though not to the exclusion of all traditional forms of relief. But the massive extensions to the operations of the poor-law system, and the charities, extended beyond the challenges to the sociology of food; they destroyed plebeian hierarchies.

The process of relief proved to be the great leveller, equalising elite craftsmen with the less-skilled, and the labouring masses; famine-relief reduced most workers to the lowest common denominator. Traditional independence, the prized social positions in which status was underpinned by greater consumerism, including command of the richest diets, was a victim, as skilled men and their families were forced into the same supplicatory postures as the meanest labourers. Such degradation was universal in working-class communities and the resultant humiliation was bitterly resented. As the second famine intensified in 1800 and 1801, many middle-class people began to fear that a combination of market forces and the relentless fiscal demands of the state, would involve them in this horrific downward social mobility.

While popular acceptance of the power structure was preserved by some forces, it was manifestly shaken by others in most regions, and on the point of evaporation, if not quite extinct, in certain localities. Hostility to authority was expressed everywhere. The range of expression impresses, from the threatening letters sent to pilchard-dispensing Cornish parsons, the firing of mean Sussex overseers' barns, the crowd's attacks on JPs and troops in scores of places, to the highly politicised challenges to northern authorities who tenaciously adhered to retrenchment. But the very disunity of the English ruling class, permitted by the peculiar system of power, was in fact one of the elusive strengths of the regime. In some ways this disunity, this lack of cohesion, protected the government itself; where magisterial indifference to all or parts of ministerial policies negated or mollified their harsher effects, be it unconventional foods or vigorous troop deployments, hostility to all arms of the state was dampened. The absence of uniform activity by a united ruling class, ensured that no grievance generated directly by government policies assumed universal dimensions. Thus there was no nationwide confrontation between governors and governed. Where it came closest it remained regionalised; examples include the principally radical and politically-inspired confrontation in the industrial North, and the more orthodox variety in the principally traditional revolt of the South-west. Here social equilibrium collapsed. The resultant confusion was controlled, especially in the latter, by the regular army which could not have fulfilled this function simultaneously across the entire country. The potentially most explosive and dangerous locality, London itself, was preserved by a combination of favouritism whereby the capital got a constant supply of grain, a stronger military presence, greater police protection from the only professional force in the country, backed by an advanced political intelligence-gathering agency and presided over by the unique stipendiary magistracy: finally considerable injections of government finance preserved subsistence when even the metropolis's enormous aggregate wealth failed to prop up the giant tandem of statutory and charitable public aid. Ironically, even under the direct eye of the Home Office, a Lord Mayor was able to mitigate the increasingly ruthless response of the government to disorder, which was fortuitous considering the devastating impact policing had on the Home Secretary's almost personalised Light Horse Volunteer Corps. If rioters were finally driven off London streets in 1800 without numerous broken heads, and if the LCS was roughly prevented from relaunching its offensive after the style of 1795, metropolitan trade unionists went on campaigning apparently little affected by Combination Acts, policemen, police magistrates, and the Home Secretary. Can all this be written off as 'disordered cohesion'? Cohesive elements were present in abundance; disorders were multifarious. There was much governance by consent, much governance without consent, and some localised safety valves with no governance at all. There are too many paradoxes, too many exemplars of muddling through, too many inconsistencies, and too much confusion, to warrant any finite or structured conclusion. Nor can the historian take refuge in Malthus's dictum that the preservation of order must be ascribed to 'the very great organised force in the country' to explain why his nightmare never happened:

> If political discontents were blended with the cries of hunger, and a revolution was to take place by the instrumentality of a mob clamouring for want of bread, the consequence would have been unceasing change and unceasing carnage, the bloody career of which nothing but the establishment of a complete despotism would arrest.[9]

It came perilously close, but the English ruling class, often in spite of itself, and even more regularly owing to itself, proved to be the world's premier successful example of its genre.

Here lies one reason for the survival of the riot as the most common response to subsistence problems. The state was simply too weak to ensure its suppression. The political radicals proved equally incapable of mobilising the crowd behind their cause. For there could be no simple replacement of the food riot by any other form of protest; no alternative mode could be geared, first to act against the targets identified by the 'moral economy', and secondly as a response to the concepts of 'artificial scarcity' with its heavy emphasis on the exploitation of the majority by a minority. The food riot in its various forms facilitated immediate and tailored responses. Two examples will suffice. When the inhabitants poured out of South-western towns to tour the farmers, they did so because they attributed empty markets and bakers' shops to withholding agriculturalists. When crowds seized grain shipments their main concern was to prevent the apparent certainty of starvation. Invariably desperation was evinced. Moreover, as R.B. Rose commented long ago, the riot cut across plebeian hierarchial and occupational divides; the crowd represented 'an incohoate working class', 'it united many different strata in a joint struggle to resist worsening experiences'.[10] The fact that workers capable of a high degree of organisation, not necessarily of the formal trade union format, as shown by the miners, or with the refined trade unionist experience of many groups of textile workers and the smaller numbers of dockyard employees, repeatedly led or dominated the food riot, may be ironic, but only for historians addicted to a labourist perversion of Whiggism. Rising union mentality, with its increasing emphasis on the wage as opposed to prices, is certainly revealed by the industrial struggles in the nineties. But even the most successful campaigners appreciated that employers were neither altruistic nor even humane;

wage increases had to be fought for even during the most desperate times. Many employers tried to absolve themselves and switch responsibilities firmly to public authorities. Employer attitudes were also responsible for the continued relevance of the riot. Dr. Bohstedt, reviewing historical explanations for the decline of the food riot, notes correctly that 'a much more obvious reason . . . after 1820 is simply that food crises ceased to be so acute and general as they had been before'.[11]

The riot as protest showed no decline at all in the early nineteenth century because it proved a vehicle adequate to community expression and action; 'the cry "All in a mind" . . . often preceded collective action' writes the historian of the sacking of the Sheffield School of Anatomy in 1835. Moreover, echoes of 'moral economy' are found in many riotous episodes including the notorious Reform Bill riot at Derby in 1831, when the crowd also attacked unpopular provision dealers and millers in addition to opponents of constitutional reform.[12] Food riots continued to occur in many places during the nineteenth century; West Country examples in 1832, 1847 and 1854 reflected the long regional tradition, but this could not have conditioned the socialists who engineered a food riot at Norwich in 1887, nor the Glaswegian bread rioters of 1919.[13] Food rioting was much more prevalent in 1847 than the south-western and north-east Scottish theatres identified by a recent authority.[14] On 14 May 1847 a huge assembly of the unemployed convened at Nottingham under Chartist auspices; the main speaker attributed high grain prices to 'speculators buying up corn . . . while . . . the people are starving'. Sections of the audience argued that they had 'better get corn where it is to be had', though the speaker 'dare not advise them to fetch it'; he acknowledged that 'every man had a right to a bellyful'. In the event, the crowd methodically called at most provision and bakers' shops to virtually extort contributions of bread and money; they returned with a waggon filled with 'half quartern, quartern and half-stone loaves' which were shared with the cash. More traditional implementation of the 'moral economy' occurred when a fall in wheat prices at the end of May was not immediately reflected in bread prices. In a series of disturbances lasting for three days in many of the surrounding villages, bakers were forced to abate their prices in a thoroughly orthodox outbreak of *taxation populaire*.[15]

The statements made and the actions taken at Nottingham in 1847 could have belonged to the 1790s, and reveal the depth of the tradition of 'moral economy'. For the tenets, and the identification of the confrontational interests of consumers, and producers, manufacturers and retailers, were central to nineteenth-century working-class cultural perceptions. Earlier eighteenth-century identifications of exploitive traders underlay co-operative developments before the 1790s; for example, the Mansfield Mill Club was founded in the 1770s. The famines in the nineties proved a major stimulant to later working class co-operation. Friendly Societies entered the wholesale grain market and began to erect their own facilities. Forty-three Sheffield sick-clubs combined resources to build a 'corn-mill . . . for their common use' in November 1795, and in 1800 a larger union of Mancunian Friendly Societies reputedly saved their membership £5000 through bulk purchases. The close links between these forms of co-operation and the 'moral economy' are rarely recognised, but it is very clear in the co-operative mills founded in many places during the famines. The Birmingham Flour and Bread Company was set up in 1796 in response to the 'various causes and circumstances' behind the inflation of bread prices to 'unexampled and exorbitant heights', aggravated by 'shameful adulteration . . . by various People'. Its Bath counterpart, modelled on Birmingham, noted that the latter's function 'destroyed the many-headed Hydra, wicked monopoly' by 'beating the enemy with their own weapon'.[16]

The wealthy bourgeoisie provided much of the capital, especially in the bigger centres where the grandest proposals were made. The Manchester concern commenced with £6000 subscribed in fifty pound lots, though no subscriber could invest more than £150. In lesser places, including Bridlington, all the capital came from one philanthropist. At Whitby, freemasons provided the initiative. Most followed the Birmingham mode by inviting small subscriptions from ordinary folk; at York and Hanley a share could be purchased in weekly shilling instalments. Many Friendly Societies bought shares on behalf of their members. The movement escalated, naturally enough, in September 1800, when, according to Sir Joseph Banks, 'subscriptions are handed about in all our Towns for the erecting of Mills'; he added, sagely, 'what their success will be time must shew, but they are approved in Conversation'. The Birmingham concern was possibly the most successful. Initially it sold only to subscribers, the largest of whom could philanthropically distribute their entitlement. Matthew Boulton bought four hundred shares for his workmen. The mill functioned throughout the inter-famine years and, bolstered by a further injection of bourgeois capital in September 1799, its economic success enabled it to sell to the public. By March 1800 it had cornered fourteen percent of the market, which was not surprising as it undercut competitors by twenty percent, and they were preserved in business only through the co-operative's refusal to permit sales on credit. There were permutations. At Norwich a quarter of the original share capital of £12,000 was reserved for bakers in units of twenty-five pounds. Conversely, bakers and millers were expressly excluded at York. The movement began to penetrate the countryside. Subscribers to a fund at Kilham, East Yorkshire, explained that their scheme would counteract the extortions and frauds of the millers. At Wanstead in Essex the vestry investigated funding a communal mill, but proposals proved too costly, and the village baker was the victim of vestrymen's adoption of co-operative principles, once the parish bakehouse commenced operations.[17] Although some of these concerns survived into the second half of the nineteenth century, and many of the humbler initiatives possibly continued unobtrusively under Friendly Society auspices for many years, the majority of schemes launched either failed to get off the ground, or had a transitory existence which terminated on the return of normal conditions later in 1801. The York venture collapsed as early as April 1801, once the full costs proved beyond resources. As a nineteenth-century historian of Bristol remarked in the 1880s, only one of the concerns started in that city in 1800 was 'still an existing relic of a movement which for the most part passed away with the dearth'. Where they survived, working-class members gradually took control as the bourgeoisie lost interest; this occurred at Birmingham, and provided a link with the early nineteenth century working-class movement's interest in co-operative trading. This mode of self-help ameliorated the problems of thousands, but its limited scale meant that millions were excluded and relied on aid from the charities and the state.[18]

These details on the co-operative movement, especially the role of the urban and industrial middle classes, together with the vociferous articulation of 'moral-economy' tenets from the same ranks, should serve as cautionary considerations in the assessment of middle-class consciousness. Dale Williams asserts that the 1766 subsistence crisis generated 'a growing awareness of the community of middling interests'. This appears to be distinctly unlikely, despite the fact that the issue of a royal proclamation condemning traditional marketing offences was thought to be a prime cause of intense food rioting, and shortly inspired a backlash played out in parliamentary lobbying by some, including the odd industrialist, for the repeal of the sixteenth-century anti-forestaller legislation, which triumphed in 1772. The 1766 crisis was also complicated by ministerial incompetence behind the opening of the ports for cereal exports under the bounty, and the subsequent rapid movement of considerable stocks across the internal communication systems to the ports. This pushed prices up and produced severe literal shortages for consumers. The Corn Laws were certainly not a victim of Williams's 'incident in the development of middle-class consciousness', which is largely mythical.[19] The 1766 famine, like those during the French wars, which includes that of 1810–2, reveal fierce polarisations between town and country, themselves overlaid by the formation of class consciousness, and disintegrations. The later famines served to emphasise the identical interests of urban and rural workers, reflected directly where the latter joined the former in demonstrations, and where trade unionism began to penetrate the countryside. Sections of the urban bourgeoisie, including retailers, and more especially, wholesalers of foodstuffs – none more so than the thousands of entrepreneurs in the massive milling trade – were essentially part of the agrarian capitalist structure. This is not to suggest an absolute harmony, for the activities of the big grain importers introduced conflicts, the full potential of which was not realised until after the war. But these capitalists, many of them urban, had by the 1760s, and more so by the 1790s, very different economic, and socio-political interests, from the majority of the industrial and urban bourgeoisie. Most employers in non-foodstuffs trades came under pressure to increase wages, and others whose professional activities like the medics exposed them to the realities of proletarian conditions, would be unable to perceive identical class interests with millers, corn-merchants and potato-dealers. Even the affluent took umbrage at escalating butchers' bills, and the greatest but not the only expression of this, was the 1795 scandal over the metropolitan meat trade. Recurrent wartime famines spawned conflict between capitalists, and retarded the development of middle-class solidarity. But in the final analysis, famine was attributable to the war itself. The causes of severe postwar economic problems – notably under – and unemployment, industrial recession and agricultural depression – were essentially very different. Low and relatively stable food prices, buttressed by confidence in the availability of overseas supplies in the event of harvest failures, almost eradicated the fear of famine, and in the 1820s this key source of middle-class conflict largely evaporated.[20]

If there was any truth in the assertion that the actions of the relevant Quarter Sessions meant more to most eighteenth-century people than parliamentary proceedings and government decisions,[21] then the nineties terminated the tradition. The famine-induced major swings against the war in 1795, and more fundamentally in 1800–1, had a longer-term significance, despite the very clear populist majority in favour of the war's renewal in 1803. The commitment of the country to unprecedented mobilisation and public expenditure in the gladiatorial struggle against revolutionary, as opposed to Napoleonic imperialist France, was opposed from the start by a significant minority of the enfranchised. This fundamental socio-political rift was not papered over by the formation of a broader-based conservative front, with the conjunction of the Portland Whigs with the Pitt ministry. The isolation of the Foxite opposition was principally parliamentary, though the advocacy of reform and peace weakened Fox's electoral appeal. The war never commanded mass support in spite of Pitt's attempts to conflate war objectives with suppression of the indigenous democratic movement. In passing it is worth pondering why Church and King was first so dependent on middle and upper class manipulation, secondly so ephemeral as an observable force, and thirdly why its demise at the populist level was so absolute? In an incisive article, Professor Western argued that the manipulation of a conservative patriotism, behind the war and against the political reformers, through the creation of the Volunteers, was a major achievement of key anti-revolutionary significance. Western acknowledged that the government changed its policy of 'arming the urban poor' in 1798, though explanation was restricted to implied ministerial residual nerves; he ignored the beginnings of Volunteer desertion in 1795, and made no reference to the much more portentous repetitions in 1800–1. The later desertions had a manifold significance. They weakened the patriotic politics which radiated from the Volunteers into the community as well as eroding confidence at the local level in their policing function. They represented the ruin of a major Pittite propaganda programme, and the collapse occurred in direct response to the failure of the government's public relations exercise in 1800–1. Urban Volunteers repeatedly refused to subscribe to the government's prescriptions of the free market overcoming subsistence problems. They were alienated by their role of policing the crowd; they abhorred their apparent duty to protect agrarian capital while it exploited millions of consumers. This reflected the conjunction of two moralities. The first, a genuine humanitarianism which was offended by repeated policing functions – despite the original, patriotic motivation behind enthusiasm and recruitment, and the second, a powerful tradition of 'moral economy' which was resurrected to a paramountcy by repeated experiences, climaxed by the depth of public conviction in a *pacte de famine* in the autumn of 1800.

The resultant crisis of confidence threatened to bring Pitt to his knees, independently of the inevitable furore over Pitt's intention to honour his semi-veiled promises to Irish Catholics. Potential, politically-motivated insurrection, principally in the Midlands, was contained only through

saturating extensive districts with troops. The LCS's attempted relaunch on
orthodox lines was crushed by the police and the army in the capital.
Dangerous opposition from the enfranchised, represented by the petitioning movement was headed off, perhaps only temporarily, by Pitt's capitulation to demands for the emergency parliamentary session. Home Office
fears for the physical security of parliament itself led to the Life Guards
remaining on permanent alert in nearby barracks for the duration of that
session.[22] And in all these circumstances Pitt owed his survival at the crisis
to two closely inter-twined factors determined principally by Charles James
Fox. First, Fox's own sustained secession denied his party the potent
leadership it so manifestly lacked, and infuriated his own supporters.
Secondly, the Whig opposition's studied refusal to make a bid for power
through vigorous advocacy of the people's 'moral economy' remedies
during that session, was clearly crucial. Fox's theoretical belief in free trade
was genuine, but his parliamentary supporters' subsequent disdain for any
opportunism which compromised laissez-faire principles, is an unconvincing explanation for their conduct at this juncture. Principles provide
political autobiographies and partisan accounts with the veneer of philosophical consistency, but they cannot account for the inaction on which the
balance between war and peace turned in the former's favour. Fox had
neither the political will, nor the psychological fortitude to go for office.
His continued seccession, for once became what his detractors consistently
and wrongly said it was all along – cowardice. The Foxites sustained Pitt in
power and actively supported his strategies and policies. This unity
compromised both government and opposition, and not just in plebeian
estimations; it generated much middle-class scepticism of the competence of
the entire political edifice. 'The steps taken by Parliament have increased the
rise' in prices, asserted Joseph Farington, typically; 'Had Parliament only
declared for importation and taken no further notice of the business it
would . . . have made great difference in the market'.[23] The ruling class
rallied, but only to the extent of partial silence in support of the 'moral
economy'; only a minority were genuinely convinced in Pitt's economics,
and the degree of *volte face* was conditioned by fears that continued
castigation of the agricultural and provision trade interests would generate a
revolutionary ferment, which might explode in conformity to Malthus's
vision.

Multifarious interactions fuelled the famines' increasingly heavy political
overtones. The war's role in these processes fluctuated but it was particularly significant in 1799–1801. That famine's early unfolding coincided with
the debacle of the invasion of Holland, and Pitt's arrogant rejection of
Bonaparte's peace initiative at the very end of 1799, to create a fertile
environment for political analysis and speculation. John Rickman, who
initially thought that Hadfield's attempt on the king's life 'was another
scheme of Dundas's to revive the expiring flame of loyalty', opined less
cynically that the assassination bid 'has not had that effect; the proposal of
Bonaparte for peace has sunk deep into the public mind and the minister is
at his wit's end'. When the Middlesex freeholders convened in October
1800, *all* speakers argued that 'war is the cause of the alarming high price of
provisions'. In such a climate, public conviction in the government's direct

and central responsibility for a whole range of socio-economic ills was repeatedly if variously evinced. It was said that

> the Farmers taunt to the poor is Government must have Money and we assist them, therefore they will protect us. This throws Government totally in the blame and makes the lower Class of People . . . disaffected.

In Lancashire in 1801 'the odium rests on Govermt for every evil. Even the prevalence of the Fever is ascribed to Mr Pitt as he is said to cause the dearness of Provisions, and Want produces illness'. War, fiscal exactions, the national debt, economic difficulties and inflation, came together even in working-class perceptions. Why else should a weaver confide to his diary that

> the following was taken from the Manchester Gazette of August 19th 1797 the National Debt of Great Britain is £409,665,570 yearly interest £16,272,597. Expense of the war for last year only £62,357,212.[24]

However tempered by obstructions at the hands of obdurate local officialdom, the machinery of state intruded into the lives of ordinary folk to a quite unprecedented degree in the nineties in general, and during the famines in particular. These intrusions, be they legally-inspired dietary changes or government-inspired law and order campaigns, were bitterly resented. But if the enhanced presence of the state played straight into the hands of the popular democrats, whose politicisation campaigns could marshall very real evidence why the restoration and maintenance of working-class welfare depended on their admission to the structure of governance, famine conditions activated deeply-ingrained, orthodox modes of protest, notably the food riot. Tradition firmly proved that the latter could achieve immediate remedial results, and recent experiences ironically demonstrated that even the greatly augmented repressive organs of the state could not divert, let alone terminate, that tradition in the 1790s. Food rioters chalked up many clear victories and, given the desperate circumstances, the price exacted was rarely severe, and there was always the semi-anonymity of the crowd bestowing a modicum of protection. Documentary deficiencies doubtlessly conceal many more petty and localised triumphs which were well-known to participants but remote from historians unable to penetrate the opaque atmosphere of the day. Indeed, a combination of riotous customs and the ostensible nature of the new laws against plebeian politicking, might have given the appearance that a thundering great riot would be tolerated to degrees, whereas mammoth, political meetings would galvanise a fearsome, repressive reaction. In these very real senses democratic politicisation could not easily compete with traditional forms of protest; at best, radical reform – unless the product of insurrection, or invasion, or both – was a medium or long term solution, devoid of any immediate prospect of success. This is not, however, a subscription to the 'compartmentalist' vision of the early history of the English labour movement, which asserts that 'the widespread food riots in 1800 . . . remained quite apart from the political movement, which made no attempt to exploit social and economic discontent for political advantage'. As we have seen, such statements are a manifestation of nonsense, though hammering nails into the coffin of such a defunct historiographical tradition is a banal luxury.[25]

Other forms and sources of alienation owed less to government, though they too had a key socio-political effect. Workers' experiences of the sheer exploitive capacity of capitalism were not restricted to their treatment at the hands of the agricultural interest, and its close allies in the food processing and commercial spheres. In some key industries, notably textiles and especially where technological innovations were being implemented, the adverse effects on labour were thrown into sharper relief as living standards came under additional pressure from price increases. Indeed, the agitations in both cotton and woollens during the 1790s were an initial reaction to the devastating conjunction of high living costs and industrial recession which was to dominate recurrent early nineteenth-century crises. Rapid inflation during the famines reinforced the effects of the general inflation which characterised the nineties. These conditions sufficed to extend the necessity for action to safeguard living standards, irrespective of the technology issue. Many struggles over wages transpired which in aggregate represented a very marked adoption of trade unionist activity, a response which we have encountered penetrating the countryside, and extending even to farmworkers. Many employers evoked a marked reluctance to shoulder the burdens of increased living costs by upping wages, even during the famines; this antagonised industrial relations. Employer reticence was at its most pronounced in agrarian communities, but many industrial and urban workers also experienced the direct relationship between their master's attitude and the degree of dependency on poor-law and charitable agencies. Many workers received limited charitable donations from their employers who used this manoeuvre to stave-off permanent wage rises and derive kudos from their commonly much-publicised benevolence. Niggardliness repeatedly dissolved the latter, *and* failed to avert recourse to the poor law. As a class of employers, the farmers were clearly the worst offenders, and they were numerically the largest too. Multifarious tensions developed directly from these scenarios, two of which are revealed by the contrasting sentiments of one Wiltshire clergyman, and a Yorkshire poor-law overseer, William Fawcett. The former gratuitously added a rider to his 1801 acreage return denouncing

> the very impolitic measures adopted by the magistrates of relieving . . .
> the lower classes . . . distresses out of the Poors Rate rather than by
> increasing their wages which has hurt their laudable pride, destroy'd their
> Independence and put an End to their future Exertion and Industry for
> they found that the more they appeared to earn themselves the less they
> received from the parish.

Fawcett denounced the 'Complaints' that

> come before me almost every day . . . from the Poor within this
> Jurisdiction and I am sorry that I have little to say in their favour, as they

are most of 'em, an idle indolent set of people who do not use their
endeavours to earn their bread, as long as they can be maintained in
Idleness.

By 1805 one agricultural specialist was identifying the recent famines as the
key to the apparently permanent 'broken . . . pride' which underlay the
demise of the 'disgrace' customarily attached to receiving parochial aid. It
was however, Fawcett's type of argument which increasingly prevailed; it
symbolised a form of alienation, and in the medium term fertilised the
ground for the growth of ruthless and hostile utilitarian ideology. This was
one dimension of the developments during the famines which accelerated
the growth of class ideologies, polarisations which engendered class consciousness. Even in rural East Anglia an Anglican clergyman was detecting
unmistakable signs by 1805; earlier, 'labourers were more content with their
wages, less ready to murmur in accidental advances in the price of
provisions, and more willing to work extraordinary hours as the exigencies
of their masters might require, than they are at present'. Similar evidence
abounds, including developments at York, one of the northern towns
expressly identified as free from the industrial struggles engulfing Leeds in
1801–2, but the scene of fierce conflict in 1803, with employers publicly
promising to resist the 'growing and alarming . . . Evil' of worker
combination.[26]

Several principal reasons can be advanced to explain why alienation on
these in conjunction with other scores did not finalise the consolidation of
class consciousness, which might permit an argument to be made for the
1793 to 1801 period parallel to that contrived by Harold Perkin for the years
1815 to 1819. First, the *relative* stability of the English economy in the 1790s
ensured that conditions deriving from seriously sub-standard harvests,
especially the longer-term recessions earlier in the eighteenth century,
identified by Professor Ashton, no longer obtained. In late eighteenth-
century England there could be no parallel with seventeenth-century
Scottish experiences:

> When harvests failed, not only would tenants starve, but there would be a
> total cessation of all industry. Textiles, brewing and tanning and all other
> industrial activities would cease because there would be no-one with the
> spending power to buy these products.[27]

The English economy in the nineties was too mature, too dynamic, even
explosive, to collapse in this *immediate* fashion. Moreover, for much of the
decade it was stimulated by the material demands of war. Unprecedented
mobilisation acted as a safety valve against the full expression of the
over-supply of labour, which was delayed until the immediate post-war
years. But the tertiary sector was clearly vulnerable to famine-induced
contraction, and such sectors which served a great working-class demand,
notably shoe-making and repair, probably experienced severe dislocation.
Ironically, the most dynamic sectors of the economy, especially the textile
industries with their considerable influence over other sectors, rested on
essentially shaky foundations, and these were dramatically exposed notably

by the second famine. But even here, the recession did not bite suddenly; there was no violent collapse in demand, and only sectors of the industry were seriously affected by wartime dislocations to export markets at any one time. Secondly, this very bouyancy permitted the economy to climb relatively speedily out of the 1800–1 depth of the recession, a process accelerated further by the short-lived peace, and maintained by renewed demand deriving from the opening of the second stage of the war. A vivid testimony to the rapidity and scale of the recovery, even in those regions which bore the brunt of the economic dislocations of 1800–1, is provided by Oldham weaver Rowbottom's account of Christmas 1802:

> Such a Cristmas for Roast Beff pies and Ale etc as was never witnessed by the oldest person living for Such was the power of All Familey by the Goodness of all Sorts of Trade that one family vied with A nother wich could Give the Greatest treat to its neighbour and nothing but mirth Glee and Harmony was Seen during this Great Festivity.

Moreover, the dietary horrors of famine-induced expediency were speedily reversed; even the wheaten revolution recommenced immediately, as revealed by an 1803 report which ignored the experiences of recent years:

> The food of the inhabitants of the West Riding has undergone a very material change within these two years. The lower orders . . . now no longer eat oat-cakes, but from constant employment and the increase of wages, are enabled to enjoy the indulgence of Wheat bread.

So while neither the duration of famine, with its cumulative, quantative and qualitative impact, can be ignored, nor the socio-political ramifications overlooked, the rapid return to normality with the restoration of the grain supply's critical equilibrium must be acknowledged.[28]

The first famine was as devastating as it was unexpected. It threatened to compromise Pitt's paramount policy of eradicating the French revolutionary menace. Yet Pitt's cabinet eschewed confronting the problem to try to prevent recurrence. Policies which emerged initially as exigency measures during 1794–5, were readopted, refined and advanced to a degree after 1799. But it took the second famine to create the political will even to grasp the nettle of establishing reliable population statistics. The enquiry into agrarian productivity started through the acreage returns made by the clergy, represented only an initial foray into data collection which was of obvious importance for any government faced with with major decisions over war or peace. Despite the propagandist county surveys under the auspices of the still semi-official Board of Agriculture, with their emphasis on archaic agrarian practices and the desperate need to increase acreages through facilitating enclosure, parliamentary attempts to frame appropriate legislation were effectively torpedoed by the narrowest of vested interests. And, in spite of what could be called the first time any government tried to convince the populace that there was such a thing as the national interest – for that was the real component of its public relations exercises during the famines – *the* key dimension, national subsistence in wartime, was the renewed topic of government torpor and indifference after 1801. Only the odd member of the political elite tried to overcome this remarkable indifference. 'When the difficulty has been in any degree suspended', complained Lord Sheffield, 'we neglect all those measures which might prevent the recurrence of the calamity'. With the war clearly reaching a crucial stage, and the subsistence problem threatening to recur in 1804, Sheffield lobbied Pitt, again at the head of affairs, to act decisively. Sheffield reviewed the history of British grain imports to prove the inadequacies of indigenous agrarian productivity, and the resultant export of specie to remedy them. He argued that wheat consumption must be reduced, but that the first hurdle derived from the increasingly common practice of wage supplementation under the poor law which 'counteracts the most essential of all good management viz. the use of substitutes'. Sheffield's experiences in Sussex made him too worldly-wise to expect poor-law authorities to dismantle dietary customs even in an emergency:

> We have learned from experience that neither Law, regulation nor recommendation will effectively turn the people from the Use of Wheaten Bread, and that the high price of Wheat alone will introduce Substitutes, economy and good management.

Pitt's half-hearted response produced the 1804 amendments to the corn laws. These simply altered the prices last changed in 1791; the previous ban on wheat exports was raised from 46/– to 54/–, and the low duty on imports became operative when the home price reached 66/–, a considerable increase on the 1791 figure of 54/–. As wheat prices had averaged nearly 59/– in 1803, and 62/3 in 1804, the new figures represent a minor concession to Sheffield's argument, and in reality were little more than an adjustment safeguarding the degree of agrarian profitability and equilibrium, themselves founded on consolidated inflation since 1791.[29] Sheffield's apprehensions of another famine in 1804–5 were not realised, and successive governments' prosecution of the war went unhindered by subsistence crises until 1810–3; that crisis's 1812 trough, with an industrial depression again coinciding with famine food prices, was probably more severe than its predecessor of 1800–1, though it awaits its social historian, whose previous concentration on Luddism has militated against an holistic study. The corn law of 1804 formed a precedent for 1815, though the latter could not, in some contrast to its predecessor, be legitimised as essential to national survival in difficult wartime conditions.

Dr Rule's claim that 'the structural re-ordering of class relations and ideology' during the 1790s turned on worker resistance to 'an ever-encroaching capitalism', to fuel the development of class consciousness, is only a part of the process.[30] The nineties in general, and the famines in particular, witnessed recurrent crises in the relationship between society and the state. These, and subsequent crises between society and the state, constitute the second central ingredient in the genesis of class consciousness. The new and key component is the intrusive action on the part of the state, and the nature of those intrusions. In the 1766 famine, the government, through the issue of a royal proclamation, ordered the enforcement of the

Tudor marketing laws, thereby officially sanctioning populist remedial ideology based on 'moral economy'.[31] Thirty years later, the state leant increasing weight to major dietary expedients, and obtained legislation aimed at foisting the policy on unwilling consumers; the state also advanced laissez-faire principles, and castigated and negated populist ideology, thereby laying the basis for the early nineteenth-century labour movement's loathing of classical economics, which was shared by all except an idiosyncratic, unrepresentative minority.[32] The state also obtained new, draconian laws to underpin repression, and then visibly orchestrated the conservative counter-offensive against the rapid development of a new and aggressive working-class, political ideology; the state deployed these powers against both trade unionism and the popular democratic movement. The fact that these laws were used unevenly across the regions and localities, thereby roughly paralleling the impact of retrenchment policies, matters less in this context than their addition to the statute book. In the nineties, the processes fuelling emergent class consciousness are clearer in those regions where industrial conflict, especially where technological factors were present, and populist political activities were fiercest. Developments towards regional labour movements are at their most pronounced notably in the capital, the textile belts of Lancashire and the West Riding, and in the industrial West and East Midlands. In these locations there was no division between workers engaged on the political and industrial fronts. Metropolitan trade unionists formally co-operated to campaign against the Gagging Acts in 1795. The Lancastrian authorities were incapable of demarcating between trade union movements and democratic political activities, because the same people were repeatedly involved in both. West Riding converts to physical-force politics anticipated that their seizure of power would precede reversals of current technological revolutions. Parallel conjunctions between trade unionism and democratic politicisation is found in lesser and more isolated centres of the emergent labour movement, as at Devonport where royal dockyard workers with a long and virile tradition of collective action were avid proponents of democratic political principles. The experiences of some communities at the hands of capital and the state advanced working-class consciousness much more rapidly than in others.

Only London outpaced the textile regions, especially the East Midlands and the North. Historical perceptions of the Luddite period should not be dominated exclusively by machine-breaking, for this was neither the sole response, nor an immediate reaction. Textile workers mounted a number of campaigns for the statutory regulation of their industries; they failed, and no element in their failure was more profound than the fight to retain the legal system of apprenticeship. These experiences demonstrated that the unreformed state would continue to negate the demands of labour in order to advance the opposing interests of capital. When labour in its political and industrial frustration resorted to direct action against the unacceptable innovations of capital, in the various forms of Luddism, the state intervened again with its army and revealed the reality of aristocratic monopoly of political power by designing new capital offences tailored to facilitate the prosecution of activists: executions, specifically ordered by government, followed. All of these, and other experiences, served to prove to workers caught up in these struggles that political reform was the prerequisite for the protection of labour, and the message, substantiated by empirical evidence, was extended through propaganda to a much broader plebeian constituency. From the 1790s campaigns for democracy always involved conflict between advocates of the open constitutional model pioneered by the LCS, and the revolutionary insurrectionary alternative advanced by an ultra-militant minority. All of this, industrial organisation and parliamentary lobbying through the trade unions, politicisation campaigns, and the competing strategies for a democratic triumph, was reflected by Gravenor Henson, the most famous leader of one regional labour movement, centred on Nottingham. In the 1810s Henson was concerned in all the agitations, including those for the statutory regulation of industry and the radical reform of the political system; he was at least in the secrets of the innermost Luddite councils, and aware of, if not directly involved in the revolutionary plottings which produced the abortive Pentrich rising. Neither Hanson, nor his East Midland labour movement was typical; but they comprised the avant-garde of the process of class struggle against unrestrained capitalism and against its premier supporter, the English state; capital and the state became inseperable bedfellows, and the fight against that alliance galvanised class consciousness.[33]

Nottingham's position in the vanguard of this phenomenon also testifies to its dispirate development. The degree of plebeian alienation varied across time, and geographically. For class-consciousness was not born automatically from a uniform series of experiences. Its emergence derived from both the multifarious struggles between labour and capital, and repetitive crises in the relationship between society and the state. Many of the former had but a sectoral significance, though overall the conflict broadened. We have seen the beginnings of its extension into the English countryside, the shrinking bastion of the ancien regime itself. The inroads made by the threshing machine also took the technology issue to the agricultural sector, where it aggravated a worsening post-war situation, as the over-supply of labour produced increasingly serious under- and unemployment, which in turn intensified conflict in the central theatre of poor-relief administration. Radical politics penetrated the countryside as these struggles unfolded, and accelerated working-class consciousness too.[34] Further crises of universal import between the state and society included the corn bill furore of 1815, which reaffirmed the partisan use of power deriving from the aristocracy's monopoly of the political machinery of the state, and the strange but widespread anti-governmental explosion of hostility during the celebrated Queen Caroline affair.[35] Major long-term issues, notably the National Debt and the taxes levied on plebeian consumers to finance it, also directly involved the state in the escalating postwar poverty problem. The state remounted its counter-offensives against resurgences of the democratic movement, none more fiercely than that between 1816 and 1820, with its climax in Peterloo and the passing of the notorious Six Acts. The resultant taxes on knowledge provided one direct link, and an arena for struggle between 1820 and 1830. But the final consolidation of working-class consciousness literally needed the Reform Bill Crisis of 1830–2 *and* the utilitarian legislation of the Whig government carried to power by the reformed system.[36] The prolonged rearguard action fought by the die-hard sector of the ancien regime, ironically against its own order and the people, was of central importance because the politics of the crisis penetrated even the most serene backwater of rural England. Moreover, the crisis of 1830–2 was not exclusively political as the Whigs, backed by the people, confronted aristocracy's residual deployment of power by obstructionism in the House of Lords; for it was superimposed on industrial and agrarian crises. Almost every major trade, and every urban and great industrial location, experienced labour disputes, as unionism surged forward. In the countryside a less clear-cut struggle between labour and capital exploded with the Swing revolt. The vicious reaction of Grey's ministry to Swing, the executions and the mass transportations, terminated the Whigs' popular standing, as the cause of the victims was taken up by radicals everywhere. The failure of the 1832 compromise, from a democratic perspective, was rammed home by the state's subsequent postures, notably its vicious and intimidatory action over the Tolpuddle Martyrs. The trade unions and the popular democrats took up the Martyrs' cause, and urban, industrial and rural workers united against the state, as the Grand National Consolidated Trades Union spread its tentacles into the countryside in the last stages of the formation of working-class consciousness.[37]

And if further proof of Whig treachery and the reformed state's devotion to the partisan use of power against labour was needed, it came almost immediately in the form of the 1834 Poor Law Amendment Act, which Dr Bohstedt rightly stresses 'brought the concrete significance of national policies right to the doorsteps of the working poor':[38] the rural regions bore the brunt of the act's implementation, and these experiences consolidated the process of politicisation here, commenced during the 1790s, accelerated by the struggles during the post-war depression, and further advanced by the Swing episode.[39] This Whig adoption of utilitarian ideology was not as is commonly asserted, part of their reaction to Swing.[40] For the Whigs' identification of the need to contain the popular democratic movement by limited parliamentary reform, through incorporation of a slightly broader sector of the populace in the political system, a policy implemented in 1832, was not the sole legacy bequeathed to them by events in the 1790s. For some of the Whig leaders advocated abolition of the poor law at this time. In December 1800, Lord Holland admitted that in the current famine conditions 'the people consider' the poor law 'as their only immediate recourse'; only those conditions and assumptions meant that 'a sudden abolition of the law, if practicable in Parliament would be attended with much danger': as 'Improvements on it are next to impossible', Holland as yet restrained himself to 'driving into the heads of all my acquaintance . . . [that] the whole System is radically bad'.[41] The scale and costs of relief during the famines, and the subsequent apparently irreversible enhanced profile of the social security system, intensified the hostility accruing to it. But this hostility cannot be attributed entirely to the likes of Malthus, his utilitarian disciples and those party politicians who accepted this ideology. It was also in part generated by the bourgeoisie as a direct reaction to their experiences, married with their work-ethic inspired prejudices. Francis Horner was among those young Whig politicians who detected potentially major electoral advantages through capitalising on this scenario;

> There is in the middling order of people in this country a broad foundation for a popular party, constituted by the opinions, interests and habits of those numerous families who are characterised by moderate but increasing incomes, a careful education in their youth, and a strict observance of the great common virtues.[42]

Overseer Fawcett, whom we encountered denigrating workers in general and relief claimants in particular, was an early representative of this rapidly expanding sector, whose growth helped to fuel a middle-class consciousness and all its aspirations; it operated in key support of the Whigs in 1830–2, and part of the reward comprised the reform of the poor law on utilitarian principles. And the final irony derives from both the short and long-term consistencies of those self proclaimed Friends of the People in the 1790s, and their political heirs. Their rejection of the 'moral economy' and fervent advocacy of free trade was, historically, their first major negation of the popular will. Whig attitudes towards labour were revealed by the fact that only one, Hobhouse, opposed the Combination Acts on the floor of the House of Commons.[43] Subsequent negations include the transparent tactics to prise the temporary middle and working-class alliance apart in 1832, the confrontation with tumescent trade unionism in the early 1830s, and the incorporation of the working class in an untrammelled laissez-faire labour market through the Poor Law Amendment Act. Prejudices and principles which were firmly established among the Whigs by 1800, owed much to their perceptions of developments for which the famines of the 1790s were principally but not exclusively responsible; their translation into state policy in the early 1830s, inadvertantly yet finally, cemented working-class consciousness.

NOTES

Chapter 1   Introduction

1. E.H. Phelps Brown and S.V. Hopkins, 'Seven centuries of the prices of consumables, compared with builders' wage rates', in E.M. Carus-Wilson (ed), *Essays in Economic History*, 3 vols. (1954–62), II, p. 186. E.A. Wrigley and R.S. Schofield, *The Population History of England 1541–1871; a Reconstruction*, (Cambridge, Mass., 1981), table 8/8. L.D. Schwarz, 'The standard of living in the long run: London 1700–1860', *Ec.His.Rev.*, 2s XXXVIII (1985). K.D.M. Snell, *Annals of the Labouring Poor. Social Change and Agrarian England 1660–1900*, (Cambridge 1985), appendix.
2. Liverpool to Dundas, 11 Oct. 1800, BL.Add.Mss. 38311, ff. 166–9.
3. Which did not enter the top twenty in the above calculations.
4. See below Ch. 3.
5. J.D. Chambers and G.E. Mingay, *The Agricultural Revolution, 1750–1880*, (1966), pp. 112–3.
6. A.H. John, 'Farming in wartime: 1793–1815', in E.L. Jones and G.E. Mingay (eds), *Land Labour and Population in the Industrial Revolution*, (1967).
7. G. Hueckel, 'English farming profits during the Napoleonic Wars 1793–1815', *Expl.Ec.His.*, XIII (1976).
8. C. Emsley, *British Society and the French Wars 1793–1815*, (1979), p. 85. But cf. the surprisingly unanalytical coverage in A.D. Gayer, W.W. Rostow and A.J. Schwarz, *The Growth and Fluctuation of the British Economy, 1700–1850*, 2 vols. (1953), I, p. 43 and esp. note 2.
9. R.R. Palmer, *The Age of the Democratic Revolution*, 2 vols. (Princeton, 1959–64), II, pp. 480–1. E.P. Thompson, *The Making of the English Working Class*, (1968 edition), pp. 156 ff. Cf. G.S. Veitch, *The Genesis of Parliamentary Reform*, (1965 edition), pp. 325–6, and E.J. Evans, *The Forging of the Modern State. Early Industrial Britain 1783–1870*, (1983), p. 71.
10. J. Steven Watson, *The Reign of George III*, (Oxford, 1960), pp. 360, 407.
11. P. Mackesy, *War Without Victory; the Downfall of Pitt, 1799–1802*, (Oxford, 1984), esp. pp. 179–82, 202.
12. A. Briggs, *The Age of Improvement 1783–1867*, (1962 edition), p. 168; cf. p. 182.
13. J. Tann, 'Co-operative corn milling; self-help during the grain crises of the Napoleonic Wars', *Ag.His.Rev.* 28 (1960). J.R. Poynter, *Society and Pauperism. English Ideas on Poor Relief, 1795–1834*, (1969), ch. III. M. Neuman, 'A suggestion regarding the origins of the Speenhamland plan', *EHR*, LXXXIV (1969). *Idem, The Speenhamland County. Poverty and the Poor Laws in Berkshire 1782–1834*, (1982).
14. W.M. Stern, 'The bread crises in Britain, 1795–6', *Economica*, n.s. XXXI (1964).
15. Emsley, *op. cit.*, ch. 3.
16. G.A. Williams, *Artisans and Sansculottes*, (1968), ch. 6, note 5.
17. Chambers and Mingay, *op. cit.*, pp. 206–7. Cf. B. Thomas, 'Feeding England during the industrial revolution; a view from the Celtic fringe', *Ag.His.*, 56 (1982).
18. A.B. Appleby, 'Grain prices and subsistence crises in England and France, 1590–1740', *Jnl.Ec.His.*, XXXIX (1979), *passim*, but cf. *idem*, 'Epidemics and famine in the little ice age', *Jnl.Int.His.*, X (1980), esp. p. 644. Appleby's confidence that the crisis in the late 1720s was confined to 'a few Midland parishes' was clearly based on J. Gooder, 'The population crisis of 1727–30 in Warwickshire', *Mid.His.* I (1972); however, it now seems that this crisis was geographically more diverse. Thirteen out of twenty-one Buckinghamshire parishes studied, experienced severe mortality, which was also found on the

Somerset–Wiltshire border. The latter was identically affected in the 1740–1 grain crises, which was also more widespread in its demographic impact. J. Skinner, 'Crisis mortality in Buckinghamshire, 1600–1750', *LPS*, 28, pp. 274–6, 281, 286. S. Jackson, 'Population change in the Somerset–Wiltshire border area 1701–1800; a regional demographic study', *Southern History*, 7, (1985), pp. 123, 135. D. Ormrod, *English Grain Exports and the Structure of Agrarian Capitalism 1700–60*, (University of Hull, 1985), pp. 90–1.

19. Wrigley and Schofield, *op. cit.*, pp. 325–6, 372. R.S. Schofield, 'The impact of scarcity and plenty on population change in England 1541–1871', *Jnl.Int.His.* XIV (1983), pp. 274–6, 281, 286.

20. Wrigley and Schofield, *op. cit.*, pp. 404–6, and cf. p. 412. J. Mokyr, 'The industrial revolution and the new economic history', in *idem* (ed), *The Economics of the Industrial Revolution*, (1985), pp. 20–1. Incredible contortions are encountered. The nature of contemporaneous 'good reason to fear that the rate of population growth had risen beyond the level at which it was balanced by economic growth' is never explained. Instead we are assured that Malthus and Ricardo cannot be blamed when developments (some time after 1820?) confounded them: the fact that the ancient relationship between population and the economy evaporated 'about the end of the eighteenth century . . . can be clearly demonstrated' only by the historian. E.A. Wrigley, 'The growth of population in the eighteenth century; a conundrum resolved', *P&P*, 98 (1983), pp. 146, 148–9.

21. P.H. Lindert and J.G. Williamson, 'English workers' living standards during the industrial revolution; a new look', *Ec.His.Rev.*, 2s XXXVI (1983). Snell, *op. cit.*, p. 27 note 13.

22. J.D. Post, *The Last Great Subsistence Crisis in the Western World*, (1977), pp. 48–9.

23. J. Stevenson, *Popular Disturbances in England, 1700–1870*, (1979), p. 95.

24. Emsley, *op. cit.*, pp. 43, 49–50.

25. M.W. McCahill, *Order and Equipoise. The Peerage and the House of Lords 1783–1806*, (1978), pp. 75–6.

26. J. Norris, 'British wartime inflation 1793–1815; the beginnings of a pragmatic tradition', in B.M. Gough (ed), *In Search of the Visible Past*, (Waterloo, Ontario, 1975), pp. 16–7.

27. Editor's introduction, and R. Hole, 'British counter-revolutionary popular propaganda in the 1790s', in C. Jones (ed), *Britain and Revolutionary France: Conflict, Subversion and Propaganda*, (University of Exeter, 1983), esp. pp. 8, 55–64, Cf. A. Booth, 'Popular loyalism and public violence in the north-west of England 1790–1800', *SH*, 8 (1983).

28. E.P. Thompson, 'The "moral economy" of the English crowd in the eighteenth century', *P&P*, 50 (1971), pp. 129–31. See also A.W.Coats, 'Plebs, paternalists and political economists', *ibid.*, 54 (1972), and his analysis of Thompson's theme in *The Making of the English Working Class*.

29. J.M. Martin, 'An investigation into the small size of the household as exemplified by Stratford-upon-Avon', *LPS*, 19 (1977), p. 22 note 27. Cf. G. Talbot Griffiths, *Population Problems in the Age of Malthus*, (new edition, 1967), p. 129.

30. T.R. Malthus, *An Essay on the Principle of Population*, 2 vols. (Everyman edition, W.T. Layton (ed), 1914), I, p. 1. Poynter, *op. cit.*, p. 46 and p. 149 note 177, claims that the first edition 'Was not inspired by the scarcity', and was 'not stimulated by the observation of contemporary English population growth'. Cf. D.V. Glass, 'Malthus and the limitation of population growth', in Glass (ed), *Introduction to Malthus*, (1953), p. 27. For our ignorance of Malthus's early life, see P. James, *Population Malthus: His Life and Times*, (1979), esp. p. 40, but cf. B. Stapleton, 'Malthus: the Origins of the Principle of Population?', in M. Turner (ed), *Malthus and His Time*, (1986), pp. 20–2.

31. T.R. Malthus, *An Essay on the Principle of Population*, (1798 edition, Pelican reprint, A. Flew (ed), 1970), pp. 103, 115.

32. J.J. Spengler, *French Predecessors of Malthus*, (New York, 1942), pp. 366–9. Malthus, first edition, *loc. cit.*, ch. VIII.

33. T.R. Malthus, *An Investigation of the Causes of the Present High Price of Provisions*, (1800), pp. 26–8.

34. In the first edition, *loc. cit.*, p. 69, Malthus claimed no originality for his thesis; the subject had not 'been advanced with its proper weight', and 'may probably have been stated by many writers that I have never met with'.

35. Malthus to the Rev. G. Turner, 28 Nov. 1800, cited J. Bonar, *Malthus and His Work*, (2nd edition, 1924), pp. 418–9. *Idem, Hungry Generations: the Nineteenth Century Case against*

Malthusianism, (New York, 1955), pp. 23–4. D.V. Glass, *Numbering the People. The Eighteenth Century Population Controversy and the Development of Census and Vital Statistics in Britain*, (Farnborough, 1973), pp. 96–8.

36. Later editions reiterated the references to 1800 and 1801, and used Rickman's calculations on the census to prove earlier assertions of demographic disturbances at this time. Everyman edition, *op. cit.*, I., pp. 250–2; II, pp. 38, 40–1, 60, 183, 257.

37. *Ibid.*, I, pp. 250–2.

38. Even by Stapleton, *op. cit.*, and H.L. Beales, 'The historical context of the Essay on Population', in Glass (ed), *op. cit.* Norris, *op. cit.*, p. 24 is almost alone in appreciating that the 'theory of population in its later version was largely inspired by the privations caused by the famine prices of 1799–1801'. However, Norris manages to misdate the second edition's publication.

39. T.H. Hollingsworth, editorial introduction to the 1973 Everyman edition of the *Essay*, p. xxix. P. Appleman (ed), *An Essay on the Principle of Population: Text, Sources and Background Criticism*, (New York, 1976), p. xx. S.M. Lewin, 'Malthus and the idea of progress', *Journal of the History of Ideas*, 27 (1966), p. 93. Cf. K. Smith, *The Malthusian Controversy*, (1951), p. 37.

40. D.E.C. Eversley, *Social Theories of Fertility and the Malthusian Debate*, (1975 edition, Westport, Conn.), pp. 210, 236–7, 256. Cf. Poynter, *op. cit.*, p. 155.

41. I.R. Christie, *Stress and Stability in Late Eighteenth-Century Britain: Reflections on the British Avoidance of Revolution*, (Oxford, 1984).

42. Indeed, it was extended on occasion; new legislation, to extend bounty payments to corn exported in neutral ships, was rushed through to facilitate disposal of the bumper 1779 crop. D.G. Barnes, *A History of the English Corn Laws from 1660 to 1846*, (1930), pp. 69–70.

43. J. Stuart, *An Enquiry into the Principles of Political Oeconomy*, (1767), cited by Ormrod, *op. cit.*, p. 20. A recent historian noted that 'per capita food consumption may have fallen' between 1740 and 1820. P. O'Brien, 'Agriculture and the home market for English industry, 1660–1820', *EHR*, C (1985), p. 784.

44. B.R. Mitchell, *Abstract of British Historical Statistics*, (Cambridge, 1962), pp. 94–5. W.F. Gilpin, *The Grain Supply of England during the Napoleonic Period*, (New York, 1925), esp. chs. I, II and IX.

45. In effect this represented a return to conditions last experienced in the sixteenth and seventeenth centuries. J.D. Gould, 'Agricultural fluctuations and the English economy in the eighteenth century', *Jnl.Ec.His.*, XXIII (1962), p. 316.

46. Introduction to C. and L. Tilley (eds), *Class Conflict and Collective Action*, (1981), p. 20.

47. Mokyr, *op. cit.*, pp. 20–1, 38.

48. R. Wells, *Insurrection: the British Experience 1795–1803*, (Gloucester, 1983).

Chapter 2   The Sociology and Economics of Food

1. The subtitle derives from an anonymous letter, received at Lewes, and published in the *Sussex Weekly Advertiser*, 24 Nov. 1800. W.N. Hargreaves-Mawdsley (ed), 'Woodforde at Oxford 1759–1776', *Publications of the Oxford History Society*, ns XXI (Oxford, 1969), pp. 152–3.

2. D. Davies, *The Case of the Labourers in Husbandry*, (1795). F.M. Eden, *The State of the Poor*, 3 vols. (1797). The paucity of alternative evidential sources necessitates a heavy dependency on the specimen diets and budgets published by these authorities. They cannot be mathematically accurate, but careful and critical use, especially in conjunction with other sources, permits an identification of the key characteristics of working-class dietary and budgeting practices.

3. E.g. J. Burnett, 'Trends in bread consumption', in T.C. Barker, J.C. Mackenzie and J. Yudkin (eds), *Our Changing Fare*, (1966), pp. 61–2.

4. E.J.T. Collins, 'Dietary change and cereal consumption in Britain in the nineteenth century', *Ag.His.Rev.*, 23 (1975), esp. pp. 97–106. Collins' estimation of approximately thirty per cent of the population of England and Wales subsisting on non-wheaten cereals is probably too high, and derives from his uncritical use of source materials. Collins fails to appreciate that his main source, the replies to government enquiries made during the

famines, over-stated non-wheaten consumption, in order to convince ministers that their policy of increasing dependency on non-wheaten cereals was being observed in the localities. See below, pp. 212–3.

5. 'The bread I eat in London is a deleterious paste, mixed up with chalk, alum, and bone ashes', said Mathew Bramble. T. Smollett, *Humphrey Clinker*, (Penguin edition, 1967), p. 152. Cf. Anon., *Poison Detected; or Frightful Truths; and alarming to the British Metropolis*, (1757).

6. Evidence of Tottenham miller Pratt, *Minutes*, 24 Nov. 1795. 'Report of the select committee of the House of Commons on the high price of provisions', 1773, Hansard's, *Parliamentary History*, Vol. XVII, pp. 555–6. *DPD*, 1st ser. vol. 6, p. 422. G. Pownall to W. Fawkener, 15 July 1795, BL.Add.Mss. 38230, ff. 230–1. Collins, *op. cit.*, is typically unaware of the distinction.

7. Even this distinction was not universal; the 'almost' total dependency of East Riding Wold villages on barley was replaced by wheat between 1770 and 1800.

8. This paragraph draws heavily on the returns respecting the consumption of wheat substitutes in March 1796 (especially those from the mayors of Ripon and Preston), PC. 1/33/A87–8, and the Autumn 1800 harvest returns, HO. 42/52–4. Collins, *op. cit.*, p. 108. Smollett, *op. cit.*, p. 237. M.F. Pickles, 'Mid-Wharfedale, 1721–1812; economic and demographic change in a Pennine dale', *LPS*, 16 (1976), p. 37. D.E.C. Eversley, 'The home market and economic growth in England, 1750–1780', in E.L. Jones and G.E. Mingay (eds), *Land, Labour and Population in the Industrial Revolution*, (1967), pp. 212–3.

9. Davies, *op. cit.*, pp. 8–13, 19, 28–36. Burnett, *loc. cit.*

10. Davies, *op. cit.*, pp. 36, 140–1. R. Fraser, *A General View of the Agriculture of . . . Cornwall*, (1794), pp. 26–7, 40. C.B. Worgan, *A General View of the Agriculture of . . . Cornwall*, (1811), pp. 9, 72–5.

11. Davies, *op. cit.*, pp. 146–7. T. Brown, *A General View of the Agriculture of the County of Derby*, (1794), p. 38. Eden, *op. cit.*, II, pp. 14, 73, 97–9. G. Shammas, 'The eighteenth-century English diet and economic change', *Expl.Ec.His.*, 21 (1984), p. 256.

12. Fraser, *op. cit.*, p. 21. Rev. J. Howlett, Great Dunmow, to Moore, 1 Dec. 1792, BL.Add.Mss. 16920, ff. 17–20.

13. Newbold Corn Committee administration accounts, 1795, 1800. Notts. CRO. DD. CW. 8f/1. Here workers' weekly incomes and occupations are recorded together with the names of their employers, if they were not piece or day-labourers.

14. Details on West Riding wages from Battie-Wrightson, and Harewood estates: LCA, Battie-Wrightson Cusworth wages book, 1780–1813, A/200. Harewood dep. Box 223. Rev. J. Forth's account books, and Forth to Lord Carlisle, 17 Dec. 1800, YCA, Acc. 54/5–7, 112. G. Rennie, *et al.*, *A General View of the Agriculture of the West Riding of Yorkshire* (1794). I. Leatham, *A General View of the Agriculture of the East Riding of Yorkshire*, (1794), J. Tuke, *A General View of the Agriculture of the North Riding of Yorkshire*, (1794). K.D.N. Snell, *Annals of the Labouring Poor. Social Change and Agrarian England 1660–1900*, (Cambridge, 1985).

15. 'The particulars of the Arrest and Imprisonment of T. Evans . . .', Bod.Lib. Burdett Mss. Ms. Eng.Hist. c.296, ff. 63–6. Eden, *op. cit.*, III, p. 829. LCA, Cusworth wage book, *op. cit.* Harewood dep. Box 223. W.G. Rimmer, 'Working men's cottages in Leeds 1770–1840', *Publications of the Thoresby Society*, XLVI (1963). The figures for the Kirkstall employees and the wages paid at Nowill's are taken from those firms ledgers, LCA. KF. 5/1. SCL. Nowill Dep. LD. 204. L.D. Schwarz, 'The standard of living in the long run: London 1700–1870', *Ec.His.Rev.*, 2s XXXVIII (1985), appendix 1.

16. *Annals of Agriculture*, 26 (1796), p. 136.

17. The rector of Tideswell employed a shoemaker among others for sundry tasks, including slaughtering pigs and in unloading coal supplies; he had free meals while at the rectory. The employer of a Lancashire quarryman earning eight shillings for a seventy-two hour week in 1801, had the temerity to 'grumble' when the employee did 'other work'. Diary of Rev. T. Brown, 1795, SCL Bag. Coll. 521/4. Settlement case, Lancs. CRO., Quarter Sessions roll, QSP. 1801 (Midsummer).

18. N. McKendrick, 'Home demand and economic growth; a new view of women and children in the industrial revolution', in *idem*. (ed), *Historical Perspectives: Studies in English Thought and Society*, (1974), pp. 185–8. D. Levine, 'Industrialization and the proletarian family in England', *P&P*, 107 (1985) pp. 176–9 and note 40. J. Tann, 'The employment of

power in the West of England wool textile industry, 1790–1840', in N.B. Harte and K.C. Ponting (eds), *Textile History and Economic History*, (Manchester, 1971), pp. 210–1. LCA. KF. 5/1; Cusworth wages book, A/200; Harewood dep. Box 223. W. Marshall, *The Rural Economy of Yorkshire*, 2 vols. (1787), I, p. 339. Diary of a tour to London by J. Sutcliffe of Halifax, 1797, HPL. A. Young, *A General View of the Agriculture of . . . Sussex*, (1813), p. 408. YCA, Munby dep. Acc. 54/5–7, Forth's account books, and Forth to Carlisle, 17 Dec. 1800.

19. F. Collier, *The Family Economy of the Working Classes in the Cotton Industry 1784–1833*, (Manchester, 1964, F.S. Fitton (ed)), Appendix D. McKendrick, *op. cit.*, pp. 173, 185–8, 201. J. Benson, *The Penny Capitalists: a Study in Nineteenth-Century Working-Class Entrepreneurs*, (1983), pp. 4–5, 130, 134. A.W. Dyson (ed), *William Metcalfe – His Book*, (Leeds, 1931), p. 40. *BPP*, H. of C. SC. 'Poor Law Amendment Act' (1837–8), Vol. XVII, Questions 14905, 14907–10. LCA, Cusworth wages, A/200.

20. E.W. Gilboy, *Wages in Eighteenth Century England*, (Cambridge, Mass. 1934), pp. 176 ff. LCA., KF 5/1; Harewood dep. Box 223; Cusworth wages, A/200. R.S. Neale, 'The standard of living, 1780–1844: a regional and class study', in A.J. Taylor (ed), *The Standard of Living in Britain in the Industrial Revolution*, (1975), pp. 167–9. SCL. Nowill Dep. LD 204–5. *The Iris*, and *Billinge's Liverpool Advertiser*, 8 and 12 Jan., 1801. Home Office clerks to Portland, 16 Dec. 1800, HO. 42/55. YCA. Munby Dep. Acc. 54/5–7, 112. *Annals of Agriculture*, vols. 23–29 (1794–1800), *passim*. Schwarz, *loc. cit.*

21. J. Stevenson, *Popular Disturbances in England 1700–1870*, (1979), p. 112.

22. C. Shammas, 'Food expenditure and economic well-being in early modern England', *Jnl. Ec.His.*, 43 (1983), p. 92. Neale, *op. cit.*, 165 and note 2, p. 171. Eden, *op. cit.*, II, pp. 97–9, 660–1; III, pp. 709–11. J. Burnett, *Plenty and Want. A Social History of Diet in England from 1815 to the Present Day*, (1966), p. 48. J.C. Drummond and A. Wilbraham, *The Englishman's Food*, (revised edition, 1959), pp. 218–9, 337. H. Perkin, *The Origins of Modern English Society, 1780–1880*, (1969), pp. 24–5. L.H. Lees, 'Getting and spending: the family budgets of English industrial workers in 1890', in J. Merriman (ed), *Consciousness and Class Experience in Nineteenth-Century Europe*, (New York, 1979), pp. 179–80.

23. Snell, *op. cit.*, ch. 4. M. Turner, 'Parliamentary enclosure and land ownership change in Buckinghamshire', *Ag.His.Rev.*, 21 (1973).

24. And, eighty per cent of English land was already enclosed by 1780, primarily by means other than Acts of Parliament. J.R. Wordie, 'The chronology of English enclosure 1500–1914', *Ec.His.Rev.*, 2s XXXVI, (1983), p. 503. Cf. R.A. Butlin, 'The enclosure of open fields and the extinction of common rights in England, c. 1600–1750; a review', in H.S.A. Fox and R.A. Butlin (eds), *Change in the Countryside: Essays on Rural England, 1500–1900*, (1979), pp. 66, 75. D.R. Mills, 'The quality of life in Melbourne, Cambridgeshire in the period 1800–1850', *Int.Rev.SH*, 23 (1978), p. 398. Eden, *op. cit.*, I, p. 574. ESCRO, Quarter Sessions minutes re relief schemes, 1801, Q/QV/EW1.

25. Small farmers, even in arable regions were forced on to the market for flour, notably in the midsummer hypercrisis of 1795. They seem to have had few problems in obtaining seed corn, and whether they financed its purchase by loans from richer neighbours (or even country banks), by barter, or by promising repayment through future labour services, is immaterial. One permutation, at Buckland, South Devon, involved big farmers supplying subsidised barley to both small farmers and labourers in the spring of 1801. Trouble flared on the refusal to extend this concession to sales of seed corn needed for immediate sowing. Mr. Black to Huntingdonshire Clerk of the Peace, c. 4 July 1795, ECRO. D/DBy/012. J.J. Fortescue to Lord Rolle, 4 Apr. 1801, DCRO. FLP. D1262M/L59. M. Reed, 'Social change and social conflict in nineteenth-century England; a comment', *Jnl.P.S.*, 12 (1984). *Idem*, 'The peasantry of nineteenth-century England; a neglected class?', *H.W.J.*, 18 (1984). J.M. Neeson, 'The opponents of enclosure in eighteenth-century Northamptonshire', *P&P*, 105 (1984), pp. 121–2. Cf. J.V. Beckett, 'The pattern of landownership in England and Wales, 1660–1880', *Ec.His.Rev.*, 2s XXXVII (1984), pp. 17–8.

26. Eden, *op. cit.*, I, p. 574. R. Claridge, *A General View of the Agriculture of . . . Dorset*, (1793), pp. 24–5. Vicar of Richmond, harvest return, 1800, HO. 42/54. Gilboy, *op. cit.*, pp. 153–6. W. Marshall, *The Rural Economy of the Midland Counties*, (1796), p. 97. For the extension of the practice, see below, ch. 17.

27. See below, p. 29.
28. J.M. Martin, 'Village traders and the emergence of a proletariat in south Warwickshire, 1750–1850', *Ag.His.Rev.*, 32 (1984), esp. pp. 180–1. However, Martin ignores the probability that his specialist purveyors of cheese and bacon, and his pig-dealers, were principally concerned with the supply of larger, urban markets. Cheshire window-surveyor, harvest return 1800, PRO, 30/8/291, f. 73. Eden, *op. cit.*, I, p. 491. W. Hasbach, *A History of the English Agricultural Labourer*, (1908), p. 233. J.D. Chambers, *Nottinghamshire in the Eighteenth Century*, (1968 edition), p. 289. G. Bourne, *Change in the Village*, (1912 edition), pp. 30–1, 88–9. D. Baker, 'The inhabitants of Cardington in 1782', *Publications of the Bedfordshire Historical Records Society*, 52 (1973).
29. S.D. Chapman, 'Memoirs of two eighteenth-century framework knitters', *Textile History*, I (1968–70), p. 111. *Idem*, 'Working-class housing in Nottingham during the industrial revolution', and S.D. Chapman and J.N. Bartlett, 'The contribution of building clubs and freehold land societies to working-class housing in Birmingham', in Chapman (ed), *The History of Working Class Housing*, (Newton Abbot, 1971), pp. 138, 140, 233 ff. J. Holt, *A General View of the Agriculture of the County of Lancaster*, (1795), p. 19. Settlement case, Lancs. CRO, QSP (Midsummer, 1801). Rev. Goodenough, acreage return, autumn 1801, HO. 67/23. C.W. Chalklin, *The Provincial Towns of Georgian England*, (1974), Appendix 1.
30. For example, when the Rev. Forth 'settled' with his miller for 1798 – on 28 Dec. – he paid for 6¼ quarters of wheat 'after the Rate of 6s/6d a Bushel', which was exactly the yearly average wholesale price, YCA. YL/Mumby, Acc. 54/5, f. 64, housekeeping accounts.
31. Claridge, *loc. cit.* G. Turner, *A General View of the Agriculture of the County of Gloucester*, (1794), p. 26, D. Walker, *A General View of the Agriculture of the County of Hertford*, (1795), pp. 9, 70. Eden, *op. cit.*, I, p. 491. Hasbach, *op. cit.*, p. 128. Derbys. CRO. Quarter Sessions minute books, 1795–8, pp. 156–7; 1798–1800, pp. 414, 541–2, 608–9. Portland to F. Adams, 23 Oct. 1795, HO. 43/7, pp. 226–8. *Reading Mercury*, 21 Dec. 1795. A.D. Leadley, 'Some villains of the eighteenth-century market place', in J. Rule (ed), *Outside the Law: Studies in Crime and Order, 1650–1850*, (University of Exeter, 1982), p. 27.
32. See Appendix 5.
33. F.J. Fisher, 'The development of the London food market, 1540–1640', *Ec.His.Rev.* 1st ser. (1934–5), p. 51. E.A. Wrigley, 'A simple model of London's importance in changing English society and economy 1650–1750', *P&P*, 37 (1967), pp. 54–5. O.H.K. Spate, 'The growth of London, A.D. 1600–1800', in H.C. Darby (ed), *An Historical Geography of England Before 1800*, (Cambridge, 1961 edition), p. 541. A. Everitt, 'The marketing of agricultural produce', in J. Thirsk (ed), *The Agrarian History of England and Wales 1500–1640*, (Cambridge, 1967), p. 564.
34. D.C. Coleman, *The Economy of England*, (Oxford, 1977), p. 121.
35. T. Allen, *History of the County of York*, 6 vols. (1828), I, p. 234. Holt, *op. cit.*, p. 198. D. Defoe, *A Tour through the Whole Island of Great Britain*, 2 vols. (1962 edition), II, p. 199. J. Aitken, *A Description of the Country from Thirty to Forty Miles around Manchester*, (1795), p. 574. Rennie, *op. cit.*, p. 25. Warwickshire tax-collector's harvest return, 1800, PRO 30/8/291, f. 73.
36. For our purposes the South-west comprised Cornwall, Devon, and those parts of Somerset south and west of a line from Wincanton to the mouth of the Perrot.
37. This and the following paragraph are based on: Fraser, *op. cit.* Worgan, *op. cit.* J. Rowe, *Cornwall in the Age of the Industrial Revolution*, (Liverpool, 1955). J.G. Rule, 'Some aspects of the Cornish industrial revolution', in R. Burt (ed), *Industry and Society in the South-west*, (University of Exeter, 1970). M. Overton, 'The 1801 crop returns for Cornwall', in M. Havinden (ed), *Husbandry and Marketing in the South-west*, (University of Exeter, 1973). W.G. Hoskins, *Devon*, (1954). W.W. White, *History, Gazeteer and Directory of Devon*, (1850, 1968 edition, introduced W.E. Minchinton, Newton Abbot). C. Vancouver, *A General View of the Agriculture of . . . Devon*, (1808). M. Overton and W.E. Minchinton, 'The 1801 crop returns for Devon', *Devon and Cornwall Notes and Queries*, XXXII (1973). VCH, *Somerset*, Vol. II (1911). J. Billingsley, *A General View of the Agriculture of . . . Somerset*, (2nd edition, 1798). T. Davis, *A General View of the Agriculture of . . . Wiltshire*, (1794). Market returns, MAF 10/278–85. Customs, Padstow, harvest return, 31 Oct. 1800, BT 6/139. W. Giddy, Tredea, to Addington, 20 Apr. 1801, DCRO. SP.D152M/ Corr. 1801.

38.   G.E. Fussell, 'Agriculture and economic geography in the eighteenth century', *Geographical Journal*, 74 (1929), p. 173. P. Rashleigh to R. Pole-Carew, 24 Apr. and 25 Nov. 1795, CCRO, Carew Mss. CC/K/25. Petitions from Devon Grand Jury, 21 June and 12 Oct. Letters to Portland from, Mr. Gunter, Ashburton, and the Mayor of Plymouth, 4 and 6 May, Major Elford, Brixham, and S. Cox, Bridport, 11 and 19 Oct. 1795, and De Dunstanville, 11 Feb. 1800. J. Drowas, Bristol, to E.F. Hatton, 14 Apr. 1800, HO. 42/34–6, 49; PC. 1/30/A68, 1/3477.
39.   A. Rennie, *op. cit.*, pp. 25, 103–5, 157–8. A. and E. Raistrick, *Skipton; a Study in Site Value*, (1930), p. 8. W. Harbutt-Dawson, *History of Skipton*, (1882), pp. 271–3. J. Thirsk, *English Peasant Farming*, (1957), p. 105. M.L. McCutcheon, 'Fairs and markets in Yorkshire until the eighteenth century', *Publications of the Thoresby Society*, XXXIX (1940), pp. 153–6. W.G. Rimmer, 'The evolution of Leeds to 1700', *ibid.*, L (1968), pp. 127–8. J.W. Walker, *Wakefield. Its History and People*, 2 vols. (private print, 2nd edition, Wakefield, 1938), II, pp. 520–1. Allen, *op. cit.*, VI, p. 153. E.M. Sigsworth, 'The industrial revolution', in M.W. Beresford and G.R.L. Jones (eds), *Leeds and its Region*, (Leeds, 1967). Tuke, *op. cit.*, esp. p. 38. Marshall, *Rural Economy of Yorkshire* . . ., II, pp. 256–7. R.G. Wilson, 'The navigation in the second half of the eighteenth century' (Aire and Calder), *Bradford Antiquary* ns, XLIV, (1969), p. 218 note. YCA. Foss Trustees Minute book, 11 Feb. 1806.
40.   J.A. Chartres, 'The marketing of agricultural produce', in J. Thirsk (ed), *The Agrarian History of England and Wales, 1640–1750*, 2 vols. (Cambridge, 1985), II, pp. 459–65. P. Bowden, 'Agricultural prices, farm profits, and rents', in Thirsk, *Agrarian History* . . . *1500–1640*, pp. 614–5. Fisher, *op. cit.*, p. 51. N.S.B. Gras, *The Evolution of the English Corn Market from the Twelfth to the Eighteenth Centuries*, (Cambridge, Mass., 1926), p. 123. R.B. Westerfield, *Middlemen in English Business, particularly between 1660 and 1760*, (re-issue, Newton Abbot, 1968), pp. 421–2. E.L. Jones, *Seasons and Prices. The Role of the Weather in English Agricultural History*, (1964), p. 58. G.W.J. Grainger and C.M. Elliott, 'A fresh look at wheat prices in the eighteenth century', *Ec.His.Rev.*, 2 s XX (1967), pp. 260–2. R. Mitchison, 'The movement of Scottish corn prices in the seventeenth and eighteenth centuries', *ibid.*, XVIII (1965), pp. 282–3. W.E. Minchinton, 'Bristol – metropolis of the west in the eighteenth century', *Trans. RHS*, 5th ser. IV (1954), pp. 73–4, 88. Winchester harvest return, autumn 1800, PRO. 30/8/291, f. 65. *Seventh Report*, pp. 3, 17. Liverpool to Fawkener, 23 Oct. 1800, BT. 6/139. Sir C. Willoughby, Oxfordshire, to Portland, 21 Sept. 1800; vicar of Wormald, acreage return, autumn 1801, HO. 42/51; 67/15. Rev. Heber, Cheshire, to E. Heber, 15 Aug. 1801. R.H. Cholmondeley (ed), *The Heber Letters 1783–1832*, (1950), p. 132. D. Baker, 'The marketing of corn in the first half of the eighteenth century; North-east Kent', *Ag.His.Rev*, 18 (1970). N. Goddard, 'The development and influence of agricultural periodicals and newspapers, 1780–1880', *ibid.*, 31 (1983), p. 129. R.S. Schofield, 'The impact of scarcity and plenty on population change in England, 1541–1871', *Jnl.Int.His.*, XIV (1983), p. 289. W.K. Parker, 'Wheat harvests and supplies in Herefordshire 1793–1815', *Transactions of the Woolhope Naturalists' Field Club*, XLIII (1979), p. 51. *Newcastle Journal*, 19 July 1740.
41.   S.G. Checkland, 'Corn for south Lancashire and beyond, 1780–1800; the firm of Corrie, Gladstone and Bradshaw', *Business History*, 2 (1960), pp. 4–14. G. Jackson, *Hull in the Eighteenth Century*, (1972), p. 125. Grainger and Elliott, *loc. cit.*, D. Durell, Chairman, Oxford Canal Company, to J. King, 17 July 1795, PC. 1/27/A55. SCL. WWM, estate correspondence, stewards' papers, vols. I to III.
42.   BTHR (York), DER 23/3–16. L.S. Pressnell, *Country Banking in the Industrial Revolution*, (Oxford, 1956), p. 360. A.H. John, 'Farming in wartime, 1793–1815', in Jones and Mingay, *op. cit.*, pp. 45–6. J.C. Hodgson (ed), 'North country diaries, I', *Surtees Society*, 118 (1910), pp. 321–2.
43.   A. Young, *The Question of Scarcity Plainly Stated*, (1800), pp. 52–6. Cf. A. Smith, *The Wealth of Nations*, 2 vols. (Everyman, 1961 edition), II, pp. 30–1.
44.   Spate, *op. cit.*, p. 542. Vicar of Stokesley, 1800 harvest return, HO. 42/54. *Minutes*, 2 Feb. and 20 Oct. 1795. Various written statements, Feb. 1795, BT. 5/9, ff. 379–81. President of the Board of Trade, memo., 4 Aug. 1795, BL.Add.Mss. 38353, ff. 316–35. S. Garbett to Hawkesbury, 15 July 1795, PC. 1/27/A55. *The Iris*, 14 and 21 Aug. 1795. R. Trow-Smith, *A History of British Livestock Husbandry 1700–1900*, (1959), pp. 14, 23–4.

45. Monopolistic tendencies were observable at the end of the seventeenth century. Chartres, *op. cit.*, pp. 448–65. *Seventh Report*, pp. 7–8, 18–30, 39–42, 45–9, 52–7. Baker, 'North-east Kent', pp. 142–4. Rev. Wise, 1800 harvest return, HO. 42/54. L.V. Harcourt (ed), *The Diaries and Correspondence of the Rt. Hon. George Rose*, 2 vols. (1860), I, pp. 281–5. *Gentleman's Magazine*, Aug. 1800, pp. 788–9. P. Mathias, *The Brewing Industry in England 1700–1830*, (Cambridge, 1959), p. 464.

46. Customs officers, outports, to the Board of Trade, autumn 1800; Messrs Hill, Bristol, to the Privy Council, 20 Oct. 1800, BT. 6/139. Liverpool and Bristol merchants dealt extensively in North American grain, but normally sold it directly in the Iberian Peninsular, Checkland, *op. cit.*, p. 7.

47. Poole to S.T. Coleridge, n.d. but Sept. or Oct. 1800, Mrs H. Sandford (ed), *Thomas Poole and His Friends*, 2 vols. (1888), II, p. 13. *Seventh Report*, pp. 25–6, 31, 47–8. Liverpool to Portland, 9 Oct. 1800, BL.Add.Mss. 38311, ff. 158–65. Harcourt, *op. cit.*, I, p. 284.

48. Clergy's and taxmen's 1800 harvest returns, HO. 42/52, 54–5; PRO 30/8/291, f. 50.

49. T. Batchelor, *A General View of the Agriculture of the County of Bedford*, (1808), pp. 591–2. W. Mavor, *A General View of the Agriculture of . . . Berkshire*, (1808), pp. 450, 458–9. N. Kent, *A General View of the Agriculture of . . . Norfolk*, (1794), pp. 46–7. W. Holland, *A General View of the Agriculture of the County of Chester*, (1808), pp. 314–5. Mayor of Banbury, and Boyne, to Portland, 12 and 27 Sept. 1800; Rev. Frankland, Yarlington, 1800 harvest return, HO. 42/51, 54. Deposition of Collier Church, 20 June 1740, State Papers Domestic, 36/51, ff. 258–9. S.I. Mitchell, 'Food shortages and public order in Cheshire 1757–1812', *Transactions of the Lancashire and Cheshire Antiquarian Society*, 81 (1982), pp. 46–7.

50. This point is made by many of the authors of the British Library's 'Tracts on Scarcity 1792–1800'. Cf. Mayor of Wootten Bassett, to Portland, 3 Apr. 1796, PC. 1/33/A87.

51. C.R. Fay, *The Corn Laws and Social England*, (Cambridge, 1932), p. 45. Charles Smith, *Three Tracts on the Corn Trade*, (1756), pp. 136–7. *Minutes*, 29 Oct. 1795. Vicar of Bowden, 1800 harvest return, HO. 42/54. *York Courant*, 28 Sept. 1801. Notts. CRO, Quarter Sessions order book 1796–1803, f. 52. S. and B. Webb, 'The Assize of Bread', *Economic Journal*, XIV (1904), pp. 216–7. J. Tann, 'Marketing methods in the international steam engine market; the case of Boulton and Watt', *Jnl.Ec.His.*, 38 (1978), p. 381. *Idem*, 'Co-operative corn milling; self-help during the grain crises of the Napoleonic Wars', *Ag.His.Rev.*, 28 (1980), pp. 45, 59.

52. Westerfield, *op. cit.*, p. 171. Lovell's petition, 22 July; Colquhoun to Portland, 7 Aug. 1795, PC. 1/27/A56; 1/29/A64. Liverpool to Lord Sheffield, 30 July, 1800, BL.Add.Mss. 38311, ff. 136–40. Flour stocks, Nottingham bakers, Sept. 1800, NCA. 3990, II. Webb, *loc. cit.* Eden, *op. cit.*, III, pp. 705–9. B. Hilton, *Cash, Corn and Commerce*, (Oxford, 1977), p. 27. *Morning Chronicle*, 15 Sept. 1800. *Leeds Mercury*, 1 Dec. 1804.

53. This and the following paragraph draw heavily on the replies by corporate authorities to a government enquiry into the use of coarser breads and cereal substitutes in the spring of 1796, PC. 1/33/A87–8. *DPD*, 3rd ser. X, pp. 536–9, 615–7. Collins, *op. cit.*, pp. 108–9. Burnett, *Plenty and Want . . .*, pp. 3–5. C. Mackie, *Norfolk Annals*, 2 vols. (1901), I, p. 223. Baker Smith's deposition, 18 Nov. 1795, ECRO. Q/SBb/361; 362/84. *Aris's Birmingham Gazette*, 7 July 1800. *The Iris*, 16 Dec. 1796.

54. Petition of Robert Hall re conviction for forestalling at Middlesex Sessions, Oct. 1800, and trial judge's report, HO. 47/24. *BPP*, 'Report of the select committee of the House of Commons on the petitions of the London cutting butchers', (1795), *passim*. Defoe, *op. cit.*, I, p. 343. J. Comber, *Real Improvements in Agriculture*, (1772), p. 59. *York Courant*, 20 June, 1795. YCA, K.125, Petition of the Users of York Cattle Market, 1826. J. Blackman, 'The food supply of an industrial town', *Business History*, V (1963), p. 88. C.E. Whiting (ed), 'Two Yorkshire diaries', *Transactions of the Yorkshire Archaeological Society Record Series*, CXXVII (1958), pp. 52, 148, 150. R.A.E. Wells, 'Sheep-rustling in Yorkshire in the age of the industrial and agrarian revolutions', *Northern History*, XX (1984), pp. 128–33.

55. Holland, *op. cit.*, pp. 315–6. Westerfield, *op. cit.*, pp. 204–8. YCA, York Corporation House Books, vol. 44, f. 204; 45, ff. 258, 268, 307–8; 46, ff. 68, 87, 98. W. Hargrove, *History of York*, 3 vols. (York, 1818), II, p. 174. Marshall, *Yorkshire . . .*, II, pp. 199–200. Letter dated Cullompton, 30 June 1795, NUL. Portland dep., PWF. 298. W.M. Stern,

'Cheese carried coastwise to London towards the middle of the eighteenth century', *Guildhall Miscellany*, IV (1973), pp. 207–21.

56.   J. Blackman, 'The cattle trade and agrarian change on the eve of the railway age', *Ag.His.Rev.*, 23, (1975), pp. 52–3. Thirsk, *Peasant Farming . . .*, p. 91. G.E. Mingay, 'The size of farms in the eighteenth century', *Ec.His.Rev.*, 2 ser. XVII (1961–2). *Idem.*, *Enclosure and the Small Farmer in the Age of the Industrial Revolution*, (1968). D. Hey, 'The 1801 crop returns for Yorkshire', *Yorkshire Archaeological Society Journal*, XLII (1971), pp. 457–8. A. Harris, 'The agriculture of the East Riding of Yorkshire before parliamentary enclosures', *ibid.*, XL (1959–64), p. 127. J.R. Wordie, 'Social change on the Leveson–Gower estates, 1714–1832', *Ec.His.Rev.*, 2nd ser. XXVII (1974), esp. pp. 597–8. F. Beavington, 'The development of market gardening in Bedfordshire', *Ag.His.Rev.*, 23 (1975), pp. 23–31. K.A. MacMahon, 'Roads and turnpike trusts in the East Riding of Yorkshire', *East Riding Local History Series*, 18 (1964), p. 20. Holt, *op. cit.*, pp. 6–7, 79–80, 149. Rennie, *op. cit.*, p. 114. Chambers, *op. cit.*, pp. 161, 289. G.E. Fussell, *The Dairy Farmer, 1500–1900*, (1968), p. 303. C. Hadfield, *The Canal Age*, (Newton Abbot, 1968), p. 90. Mitchell, *op. cit.*, pp. 45–6.

57.   Holt, *op. cit.*, p. 198. Defoe, *op. cit.*, I, p. 344. I. Pinchbeck, *Women Workers and the Industrial Revolution*, (1969 edition), pp. 293–4. V. Smith, 'The Lewes Market', *Sussex Archaeological Collections*, CVII (1969), pp. 92–3, 98. DCRO, City of Exeter, Quarter Sessions minute books, 73B, 73C. W. Marshall, *Review of the Reports to the Board of Agriculture. The Northern Department*, (York, 1818), p. 270. D. Davis, *A History of Shopping*, (1966), pp. 181–216. W.G. Rimmer, 'The industrial profile of Leeds 1740–1840', *Publications of the Thoresby Society*, L (1968), pp. 130 ff., esp. 137. Mitchell, *op. cit.*, p. 46. Eden, *op. cit.*, I, p. 491. Burnett, *op. cit.*, p. 35. D. Vincent (ed), *Testaments of Radicalism: Memoirs of Working-Class Politicians 1790–1885*, (1977), pp. 161–2. R. Roberts, *The Classic Slum*, (Manchester, 1971), p. 6 esp. note 5.

58.   A.W. Coats, 'Plebs, paternalists, and political economists', and E.F. Genovese, 'The many faces of moral economy; a contribution to a debate', *P&P*, 54, pp. 130–3; 58, pp. 165–7 (1972 and 1973). Cf. J. Norris, 'British war-time inflation 1793–1815; the beginnings of a pragmatic tradition', in B.M. Gough (ed), *In Search of the Visible Past*, (Waterloo, Ontario, 1975), p. 16.

59.   Certain partial exceptions, in addition to the benefits of allotments and exploitation of common rights, deserve recognition. It is possible that workers employed on short-term, but intense projects, like canal-building, earned sums adequate to medium-term provisioning. Sums earned in harvesting, by agricultural labourers and that diminishing proportion of non-agrarian workers who still participated, could also be spent on stocks, especially potatoes. Conversely, much of this cash went on clothes, shoes and rent. Although contemporary claims of workers' proverbial improvidence are doubtlessly exaggerations, recent historical recognition of leisure preferences suggest that these criticisms were not unreal. Gleaners could certainly collect cereals adequate to a month's consumption of a small family, and some claimed, much, much more. Snell, *op. cit.*, p. 179.

60.   Hilton, *op. cit.*, pp. 26–30. A. Booth, 'Food riots in North-west England 1790–1801', *P&P*, 77 (1977), p. 93. Webbs, *op. cit.*, pp. 200–3. *Minutes, passim*.

61.   This, and the following paragraph are principally based on *Seventh Report*, pp. 3–6, 16, 18–21, 24, 31, 34, 43, 48, 51, 54. John Brickwood, merchant-importer, to the Privy Council, Mar, 1796, PC. 1/33/A86. Goddard, *loc. cit.*

62.   *Seventh Report*, p. 20. D.G. Barnes, *A History of the English Corn Laws from 1660 to 1846*, (1930), pp. 26–7. Fay, *op. cit.*, p. 66. BPP, 'Report of the select committee of the House of Commons on petitions complaining of agricultural distress', (1820), pp. 17, 37, 48. W. Vamplew, 'A grain of truth: the nineteenth-century corn averages', *Ag.His.Rev.*, 28 (1980).

63.   One merchant-importer, Brickwood, argued that the scale on which the 'principal Factors' dealt in foreign grain, was so great that two or three of them could 'colleague . . . to depress or raise the market', and then promptly denied that 'they are on those particular Terms together'. *Seventh Report*, pp. 25, 31, 47–8. Liverpool to Portland, 9 Oct. 1800, BL.Add.Mss. 38311, ff. 158–65. Harcourt, *op. cit.*, I, p. 284.

Chapter 3   Harvests and Markets in Wartime 1794–1801:
'called Famine . . . in any other Country than this'

1. A. Smith, *The Wealth of Nations*, 2 vols. (1961 edition), II, p. 33. A. Young, *The Question of Scarcity Plainly Stated*, (1800), p. iv. *Morning Chronicle*, 15 Sept., and *Gentleman's Magazine*, Sept. 1800, pp. 835–6. Portland to the Duke of Marlborough, 29 Sept. 1800, HO. 42/51. Clinton to Lord William Bentinck, in Austria, 23 Dec. 1800, NUL. Portland dep. PwJa.112.
2. J.M. Stratton, *Agricultural Records*, A.D. 200–1968, (1969), pp. 6–9. E.L. Jones, *Seasons and Prices. The Role of the Weather in English Agricultural History*, (1964), p. 48.
3   The *Kentish Chronicle* gave four reports on key summertime progress in 1793, on 21 June, 2 and 5 July, and 27 Aug., and the *Stamford Mercury*, three, on 17 May, 19 July and 16 Aug.
4. *Oxford Journal*, 8 Sept. 1798. *Kentish Chronicle*, 5 July 1793.
5. The latest agrarian historian to use governmental surveys is M.E. Turner, 'Agricultural productivity in England in the eighteenth century: evidence from crop yields', *Ec. His. Rev.*, 2 s. XXXV, (1982). If Turner is insufficiently critical of these sources, and surprisingly has not used additional evidence – notably of meteorological conditions – I have utilised his calculations here, as the best available from an agricultural specialist.
6. Harvest returns in HO. 42/36–7. PC. 1/30/A71. J.W. Emmerton, Nottinghamshire, to his brother, 20 July and 31 Aug. 1794, Notts. CRO. DD. Sy 168/XI, XLI. Auckland to Lord Henry Spencer, 14 Aug. and 18 Sept. 1794, Bishop of Bath and Wells (ed), *Journal and Correspondence of Lord Auckland*, 4 vols. (1862), III, pp. 229, 240. *Hereford Journal*, 14 Jan. 1795.
7. T.S. Ashton, *Economic Fluctuations in England 1700–1800*, (Oxford, 1959), p. 25. *York Chronicle*, Jan. to March 1795. *York Herald*, 14 and 21 Feb., and *York Courant*, 16 Feb. 1795. *Sherborne Mercury* and *Hull Advertizer*, 2 and 14 Mar. 1795. Stratton, *op. cit.*, p. 91. Rev. W. MacRitchie, *Diary of a Tour through Great Britain in 1795*, (1897), pp. 127, 130–1, 149–50. R.C. Broadley to Sir C. Sykes, 19 May 1795, HCRO, DD SY. 101/67. Jones, *op. cit.*, p. 153. K.C. Balderstone, (ed), *Thrailania: the Diary of Mrs. Hester Lynch Thrale 1776–1809*, 2 vols. (Oxford, 1942), II, p. 932. Diary of William Harwood, Bilborough, Nottinghamshire, NCA. M21211. J. Jeffreys, Plymouth, and J.J. Butt, Salisbury, to Pole-Carew, 29 June and 7 July 1795, CCRO, Carew Mss. CC/K/25. Estate-agent Black, to Huntingdonshire Clerk of the Peace, c.4 July 1795, ECRO. D/DBy/O12. Mr. Grenville, Pembrokeshire, and Sir C. Willoughby, Oxfordshire, to Portland, 18 and 28 June 1795, HO. 42/35. Mayor of Richmond, to Pitt 16 July, Banks to Hawkesbury, 30 Aug. 1795, PC. 1/27/A55; 1/29/A64. E. Gray (ed), *Man Midwife: The Further Experiences of John Knyveton . . . 1763–1809*, (1946), p. 149. J.C. Godfrey, *The History of the Parish and Priory of Lenton in the County of Nottingham*, (1884), pp. 463–4.
8. Returns, HO. 42/36–7. J. Porter, Lincolnshire, to the Home Office, 29 Oct. 1795, PC. 1/30/A68. Emmerton to his brother, 30 Aug. 1795, Notts. CRO. DD.SY. 169/IX. *Sussex Weekly Advertiser*, 21 Sept. 1795. W. Pitt, *A General View of the Agriculture of the County of Stafford*, (2nd edition, 1795), p. 161.
9. See below pp. 192–4 for details.
10. Jones, *op. cit.*, pp. 153–4. Stratton, *op. cit*, p. 92. Sir J. Sinclair, *Address to the Board of Agriculture*, (1796), p. 2. Pitt, *op. cit.*, p. 161.
11. Rev. R. Heber, Malpas, to E. Heber, 20 Apr. 1799, R.H. Cholmondeley (ed.), *The Heber Letters, 1783–1832*, (1950), pp. 110–1. Emmerton to his brother, 20 June and 4 Oct. 1799, Notts. CRO. DD. SY. 169/LII, LIV. *Commercial and Agricultural Magazine*, Aug. 1799, p. 71; Sept. 1799, p. 41; Oct. 1799, p. 217; Nov. 1799, pp. 221–2. Letters to Sykes from, R.H. Beaumont, 6 Sept, and G. Britton, Sledmere, 23 June, 23 July, 25 Aug, 1 and 15 Sept., 27 and 30 Oct., 3, 10 and 19 Nov. 1799, HCRO. DD. SY. 101/54, 66. F. Bamford (ed), *Dear Miss Heber. An Eighteenth-Century Correspondence*, (1936), pp . 188, 191, 193. *DPD.*, 3rd. ser. vol. 10, p. 717. *Lincoln, Rutland and Stamford Mercury*, 23 and 30 Aug., and 11 Nov. 1799. *Sussex Weekly Advertiser*, 19 and 26 Aug. 1799. T. Lack, Soho, to Liverpool, 6 Oct. 1799, BL. Add. Mss. 38233, ff. 240–1. *Exeter Flying Post*, 3 and 10 Nov, 1799. *The Times*, 8 and 16 Jan. and 28 Feb. 1800. A.W. Dyson (ed), *William Metcalf – His Book*, (Leeds, 1931), pp. 81–2. *Brighton Patriot*, 6 June 1837. J. Ayres (ed), *Paupers and Pig Killers: the Diary of William Holland a Somerset Parson 1799–1818*, (1986 edition), p. 17.

12. A. Young to Pitt, 28 Nov. 1799, PRO. 30/8/193, ff. 155–6. London merchant, Philipps, to the Board of Trade, 24 Feb. 1800; Sir. J. Sinclair to Dundas, 26 June and 3 July 1800, BT. 1/18, ff. 187–9, 335–7. *Sussex Weekly Advertiser*, 21 Oct. and 18 Nov. 1799. *Commercial and Agricultural Magazine*, Oct. 1799, pp. 218–9; Jan. 1800, p. 66; Mar. 1800, pp. 216–7; May 1800, pp. 369–70; June 1800, p. 443; July 1800, p. 66; Oct. 1800, pp. 304–5. *The Times*, 8 Jan., 8 Aug. and 4 Sept. 1800. Mary Sturge to her father, 3 Oct. 1800, OCRO. Marshall Mss., XVII/i/i/75. *Hull Advertizer*, 18 Apr. 1800. Ashton, *op. cit.*, p. 9. B.L.H. Horn (ed), 'Letters of John Ramsay 1799–1812', *Publications of the Scottish Historical Society*, 4th ser. 3, (Edinburgh, 1968), p. 19. *Norfolk Chronicle*, 16 Aug. 1800. *Kentish Chronicle*, 8, 15 and 22 Aug. 1800. F. Grimston, Kilnwick, to T. Grimston, 25 June, 1800. HCRO. DD. GR. 43/20. Letter from Canning, 1 Aug. 1800, *Later Corr.*, III, p. 379 note 2. Ayres, *op. cit.*, pp. 17–8.
13. A. Freemantle (ed), *The Wynne Diaries*, 3 vols. (1940), III, pp. 20–1. Lancs. CRO. Dickenson diary, DDX 274/15. T. Batchelor, *A General View of the Agriculture of the County of Bedford*, (1808), p. 390. *Commercial and Agricultural Magazine*, Aug. 1800, p. 145; Sept. 1800, p. 226; Oct. 1800, p. 281. *Sussex Weekly Advertiser*, 8 Sept. 1800. *Newcastle Courant*, 13 Sept. 1800. Rashleigh to Pole-Carew, 23 Aug. 1800, CCRO. Carew Mss. CC/L/32. Banks to Liverpool, 25 Sept. 1800, BL. Add. Mss. 38234, ff. 152–3.
14. Only four of the scores of clergymen who commented on productivity in their acreage returns, claimed any deficiency, HO. 67/series. *Commercial and Agricultural Magazine*, Oct. 1800, pp. 304–5. *The Times*, 1, 27 and 30 July, 6, 10 and 17 Aug. 1801. Hawkesbury to Liverpool, 9 Aug. 1801, BL. Add. Mss. 38235, ff. 172–3. S. MacDonald, 'Agricultural response to a changing market during the Napoleonic Wars', *Ec. His. Rev.*, 2 s. XXXIII, (1980), esp. pp. 62–3.
15. Gould, *op. cit.*, pp. 325–6.
16. Mark Lane reports in the *Lincoln, Rutland and Stamford Mercury*, for Oct., Nov., and Dec., 1794 and 1799. 'True Briton', Brighton, to the Lord Mayor of London, 6 Jan. 1795, HO. 42/34. R.C. Broadley to Sykes, 10 May 1795, HCRO. DD. SY. 101/67. Mss., 'Report of the Sub-Committee of the Corporation of London on Public Mills', 10 May 1798, BT. 1/18, ff. 313–23. Mayor of Bristol to Lord Sheffield, 21 Jan, 1795, PRO. 30/8/177, ff. 216–23. *The Times*, 7 Feb. 1795. MAF. 10/284.
17. *The Times*, 2 Jan. 1795. *Report of the Committee of the Board of Agriculture concerning the Culture and Use of Potatoes*, (1795). Diary of T. Howes, Manningthorpe, NNRO. Holmes dep. Houghton to his brother, 4 Feb. 1795, Lancs. CRO, DD. Ht., 11/20.
18. Scruton and Tysoe, vestry minutes, NYRO, PR/SCR/2/1: WCRO, DR.288. Newcastle Corporation Council Minutes, 1785–99, f. 268, Newcastle City RO. *Norfolk Chronicle*, 21 Dec. 1794. *Aris's Birmingham Gazette*, 24 Dec. 1794 and 16 Feb. 1795. *Reading Mercury*, 26 Jan. and 23 Feb. 1795. *Newcastle Advertiser*, 24 Jan., 7 and 28 Feb. 1795. *Gloucester Journal* 23 Feb. 1795. *Sherborne Mercury*, 9 Mar. 1795. *Hull Advertizer*, 6 June 1795.
19. *Reading Mercury*, 14 Jan, 1795. *Hereford Journal*, 19 Jan. 1795. *The Times*, 7 Feb. 1795.
20. *Norfolk Chronicle*, 9 Oct. 1799. *Agricultural and Commercial Magazine*, Oct. 1799, pp. 1079–81. *Gentleman's Magazine*, Dec. 1799, p. 217. *The Times*, 21 Jan. 1800. *Oxford Journal*, 21 Dec. 1799. *DPD.*, 3rd ser. vol. X, pp. 653–60, 711.
21. *DPD.*, 3rd ser. vol. X, p. 710; vol. XIII, p. 42. Mr. Henson, Hazely, Yorkshire, to J.B. Lacy, Ascot, 15 June 1800, BT. 1/18, ff. 333–4. *The Times*, 12 Nov. 1800.
22. E.g. H. Holland, *A General View of the Agriculture of the County of Chester*, (1808), p. 153.
23. *Hull Advertizer*, 8 Aug. 1795. *Newcastle Advertiser*, 9 May 1795. Mayor of Canterbury, and Marquis of Hertford, to Portland, 21 Mar., and 23 Apr. 1795, HO. 42/34. Sir J. Sinclair to the Home Office, with enclosure, 28 Mar. 1795, PC. 1/24/A47. *Kentish Chronicle*, 24 Apr. 1795.
24. Devizes handbill, 20 Apr. 1800, DCRO. SP. DI52M/Corr. 1800. Cf. Lt. Col. Cockell to Windham, 7 May, WO. 40/17, and M. Burgoyne to Portland, 2 May 1800, HO. 42/50.
25. Heathcote to Lord Gower, 29 Apr. Legge to Portland, 13 May 1800, HO. 42/49–50.
26. See below pp. 187–9.
27. YCA. York Corporation House Books, vol. 46, pp. 340–1. *York Courant*, 26 May 1800. Bristol Corporation bought grain at Hamburg, but authorities at Manchester and Liverpool paid cash prizes to auspicious suppliers of town markets. J. Latimer, *Annals of Bristol in the Eighteenth and Nineteenth Centuries*, 2 vols. (reprinted, Bath, 1970), I, p. 531; II, p. 6. *Manchester Gazette*, 7 Dec. 1799 and 8 Mar. 1800. J.A. Picton, (ed), *Municipal*

Archives and Records. City of Liverpool, (1903), p. 153.

28. For the crisis and horse-owners see below, pp. Ayres, *op. cit.*, p. 51.

29. C. Atkinson, report on London flour supply, 2 July 1795. Nottingham Bench, and chairman of relief committee, to Portland, both 18 July: Mayor of Coventry to Portland, 22 July; Legge to Portland, 16 and 29 July, and 8 Aug. with enclosure; Mayor of Leicester to S. Smith MP, 17 and 20 July 1795, HO. 42/35: PC. 1/27/A56; 1/29/A64. *Minutes*, 5 Aug. 1795.

30. *Newcastle Courant*, 25 July, 1, 8 and 15 Aug. *Newcastle Chronicle*, 1 Aug. 1795. *The Iris*, 29 July 1795. Mayor of Newcastle-upon-Tyne to Dundas, 20 and 21 July; Lord Darlington, and Etherington (with enclosures), to the Privy Council, 26 July and 5 Aug: letters and petitions to the Privy Council from Manchester Bench, 27 July, Whitehaven, 31 July, J.C. Curwen, 4 Aug., and Lord Lonsdale, 19 Aug. 1795, PC. 1/27/A55–6; 1/29/A64, A66. *Leeds Intelligencer*, 13 and 20 July 1795.

31. Mayor of Chester to the War Office, 31 May 1795, WO. 1/1084, ff. 549–50. Letters to Portland from Mr. Grenville, Pembrokeshire, 19 June, and Scarborough Town Clerk, with enclosures, 17 July; Sunderland relief committee to Major Napier, 10 July; petitions from authorities at Bristol, and King's Lynn, 7 and 26 July 1795, HO. 42/35: PC. 1/27/A54–6.

32. Undated, unsigned, memorandum respecting bread, forage and fuel contracts for Home Encampments, PRO. 30/8/231, ff.45–7.

33. Petitions of Mr. Lindsey, 18 July, and Edward Wood, 5 Aug.; Commissary-general, Southampton, to the Privy Council, with enclosures, 10 Aug. 1795, PC. 1/27/A56; 1/29/A64.

34. As Norwich bakers ran out of flour, an emergency committee bought 'sundry portions . . . from millers who were not in the habit of supplying Norwich', NNRO., Norwich Guardians of the Poor, Minutes 1789–96, Case 20 Shelf e.

35. Even tiny places within regions of consumption were forced to purchase on behalf of at least the poorer inhabitants, as represented by those made by poor-law authorities at Kenilworth and Heath in the Midlands. Parochial records, WCRO., DR. 296/50. Derbys. CRO, D703A/PO/1.

36. *Aris's Birmingham Gazette*, 13 July 1795. *Derby Mercury*, 23 July 1795. Nottingham Common Hall Order Book, 9 July 1795, NCA., A. 3554, f. 42. *The Iris*, 10 and 24 July 1795. *Newcastle Advertiser*, 4 July 1795. *Hull Advertiser*, 18 July 1795. *Manchester Mercury*, 4 and 11 Aug. 1795. Picton, *op. cit.*, pp. 192–3. T.C. Barker and J.R. Harris, *A Merseyside Town in the Industrial Revolution: St. Helens 1750–1850*, (1954), p. 93. R. Browne, Sheffield, to Fitzwilliam, 19 July 1795, SCL. WWM. F47/2/10–1. Rev. J. Wilkinson, Sheffield, to Richard Ford, 6 Aug. 1795, NUL. Portland dep. PwF. 3942–3. P. Ward to the War Office, 12 July 1795, WO. 1/1084, ff. 669–73. S. Garbett, Birmingham, to Hawkesbury, S. Smith, Nottingham, and W. Crawshay, South Wales, to Fawkener, 12, 18 and 20 July; letters to Portland, from Earl of Stamford 27 June and 4 July, and chairman, Nottingham relief committee, 18 July; E.J. Stuart to Pitt, with enclosure, 11 July 1795, BL. Add. Mss. 38230, f.236: HO 42/35; PC. 1/27/A55–6.

37. Petitions to the Privy Council from, the 'Millers, Bakers and Others of Manningtree Essex', and T. Barley, both 15 July, four Dover millers, and Lovell, 17 and 22 July; deposition of miller W. Carter, Willsbridge, and baker S. Davis, Keynsham, both 18 July; letters to Portland from Sir C. Willoughby, Oxfordshire, 28 June, A. Curzon, and Knox, 5 and 14 July 1795, and Lonsdale with enclosures, 2 Aug: corndealer Hewitt to surgeon Hunt, 20 July 1795, HO. 42/35; PC.1/27/A55–6.

38. *Kentish Chronicle*, 24 Apr. 1795. *Sherborne Mercury*, 4 May 1795.

39. Mr. Black to Huntingdonshire Clerk of the Peace c.4 July 1795, ECRO, D/DBy/012. R.J. Buxton MP, to Charles Long, under-secretary, Treasury, 7 July; Heathcote to the Privy Council, 26 July 1795, PC. 1/27/A54, A56. A. Baker MP, Bayfordbury, to Portland, 11 July 1795, NUL, Portland dep. PwF. 233a–b. Birdchanger vestry minutes; cf. decisions taken between 29 June and 21 July in other Essex parishes, Terling, Dagenham, Chelmsford, Rydon, and Billericay, ECRO, DP. 25/8/1; 60/8/3; 69/8/1; 94/12/11; 139/8/1; 299/8/2. *The Times*, 24 July 1795.

40. Great Parndon and Great Sampford vestries, ECRO. DP. 184/8/2; 289/8/2. *Reading Mercury*, 29 June 1795.

41. J. and W. Squire, Peterborough, to Pitt, 20 July; Mayor of Leicester to S. Smith, 23 July;

Rev. Knollis, Burford, and Mayor of Bedford, to Portland, 20 and 24 July 1795, HO. 42/35: PC/1/27/A55; 1/29/A64. Youell diary, 14 July 1795, NNRO. D87. *Lincoln, Rutland and Stamford Mercury*, 31 July 1795.

42.   S. Garbett to H. Legge, 25 and 28 July, and 4 Aug; Lovell to P. Colquhoun, 5 Aug. 1795, PC. 1/27/A56; 1/29/A64. *Minutes*, 5 Aug. 1795. Mark Lane inspector Atkinson, report, 2 July 1795, HO. 42/35.

43.   See below.

44.   F. Adams and A.A. Baker, Keynsham, to Portland, with enclosures, 18 July 1795, PC. 1/27/A55. Atkinson's report, *loc. cit.* Howard's printed bill, 16 July 1795, BL. Add Mss. 35642. f.126. Quarter Sessions minutes. Berkshire, 15 July, Oxfordshire, 1 Aug. 1795, BCRO. Q/508, ff. 8–9: OCRO. QSM 1/5. Black to Huntingdonshire Clerk of the Peace, *loc. cit. Exeter Flying Post*, 16 July 1795. *Bath Journal*, 22 July 1795. *Blackburn Mail*, 12 Aug. 1795. *Manchester Mercury*, 4 and 11 Aug. 1795. *Derby Mercury*, 5 Nov. 1795.

45.   *Reading Mercury*, 14 Sept. 1795. Deposition of W. Carter, 18 July, 1795; Messrs. Kerey, Jane and Turton, to a Monmouth correspondent, 14 July 1795, PC. 1/27/A55. Earl of Warwick to Portland, 29 July 1795, HO. 42/35. *Lincoln, Rutland and Stamford Mercury*, 18 Sept. 1795. Norwich Guardians of the Poor Minute, 1 July 1795, NNRO., Case 20 shelf e. *Hull Advertiser*, 25 July 1795. Documents re riot at Saffron Walden, ECRO. D/DBy/012. *Leeds Intelligencer*, 25 Jan. 1796.

46.   A. Smith, *The Wealth of Nations*, 2 vols. (1961 edition), I. p. 40. Henry Duncombe to W.A. Miles, 2 Aug. 1795, C.P. Miles (ed). *The Correspondence of William Augustus Miles on the French Revolution, 1789–1817*, 2 vols. (1890), I. pp. 243–4. MacRitchie, *op. cit.*, pp. 108, 113. *Lincoln, Rutland and Stamford Mercury*, 21 Aug. 1795. J.W. Emmerton to his brother, 30 Aug. 1795, Notts. CRO. DD. SY 168/ix. W. Baker to Portland, 17 Aug: Rev. T. Dalton, Carisbrook, harvest return, Nov. 1800, HO. 42/50, 54. Messrs. Hill, Bristol, to Fawkener, 28 Oct. 1800, BT. 6/139. Sir Joseph Banks to Liverpool, 15 Aug. 1800, BL. Add. Mss. 38234, ff. 130–1. *Seventh Report*, p. 23.

47.   PRO. 30/8/291, ff. 43, 58, 60, 66, 71. HO. 42/54.

48.   Market reports in the *Lincoln, Rutland and Stamford Mercury*, 18 and 25 July, 6, 13, 20 and 27 Aug. and 1 Sept. 1800. Letters to Portland from, J. Giffard, London stipendiary, and J.B. Head, both 2 Sept; E. Monckton, Somerton, 14 Sept; the Birmingham Bench, 23 Sept; and the Earl of Warwick, 5 Oct; vicar of Rochford, harvest return, Oct. 1800, HO. 42/51–2, 55. Sheffield handbill, 8 Sept. 1800, YML. HH. 3(I).

49.   Sheffield to Liverpool, and reply, 24 and 30 July 1800, BL. Add. Mss. 38234, ff. 115–7, 38311, ff. 136–40. Reports, *Lincoln, Rutland and Stamford Mercury*, Oct–Nov. 1800. Harvest returns, 1800, PRO. 30/8/291, ff. 4, 44, 49, 51–2, 55, 60–1, 64–5, 73–6. *Commercial and Agricultural Magazine*, Oct. 1800, pp. 262–4, 304–5. W. Salmon, Devizes, to Addington, 14 Dec. 1800, DCRO, SP. D152M/Corr. 1800. Rev. R. Dyneley, acreage return, 30 Nov. 1801, HO. 67/26, f. 448.

50.   Lord Crumore to the Privy Council, 26 July 1795, PC. 1/27/A56. W. Hill, Ormskirk, and T. Abdy Abdy, to Portland, 8 and 13 Aug. 1795, HO. 42/35. Signed confession exacted from an Essex farmer by estate-agent Black, ECRO. D/DBy/012. *Derby Mercury*, 29 Oct. and 5 Nov. 1795. *Reading Mercury*, 21 Dec. 1795. J. Howsham, Wakefield, to W. Spencer-Stanhope MP, 28 Feb. 1796, SCL. SS.60586/9. *Lincoln, Rutland and Stamford Mercury*, 11 Sept., 9, 16 and 30 Oct., 6 Nov. and 4 Dec. 1795.

51.   Mark Lane reports, *Lincoln, Rutland and Stamford Mercury*, Jan. and Feb., 1796 and 1801. *Seventh Report*, p. 57. A. Graham to J. King, 1 Jan. 1801; Rev. Courthope, Glynde, acreage return, 1801, HO. 42/61; 67/4. R.A. Harrison, Hull, to Fitzwilliam, 27 Dec. 1800, SCL. WWM. F.47/25/1. Rev. J. Foley, to Mr. Blagg, 11 Apr. 1801, GCRO., 149X/5/4. *Aris's Birmingham Gazette*, 22 and 29 Sept. and 20 Oct. 1800.

52.   Mayor of Plymouth, with enclosure, 6 Apr., and Sir F. Bassett, with enclosure, to Portland, 2 July 1795, HO. 42/34; PC. 1/24/A47; 1/27/A54.

53.   T. Colewell to Sir J. Morshead, 12 July, and Messrs. Gribble, Barnstaple, to Mr. Mitford, 18 July 1795, PC. 1/27/A55–6. Giddy Diary, CCRO., DD. DG. 14. W.G. Hoskins, *Industry, Trade and People in Exeter 1688–1800*, (Manchester, 1935), pp. 146–7.

54.   D. Yonge to Pole-Carew, 25 Oct. 1800, CCRO, Carew Mss. CC/L/31. Rodd to Portland, 28 Oct. 1800; Welsford, Totnes, to Fortescue, 4 Apr. 1801, HO. 42/61. Col. Bastard MP., CO. Devon Militia, to Addington, 4 May 1801, DCRO., SP. D152M/ Corr. 1801.

55. Mayor of Penzance, 10. Mar., and W. Elford, 6 Apr. 1795, to Portland; Mr. George, St. Austle, to Bassett, 30 Mar. 1795, HO. 42/34. P. Rashleigh to Henry Dundas, with enclosure, 27 Mar. 1795, PC. 1/24/A47. Letters to Fortescue from, Elford, 11 Apr. 1795 and J. Willcock, 1 and 15 April 1801: deposition of J. Bate, 15 Apr. 1801: statement of stocks in Plympton and Ermington Hundreds, signed by the magistrates, 11 Apr. 1801: Bastard to Addington, 3 Apr. 1801, DCRO., FLP. D1262M/F7; L52–3: SP. D152M/Corr. 1801.

56. R. Wells, 'The revolt of the south-west, 1800–1; a study in English popular protest', *SH.*, VI, (1977).

57. This is not however to deny that serious subsistence problems were experienced between 1750 and 1790. It is surely significant that the most riotous response to earlier dearth conditions came during the harvest period of 1766, when expectations of a reduction in previous high prices were unfulfilled owing to governmental ineptitude in permitting the ports to be opened for exportation. This had the effect of driving home prices still higher while grain traders strove to maximise profits through collecting the export bounty in addition to the advantages derived from supplying desperate continental markets. Crowds mobilised principally to stop the massive consignments being moved rapidly along the communication systems to the ports. D.E. Williams, 'Morals, markets and the English crowd in 1766', *P&P*, 104, (1984). Other later eighteenth-century riotous episodes prior to the nineties have distinctly localised and/or regionalised characteristics. A. Charlesworth (ed), *An Atlas of Rural Protest in Britain 1548–1900*, (1983), pp. 86–8, 92–5.

58. Oats are a partial exception; their low average price for 1797 possibly only reflects a relative abundance deriving from the 1796 importation, above-average yields, and an inter-famine restoration of the trend away from their consumption by people.

Chapter 4 'Many an honest man doeth not know how to get one Week or Day over': the Reality of Famine in Wartime

1. T. Hayter, *The Army and the Crowd in mid-Georgian England*, (1978), p. 49. Ironically, Hayter appears to believe that 1789 is the terminal date.

2. R. Mitchison, 'The movements of Scottish corn prices in the seventeenth and eighteenth centuries', *Ec. His. Rev.* 2s. XVIII, (1965), p. 286.

3. T.C. Smout, 'Famine and famine relief in Scotland', in Smout and L.M. Cullen (eds), *Comparative Elements of Scottish and Irish Economic and Social History, 1600–1900*, (Edinburgh, 1977), p. 3.

4. A.B. Appleby, 'Famine, mortality and epidemic disease; a comment', *Ec. His. Rev.*, 2 s. XXX, (1977), pp. 508–12.

5. J. Stevenson, *Popular Disturbances in England 1700–1870*, (1979), pp. 110–2.

6. D.J. Oddy, 'Urban-famine in nineteenth-century Britain; the effects of the Lancashire cotton famine on working-class diet and health', *Ec. His. Rev.*, 2.s. XXXVI, (1983), esp. pp. 68–72. This paragraph draws heavily on Oddy's article, and the argument in this chapter is reinforced strongly by Oddy's thesis; his work has refined, but not altered my own views, first developed in 1978.

7. M.W. Flinn, (ed), *Scottish Population History from the 17th Century to the 1930s'*, (Cambridge, 1977), pp. 4–5.

8. Charges of idleness on the part of agrarian workers reached a crescendo in the years before the 1834 Poor Law Amendment Act, and possibly derive from mistaking mental attitudes as the cause, instead of physical inertia, induced by malnutrition.

9. N.J. Silberling, 'Financial and monetary policy of Great Britain during the Napoleonic Wars', *Quarterly Journal of Economics*, XXXVIII, (1924). E.B. Schumpeter. 'English prices and public finance, 1660–1822', *Economic Statistics*, XX, (1938). E.V. Morgan, 'Some aspects of the Bank Restriction period, 1797–1821', *Economic History*, IV, (1939). J.L. Anderson, 'A measure of the effect of British public finance, 1793–1815', *Ec. His. Rev.*, 2 s. XXVIII, (1974).

10. T.S. Ashton, *Economic Fluctuations in England 1700–1800,* (Oxford, 1959), ch. 2. J.D. Chambers and G.E. Mingay, *The Agricultural Revolution 1750–1880*, (1966), p. 109. Anderson, *op. cit.*, p. 617.

11. Anderson, *loc. cit. Idem.*, 'Aspects of the effect on the British economy of the wars with France 1793–1815', *Australian Economic History Review*, XII, (1972). C.K. Harley, 'British industrialization before 1841; evidence of slower growth during the industrial revolution', *Jnl. Ec. His.*, XCII, 2, (1982), p. 283.

12. D.T. Jenkins, *The West Riding Wool Textile Industry 1770–1835; a study in Fixed Capital Formation*, (Edington, 1975), esp. pp. 175–7. S. Shapiro, *Capital and the Cotton Industry in the Industrial Revolution*, (Ithica, N.Y. 1967), *passim*.

13. J. Beckett, Barnsley, to W. Spencer-Stanhope, 1 May 1802, SCL. SS. 60588/40. *The Iris*, 23 Apr. 1803. J.G. Williamson, 'Why was British growth so slow during the industrial revolution', *Jnl. Ec. His.*, XLIV, 3, (1984) p. 703.

14. *Aris's Birmingham Gazette*, 22 Dec. 1794. *The Iris*, 30 Jan. 1795.

15. *Leicester Journal*, 8 Apr. 1796. A. Temple-Patterson, *Radical Leicester*, (Leicester, 1954), p. 57. R.A.E. Wells, *Riot and Political Disaffection in Nottinghamshire in the Age of Revolutions 1776–1803*, (University of Nottingham, 1984), pp. 16–7.

16. Leeds Corporation Court book, LCA., LC/M3. *BPP*, 'Report of the select committee of the House of Commons on the woollen manufactury', (1802–3), p. 223. West Riding acreage returns, 1801, HO. 67/26.

17. Coventry tax-office to the Treasury, enclosing petitions, 13 Mar. 1801. T. 1/857. J. Bohstedt, *Riot and Community Politics in England and Wales, 1790–1810*, (1983), pp. 39–40. G. Jackson, *Hull in the Eighteenth Century*, (1972), p. 19. P.C. Garlick, 'The Sheffield Cutlers and the Allied Trades in the Eighteenth Century', (Unpublished MA thesis, University of Sheffield, 1951), Appendix II.

18. Close to Wentworth Woodhouse steward Hall, 2 Apr. and 12 June 1795, SCL. WWM, stewards' papers, vol. 6 (iv). K.P. Bawn, 'Social Protest, Popular Disturbances and Public Order in Dorset, 1790–1838', (Unpublished Ph.D. thesis, University of Reading, 1984), p. 246.

19. A. Young, *The Question of Scarcity Plainly Stated*, (1800). p. iv. *Manchester Gazette*, 28 Dec. 1799. *Morning Chronicle*, 15 Sept. 1800. *Gentleman's Magazine*, Sept. 1800, pp. 835–6. Portland to Marlborough, 29 Sept.; J. Walker to Addington, 13 July 1801, HO. 42/51; 61. Clinton to Lord George Bentinck, in Austria, 23 Dec. 1800, NUL. Portland dep., PwJa. 112. Rowbottom diary entries, 1 Jan. and 2 May 1801, OPL. Fitzwilliam to C. Hudson, 31 Dec. 1800; Crowder, and B. Frank, to B. Cooke, 31 Mar. and 12 Apr. 1801, SCL. WWM., F49/9, 11; F127/57. Lord Morely's diary, 28 Jan 1800, BL. Add. Mss. 48246, ff. 28–9.

20. The specimen figures in the text derive from Appendix 4, where calculations of living costs based on prices in each of six selected markets, are given.

21. It should be emphasised that these figures, and those in the next paragraph, relate to the cereal component of the full diet; they have not been weighted to reflect the fact that workers economised by the reduction of non-cereals; attempts would be made to cover the resultant dietary deficiency through increased cereal consumption.

22. See Appendix 5. This section also draws upon statistical evidence in R.A.E. Wells, 'The Grain Crises in England 1794–6, 1799–1801', (Unpublished D. Phil thesis, University of York, 1978), pp. 972–4.

23. Returns, spring 1796 and autumn 1800, PC. 1/33/A87–8: HO. 42/53–5. Cf. Rashleigh to Pole-Carew, 10 Mar. 1800, CCRO, Carew Mss., CC/L/33, *The Times*, 29 Oct. 1800. J. Ayres (ed), *Paupers and Pig Killers: the Diary of William Holland a Somerset Parson 1799–1818*, (1986 edition), p. 28, and A. Kussmaul (ed), 'The Autobiography of Joseph Mayett of Quainton 1783–1839', *Buckinghamshire Record Society*, 23, (1986), pp. 10–1.

24. *Minutes*, 20 Oct. 1795. Clergy's 1800 harvest returns, Malton, Cardiff, Winterslow, Wrenbury (Cheshire), Waterbeach and Bottisham (Cambridgeshire), HO. 42/54. D.H. Kennett, 'Wheat and malt prices in Cambridge in the late eighteenth century', *Ag. His. Rev*, 20, (1972), p. 62. Ayres, *loc. cit.*

25. F.M. Eden, *The State of the Poor*, 3 vols. (1797), III, pp. 814–5. Ashton, *op. cit.*, p. 26. Rowbottom diary, 20 Apr. 1800, and 6 Feb. 1801, OPL. Ayres, *op. cit.*, p. 53. Clergy's 1800 harvest returns from Catterick and East Brent, HO.42/54–5.

26. E.g. wills of Palmer, and Gould, made in Devon in 1795 and 1801 respectively. J. Lock, *Records of South Molton*, (South Molton, 1893), p. 167.

27. Rowbottom diary, 17 Feb., May, 8 June 1795, and 19 Mar. 1800, OPL. Portland to the Marquis of Salisbury, 24 Mar. 1795, HO. 43/6, p. 298. J. Carpenter, Tavistock, to

Portland, with enclosures, 22 June 1800, HO. 42/50.
28. A.B. Haden to Portland, 27 Sept, W. Hall to P. Colquhoun, 21 Oct. 1800, HO. 42/51–2. W. Milnes to Sir J. Banks, 9 Sept. 1800, BL. Add. Mss. 38234, ff. 146–7. Rowbottom diary, 'Select observations', May 1800, OPL. Bowns to Hall, 10 and 27 Dec. 1800, SCL. WWM, stewards' papers, vol. 6 (VI). *The Iris*, 8 and 29 Jan., 5 Mar., 29 Oct., and 17 Dec. 1801.
29. *Norfolk Chronicle*, 24 May 1800. *Aris's Birmingham Gazette*, 2 Feb, 1801. *London Gazette*, 15 Nov. 1800. *Manchester Gazette*, 14 and 21 Feb. 1801. Annotated mss., 'Minutes of the Trial of Montgomery', nd. but 1796, SCL. MD. 1092, f. 31.
30. Sampson to a Mr. Foster, Harewood, 5 Nov. 1795; Legge, 13 May, and Mayor of Portsmouth, with enclosure, 18 Sept. 1800, to Portland, HO. 42/36, 50–1. *London Gazette*, 13 Sept. 1800. BL. Place Newspaper Collection, vol. 37, f. 45. Indictment of Crook, PL. 27/8 pt. II.
31. Letters to Portland, each with enclosures from, W.H. Baker, Stroud, Oct. 1795; Lord Aylesford, Warwickshire, 31 Aug., and Mr. Bracebridge, Atherstone, 19 Sept. 1800, HO. 42/36, 50–1. Liverpool to Banks, 25 Sept., and Dundas, 11 Oct. 1800, BL. Add Mss. 38311, ff. 150–6, 166–9.
32. *Kentish Chronicle*, 19 Sept. 1800. Rev. B. Burnaby, to the Bishop of Lincoln, 8 Nov. 1800, HO. 42/52. W. Wyatt, diary, 31 Dec. 1800. SCL. Bag. Coll. 655/2. Rowbottom diary, 31 Dec. 1800, OPL.
33. A. Fremantle (ed), *The Wynne Diaries*, 3 vols. (1940), III, p. 34. Ainsworth to Peel, Wilberforce to W. Hey, and J.A. Busfeild to Earl Fitzwilliam, 12, 17 and 20 Mar. 1801, HO. 42/61: R.I. and S. Wilberforce (eds), *The Correspondence of William Wilberforce*, 2 vols. (1840), I., pp. 224–5.
34. Black to Huntingdonshire Clerk of the Peace, c. 4 July 1795, ECRO. D/DBy/012. Overseers' accounts, Plympton, St. Mary, PCA., PSM/4. Rev. J. Monypenny, Rolvenden, Kent, to Portland, with enclosure, 12 Nov. 1795; Lt. Col. Elford, memo., 22 Apr. 1800, HO. 42/36, 49.
35. Clergy's 1800 harvest returns, esp. from Leicester, Woodchurch, Cheshire, Howshead, Lancashire, and Barham, Berkshire; clergy's 1801 acreage returns, esp. West Riding, HO. 42/53–5; 67/26. Petitions from London parishes, Nov. 1800, *JHC*. vol. 55, pp. 797–9, 827–8, 864. Rolle to Fortescue, 28 Dec. 1800, DCRO.FLP. D1262M/L46. *York Herald*, 11 Jan. 1800. *Leeds Intelligencer*, 27 Jan. 1800. *Newcastle Courant*, 4 Nov. 1800. J. Howard, Wakefield, to W. Spencer-Stanhope, 18 Mar. 1800, SCL. SS. 60586/43. Exeter Bread Committee Minutes, 28 Mar. 1801, DCRO. Exeter city archives, Misc. Papers Box 10. Bohstedt, *op. cit.*, pp. 39–40. Ayres, *op. cit.*, pp. 23, 26, 47, 53.
36. For the rate-crisis, see below, pp. 311–4 *The Iris*, 10 Jan. 1801. Rolle to Fortescue, 28 Dec. 1800, DCRO. FLP. D1262M/L46. *Leeds Mercury*, 18 July 1801. Wilton petition, spring 1801, *JHC*, vol. 56. p. 234. T.C. Barker and J.R. Harris, *A Merseyside Town in the Industrial Revolution. St. Helens 1750–1850*, (1954), p. 165. Gulval vestry minutes, 21 Sept 1800, CCRO. DDX. 173/77/2. Gloucestershire Quarter Sessions minute, Epiphany 1801, GCRO. Q/SO/12, pp. 247–58. *BPP*, 'Bills', (1801), I. pp. 1, 91 (as amended), 41 Geo. III, cap. 23. W.E. Tate, *The Parish Chest*, (Cambridge, 1960 edition), p. 28.
37. Rev. J. Isaacs to Pole-Carew, 7 Jan. 1801, CCRO. Carew mss. CC/1/33.
38. S. Catts and E. van de Walle, 'Nutrition, mortality and population size; Malthus's court of last resort', and N.S. Scrimshaw, 'The value of contemporary food and nutrition studies for historians', *Jnl. Int. His.*, XIV, (1983), pp. 225, 529.
39. See ch. 1, introduction, above.
40. E.A. Wrigley and R.S. Schofield, *The Population History of England 1541–1871; a Reconstruction*, (Cambridge, Mass. 1981), pp. 320–325.
41. Whether the rise belongs to 1800 or 1801 seems to depend on whether the calendar or harvest year is used. Cf. Wrigley and Schofield, *op. cit.*, p. 285. B.R. Mitchell, *Abstract of British Historical Statistics*, (Cambridge, 1962), p. 28.
42. Mitchell, *loc. cit.* W.M. Stern, 'The bread crisis of 1795–6', *Economica*, new ser. XXXI, (1964), p. 173. J.S. Taylor, 'Poverty in a West Devon parish', *Reports of the Devonshire Association*, C1, (1969), pp. 176–7. R.A.E. Wells, 'Dearth and distress in Yorkshire, 1793–1802', *Borthwick Papers*, 52, (University of York, 1977), pp. 23–4. Yorkshire statistics derive from *idem.*, thesis, Appendix 13. Wrigley and Schofield, *op. cit.*, p. 310.
43. J.F.D. Shrewsbury, *A History of the Bubonic Plague in the British Isles*, (1970), p. 50.

Portland to Bosanquet, and reply, 1 Aug. and 2 Dec. 1800; petition from Christ Church, Spitalfields, 30 July 1801, T. 1/853; 865. P. Colquhoun, report on East London, n.d. but Nov. 1800, HO. 42/53.

44. P.E. Razzell, 'Population growth and economic change in eighteenth-century and early nineteenth-century England', in E.L. Jones and G.E. Mingay (eds), *Land, Labour and Population in the Industrial Revolution*, (1967), p. 265. *The Iris*, 17 Dec. 1801. Many entries in Rowbottom diary for 1801, OPL. For causes of deaths in Leeds, see some of the entries in G.D. Lumb (ed), 'The registers of the Chapels of St. John, Holy Trinity, Headingly, Bramley, Beeston, Chapel Allerton, and Farnley in Leeds', and *idem*. (ed), 'The registers of the Chapels of the Church of Leeds 1764–1812, Holbeck, Armley and Hunslett', *Publications of the Thoresby Society*, XXIX and XXXIV, (1928 and 1934). J.D. Chambers, 'The Vale of Trent, 1670–1800', *Ec. His. Rev. Supplement*, III (1957), pp. 28–9. N. Nutcombe to Fortescue, 28 Dec. 1800, DCRO. FLP. D1262M/L48. Simcoe to Portland, 5 Apr. 1801, HO. 42/61. *Billinge's Liverpool Advertiser*, 5 Oct. 1801. T. Bailey, *Annals of Nottingham*, 4 vols. (1855), IV, p. 187. Ayres, *op. cit.*, p. 55.

45. Colquhoun's report, *loc. cit.* Haden to Portland, 16 May and 27 Sept; anon. to Portland, 3 Nov. 1800; Websey acreage report 1801, HO. 42/50–1: 67/26. Rowbottom diary, 26 Mar. 1801, OPL. *Manchester Gazette*, 28 Mar. 1801. M.D. George, *London Life in the Eighteenth Century*, (1965 edition), pp. 173–4. R.S. Schofield and C. Barham, 'Extracts from the parish registers of Barming, Kent'. *LPS*, 33, (1984), p. 59.

Chapter 5 'Extreme Avarice and Rapaciousness': Contemporary Analysis and Popular Prejudice

1. B. Harrison and P. Hollis (eds), *Robert Lowery; Radical and Chartist*, (1979) , p. 121.
2. 1812, cited by F. Peel, *The Risings of the Luddites, Chartists and Plug-Drawers*, (4th edition, 1968), p. 73.
3. J. Stevenson, *Popular Disturbances in England 1700–1870*, (1979), ch. 3 R.B. Rose, 'Eighteenth century price riots, the French Revolution and the Jacobin Maximum', *Int. Rev. SH*. IV, (1959), p. 435. J. Rule, *The Experience of Labour in Eighteenth-Century Industry*, (1981), p. 212. Cf. G. Rudé, *The Crowd in History 1730–1848*, (New York, 1964), pp. 5–6, 35–6. E.P. Thompson, *The Making of the English Working Class*, (1968 edition), pp. 68–72. C.R. Dobson, *Masters and Men. A Pre-History of Industrial Relations 1717–1800*, (1980), p. 114.
4. E.P. Thompson, 'The "moral economy" of the English crowd in the eighteenth century', *P&P*, 50, (1971), pp. 128–9. E.F. Genovese, 'The many faces of moral economy; a contribution to a debate', *P&P*, 58, (1973), pp. 164–5.
5. Rule, *op. cit.*, esp. pp. 150–1, 185–6. E.J. Hobsbawm, *Labouring Men*, (1968 edition), p. 7.
6. Dobson, *op. cit., passim*. Cf. M.I. Thomis, *Politics and Society in Nottingham 1785–1835*, (Oxford, 1969), pp. 50–1. G. Henson, *History of the Framework Knitters*, (1970 edition, Newton Abbot), p. 116. S.D. Chapman, 'Memoirs of two eighteenth-century framework knitters', *Textile History*, I., (1968–70), p. 115.
7. M.D. George, *London Life in the Eighteenth Century*, (1966 edition), chs. 4 and 6. Rudé, *op. cit.*, ch. 4. J.L. and B. Hammond, *The Skilled Labourer*, (1979 edition), pp. 10–4. W.J. Shelton, *English Hunger and Industrial Disorders*, (1973), part II.
8. I.R. Christie, *Stress and Stability in Late Eighteenth Century Britain; Reflections on the Avoidance of Revolution*, (Oxford, 1984), pp. 143–8.
9. Dobson, *op. cit.*, esp. p. 29. Cf. A. Aspinall (ed), *The Early English Trade Unions*, (1949), esp. p. xxii.
10. Stevenson, *op. cit.*, pp. 130, 134. Rule, *op. cit.*, p. 190.
11. J. Bohstedt, *Riots and Community Politics in England and Wales 1790–1810*, (1983), pp. 99, 126–7. A. Charlesworth (ed), *An Atlas of Rural Protest in Britain 1548–1900*, (1983), p. 70. J. Foster, *Class Struggle and the Industrial Revolution*, (1974), pp. 19–20, 38.
12. Thompson, *The Making. . .*, p. 70. *Idem.*, 'moral economy. . .', pp. 79, 128–31. Stevenson, *op. cit.*, p. 110.
13. Portland to the Rev. Bancroft, 8 Aug. 1799, Aspinall, *op. cit.*, pp. 26–7. R. Wells, *Insurrection: the British Experience 1795–1803*, (Gloucester, 1983), pp. 51–3. *The Times*, 28 Jan. 1800.

14. R.A.E. Wells, 'The development of the English rural proletariat and social protest 1700–1850', *Jnl PS.*, 6, (1979). E.P. Thompson, 'The crime of anonymity', in D. Hay, P. Linebaugh and Thompson, (eds), *Albion's Fatal Tree*, (1975), pp. 277–8, 298.

15. Wells, *loc. cit.* A. Charlesworth, 'The development of the English rural proletariat and social protest 1700–1850; a comment', *Jnl. PS*, 8, (1980). Wells, 'Social conflict and protest in the English countryside in the early nineteenth century; a rejoinder', *Jnl. PS*, 8, (1981). Charlesworth, *An Atlas. . . ,* pp. 140–5.

16. Rudé, *op. cit.* ch. 13. K. Logue, *Popular Disturbances in Scotland 1780–1815*, (Edinburgh, 1979), ch. 9.

17. M.I. Thomis and J. Grimmett, *Women in Protest 1800–1850*, (1982).

18. J. Stevenson, 'Food riots in England 1792–1818', in Stevenson and R. Quinault (eds), *Popular Protest and Public Order*, (1974), pp. 35–7, 56, 67. Charlesworth, *An Atlas. . . ,* p. 63.

19. E.J. Hobsbawm and G. Rudé, *Captain Swing*, (1973 edition), p. 34.

20. For various permutations of Thomis's opinion see M.I. Thomis, *The Luddites*, (Newton Abbot, 1971), *passim. Idem.*, *The Town Labourer and the Industrial Revolution*, (1974), p. 186. *Idem.*, *Responses to Industrialism: the British Experience 1780–1850*, (1976), pp. 82 ff. For a superb critique, see F.K. Donnelly, 'Ideology and early working-class history; Edward Thompson and his critics', *SH*, 2. (1976).

21. J. Walvin, 'English Democratic Societies and Popular Radicalism 1791–1800', (Unpublished DPhil. thesis, University of York, 1969), p. 603. A. Booth, 'Food riots in the North-west of England 1790–1801', *P&P*, 77, (1977), pp. 104, 107. Stevenson, 'Food riots. . .', pp. 55–6.

22. Stevenson, *Popular Disturbances. . . ,* pp. 106–8. Cf. Bohstedt, *op. cit.* pp. 16–9.

23. A. Fremantle (ed), *The Wynne Diaries, 3* vols. (1940), III, p. 20. *Annals of Agriculture*, XIV, (1790), pp. 65–6. Diary entry, 28 July 1800, K.C. Balderstone (ed), *Thrailiana: The Diary of Mrs. Hester Lynch Thrale 1776–1809*, 2 vols. (Oxford, 1942), II, p. 932. *The Times*, 4 Aug. 1800. *Gentleman's Magazine*, July 1800, p. 688. *Chelmsford Chronicle*, 27 June 1800. *Norfolk Chronicle*, 26 Oct. 1799. Shelton, *op. cit.*, p. 116. J.D. Post, *The Last Great Subsistence Crisis in the Western World*, (1977), pp. 16–7, 58, 80.

24. *Kentish Chronicle*, 29 Aug. 1800. *Sussex Weekly Advertiser*, 8 Sept. 1800. *The Times*, 19 July and August, esp. 27 Aug. 1800. *Aris's Birmingham Gazette*, 18 Aug. 1800. *Derby Mercury*, 21 Aug. 1800. *Hull Advertizer*, 23 and 30 Aug. and 13 Sept. 1800.

25. Thompson, 'Moral economy. . .', p. 93.

26. This episode can be followed in letters from a number of Yorkshiremen in the Malton area, Banks, and Lord Carlisle, who were asked to report, PC. 1/27/A54, A56. For local press coverage see the relevant issues of the *York Courant, York Herald*, and *Hull Packet*; for provincial coverage, see *Sussex Weekly Advertiser, Gloucester Journal*, and *Reading Mercury*, and metropolitan coverage in *The Times*.

27. HO. 67/series.

28. Mrs. Berry to the Earl of Orford, 18 Aug. 1795, W.S. Lewis (ed), *Horace Walpole's Correspondence*, 12 vols. (in progress, 1937 –), 12, p. 142. G. Galbraith (ed), *The Journal of the Rev. William Bagshaw-Stevens*, (Oxford, 1965), p. 303. H. Grimston to Capt. Grimston, 15 Aug. 1800, HRO. DD. GR. 43/20.

29. Cf. T.S. Ashton, *Economic Fluctuations in England 1700–1800*, (Oxford, 1959), pp. 11, 33, and P. Bowden, 'Agricultural prices, farm profits and rents', in J. Thirsk (ed), *The Agrarian History of England and Wales 1500–1640*, (Cambridge, 1967), p. 620, with E.L. Jones, *Seasons and Prices. The Role of the Weather in English Agricultural History*, (1964), pp. 51, 56.

30. *Commercial and Agricultural Magazine*, Oct. 1800, pp. 280–1.

31. Thompson, *The Making. . . ,* pp. 66–73, developed in *idem.*, 'Moral economy. . . .'. The following discussion is inspired by this essay, and A.D. Leadley, 'Some villains of the eighteenth-century market place', in J. Rule, (ed), *Outside the Law: Studies in Crime and Order 1650–1850*, (University of Exeter, 1982).

32. *Gloucester Journal*, 2 Nov. 1795. In 1813 Manchester bakers were 'not so obnoxious to the mob as the corn and flour dealers', C.R. Fay, *The Corn Laws and Social England*, (Cambridge, 1932), p. 52.

33. Letters to Portland from Lonsdale, with enclosure, 2 Aug., Sir. C. Willoughby, 7 Aug., and the Duke of Richmond, with enclosure, 19 Nov. 1795: Rev. Frankland's 1800 harvest

return, HO. 42/35–6, 54. Wells customs, 1800 harvest return, BT. 6/139. *Sussex Weekly Advertiser*, 18 Jan. 1796. *Reading Mercury*, 21 Dec. 1795. P. Pashleigh to Pole-Carew, 25 Nov. 1795, CCRO. Carew Mss. CC/K/25.

34. Unsigned Cheshire harvest return, 1800: letters to Portland from Salisbury Town Clerk, with enclosure, 6 Apr., a Hampshire JP, 14 Aug., Lord Spencer, 31 Oct., and Lord Bateman, 5 Nov. 1795, HO. 42/34–6, 54.

35. Customs officer Hume to the Treasury, 22 July 1795, T.1/751/2652. Mayor of Leicester to S. Smith, 25 July 1795, PC. 1/27/A56. *Gloucester Journal*, 8 Feb. 1796. 1800 harvest returns from vicars of Colne and Colmer, HO. 42/53–4. Hampshire window-surveyor's 1800 harvest return, PRO. 30/8/291, ff. 45, 65.

36. For example, the campaign by the crusty Maidenhead JP (who went on to write a tract against speculative trading) against traditional market offences can be followed in the *Reading Mercury*, 27 Apr., 20 July and 31 Aug. 1795. Thompson, 'Moral economy. . .', pp. 81 and 97. Fortescue to Portland, 11 Apr. 1795, HO. 42/34. Undated paper among Staffordshire Quarter Sessions papers, Staffs. CRO. Q/SB/1795. G.C. Miller, *Blackburn, the Evolution of a Cotton Town*, (Blackburn, 1951), p. 61. J. Ayres (ed), *Paupers and Pig Killers: the Diary of William Holland a Somerset Parson, 1799–1818*, (1986 edition), pp. 16, 43, 47–8, 51

37. *Sussex Weekly Advertiser*, 24 and 31 Mar. 1800. *Kentish Chronicle*, 20 Jan. 1801.

38. *Sussex Weekly Advertiser*, 5 Nov. 1795. Letter from R. Eascott, forwarded to Portland, Mar. 1795, PC. 1/24/A47. *Gloucester Journal*, 23 Nov. 1795. Haden to Portland, 10 May and 14 Sept. 1800, HO. 42/50–1. Gloucestershire Quarter Sessions to the War Office, May 1800, WO 40/17. *Sherborne Mercury*, 6 Apr. 1795. Oxfordshire Quarter Sessions minutes, 1 Aug. 1795, OCRO, QSM/I/5. *Norfolk Chronicle*, 21 Nov. 1795. *Newcastle Courant*, 5 Mar. 1796.

39. *Oxford Journal*, 18 Oct. 1800. Petition to the House of Commons, 17 Feb. 1800, *JHC*, vol. 55, pp. 188–9.

40. Devaynes to Pitt, 13 Mar. 1795, PRO. 30/8/129, ff. 190–1. *The Times*, 17 Apr. 1795. *Minutes*, 27 Apr. 1795.

41. T. Pennant, Liverpool, to Kenyon, 8 Mar. 1795, G.T. Kenyon, *The Life of Lloyd the First Lord Kenyon*, (1873), pp. 323–4, 388.

42. *Annals of Agriculture*, XXV, (1795), pp. 110–1. *Blackburn Mail*, 7 Oct. 1795. Unsolicited information of T. Smallwood, 12 Sept. 1795; bail form of Sarah Reeves, 23 Sept., and Staffordshire jail list 8 Oct; conviction of E. Load, Staffs. CRO. Quarter Sessions files and minutes, Michaelmas Sessions, 1795, Q/SB, 1795: Q/SO/21, f.57. *The Times*, 19 Oct. 1795.

43. Among the many examples:–
Birmingham: several prosecutions ordered by a special association to prosecute offenders, WCRO. QS. 39/10; 42/1.
Warwick: two farmers fined for regrating in the borough market, 17 Sept., WCRO. Warwick Corporation Records, W/7/65.
Sheffield: indictments against S. Fowler, and J. Saunders, 'Brokers', for buying eels en route for market, 30 June 1796, WYRO. Quarter Sessions Roll, Michaelmas, 1796.
Newcastle-upon-Tyne: conviction of T. Simpson, Easter 1796, Newcastle City Archives, Borough Quarter Sessions minutes 1762–96, p. 307.
Chesterfield: conviction, Michaelmas 1796, of R. Melward, Longuer, Staffordshire, for regrating cheese, Derby CRO. Quarter Sessions Orders 1795–8, ff. 116–7.
Salisbury: guilty pleas of J. Game, and R. Looke, for forestalling, and J. Shergold, for regrating, summer Assizes, Ass. 23/8.

44. E.g. alleged regrating offences at markets at Ancaster, Lincolnshire, and Cheriton Fitzpaine, Devon, both committed by butchers; Lincs. CRO., Kesteven Division, Quarter Sessions minutes, 1795–1802, ff. 27–8; DCRO, Quarter Sessions Roll, 1796, 3/4A/10G.

45. E.g. indictment of J. Higgins of Wells, Somerset, for purchasing 100 lbs of cheese, for £21, while en route to Wincanton market, SCRO, Quarter Sessions Order Book QO.1. 2/4(2), p. 335.

46. Five unconnected cases, involving wheat and potatoes, heard at the Michaelmas 1795 and Easter 1796 Quarter Sessions, Dur. CRO, QOB. 15, pp. 577, 596–7.

47. Twenty-two in Gloucestershire by Jan. 1796; *Gloucester Journal*, 18 Jan. 1796.

48. The Birmingham Association's informer proved incompetent; he pleaded for reinstatement, 'being confident the failure of their last attempts was not owing to him': one indictment was 'withdrawn by the prosecutor being wrong'; WCRO. QS. 32/2 (Epiphany 1796).
49. E.g. J. Wooten, fined £10 and imprisoned for regrating eggs in Weymouth market. This severity may derive from another outstanding case against him for an offence at Dorchester. *Exeter Flying Post*, 21 July, 1796. J. Pattinson of Durham was fined five guineas, and imprisoned for five months for engrossing wheat, Dur. CRO. QOB. 15, p. 597.
50. Watson and Son, Warren House, to Hawkesbury, 5 Nov; Cawthorne to the Lord Mayor of London, 16 Nov; Pownall, 25 Sept, and Rose, 27 Oct. 1795, to the Privy Council, PC. 1/29/A66; 1/30/A63, A71.
51. Lancs. CRO. PR. 2067. Bowes to Portland, and J. King's reply, 17 and 20 May 1800, HO. 42/50; 43/11, pp. 488–9.
52. Kenyon developed a personal hatred of Waddington, whose subsequent 'very reduced circumstances' were gleefully reported in a letter from the judge to his son, 30 July 1801, Kenyon, *op. cit.*, pp. 38–7. *Kentish Chronicle*, 11 Feb. 1800. *The Times*, 14 Feb. 1800. *Gentleman's Magazine*, Aug. 1800, pp. 788–9.
53. *The Times*, 17 May 1800. *Hull Advertizer*, 26 July 1800. *Nottingham Journal*, 19 July and 9 Aug. 1800.
54. L. Horner, *Memoirs of Francis Horner*, (Edinburgh, 1849 edition), pp. 71, 79–80, 90–3.
55. Elizabeth to Rev. Heber, 5 July 1800, R.H. Cholmodeley (ed), *The Heber Letters 1783–1832*, (1950), p. 119. Ayres, *op. cit.*, p. 41. Portland to W. Baker, MP, 24 Aug. 1800, HO. 43/12, pp. 78–82. *DPD*, 3rd. ser. vol. XII, pp. 251–72, 427–49. The Board of Trade's enquiry and the London Flour Company Act are examined below, pp. 196–8, 217–8.
56. *DPD, loc. cit.* Sheffield to Liverpool, and reply, 24 and 30 July 1800, BL. Add. Mss. 38234, ff. 115–7; 38311, ff. 136–40. Hawkesbury, 5 July 1800, and Grenville n.d. to Pitt, PRO 30/58/3, ff. 45, 50.
57. Fawkener to Liverpool, 9 Aug. 1800, BL. Add. Mss. 38234, ff. 141–3.
58. E.g. Walsall petition, Folliott, and C. Preston, to Portland, 13, 19 and 21 Sept. 1800, HO. 42/51.
59. *Hull Advertizer*, 20 Sept. 1800.
60. HO. 42/52
61. 1800 harvest return; cf. those from vicars of Bowden, and Haslingden, HO. 42/54–5.
62. L.V. Harcourt (ed), *The Diaries and Correspondence of the Rt. Hon. George Rose*, 2 vols. (1860), I, p. 282. Erskine to Kenyon, 15 Oct. 1800, *HMC*, 'Fourteenth Report', (1894), Kenyon Mss. appendix part iv, pp. 554–5. Wilberforce to Lord Muncaster, 5 Nov. 1800, R.I. and S. Wilberforce (eds), *The Correspondence of William Wilberforce*, 2 vols. (1840), I, pp. 217–8. Banks to Liverpool, 16, 28 and 29 Sept; Liverpool to Banks, 25 Sept. 1800, BL. Add. Mss. 38234, ff. 152–3, 164–7; 38311, ff. 158–65. Pitt to Addington, 29 Sept. and 9 Oct. 1800; Grenville to Pitt, 24 Oct. 1800, DCRO, SP. D152/Corr. 1800–1; Lord Stanhope, *Life of Pitt*, 4 vols. (1862), III, pp. 245–50.
63. (Grant), *The Great Metropolis*, 2 vols. (1836), II, p. 39. I.R. Christie, 'James Perry of the *Morning Chronicle*, 1756–1821', in *idem., Myth and Reality in Late Eighteenth-Century British Politics and Other Papers*, (1970). Perry's Morton estate was auctioned on 24 July 1824 following his death. It comprised a considerable number of fields on both sides of the river, a small country house, and a variety of outbuildings, one of which had been converted into a calico factory. The central feature, Lot 1, was his mill, 'for many years past considered as one of the best in the country'. Although it was water-powered, it cost £20,000 to build. On three floors, each with a storage capacity of 1,000 quarters, it could grind 300 per week. Sale catalogue, 'The Morton Estate', BL. pressmark, 799 m.26.
64. Lowndas to Liverpool, 1 Nov. 1800, BT. 6/139. *Morning Chronicle*, 22 and 29 Oct. 1800.

Chapter 6 *'A more honourable death than to be starv'd alive':* Taxation Populaire *and the 'Early Phases' of the Famines*

1. E.P. Thompson, 'The "moral economy" of the English crowd in the eighteenth century', *P&P*, 50, esp. pp. 76–9, and 120 note. *Idem.* 'The crime of anonymity', in D. Hay, P.

Linebaugh and Thompson (eds), *Albion's Fatal Tree,*. (1975), p. 263.

2. J. Walter and K. Wrightson, 'Dearth and the social order in early modern England', *P&P*, 71, (1976), pp. 26–7, 36.

3. J. Stevenson, 'Food riots in England, 1792–1818', in Stevenson and R. Quinault (eds), *Popular Protest and Public Order*, (1974), pp. 35–6, 56, 67.

4. D.E. Williams, 'Were "hunger" rioters really hungry? Some demographic evidence', *P&P*, 71, (1976), pp. 70–5. J. Bohstedt, *Riots and Community Politics in England and Wales 1790–1810*, (1983), p. 11.

5. Bohstedt, *op. cit.*, p. 12, and ch. 1 note 6; ch. 6, notes 138 and 151. Cf. the assumptions made by another North American scholar, F. Munger, 'Contentious gatherings in Lancashire England', in C. and L. Tilly (eds), *Class Conflict and Collective Action*, (1981), esp. p. 76 and note 5; Munger asserts that the scale of 'contentious gatherings' will emerge from three newspapers; greater 'supplementary' detail can then be amassed from 'whatever information is available from archival and secondary sources'. The former include the Home Office papers, but not the Palatinate's Assize records also held in the PRO. Munger's methodological muddle derives partly from this all too common ignorance among overseas scholars of English juridical idiosyncracies, and is aggravated by the use of unexplained 'annual data' for a mere nine sample years. The resultant findings are worthless.

6. Bohstedt, *op. cit.*, pp. 20–1, 41; cf. ch. 9, note 72.

7. *Ibid*, p. 166 and ch. 8 note 7. Cf. R.A.E. Wells, *Riot and Political Disaffection in Nottinghamshire in the Age of Revolutions 1776–1803*, (University of Nottingham, 1984).

8. Bohstedt, *op. cit.*, p. 204. *Norfolk Chronicle*, 6 Sept. 1800. Deputy-mayor Herring to Portland, 22 Sept. 1800, HO. 42/51. NNRO, Quarter Sessions minutes, Case 20 shelf 6, f. 25; Mayoralty Court Book, Case 16, Rep. 128, 37. For other examples of the mass mobilisations of the Norwich populace see below pp. 108–9.

9. Bohstedt, *op. cit.*, ch. 6 note 115. Depositions, 'The King on the Prosecution of the Constables of Great Bolton against William Crook', PL. 27/8, part ii; 28/40/3.

10. D.E. Williams, 'Morals, markets and the English crowd in 1766', *P&P*, 104, (1984), p. 70. Bohstedt, *op. cit.*, p. 154.

11. E. Moir, *The Justice of the Peace*, (1969), p. 122. Dawson to Fitzwilliam, 27 July 1801, SCL. WWM. F.45/20. Legge to J. King, 2 Sept. 1801, HO. 42/62. Taylor to J. Brooke, steward to the Duke of Marlborough, 22 Sept. 1800, BCRO. D/Esv (M), B.

12. P. Storey, 4 May, and Messrs. Gunter and Abrahams, 26 July 1800, to the War Office, WO. 40/17. Portland to W.E. Taunton, 8 Sept. 1800, and anon. to Portland, 12 Apr. 1801, HO. 42/51, 61. Cf. Bohstedt, *op. cit.*, ch. 1.

13. T. Hayter, *The Army and the Crowd in Mid-Georgian England*, (1978) esp. pp. 9–15. L. Radzinowicz, *A History of English Criminal Law*, 4 vols. (1948–68), IV, pp. 146–52. Capt. Alexander to Windham, 6 May 1795, and endorsement by Adjutant-General Brownrigg; Whyte to the War Office, and to Lord Howard, 3 and 6 Aug. 1795; legal opinion, 1796, WO. 1/1082, ff. 99–102; 1/1094; 4/167: ECRO. D/DBy/012.

14. For magisterial attitudes see below pp. 260–65 and for Portland's pp. 254–58 below.

15. For example, George Lewis was listed as charged with assault in the Ilchester jail Calendar; in his case, three extant depositions prove that the offence occurred during a riotous sortie from the City of Bath, SCRO, Sessions Roll, CQ/3/168.

16. *Derby Mercury*, 8 Apr. 1801. J. Hopps to B. Gott, 29 Apr. 1800, W.B. Crump, 'The Leeds woollen industry, 1780–1820', *Publications of the Thoresby Society*, XXXII, (1931), p. 255. *Leicester Journal*, 24 Apr. 1795. Cf. the much more simplistic interpretation in Bohstedt, *op. cit.*, p. 12.

17. A.W. Dyson (ed), *William Metcalfe – His Book*, (Leeds, 1931), p. 29. *Leeds Intelligencer*, 4 Aug. 1800. *Cambridge Intelligencer*, 13 Sept. 1800.

18. Lonsdale, 2 Aug. 1795, Legge, 13 May, and Fitzwilliam, 3 Sept. 1800, to Portland; J. King to Bow St. magistrates, 23 Jan. 1795, HO. 42/35, 50–1; 43/6, p. 170. Sir Charles Graham and others to the War Office, 29 July 1795, WO. 1/1087, ff. 377–82. Rowbottom diary, 28 and 31 Oct 1799, OPL. *Newcastle Chronicle*, 1 Aug. 1795.

19. Bohstedt, *op. cit.*, pp. 4–7 and ch. 1 note 31. C. Tilley, in his 'Introduction', in Tilley, *loc. cit.*

20. J. Turner, 4 Aug, and Marquis Townsend, 10 Dec. 1795, to Portland; letters to the Home Office from Town Clerk Nottingham (draft), Fitzwilliam, the Birmingham Bench, and

D. Harris, 1, 3, 11 and 16 Sept. 1800, NCA. 3990, I.3: HO. 42/35, 37, 51; 48/20, ff. 234–5.

21. WYRO, Quarter Sessions Roll, Midsummer 1795. Chairman Taylor to Fitzwilliam, 29 July 1795, SCL. WWM. F44/45.

22. E.g. *Derby Mercury*, 15 May, 1800. A reward notice was issued in consequence of a riot on the 3rd, when a woman was assaulted and 'robbed' of her butter.

23. *Aris's Birmingham Gazette*, 29 Jan. 1800. *Staffordshire Advertiser*, 19 Apr. 1800.

24. A Lancaster diarist noted in Jan. 1796 that during 'this winter there has passed through Lancaster many hundred loads of meal every week which gives great disturbance to Lancaster mobs', though the historian of North-western food riots tabulates only one for the whole year. A. Booth, 'Food riots in the North-west of England, 1790–1801', *P&P*, 77, (1977), pp. 90, 96.

25. Mr. Charlesworth uses my 'patterning of the development of the crises in England', to map food riots to illustrate the 'composition of the various stages of the *crises de subsistence*'. A. Charlesworth (ed), *An Atlas of Rural Protest in Britain 1548–1900*, (1983), pp. 97–103.

26. G. Britton, Sledmere, to Sir C. Sykes, 3 Nov. 1799, HRO. DD. SY. W.1/66. Rowbottom diary, 28–31 Oct. 1799 and 3 Feb. 1800, OPL. *York Herald, The Iris*, and *Staffordshire ADvertiser*, 1, 14, and 15 Feb 1800. WYRO, Quarter Sessions Roll, Epiphany 1800, and minutes 1799–1801. Holland Watson, Stockport, to Windham, 2 Feb. 1800, WO. 40/17. Lord Chief Justice Mansfield to Portland, 27 Jan. 1801, HO. 47/26. Booth, *op. cit.*, pp. 89–90.

27. *Aris's Birmingham Gazette*, 10, 17 and 24 Feb. 1800. J. Sneyd, Belmont, to the War Office, 6 Feb. 1800, WO. 1/1105, ff. 441–4. Depositions, Staffordshire Lent Assize, 1800, Ass. 5/120, part iv.

28. *Aris's Birmingham Gazette*, 6 Apr. and 4 May 1795. *Derby Mercury*, 23 and 30 Apr. 1795. *Leicester Journal*, 24 Apr. 1795. Letters to the War Office from Capt. Sinclair, CO 22nd Light Dragoons, Coventry, J.G. Norbury, and J. Falconer, 19, 23 and 24 Apr. 1795, WO. 1/1092, ff. 33–6; 1/1093, ff. 267–8. J. Burnaby to Pitt, 6 Apr; Portland to the Duke of York, 9 and 14 Apr; Brownrigg to J. King, 10 Apr; Marquis of Hertford to Portland, 23 and 24 Apr. 1795, HO. 42/34; 51/147, ff. 75–6; 50/4, f. 197. J. Blackner, *A History of Nottingham*, (Nottingham, 1815), p. 391.

29. *Newcastle Chronicle*, 23 Apr. 2, 9 and 30 May 1795. *Newcastle Advertiser*, 9 and 23 May 1795. *The Iris*, 1 and 8 May 1795. *London Gazette*, 19 May 1795. *The Times*, 5 and 13 May 1800. For this major extension of truck, see below, and for the strike, pp. 294, 169–70.

30. Wells, *op. cit.*, pp. 13, 16, 26–7. Indictments, Salford Easter 1800 Quarter Sessions, Lancs. CRO. QSI/2/175. T. Ainsworth, Bolton, to Sir R. Peel, 12 Mar. 1801, HO. 42/61. *Billinge's Liverpool Advertiser*, 30 Mar. 1801. A.A. Shuttleworth, Hathersage, near Sheffield to W. Spencer-Stanhope, 19 Mar. 1801, SCL. SS 60588/595.

31. Rowbottom diary, 7 Nov. 1795, OPL. Printer's bill, Lancs. CRO, Quarter Sessions file, Epiphany 1800. Mayor of Plymouth to Fortescue, with enclosure, 2 May 1801, DCRO, FLP. D1262/L53. Depositions of 'Gardener' Heason, butchers Cantrill and Tomkins, and W. Hill; various invoices for repairs, WCRO, Quarter Sessions Files, Midsummer 1800 and Epiphany 1801, QS. 32/2. Birmingham Postmaster to J. Freeling, 2 and 3 May; Birmingham Bench, with enclosures, and Legge, to Portland, 5 and 13 May 1800, HO. 42/50, 215; 48/9, ff. 80–3.

32. For which see E.J. Hobsbawm and G. Rudé, *Captain Swing*, (1973 edition), p. 39.

33. Earl Gower, with enclosure, to Portland, 29 Apr. and 1 May 1800: T. Dudley, Dudley, to Dundas 7 Nov. 1800, HO. 42/49–50; 50/48. Letter from F.M. Sparrow, n.d. but Apr/May 1800, Shropshire CRO, 665/5968. Indictments, Staffordshire Summer Assize 1800, and numerous depositions by farmers, their wives, and servants, 1 and 2 May 1800, Ass. 5/120, part iv. Indictments, and Warwick county jail register, WCRO, Quarter Sessions File, Midsummer 1800, QS. 32/2. *The Times*, 1 and 2 May 1800. *Staffordshire Advertiser*, 3 May 1800, 3 and 17 Apr. 1801. *Aris's Birmingham Gazette*, 5 May and 21 July 1800, and 30 Mar. and 6 Apr. 1801. *Derby Mercury*, 2 Apr. 1801.

34. See below, pp. 116–19.

35. R. Wells, *Insurrection: the British Experience 1795–1803*, (Gloucester, 1983), pp. 79–83. *Idem.*, 'The Militia mutinies of 1795', in J. Rule, (ed), *Outside the Law: Studies in Crime and Order 1650–1850*, (University of Exeter, 1982), pp. 35–40 and sources cited therein.

36. R. Eastcott to Lord Rolle, 28 Mar. 1795, NUL., Portland dep. PwF. 9847. Anon. to the
     Home Office, 30 Mar; D. Foulkes, Medland, and W. Elford, to Portland, both 6 Apr.
     1795, HO. 42/34: PC. 1/24/A46. Fortescue to Portland (draft), 11 Apr; Elford, and J.B.
     Cholwich, Tiverton, to Fortescue, 11 and 19 Apr. 1795: indictment of Mary Plymsell, for
     riot and assault at Crediton, DCRO, FLP. D1262M/L3, L7: Quarter Sessions Roll,
     Midsummer 1795, 3/4A/10G. W. Smith, St. Budeaux, to R. Pole-Carew, 17 Apr. 1795,
     CCRO, Carew Mss. CC/K/25. *Exeter Flying Post*, 30 Apr. 1795.
37. Indictments, Ass. 23/8. Mr. Gunter, Ashburton, and W. Byrne, to Portland, 4 and 6
     May, 1795, HO. 42/34. *Exeter Flying Post*, 16, 23 and 30 Apr., 7 May and 6 Aug. 1795. A.
     Jenkins, *A History of Exeter*, (2nd edition, 1841), pp. 222–3. Cf. the account in Bohstedt,
     op. cit. pp. 37, 39, 43, 65 and esp. ch. 2 note 98.
38. Mayor of Plymouth to Portland, 6 Apr. 1795, HO. 42/34. J. Sabine, Lennox's secretary,
     to Windham, 5 Apr. 1795, WO. 1/1093, ff. 245–7. Elford to Fortescue, 4 Apr. 1795,
     DCRO, FLP. D1262M/L7.
39. These 1795 disturbances in the Kingswood community were caused by an attempt by a
     tithe owner to increase it on coal. See correspondence of William Blathwayt, Mar. and
     Apr. 1795, GCRO, D1799/C170. General Rooke, Bristol, to Portland, 15 and 19 Mar,
     Mayor of Bristol to J. King, 17 Mar. 1795, HO. 42/34. Rooke to Windham, 16 and 17
     Mar. and 17 Apr. 1795, WO.1/1092, ff. 75–6, 83, 155, 161–2. J. Small to Rooke, 16 Apr.
     1795, HO. 50/23. *Sherborne Mercury*, 30 Mar. 1795. *Gloucester Journal*, 27 Apr. 1795. See
     also R.W. Malcolmson, '"A set of ungovernable people"; the Kingswood Colliers in the
     eighteenth century', in J. Brewer and J. Styles (eds), *An Ungovernable People, The English
     and their Law in the Seventeenth and Eighteenth Centuries*, (1980).
40. Archdeacon Turner to Portland, with enclosed depositions, 25 Apr; Portland to the War
     Office, and reply, both 29 Apr, and to Turner, 7 May; Duke of York to Lt. Col. Shaw, 29
     Apr. and reply, 1 May 1795, HO. 42/34; 43/6, pp. 400–1; 50/4, ff. 297, 313–4, 317–24.
41. Abingdon petition, 11 Feb; Mr. Lovedon, to Charles Dundas MP, Chairman Berkshire
     Sessions, and to the War Office, both 8 Apr; Rev. Watts to Dundas, 8 and 13 Apr;
     Dundas to Windham, 8 Apr; CO 122nd Regiment to Windham, 28 Mar, and unknown to
     Windham, 6 June 1795, WO. 1/1089, ff. 683–4; 1/1090 ff. 94–5; 40/17.
42. *Kentish Chronicle*, 6 Feb. and 3 Apr. 1795. *Sussex Weekly Advertiser*, 23 Feb, 9 and 16 Mar.
     1795. Miller Jacques, Lamberhurst, to the Home Office, 22 Jan. 1795, HO. 42/34. E.
     Hussey, 25 Jan, and Chatham Bench 25 Mar, to the War Office; Chatham Bench to
     Dalrymple, 26 Mar; Dalrymple to the War Office, 6 Apr. 1795, WO. 1/1084, ff. 241–2;
     1/1085, ff. 151–4, 175–7; 1/1088, ff. 33–4.
43. *Sussex Weekly Advertiser*, 16, 23 and 30 Mar, and 20 Apr. 1795. *Kentish Chronicle*, 31 Mar,
     17 and 24 Apr. 1795. *The Times*, 11 Apr. 1795. Mayors of Canterbury, 31 Mar, and
     Portsmouth, 12 Apr. 1795, to Portland, HO. 42/34. Mayor of Arundel to the War Office,
     Mayor of Chichester to Richmond, and Richmond to Windham, all 13 Apr; Bishopp to
     the War Office, 15 Apr. 1795, WO. 1/1082, ff. 27–8, 87; 1/1092, ff. 139–47.
44. *Sussex Weekly Advertiser*, 20 Apr. 1795. Richmond to Windham, 13 Apr; Bishopp to the
     War Office, 15 Apr. 1795. Major Atherstone's evidence, Court Martial of Oxfordshires,
     WO. 1/1082, ff. 27–8, 1/1092, ff. 139–47; 71–170.
45. This account is based on the very full transcript of the Court Martial proceedings, WO.
     71/170, supplemented by Capt. Harben, to the War Office, 17 Apr, WO. 1/1088, ff.
     117–9, the report of Mr. Justice Buller on the Special Commission and the clemency pleas
     from civilians sentenced to death, Richmond to York, 21 Apr, H. Shelley, and W.B.
     Langridge, to Portland, both enclosing claims for damages from local publicans and
     others, 15 and 20 June 1795, HO. 42/35; 47/18; 40/4, ff. 273–83, and petition of J. Inskip
     for damages, 27 June 1796, T. 1/770/3196; other accounts of the mutiny and trials,
     Sheffield to Portland, 29 July 1795, NUL, Portland dep. PWF.5181; *Sussex Weekly
     Advertiser*, 20 Apr, 25 May and 1 June 1795. *The Times*, 21 Apr. 1795.
46. *Sussex Weekly Advertiser*, 20 and 27 Apr. and 1 June 1795. *Kentish Chronicle*, 24 and 28
     Apr. 1795. *The Times*, 25 Apr. 1795. *Reading Mercury*, 27 Apr. 1795. Richmond to York,
     and reply, 21 and 22 Apr. 1795, HO. 50/4, ff. 273–88. E. Milner Jnr. to the War Office,
     21 Apr. 1795, WO.1/1088. ff. 133–6. Rowbottom diary, 12 June 1795, OPL. W. Lee,
     Lewes, to Richmond, with enclosure, 15 June 1795, HO. 42/35. DCRO., Exeter City
     archives, Box 11, Quarter Sessions papers, 1794–1802, indictment of Thomas Goss.
47. *DPD*, 2nd ser. vol. 41. pp. 206, 333–47. Unsigned memo n.d. WO. 1/1092, f. 149.

Kentish Chronicle, 24 Apr. 1795.
48. For the prosecutions of the Oxfordshire militiamen and the civilians, see below pp.
49. WO. 71/170. Indictments, Ass. 35/235. *DPD, loc. cit. Sussex Weekly Advertiser,* 20 Apr, 1 June and 27 July 1795. *Kentish Chronicle,* 24 Apr. 1795. *Reading Mercury,* 27 Apr. 1795. Mayor of Hastings to the War Office, 26 Apr. 1795, WO.1/1088, ff. 151–4. Prosecution briefs, TS. 11/944/3431–2. Lt. Col. Sneyd, 23 May, and Portland, 19 June 1795, to Lord Uxbridge, HO. 42/34; 43/6, p. 437.

Chapter 7 *'Taking Bread out of our Mouths' : the Crowd, Food Transportation, and the Midsummer Hypercrisis of 1795*

1. Cf. Rev. Knollis, 20 July, and Sir. C. Willoughby, 7 Aug. 1795, to Portland, HO. 42/35.
2. Willoughby to Portland, 28 June; Mr. Sparrow to the Home Office, n.d; Mark Lane Inspector Atkinson, report, 2 July 1795, HO. 42/35. Lord Cadogan, Thetford, to Windham, 14 May 1795, WO. 1/1084, ff. 515–6. Rous to Pitt, 7 July 1795, PRO. 30/8/171, ff. 108–9. *The Times,* 8 July 1795. *Reading Mercury,* 11 July 1795.
3. The reported exceptions comprise crowds demanding a combination of price reductions and wage increases in the Thetford district in Dec. 1794, in the Norwich area in Jan, and at West Dereham in Mar. 1795. Minor *taxation populaire* incidents occurred at Bury St. Edmunds and Norwich on 29 Apr. and 2 May, respectively, and a London-bound consignment of meat was stopped and sold off at reduced prices at Newmarket on 14 May 1795. R.J. Buxton to B. Gurney, 4 Dec. 1794, IESRO, Gurney Coll. (temporary deposit, 1972), vol. 7, No. 22. Buxton to Portland, 4 Dec. 1794, HO. 42/33. Mayor of Norwich to the War Office, 31 Jan. 1795, WO.1/1091, ff. 7–8. *Lincoln Rutland and Stamford Mercury,* 27 Mar. and 22 May 1795. *Norfolk Chronicle,* 9 May 1795. Prosecution cases, Norfolk Easter Quarter Sessions 1795, NNRO. Quarter Sessions Minutes, 1791–5.
4. *Bath Chronicle,* 22 July 1795. *The Times,* 22 July 1795. Hardwicke to Portland, 19 July 1795, HO. 42/35. A Gray, *The Town of Cambridge. A History,* (1925), p. 164.
5. Handbills issued by Saffron Walden authorities, 26 June, 10, 13, 18 and 28 July; Lord Howard to Cornwallis, and reply, and to the Mayor, all 27 July; R. Whyte, CO Lexden Camp, and Hall, to Howard, both 28 July 1795, and numerous depositions by witnesses, ECRO., D/DBy/012. Notice issued by Howard, 16 July 1795, BL. Add. Mss. 35642, f.126. Indictments of seventeen people, Essex Lent Assize, 1796, Ass. 35/236. 'Journals of the Hon. William Hervey 1755–1814', *Suffolk Green Books,* No. XIV, vol. 16, (Bury St. Edmunds, 1906), p. 410.
6. Hardwicke to Portland, 27 July 1795, HO 42/35. Draft brief, trial of Mary Killingbeck, ECRO, Michaelmas 1795 Quarter Sessions file, Q/SBb/361.
7. Letters to Portland from, Buckingham, 9 July, and Mayor of Bedford, 24 July and 7 Aug. 1795, HO. 42/35. Messrs. Fisher, Yarmouth, to C. Scott, government corn-agent, 14 July; aide-de-camp Yarmouth, to Commissary-general Bissett, 15 July; W.E. Taunton, Oxford, to Portland, with enclosure, 6 Aug. 1795, PC. 1/27/A55; 1/29/A64. Resolutions of Oxford Corporation, *Reading Mercury,* 13 July and 3 Aug. 1795. Rev. Bagshaw-Stevens, diary 17 July, and letter to G. Greaves, 7 Aug. 1795, G. Galbraith (ed), *The Journal of the Rev. William Bagshaw-Stevens,* (Oxford, 1965), pp. 271, 276–7.
8. Paul to the War Office, 20 and 21 July 1795, WO.1/1091. Depositions, Herefordshire, T. Moore 24 June; Oxfordshire, Higgens and others, Ass. 5/116, part i. Town Clerk Tewkesbury, 25 June, and Willoughby, 7 Aug, to Portland; Baron Thompson's report on trial of five women at Gloucestershire Summer Assize 1795, HO. 42/35; 47/18. *The Times,* 2 July 1795. *Derby Mercury,* 30 July 1795.
9. *The Times,* 8 July 1795. Kay's deposition, Ass. 5/116, part i. W. Villiers to the Privy Council, 27 Aug. 1795, PC. 1/30/A68. Paul to the War Office, 20, 21 (twice) and 26 July, and 4 Aug. 1795, WO. 1/1091.
10. Indictments and examinations, NYRO, Quarter Sessions Michaelmas 1795 file. Buxton to Sir J. Woodhouse, July 1795, PC. 1/27/A56. *Norfolk Chronicle,* 8 Aug. 1795.
11. Miller Youell, diary 15 July 1795, NNRO, D87. Messrs. Fisher to Scott, 14 July; J. Lance to Bissett, 15 July; letters to Portland from Rev. Knollis, 20 July, Mayor of Coventry, with enclosures, 22 July, Mayor of Bedford, 24 July, and Mayor of Nottingham, 6 Aug;

petitions to the Privy Council, from the 'Principal Inhabitants' of Wells, 20 July, and Lovell, 22 July; Lovell to P. Colquhoun, 5 Aug; complaint of baker Charlwood of Woodstock, 14 Aug; J. and W. Squire, Peterborough, to Pitt, 22 July 1795, HO. 42/35: PC. 1/27/A55–6; 1/29/A64. R.H. Gretton, *The Burford Records*, (Oxford, 1920), pp. 129–30.

12. BL. Place Newspaper Coll., vol. 37, f.41. R.A.E. Wells, 'Dearth and distress in Yorkshire 1793–1802', *Borthwick Papers*, 52, (University of York, 1977), p. 26.

13. The government's policies respecting the distribution of its own corn supplies are considered below, ch. 11.

14. Mayor of Chester to the War Office, 31 May 1795, WO. 1/1084, ff. 549–50. W. Villiers, Birmingham to the Burford Bench, 8 Aug; Mayor of Leicester to S. Smith MP, 25 July; Knollis to Portland, 28 July 1795, PC. 1/27/A56; 1/29/A64. *Minutes*, 28 July 1795. T. Deverill, Thoby, to Major Frewen-Turner, 1 Aug. 1795, ESCRO, Frewen Mss. 1477. *Leicester Journal*, 13 Aug. 1795. *York Herald*, 17 Aug. 1795. P. Storey, Loughborough, 9 Aug., and W. Sheffingham, Leicester, to Windham, 12 Nov. 1795, WO.1/1093. J. Bohstedt, *Riots and Community Politics in England and Wales, 1790–1810*, (1983), pp. 1–3.

15. *Staffordshire Advertiser*, 6 and 13 June 1795. *Aris's Birmingham Gazette*, 8 June, 3 and 10 Aug. 1795. *The Times*, 25 June and 8 Aug. 1795. *Hull Packet*, 22 June 1795. Callow to the War Office, 22 and 24 June, 7, 30 and 31 July 1795, WO 1/1084, ff. 627–30, 635–6, 655, 693–6. Warwick to Portland, Garbett to Legge, both 29 July; Messrs. Spencer, Hicks and Villiers to Portland, 23 June 1795, HO. 42/35; PC. 1/29/A64. J. Randall, *A History of Madeley*, (1880), pp. 108–9. B. Trinder, *The Industrial Revolution in Shropshire*, (1973), pp. 380–1.

16. Like many other millers, Pickard also dealt in coal; he owned Snow Hill wharf, and had seven barges and thirteen carts. Sale notice, *Aris's Birmingham Gazette*, 15 Sept. 1800.

17. The question of radical participation in popular disturbances is reserved for ch. 9.

18. *Aris's Birmingham Gazette*, 29 June 1795. *The Times*, 25 and 26 June, 1795. *Annual Register*, 1795, pp. 25–6. Callow to the War Office, 23 June 1795, WO. 1/1084, ff. 627–30. Birmingham Bench to Portland, 23 June; I. Spooner to Morduant, 25 June 1795, HO. 42/35. Garbett to Hawkesbury, 3 July 1795, BL Add. Mss. 38230, f.200. W. MacRitchie, *Diary of a Tour through Great Britain in 1795*, (1897), p. 19.

19. R.A.E. Wells, *Riot and Political Disaffection in Nottinghamshire in the Age of Revolutions, 1776–1803*, (University of Nottingham, 1984), pp. 14–5.

20. Mayor of Richmond to the War Office, 7 June 1795, WO 1/1092, ff. 213–6. For disturbance in the West Riding outside Sheffield, see Wells 'Dearth and distress . . .', pp. 25–6.

21. WYRO, bail forms and indictments, Quarter Sessions files, Midsummer and Michaelmas 1795. M.A. Taylor, Sessions chairman, to Fitzwilliam, 29 July 1795, SCL, WWM. F44/45. *The Iris*, 26 June 1795.

22. *The Iris*, 7 and 14 Aug. 1795, and 29 Jan. 1796. *Hull Advertizer*, 6 Aug. 1795. *York Courant*, 17 Aug. 1795. Rev. Wilkinson to R. Ford, 8 Aug. 1795, NUL, Portland dep. PwF. 3843. J. Biran, Tontine Inn, Sheffield, to W. Hall, 5 Aug. (thrice); Fitzwilliam to Hall, 5 Aug. 1795: Mss. 'Minutes of the Trial of Montgomery', SCL, WWM Stewards' papers, 3 (vi), 1793–5; 6 (V), 1795–7: MD 2104, f. 58. JP's handbill, Sheffield, 5 Aug. 1795, YML, HH 3(2). W.E. Spencer, 'An Account of the Relief of Distress in Sheffield. . .1795', (Unpublished Mss. SCL). MacRitchie, *op. cit.*, p. 109.

23. Letters to Windham from, General Musgrave, 13 Aug. and Holland Watson, 1 and 5 Aug. 1795, WO. 1/1090, ff. 455–6; 1/1094. W. Hill, Ormskirk, to Portland, 8 Aug. 1795, HO. 42/35. Indictments for riotous assembly, Manchester, 27 July 1795, Lancs. CRO. Quarter Sessions file, QSO. 2/104. *Manchester Mercury*, 4 and 11 Aug. 1795. *The Times*, 8 Aug. 1795. W.E.A. Axon, *The Annals of Manchester*, (1886), p. 122.

24. Rowbottom diary, 30 July to 4 Aug. 1795, OPL. *Blackburn Mail*, 12 Aug. 1795. Letters to the War Office from Rev. T. Drake, Col. J. Entwisle, and Col. J. Hunt, 3, 5 and 9 Aug. 1795, WO 1/1086, ff. 99–102; 1/1088, ff. 393–4.

25. J. Latimer, *Annals of Bristol in the Eighteenth and Nineteenth Centuries*, 2 vols. (Reprinted, Bath, 1970), II, p. 516. Rooke to Windham, 7 June; Cerjal to the War Office, 21 July 1795, WO 1/1084, ff. 683–4; 1/1092, ff. 221–2. *Leicester Journal*, 24 July 1795. *Hull Packet*, 8 Aug. 1795. *Hull Advertizer*, 11 Aug. 1795.

26. J. Stevenson, 'The London "Crimp" riots of 1794', *Int. Rev. SH*, XVI, (1971). For

metropolitan disturbances in the summer of 1795, see below pp. 136–38.

27. A series of disturbances in several market towns, which extended to the villages, with seizures of road shipments, intermixed with price-fixing, came to a climax with the temporary closure of the port of Wells in December. Letters to the War Office from Rev. W. Butts, 25 Sept, Lord Cadogan 22 Oct. and 3 Nov, R.J. Buxton, 23 Oct, J. Frere 20 and 25 Oct, and C. Yorke, 31 Oct. 1795, WO 1/1083, ff. 343–6, 405–6; 1/1086; 1/1094. Letters to Portland from Lord Hardwicke, 19 Sept, Viscount Townsend, 16 and 22 Dec. 1795, and 5 Jan. 1796; Mr. Jodrell to Townsend, and Portland to York, both 23 Dec. 1795, HO. 42/36–8, 51/148, pp. 254–5. *The Times*, 16 Sept. 1795. *Norfolk Chronicle*, 24 Oct. 12 and 19 Dec. 1795. *London Gazette*, 2 Jan. 1796. B. Cozen-Hardy (ed), 'Mary Hardy's diary', *Norfolk Record Society*, 37, (1968), pp. 90–1.

28. For incidents in the 1795–6 season in Lancashire and Yorkshire, see depositions of G. and M. Brown, Kendal, 22 Jan. 1796, Ass. 45/39. T. Gill, Lancaster, to the War Office, 27 Jan. 1796, WO 40/17. *The Times*, 1 and 20 Oct. 1795. H. Cholmondeley, Howsham, to Portland, 5 Nov. 1795, HO. 42/36. Cart driver's deposition against Topcliffe women, NYRO, Quarter Sessions file, QSB/Epiphany 1796. T. Lister, Kettlelwell, to Fitzwilliam, 13 Feb. 1796, SCL. WWM. Y.17, and for attempts to deter Somerset merchants sending cargoes to South Wales in the spring of 1800, see various depositions, SCRO, Quarter Sessions files, Easter and Summer 1800, CQ/3/1/368–9, and threatening letter, Minehead, 23 Apr. 1800, HO. 42/49.

29. For the shift in Cornish farmers' marketing patterns, see above pp. 48–50.

30. E.G. Ross petition, 26 Apr. 1756, State Papers Domestic, 36/136, f. 107.

31. Mayor of Bristol to Richmond, with enclosure, 24 Feb. 1795, PRO. 30/8/177, ff. 216–33. P. Rashleigh to Pole-Carew, 25 Nov. 1795, CCRO, Carew Mss. CC/K/25.

32. J. Drowas to Hatton, 14 Apr. 1800, HO.42/49. Rev. J. Foley to Mr. Blagg, 31 Mar. 1801, GCRO, 421x/5/3.

33. *The Times*, 2 and 27 July, 1795. *Gloucester Journal*, 29 June, 2 and 16 Nov, 7 Dec. 1795, and 4 Apr. 1796. *Hereford Journal*, 4 and 18 Nov. 1795. *London Gazette*, 20 Nov. 1795 and 26 July 1796. Mayor of Gloucester to the War Office 24 July and 4 Aug; Mayor of Monmouth memorandum, 28 Nov. 1795, WO.1/1087, ff. 251–4; 1–1090, ff. 599–600; 1/1094. Sir G. Cornewall, 1 July, and Mayor of Gloucester, 4 Aug. 1795, and Mr. Justice Lawrence, reporting on the trials at Gloucestershire Lent Assize, 5 April, 1796, to Portland, HO. 42/35; 47/20. J. Matthews, to the Privy Council, 20 July 1795, PC. 1/27/A55.

34. Gloucestershire Quarter Sessions to the War Office, May 1800, WO. 40/17. Chepstow Bench, 16, 17 and 18 Mar., and Foley, 4 Apr. 1801, to Portland, HO. 42/61. GCRO, Quarter Sessions file, jail calendar, Midsummer 1801, Q/SG. *Gloucester Journal*, 7 Apr. 1800 and 6 Apr. 1801.

35. Letters to Portland from Mayor of Falmouth 10 Jan. and 10 Apr, Capt. Tremeneere, 11 Mar, Mayor of Penzance, 13 Mar, and Sir F. Bassett, 1 May: Rashleigh to Dundas, with enclosure, 31 Mar; J. James, Truro, to General Halse, 30 Mar; Mr. George, St. Austle, to Bassett, 27 and 30 Mar; reward notice, 14 Mar; Portland to the Mayor of Falmouth, 6 Jan. 1795, HO. 42/34; 43/6. Sir W. Moles to Lemon, with enclosure 27 Mar, and Bassett to J. King, with enclosures, 27 July 1795, PC. 1/27/A47; 1/27/A54. Rashleigh to Pole-Carew, 12 Apr; W. Wilson, Truro agent, to James Watt, 4 Aug; Giddy diary, 14 Mar. and 9 July 1795, CCRO, Carew Mss. CC/K/25; DDX. 3/8/8; DD. DG14. *Sherborne Mercury*, 30 Mar. and 20 Apr. 1795.

36. Helston Bench to Portland, Apr. 1796, HO. 42/39. *London Gazette*, 30 Apr. 1796. A.K. Hamilton-Jenkin, *The Cornish Miner*, (1927), pp. 163–4.

37. Rashleigh to Dundas, 30 Mar. 1795, PC. 1/24/A47. Sampson to Foster, 5 Nov. 1795; Major St. John, to General Morris with enclosure, 10 Apr. 1796; High Sheriff of Cornwall, 27 Apr, and Rev. Giddy, with enclosure, 16 Apr. 1796, to Portland: Drowas to Hatton, 14 Apr. 1800; T. Gregor, Grampound, to Portland, 31 Jan. and 4 Feb. 1801; J. King to Brownrigg, 21 and 22 Apr. 1796, HO. 42/36, 38, 49, 61; 51/148, pp. 308–11. Giddy diary, 6 Apr. and 6 June 1796, CCRO, DD. DG. 15. Giddy to Addington, 20 Apr. 1801, DCRO. SP. D152M/Corr. 1801. Indictments, Cornwall Summer Assize 1796, Ass. 23/8. *London Gazette*, 9 Jan. 1796. *Exeter Flying Post*, 14 and 21 Apr. 1796. *Gloucester Journal*, 25 Apr. 1796. *The Courier*, 20 Apr. 1801. *Bonner and Middleton's Bristol Journal*, 25 Apr. 1801.

38.   For importation policies, see below, ch. 11.

Chapter 8 'Glorious tho' Awfull Weeks'; the Hypercrisis of September 1800

1.   For public opinion at this juncture, see above pp. 86–9.
2.   Watson to Portland, 31 Aug, J. Golby, Nottingham, to John Stockley, White Lion, Lower Middleton Cheyney, Northamptonshire, 7 Sept. 1800, HO. 42/50–1. Coldham to Portland (draft), 1 Sept. 1800, D. Gray and V. Walker (eds), *Records of the Borough of Nottingham*, vol. 7 (Nottingham, 1948), pp. 395–6. J. Blackner, *A History of Nottingham*, (Nottingham, 1815), p. 393. *The Times*, 5 Sept. 1800.
3.   Capt. Boultby to Portland, 5 Sept. 1800, HO. 42/51. *The Times*, 5 Sept. 1800.
4.   *The Times*, 5 Sept. 1800. *Nottingham Journal*, 6 Sept. 1800. Mayoral handbills, 1 and 2 Sept, and draft letter to named householders, 2 Sept; C.H. Flinn to the Mayor, 6 Sept. 1800, NCA., 3990, I, 2i; 4ii; 20. Coldham to Portland (draft), 1 Sept., Gray and Walker, *loc. cit.* Blackner, *op. cit.*, p. 394. Watson to Portland, 3 Sept. 1800, HO. 42/51.
5.   Coldham to Portland, (draft) 3 Sept. 1800, NCA., 3990, I, 3. Watson, 3 Sept. and Mr. Bingham, Calverton, 15 Nov. 1800, to Portland, HO. 42/51, 53. *The Times*, 5 Sept. 1800.
6.   Nottingham Mayoral handbills, 2, 3, and 7 Sept; Coldham circular letter, 1 Sept, and replies from J. Bettison, Boultby, Clifton, and W.G. Williams, all 2 to 5 Sept. Davidson to committee established to record details of sales to millers, 3 Sept. 1800, NCA., 3990, I, 6–8, 14, 16i; IV, 4i and ii: M/479/231–2. *Nottingham Journal*, 6 Sept. 1800. Blackner, *op. cit.*, p. 374. Gray and Waller, *op. cit.*, pp. 398–9. Mansfield Bench handbill, YML., HH. 3(2). Watson to Portland, and Golby to Stockley, both 7 Sept. 1800, HO. 42/51.
7.   Emmerton to his brother, 11 Sept. 1800, Notts. CRO. DD. SY. 284/4. Letters to Coldham from Boultby, Flinn, Anna Newcastle, Isabel Wright, H. Breedon, J. Bettinson, J. Strong, J. Newton, and S. Davarell, all 3–11 Sept: Davison to Mayor Oldknow, 8 Sept; returns of corn sold, 4 to 9 Sept. 1800, NCA., I, 16i, 20–1, 22–4, 26–7, 31; II, 4–10; III, 6. Watson to Portland, 7 Sept. 1800, HO. 42/51. Mansfield handbill, *loc. cit. Nottingham Journal*, 4 Oct. 1800.
8.   For government policy at this juncture, see below pp. 237–243.
9.   Letters to Portland from, Watson, 7 and – with enclosure – 17, Smith 13, and Coldham, 16 Sept. 1800, HO. 42/51. Boultby to Coldham, 5 Sept. 1800, NCA., 3990. I, 16i. Emmerton to his brother, 11 Sept. 1800, Notts. CRO, DD. SY. 284/4. *Nottingham Journal*, 4 Oct. 1800.
10.   *The Times*, 13 Sept. 1800. *Nottingham Journal*, 4 Oct. 1800. Emmerton to his brother, *loc. cit.* Letters to Portland, from Watson, 13 and 19, Smith 13, 16, 17 and 22, and Coldham, with enclosures, 22 Sept. 1800, HO. 42/51. Diary of Abigail Hawthorne: Nottingham Borough Quarter Sessions, bail forms, Michaelmas 1800 file: various handbills and related documents: Nottingham Corporation Minutes, 7 Nov. 1800. and 6 Jan. 1801, NCA. M23904: 193A: 3990, I, 35: CA. 3580, ff. 13, 20–1.
11.   *The Times*, 6, 13 and 15 Sept. 1800. *Blackburn Mail*, 27 Sept. *Derby Mercury*, 4 Sept. 1800. Sir. J. Banks to Liverpool, 3 and 6 Sept; W. Milnes to Banks, 9 Sept. 1800, BL. Add. Mss. 38234, ff. 138–47. Mayor of Chesterfield, Mr. Jefferend, Leicester, and Capt. Gebb, to Portland, 7, 8 and 29 Sept. 1800, HO. 42/51. P. Storey, Loughborough, and Abney, to the War Office, 11 and 16 Sept. 1800, WO. 40/17. A Temple-Patterson, *Radical Leicester*, (Leicester, 1954), pp. 83–4.
12.   Anon, Stourbridge, to Lord Aylesford, 26 Aug; Birmingham Bench to Portland, 11 Sept. 1800, HO. 42/50–1. Indictment of printer William Pearsall, WCRO, Michaelmas 1800 Quarter Sessions file, QS. 32/2. *Aris's Birmingham Gazette*, 15, 22 and 29 Sept. 1800. *The Times*, 16 Sept. 1800. *Morning Chronicle*, 23 Sept. 1800.
13.   Pearsall's indictment; depositions of C. Hide, E. Griffiths, constable Millward, and R. Smith, all of Birmingham, 15 Sept. 1800, WCRO, QS 32/2. *The Times*, 16 Sept. 1800. *Aris's Birmingham Gazette*, 15 Sept. 1800.
14.   *Aris's Birmingham Gazette*, 8, 15, 22 and 29 Sept., and 13 Oct. 1800. *The Times*, 18 and 23 Sept. 1800. *London Gazette*, 7 Oct. 1800. Birmingham Bench to Portland, 19 Sept. 1800, HO. 42/51.
15.   Wrottesley, 14 Sept, and Mayor of Walsall, 12 and 16 Sept. 1800, to the War Office, WO.

40/17. Petition of the Capital Burgesses of Walsall, 13 Sept: Kidderminster Bench, 13 Sept, and E. Monckton, with enclosures, 14 and 19 Sept. 1800, to Portland, HO. 42/51. Derbys. CRO, Quarter Sessions Minutes, 1798–1800, pp. 646–50; 1801–3, p. 3: gaol calendar, 1x/7. *Aris's Birmingham Gazette*, 15 and 22 Sept. 1800. *Staffordshire Advertiser*, 13 and 20 Sept. 1800. *The Times*, 22 Sept. 1800. P.C.G. Webster, *The Records of the Queen's Own Regiment of Staffordshire Yeomanry*, (1870), p. 16. J.L. Cherry, *Stafford in Olden Times*, (1890), p. 10.

16. Rev. Dr. Hughes, to Portland, 4, 7, 14 and 15 Sept. 1800, HO. 42/51. J. King to the War Office, 9 Sept. 1800, WO. 40/17. *Oxford Journal*, 6 and 13 Sept. 1800.

17. Letters to Portland from, Mayor Walford of Banbury, enclosing Golby's letter, Hughes, and High Sheriff Williams of Oxfordshire; Bignell to Butler; Walford to Williams, all 12 to 24 Sept. 1800, HO. 42/51.

18. This and the following paragraph are based on witnesses' statements taken by the county magistracy after the Home Office ordered an inquiry prior to the intended prosecution of the outgoing Mayor; depositions of jailer Harris, turnkey Harris, prison porter Ecles, S. Field of the Banbury Volunteers, J. Lock jnr., and Rev. J. Graham; additional information from jailer to J. King, 16 Sept, Bignell to Butler, 15 Sept; statement of Town Clerk Taunton, 27 Sept; letters to Portland from, Cooke, 21 Sept, Willoughby, 17 and 21 Sept, and 3 Oct, and Dr. Marlow, 6 Oct. 1800, HO. 42/51–2; 48/9, ff. 238–65. *Oxford Journal*, 11 Oct. 1800.

19. R. Taylor, Witney, to J. Brook, Marlborough's steward, 22 Sept. 1800, BCRO., D/ESv/(m), B. 13, 15. 'An account of the proceedings of John Cobb, DD', sent to Portland, 26 Sept; deposition of miller Paine, 23 Sept; Hughes, 14 Sept, and Rev. J. Knollis and A. Gabell, 22 Sept. 1800, to Portland, HO. 42/51. *Oxford Journal*, 11 Oct. 1800.

20. Letters to Portland from, J. Latham, Romsey, 2 and 4 Sept, J. Jeffrey, Poole, 8 Sept, Mayor of Southampton, 9 Sept, and Bailiff of Blandford, 11 Sept. 1800, HO. 42/41. *The Times*, 8 Sept. 1800. *London Gazette*, 13 Sept. 1800. Romsey indictments, and Overton borough records, HCRO., QR/Michaelmas 1800.

21. East Anglian riots in Sept. include Stamford and Norwich (1st), King's Lynn (9th), Dereham (12th), and Cambridge (13th). Riots after the start of metropolitan disorders include Harwich and Chelmsford (18th), and Norwich (19th). *The Courier*, 9 Sept. 1800. *The Times*, 12, 19 and 22 Sept. 1800. *Norfolk Chronicle*, 6 and 20 Sept. 1800. *Chelmsford Chronicle*, 26 Sept. 1800. NNRO., City of Norwich Quarter Sessions minutes, Case 20, shelf b/25. Capt. Gebb, Chelmsford, and T. Herring, Norwich, to Portland, 18 and 19 Sept. 1800, HO. 42/51.

22. The physical-force radical faction's initial role was critical; for the relationships between popular political activists, and riot see below ch. 9.

23. Combe to Portland, 14 (with enclosures) and 15 Sept; J. King to J. Gifford, 15 Sept. 1800, HO. 42/51; 43/11, p. 87. *The Times*, 16 Sept. 1800. R.R. Sharpe, *London and the Kingdom*, 3 vols. (1892–5), III, pp. 241–2.

24. J. Somerby to Liverpool, 16 Sept. 1800, BL. Add. Mss. 38234. f. 155. Combe to Portland, 15 and 16 Sept. 1800, HO. 42/51. Sharpe, *loc. cit.* *Kentish Chronicle*, 19 Sept. 1800. *The Times*, 16 and 17 Sept. 1800.

25. Letters to the Home Office from, Combe, 16, 18 (with enclosure), and 20 Sept; R. Baker, 17 Sept, Sir. R. Ford n.d. (16 Sept.), Mr. Mares, 22 Sept. 1800 and Gifford, 9 Jan. 1801. HO. 42/51, 55, 61. M.D. George (ed), *Catalogue of Political and Personal Satires*, vol. VIII, (1950), pp. 624–6. J.J. Green, 'Some extracts from the diary of Susanna Gray', *Essex Review*, XVIII, (1909), pp. 153–4. *The Times*, 15 Sept. 1800.

26. *The Times*, 17 Sept. 1800. Combe, 16 and 17 Sept., and chief clerk, Union Hall Police Office, 16 Sept. (twice), to Portland; Whitechapel Bench to J. King, 17 Sept; Messrs Fyrrh and Wood, to Ford, n.d. but 16 Sept. 1800, HO. 42/51, 55. Sharpe, *loc. cit.*, pp. 242–5. *Kentish Chronicle*, 19 Sept. 1800.

27. *Kentish Chronicle*, 19 and 22 Sept. 1800. Combe to Portland, 16, 17 and 18 (twice) Sept. 1800, HO. 42/51. War Office to CO. Tower Hamlets Militia, 17 Sept. 1800, WO. 5/105, f. 187.

28. G. Story, Shadwell Police Office, 18 Sept, and Combe, 18 and 19 Sept. 1800, to Portland, HO. 42/51. *Kentish Chronicle*, 23 Sept. 1800. *The Times*, 20 Sept. 1800. Grimston to T. Grimston, 20 Sept. 1800, HRO, DD. G.R. 43/20. Smith to Spencer-Stanhope, 18 Sept.

1800, SCL., SS. 60556/4.

29. Loughborough to Auckland, 20 Sept. 1800, BL. Add. Mss. 34455, ff. 313–5. J. King to
     Major Elliott, Westminster Volunteer Cavalry, 16 and 18 Sept, and M. Lewis, War
     Office, 19 Sept; Combe to Portland, 19 and 20 Sept; Combe and various magistrates to
     the Home Office, 20–24 Sept; London stipendiaries, letter of thanks to all London
     Volunteer Corps, 24 Sept; Portland to Col. Herries, 22 Sept. 1800, HO. 42/51; 43/12, pp.
     139–40, 170; 51/154, p. 54. Portland to George III, 20 Sept. 1800, *Later Corr.* III, p. 415.
     The Times, 20 and 23 Sept. 1800.

30. *The Times*, 22 Sept. 1800. *Kentish Chronicle*, 26 Sept, 3 and 17 Oct. 1800. *Sussex Weekly
     Advertiser*, 22 and 29 Sept. 1800. *E. Johnson's British Gazette and Sunday Monitor*, 28 Sept.
     1800. 'Extract of a letter from Margate', in *Staffordshire Advertiser*, 4 Oct. 1800. Letters to
     Portland from, the Mayor of Rochester, A. Graham, Sheerness, Sir. E. Baker (with
     enclosures), W. Slaughter, Sandwich, Town Clerk of Southampton, Mayor of Ports-
     mouth (with enclosures), Lord Boyne (with enclosures), Tunbridge Wells, Duke of
     Richmond, Chichester, and W. Mitford (with enclosures), Petworth, all 18–29 Sept.
     1800, HO. 42/51. WSCRO, indictments, Michaelmas 1800, QR. W/631. A Fremantle
     (ed), *The Wynne diaries*, 3 vols. (1940), III, pp. 22–3. 'Journals of the Hon. William
     Hervey 1755–1814', *Suffolk Green Books*, no. XIV, vol. 16, (Bury St. Edmunds, 1906), p.
     436.

31. Letters to Portland from Fitzwilliam, 2 and 9 Sept., Rev. Wilkinson, 8 Sept, and W. Gott,
     21 Sept. 1800, HO. 42/51. H. Parker to Fitzwilliam, 2 Sept. 1800, SCL. WWM. F.44/50.
     The Iris, 28 Aug. and 25 Sept. 1800. *Hull Advertizer*, 27 Sept. 1800. *Newcastle Courant*, 27
     Sept. 1800. A. Booth, 'Food riots in the North-west of England 1790–1801', *P&P*, 77,
     (1977), p. 90.

32. Earl of Berkeley, 16 and 25 Sept., and Gen. Rooke, 18 Sept. 1800, to Portland, HO.
     42/51. Indictments, Ass. 25/1/3; 25/1/12. W. Salmon to Addington, 14 Sept. 1800,
     DCRO., SM. D152M/Corr. 1800. SCRO., Quarter Sessions Minutes, CQ. 2, 2/4/(3),
     pp. 194, 251.

33. Booth, *op. cit.*, p. 104.

Chapter 9 *'Promoting General Confusion': Popular Political Radicalism and Protest*

1.   The geography of the democratic presence is illustrated by Map 1 which is based on
     evidence contained in a considerable range of primary and secondary sources.

2.   H. Frensgrouse (sic) to T. Ashley, 30 Apr. 1796, BL. Add. Mss. 27815, ff. 53–4. E.P.
     Thompson, *The Making of the English Working Class*, (1968 edition), p. 201.

3.   H. Nicholas (ed), *The Letters of Joseph Ritson Esq.*, 2 vols. (1833), II, pp. 22–3.

4.   Buxton to Gurney, 11 Dec. 1794, IESRO, Gurney Coll. (temporary deposit 1972), vol.
     7, f. 22. *Leeds Intelligencer*, 17 Aug. 1795. C. Rashleigh to Dundas, with enclosures, 31
     Mar. 1795, HO. 42/34. Rashleigh to Pole-Carew, 12 Apr. 1795, CCRO, Carew Mss.
     CC/K/25. Mr. George, St. Austell, to Sir F. Bassett, 30 Mar. 1795, PC. 1/24/A47.

5.   For the Court Martial see below pp. Chatham Bench, 25 Mar, and Bishopp, 25 Apr.
     1795, to the War Office, WO. 1/1082, ff. 627–8; 1/1084, ff. 241–2.

6.   *Blackburn Mail*, 29 Apr. 1795. Black to Lincoln, July 1795, ECRO. D/DBy/012. Buxton
     to Gurney, *loc. cit.* Paul to the War Office, 21 July and 7 Aug. 1795, WO. 1/1091: PC.
     1/29/A64.

7.   Information of pilot James Holland and others, Sept. 1795, PL. 27/7, part i. For radical
     activity at this hostelry see deposition of jeweller John Hayes and others, July 1797, PL.
     27/7, part ii.

8.   A reference to the town's relief organisation, which had just increased the price of its
     subsidised bread.

9.   A reflection of the campaign to encourage new army recruits to intervene on behalf of the
     populace.

10. *Reading Mercury*, 27 Apr. 1795. *Sussex Weekly Advertiser*, 26 Apr. 1802. DCRO, City of
     Exeter Quarter Sessions Papers, 1794–1892, Box 11. W. Lee, Lewes, to the Duke of
     Richmond, with enclosure, 15 June; J. Spooner to Sir J. Morduant, 25 June 1795, HO.

42/35. For the full text of the Lewes Bill see E.P. Thompson, 'The crime of anonymity', in D. Hay, P. Linebaugh and Thompson (eds), *Albion's Fatal Tree*, (1975), pp. 337–8. *Gentleman's Magazine*, (1795), pp. 26–7. *The Times*, 26 June 1795. *York Courant*, 17 Aug. 1795. *Manchester Mercury*, 18 Aug. 1795.

11. Sheffield handbill, 5 Aug. 1795, YML., HH. 3(2). Birmingham reformers to the LCS, 10 July 1795, BL. Add. Mss. 27813, ff. 73–5. C. Jewson *The Jacobin City: A Portrait of Norwich 1788–1802*, (1975), pp. 63–4. Sir J. Carter to Portland, 25 July 1795, HO. 42/35.

12. A. Goodwin, *The Friends of Liberty*, (1979), pp. 372–4. Thompson, *The Making . . .*, pp. 153–4. Seized LCS documents and spy reports, PC. 1/23/A38.

13. For the nature and power of this sector of the press, esp. *after* 1795, see below pp. 143–4.

14. Sir J. Turton to Portland, 16 July 1795, HO. 42/35. Pamphlet advertisement, BL. Place Newspaper Coll. Vol. 37, f. 147. M.D. George, *Catalogue of Political and Personal Satires*, Vol. 7, (1942), pp. 184–5.

15. Portland to George III, 18 July 1795, *Later Corr.* II, p. 359. E. Heber to her father, 15 July 1795, R.H. Cholmondeley (ed), *The Heber Letters 1783–1832*, (1950), pp. 92–3. Letters to Portland from, Mr. Andrews JP, Westminster, Anon., Volunteer CO Le Meusieur (twice), D. Williams, Spitalfields, and Middlesex Sheriffs, all 15–17 July; J. King to Brownrigg, 14 July; Home Secretary, and various Home Office officials, to several London authorities, 27 June to 11 July 1795; J. Nares to J. King, 25 Apr. (and endorsement) and 1 May 1800, HO. 42/35, 49–50; 65/1, pp. 20–30. *Morning Chronicle*, 30 July 1795. BL. Place Newspaper Coll., vol. 37. f. 40. J. Ehrman, *The Younger Pitt: the Reluctant Transition*, (1983), p. 454.

16. Sheffield Constitutional Society, *Proceedings of a Public Meeting*, (Sheffield, 1795). LCS. General Committee Minutes, 20 Aug. 1795, BL. Add Mss. 27813, ff. 109–10. J.A. Busfeild, with enclosures, 9 Oct, and the Rev. Coulthurst, 16 Oct. 1795, to Portland, HO. 42/35. M. Thale (ed), *Selections from the Papers of the London Corresponding Society*, (Cambridge, 1983), p. 347.

17. Jewson, *op. cit.*, pp. 38–9, 46–8, 65. Norwich Patriotic Society to the LCS, 16 Sept. 1795, PC. 1/23/A38. Sir. J. Rous to Pitt, 7 July 1795, PRO. 30/8/178, ff. 108–9. R. Fellows to Portland, with enclosure, 19 Oct. 1795, HO. 42/36. Indictment of Breezer, NNRO, Quarter Sessions roll, Epiphany 1796. *Norfolk Chronicle*, 23 Jan. 1796.

18. W.H. Baker to Portland, with enclosure, c. 19 Oct. 1795, HO. 42/36. Powell's reports on LCS. General Committee, Aug. to Oct. 1795, PC. 1/23/A38. LCS. committee minutes, Aug to Oct. 1795, BL. Add. Mss. 27813, ff. 54–141. *Sussex Weekly Advertiser*, 19 Oct. 1795.

19. Powell reports, Sept. and Oct. 1795, PC. 1/23/A38. *Morning Chronicle*, 22 and 27 Oct. 1795. Unsigned report on Thelwall lectures, 25 Oct. 1795, HO. 42/37. Thelwall speech, cited E. Royle and J. Walvin, *English Radicals and Reform 1760–1848*, (1982), p. 76. *Tribune*, XXIX, 23 Sept. 1795. E. Gray (ed), *Man Midwife. The Further Experiences of John Knyveton MD . . . 1763–1809*, (1946), p. 156. A.D. Harvey, *Britain in the Early Nineteenth Century*, (1978), pp. 81–2.

20. Based on a series of detailed intelligence reports of debates and lectures at a number of metropolitan venues, Oct. to Dec. 1795, HO. 42/37.

21. Powell report, 23 Nov. 1795, PC. 1/23/A38. LCS bill signed Ashley, 12 Nov. 1795, and undated handbill, 'United Meeting of the Journeymen', BL. Place Newspaper Coll. Vol. 37. ff. 93, 97. Draft reply, LCS to Portsmouth Corresponding Society n.d. but Nov. 1795, BL. Add. Mss. 27815, f. 12.

22. Powell reports, 12 Dec. 1795, 7, 15 and 26 Jan, 13 and 15 Feb, 8 Mar, 21 Apr. and 23 Nov. 1796, PC. 1/23/A38. Letters to the LCS from, T. Jackson, Portsmouth, 9 Mar, R. Cooke, Gravesend, 15 Mar, and Melbourne Corresponding Society, 12 July; C. Clay, Selby, to watchmaker Edwards, 5 Sept. 1796; C. Bent, Salford, to M. Goodyear, n.d. (1796), BL. Add. Mss. 27815, ff. 29, 33, 49–50, 85–6, 120–1. *Manchester Mercury*, 1, 8 and 15 Dec. 1795. J. Bohstedt, *Riots and Community Politics in England and Wales 1790–1810*, (1983), pp. 120–4.

23. Goodwin, *op. cit.*, pp. 401–2. Deposition of constable Halliley, Dewsbury, 12 May 1796, WYRO, Midsummer 1796 Quarter Sessions file. *The Iris*, 3 Feb. 1797.

24. Draft LCS letter to Norwich, n.d. (1796), BL. Add. Mss. 27815, ff. 132–3.

25. Smallfield, Rochester, to the LCS, 3 July 1796: cf. Bent to Goodyear, (1796), BL. Add. Mss. 27815, ff. 49–50, 76. J. Money, *Experience and Identity. Birmingham and the West*

Midlands 1760–1800, (Manchester, 1977), pp. 268–9.

26. R.A.E. Wells, *Riot and Political Disaffection in Nottinghamshire in the Age of Revolutions 1776–1803*, (University of Nottingham, 1984), p. 20. Goodwin, *op. cit.*, pp. 375–8, 471–2. Jewson, *op. cit.*, pp. 71–3. F. Grace, 'Food riots in Suffolk in the eighteenth century', *Suffolk Review*, V, (1980), p. 41.

27. R. Wells, *Insurrection: the British Experience 1795–1803*, (Gloucester, 1983), ch. 3. Anon. to R. Ford, 10 Jan; Powell reports, 1 Nov. and 8 Dec. 1796, PC. 1/23/A38. J.G. Jones, *Sketch of a Political Tour through Rochester, Chatham, Maidstone, Gravesend*, (1796), pp. 25–6.

28. Powell to Ford, 28 Oct, 1796, PC. 1/23/A38. Draft, LCS. to Rochester Corresponding Society, n.d. (1796), BL. Add. Mss. 27815, ff. 51–2.

29. W. Goldson to Portland, with enclosures, including 'Promise to pay to Sir Timothy Takeall, or bearer the sum of Two Pence on the Abolition of Slavery and Establishment of Freedom', (also depicting John Bull groaning under the weight of the Salt Tax and Triple Assessment), HO. 42/50.

30. See above, pp. 124–5.

31. SCL, handbill collection, no. 1553. Information of J. Phillips, shoemaker, S. Benson, bookbinder, and R. Tackeray, tin-plate worker 7 July 1797, PL. 27/7, part i. General Rooke to Windham, 13 Nov. 1795. WO. 1/1092, ff. 401–2.

32. A reference to the illegalisation of the sale of fresh bread, see below, pp. 216–17.

33. *Leicester Journal*, 7 Mar. 1800. Letters to Portland from, H. Shadwell, Lewes, Sir. J. Heathfield, Staffordshire, both with enclosures, Mayor of Banbury, and High Sheriff of Oxfordshire, all 26 Apr. to 2 May, and Mayor of Ramsbury, with enclosure, 12 June; W. Wilshere, Hitchen, to the Marquis of Salisbury with enclosure, 13 Feb; Heathfield to Lord Gower, 30 Apr; and J. Gottswatt, Birmingham, to Sir. F. Freeling, 2 May 1800, with enclosure, HO. 42/49, 215. Mr. Lee, Malden, to Windham, with enclosure, 6 Feb. 1800, WO. 40/17. W. Sandley, Trowbridge, to Rooke, with enclosure, 18 May 1800, PC. 1/3490.

34. Town Clerk to Portland, 11 July 1797, HO. 42/41. For Whitehall's attitude to prosecutions see Wells, *Insurrection . . . ,* esp. p. 43; cf. C. Emsley, 'An aspect of Pitt's "Terror": prosecutions for sedition during the 1790s', *SH*, 6. No. 2. (1981).

35. Documents seized on Joseph Bacon, Apr. 1801, PC. 1/3526. Deputy Town Clerk, Bath, to the Master of the Rolls with enclosures, 13 and 16 Mar; letters to Portland from, Bowen, 17 May, and Mayor of Bath, 21 Oct. and 11 Nov. (with enclosures) 1800, HO. 42/49–50, 52–3.

36. Legge to Portland, 13 May; J. Golby to J. Stockley, 7 Sept. 1800, HO. 42/50–1.

37. Hodgson to Bacon, 14 May 1798; W.H. Reid, 21 May 1800, and J. Nares, 14 Feb. 1803, to R. Ford, PC. 1/3490; 1/3526; 1/3564. 'Declaration of the New Union of United Societies of England, Scotland, Wales and Ireland to the Parliament of the Aristocracy of those Countries', handwritten bill, sent to the Home Office, 2 Aug. 1800, HO. 42/50. For details see Wells, *Insurrection . . . , passim.* and M. Elliott, *Partners in Revolution. The United Irishmen and France*, (Princeton, 1982), *passim.*

38. York to Windham, 30 Jan. and 2 Feb., and reply, 1 Feb. 1800, WO. 40/13. York, memorandum, 1 Nov. 1801, *Later Corr.*, III, pp. 620–5. *The Times*, 11 Apr. 1800. Examination of Private J. Bark, Coldstream Guards, 20 May 1800, PC. 1/3490.

39. 'Secret Informat(ion)', stipendiary magistrate Nares, to Ford, with enclosure, 19 May; unidentified London stipendiary to Ford, n.d., and secret reports by 'R.B.' 19 and 21 May; depositions of S. Hopkins, 20 May 1800, PC. 1/3490.

40. *The Times* made an opaque reference to this, but not until 20 May 1800. Index to intelligence reports, 28 and 29 Apr. 1800, PRO. 30/58/8, f. 148. Examinations of Jackson and Bark, 18 and 20 May 1800, PC. 1/3490. Examinations of J. Howe, 21 and 24 July, and A. Howard, 25 July 1800, HO. 42/50.

41. *The Times*, 22 May 1800. T. Ellison, Dublin to E. Crocker, 23 May 1800, PC. 1/3490. Sir James Crauford to Grenville, with enclosures, 17 June 1800, HO. 42/50.

42. Unidentified stipendiary to Ford, *loc. cit.*

43. *Ibid.* As a result of his investigation with the firing party's captain, the stipendiary opined that 'we think it not best to make the matter public'.

44. The firing party immediately reloaded and fired again, 'which precluded the possibility of tracing the musquet from whence the ball came . . . the muzzle would have exhibited the

same mark'; *The Times*, 16, 17 and 26 May 1800. *The Times* also queried 'how a ball cartridge could be fired from a musquet ignorantly, as its weight is so very different from . . . a powder cartridge'. Although the firing party's cartouches had all been previously inspected by the officers in the prescribed fashion, the military privately convinced the unidentified stipendiary that after 'all the searching possible in Cartouch or other situations it will never be discovered who has a Ball Cartridge'; to Ford, *loc. cit.*

45. Lt. Col. Brownrigg to Field Officers, Guards, 3 June; Horse Guards orders, 16 and 23 May 1800, WO.3/22, p. 287; 3/33, pp. 7, 25–6. Circular from deputy adjutant-general to all officers, 16 May, published in *The Times*, 19 May: later reports in *The Times*, 23 and 26 May 1800, alleged that recent changes in the packaging of blanks and the use of old ammunition, had led to the wrongful issue of live rounds. This story, of course, failed to confront the key question of the considerable differences in cartridge weights. Nevertheless, this propaganda succeeded to an extent. Lord Morely was assured that there was 'every probability that it was accidental', while dining at the Marquis of Salisbury's house, in the company of senior government figures, including Westmoreland, Chatham and Wellesley: diary, 18 May 1800, BL. Add. Mss. 48246, ff. 79–80.

46. Anon. letter, 'For the King', 16 May; 'A Faithful Soldier' to stipendiary Sir. W. Addington, 17 May; Nares to Ford, 19 May; 'R.B.' report, 21 May; Bow St. Runner Amsden's report, and D. Collins to Portland, both 21 May; R. Wills, deposition, 22 May 1800, PC. 1/3490.

47. Col. Lennox to Portland, and draft, Home Office to Ford (?), both 17 May; examination C. Jackson, 18 May; J. Kirkby to J. King, and King to Dr. Munro, both 22 May; report of psychiatric doctors, Munro, Willis and Simmons, 12 June 1800, PC. 1/3490. Examination, Hadfield, 15 May 1800, TS. 11/937/223.

48. The main documentation is in PC. 1/3490; like other collections of its genre, further materials are contained among the relevant Treasury Solicitor's papers (TS. 11/937/223, for Hadfield), but the remainder have been deliberately removed. See Wells, *Insurrection . . .*, Ch. 2.

49. My italics, Buckingham to Grenville, 18 May 1800, HMC, 'Dropmore Mss', vol. 7, (1908), p. 231. Lord Morely's diary, 23 June 1800, BL. Add. Mss. 48246, ff. 94–5.

50. N. Walker, *Crime and Insanity in England: The Historical Perspective*, vol. I, (Edinburgh, 1968), pp. 74–83. *The Times*, 27 June 1800. Prosecution and defence briefs, TS. 11/937/223.

51. *The Times*, 17 May 1800. Evidence of Bow St. Runner Dowsett, 18 May 1800, PC. 1/3490. Truelock's examination, 16 May 1800, TS. 11/937/223.

52. *The Times*, 19 May 1800. J.F.C. Harrison, *The Second Coming*, (1979), p. 201. W.H. Reid to G. Canning, 17 May, and Ford, 21 May; deposition of S. Cook, 24 May 1800, PC. 1/3490.

53. Reid to Canning, n.d., 17 and 18 May, and to Ford (?) n.d. and 20 May; deposition of H. Howard, 19 May 1800, PC. 1/3490. Examination of Mrs. E. Hadfield, 16 May 1800, TS. 11/937/223. Hadfield went to Bedlam, where he remained despite some 'very sane' lobbying for his release, till his death in 1829. Truelock, who was also incarcerated for life, developed his millenarian fantasies in Bedlam, where he too stayed until the 1820s. J.A. Hone, *For the Cause of Truth; Radicalism in London 1796–1821*, (Oxford, 1982), p. 251 note. *Sketches in Bedlam*, (1823), pp. 16–25. *Sussex Advertiser*, 1829.

54. *The Times*, 17 May, 17 June and 11 July 1800. T. Curry, Portsmouth, with enclosure, 31 May, and G. Maxwell, Huntingdonshire, 15 June 1800, to Portland, HO. 42/50.

55. Brownrigg to Ford, and Ford's report, both 23 May; John Wilson, deposition, and undated notes, May to June, 1800, by Ford, J. King, and Portland, PC. 1/3490. Docket, endorsed by Ford, c. 22 July; Nares to Ford, 24 July 1800, HO. 42/50.

56. For Despard see Wells, *Insurrection . . .*, Ch. 11. M. Elliott, 'The "Despard Conspiracy" reconsidered', *P&P*, 75, (1977).

57. Lord Mayor of London, to Portland, with enclosures, 10 June; Bow Street Runner Amsden's report, 9 Dec. 1800, HO. 42/50, 55.

58. R. Laing, with enclosure, 11 Nov, and Bayley, 30 Nov, to Portland; Mr. Pearson to F. Freeling, 11 Oct. 1800, HO. 42/52–3. *The Times*, 18 Nov. 1800.

59. Home Office correspondence with the War Office, and London stipendiaries, Sept. to Dec. 1800, HO. 51/154, pp. 53–4, 57, 68–9, 83; 65/1.

60. Amsden's report, 9 Dec; Portland to the Birmingham Bench, c 24 (draft) and 30 Sept., to

the Rev. Corbett, 30 Sept. and Sir J. Wrottesley, 7 Oct. 1800, HO. 42/51, 55; 43/12, pp. 191–3, 217–8.

61. For a more detailed picture of the crisis of confidence, see below pp. 240–47. C. Lush, Shoreditch, 14 Oct., and Bayley, 18 Nov. both with enclosures, to Portland: Poster, 'Fellow Country Men', Cornhill, London, 17 Oct. 1800, HO. 42/52–3.

62. Index to intelligence reports, PRO. 30/58/8, f. 148. Wells, *Insurrection . . . , pp. 184–7. Idem., Riot and Political Disaffection . . . ,* pp. 32–4.

63. Letters to Portland, all with enclosures, from Equerry-in-Waiting, 13 Dec, Bailiff of Kidderminster, 17 Dec. 1800, and Mr. Lloyd, Lenham, Kent, 2 Jan. 1801, HO. 42/55, 61. *London Gazette*, 27 Dec. 1800.

64. I have to thank Dr Malcolm Chase of the University of Leeds, for providing several references to Spence's activities. T. Spence, *The Restorer of Society to its Natural State*, (1801). W. Hone to F. Place, 6 Nov. 1830, bound with a volume of Spencean tracts, including 1801 broadside, issued by 'The Real Friends to Truth, Justice and HUMAN HAPPINESS', London School of Economics, pressmark, R(SR) 422.

65. Amsden's report, 9 Dec. 1800; J.A. Busfeild to Fitzwilliam, with enclosure, 21 Mar, and Mayor of Leeds to the Home Office, with enclosure, 1 Aug 1801; letters to Portland from, justices Breton and Maxwell, with enclosures, Ashford, Kent, 1 Jan, T. Lamb, Rye, with enclosures, 14 Feb, T. Bancroft, Oldham, 7 Mar, and Fitzwilliam, 18 Apr. 1801, HO. 42/55, 61. Anon., Wolverhampton, to Lady Glynne, *London Gazette*, 13 Jan. 1801. T. Hardy to Major Cartwright, 24 Jan. 1801, BL. Add. Mss. 27818, ff. 16–9. M. Bethan-Edwards (ed), *The Autobiography of Arthur Young*, (1898), p. 366. Spence, *op. cit.*, p. 20.

66. Wells, *Insurrection . . . ,* chs. 10 and 11.

67. Simcoe to Fortescue, 28 Mar; memorandum, 'Force actually in the western District', 3 Apr. 1801, DCRO, FLP. D1262M/L59, L63. Simcoe to Addington, 30 Mar. 1801, cited G. Pellow, *The Life and Correspondence of Henry Addington, First Lord Sidmouth*, 3 vols. (1847), I, pp. 362–3. Simcoe to Portland, 28 Mar. and 3 Apr; Brownrigg to E.F. Hatton, 3 Apr; Portland to Fortescue, 12 Apr. 1801, HO. 42/61; 43/12, pp. 513–6.

68. For the development of the south-western crisis, see above pp. 48–50.

69. Letters to Fortescue from, R. Eales, Exeter, 23 Mar, Simcoe, 28 Mar, Mayor of Bideford, 15 Apr, and justice Montague, 4 May; Col. Taylor to Simcoe, 1 May 1801, DCRO, FLP. D1262M/L48, L52–3, L59. Simcoe to Portland, 27 Mar. 1801, HO. 42/61.

70. For details see R. Wells, 'The revolt of the south-west 1800–1; a study in English popular protest', *SH*, 1, no. 6. (1977), pp. 714–6 and sources cited there.

71. A policy developed after pressure from the Cornish Bench in 1796; *ibid.*, p. 720.

72. Anon. to J. Reeves, 9 Nov. 1792, BL. Add. Mss. 16927, ff. 41–2. Navy Board minute, 1 Apr; Commissioner Franshawe to the Board, 11 Apr. 1801, Adm. 106/1916, 2664. Franshawe to Fortescue, 27 Apr; Devonport JPs to Portland, 23 Apr; informer's report on Central Committee meeting, 15 Apr. 1801, HO. 42/61.

73. Much of this material was never forwarded to the Home Office, though some turns up in antiquarian collections; E.P. Thompson, 'The crime of anonymity', in D. Hay, P. Linebaugh and Thompson (eds), *Albion's Fatal Tree*, (1975), pp. 295, 340–1. Letters to Fortescue from, J.B. Cholwick, 24 Mar, CO's Dartmouth and Ippleden Volunteers, 7 and 18 Apr, Simcoe, 18 Apr, and W. Foot, 23 May 1801, DCRO, FLP. D1262M/L52–3, L59. Letters to Portland from, Fortescue, 14 and 24 (with enclosure) Apr, Mayor of Bideford, 8 Jan, and W.A. Sandford, 23 Mar: letter to Lt. Williams, enclosed S. Franshawe to Simcoe, 26 Mar; Eales to Rolle, with enclosure, 25 Apr. 1801, HO. 42/61.

74. MAF. 10/285. Simcoe to Portland, 5 Apr. 1801, HO. 42/61. J.J. Fortescue to Fortescue, 23 Mar. and 4 Apr. 1801, DCRO., FLP. D1262M/L53, L59. Wells, *op. cit., passim.*

75. Wells, *op. cit.*, pp. 742–3.

76. *Ibid*, pp. 726–7. Bastard to Addington, 4 May 1801, DCRO, SP. D152M/Corr. 1801.

77. Wells, *op. cit.*, pp. 726–7.

78. As argued by E.F. Genovese, 'The many faces of moral economy: a contribution to a debate', *P&P*, 58, (1973), p. 165.

79. Wells, *op. cit.*, pp. 734–8. J. Ayres (ed), *Paupers and Pig Killers; the Diary of William Holland a Somerset Parson 1799–1818*, (1986 edition), p. 71.

80. Ainsworth to Peel, 12 Mar. 1801, HO. 42/61. J. Bland, *The Average Depression of the Price of Wheat in War below that of the Preceeding Peace*, (1800), p. 2. Anon., Kingsbridge, to

Fortescue, 4 May 1801, DCRO, FLP. D1262M/L53.
81. *Cambridge Intelligencer*, 13 and 20 Sept. 1800.
82. Spence, *op. cit.*, esp. pp. 15–22.
83. R. Spillman to the Home Office, 25 Aug. 1793; Mayor of Banbury to Portland, 12, 17 (with enclosure), and 24 Sept, and to High Sheriff Williams, 11 Sept; R. Bignell to R. Butler, 15 Sept. 1800. HO. 42/26, 51. Mayor of Banbury to the War Office, 18 Sept. 1800, WO. 40/17.
84. J. Dixon to Fitzwilliam, 10 May 1802, SCL. WWM. F. 51/13.

Chapter 10   Conclusion: Famine, the Defences of the Poor, and the Threat to Public Order

1. See below p. 294.
2. See below pp. 290–94.
3. Indictments and jail calendar, West Sussex Midsummer Sessions, 1795, WSCRO., QR. W/610, ff. 18, 21, 84–5. HCRO., QR. Easter 1800. Lincs. CRO. Kesteven division, Quarter Sessions minutes 1798–1802, pp. 454–6.
4. Indictments and jail calendar, Somerset Lent Assize 1801, Ass. 25/1/3; 25/1/12. SCRO., Easter 1800 Quarter Sessions roll, CQ. 2. 3/1/368. Lt. Col. Elford, memorandum, 22 Mar. 1800, HO. 42/49. Smith's deposition, 18 Nov. 1795, and prosecution brief notes, Quarter Sessions files and papers, ECRO., 362/84; Q/SBb/361. *Sherborne Mercury*, 20 July 1795.
5. Richmond to Windham, 13 Apr. 1795, WO. 1/1092, ff. 139–47. *Sussex Weekly Advertiser*, 20 Apr.1795. *The Times*, 30 Sept. 1800. Rev. North, harvest return, 1800, HO. 42/54. HCRO., QR. Michaelmas 1800. R.J. Buxton to B. Gurney, 4 and 11 Dec. 1794, HO. 42/33; IESRO., Gurney Coll. vol. 7 (temporary deposit, 1972). *Bath Chronicle*, 22 July 1795.
6. 'Journals of the Hon. William Hervey 1755–1814', *Suffolk Green Books*, no. XIV, vol. 16, (Bury St. Edmunds, 1906), pp. 410–1. Ass. 31/17, p. 209; 25/236. Files of papers 'Commitment of Walden Rioters', and correspondence of Lord Howard re. riot, ECRO., D/DBy/012.
7. Indictments of rioters at Romsey and New Alresford, 1 and 25 Sept. 1800, HCRO., QR. Michaelmas 1800.
8. Documented disturbances are listed in Tables 1 to 5.
9. Including the example in the Baldock district of Hertfordshire, where a group went through 'several villages . . . Compelling the Labourers to joyn them under pretence of Reducing the Price of Bread and increasing their Wages'. P. Monoux, Sandy to ? 21 Mar. 1793, HO. 42/25.
10. Hurstpierpoint parish records, and West Sussex Quarter Sessions rolls, Epiphany and Easter 1795, WSCRO., Par. 400/37/33–62: QR. 608, ff. 58, 62; 609, ff. 51–3. *Reading Mercury*, 30 Mar. 1795. Indictments, Ass. 25/235. Sir. A. Hume, 11 July 1795, and H. Shadwell, 15 Feb. 1801, to Portland, HO. 42/35, 61.
11. *Sussex Weekly Advertiser*, 8 Feb., 8 Mar. and 25 Apr. 1796. J. Bohstedt, *Riot and Community Politics in England and Wales, 1790–1810*, (1983), pp. 188–92. A.F.J. Brown, *Essex at Work 1700–1815*, (Chelmsford, 1969), pp. 131–2. F. Grace, 'Food riots in Suffolk in the eighteenth century', *Suffolk Review*, V, (1980), p. 38.
12. Norfolk campaign; notice issued in *Norfolk Chronicle*, 14 Nov. 1795, and printed by Arthur Young without comment, *Annals of Agriculture*, XV, (1796), p. 503. On the local democratic campaign, see above pp. Two Hertfordshire MPs, Hume and Baker, wrote independently to Portland to complain at the effects of Whitbread's crusade, on 6 July 1795; HO. 42/35: NUL., Portland dep. PwF. 233. J. Uskerne, Hertford Loyalist Society, to John Reeves, 8 Jan. 1793, BL. Add. Mss. 16928, ff. 16–7.
13. For example, the high cost of food and the increased wages paid by farmers in the locality, was advanced by the labourers on one East Cornwall estate in support of a demand for more cash: the claim was initially resisted, but later granted by the landowner; manager W. Smith to R. Pole-Carew, 6 Dec. 1799 and later letters, CCRO., Carew Mss. CC/K/30.

14. W. Wilshire, Hitchen, to Marquis of Salisbury, 13 Feb, and Lord Leslie, Dorking, 7 Mar.
     1800, to Portland, HO. 42/49. *Sussex Weekly Advertiser*, 21 Apr. 1800 and 16 Mar. 1801.
     The Times, 14 Feb. 1801.
15. Essex; *The Times*, 14 June, 9 and 13 Aug. 1800. *Chelmsford Chronicle*, 13 June 1800.
     Morning Chronicle, 26 June 1800. Ass. 31/8. Essex Quarter Sessions papers, ECRO.,
     Q/SMf/29; Q/SBb/381/20. Berkshire: Newbury Bench to Windham, 10 June 1800, WO.
     40/17. *Reading Mercury*, 16 June 1800. Kent: Ass. 31/17, p. 158. E. Melling (ed), *Kentish
     Sources: Crime and Punishment*, (Maidstone, 1969), p. 152. Hampshire: HCRO, Quarter
     Sessions roll, Michaelmas 1800.
16. *DPD.*, 2nd. ser. vol. 43, pp. 247–8.
17. Prosecutor's brief, TS. 11/914. Indictments, Devon Epiphany 1801 Quarter Sessions roll,
     DCRO., 3/4B/1b.
18. *Reading Mercury*, 30 Mar. 1795. Mr. George, Bath, to the Master of the Rolls, 13 and 16
     Mar; Mr. Elws. Clare, to Dundas, 28 Jan; Poulett to Portland, 15 May 1800, all with
     enclosures, HO. 42/49–50; 50/47.
19. L. Edwin to Portland, 30 Aug. 1800, HO. 42/50. *London Gazette*, 1 Mar. 1800. *Derby
     Mercury*, 20 Feb. 1800 and 30 July 1801.
20. Sheffield to Pitt, 18 Dec. 1799, PRO. 30/8/177, ff. 233–5. G.Y. Fort to W. Hussey, 19
     Feb, and Mildmay to Hawkesbury, 2 and 4 Mar. 1800, HO. 42/49. *London Gazette*, 22
     Mar. 1800.
21. *London Gazette*, 22 Mar. 1800 and 13 Jan. 1801.
22. *Norfolk Chronicle*, 5 Dec. 1795. *Reading Mercury*, 2 Feb, 6 Apr, and 20 July 1795.
23. *Lincoln, Rutland and Stamford Mercury*, 10 Jan. 1796. *London Gazette*, 24 Jan. 1796.
24. *London Gazette*, 14 Apr. 1795 and 22 Jan. 1796.
25. *Ibid.*, 9 Apr. 1796. *The Iris*, 1 Apr. 1796.
26. Sheffield to Pitt 18 Dec. 1799, *loc. cit. London Gazette*, 23 Dec. 1799, 1 and 22 Mar, 10
     May, 12 and 19 July, and 16 Aug. 1800. *Sussex Weekly Advertiser*, 10, 24 and 31 Mar, 7
     and 21 Apr. and 12 May 1800. Letters to Portland from Mayor of Southampton, 26 Feb,
     Mayor of Romsey, 5 Mar, H. Shelley and W. Green, Lewes, 31 Mar, H.T. Shadwell,
     with enclosures, 17 Apr, M. Burgoyne, 2 May, T. Ruggles, 24 June and 6 July, and T.
     Hall, 14 July 1800, HO. 42/49–50. Hall to Braybrooke, 14 July, and Braybrooke to Essex
     Clerk of the Peace, with enclosures, 18 July 1800, ESCRO., Q/SBb/380/66/1–4.
     Chelmsford Chronicle, 27 June 1800. *Gentleman's Magazine*, Aug. 1800, p. 784.
27. Letters to Portland from, J. Sprude, 24 Oct, R.C. Barnard, 26 Oct, and Mr. Watts, Sun
     Fire Office, with enclosure, 1 Nov. 1800, HO. 42/52–3. HCRO., QR Midsummer 1800
     and Epiphany 1801. M. Thomas, 'The rioting crowd in Derbyshire in the eighteenth
     century', *Derbyshire Archaeological Journal* XLV, (1975), p. 41.
28. Buckingham to Portland, 2 Nov. 1800, HO. 42/53.
29. A. Charlesworth, 'The development of the English rural proletariat and social protest
     1700–1850; a comment', *Jnl. PS*, 8, 1, (1980), pp. 107–8. R.A.E. Wells, 'Social conflict
     and protest in the English countryside in the early eighteenth century; a rejoinder'. *Ibid.*,
     8, 4, (1981), pp. 526–7. Cf. Bohstedt, *op. cit.*, pp. 192–3.
30. Letters to Portland from, E. Greathead, 2 May, Burgoyne, 19 June, and Buckingham, 2
     Nov. 1800. HO. 42/50, 53.
31. See below pp. 166–67. Cf. Bohstedt, *op. cit.*, p. 195.
32. *DPD.*, 3rd ser. vol. 10, p. 234. Reddlesdale to Fitzwilliam, 12 June 1801, SCL., WWM.
     F.51/3. *Manchester Mercury*, 17 Jan. 1801. Bedford to Pelham, 4 May 1801, BL. Add. Mss.
     33107, ff. 45–6. Lansdowne to Portland, 25 Dec. 1800, HO. 42/55. P. James, *Population
     Malthus*, (1979), p. 86. M.W. McCahill, *Order and Equipoise. The Peerage and the House of
     Lords 1783–1806*, (1978), p. 46 note 1.
33. Stockland overseers' accounts, 2 July 1801, DCRO., D1251A/PO.3. Cf. Gulval vestry
     minute, 6 July 1801, CCRO., DDX. 173/85.
34. Mr. Palmer, Uppingham, to Portland, 8 and 27 Nov. 1800, HO. 42/53. *Nottingham
     Journal*, 18 Mar. 1801. Cf. R.A.E. Wells, 'Sheep rustling in Yorkshire in the age of the
     agrarian and industrial revolutions', *Northern History*, XX, (1984).
35. P.B. Munsche, *Gentlemen and Poachers: the English Game Laws 1671–1831*, (Cambridge,
     1981), pp. 99–100, 115–6, 126–7, 150.
36. Information of H. Dawson, 21 Jan. 1801, WYRO, Quarter Sessions roll, Easter 1801. Cf.
     depositions of Funtingdon yeoman Martin, and labourer Redman, 10 Oct. 1800,

WSCRO. QR. W/632.
37. E.g. deposition of E. Peskett, 7 Aug. 1799, WSCRO. QR. W/627 f. 41.
38. *Reading Mercury*, 20 Jan. 1800. *Newcastle Advertiser*, 22 Nov. 1800.
39. WSCRO, indictments, QR. W/632. Deposition of J. Lidden, 20 Sept. 1800, DCRO, Michaelmas Quarter Sessions file, 3/4B/1b. Threatening letter, 18 June, enclosed by J. Hall, Essex, to Portland, 14 July 1800, HO. 42/50. J. Ayres (ed), *Paupers and Pig Killers; the Diary of William Holland a Somerset Parson 1799–1818*, (1986 edition), p. 25.
40. J. Rule, *The Experience of Labour in Eighteenth-Century Industry*, (1981), esp. pp. 177–8, 182–3; cf. C.R. Dobson, *Masters and Journeymen. A Pre-History of Industrial Relations 1717–1800*, (1980), ch. 9. and J. Stevenson, *Popular Disturbances in England 1700–1870*, (1979), esp. pp. 127–9. J. Ehrman, *The Younger Pitt. The Reluctant Transition*, (1983), p. 154 note 3. *York Courant*, 13 July 1800.
41. *Newcastle Advertiser*, 3 and 10 May 1795. E. Walls, Spilsby, to Sir. J. Banks, 30 May 1795, cited J.W.F. Hill, *Georgian Lincoln*, (Cambridge, 1966), pp. 167–8. E. Sykes, Hull, to T. Grimston, 29 Apr. 1796, HRO., DD. DR. 23/16. *Reading Mercury*, 23 June 1800.
42. D. Vincent, (ed), *Testaments of Radicalism: Memoirs of Working Class Politicians 1790–1885*, (1977), pp. 52, 77–8. Devaynes, with enclosures, 12 Jan, and D. Williams, 17 July, to Portland; Exeter journeymen fullers' handbill, 28 Mar; R. Eastcott, Exeter, to ? 30 Mar; anon., Cumberland, to Lord Lonsdale, 28 July 1795, HO. 42/34–5. P. Colquhoun to Portland, 9 July 1795, PC. 1/27/A54. *Nottingham Journal*, 4 and 25 July 1795. R.A.E. Wells, *Riot and Political Disaffection in Nottinghamshire in the Age of Revolutions 1776–1803*, (University of Nottingham, 1984) pp. 14–7. Bohstedt, *op. cit.*, pp. 128–9. Dobson, *op. cit.*, p. 138. Stevenson, *op. cit.*, pp. 129, 132. A. Plummer, *The London Weavers' Company 1600–1970*, (1972), p. 330. R. Challinor, *The Lancashire and Cheshire Miners*, (Newcastle-upon-Tyne, 1972), p. 22.
43. *Leeds Intelligencer*, 25 Jan. 1796. Bowns to Fitzwilliam, 18 Dec. 1797, 29 May and 13 Sept. 1799, SCL., WWM. F40/93, 95; stewards' papers, vol. 6 (VI), 1798–1800.
44. One of the bills published by the miners gave the prices enforced by the populace at Taunton, which the miners said, were acceptable.
45. Correspondence of Delaval with his Hartley agent, and others, 26 Apr. to 10 May 1800, NCRO, ZDE. 24/7–16. *Newcastle Advertiser*, 3, 10 and 17 May 1800. *Newcastle Chronicle*, 3, 10 and 17 May 1800. *The Times*, 5 and 13 May 1800. Correspondence of W. Braithwayt, Mar. 1795, GCRO, D1799/C170. Major-General Rooke, Bristol, to Portland, 15 Mar. 1795 and 7 Apr. 1801; Rooke to J. King, 17 Mar. 1795; Dr. Small to Portland with enclosures, 15 Apr. 1801, HO. 42/34, 61. Rooke to Windham, 17 Mar. 1795, WO. 1/1092, ff. 75–6. *Sherborne Mercury*, 30 Mar. 1795.
46. A.J. Randall, 'The shearmen and the Wiltshire outrages of 1802: trade unionism and industrial violence', *SH.*, 7, (1982), pp. 285–6. R.A.E. Wells, 'Dearth and distress in Yorkshire 1793–1802', *Borthwick Papers*, 52, (University of York, 1977), pp. 7–10. Letters to the War Office from J. Ainstie, Devizes, 28 May, W. Seymour and R. Long, 7 Aug, and R. Stevens, 1 and 29 Oct. 1795, WO. 1/1082, ff. 119–22; 1/1093. *Leeds Intelligencer*, 14 Sept. and 7 Dec. 1795.
47. Wells, *loc. cit.*, pp. 40–1. Randall, *op. cit.* K.G. Ponting, *The Woollen Industry of South-west England*, (1971), part III. Beckett to W. Spencer-Stanhope, 17 May 1802, SCL., SS. 60564, f. 642.
48. Master-shoemaker Cook, Lancaster to J. Moore, 5 Jan. 1793, BL. Add. Mss. 16928, ff. 9–10. A. Temple-Patterson, *Radical Leicester*, (Leicester, 1954), p. 28. Mayor of Newcastle to Portland, 13 Jan. 1800, HO. 42/49. A. Aspinall (ed), *The Early English Trade Unions*, (1949), pp. 25–7. Randall, *op. cit.*, pp. 292, 300. Dobson, *op. cit.*, pp. 141, 149–50. *The Times*, 23 Dec. 1800. *The Iris*, 8 Jan. 1801. *Billinge's Liverpool Advertiser*, 5 and 12 Jan. 1801. *The Gorgon*, 26 Sept. and 10 Oct. 1818.
49. *The Iris*, 5 and 15 July 1797. Sheffield silversmith's handbill, 20 Feb. 1798, YML., HH.3(2). Randall, *op. cit.*, p. 290. W. Cookson to Fitzwilliam, 18 Aug. and 8 Sept. 1802; W. Beckett to Fitzwilliam, 28 Jan; Fitzwilliam to Pelham, 30 Jan. 1803; 'J.R.', Sheffield to C. Thomas, Bristol, 28 Dec. 1802, and to G. Palmer, Leeds, 17 Mar. 1803; Aspinall, *op. cit.*, pp. 52–3, 59–61, 65–9; SCL., WWM, F.45/114, 117. *Leeds Intelligencer*, 22 Jan. 1802.
50. Conspiracy indictments, 30 June 1796, WYRO. Midsummer 1796 Quarter Sessions file. W. Butts to Windham, 28 Sept. 1795, WO. 1/1083, ff. 343–6. *Newcastle Courant*, 2 May 1800. *Leeds Intelligencer*, 21 Oct. 1799. *Newcastle Advertiser*, 29 Mar. 1800. City of

Norwich, summary conviction returns to Epiphany City Quarter Sessions 1796, NNRO., Shelf b. Case 20. W. le Hardy (ed), *Hertfordshire County Records. Calendar to the Quarter Sessions Minute Books*, VII, (Hertford, 1935), pp. 457–8.

51. Butts to Windham, 25 Sept. 1795, WO. 1/1083, ff. 343–6. H. Sedley, Nuttal Temple, to Portland, 2 Aug. 1795, NUL., Portland dep. PwF. 8254. D. Hay, 'Manufacturers and the criminal law in the later eighteenth century: crime and "police" in south Staffordshire', *Police and Policing*, (P&P Colloquium papers, 1983), p. 8.

52. T. Hall to Braybrooke, 14 July, and Braybrooke to Essex Clerk of the Peace, 18 July 1800, ESRO., Q/SBb/380/66/1–4. Adams, 2 June, and Hall, with enclosures, 14 July 1800, to Portland, HO. 42/50. *Chelmsford Chronicle*, 27 June 1800.

53. *The Iris*, 2 July 1801.

54. Stevenson, *op. cit.*, pp. 105–6. Bohstedt, *op. cit.*, p. 3.

55. *Bonner and Middleton's Bristol Journal*, 25 Apr. 1801. Rev. D. Hughes, Oxford, to Portland, 7 Sept. 1800; deposition n.d. (1801) of farmer Fromlett; Totnes 'Committee of the People' bill, 3 Apr: anon., Yeovil, to Portland, 31 Mar; farmer Honeybeare's deposition, 3 Apr. 1801, HO. 42/51, 61. Savery's deposition n.d., and Honeybeare's statement, forwarded by Eales to Fortescue, 28 July 1801: abstract n.d. of events at Modbury, DCRO., FLP. D1262M/L50, L53–4. John Harris, 'A History of Plymouth', 2 vols. (unpublished mss. 1808, copy in City of Plymouth Library), II, pp. 141–2.

56. See below pp. 263, 277, 280–1.

57. For examples see E.P. Thompson, 'The "moral economy" of the English crowd in the eighteenth century', *P&P*, 50, (1971), pp. 112–4.

58. Truro respondent to the LCS, 6 Apr. 1796, BL. Add. Mss. 27815, ff. 41–2. Observation of J. Buckingham of Flushing, cited Rule, *op. cit.*, pp. 206–7. Depositions re Ellesmore crowd, 8 Nov. 1800, Ass. 5/121, part ii. Bettison to a Newark lawyer, 15 Sept. 1800, Notts. CRO., CA. 5/2/114. Paul to the War Office, 21 July 1795, WO. 1/1091.

59. Wrottesley to Portland, 1 May 1800, HO. 42/50. Numerous depositions by Staffordshire farmers, wives and servants, 1 to 2 May, 1800, Ass. 5/120, part iv.

60. *Staffordshire Advertiser*, 30 Aug. 1800. *Aris's Birmingham Gazette*, 21 July, 1800. Cf. the exploitation of metropolitan Chartist rallies by vagabonds and criminal elements, D. Goodway, *London Chartism 1838–1848*, (1982), pp. 126–7.

61. Depositions of R. Honey and family, and reward handbill, 23 Apr; Devonport Bench to Fortescue, 15 and 18 July 1801, HO. 42/61: DCRO, FLP. D1262M/L54 L55–6. *Exeter Flying Post*, 30 Apr. 1801, 25 Mar, 19 Aug. and 2 Sept. 1802.

62. Bohstedt, *op. cit. passim*.

63. Rashleigh to Pole-Carew, 24 Apr. 1795, CCRO., Carew Mss. CC/K/25. Elford to Fortescue, 11 Apr. 1795, DCRO., FLP. D1262M/F7. H. Legge, Birmingham, 13 May, and Bowen, Bath, 17 May 1800, to Portland, HO. 42/49. *The Times*, 27 Apr. 1800.

64. For examples at Norwich, Belper and Wakefield, see Norwich Mayoralty Court minute, 2 May 1795, NNRO, Case 16, Rep. 128, 36. *Norfolk Chronicle*, 9 May 1795. *Leeds Intelligencer*, 12 May 1800. *Derby Mercury* 15 May 1800.

65. Thompson, *op. cit.*, p. 120. *Sherborne Mercury*, 6 Apr. 1795. *Blackburn Mail*, 24 Sept. 1800. A. Graham to J. King, 25 Sept; Mayor of High Wycombe to Portland, 26 Sept. 1800, HO. 42/51. Hervey, *Journal . . .* , p. 436.

66. Willoughby, and Rev. J. Cooke, to Portland, both 21 Sept. 1800, HO. 42/51. J. Willcock, 15 Apr, and A. Montague, 4 May, to Fortescue; Bastard to Addington, 4 May 1801, DCRO, FLP. D1262M/L52–3; SP. D152M/Corr. 1801.

67. Bruden to Windham, 22 Sept. 1800, WO. 40/17. Nottingham handbill, 13 Sept; letters to Portland from Smith, 13 Sept, Coldham, 16 Sept. 1800, Devonport Bench, 18 Apr. and Bastard, 10 Apr; J. to W. Pulling, 6 Apr; Plymouth bakers' handbills, 6 and 10 Apr. 1801, HO. 42/51, 61. Emmerton to his brother, 11 Sept. 1800, Notts. CRO., DD. SY. 284/4. Bastard to Addington, 4 May; undated memorandum (1801), DCRO, SP. D152M/Corr. 1801: FLP D1262M/L52.

68. Stevenson, *op. cit.*, p. 110, but cf. p. 239.

69. *The Times*, 13 Sept. 1800. J. Barker, and Coldham, to Portland, both 23 Sept. 1800, and with enclosures, HO. 42/51.

70. *Aris's Birmingham Gazette*, 18 Sept. 1800, and cf. Giddy diary, 9 July 1795, CCRO., DD. DG. 14. Board of Trade Minute, 24 Oct. 1800, BT. 5/12, ff. 59–62. Messrs. Gibson, Danzig, to J. Crawford, London, 18 Nov. 1800, BL. Add. Mss. 38234, ff. 248–53. *Annals*

of Agriculture, 24, (1795), pp. 540–1.

Chapter 11   *Intervention Versus Free Trade: Securing Imports in Wartime 1794–1801*

1. See esp. Auckland to Pitt, 8 Nov. 1795, PRO. 30/8/110, ff. 279–80. J. Ehrman, *The Younger Pitt. The Reluctant Transition*, (1983), pp. 513–4. M.W. McCahill, *Order and Equipoise. The Peerage and the House of Lords 1783–1806*, (1978), pp. 132–3.
2. BT. 3/5, ff. 44–6; 5/9, f. 290. PC. 2/142, pp. 105–7; 2/143, pp. 529–30. Scott to Long, 13 Dec. 1794, PRO. 30/8/176, ff. 70–1. J. Brickwood to J. King, 14 and 15 Nov., and 7 Dec. 1794, BL. Add. Mss. 58792, ff. 28–33. *Minutes*, 31 Jan. 1795.
3. *DPD.*, 2nd. ser. vol. 40, pp. 199–200, 338–9, 362–3; vol. 41, pp. 70, 73–117, 129–34, 208, 290–329. *JHC.*, vol. 50. pp. 120, 467, 541. *The Times*, 2 Jan. 1795. Lord Mayor of London to Portland, 6 Jan. 1795, HO. 42/34. Buxton to B. Gurney, 20 Jan. 1795, IESRO., Gurney Coll., vol. 7. no. 27 (temporary deposit, 1972). *Hull Advertizer*, 21 Mar. 1795.
4. *Minutes*, 31 Jan, 4 and 20 Feb, 1795. Brickwood to Board of Trade, 26 Nov. 1795, PC. 1/25/A48. Board of Trade minute 4 Feb. 1795; Canada merchants Henry, and Inglis, to Hawkesbury, 7 and 16 Feb. 1795, BT. 1/12, ff. 221, 256–80 3/5, f. 62; 5/9, f. 394. Privy Council orders, T. 1/744/526.
5. *Minutes*, 2 and 4 Feb. 1795. PC.2/142, pp. 367–8. Messrs. Gibson and Atkinson to Messrs. Baxter, 23 Jan; Scott's report, 24 Feb. 1795, BT. 1/12, ff. 262–3, 266–8. Brickwood to the Privy Council, 26 Mar; Scott to Lord Spencer, 2 Apr. 1795, PC. 1/25/A48. Auckland to Spencer, 6 Mar 1795, Bishop of Bath and Wells (ed), *The Journal and Correspondence of Lord Auckland*, 4 vols. (1861–2), III, pp. 291–2.
6. Canada merchant Glenny to the Home Office, 7 Jan. 1795, HO. 42/34. Mercantile proposals; Scott to Spencer, 2 Apr; lists of ships for despatch, 14, 20 and 21 Apr. 1795, PC. 1/33/A47–8. Brickwood, 29 May, and Scott, 12 June and 18 Aug. 1795, to Hawkesbury, BL. Add. Mss. 38230, ff. 173, 179–80, 265. A. Aubert to Banks, 2 Feb; S. Cotterell to Bosanquet, 2 Apr. 1795, BT. 1/12, f. 219; 3/5, f. 80. Turnbull Forbes to the Privy Council, 15 July 1795, T. 1/751/2587. *Minutes*, 2 and 14 Apr., and 2 and 10 July 1795.
7. PC. 2/143, p. 522. *Minutes*, 10 July 1795. Brickwood to Hawkesbury, 29 May; Hawkesbury to Sinclair, 13 June 1795, BL. Add. Mss. 38230, f. 173; 38310, f. 275. Brickwood to the Privy Council, 18 and 26 July 1795, PC. 1/26/A51; 1/27/A55. Turnbull Forbes to the Privy Council, 15 July; Privy Council to Rose, 20 July; Bond to the Foreign Office, 13 July 1795, T. 1/751/2587, 2621; 1/753/3298.
8. *Minutes*, 26 June, 5 July and 19 Aug. 1795. Privy Council to Scott, Brickwood, and the admiralty, all 24 June 1795, PC. 2/143, pp. 332–4. Scott to Hawkesbury, 27 July 1795, BL. Add. Mss. 38230, ff. 254–5. Treasury to Plymouth customs, 8 Apr, and to Scott, 21 May 1795, T.11/38, pp. 77–8; 27/45, f. 413. Scott's sales return, 8 July 1795, HO. 42/35. Portland to Sir. F. Bassett, 9 Mar. 1795, NUL., Portland dep. PwW. pp. 73–4. Portland to George III, 21 Aug. 1795, *Later Corr.* II, pp. 389–90.
9. *Minutes*, 26 June, 1, 7, 23 and 29 July, and 19 Aug. 1795. Letters to Hawkesbury from, Brickwood, 23 July, and Scott, 27 July and 8 Aug; Hawkesbury to Banks, 20 Aug. 1795, BL. Add. Mss. 38230, ff. 238–9, 263–4, 294–5; 38310, p. 277. Sir G. Yonge to Pitt, 29 June 1795, PRO. 30/8/193, ff. 90–1. Earl of Stamford to Portland, and reply, 4 and 9 July 1795; undated Home Office memorandum, HO. 42/35; 43/6, p. 535. Hawkesbury to Portland, c. 6 Aug; Messrs. Lewin and Norwood to the Privy Council, 23 July 1795, PC. 1/27/A56; 1/29/A64. Sheffield to Portland, 29 July 1795, NUL., Portland dep. PwF. 5181.
10. *Minutes*, 2, 17, 22, 27 and 29 July, 5 and 9 Aug. 1795. Nottingham relief committee, 18 July, and Sir. H. Etherington, Hull, 5, 10 (with enclosure) and 13 Aug., to Portland; Mayor of Norwich to H. Hobart MP, 12 and 15 July; Hawkesbury to Garbett, 10 Aug. 1795, PC. 1/27/A55–6; 1/29/A64. *Norfolk Chronicle*, 18 July 1795. J. Norris, 'Samuel Garbett and the early development of industrial lobbying in Great Britain', *Ec. His. Rev.*, 2s. X, (1958).

11. *Minutes*, 5 Aug. 1795. Mayor of Gloucester, 1 July, and Lonsdale, with enclosure, 2 Aug. 1795, to Portland, HO.42/35. Letters to Pitt from E.J. Stuart, 11 July, Mayor of Richmond, 13 July, and J. and W. Squire, 20 July; Scarborough petition, 12 July 1795, PC. I/27/A55. *Gloucester Journal*, 29 June and 13 July 1795. Giddy diary, 2 July 1795, CCRO, DD. DG. 14.

12. Baker to Portland, 11 July 1795, NUL., Portland dep. PwF. 233. *Sussex Weekly Advertiser*, 20 July 1795.

13. *Minutes*, 5 Aug. 1795. Lonsdale to Portland, 2 Aug. 1795, HO. 42/35. Curwen's letter endorsed by Hawkesbury, PC. 1/29/A64. Portland's reply, cited in full by E. Hughes, *North Country Life in the Eighteenth century*, 2 vols. (1952 and 1965), II, ch. VIII and esp. pp. 280–1.

14. Memorandum, 4 Aug. 1795, BL. Add. Mss. 38353, pp. 316–35.

15. Letters to Hawkesbury from Banks, 30 Aug, Sheffield, 13 Sept, and Fawkener, 29 Sept. 1795, PC. 1/29/A66: BL. Add. Mss. 38230, f. 328. Portland to George III, 21 and 29 Aug. and 2 Oct. *Later Corr.* II, pp. 389–90, 394, 407–9, and replies 30 Aug. and 4 Sept. 1795, NUL., Portland dep. PwF. 4095, 4098. J. Sinclair, *Address to the Board of Agriculture*, (1796). PC. 2/144, pp. 241, 254.

16. Fawkener to Rose, 8 and 16 Oct: Mr. Berwicke to the Privy Council, 7 Oct. and 11 November; extracts from correspondence between Sir W. Hippersley, Ambassador at Naples, and Sir. W. Hamilton, 1795, T. 1/754/3662: PC. 1/29/A67; 1/30/A71; 1/32/A81. Fawkener to Hawkesbury, 16 Oct. 1795, BL. Add. Mss. 38230, f. 350. Portland to Sir G.O. Paul, 10 Oct. 1795, NUL., Portland dep. PwF. 7394.

17. Messrs. Helicar to the Privy Council, 8 Oct; resolutions of the Gloucestershire Bench, 6 Oct; Hawkesbury to Fawkener, 16 Oct; Paul to Portland, 21 Oct. 1795, PC. 1/27/A67; 1/30/A68. Penwick Bench to Portland, 24 Nov. 1795, HO. 42/36. Letters to Hawkesbury from, Sheffield, 13 Sept, Brickwood, 7 Oct, and Scott, 8 Oct. 1795, BL. Add. Mss. 38230, ff. 304–9, 340–1; 38393, p. 336. Foster to Sheffield, 22 Oct. 1795, ESCRO, Add. Mss. 4550/2.

18. Paul to Portland, 21 Oct. 1795, PC. 1/30/A68. Draft bounty schemes, PRO. 30/8/197. ff. 1–2. *DPD.*, 2nd. ser. vol. 43, pp. 3–4, 57–8, 69–70. Hansard, *Parliamentary History*, vol. XXXII, (1818), pp. 236–42. *The Times*, 4 Nov. 1795.

19. Messrs. Gibson and Atkinson, Danzig, to Messrs Baxter and Mair, London, 15 Sept; J. Balfont, Pilrig, to Dundas, 13 Oct; Brickwood, and Scott, to the Privy Council, both 12 Oct; Danzig market report, 26 Nov. and Turnbull Forbes to D. Ryder, 9 Dec. 1795, PC. 1/29/A68; 1/30/A68; 1/31/A73. Ex-Mayor Smith, Bristol, to Hawkesbury, 15 Oct. 1795, BL. Add. Mss. 38230, ff. 347–9. Sheffield to Auckland, 26 June 1796, Bath and Wells, *loc. cit.* pp. 349–50.

20. *BPP.*, 'First and Second Reports of House of Commons Select Committee on the High Price of Corn', (16 Nov. and 8 Dec. 1795). *DPD, loc. cit.*, pp. 349–50.

21. *The Times*, 14 Nov. 1795. 2nd Earl of Colchester (ed), *The Diary and Correspondence of Charles Abbot, Lord Colchester*, 2 vols. (1861), II, p. 6. Privy Council directives to consuls in Baltic countries, the 'Barbary States', Italian states, Prussia, Russia, Pomerania, and the USA., Brickwood, 22 Dec, Scott, 28 Oct, 19 and 28 Dec, and Turnbull Forbes, 1 Dec. 1795, 11 Mar. and 20 July 1796; Fawkener to C. Hamilton, and Turnbull Forbes, both 9 Dec, and to Scott, Turnbull Forbes, and B. Berwicke, all 21 Nov; G.S. Farrington to Hawkesbury, 12 Nov. 1795: Privy Council draft minutes, 16 Jan. 1796, PC. 1/30/A71; 1/31/A73; 1/32/A80; 1/33/A86, 1/34/A92: 2/144, pp. 450–2, 557, 571, 573–4. Scott to the Treasury, 15 June 1796, PRO. 30/8/176, ff. 72–5.

22. Mayor of Newcastle to Portland, 12 Jan. 1796: J. King to the Mayor of Plymouth, 15 and 21 Oct, and Portland to H. Cholmondeley, 26 Nov. 1795, HO. 42/38; 43/7, pp. 212, 241, 284–5. Sir F. Bassett, memorandum, 10 Nov; Fawkener to Scott, 16 Nov. 1795, PC. 1/31/A73; 2/144, pp. 446/7.

23. Memorandum from Bassett, 10 Nov; Fawkener to Scott, 16 Nov, to Brickwood, 28 Nov, and replies 5 and 14 Dec; N. to J. Brickwood, 22 Oct; Privy Council to Scott, 5 Dec. 1795, to Brickwood, 27 Jan., and to the Victualling Board 28 Jan; Scott to the Privy Council, 7 and 22 Mar; account of sales in London by J. Brickwood, 1 Jan. to 22 Mar. 1796, PC. 1/30/A68, A70; 1/31/A71, A73; 1/32/A80; 1/33/A86; 2/144, pp. 446–7. Hawkesbury to Col. Wood, 6 Feb 1796, Add. Mss. 38310, pp. 299–300. *BPP*, 'Report of the select committee of the House of Commons on the Causes and Extent of the Losses

sustained by British Merchants', (20 June 1797), pp. 2–3. *Sussex Weekly Advertiser*, 14 Mar. 1796.

24. Privy Council draft orders, 7 and 25 July, 8 and 16 Aug; Privy Council to Scott, 5 May, and Rose, 6 May; Turnbull to the Privy Council, 11 Mar; Scott to the Privy Council, 18 and 25 July, 8 and 16 Aug. 1796, PC. 1/32/A80; 1/33/A86; 1/34/A91–2; 1/35/A95: 2/145, p. 527. Scott to the Treasury, 15 June 1796, PRO. 30/8/176, ff. 72–5. *BPP*, 'Merchants losses . . .', p. 6.

25. B.R. Mitchell, *Abstract of British Historical Statistics*, (Cambridge, 1962), p. 97. Scott to the Privy Council, 30 June, 8, 16 and 24 Aug. 1796, PC. 1/33/A86; 1/34/A92; 1/35/A95.

26. B.T. 5/10, f. 419, Hawkesbury's endorsement refusing Liverpudlian merchant's request for a letter of introduction to Pitt, 20 July 1797. *BPP.*, 'Merchants losses . . .', *passim*, including appendices. *DPD.*, 3rd. ser. vol. 1, pp. 624–5. 'Petition of the London Merchants engaged in importing Corn', 17 May 1797, and Hawkesbury's rejection of two further requests, May 1798, BL. Add. Mss. 38230, ff. 170–5; 38232, f. 47.

27. *Newcastle Advertiser*, 2 Nov. 1799. *Blackburn Mail*, 20 Nov. 1799. *Hull Advertizer*, 15 Mar. 1800. *The Times*, 10 May 1800. Haden to Portland, 16 May 1800, HO. 42/50. E. to R. Heber, 5 July 1800, R.H. Cholmondeley (ed), *The Heber Letters 1783–1832*, (1950), p. 119. Liverpool to Pitt, 17 Aug. 1800, BL. Add. Mss. 38311, pp. 37–8. D. Scott, Chairman, East India Co., to Pitt, 21 Nov. 1799, reporting on request for harvest and market 'prices and prospects' in England and Scotland, C.H. Philipps (ed), 'The correspondence of David Scott, Director and Chairman of the East India Company relating to Indian affairs 1787–1805', *Publications of the Camden Society*, 3rd. ser. no. 76, 2 vols. (1951), I, pp. 221–2.

28. 39 Geo. III, cap. 87.

29. *DPD.*, 3rd. ser. vol. 10, pp. 1–3, 16, 71, 95–6, 540–3. *JHC*, vol. 55, pp. 35–8, 49. *The Times*, 15 Feb. 1800. *Morning Chronicle*, 22 Feb. 1800. Fox to Grey, 1 Dec. 1800, Lord John Russell (ed), *Memoirs and Correspondence of Charles James Fox*, 4 vols. (1854), III, pp. 316–7.

30. Privy Council to the Foreign Office, 11 Oct. and 16 Dec; to the Treasury, 25 Oct. 1799, and to Turnbull Forbes, 31 Jan. 1800; Privy Council order, 6 Dec. 1799, PC. 2/153, pp. 415, 567–8, 620–1, 688–9. Liverpool to Hellicar, 16 Sept, and to Sheffield, 23 Dec. 1799, BL. Add. Mss. 38311, pp. 53, 73–6. Board of Trade minutes, 12 and 13 Dec. 1799, and 24 Feb. 1800, BT. 1/18, ff 187–9; 5/12, ff. 380–98. Rose to Wilberforce n.d. (but Nov. 1799), in A.M. Wilberforce (ed), *Private Papers of William Wilberforce*, (1897), pp. 86–9. A. Young to Pitt, 28 Nov. 1799, PRO. 30/8/193, ff. 155–6. Sir G. Barclay to Grenville, 8 Mar. and 13 May 1800, BL. Add. Mss. 59375, ff. 89–90, 124–5. *Lincoln, Rutland and Stamford Mercury*, 18 Oct. 1799. *York Courant*, 9 Dec. 1799.

31. Both reports are reprinted in *DPD.*, see 3rd. ser. vol. 10, esp. p. 536, and vol. 11 esp. pp. 359, 362, 371, 373–4, 410, 543, 550–1, 587–8, 641. Rose to Wilberforce, *loc. cit.* Privy Council, 8 Feb, and the Home Office, 21 Mar. 1800, to Liverpool, PC. 2/154, pp. 216–7: HO. 43/11 p. 414. *The Times*, 8 and 11 Mar. 1800.

32. See above pp. 25–6 for London's customary consumption of the best wheat from many regions.

33. Liverpool to Portland, 9 Oct. 1800, BL. Add. Mss. 38371, pp. 158–65. Board of Trade correspondence with customs, late May 1800, BT. 1/18, ff. 296–9, 331–2, 362–7; 6/3, ff. 164–5.

34. This survey is based on the customs returns, BT. 6/139, the taxmen's, PRO. 30/8/291, ff. 42, 64, 71, and the clergy's, HO. 42/52, 54–5.

35. Returns, *loc. cit.* Liverpool's memorandum on corn, 23 Oct. 1800, BL. Add. Mss. 38234, ff. 191–212. *Manchester Mercury*, 11 Feb. 1800. *York Herald*, 1 Mar. 1800. *York Courant*, 29 June 1800.

36. Portland to W. Baker MP, 24 Aug 1800, HO. 43/12, pp. 78–82. Mr. Philipps, London, 24 Oct, and T. Hill, Bristol merchant, 28 Oct, to Liverpool: Board of Trade minutes, 24 Oct. 1800, BL. Add. Mss. 38234, ff. 219–20: BT. 5/12, ff. 59–75; 6/139.

37. Customs returns, BT. 6/139. Board of Trade Minute, 24 Oct. 1800, BT. 5/12, ff. 59–75. W. Bryers, Hartley, to Lord Delaval, 31 Jan. 1801, NCRO, ZDE. 4/24/41. L.V. Harcourt (ed), *The Diaries and Correspondence of George Rose*, 2 vols. (1860), I, pp. 281–5. E.P. Thompson, 'The "moral economy" of the English crowd in the eighteenth century', *P&P*, 50, (1971), p. 94.

38. Pitt to Rose, 22 Sept. 1800, BL. Add. Mss. 42772, f. 120. S. Maccoby, *English Radicalism 1785–1832*, (1955), p. 141.

39. Liverpool to Sheffield, 30 July; Fawkener to Liverpool, 22 Sept. 1800, BL. Add. Mss. 38234, ff. 156–7; 38311, p. 140. Henry to Phillip Addington, 1 Sept. 1800, DCRO, SP. D152M/Corr. 1800–1. Grenville to Buckingham, 15 Sept. 1800, Duke of Buckingham and Chandos (ed), *Memoirs of the Court and Cabinets of George III*, 4 vols. (1853–5), III, pp. 93–4. Grenville to Pitt, 24 Oct. 1800, Earl of Stanhope, *Life of Pitt*, 4 vols. (1862), III, pp. 247–50. Liverpool memorandum, and Pitt to Rose, both 22 Oct; Rose to the Board of Trade, 23 and 28 Oct. 1800, BT. 6/139.

40. Liverpool's memorandum, 22 Oct. 1800, BT. 6/139. Fawkener to Liverpool, 25 Oct. 1800, BL. Add. Mss. 38234, f. 225.

41. Scott to the Board of Trade, 3 Nov. 1800, and his examination, BT. 5/12, ff. 59–75, 126–34.

42. Gibson and Co., Danzig, to J. Crawford, London, 18 Nov, in reply to an enquiry, made 29 Sept. 1800, BL. Add. Mss. 38234, ff. 248–53. Examinations before the Board of Trade, 24 Oct. and 4 Nov: Board of Trade Minutes, 29 and 31 Oct. and 1 Nov; written replies by J. Brickwood jnr., 31 Oct, and J.C. Ruding, 6 Nov. 1800: customs' replies re. working of 1800 Importation Act, BT. 5/12, ff. 59–92, 102–24, 135–41, 149–50; 6/139.

43. *The Times*, 13 Oct. 1800. *JHC.*, vol. 55., pp. 802–3. *DPD.*, 3rd ser. vol. 14, pp. 81–4. Board of Trade Minutes, 12 and 18 Nov. 1800, BT. 5/12, ff. 148–9, 151–5.

44. Mitchell, *loc. cit.* The wheat import figure for 1800 in this table is a misprint and should be increased by one million.

45. Mark Lane reports in the *Lincoln, Rutland and Stamford Mercury*, Feb. to Aug. 1801, esp. 6 and 13 Feb. 1801. J. Porter to Liverpool, 9 Sept, 1801, BL. Add. Mss. 38473, ff. 60–1.

46. Harcourt, *loc. cit. JHC*, vol. 55, pp. 799, 874.

47. Pitt to Grenville, 2 Nov. 1800, *HMC.*, 'Dropmore Mss.', vol. 7, (1908), pp. 371–2. 'Sixth report of the select committee on the high price of corn', *DPD*, 3rd ser. vol. 14. pp. 584–97, esp. p. 592.

Chapter 12   Dietary Expedients and Vested Interests: Recommendation versus Compulsion June 1795 to July 1800

1. *Minutes*, 31 Jan, 2 and 20 Feb. 1795. Sinclair to Hawkesbury, 18 Feb. 1795, and various written statements, BT. 1/12, ff. 254–5; 5/9, ff. 379–91.

2. *Minutes*, 27 April, 1 and 2 July 1795. Flour contractor Bailey to Portland, 16 May 1795, endorsed by Hawkesbury, HO. 42/34. Sub-committee report, 27 Apr. 1795, PC. 1/25/A59. Lord Mayor of London to Portland, 29 April 1795, BL. Add. Mss. 38230, f. 158.

3. DCRO., Bideford Borough Quarter Sessions minutes, 1787–1818, 1064, QSO. 4; Devon General Sessions Minute, 19 April 1795, Q/SO/22. Sheffield to Portland, 28 June 1795, HO. 42/34. Pitt to Hawkesbury, 1 July 1795, BL. Add. Mss. 38353, ff. 309–10. *Minutes*, 1 and 2 July 1795.

4. *Minutes*, 1 and 2 July 1795.

5. *The Times*, 4 July 1795. Sheffield to Hawkesbury, 'Copy of a Paper transmitted to the Lord Mayor', Lord Justice Eyre to the Privy Council, and Privy Council to Kenyon, all 5 July: Privy Council minutes, PC. 1/27/A54; 2/142, pp. 361–2: BL. Add. Mss. 38230, ff. 210–1, 219–20. *Minutes*, 6 July 1795.

6. *Minutes*, 10 July 1795. Privy Council minute, signed by thirty-nine persons, PC. 2/143, p. 379. George III to Pitt, 17 July 1795, PRO. 30/8/104, f. 44.

7. *Minutes*, 5, 10, 15, 16 and 17 July 1795.

8. Lord Mayor to Hawkesbury, 18 July 1795, BL. Add. Mss. 38230, ff. 233–4.

9. McEwan's petition, 23 July, *Minutes*, 29 July 1795.

10. Privy Council minute, 11 July; Sinclair to the Privy Council, with enclosures, 5 and 12 July, and reply 9 July 1795, PC. 1/27/A54–5; 2/143, pp. 418, 445–6. *The Times*, 19 Mar. 1795.

11. Letters from Portland to various correspondents, 1 to 10 July 1795, HO. 42/35; 43/6, pp. 509–35. *Minutes*, 16 and 29 July 1795. General orders, WO. 4/773.

12. NCA., Nottingham Borough Sessions order book, CA. 355. SCRO., Quarter Sessions order book, CQ.2, 2/4(2), f. 253. BCRO., Quarter Sessions order book, Q/508, pp. 8–9. Chairman, Devon Sessions to Portland, 29 July 1795, PC. 1/27/A56. ESCRO., Par. 236/12/1. ECRO., DP. 69/8/1. *Reading Mercury*, 20 and 27 July 1795. *Newcastle Courant*, 25 July, 1 and 8 Aug. 1795. *Hull Advertizer*, 18 July 1795. *Newcastle Advertiser*, 25 July 1795. *Manchester Mercury*, 4 Aug. 1795. Mrs. H. Sandford (ed), *Thomas Poole and His Friends*, 2 vols. (1888), I. pp. 134–6.
13. *Leeds Intelligencer*, 13 and 20 July 1795. *The Iris*, 22 July 1795. *Manchester Mercury*, 25 Aug. 1795. T. Escourt to Lord Verulam, 12 Aug. 1795, *HMC*, 'Earl of Verulam mss.', (1906), p. 158. Chairman, Sheffield relief committee, to Fitzwilliam, 16 July 1795, SCL., WWM. F. 47/9–11. Rev. Wilkinson, Sheffield, to R. Ford, 6 Aug. 1795, NUL., Portland dep. PwF. 3943. S. Garbett, 15 July, and Banks, 30 Aug. 1795, to Hawkesbury, PC. 1/27/A55; 1/29/A66. Quarter Sessions order books, BCRO., Q/508, pp. 8–9: OCRO, QSM. I/5.
14. *Sussex Weekly Advertiser*, 20 July 1795. Carnarvon to Portland, 29 July 1795, NUL., Portland dep. PwF. 5067. Holland Watson, Stockport, 5 Aug, and Mr. St. John, Hartfordbridge, 15 Aug. 1795, to Windham, WO. 1/1094. Chairman, Stockport relief committee, to the Privy Council, 30 Aug. 1795, PC. 1/29/A66.
15. W. Belsham to Portland, 7 Aug. 1795, HO. 42/35. Mr. Lee, Exeter, to Addington, 25 July 1795, DCRO, SP. D152M/Corr. 1789–1795. *The Iris*, 14 and 21 Aug. 1795. Butt to Pole-Carew, 4 July 1795, CCRO., Carew Mss. CC/K/25. Hawkesbury's memorandum on corn, 4 Aug 1795, BT. 6/139. A. Booth, 'Food riots in North-west England 1790–1801', *P&P*, 77, (1977), p. 87.
16. Sheffield to Hawkesbury, 13 Sept; Hawkesbury's memorandum on corn (draft), 4 Aug. 1795, BL. Add. Mss. 38230, ff. 304–9; 38353, ff. 316–35.
17. *Minutes*, 20, 23, 24 and 27 Oct. 1795.
18. G. Rose to the Privy Council, 29 Oct. 1795, PC. 1/30/A68. *Minutes*, 29 Oct. 1795. Portland to George III, 2 Oct. 1795, *Later Corr.*, II, pp. 407–9. 'Report of the Sub-Committee of the Corporation of London . . . for erecting Public Mills on the Banks of the Thames', 10 May 1798, BT. 1/18, ff. 313–23.
19. *Minutes*, 2 Nov. 1795. The greatly amended working draft is in PC 1/30/A71.
20. *DPD.*, 2nd ser. vol. 43, pp. 70–7, 786. Hansard's, *Parliamentary History*, vol. XXXII, pp. 235–6. *The Times*, 4 Nov. 1795. Auckland to Pitt, 8 Nov. 1795, PRO. 30/8/110, f. 279.
21. *BPP*, 'First report of the select committee of the House of Commons on high price of corn', (1795). Auckland to Pitt, 15, 18, 23 and 24 Nov, and 8 Dec. 1795, PRO. 30/8/110, ff. 279–80, 283–4, 287–92. *The Times*, 14 Nov. 1795.
22. Undated memorandum, calculations and draft speeches in Pitt's papers, PRO. 30/8/197, ff. 1–2; 30/8/291, ff. 38–9. *BPP.*, 'Third report of the select committee of the House of Commons on the high price of corn', (1795). *DPD., loc. cit.*, pp. 730–2. Hansard, *loc. cit.*, pp. 687–96. Debrett's, *Parliamentary Register of the House of Lords*, vol. XLV, pp. 180–3, 209–13. Fitzwilliam to Wentworth steward Hall, 24 Dec. 1795, SCL., WWM. stewards' papers, 3 (VI).
23. Draft Privy Council Minutes, 18 Nov. and 5 Dec; Lord Mayor to the Privy Council, 2 Dec. 1795, PC. 1/30/A71; 1/31/A73. *DPD., loc. cit.*, pp. 110, 783–9, 793–4. *BPP*, 'Bills', vol. XXVI, (1795–6), no. 758.
24. *DPD., loc. cit.*, pp. 786, 789. Privy Council minute, PC. 2/144, pp. 542–3. Lancs. CRO., Quarter Sessions minute, 12 Jan. 1796, QSO/2/165. Wapentake of Barkstone Ash, Court of Sewers, printed notice, 26 Dec. 1795, SCL. WWM. F. 47/34. St. Nicholas, Newcastle, vestry minute, 2 Feb. 1796, Newcastle City Archives, MA. 183.
25. For example, Charfield, Gloucestershire, vestry minute, 26 Jan. 1796, GCRO., D74/VE/ 2/2, and Boxwell and South Weald, Essex, ECRO. DP. 288/8/2; 128/8/4.
26. Board of Agriculture, *Account of the Experiments tried . . . in the Composition of Various Sorts of Bread*, (10 Nov. 1795).
27. J.W. Emmerton to his brother, 30 Aug. 1795, Notts. CRO, DD. SY 169/IX. Probus vestry minute, 11 Jan. 1796, CCRO. DD. P.194/12/5. DCRO, Quarter Sessions orders book, Q/SO/22. *Gloucester Journal*, 8 Feb. 1796. *Sussex Weekly Advertiser*, 18 and 25 Jan. and 8 Feb. 1796. Reading St. Giles vestry minute, 25 Jan. 1796, BCRO, DP. 96/8/3. *Norfolk Chronicle*, 30 Jan. 1796. Lady Forrester to Verulam, 18 Dec. 1795, HMC., *loc. cit.*, p. 162.

28. The replies are in PC. 1/33/A87, part i and ii. Privy Council to the Home Office, 18 Mar.
     1796, PC. 2/145, p. 324. *DPD*, 2nd ser. vol. 44, pp. 225–6.
29. Rose to Wilberforce, n.d. (but Nov. 1799), A.M. Wilberforce, (ed), *The Private Papers of
     William Wilberforce*, (1897), pp. 86–9. *DPD*, 3rd ser. vol. 10, pp. 536–7. *BPP*, 'First report
     of the select committee of the House of Commons on bread corn'. (10 Feb. 1800).
     Liverpool to Sheffield, 23 Dec. 1799, BL. Add. Mss. 38311, pp. 73–6.
30. BT. 1/14, f. 35; 3/5, ff. 175–6. J.H.F. Brotherstone, *Observations on the Early Public Health
     Movement in Scotland*, (1952), pp. 19–22.
31. 37 Geo. III, cap. 98. C.R. Fay, *The Corn Laws and Social England*, (Cambridge, 1932), p.
     46.
32. W. Thornby and E. Walford, *Old and New London*, 6 vols. (n.d.), VI, p. 382. Anon.
     Albion Mills. State of Facts, (1791 – copy in BL. pressmark, 8227, f. 11). BT. 1/18. ff.
     313–28.
33. G.E. Ellis, *Memoirs of Benjamin Thompson, Count Rumford*, (Boston, Mass., 1870), pp.
     188–96. Count Rumford, *Complete Works*, 4 vols. (American Academy of Art and
     Science, Boston, Mass, 1870–4), IV, pp. 398 ff. F. Redlich, 'Science and charity. Count
     Rumford and his followers', *Int. Rev. SH.*, XVI, (1971). *Newcastle Advertiser*, 28 Dec.
     1799. *The Iris*, 10 Jan. 1800. *Gloucester Journal*, 6 Jan. 1800. *York Courant*, 25 Nov., 2, 23
     and 30 Dec. 1799, and 20 Jan. 1800. *Sussex Weekly Advertiser*, 9 Dec. 1799. *Manchester
     Gazette*, 21 Feb. 1801.
34. *Sussex Weekly Advertiser*, 9 Dec. 1799. *Blackburn Mail*, 20 Nov. 1799. Sheffield to
     Liverpool, 19 Dec. 1799, BL. Add. Mss. 38233, ff. 352–3. *Norfolk Chronicle*, 9 Nov. 1799.
     'The journals of the Hon. William Hervey, 1755–1814', *Suffolk Green Books*, no. XIV,
     vol. 16, (Bury St. Edmunds, 1906), p. 433. *Oxford Journal*, 30 Nov. 1799.
35. For examples of ministers' private correspondence to this effect, see letters to Pitt from
     D. Scott, 21 Nov. and A. Young, 28 Nov. 1799, C.H. Phillips (ed), 'The correspondence
     of David Scott, Director and Chairman of the East India Company relating to Indian
     affairs 1787–1805', *Publications of the Camden Society*, 3rd ser. 76, 2 vols. (1951), I, pp.
     221–22: PRO. 30/8/193, ff. 155–6. Liverpool merchant Walker to Lord Liverpool, 25
     Nov. 1799, BL. Add. Mss. 38233, ff. 289–90.
36. Rose to Wilberforce n.d. *loc. cit.* Sheffield to Pitt, 18 Dec. 1799, PRO. 30/8/177, ff.
     233–5. Sheffield to Liverpool 19 Dec.: Wycombe to Holland, 13 Nov. 1799, BL. Add.
     Mss. 38233, ff. 352–3; 51685, f. 103.
37. Sheffield to Pitt, 18 Dec. 1799, *loc. cit.* Liverpool to Sheffield, 23 Dec. 1799, BL. Add.
     Mss. 38311, pp. 73–6. Draft engagement, Dec. 1799, HO. 42/48.
38. Portland to Kirkwall, 17 Feb. 1800; cf. Portland to Salisbury, 30 Dec. 1799, and J. King
     to Mayor of Boston, 15 Jan. 1800, HO. 43/11, pp. 324, 329, 365–6.
39. NNRO, Quarter Sessions minute, 16 Jan. 1800, QOB.15, administration order book,
     1799–1811, ff. 7–8. W.M.Hartwell, and C. Frenshawe, to Fortescue, both 8 Feb. 1800,
     DCRO., FLP. D1262M/L43. W. Hastings to Fitzwilliam, 31 Dec. 1799, SCL.,
     WWM.F.47/15. Wanstead vestry minutes, 12 Jan. 1800, ECRO., DP. 392/8/2. M.
     Tibbets to her sister, 9 Jan. 1800, Derby Public Library, Pares Collection. GCRO.,
     Quarter Sessions orders, 14 and 29 Jan. 1800, Q/SO/12, ff. 100–4. Cheshire CRO,
     Quarter Sessions orders, 14 Jan. and 11 Feb. 1800, QSM. 28a, ff. 135, 139. WYRO.,
     Quarter Sessions order book, 1798–1801, pp. 111, 113. BCRO., Quarter Sessions orders,
     Q/SO/12, ff. 411–3. Earl of Mt. Edgecumbe to Portland, 21 Jan. 1800, HO. 42/49.
40. *Morning Chronicle*, 22 Jan. 1800. *The Times*, 9 and 17 Jan. 1800.
41. Draft Bill; Haden to Portland, 10 and 16 May, and reply 14 May 1800, HO. 42/49–50.
     DPD., 3rd ser. vol. 10, pp. 536–9, 601–17, 711–22; vol. 11, pp. 6–9, 14–29, 174–6, 520–1.
     JHC., vol. 55, pp. 362, 371–2, 400, 445, 476, 495. *The Times*, 31 Jan. and 20 Feb. 1800.
     Sussex Weekly Advertiser, 12 May 1800. *Kentish Chronicle*, 7 Feb. 1800. Pitt to Grenville,
     11 Dec. 1799, *HMC.*, 'Dropmore mss.', vol. 7 (1908), p. 406. Staffs. CRO., Quarter
     Sessions minutes, Q/SB, 1800. NCRO., Quarter Sessions minutes, QOB.15. Sheffield
     to Pelham, 10 Mar. 1800, BL. Add. Mss. 33124, ff. 23–37.
42. J. Tann, 'Co-operative corn-milling; self-help during the grain crises of the Napoleonic
     wars', *Ag. His. Rev.*, 28, (1980), pp. 49–50. BT. 1/18, ff, 313–23. Details on Southwell
     Mills collected by Liverpool, BL. Add. Mss. 38234, f. 176.
43. Liverpool to Fawkener, 23 Oct. 1800, BT. 6/139. Liverpool to Sheffield, 30 July 1800,
     BL. Add. Mss. 38311, pp. 136–40.

44. *Morning Chronicle*, 4, 9, 12, 16 and 18 June, and 7, 16, 18, 22, 24 and 25 July, 1800. *DPD.*, 3rd ser. vol. 12. pp. 118–24, 251–72, 427–49. *JHC.*, vol. 55, pp. 691, 704, 706, 727, 731–2. Sheffield to Liverpool and reply, 24 and 30 July; Liverpool to Dundas, 11 Oct. 1800, BL. Add. Mss. 38234, ff. 115–7; 38311, pp. 136–40, 166–9. Board of Trade minute, 24 June 1800, BT. 5/12, f. 27. *London Millers' Observations on the Birmingham Union Mill*, (1800). 40 Geo. III, cap. 97.
45. *JHC.*, vol. 55, pp. 663–4, 675, 684, 715–6
46. For examples of convictions see *Hull Advertizer*, and *Blackburn Mail*, 12 and 16 July 1800, and a letter from a Stroud baker to a JP, GCRO., D.149, F.44/12a; returns of summary convictions, SCRO., CQ2, 2/4(3). *JHC.*, vol. 55, pp. 622, 666, 702, 707. *DPD.*, 3rd. ser. vol. 11, pp. 9, 13–4, 21–2.
47. *DPD.*, 3rd ser. vol. 10, pp. 601–14, 617–9; vol. 11, pp. 4–29, 43–6, 61–5. Sir W. Pulteney MP to Addington, 2 and 15 Mar. 1800, DCRO., SP. D152M/Corr. 1800. Portland to W. Baker MP, 24 Aug. 1800, HO. 43/12, pp. 78–82. Sheffield to Liverpool, 24 July 1800, BL. Add. Mss. 38234, ff. 115–6.

Chapter 13   *'Brown George': Compulsion Versus Vested Interests,
September 1800 to July 1801*

1. The clergy's returns, on which this paragraph is partially based, are in HO. 42/52–5. W.H. Chaloner (ed), *The Autobiography of Samuel Bamford*, 2 vols. (1967), I, pp. 174–5. Returns, ESCRO., Q/AV/EW1.
2. Mayor of Romsey, 26 Feb, and J. Carpenter, Tavistock, 22 June, enclosing a 'Copy of a Paper affix'd to Rd. Walter's shop door . . . June 17th 1800', to Portland; Birmingham postmaster to F. Freeling with enclosure, 2 May 1800, HO. 42/49–50, 215. Mr. Lea to Windham, with enclosures, 6 Feb. 1800, WO. 40/17.
3. Rev. Dr. Cleaver, 8 Dec, and W. Hastings, with enclosure, to Fitzwilliam, and reply, 21 to 27 Dec. 1800, SCL., WWM. F.47/17–8, 20–4. Sheffield to Liverpool, 24 July 1800, BL. Add. Mss. 38234, ff 115–7.
4. *Worcester Journal*, Sept. 1800. *Aris's Birmingham Gazette*, Sept. 1800. *York Courant*, 15 Sept. 1800.
5. E.g. 'Crises' to *The Times*, 23 Oct. 1800.
6. E.g. Hertfordshire; W. le Hardy and G. Reckett (eds), *Hertfordshire County Records. Calendar to the Quarter Sessions, 1799–1833*, (Hertford, 1939), pp. 19–20.
7. E.g. Banbury and Bingfield, Berkshire. *Oxford Journal*, 11 Nov. 1800. BCRO., DP. 18/8/1.
8. E.g. *Blackburn Mail*, 22 Oct. 1800.
9. For the concensus of public opinion over a 'pacte de famine', see above pp. 85–8 and for the crisis of confidence in the government, see below pp. 237–47 Portland to W. Watson, Southwell, 4 Sept, and to the Birmingham Bench 8 Oct. 1800, HO. 42/52; 43/11, pp. 99–101. Col. W.H. Clinton to Lord William Bentinck, 16 Oct. and 3 Nov. 1800, NUL., Portland dep. PwJa.106–7. T. Grenville to Marquis of Buckingham, 20 Oct. 1800, The Duke of Buckingham and Chandos (ed), *Memoirs of the Courts and Cabinets of George III*, 4 vols. (1853–5), III, pp. 97–9.
10. 'First report of the select committee of the House of Commons on the high price of corn', 24 Mar. 1800 in *DPD.*, 3rd ser. vol. 13, pp. 225–62, esp. 230–1, 235–6. *BPP.*, 'First report of the select committee of the House of Lords on the dearth of provisions', 10 Dec. 1800, p. 47. Portland to George III, 2 Dec. 1800, *Later Corr.*, III, pp. 444–5. Royal Proclamation; S. Cottrell to the king's printer, 4 Dec. 1800, PC. 2/156, pp. 211–2, 233–4. Draft circular, HO. 42/55. *Norwich Chronicle*, 13 Dec. 1800. *Hull Advertizer*, 27 Dec. 1800.
11. R. Wells, *Insurrection; the British Experience, 1795–1803*, (Gloucester, 1983), pp. 188–94.
12. Pitt to Grenville, 23 Oct. 1800, *HMC.*, 'Dropmore Mss.', vol. 7, (1908), pp. 357–8. *DPD.*, 3rd ser. vol. 13, pp. 245, 406–8, 471–87, 521–9. *The Times*, 29 Nov. and 20 Dec. 1800. Auckland to Pitt, 27 Dec. 1800, PRO. 30/8/110, part ii, ff. 411–2. *BPP.*, 'Second report of the select committee of the House of Lords on the dearth of provisions', 15 Dec. 1800.

13. 41 Geo. III, cap. 12. *DPD., loc. cit.*, pp. 84–5, 225–36, 384–9, 425–31, 445–9, 537–9. *JHC.*, vol. 55, pp. 900, 906. Fox to Grey, 1 Dec. 1800, Lord John Russell, (ed), *Memorials and Correspondence of Charles James Fox*, 4 vols. (1853–7), III, pp. 316–7.

14. *DPD., loc. cit.*, pp. 229, 418–23, 468–9, 503. *JHC.*, vol. 55, pp. 875, 878, 881. 896, 917, 921. Hull committee handbill, SCL., WWM. F.45/25/2.

15. *JHC.*, vol. 55, pp. 905–6, 923. *DPD., loc. cit.*, pp. 496–550, 589. Fox to Grey, n.d., Russell, *loc. cit.*, p. 310. Buckingham to Grenville, 23 Dec. 1800, *HMC., loc. cit.*, pp. 413–4. *The Times*, 19 Dec. 1800.

16. *Manchester Gazette*, 14 Feb. 1801. *Lincoln, Rutland and Stamford Mercury*, 6 and 13 Feb. 1801. Turton, and Richmond, to Portland, both 7 Feb; Shadwell to Richmond, 15 Feb. 1801, HO. 42/61. W. Branch-Johnson (ed), *The Carrington Diary*, (1956), p. 31. *Sussex Weekly Advertiser*, 26 Jan, 9 and 16 Feb. 1801. J. Ayres (ed), *Paupers and Pig Killers: the Diary of William Holland a Somerset Parson 1799–1818*, (1986 edition), p. 58. Icklesham vestry minutes, 16 Feb., 11 Dec. 1800, 21 and 26 Jan., and 17 Feb. 1801, ESCRO. Par. 401/12/2. Cf. the account in E.P. Thompson, 'The "moral economy" of the English crowd in the eighteenth century', *P&P.*, 50, (1971), pp. 81–2 and note 19.

17. *DPD.*, 3rd ser. vol. 14, pp. 137, 142–3, 168, 179–83, 267. *JHC.*, vol. 56, p. 83. *Kentish Chronicle*, 17 Feb. 1801. *The Times*, 18 Feb. 1801. Lord Holland, *Memoirs of the Whig Party*, 2 vols. (1852), I, pp. 176–7. Fox to Lauderdale, 9 Apr. 1801, Russell, *loc. cit.*, p. 336. I. MacAlpine and R. Hunter, *George III and the Mad Business*, (1969), pp. 115–6. Third Earl of Malmesbury (ed), *Diaries and Correspondence of James Harris, 1st Earl of Malmesbury*, 4 vols. (1844), IV, p. 16. *Hull Advertizer*, 7 Mar. 1801.

18. *Aris's Birmingham Gazette*, 22 and 29 Dec. 1800. GCRO., Quarter Sessions orders, Q/SO/12, ff. 247–50. Handbills, Rotherham, 8 Dec., and Halifax, 15 Dec. 1800, SCL., WWM. F.47/38–41.

19. Emmerton to his brother, 22 Dec. 1800, Notts. CRO., DD. SY. 284/5. Terling and Woodford vestry minutes, ECRO., DP. 167/8/3; 299/8/3. *Oxford Journal*, 27 Dec. 1800.

20. *York Herald*, 20 and 27 Dec. 1800. *Leeds Mercury*, 18 July 1801. *Kentish Chronicle*, 2 and 6 Jan. 1801. *Oxford Journal*, 24 and 31 Jan. 1801. Moreton vestry minute, 30 Dec. 1800, ECRO., DP. 72/8/1. St. Branwell, churchwardens' accounts, audited Feb. 1801, CCRO., DD. P.212/8/1. Rev. Harcup to Lord Rous, 5 Jan, enclosed Rous to Portland, 26 Jan. 1801, HO. 42/61.

21. Portland to Bayley, 6 Apr. 1801, HO. 43/12, p. 503.

22. E.g. Portland to Rev. Hewett, Worksop, 27 Dec. 1800, NUL., Portland dep. PwV. III.

23. Portland to the Plymouth Bench, 4, 14 and 20 Apr, to H. Tucker, Honiton, 6 Apr, to the Lord Lieutenants of Devon and Cornwall, 30 Mar. and 3 Apr, and to Fortescue, 16 Apr; E.F. Hatton to the Mayor of Exeter, 25 Mar, and to Rev. Giddy, 20 Apr. 1801, HO. 42/61; 43/12, pp. 478–9, 487–93, 495–6; 43/13, pp. 1–2, 7, 9–10, 13–5.

24. E.g. at Great Pandon, Essex, 8 Dec., and Shinfield, Berkshire, 17 Dec. 1800, ECRO., DP. 184/8/2: BCRO., DP. 110/8/1.

25. Branch-Johnson, *loc. cit.*

26. One Sussex Sessions used a special minute book to record their proceedings, ESCRO., Q/AV/EW1. The order books for two Lincolnshire General Session divisions make no mention of the Act; Holland, 1799–1807, and Kesteven, 1795–1802, Lincs. CRO; nor does the North Riding minute books, but constituent parish records, Northallerton, Great Ayton, Bagley and Newton-under-Roseberry, indicate non-implementation, and five more, Catterick, Rosedale, Thirsk, Topcliffe and Yafforth, record implementation. NYRO., Quarter Sessions minutes, QSM. 2/30: PR. No. 3/6 and 12/1; AYG/9/1; NeC/3/1; 13A/1; ROS/3; TH/6/1/5; YAF/2/1; TOP/2/1. Derbyshire Sessions recorded their formal sittings, but no orders, and the eight parishes with extant records reveal non-implementation; Barlow, Bradbourne, Church Brompton, Mappleton, Marston-on-Dove, Netherseal, Repton and Whitwell, Derbys. CRO., Quarter Sessions minutes, 1801–3, ff. 76–9: D.957A, PO/22; 944A, PO/1: 854A, PO/1; 813A, PP/1; 809A, PO/1; 638A, PO/2; 705A, PW/1.

27. ESCRO., Q/AV/EW1. Petty Sessions returns, Thurgaston, 7 Jan, and Williton, 8 Apr. 1801, Notts. CRO., QSV. 21: SCRO., CQ. 3/1/369.

28. Rev. D. Durrell, 22 Nov. 1800, to *Reports of the Society for Bettering the Condition of the Poor*, vol. III, (1802), pp. 43–50. BCRO., Quarter Sessions orders, Q/SO/9, ff. 34, 46; overseers' accounts, Sulham, Kingston-Lisle, Westfield, Old Windsor and Uffington,

DP. 123/12/2–3; 115B/12/3–4; 144/12/4; 150/12/2; 134/12/2–3. NNRO., Quarter Sessions administration orders, 1799–1811, ff. 15–23.

29. Birmingham vestry to the Clerk of the Peace, Warwickshire, 7 Feb; J. Price to Quarter Sessions Chairman, 9 Feb. 1801, WCRO., Quarter Sessions file, QS. 32/2 (Easter 1801). Norwich Guardians minutes, 1796–1804, ff. 289–90, NNRO., Case 20 shelf e. NCRO., returns Newcastle-upon-Tyne wards of Tindale, and Castle, to the County Sessions, QOB. 15.

30. J. Sudford to Lord Aylesford, 9 Jan. 1801, and returns to Warwickshire Sessions, WCRO., QS. 32/2 (Easter 1801). Staffordshire handbills, and letters to Clerk of the Peace from, Rev. E. Powys and W.H. Cogny, and J. Jackson, both, 16 Feb, J. Sparrow, 30 Jan, and J. Williams, 13 Feb. 1801, Staffs. CRO., Quarter Sessions file, Q/SB, 1801. *Staffordshire Advertiser*, 7 Feb. and 11 Nov. 1801. Worcs. CRO., Quarter Session file for 1801, and minutes, QS. b118, vol. 7, ff. 287–9. *Gloucester Journal*, 12 Jan. 1801. Clitheroe vestry minutes, Lancs. CRO., PR. 1963.

31. Plymouth; committee poster, PCA, W646, bundle 1. Exeter Committee minutes and papers, DCRO. Exeter City Records, Misc. papers box 10. *Exeter Flying Post*, Dec. 1800 to Feb. 1801. Customs officials to Treasury, T.1/860. Various letters to Fitzwilliam, and handbills, Dec. 1800 to Jan. 1801, SCL., WWM. F.47/19, 23, 25. T.B. Bayley, to Portland, 27 Nov. 1800, HO. 42/53. *York Courant*, Dec. 1800 to Feb. 1801. *Blackburn Mail*, Dec. 1800 to Feb. 1801. Eden in *Reports of the Society for Bettering the Condition of the Poor, loc. cit.*, pp. 157–69. *Newcastle Advertiser*, 4 July 1801. John Dickenson II, diary, 13 May 1801, Lancs. CRO. DDX. 274/15. Rev. Karslake to Fortescue, 29 Apr. 1801, DCRO., FLP. D1262M/L51. A. Wrigley, *Saddleworth Chronological Notes, 1200–1900*, (2nd edition, Staleybridge, 1941), p. 33. *JHC.*, vol. 56 p. 494 and Appendix 41. W. Bryce, Aberdoir, to James Loch, 18 Dec. 1800, R.M. Buddle-Atkinson and G.A. Jackson, (eds), *Brougham and His Early Friends: Letters to James Loch, 1798–1809*, 3 vols. (private print, 1908), I, pp. 211–3.

32. For the crisis in poor relief, see below pp.   Letters to Portland, all with enclosures from, Rev. Wood, 26 Dec. 1800, Mayor of Bideford, 8 Jan, W.A. Sandford, 23 Mar. 1801, HO. 42/55, 61. *London Gazette*, 27 Dec. 1800 and 13 Jan. 1801.

Chapter 14   Public Relations: the State and Society, and Famine

1. Haden to Portland, 10 May 1800, HO. 42/50.
2. Board of Trade minutes, 2 and 20 Jan, and other documents, Jan. 1794; endorsement on petition of Dumfries bakers, 18 Feb. 1795, BT. 3/5, ff. 66–7, 123–30, 156.
3. E.g. Portland to the Mayor of Falmouth, 6 Jan, and Fortescue, 8 Mar; J. King to Capt. Tremenheere, Penzance, 18 Mar, and P. Milnes, Wakefield, 24 June 1795, HO. 43/6, pp. 275–6, 338, 481.
4. *Minutes*, 26 June and 17 July 1795. Portland to the Birmingham Bench, and H. Curzon, 9 and 10 July 1795, HO. 43/6, pp. 533–7.
5. *Minutes*, 22 July 1795. Grafton to Portland, 5 Aug. 1795, and Hawkesbury's endorsement, PC. 1/29/A64. C. Willoughby to T. Carter, 7 Aug. 1795, HO. 42/35.
6. Portland to Willoughby, 9 Aug. 1795, HO. 43/6, p. 536. Portland's endorsement on petition from R. Charlwood, 14 Aug. 1795, PC. 1/29/A64.
7. *Minutes*, 20, 23 and 24 Oct. 1795. Circular, 25 Oct. 1795, HO. 42/36. Pitt to Stafford, 6 Nov. 1795, L.V. Harcourt (ed), *The Diaries and Correspondence of the Rt. Hon. George Rose*, 2 vols. (1860), I, pp. 203–4.
8. The difficulties caused by obstructive farmers are discussed above pp.   BPP., 'House of Commons select committee on the high price of corn', (1795), first report, pp. 3–4, third report, pp. 3–4.
9. *Minutes*, 30 Sept, 1, 20, 23, 24, 26 and 29 Oct. 1795. Portland to George III, 2 Oct. 1795, *Later Corr.*, II, pp. 407–9. Brickwood, and Scott, to Hawkesbury, 7 and 8 Oct. 1795, BL. Add. Mss. 38230, ff. 340–1; 38353, f. 336.
10. For a recent, but traditional account of this episode, see J.R. Poynter, *Society and Pauperism. English Ideas on Poor Relief 1795–1834*, (1969), pp. 55–76.
11. *DPD.*, 2nd ser. vol. 43, pp. 4–83, esp. pp. 9–10, 22–6, 75–7.

12. *Ibid.*, pp. 70–5. *BPP.*, 'Third report. . .', Appendix 4.
13. 36 Geo. III, cap. 9, 'An Act to prevent Obstructions to the free passage of Grain within the Kingdom'; the Act also introduced a non-capital alternative to existing legislation against breaking into granaries, and stealing the contents; the penalty was seven years transportation. Law Officers' report, PC. 1/30/A71. *DPD., loc. cit.*, pp. 83–4, 349–50. Portland to the Bishop of Exeter, 21 Jan. 1796, NUL., Portland dep. PwV. III. Endorsement on Lord Milford to Portland, 24 Mar. 1796, HO. 42/38.
14. *DPD.*, 2nd ser. vol. 44, pp. 56–8, 213–6, 430, 700–2.
15. E.P. Thompson, 'The "moral economy" of the English crowd in the eighteenth century', *P&P.*, 50, (1971), p. 129.
16. *DPD.*, 3rd ser. vol. 10, pp. 536–9; vol. 11, p. 5. Portland to the Duke of York, and circular, 1 and 4 Mar; Portland to Haden, 14 May; Portland's endorsement on letter from deputy Mayor Bowden of Bath, and J. King's reply, 17 and 20 May 1800, HO. 42/49–50; 43/11, pp. 498–9; 51/153.
17. Portland to J. King, 23 Oct. 1800, BL. Add. Mss. 58972, f.55. J. King to Liverpool, 9 Sept. 1800, HO. 42/51.
18. Portland to G. Coldham, Dr. Hughes, the Birmingham Bench, and D. Mangewell; J. King to S. Smith, Liverpool, and the town clerk of Blandford, all 9 to 19 Sept. 1800, HO. 42/51; 43/12, pp. 110–1, 116–7, 121, 127–8, 144–5: NUL., Portland dep. PwV. III.
19. J. King to the War Office, 9 Sept. 1800, WO. 40/17. Dr. Hughes to Portland, and reply, 4 and 14 Sept; Portland to Taunton, Marlow, and Foljambe, 8, 12 and 13 Sept. 1800, HO. 42/51: NUL., Portland dep. PwV. III.
20. Hughes to Portland, 14 Sept., J. King to Taunton, 18 Sept. 1800, HO.42/51; 43/12, p. 146. *Oxford Journal*, 6, 13 and 27 Sept, and 4 Oct. 1800.
21. Letters to Portland from, General Rooke, Bristol, Earl of Berkeley, Monmouthshire, and E. Morgan and S. Homfray, Merthyr Tydfil, 22 to 25 Sept. 1800, HO. 42/51. D.J.V. Jones, *Before Rebecca*, (1973), pp. 23 ff. Portland to George III, 23 Sept. 1800, *Later Corr.* III, p. 415.
22. Portland to Marlborough, 22, 29 (draft), and 30 Sept. 1800, HO. 42/51: NUL., Portland dep. PwV III. Steward E. Lock to Marlborough, 17 Sept. 1800, BCRO., D/ESv(M), BB. *Oxford Journal*, 27 Sept. 1800. Portland to J. King, 23 Oct. 1800, BL. Add. Mss. 58972, f. 55. Portland to George III, 27 Sept. 1800, *Later Corr.*, III, p. 418.
23. Portland to Haden, Monckton, Mr. Wakefield and Capt. Lemmon, 30 Sept. to 10 Oct. 1800, HO. 42/51–2; 43/12, pp. 194–6, 212: NUL., Portland dep. PwV. III.
24. Perry's *Morning Chronicle* with a series of articles in Sept. and Oct. 1800, some written by Tom Poole, defending the grain trade, was an exception. Mrs. H. Sandford, *Tom Poole and His Friends*, 2 vols. (1888), II, pp. 10–4.
25. E.g. *Anti-Jacobin Review*, vol. 7, (1801), pp. 326–7.
26. *Ibid.*, 9, (1801) review of 'J.W.', *Democracy the Cause of the Present Dearth and Suffering of the Poor*, (1801), pp. 173–5. *The Times*, 21 and 28 Oct. 1800. Acreage returns, Rector of Lawdon, 8 Sept, and Rev. Freeman, 15 Dec. 1801, HO. 67/6, 15. J. Blackner, *A History of Nottingham*, (Nottingham, 1815), p. 394.
27. Anon., *Thoughts on the Dearness of Provisions*, (Oxford, n.d. but 1800), pp. 5–6. A 'Birmingham Manufacturer', and Haden, to Portland, 19 and 27 Sept. 1800, HO. 42/51. Rashleigh to Pole-Carew, 2 Nov. 1800, CCRO., Carew Mss. CC/L/31.
28. Anon. to the Sun Fire Office, 29 Oct; anon. to Portland, received, Nov; Bailiff of Ipswich to Portland, with enclosure, 25 Nov. 1800, HO. 42/53, 55.
29. *The Times*, 4, 6 and 10 Oct. 1800. Portland to George III, 3, 6 and 10 Oct. 1800, *Later Corr.* III, pp. 421–2, 425, 427.
30. *The Times*, 4, 6 and 29 Oct. 1800. *Oxford Journal*, 18 Oct. 1800. J. Hatsell to Addington, 12 Sept. 1800, DCRO., SP. D152M/Corr. 1800–1. Worcester petition: letters to Portland from, W. Thorn and W. Gower, Kidderminster, 15 Sept., Wrottesley, Wilkinson, and Mayor of Bath, 13, 16 and 21 Oct; deposition of T. Robinson, 17 Oct. 1800; undated harvest return from Rev. Dr. Collins, HO. 42/51–2, 55. Nottingham Corporation minutes, NCA., CA. 3566, ff. 9–11. *York Courant*, 6 Oct. 1800. *Blackburn Mail*, 5 Nov. 1800.
31. See above, ch. 5.
32. Vicar of Bowden, harvest return; Portland to the Birmingham Bench, 8 Oct. 1800, HO. 42/52, 54.

33. R. Wells, *Insurrection; the British Experience 1795–1803*, (Gloucester, 1983), pp. 188–94.
34. Pitt to Addington, 8 and 9 Oct. 1800, Lord Stanhope, *Life of Pitt*, 4 vols. (1861–2), III, pp. 244–5. Pitt to George III, 10 Oct. 1800, *Later Corr.*, III, pp. 427–8. Harcourt, *loc. cit.*, pp. 281–2. Liverpool to Portland, 9 Oct. 1800, BL. Add. Mss. 38311, pp. 158–65.
35. Pitt to Addington, 9 Oct. 1800, *loc. cit.* Portland to Dundas, and Auckland, 12 and 25 Oct. 1800, NUL., PvW III. Grenville to Auckland, 20 Oct; Liverpool to Portland, and Dundas, 9 and 11 Oct; Fawkener to Liverpool, 25 Oct; Grenville to T. Grenville, 10 Oct. 1800, BL. Add. Mss. 34455, f. 321; 38234, f. 255; 38311, pp. 158–69; 41852, ff. 66–7.
36. 'Draft of His Majesty's Answer' to the London petition, n.d.; Mr. Miller to Portland, 6 Nov; Rev. Burnaby, harvest return, 8 Nov; Rev. J. Lowe to Fitzwilliam, 5 Dec. 1800, HO. 42/53–5. *The Times*, 13 Oct. 1800. *The Star*, 16 Oct. 1800. *Morning Chronicle*, 17 Oct. 1800. *York Herald*, 8 Nov. 1800. Clerkenwell petition to the Commons, 14 Nov. 1800, *JHC.*, vol. 55, pp. 827–8. Yonge, 25 Oct, and J.J. Butt, Salisbury, 13 Nov. 1800, to R. Pole-Carew, CCRO., Carew Mss. CC/L/31.
37. Portland to Auckland, 25 Oct. 1800, *loc. cit.* Pitt to Grenville, 2 and 6 Nov. 1800, *HMC.*, 'Dropmore mss.', vol. 7. (1908), pp. 371–2. Undated draft of King's speech, PRO. 30/8/234, ff. 37–9. *The Times*, 12 Nov. 1800.
38. Lord Holland (ed), *Memoirs of the Whig Party*, 2 vols. (1852), I. pp. 166–9. Grey, and Oxford, to Holland, 7 and 17 Nov. 1800, BL. Add. Mss. 51544, ff. 66–7; 51821, ff. 293–4.
39. Erskine to Kenyon, 15 Oct. 1800, *HMC.*, 'Fourteenth report', (1894), pp. 554–5. *The Times*, 12 Nov. 1800. *DPD.*, 3rd ser. vol. 13, pp. 31–4, 235–62. J. Symonds to A. Young, 30 Nov. 1800, M. Bethan-Edwards (ed), *The Autobiography of Arthur Young*, (1898), pp. 344–5.
40. Warwick to Portland, 5 and 8 Oct, and reply, 7 Oct. 1800, HO. 42/52; 43/12, pp. 220–2. Portland to Dundas, 12 Oct. 1800, NUL., Portland dep. PwV III. *The Times*, 12, 15 and 18 Nov. 1800. *DPD., loc. cit.*, pp. 8–20, 406–10. Holland to Caroline Fox, 24 Dec. 1800, and undated reply, BL. Add. Mss. 51735, ff. 231–2.
41. *DPD., loc. cit.*, pp. 225–33, 241–5, 471–87, 584–91. M.W. McCahill, *Order and Equipoise. The Peerage and the House of Lords 1783–1806*, (1978), p. 68.
42. Fox to Grey, c. 2 Dec. 1800, Lord John Russell (ed), *Memoirs and Correspondence of Charles James Fox*, 4 vols. (1854) III, pp. 315–6. Wilberforce, and George III, to Kenyon, 9 and 13 Jan. 1801, *HMC., loc. cit.* Holland, *loc. cit.* Dundas to Warwick, Dec. 1800, WO.1/1105, ff. 589–92. Lord Morely's diary, 4 and 6 June 1800, and 9 Mar. 1801, BL. Add. Mss. 48246, ff. 85–6; 48247, f. 204.
43. *Seventh Report*, pp. 3–9. J.D. Chambers and G.E. Mingay, *The Agricultural Revolution 1750–1880*, (1966), p. 121.
44. R. Willis, 'William Pitt's resignation in 1801: re-examination and document', *Trans. RHS.*, 5th ser. (1971), pp. 240–57.
45. Acreage returns, vicars of Launceston, Campden, and Faldingworth; cf. those from Blaxton, Cubbington, and Langhope, HO. 67/10, f. 45; 67/11, ff. 46, 131; 67/14, f. 81; 67/15. Morely diary, 30 Mar., 15 May, 8 and 13 June 1801, BL. Add. Mss. 48247, ff. 32–3, 53–4, 78, 85.

Chapter 15   Riot Control and the Repressive Agencies

1. King to Oswin, 5 Aug; Portland to J. Foote, 10 Nov; cf. Portland to J. Lloyd, 4 Apr. 1795, HO. 43/6, p. 313; 43/7, pp. 94–5, 254.
2. Portland to T.M. Palmer, 26 Feb, to Gower, 1 May 1800, and draft to Poulett and Fortescue, 30 Mar. 1801, HO. 42/61; 43/11, pp. 375–7, 460–1.
3. Charges of Kenyon and Mr. Justice Hardinge to Grand Juries for Worcestershire and Glamorganshire, *Reading Mercury*, 3 Aug. 1795, *Gloucester Journal*, 20 Apr. 1801.
4. Winchcombe ruefully added that he had 'no reason at present to expect' riots; draft to the War Office (?), 21 June 1799, GCRO., D149, X21/41. J.R. Western, 'The Volunteer Movement as an anti-revolutionary force 1793–1801', *EHR.*, LXXI, (1956), esp. p. 608.
5. Portland to F.J. Foljambe, 13 Sept. 1800, NUL., Portland dep. PwV III, among hundreds of examples.

6. Portland to Poulett, 8 Aug. 1795, and circular, 4 Mar. 1800, HO. 42/49; 43/7, pp. 107–8.
7. For which see L. Radzinowicz, *A History of English Criminal Law*, 4 vols. (1948–68), IV, ch. 4, esp. pp. 129–30 and note 4. T. Hayter, *The Army and the Crowd in Mid-Georgian England*, (1978), part i.
8. Portland to Hardwicke, and J. King to York, both 19 Sept. 1795, HO. 43/7, p. 185; 51/148, f. 214.
9. York's secretary, Hawgill to J. King, 19 Sept. 1795, HO. 50/4, pp. 573–4. Under-secretary Lewis, War Office, to Lord George Lennox, 31 Dec. 1796, WO. 4/167, pp. 279–80.
10. Portland to H. Sedley, 19 Dec. 1800, NUL., Portland dep. PwV. III. Portland to G. Coldham, 30 Apr, the Mayor of Banbury, S. Homfray, and Birmingham Bench, 13, 18 and 19 Sept. 1800, HO. 42/51; 43/11, pp. 479–80; 43/12, pp. 147–8. Royal Proclamation, 18 Sept. 1800, PC. 1/3505B.
11. J. King to Herries, and Major Elliott, 15 and 16 Sept; Portland to Combe, and circular to all London JPs, 16 and 19 Sept. 1800, HO. 42/51; 43/12, pp. 138–40.
12. Portland to W.E. Taunton, 9 Sept, to Dr. Marlow, and Rev. Dr. Hughes, both 12 Sept, and to Marlborough, 22 Sept. 1800, HO. 42/51. Lewis to Taunton, 7 Sept. 1800, WO. 4/180. J. King to Coldham, 14 Sept. 1800, D. Gray and V.W. Walker (eds), *Records of the Borough of Nottingham*, vol. 7, (Nottingham, 1948), p. 402.
13. R. Wells, *Insurrection; the British Experience 1795–1803*, (Gloucester, 1983), pp. 190–2.
14. E.g. R. Whyte, Lexden Camp, to the War Office, and to Lord Howard, 3 and 6 Aug. 1795, WO. 1/1094: ECRO., D/DBy/012.
15. York to George III, 10 and 17 Sept. 1800, *Later Corr.*, III, pp. 411–3. Wells, *op. cit.*, ch. 10.
16. Portland to Poulett and Fortescue, 3 Apr. 1801, HO. 43/12, pp. 491–3. R. Wells, 'The revolt of the South-west 1800–1; a study in English popular protest', *SH.*, 1, 6, (1977), p. 729.
17. Portland to the Mayor of Stafford, and to Sir J. Heathcote, 22 and 29 Sept. 1800, and to Earl Fortescue, and the Devonport Bench, 12 and 20 Apr. 1801, HO. 42/51; 43/12, pp. 184–6, 513–6; 43/13, pp. 13–5. Printed copy opinion of V. Gibbs, Recorder of Bristol, and three other lawyers, 30 Mar. 1801, SCRO., DD. TB. C/1534. *Bath Chronicle*, 9 Apr. 1801. *Felix Farley's Bristol Journal*, 11 Apr. 1801. *Reading Mercury*, 3 Aug. 1795.
18. Portland to H. Leychester, 4 Apr, the Yalding Bench, 16 May, and the Birmingham Bench, 25 June 1795, HO. 43/6, pp. 313, 414, 482–3. Simcoe, 16 May, and Bastard, 31 July 1801, to Fortescue, DCRO., FLP. D1262M/L53, L55.
19. J. King to Mayor of Portsmouth, 29 Aug; Portland to Combe, 16 and 17 Sept, to S. Homfray, 27 Sept. 1800, and Poulett and Fortescue, 30 Mar. and 3 Apr. 1801, HO. 42/51, 61; 43/12, pp. 84, 131, 133–4, 491–3.
20. For the Special Commission and the Court Martial proceedings see below pp. 281–84. Portland to Heathcote, 6 May, and Homfray, 4 Oct. 1800, HO.43/11, pp. 469–70; 43/12, p. 211.
21. Portland to Poulett, 7 Apr. 1801, HO. 43/12, pp. 497–9.
22. Portland's determination to establish that interference with the internal transit of provisions could incur capital charges conditioned his response at this time, despite the recent Act offering alternative, lesser penalties. Mr. Justice Lawrence to Portland, 5 Apr. 1796; undated petition of the Warden and Verderers of the Forest of Dean, HO. 47/20: Ass. 5/116. *Hereford Journal*, 18 Nov. 1795. *Gloucester Journal*, 28 Mar. and 4 Apr. 1796.
23. Mr. Justice Grose, 27 Aug. 1796, Deputy-Recorder of Nottingham, 10 Nov. 1800, and Chief Justice Mansfield, 27 Jan. 1801, to Portland, HO. 47/25–6; 48/20. D. Hay, 'Property, authority and the criminal law', in Hay, P. Linebaugh and E.P. Thompson (eds), *Albion's Fatal Tree*, (1975). Cf. J. Stevenson, *Popular Disturbances in England 1700–1870*, (1979), pp. 4–5.
24. On one exceptional occasion hints that financial aid might be forthcoming were made to a Nottinghamshire JP organising the prosecution of individuals for riot offences tinged with political motivation, but this appears to have been a ruse to rouse his flagging enthusiasm. J.King to Bingham, 17 Nov. 1800, HO. 43/12, p. 289.
25. T. Stone to Portland, with enclosures, and J. King's reply, 27 and 30 Sept; Portland to Buckingham, 11 July 1795, and Sir C. Willoughby, 18 Sept. and 4 Oct.; Willoughby to Portland, 3 Oct. 1800, and Attorney-General's opinion thereon; J. King to R. Mascall, 8

Notes   389

Jan. 1801, HO. 42/51; 43/6, pp. 539–40; 43/12, pp. 141–2, 190–1, 213, 387–8; 48/9, ff. 219–20. Wells, *Insurrection* . . . , p. 47.

26. Portland's private secretary to Willoughby, 5 Aug. 1795: Portland to the Bishop of Exeter, 21 Jan. 1796, NUL., Portland dep. PwV. 110, pp. 16–7; PwF. 9476. Portland to the Devonport Bench, 4 Apr. 1801, HO. 43/12, pp. 489–91.

27. Depositions and correspondence, esp. J. King to Oxford town clerk, and reply, 18 and 23 Sept, Jailer Herries to the Home Office, 16 Sept, Portland to Marlborough, 29 Sept. and 19 Nov, Portland to the Lord Chancellor, 30 Oct, Law Officers to Portland, 31 Oct. 1800, HO. 42/51; 43/12, pp. 204, 295–8; 48/9, ff. 228, 234–66, 284–5.

28. Letters to Fortescue from, Eales, and Simcoe, 23 and 24 Mar, and J. Inglitt Fortescue, 4 Apr: E. Giddy to Addington, 20 Apr. 1801, DCRO., FLP. D1262M/L59: SP. D152M/ Corr. 1801. Portland to Simcoe, 9 Apr; Fortescue to Mayor of Totnes, 9 May 1801, HO. 42/61–2.

29. Portland to Lord Rolle, 24 Dec. 1800, F. Gregor, Grampound, 6 Feb, Fortescue and Poulett, 30 Mar, and Fortescue, 16 Apr 1801, HO. 42/61; 43/12, pp. 364–5, 413–4; 43/12, pp. 1–2.

30. Wells, 'Revolt of the South-west. . .', pp. 734–6.

31. Rev. J. Phillips to Portland, 24 Aug. 1795; 'An Account of the proceedings of John Cobb', forwarded to the Home Office, 26 Sept. 1800, HO. 42/35, 61. J. Hopps to B. Gott, 5 May 1800, cited W.B. Crump. 'The Leeds woollen industry, 1780–1820', *Publications of the Thoresby Society*, LXXI, (1931), p. 238. *The Iris*, 1 May 1800. Sheffield reward handbill, 29 Apr. 1800, YML., HH.3(2). Committal of J. Groves, 8 Aug. 1795, ECRO., Q/Sb/17, f. 24; Q/SMg/27.

32. 'State of the Proceedings before . . . Viscount Boyne', forwarded by T. Stone to Portland, 27 Sept. 1800, HO. 42/51. *Sussex Weekly Advertiser*, 9 Mar. 1795. Draft warrant, 24 June 1795, CCRO., Carew Mss. PO. 34/36. Anon., Cullompton, Devon, to N. Bolton, 30 June 1795, NUL., Portland dep. PwF. 298. A. Abney, Uplowman, to the War Office, 24 June 1795, WO. 1/1082, ff. 145–6. Chairman, Devon Bench, to Portland, 29 July 1795, PC. 1/27/A56.

33. Fitzwilliam, 3 Sept. 1800, and Chepstow Bench, 17 Mar. 1801, to Portland, HO. 42/51, 61. WYRO., discharged bail forms, 2 Sept 1800, West Riding Quarter Sessions File, Michaelmas, 1800. *Aris's Birmingham Gazette*, 15 September 1800. NCA., eleven bail forms, returned to Nottingham Borough Quarter Sessions, 193A, Michaelmas 1800 file. Norwich Mayoralty Book, 29 Sept; City of Norwich, Quarter Sessions minute, Michaelmas 1800, NNRO., Case 19, Dep. 128, 37; Case 20, shelf b, 25. C.B. Jewson, *The Jacobin City; a Portrait of Norwich 1788–1802*, (1975), p. 82.

34. Hayter, *op. cit.*, pp. 1–2, but cf. pp. 16, 19.

35. *The Courier*, 2 Apr. 1801. Commissioner Franshawe to the Navy Board, 31 Mar. and 11 Apr. 1801, Adm. 106/1916. Devonport Bench to Portland, 16, 17, 18 and 23 Apr; letter to 'My Dearest Brother', signature cut away, from Plymouth, 31 Mar; J. Elford, Plymouth, to J. Elliott, 17 Apr; Eastlake to the Navy Board, 18 Apr; copies of interchange of letters between Franshawe and the Devonport Bench, 17 Apr. 1801, HO. 42/61.

36. Fitzwilliam to Portland, 3 Sept. 1800, HO. 42/51. Mayor of Plymouth to Major-General England, 30 and 31 Mar. 1801, PCA, W. 362/5/1–3.

37. Holland Watson to Windham, 2 Feb. 1800, WO. 40/17. Walford to Portland, 12 and 24 Sept, and reply 13 Sept; R. Bignell to C. Butler, 15 Sept; Mayor of Bath, 21 Oct. 1800, and Devonport Bench, 1 April, to Portland; 'My Dearest Brother', letter, 31 Mar. 1801, HO. 42/51–2, 61 *Oxford Journal*, 25 Oct. 1800.

38. Wells, *Insurrection* . . .' pp. 189–92.

39. For Haden's massives to Portland, see above pp. 230, 237. Haden committed about one third of all Staffordshire defendants for trial, D. Hay, 'Manufacturers and the criminal law in the later eighteenth century; crime and "police" in south Staffordshire', *Police and Policing*, (P&P) Colloquium, 1983), p. 48. Haden to Porland, 30 July 1801, HO. 42/62.

40. *Norfolk Chronicle*, 30 Apr. 1796. W. Villers, Birmingham, 30 Apr, and Mayor of Richmond, 7 June 1795, to Windham, WO. 1/1084; 1/1092, ff. 213–6. Rev. Huntingdon of Hampshire, to Addington, 7 Oct. 1800, DCRO., SP. D152M/Corr. 1800–1.

41. Romilly to the Duponts, 29 Sept. 1800, S. Romilly, *Memoirs of Sir Samuel Romilly*, 2 vols. (ed. by his sons, 1840), II, pp. 72–5.

42. J.G. Jones, *Sketch of a Tour through Rochester, Chatham, Maidstone, Gravesend*, (1796), p. 26. G. Weston, Birmingham, to F. Freeling, 2 May; Fitzwilliam to Portland, 3 Sept. 1800, HO. 42/51, 215.

43. *Exeter Flying Post*, 14 Apr. 1796. *Gloucester Journal*, 25 Apr. 1796. High Sheriff of Cornwall to Portland, 27 Apr. 1796, enclosing depositions, HO. 42/38. Giddy diary, 6 Apr. 1796, CCRO., DD. DR. 15. Anon., Truro, to the LCS. 6 Apr. 1796, BL. Add. Mss. 27815, ff. 41–2.

44. Rev. Dr. Phillips, Haverfordwest, 24 Aug. 1795, Haden, and Mayor of Bath, 1 and 21 Oct., to Portland; Bignell to Butler, 15 Sept. 1800, HO. 42/35, 51–2. *The Times*, 30 Sept. 1800. *The Courier*, 2 Apr. 1801. *Bonner and Middleton's Bristol Journal*, 14 Apr. 1801. *Manchester Mercury*, 4 Aug. 1795.

45. Coldham to Portland, 25 Apr. 1800, HO. 42/49. *Derby Mercury*, 30 July 1795.

46. Rev. Robinson to Portland, 15 Oct. 1800, HO. 42/52. Copy of a letter from Gloucester, 5 Dec. 1800, forwarded to Dundas, HO. 50/10, ff. 707–8.

47. York to Addington, Feb, with report of army strength in Devon; memorandum, 'Force actually in the Western District', 3 Apr; Brownrigg to Hatton, 3 Apr; Simcoe to Fortescue, 28 Mar. and 3 Apr, and to Portland, 5 Apr. 1801, DCRO., FLP. D1262M/ L48, L63: SP. D152M/Corr. 1801. Monthly returns and summaries of regimental returns, WO. 17/9, 887, 898, 919, 973, 2785.

48. Callow, 23 June, and Cerjal, 21 July 1795, to the War Office, WO. 1/1084, ff. 627–30, 683–4. Birmingham Bench to Portland 23 June 1795; Weston to Freeling, 2 May 1800, HO. 42/35, 215. Rowbottom diary, 30 July to 2 Aug. 1795, OPL.

49. *The Times*, 26 June, 11 and 12 Aug. 1795. R. Whyte, Lexden Camp, to Lord Howard, 6 Aug. and 2 Sept. 1795, ECRO., D/DBy/012. Anon., Truro, to the LCS, 6 Apr. 1796, BL. Add. Mss. 27815, ff. 41–2. *Exeter Flying Post*, 14 Apr. 1796. *London Gazette*, 23 Apr. and 3 May 1796.

50. Teesdale Cockell to Fitzwilliam, 6 Oct. 1795, SCL., WWM. Y16. Cf. M. Burgoyne, Essex to Portland, and P. Storey to the War Office, 2 and 4 May 1800, HO. 42/50: WO. 40/17.

51. Spencer-Stanhope, draft speech, 1799, SCL., SS. 60588. Rashleigh to Pole-Carew, 2 Nov. 1800, CCRO., Carew Mss. CC/L/31. Portland to George III, 1795, *Later Corr.* II, pp. T.B. Bayley to J. King, 6 May 1800, HO. 42/50. J. Bohstedt, *Riots and Community Politics in England and Wales 1790–1810*, (1983), pp. 50–1. Cf. R. Glen, *Urban Workers in the Early Industrial Revolution*, (1984), pp. 51–2.

52. Rev. T. Drake, and Col. Entwistle, to the War Office, 3 and 5 Aug. 1795, WO. 1/1086, ff. 99, 101–2. *The Iris*, 14 Aug. 1795. Lorraine to R. Heron, 9 Mar. 1800, Newcastle City Library, Archives Dept., Northumberland Lieutenancy Papers, Vol. II. Herries and Leslie, to Dundas, 23 Mar. 1800, HO. 50/47.

53. Earl Gower, with enclosures, 28 Apr, Lord Aylesford, with enclosures, 31 Aug. 1800, and T. Gregor, Grampound, 31 Jan. 1801, to Portland, HO. 42/49–50, 61. *Aris's Birmingham Gazette*, 19 May 1800. *London Gazette*, 31 Mar. 1801. *The Iris*, 21 Feb. 1800. Cf. Earl of Berkeley, Gloucestershire, to Brownrigg, 13 Oct. 1800, HO.50/10, ff. 519–21.

54. R.A.E. Wells, 'Dearth and Distress in Yorkshire 1793–1802', *Borthwick Papers*, 52, (University of York, 1977), pp. 30–4.

55. *Oxford Journal*, 25 Oct. 1800. *Nottingham Journal*, 4 Oct. 1800. *Morning Chronicle*, 15 Sept. 1800. *Kentish Chronicle*, 26 Sept. 1800. *E. Johnston's British Gazette and Sunday Monitor*, 28 Sept. 1800. Fortescue to CO. Kingsbridge Volunteers, n.d. but 1801, DCRO. FLP. D1262M/L53. Palmer, 4 Sept, J. Jeffery, 8 Sept., and Birmingham Bench, 3 Oct 1800, to Portland; Portland to Fortescue, 6 Apr. 1801; London Light Horse Volunteers, printed account, 'General Meeting of Corps', 17 Dec. 1800, HO. 42/51–2; 43/12, pp. 499–502; 44/44, ff. 80–3.

56. Rolle, with enclosures, 28 Dec. 1800, and Gregor, 31 Jan. 1801, to Portland; Sidmouth Volunteers to their CO, 18 Dec. 1800, HO. 42/55, 61. Letters to Fortescue from, Welsh, 4 and 6 Jan., J.B. Cholwick, 9 Jan. and J. Coleridge, Feb: Simcoe, 18 Jan, and W. Giddy to Addington, 20 Apr. 1801, DCRO., FLP. D1262M/L48: SP. D152M/Corr. 1801. *Exeter Flying Post*, 25 Dec. 1800, and 1 and 8 Jan. 1801. Wells, 'Revolt of the South-west. . . ', pp. 724–5.

57. Indictments against Devon officers, and relevant depositions, Ass. 25/1/13: HO.

42/61–2. *Oxford Journal*, 25 October 1800. *Exeter Flying Post*, 2 July 1795. *Sherborne Mercury*, 6 July 1795.

58. Western, *op. cit.*, p. 611. W.G. Hoskins (ed), *Exeter Militia List 1803*, (1972). Cockell to Fitzwilliam, 6, 12 and 16 Oct; Fitzwilliam to Spencer-Stanhope, 7 Aug. 1795, SCL. WWM. Y16: SS. 60564/18. *Leeds Intelligencer*, 8 Dec. 1799. Examination of cordwainer Stanley, 26 Nov. 1799, LCA. Rad. Mss. I. 578. *London Gazette*, 25 Apr. 1796. Gott, 21 Sept, and Fitzwilliam, 14 Oct. 1800, to Portland, HO. 42/51; 50/48.
59. Wells, *Insurrection. . .*, pp. 194–226.
60. T. Ainsworth to Sir. R. Peel, 12 and 14 Mar. 1801, HO. 42/61.
61. George III to Hobart, 22 July 1801, *Later Corr.*, III, p. 580. R. Glover, *Britain at Bay*, (1973), pp. 44–5.

Chapter 16   The Role of the Courts

1. HCRO., QR. Michaelmas 1800.
2. Rashleigh to Pole-Carew, 24 Apr. 1795, CCRO., Carew Mss. CC/K/25. Coldham to Portland, 25 Apr, and cf. Heathcote to Gower, 27 Apr. 1800, HO. 42/49.
3. Wrottesley, 1 May, and Bingham, 15 Nov. 1800, to Portland, HO. 42/50, 53. *Staffordshire Advertiser*, 3 May 1800. *Aris's Birmingham Gazette*, 5 May 1800. Depositions and indictments, Staffordshire Summer Assize, 1800, Ass. 5/120, part v. Staffordshire jail calendar, and other documents, Staffs. CRO., Q/AG, D. 1723/4, ff. 39–40.
4. See below, p. 281.
5. Eales to Rolle, and Portland to Fortescue, both 30 Mar; Poulett, and Fortescue, to Portland, both 4 Apr; Devon county meeting handbill, 7 Apr; anon. to Devonport JP. St. Aubyn 2 Apr., and Devonport Bench to Portland, 20 Apr. 1801, HO. 42/61. Indictments, Somerset Lent Assize 1801, and Minutes, Ass. 25/1/2–3; 25/1/12; 23/9. SCRO., Quarter Sessions File, Midsummer 1801, and minutes, CQ. 3/1/369; CQ. 2/2/4(3). CCRO., Quarter Sessions minutes, Easter and Midsummer 1801, QSM. 7, ff. 99, 128. 'D.G.', Modbury, to Col. Bastard, 5 May; A.J. Taylor, 12 Apr, and Carpenter, with enclosed handbill, 23 Apr. 1801, to Fortescue, DCRO., FLP. D1262M/L59, L62–3.
6. Various crowd victims' depositions, and amended statement by Totnes crowd leader, Halse Ley; Welsford to Roedean, n.d., 1 and 2 May, and to Fortescue, 1 and 4 May; Fortescue to Kitson, 28 Apr. and 10 May, and replies, 1, 19 and 20 May, to the Mayor of Totnes, 29 Apr. and 9 May, and replies, 29 Apr. and 10 May, and to Studdy, and Taylor, both 14 Apr; Welsford to Kitson, 10 and 28 May, and reply c.29 May; Millers Walsh and Harrison to Welsford, 23 May; Kitson, 22 Apr. and Portland, 29 May, to Eales; Portland to Bastard, 20 Apr, and to Fortescue, 22 July; Treasury Solicitor White to Hatton, 26 May 1801, DCRO., FLP. D1262M/L53, L55, L58–9, L61: HO. 42/61–2; 43/13, pp. 59–63, 78; 49/4, ff. 70–1. Devon Assize records, Ass. 25/1/13; 25/3/1. DCRO., Quarter Sessions, 3/4b/lb. *London Gazette*, 28 Apr. 1801.
7. Letters to Portland from Rev. Phillips, 24 Aug. 1795, Heathcote, with enclosures, 4 and 5 May, Mayor of Winchester, with enclosure, 4 Oct, and Bingham, 15 Nov: Mayor of Stafford to Gower, 13 May; for similar manifestations see Coldham, 25 Apr, with enclosure, and Dr. Marlow, with enclosure, 17 Oct. 1800, to Portland, HO. 42/35, 49–50, 52–3. *Oxford Journal*, 11 Oct. 1800.
8. HCRO. QR. Easter, Midsummer and Michaelmas 1800; Epiphany and Easter 1801.
9. *Leeds Intelligencer*, 16 Dec. 1799. *Blackburn Mail*, 4 Jan. 1800, 19 and 26 Aug, 2 and 9 Sept. 1801. *Derby Mercury*, 13 Feb. 1800. *The Iris*, 14 Feb 1800, and 9 Apr. 1801. *Manchester Mercury*, 8 Apr. and 17 June 1800. *Manchester Gazette*, 26 July 1800 and 4 Apr. 1801. *Staffordshire Gazette*, 11 Apr. 1801. Rowbottom diary, 11 Feb. 1800, OPL. Lancashire Assize records, PL. 27/8, part ii; 28/4, ff. 31, 38–41, 44–8. Cheshire Assize Records, Cheshire, 24/180/6. Lancashire Quarter Sessions, Lancs. CRO., QJV/1/174–5; QSO/2/169–70; QUI/1/175. Bayley, 23 June 1800, Bancroft, 14 Mar, and Stonor, 2 Apr, to Portland; Ainsworth to Peel, 12 and 14 Apr. 1801, HO. 42/50, 61.
10. The uneven preservation of legal records prevents a detailed statistical survey.
11. This account derives from depositions and indictments in the Assize rolls, Ass. 5/120, part v, Stafford jail register, Staffs. CRO., Q/AG. D.1723/4, ff. 37–40, and Wrottesley to Portland, 1 May 1800, HO. 42/50.

12. Quarter Sessions minutes, CCRO., QSM. 7, pp. 128–30: NCRO., QOB. 14: Newcastle
     City RO., vol. 1762–96, p. 297: Dur. CRO., QOB. 15. pp. 597–8. W. Mitford to
     Portland, 8 Oct. 1800, HO. 42/52.
13. Anon., n.d. but 1796, Richmond, 25 Sept, and Mitford, 8 Oct. 1800, to Portland, HO.
     42/51–2; 47/20.
14. Letters to Portland from Judges, Lawrence, 5 Apr, and Grose, 27 Aug. 1796, Rooke, 10
     Apr. 1797, and Mansfield, 27 Jan. 1801, HO. 47/20, 26; 48/20. *Gloucester Journal*, 20 Apr.
     1801.
15. Indictments, Ass. 23/8. A. Jenkins, *History of Exeter*, (2nd edition, 1841), p. 140. *The
     Times*, 5 Aug. 1795. *Exeter Flying Post*, 6 Aug. 1795. W. Byrne, Chudleigh, to Portland,
     and the War Office, 6 and 9 May 1795, HO. 42/34; WO. 1/1083, ff. 45–6. E. Gattey, 3
     and 4 Aug, and T. Taylor, 4 Nov. 1795, to De la Pole, CCRO., Carew Mss. PO/22/18.
16. A.K. Hamilton-Jenkin, *The Cornish Miner*, (1927), pp. 163–4. Rev. E. Giddy, diary, 27
     July 1796, and later annotations, CCRO., DD. DG. 15. Poulett to Portland, 4 Apr. 1801,
     HO. 42/61. *Bonner and Middleton's Bristol Journal*, 18 Apr. 1801. *Felix Farley's Bristol
     Journal*, 18 Apr. 1801.
17. Indictments, Ass. 23/8. Giddy diary, *loc. cit.* Grose to Portland, 27 Aug. 1796, HO.
     48/20. Hamilton-Jenkins, *loc. cit.* GCRO., Quarter Sessions files and minutes, jail
     register, Midsummer 1801, Q/SG (Midsummer 1801); Q/SM. (1), 3.
18. Richmond to York, 21 Apr. 1795, HO. 50/4, ff. 273–83. Sloane to Sir C. Morgan, 23
     Apr: Judge-Advocate to Richmond, 22 May 1795; Court Martial minutes, WO. 1/1090,
     ff. 295–300: 71/170: 72/17. *Sussex Weekly Advertiser*, 11 May 1795.
19. *Sussex Weekly Advertiser*, 25 May, 1 and 15 June 1795. Richmond, and Portland, to York,
     21 and 26 Apr; Portland to the Lord Chancellor, 5 May 1795, HO. 43/6, p. 395; 50/4, ff.
     273–83; 51/148, f. 97. *The Star*, 29 May 1795. *Gloucester Journal*, 8 June. 1795.
20. C-in-C, General Order, 15 May; Adjutant-General, and York, to Richmond, 22 and 25
     May 1795, WO. 3/13, pp. 211–2; 3/28, p. 104; 1/1090, ff. 295–300. George III to
     Portland, 14 June 1795, *Later Corr.*, II, pp. 305–6. *Brighton Gazette*, 18 Oct. 1855.
21. This and the following paragraphs are based on; *Sussex Weekly Advertiser*, 15 June 1795.
     Reading Mercury, 15 and 22 June 1795. Portland to George III, 14 June 1795, *Later Corr.* II,
     pp. 305–6. Trial judge to Portland, n.d., HO. 48/5. Portland to Sheffield, and reply, 28
     and 29 July 1795, NUL., Portland dep. PwV. 109, pp. 154–6; PwF. 5181. J.A. Erredge, *A
     History of Brighthelmstone*, (Brighton, 1862), pp. 170–4. *Brighton Gazette*, 18 Oct. 1855.
22. C. Calhoun, *The Question of Class Struggle; Social Foundations of Popular Radicalism during
     the Industrial Revolution*, (Oxford, 1982), pp. 168–9.
23. C. Emsley, 'An aspect of Pitt's "Terror": prosecutions for sedition during the 1790s',
     SH., 6, 2, (1981). Cf. R. Wells, *Insurrection: the British Experience 1795–1801*, (Gloucester,
     1983), pp. 44–7.
24. *Ibid.*, ch. 2. J.R. Western, 'The Volunteer Movement as an anti-revolutionary force,
     1793–1801', *EHR.*, LXXI, (1956), p. 605.
25. G.A. Williams, *Artisans and Sansculottes*, (1968), p. 189.
26. *Ibid.*, pp. 105–6. Three Cornish JPs, n.d. but 1796, to Portland; A. Graham to J. King, 26
     Dec. 1800, HO. 42/39, 55. E.P. Thompson, *The Making of the English Working Class*,
     (1968 edition), pp. 199–200.
27. Welsford to Roedean, and Fortescue, 2 and 4 May 1801, HO. 42/62.
28. The Hadfield episode revealed features of the process whereby the army began to
     sympathise with civilian subsistence problems, as shown above, pp., and if the army was
     hated, despised and feared by proletarians, the latter evinced considerable sympathy when
     soldiers were flogged – normally inflicted publicly. Cf. J.R. Dinwiddy, 'The early
     nineteenth-century campaign against flogging in the army', *EHR.*, XCVII, 383, (1982),
     and E.E. Steiner, 'Separating the soldier from the citizen: ideology and criticism of
     corporal punishment in the British Army, 1790–1815', *SH.*, 8, 1, (1983).
29. Mr Emsley's recent re-evaluation of the legal and military dimensions of Pitt's terror,
     achieves its superficially judicious conclusion through a studious separation of the
     military and legal arms of the state. C. Emsley, 'An aspect of Pitt's "Terror": prosecution
     for sedition during the 1790s', *SH*, vi, (1981); *idem.*, 'The military and popular disorder in
     England in the 1790s', *Journal of the Society of Army Historical Research*, lxi, (1983); *idem.*,
     'Repression, 'terror' and the rule of law in England during the decade of the French
     Revolution', *EHR.*, C, 397, (1985).

Chapter 17 *'I cannot work through this Time of Necessity without your Assistance': the Relief of the Working Class*

1. The citation forming the chapter title derives from blacksmith Snelling to Medfield vestry, 25 Jan. 1801, IESRO., Medfield parish papers, FC. 91. G12/16. *Annals of Agriculture*, 24, (1795), pp. 540–1. Cf. Rev. J. Foley, chairman's address to the Gloucestershire Sessions Grand Jury, *Gloucester Journal*, 27 Apr. 1801.

2. L. Radzinowicz, *A History of English Criminal Law*, 4 vols. (1948–68), IV, pp. 13, 59–60. J.R. Poynter, *Society and Pauperism: English Ideas on Poor Relief 1795–1834*, (1969), *passim*.

3. Mss. entitled 'Hayes in Kent'; Bastard to Fortescue, 4 Jan. 1800, DCRO., SP D152M/Corr. 1801; FLP. D1262M/F43. *Manchester Mercury*, 3 Feb. 1795. Audits, Charlton Adam, 27 Apr. 1795, SCRO., DP. cha. a. 13/2/1; Blything Union, 7 Apr. 1796, IESRO. ABA/AB1/1. Vestry Minutes, Cartmel, 6 Mar. 1800, Lancs. CRO., PR. 2712/2; Ludgvan, 4 May 1800; W. Smith, St. Budeaux, to Pole-Carew, 20 Mar. 1801, CCRO., DP. 129/8/1; Carew mss. CC/L/33. J. Carr, agent at Ford, to Lord Delaval, 30 Jan. 1801, NCRO., ZDE4/59/22.

4. Quantification is also seriously impeded by the failure to locate any detailed charity accounts to use in conjunction with poor-law expenditure records for any one parish or locality. Relief calculations appear in Appendices, 6, 7 and 8.

5. *Aris's Birmingham Gazette*, 15 and 22 Dec. 1794, 2 and 9 Feb. 1795. *The Iris*, 30 Jan. 1795. *Sussex Weekly Advertiser*, 26 Jan. and 2 Feb. 1795. *Reading Mercury*, 1, 22 and 29 Jan., and 19 Mar. 1795. *Hull Advertizer*, 6 June 1795. *Manchester Mercury*, 3 Feb. and 17 Mar. 1795. *Lincoln, Rutland and Stamford Mercury*, 23 Jan. and 17 Apr. 1795. *Blackburn Mail*, 28 Jan. and 4 Mar. 1795. *Sherborne Mercury*, 9 Mar. 1795. *Exeter Flying Post*, 19 Mar. 1795. NNRO., Howes diary, Holmes dep.

6. Examples include Beckley, Sussex; Werlingworth, Suffolk; Ketteringham, Norfolk; Topcliffe, North Riding; Tysoe, Warwickshire; Newbold, Derbyshire: ESCRO., Par. 237/12/2; IESRO., FC. 94/A1/2; 94/ G8/1; NNRO., PD. 42/18; NYRO., PR. TOP/2/3; WCRO., DR. 288; Notts. CRO., DD. CW. 8f/1.

7. *Newcastle Advertiser*, 21 Feb. 1795. *Sussex Weekly Advertiser*, 29 Dec. 1794.

8. Cf. the accounts by M. Neuman, *The Speenhamland County. Poverty and the Poor Laws in Berkshire, 1782–1834*, (1982), pp. 75–80, *idem.*, 'Suggestion regarding the origins of the Speenhamland plan', *EHR.*, LXXXIV, (1969), and *idem.*, 'Speenhamland in Berkshire', in E.W. Martin, (ed), *Comparative Development in Social Welfare*, (1972), pp. 89–92. J. Bohstedt, *Riots and Community Politics in England and Wales 1790–1810*, (1983), p. 193, and ch. 8, note 109.

9. Willoughby to Dundas, 19 Nov, 1794, and to Portland, 28 June 1795, SR0., Melville Mss. GD. 51/1/372: HO. 42/35. OCRO., Quarter Sessions minutes, Q/SM, 11/2. E.W. Martin, 'From parish to union', in Martin, *op.cit.*, p. 36.

10. *Reading Mercury*, 15 and 22 Jan, and 20 Apr. 1795.

11. However, no alternative explanation is given; Neuman 'Speenhamland in Berkshire', *loc. cit.*, p. 88.

12. W. Baker, MP, to Portland, 13 July 1795, HO. 42/35. *York Courant*, 13 July 1795. Sykes to Wilberforce, 27 Jan. 1796, HRO., DD. SY. 101/54. *Reading Mercury*, 11 May 1795.

13. *Reading Mercury*, 11 May 1795, formal notices and news items.

14. More efficient workers usually received higher incomes than the less able.

15. *Reading Mercury*, 11 May and 27 July 1795.

16. OCRO., Quarter Sessions minutes, QSM. I/5. Willoughby to Portland, 7 Aug. 1795, HO. 42/35. Lord Carnarvon, High Clere, Hampshire, to Portland, 15 July 1795, NUL., Portland dep. PwF. 5067. GCRO., Quarter Sessions draft orders, Q/SM. 3/1. *Gloucester Journal*, 27 July 1795.

17. *Reading Mercury*, 29 June, 13 and 20 July 1795. Overseers' accounts and vestry minutes, Brimpton, Tilehurst, Uffington, BCRO., DP. 26/12/4; 132/8/2; 134/8/1.

18. R.S. Ince, 'The Care of the Poor at Stowmarket 1780–1830', (Unpublished BA thesis, University of Oxford, n.d.), pp. 75 ff. Overseers' accounts and vestry minutes, Chelmsford, Saxted, Hoveringland, ECRO., DP. 94/12/1; IESRO., FC. 102/A1/2; NNRO., PD. 35/17.

19. E.g. vestry minutes, Great Bardfield, Clavering, ECRO., DP. 67/8/2; 332/8/2: Cohn St.

Denis, GCRO., P. 97, VE. 2/2: Martock, SCRO., DP. Mart. 134/2/5: Sibbon, Wingfield, and Loes and Wilford Gilbert Union, IESRO., HB. 10/50/20/213(4); FC. 61/G1/1, 84/8/2.

20. T. Stone, *A General View of the Agriculture of the County of Lincoln*, (1794), p. 45. G. Turner, *A General View of the Agriculture of the County of Gloucester*, (1794), p. 26. N. Kent, *A General View of the Agriculture of . . . Norfolk*, (1796), pp. 46–7. R. Fraser, *A General View of the Agriculture of . . . Devon*, (1794), p. 17. J. Monk, *A General View of the Agriculture of the County of Leicester*, (1794), p. 57. Drake Home Farm accounts, DCRO., D346M/E12. J. Jeffery, Antony, to Pole-Carew, 29 June 1795, CCRO., Carew mss. CC/K/25. *Aris's Birmingham Gazette*, 12 Jan. 1795. *Norfolk Chronicle*, 21 Dec. 1794. Werlingworth vestry minutes, IESRO., FC. 94/A1/2. *Lincoln, Rutland and Stamford Mercury*, 3 July 1795. W.K. Parker, 'Wheat supplies and prices in Herefordshire 1793–1815', *Transactions of the Woolhope Naturalists' Field Club*, XLIII, (1979), p. 48. K.P. Bawn, 'Social Protest, Popular Disturbances and Public Order in Dorset, 1790–1838', (Unpublished Ph.D. thesis, University of Reading, 1984), pp. 161–2.

21. *Blackburn Mail*, 26 Aug. 1795. Crooks, manager Seaton Sluice, 20 Apr. and 20 Aug, and J. Oxley, Hartley, 25 July 1795, to Delaval, NCRO., ZDE4, 6/58, 69: 18. NEIMME., Watson Collection, Shelf 11, vol. XV. A. Raistrick, *Two Centuries of Industrial Welfare. The London (Quaker) Lead Company 1692–1905*, (1935), p. 35. *Newcastle Advertiser*, 22 Aug. 1795.

22. J. James to General Halse, 26 Mar. 1795, HO. 42/34. *Exeter Flying Post*, 14 May 1795.

23. Carnarvon to Portland, 15 July 1795, *loc. cit. Sussex Weekly Advertiser*, 20 Apr. 1795. Sir G. Yonge, to Pitt, 23 June 1795, PRO. 30/8/193, ff. 90–1. Gunter to Portland, 4 May 1795, HO. 42/34. E.P. Thompson, 'The "moral economy" of the English crowd in the eighteenth century', *P&P*, 50, (1971), pp. 124–6.

24. F.M. Eden, *The State of the Poor*, 3 vols. (1797), III, p. 837. *Hull Advertizer*, 30 Jan. 1795 and 22 Feb. 1796. *York Courant*, 9 Feb. 1795. *Reading Mercury*, 9 Mar. 1795. M.I. Thomis, *Politics and Society in Nottingham 1785–1835*, (Oxford, 1969), pp. 5–6. Newbold charity accounts, 1795, Notts. CRO., DD. CW. 8f/1. *Annals of Agriculture*, 24, (1795), pp. 55, 76. Great Parndon vestry minutes, ECRO., DP. 184/8/2.

25. Vestry minutes, 30 June 1795, ECRO., DP. 25/8/1.

26. *Annals of Agriculture*, 25, (1796), pp. 537, 627 ff. IESRO., East Suffolk Quarter Sessions minutes, 12 and 17 Oct. 1795, B. 105/2/50, pp. 115, 120. Poynter, *op. cit.*, p. 80. *Reading Mercury*, 2 and 16 Nov, and 21 Dec. 1795. E.W. Gilboy, *Wages in Eighteenth Century England*, (Cambridge, Mass. 1934), pp. 176 ff.

27. Overseers' accounts and vestry minutes: Fillongly and Kenilworth, WCRO., DR. 296/50; 404/91. Hethersett, Hoveringland, Terrington: Great Yarmouth Mayoral order, 19 Sept. 1795; 'Papers re. the Maintenance of the Poor at King's Lynn, 1795–7', NNRO., PD. 35/17–8; 41–32: Terrington St. Clemence, town book, 1758–1823 (uncatalogued): C12/3: Bradfer-Laurence deposit, BL. 15 part iv. *Norfolk Chronicle*, 8 Aug. 1795. Mary Sturge to her father, 22 Dec. 1795, OCRO., Marshall deposit, XVII/1/1/68.

28. E.g. East Leake, Notts, CRO., PR. 2011. Burton-on-Dunsdale, Butlers Marston, WCRO., DR. 218; 458/42. Peldon, ECRO., PD. 287/8/2. Burton Agnes and Burton Pidsea, East Riding, HRO., PR. 1859; 2112.

29. E.g. Stawley, Wells, SCRO., DP. staw. 13/2/3: W. St. C. 9/1/3, 13/2/9. Great Parndon, ECRO., DP. 184/8/2. Tettenhall, Staffs. CRO., D571A/PO/3.

30. E.g. Askew, Tysoe, Wolfhamote, WCRO., DR. 156/18; 167/6; 288. Boxwell, Terling, Tolleshurst, ECRO., DP. 105/8/2; 288/2/20; 299/8/2. Cratfield, IESRO., FC. 62/G12/1/A/2/3. Ketteringham, NNRO., PD. 42/18. Edingham, Northumberland, *Newcastle Advertiser*, 16 Jan. 1796. Beckley, ESCRO., Par. 23/12/2, p. 124.

31. E.g. Luppitt, DCRO., D1302A/PV/1. Dulcoe, Lanivet, Morewenstow, St. Ginny's, CCRO., DDP. 51/12/2; 110/12/3; 158/12/2; 67/12/1.

32. E.g. Breage, Probus, CCRO., DDP. 18/8/1; 194/12/5. North Perrot, SCRO., DP. per. 13/2/6.

33. Neuman, 'Speenhamland in Berkshire', *loc. cit.* Uffington overseers' accounts, BCRO., DP. 134/12/3. OCRO., Quarter Sessions minutes, QSM. I/5.

34. GCRO., Quarter Sessions minutes, QSM. 3/1: overseers' accounts and vestry minutes, Cohn St. Denis, Frampton-on-Severn, Horsley, Charfield, P. 97/VE/2/2–3; 149/OV/2/2; 181/OV/2/6; 74/VE/2/2.

35. E.g. Sandford, and Loes and Wilford, Gilbert Unions; Sibbon, Wingfield, IESRO., ADA7/AB1/1–2; HB. 10/50/20/21/3(4); FC. 61/G1/1; 84/G6/3. Clavering, Great Sampford, ECRO., DP. 289/8/2; 332/8/2.
36. *Gloucester Journal*, 16 Nov. and 7 Dec. 1795. *Lincoln, Rutland and Stamford Mercury*, 25 Dec. 1795. *Hull Advertizer*, 21 Nov. 1795. *Exeter Flying Post*, 14 Apr. 1796. J.E. Blackett to Mrs. Beaumont, 26 Nov. 1795; R. Mulcaster and J. Bell, to Blackett, 18 Dec. 1799; Crooks to Delaval, 26 Aug. 1796, NCRO., ZDE4/22/60: ZBL/209/224–5. Messrs. Foster to W. Redhead, 9 Dec. 1795, Dur. CRO., Buddle Collection, (uncatalogued, 1972).
37. *Reading Mercury*, 25 Jan. 1796.
38. Raistrick, *op. cit.*, p. 35. Crooks to Delaval, 20 Apr; Blackett to Beaumont, 26 Nov. 1795, NCRO., ZDE4/6/58: ZBL/224. *Newcastle Chronicle*, 22 Aug. 1795. *Hull Advertizer*, 21 Nov. 1795. Sir C. Sykes to Wilberforce, 27 Jan. 1796, HRO., DD. SY. 101/54.
39. Werlingworth and Saxted vestry minutes, IESRO., FC. 94/A1/2; 102/A1/2.
40. Newman, 'Speenhamland in Berkshire', esp. pp. 88–9, 109. J.L. and B. Hammond, *The Village Labourer*, (1966 edition), pp. 159–60. 'Table of Allowance for the Poor as settled by the Magistrates', 14 July 1795, GCRO., Quarter Sessions minute, QSM. 3/1. Quarter Sessions minutes, BCRO., Q/509, ff. 36 ff. and OCRO., QSM. I/5. *Reading Mercury*, 6 July 1795.
41. Vestry minutes, ECRO., DP. 94/12/11; 105/8/1. Newbold charity account, Notts. CRO. DD. CW. 8f/1.
42. ECRO., DP. 67/8/2; 289/8/2. Terrington town book, *loc. cit.*
43. Colquhoun to Hawkesbury, 12 July 1795, PC. 1/27/A55. Great Bardfield vestry minutes, 16 June 1795, ECRO., DP. 67/8/2.
44. *York Courant*, 2 and 30 Dec. 1799. *Staffordshire Advertiser*, 22 Feb 1800. Bastard to Fortescue, 4 Jan. 1800, DCRO., FLP. D1262M/F43. Bamburgh Castle Corn Charity records; Bell to Blackett, 20 Dec. 1799, NCRO., Crewe Mss. B.117, 120: ZBL/225. Raistrick, *op. cit.*, pp. 35–6. NEIMME., London Lead Company minutes, 30 Jan. 1800, vol. 15. Heaton Colliery estimates, Watson Collection, shelf 10, vol. 43. Buddle, bills, estimates, and correspondence with Claude Scott of Mark Lane, Feb. 1800, Dur. CRO., Buddle Collection, 247, 1025, 1187. Drowas to Hatton, 14 Apr; Homfray to Rooke, 24 Sept. 1800, HO. 42/49,51. Gulval vestry minute, 18 Mar. 1800, CCRO., DDX. 173/77/1. Werlingworth and Saxted overseers' accounts, IESRO. FC.94/A1/2; 102/A1/2.
45. E.g. Yorkshire parishes, Rosedale, Scruton, Welbeck, Yafforth, NYCRO., PR. ROS/3; SCR/2/1; HRO. PR. 1459. Rempstone, Notts. CRO., PR.8. Askew, WCRO., DR. 156/18. Terling, ECRO., DP. 299/8/3. Hatfield, Hertfordshire, Salisbury to Portland, 25 Dec. 1799, HO. 42/48. East Grinstead, Sussex, *Sussex Weekly Advertiser*, 18 Nov. 1799.
46. E.g. Skipton, Rochdale, Thirsk, *York Courant*, 25 Nov. 1799, *Blackburn Mail*, 4 Dec. 1799; NYCRO. PR. TH/6/1/5.
47. E.g. Maidstone and Chatham, *Kentish Chronicle*, 10 Jan. and 7 Feb. 1800.
48. See above, pp. 215–16.
49. Neuman, *Speenhamland County...*, pp. 90–4, and cf. pp. 159–60, 166–8. BCRO., Quarter Sessions minutes, Q/SO/8, pp. 411–3. *Reading Mercury*, 20 Jan. 1800. *Oxford Journal*, 1 Feb. 1800.
50. Neuman, 'Origins ... Speenhamland...', pp. 162 ff. Stinchcombe, Frampton-on-Severn, GCRO., P. 312/OV/2/2; 149/OV/2/2. Overseers' accounts, NNRO., PD. 41/32: ESCRO., Par. 253/12/1.
51. E.g. Dagenham, Dovercourt, Great Sampford, Wrabness, ECRO., DP. 174/8; 69/8/1; 289/8/2; 6/8/1A. Benhall, Hollesley, Wingfield, IESRO., FC. 131/G1/2; 170/G1/2; 84/G16/3. Shropham, NNRO., PD. 20/30–1.
52. E.g. Carnaby, Easington, HRO., PR. 2315: NYCRO., PR. EAT/2/1. Charlton Adam, Langford Buddle, Ottery, SCRO., DP. Cha. a. 13/2/1; laf. 13/2/4–5; oth. 13/2/2–3. Bajenton, Chilvers Coton, Honiley, WCRO., DR. 251; 346; 270.
53. Wrabness, ECRO., DP. 6/8/1A. Wingfield parish; Loes and Wilford Union, IESRO., FC. 84/G6/3; HB. 10/20/21–3(5). Townsend to Portland, 5 Mar. 1800, HO. 42/49. Lord Braybrooke, to Essex Clerk of the Peace, with enclosures, 18 July 1800, ESCRO., Q/SBb. 380/66/1–4. *Chelmsford Chronicle*, 27 June 1800. *Sussex Weekly Advertiser*, 10 Mar. 1800. Cf. the collapsing *per capita* value of relief presented graphically by K.D.M. Snell, *Annals of the Labouring Poor. Social Change and Agrarian England 1660–1900*, (Cambridge,

1985), p. 89.

54. Many Cornish parishes organised supplies, including Breage, Dulcoe, Ludgvan, Roach and St. Ginney's; CCRO., DDP. 18/8/1; 51/12/1; 129/8/1; 158/12/2; 67/12/2; DDX. 173/77/1.

55. This paragraph is specifically based on the administrative records of the following parishes: Framfield, ESCRO., Par. 343/12/1, p. 12. Cropwell Butler, Notts. CRO., PR.4546. Cheadle, Hampton Ridware, Staffs. CRO., P. 233A/PV/1; 1/A/PV/3. Nether Whiteacre, Barston, Frankton, WCRO., DR(B). 27/18; 46/79: DR. 217. Medfield, Great Glenham, IESRO., FC. 91/G12/17; 121/G1/2. Queen Camal, Horsington, West Pennard, SCRO., DP. q. ca. 9/1/1; hors. 13/2/4; w. pen. 9/1/2. Stinchcombe, Eastington, GCRO., P. 312/OV/2/2; 149/OV/2/2. Scruton, NYCRO. PR. SCR/2/1.

56. Parochial administration records; Kingston Lisle, BCRO., DP. 115B/12/4. Lowton Carmel, Poulton, Lancs. CRO., PR. 359–60; 2712/2–3; 2047. Terling, ECRO., DP. 299/8/3. *Manchester Gazette*, 7 Dec. 1799, 8 Mar. and 31 May 1800. *Manchester Mercury*, 17 and 24 July 1800.

57. The broad geography of examples includes Appleton Roebuck and Castle Howard, Yorkshire, Wanstead, Essex, Upottery, Devon, Islip, Oxfordshire, and 'several . . . Villages' in rural Nottinghamshire. *York Courant*, 2 Dec. 1799. ECRO., DP. 392/8/2. Upottery estate steward to Addington, 17 Mar: Bastard to Fortescue, 4 Jan. 1800, DCRO., SP. D152M/Corr. 1800: FLP. D1262M/F43. *Oxford Journal*, 4 Jan. 1800. Bassetlaw Petty Sessions return, Jan. 1801, Notts. CRO., Quarter Sessions file, QSV. 22. W. Fawcett to Lord Howard, 6 Mar. 1800, NNRO., How. 758/29, 349X.

58. The statistics and other details come from accounts in the provincial press, especially: *Gloucester Journal*, 24 Feb. 1800. *Norfolk Chronicle*, 9 Nov. 1799. *Hull Advertizer*, 22 Feb, 13 and 20 Sept. 1800. *Sussex Weekly Advertiser*, 9 Dec. 1799. *Newcastle Advertiser*, 28 Dec. 1799. *The Iris*, 10 Jan. 1800. *Kentish Chronicle*, 14 Mar. and 1 Apr. 1800. *Aris's Birmingham Gazette*, 3 and 17 Feb. 1800. *Leeds Intelligencer*, 27 Jan. 1800. *Manchester Gazette*, 31 May 1800. *Reading Mercury*, 6 Jan. 1800. *Oxford Journal*, 11 Jan. 1800.

59. G. Warde, Bath, to R. Benyon, 10 Jan. 1796, BCRO., D/EBy/C9. *Gloucester Journal*, 17 Feb. 1800. *Sussex Weekly Advertiser*, 9 Dec. 1799. W. Hastings to Fitzwilliam, 8 Feb. 1800, SCL., WWM. F. 47/16. Ramsay to Mrs. Graham, 21 Feb. 1800, B.L.H. Horn, (ed), 'Letters of John Ramsay 1799–1812', *Publications of the Scottish Historical Society*, 4th ser. 3, (Edinburgh, 1966), p. 8. *Kentish Chronicle*, 14 Mar, 1, 8 and 25 Apr, and 20 May 1800. *Aris's Birmingham Gazette*, 17 and 31 Mar. 1800. *The Iris*, 4 Apr. 1800. *York Herald*, 12 Apr. 1800.

60. See above, p. 48.

61. *Hull Advertizer*, 13 Sept. 1800. *Aris's Birmingham Gazette*, 6 Oct. 1800 and 10 Jan. 1801. NCA., Nottingham Corporation minutes, CA. 3560, p. 14. *Oxford Journal*, 18 and 25 Oct, 29 Nov, 13 and 20 Dec. 1800, 24 and 31 Jan. 1801. W. le Hardy and G. Reckett (eds). *Hertfordshire County Records. Calendar of the Sessions Books, 1799–1833*, (Hertford, 1939), pp. 19–20. Hollesley vestry minutes, IESRO., FC. 170/G1/2. Overseers' accounts, Modbury, DCRO., D269M/PO/2 and Gnossall, Staffs. CRO. D951/5/7–8.

62. Birmingham overseers' return, WCRO., Epiphany 1801 Quarter Sessions file, QS. 32/2. Exeter subscription administration records, DCRO., Exeter City Records, Misc. Papers Box 10. *Aris's Birmingham Gazette*, 6 Oct, 3 and 17 Nov. 1800, and 23 Feb. 1801. *Manchester Gazette*, 21 and 28 Feb. and 12 Apr. 1801. *Leeds Mercury*, 18 July 1801. Shinfield vestry minute, 17 Dec. 1800. BCRO., DP. 110/8/1.

63. Poulett to Portland, with enclosures, 15 May 1800, HO. 42/50. *Aris's Birmingham Gazette*, 12 May 1800. B. Cozens-Hardy (ed), 'Mary Hardy's diary', *Norfolk Record Society*, 37, (1968), p. 109. West Pennard vestry minute, 23 Dec. 1800. SCRO., w. pen. 9/1/2.

64. *Norfolk Chronicle*, 17 Sept. and 27 Dec. 1800. *Reports of the Society for Bettering the Conditions of the Poor*, III, (1802), pp. 26–8, 157–8. Vicar of Sutton Verger, acreage return, 27 Oct. 1801, HO. 67/23, f. 245. T. Rudge, *A General View of the Agriculture of the County of Gloucester*, (1805), p. 346. Sir G.O. Paul to Portland, 7 Aug. 1795, PC. 1/29/A64. DPD., 2nd ser. vol. 43, pp. 247–8, 649–50.

65. Woodford vestry minute, 1 Dec. 1800, ESRO., DP. 167/8/3. *Sussex Weekly Advertiser*, 3 Feb. 1795. *Manchester Mercury*, 3 Feb. 1795. *Leeds Intelligencer*, 20 July 1795. *Newcastle Advertiser*, 25 July 1795. Sandford Union minute, 14 July 1795, IESRO., ADA7/AB1/2.

Huntingdonshire county meeting handbill, 30 July 1795, BL. Add. Mss. 35642, ff. 123–4.
W. Fawcett to Howard, 6 Mar. 1800, NNRO., 758/29/349x. *Lincoln, Rutland and Stamford Mercury*, 30 Jan. 1795. *Reading Mercury*, 6 July 1795. Bingfield vestry minutes; Kingston Lisle overseers' accounts; Quarter Sessions minutes, BCRO., DP. 18/8/1; 115B/12/4: Q/SO/9, ff. 36–8.

66. *Sussex Weekly Advertiser*, 2 Feb. 1795. *Newcastle Advertiser*, 13 June and 4 July 1795, and 20 Dec 1800. *Aris's Birmingham Gazette*, 22 Nov. 1794. Sheffield committee handbill, 5 Feb. 1795, SCL., JC. 1605. *Kentish Chronicle*, 2 Jan. 1801. *Reports of the Society for Bettering the Condition of the Poor*, III, (1802), pp. 60–5. E.R. Wickham, *Church and People in an Industrial Society*, (1957), pp. 20, 56. I.R. Christie, *Stress and Stability in Late Eighteenth Century Britain: Reflections on the British Avoidance of Revolution*, (Oxford, 1984), pp. 196–7. Vestry minutes: Great Parndon, 22 July 1795; Wanstead, 19 May 1800, ECRO., DP. 184/8/2; 292/8/2: Slimbridge, 15 Jan. 1796 and 23 Apr. 1801; Stroud, 20 July 1801, GCRO., P. 320a/OU/7/1; 298a/VE/2/1. Huish Episcopi, 27 Mar. 1801, SCRO., DP. h. ep. 9/1/4: Truro St. Clements, 14 Apr. and 13 May 1800, CCRO. DDP. 33/12/1. NNRO., Bradfer-Laurence Collection, 'Papers re Maintenance of the Poor in King's Lynn, 1795–7', BL. (15), part iv.

67. *Reports of the Society for Bettering the Condition of the Poor*, III, (1802), pp. 192–9. South Weald vestry minute, 14 June 1801, ECRO., DP. 128/8/4. Sandford Union committee orders, IESRO., ADA7/AB1/2. W. le Hardy (ed), *Hertfordshire County Records – Calendar to the Quarter Sessions Minute Books, 1752–98*, (Hertford, 1935), pp. 450–2. *Reading Mercury*, 16 Nov. 1795. Heathersett vestry minutes, 1795, NNRO., PD. 41/32. WCRO., Quarter Sessions minute, Epiphany 1801, QS. 39/10. Midhurst vestry minutes, June 1799, WSCRO. Par. 138/12/1.

68. *Newcastle Advertiser*, 30 Aug. 1800. Vestry minutes; Newcastle-upon-Tyne, St. Nicholas, 28 June 1800, Newcastle City Archives, MA.183: Moreton, 30 Dec. 1800; South Weald, 14 June and 4 Aug., 1801, ECRO. DP. 72/8/1; 128/8/4. South Molton, 18 Feb. 1801, DCRO., D814A/PO/3: Ludgvan, 7 Jan. 1801, CCRO., DDP. 129/8/1. Neuman, *Speenhamland County . . .*, p. 161.

69. Neuman, *Speenhamland County. . .*, p. 154. *Hull Advertizer*, 20 Mar. 1795. *Derby Mercury*, 23 July 1795. A.W. Dyson (ed), *William Metcalf – His Book*, (Leeds, 1931), p. 37. Vestry minutes; Cheadle, 21 Aug. 1795, Staffs. CRO., D. 233A/PV/1: Terling, 6 July and 12 Aug. 1795; Weatherfield, 23 Oct. 1800, ECRO., DP. 119/8/5; 299/8/2. Burtonwood, 10 Nov. 1796, Lancs. CRO., PR. 2720/2.

70. Neuman, *Speenhamland County. . .*, p. 156.

71. Vestry minutes; Werlingworth, 11 Jan. 1796, IESRO., FC. 94/A1/2: Ludgvan, 3 Jan. 1801, CCRO., DDP. 129/8/1: Chigwell, 24 Jan. 1796, ECRO., DP. 168/8/9. *Reading Mercury*, 3 Aug. 1795. J. Howson, Wakefield, to W. Spencer-Stanhope, 9 Apr. 1796: W. Hastings, Malton, to Fitzwilliam, 21 Jan. 1801, SCL., SS. 60586/10: WWM. F.47/19. Sykes to Wilberforce, 27 Jan. 1796, HRO., DD. SY. 101/54. *Leeds Intelligencer*, 16 Dec. 1799. *The Iris*, 7 Aug. 1800.

72. *Sussex Weekly Advertiser*, 2 Feb. 1795. Drowas to Hatton, 14 Apr. 1800, HO. 42/49. J. Ehrman, *The Younger Pitt. The Reluctant Transition*, (1983), p. 166. B. Trinder, *The Industrial Revolution in Shropshire*, (1973), pp. 200–6.

73. Lord Townsend, Rainham, to Portland, 1 Jan. 1796, HO. 42/38. *Cambridge Intelligencer*, 22 Nov. 1800.

74. Vestry minutes; Brewood, 16 and 20 Feb. 1800 and 24 Feb. 1801, Staffs. CRO., D. 880/2/2: Midhurst, Nov. 1794, WSCRO., Par. 138/12/1: Wansted, 19 May 1800, ECRO., DP. 392/8/2: Ludgvan, 3 Jan. and 22 Mar. 1801, CCRO., DDP. 129/8/1; Market Weighton, 14 Dec. 1800, BIHR., M/W/20. Hatfield handbill, 15 Dec. 1795, Beds. CRO., Whitbread Mss. W.1/11. Norwich Guardians of the Poor, minutes 6 and 7 Jan. 1795, NNRO., Ca.20, shelf e. G. Jackson, *Hull in the Eighteenth Century*, (1972), p. 324. J. Money, *Experience and Identity. Birmingham and the West Midlands 1760–1800*, (Manchester, 1977), p. 267. Neuman, *Speenhamland County. . .*, p. 154.

75. Neuman, *Speenhamland County . . .*, p. 107, note 60. Heathersett minute, 22 Nov. 1799: vestry minutes and overseers' accounts of Norwich parishes of St. James, St. Lawrence, St. Martin at Oak, St. Peter Hungate, NNRO., PD. 11/83; 15/39–40; 26/27–8; 41/32; 58/38; 66/45. Bradfer-Laurence Collection, BL. (15), part iv, 'Papers re Maintenance of the Poor at King's Lynn, 1795–7'. *Cambridge Intelligencer*, 22 Nov. 1800.

76. Gray to overseer Gregory, 1 Mar. 1796, WSCRO., Par. 100/37/3. Snelling to Medfield vestry, 25 Jan. 1801, IESRO., Medfield parish papers, FC. 91/G12/16. D. Lowe, *The Life, Adventures and Experience of David Lowe*, (3rd edition, Nottingham, 1823), p. 78. Scruton vestry minutes, 1 Mar. 1795, NYCRO., PR. SCR/2/1. Ashby to R. Pattenden, 1 Mar. 1800, ESCRO., Par. 284/13/12, f.8.

77. Vestry minutes; Ludgvan, 15 Mar. 1801, CCRO. DDP. 129/8/1; cf. Terling, 11 Feb. 1800, ECRO., DP. 299/8/3: Thirsk, 4, 7 and 13 Feb. 1800, NYCRO., PR. TH/6/1/5. *Sussex Weekly Advertiser*, 26 Jan. 1795. *Hull Advertizer*, 8 Mar. 1795.

78. Scruton vestry minute, 23 July 1795, NYCRO., PR. SCR/2/1. Saffron Walden handbill, 10 July 1795, ECRO., D/DBy/012. M.D. George, *London Life in the Eighteenth Century*, (1966 edition), pp. 120–31, and note 54. G. Rudé, *Hanoverian London*, (1971), p. 7. F. Sheppard, *London 1808–70: the Infernal Wen*, (1971), pp. 5–6, 14. J.A. Jackson, 'The Irish in East London', *East London Papers*, 6, (1963). S. Gilles, 'English Catholic charity and the Irish poor in London', *Recusant History*, 11. (1972), esp. p. 184. D. Hay, 'Manufacturers and the criminal law in the later eighteenth century; crime and "police" in south Staffordshire; *Police and Policing*, (P & P Colloquium, 1983), pp. 44–5.

79. E.g. St. Michael Carhays, CCRO., DDP. 24/12/1: Carlton, East Drayton, Notts. CRO., PR. 4824; 6521: Badby, NYCRO., PR. BA/2.

80. W. Pitt, *A General View of the Agriculture of the County of Stafford*, (2nd edition, 1796), p. 173. Rev. R. Walker to Fortescue, 26 Mar. 1801, DCRO., FLP. D1262M/L48. J. Howson to W. Spencer-Stanhope, 18 Mar. 1800, SCL., SS. 60586/43. *Reports of the Society for Bettering the Condition of the Poor*, III, (1802), pp. 157–69.

81. Scruton vestry minute, 5 Feb. 1795, NYCRO., PR. SCR/2/1, with additional details from *Yorkshire Poll Book*, (1807), and S. Baines, *Directory of Yorkshire*, 2 vols. (1822–3), II. Cf. with detailed lists of small subscribers for: Gulval, CCRO., DDX. 173/77/1: Upholland, Cartmel, Poulton, Lancs. CRO., PR. 2907/2/1; 2712/2–3; 2047: Newbold Corn Charity administration book, 1795 and 1800, Notts. CRO., DD. CW. 8f/1. R. Osmerod to Caroline Fox, 9 Dec. 1800, BL. Add. Mss. 51821, ff. 288–9. *Manchester Mercury*, 28 Dec. 1799. *York Courant*, 9 Feb. 1795, 30 Dec. 1799, 6 Jan, 15 and 22 Dec. 1800.

82. R. Wells, 'The revolt of the South-west 1800–1; a study in English popular protest', *SH*. 1, 6, (1977), pp. 720–1. W. Thorn and W. Gower, to Portland, 15 Sept; Bancroft to J. King, 20 Dec. 1800, HO. 42/51, 55. Dawson to Fitzwilliam, 8 Feb. 1801, SCL., WWM. F.47/13.

83. For example as implied by Bohstedt, *op. cit.* p. 97.

84. *The Iris*, 4 Apr. 1800. Printed accounts, Sheffield charity, 1800–1; Rev. Wilkinson to Fitzwilliam, 5 Feb. 1801, SCL. MP. 185L: WWM. F. 122/41. *Reports of the Society for Bettering the Condition of the Poor*, III, (1802), pp. 157–69. Osmerod to Fox, *loc. cit.* Rector of Clitheroe, harvest return, 8 Nov. 1800, HO. 42/53. *Hull Advertizer*, 24 May 1800. *Manchester Gazette*, 12 Apr. and 31 May 1800. Diary of A.A. Gawthorn, NCA., M. 23904. Emmerton to his brother, 4 Jan. 1801, Notts. CRO., DD. SY. 284/6.

85. Messrs. Gribble to Mr. Mitford, 18 July 1795, PC 1/27/A56. T. Godman to Lord Verulam, 27 July 1795, *HMC*., 'Verulam mss.', (1906), p. 157. Poole to Coleridge, May 1801, Mrs. H. Sandford (ed), *Thomas Poole and His Friends*, 2 vols. (1888), I. pp. 45–7. Simcoe to Fortescue, 15 Apr. 1801, DCRO., FLP. D1262M/L52. *Derby Mercury*, 22 Oct. 1795.

86. Pitt in the Commons, 10 June 1800; Commons corn committee fifth report, 18 Dec. 1800, and debate thereon, *DPD*., 3rd. ser. vol. 12, pp. 79–83; vol. 14. pp. 510–4, 541–7. E.N. Williams, *The Eighteenth Century Constitution*, (Cambridge, 1960), pp. 272–3.

87. Davison to Fitzwilliam, 8 Feb. 1801, SCL., WWM. F.47/13. Wilberforce to W. Hey, 17 Mar. 1801, R.I. and S. Wilberforce (eds), *The Correspondence of William Wilberforce*, 2 vols. (1840), II, pp. 224–5. *DPD*., 3rd ser. vol. 15, pp. 532–4, debate on 1801 corn committee's fourth report, 20 Mar.

88. Rev. J. Foley to C. Blagge, 11 and 31 Mar, and 11 Apr, and to the Marquis of Worcester, 1 Mar; petition of Gloucestershire Grand Jury, 25 Mar, (Lent Assize): Gloucestershire Quarter Sessions minute, 28 Feb. 1801, GCRO., D.421X/5/1–5; QSM. 3/1. *DPD*., 3rd ser. vol. 16, pp. 39–43, corn committee fifth report, Apr. 1801.

Chapter 18   *Paradoxes, Ironies and Contradictions: some Conclusions*

1. For a description and use of Oddy's model, see above ch. 5. D.J. Oddy, 'Urban famine in nineteenth-century Britain; the effect of the Lancashire cotton famine on working-class diet and health', *Ec. His. Rev.* 2s, xxxvi, 1, (1983). S. Jackson, 'Population change in the Somerset–Wiltshire border area 1701–1800; a regional demographic study', *Southern History*, 7, (1985), p. 135. J.K. Edwards, 'Norwich bills of mortality 1707–1830', *Yorkshire Bulletin of Economic and Social Research*, 21, (1970), appendix. S. Catts and E. van de Walle 'Nutrition, mortality and population size; Malthus' court of last resort', *Jnl. Int. His.*, p. 222. W. le Hardy (ed), *Hertfordshire County Records. Calendar to the Quarter Sessions Minute Books*, VIII, (Hertford, 1939), pp. 28–35. E.A. Wrigley and R.S. Schofield, *The Population History of England 1541–1871. A Reconstruction*, (Cambridge, Mass., 1981), pp. 379–82; cf. p. 372. D. Weir, 'Life under pressure; France and England, 1670–1870', *Jnl of Ec. His.*, XLIV, 1, (1983), p. 43.
2. J. Mokyr, 'The industrial revolution and the new economic history', in *idem* (ed), *The Economics of the Industrial Revolution*, (1985), p. 50, note 63, citing P.H. Lindert and J.G. Williamson, 'Reinterpreting Britains social of tables, 1688–1913', *Expl. Ec. His.*, 20, 1, (1983), p. 101, reiterated with inadequate qualification by J.G. Williamson, *Did British Capitalism Breed Inequality?*, (1985), p. 21.
3. J.D. Post, *The Last Great Subsistence Crisis in the Western World*, (1977), pp. 48–9.
4. A. Sen, *Poverty and Famine. An Essay on Entitlement and Deprivation*, (Oxford, 1981), pp. 1–8, 47–50, 162–6, and cf. the discussion of the historical applicability of entitlement in L.A. Tilley, 'Food entitlement, famine and conflict', *Jnl. Int. His.*, XIV, 2, (1983), pp. 334–9.
5. A.B. Appleby, 'Epidemics and the little ice age', *Jnl. Int. His.*, X, 4, (1980), p. 663. Wrigley and Schofield, *op. cit.*, p. 319. Post, *op. cit.*, pp. 53, 63–6, 87–9.
6. F.M. Eden, *Observations on Friendly Societies*, (1801), p. 8. D. Bythell, *The Handloom Weavers*, (Cambridge, 1969), p. 182.
7. Cornish clergyman to a Penzance merchant, 24 June 1795, PC.1/27/A54. *Exeter Flying Post*, 28 Aug. 1800. OPL., Rowbottom diary 1794–1801, *passim*.
8. T.R. Malthus, *An Essay on the Principle of Population*, 2 vols. (2nd edition of 1803, Everyman, 1914), II, pp. 187, 211–2.
9. *Ibid.*, II, p. 187.
10. R.B. Rose, 'Eighteenth-century price riots, the French Revolution, and the Jacobin Maximum', *Int. Rev. SH.*, IV, (1959), p. 435.
11. J. Bohstedt, *Riots and Community Politics in England and Wales 1790–1810*, (1983), p. 213. Cf. R. Wells, 'The revolt of the South-west 1800–1; a study in English popular protest', *SH*, 1, 6, (1977).
12. F.K. Donnelly, 'The destruction of the Sheffield School of Anatomy in 1835; a popular response to class legislation', *Transactions of the Hunter Archaeological Society*, X, 3, (1975), p. 171. J. Wrigley, 'Derby and Derbyshire during the great reform bill crisis of 1830–2', *Derbyshire Archaeological Journal*, 101, (1981), pp. 144, 148.
12. C. Mackie, *Norfolk Annals*, 2 vols (1901), II, p. 234. A.J. Coles, 'The moral economy of the crowd; some twentieth-century food riots', *Journal of British Studies*, XVIII, (1978). *Brighton Gazette*, 19 Jan. 1854.
14. E. Richards, 'The geography of food riots: 1847', in A. Charlesworth (ed), *An Atlas of Rural Protest in Britain 1548–1900*, (1983), pp. 108–11.
15. Although fourteen people were prosecuted, felony charges were dropped in a calculated display of leniency, which of course had hundreds of historical precedents. *Nottingham Review*, 14 May, 11 and 18 June, and 2 July 1847.
16. *Derby Mercury*, 19 Nov. 1795. *Manchester Mercury*, 3 Mar. 1801. J. Tann, 'Co-operative corn milling; self-help during the grain crises of the Napoleonic Wars', *Ag. His. Rev.*, 28, (1980), pp. 47–8. Birmingham Company articles, BT. 3/5, ff. 419–33. *Gentleman's Magazine*, (Feb. 1801), p. 175.
17. Tann, *op. cit.*, *passim*. Portland with enclosures re. the proposed Manchester Mill, to the Privy Council, 12 Feb. 1800, PC. 1/3477. Board of Trade minutes, 4 Mar. 1800, an investigation of the Birmingham Company personnel, BT. 5/11, ff. 419–43. Wanstead vestry minutes, 12 Jan. and 23 Mar. 1801, ECRO. DP. 392/8/2. *Aris's Birmingham Gazette*, 15 Dec. 1800. *Norfolk Chronicle*, 21 Feb. 1801. *Manchester Gazette*, 10 Jan. 1801.

York Courant, 12 May, 13 June and 15 Dec. 1800, and 16 Feb. 1801. *Staffordshire Advertiser*, 1 and 15 Nov. 1800. Banks to Liverpool, 16 Sept. 1800, BL. Add. Mss. 38234, ff. 152–3.

18. Tann, *op. cit.*, esp. pp. 52–7. J. Latimer, *Bristol in the Eighteenth and Nineteenth Centuries*, 2 vols., (1873 and 1887, reprinted Bath, 1970), II, p. 7–8. *York Herald*, 22 Nov. and 20 Dec. 1800. *York Courant*, 3 Nov. 1800 and 27 Apr. 1801.

19. D.E. Williams, 'Morals, markets and the English crowd in 1766', *P&P.*, 104, (1984), esp. pp. 66, 71–2.

20. For a local analysis of the problematic of middle-class consciousness – at Stockport – which emphasises that before 1820 'it was extremely difficult for "bourgeois" solidarity to emerge', see R. Glen, *Urban Workers in the Early Industrial Revolution*, (1984), pp. 279–80.

21. A.P. Thornton, *The Habit of Authority*, (1966), p. 79.

22. Portland to the Duke of York, 9 Nov. 1800, HO. 50/10, f.571.

23. Grey to Holland, 7 Nov. 1800, BL. Add. Mss. 51544, ff. 66–7. J. Greg (ed), *The Farington Diary by Joseph Farington R.A.*, 6 vols. (3rd. edition, 1923), I, pp. 294–5.

24. Rickman to Southey, in Lisbon, 28 May 1800, O. Williams, *Life and Letters of John Rickman*, (1911), pp. 30–1. J.A. Hone, *For the Cause of Truth; Radicalism in London 1796–1821*, (Oxford, 1982), p. 131. Anon. to T. Edmunds, Barnsley, 12 May 1800, SCL. WWM. F.47/78–80. R. Wells, *Insurrection; the British Experience, 1795–1803*, (Gloucester, 1983), p. 208. OPL. Rowbottom diary, Aug. 1797.

25. M.I. Thomis and P. Holt, *Threats of Revolution in Britain 1789–1848*, (1977), pp. 24–6. Cf. A. Booth, 'Popular loyalism and public violence in the North-west of England, 1790–1800, *SH.*, 8, (1983), pp. 302–3.

26. Acreage return, 27 Oct. 1801, HO. 67/23, f. 245. Fawcett to Howard, 6 Mar. 1800, NNRO. How. 758/29, 349X. T. Rudge, *A General View of the Agriculture of the County of Gloucester*, (1805), p. 346. A.D. Gilbert, 'Methodism, dissent and political stability in early industrial England', *Journal of Religious History*, X, (1979), p. 386. *York Herald*, 16 July 1803.

27. T.S. Ashton, *Economic Fluctuations in England 1700–1800*, (Oxford, 1959), ch. 2. R. Mitchison, 'The making of the old Scottish poor law', *P&P.*, 63, (1974), p. 72 and note 37.

28. In conversations in 1802, people commonly contrasted current prices with those in 1800–1. Rowbottom diary, 1 Jan. 1803. *York Herald*, 7 May 1803. J. Ayres (ed), *Paupers and Pig Killers: the Diary of William Holland a Somerset Parson 1799–1818*, (1986 edition), p. 75.

29. Sheffield to Pitt, n.d., but 1804, PRO.30/8/291, ff. 29–32. D.G. Barnes, *A History of the English Corn Laws 1660–1846*, (1965 edition), pp. 88–90. C.R. Fay, *The Corn Laws and Social England*, (Cambridge, 1932), pp. 29–32.

30. J.G. Rule, *The Experience of Labour in Eighteenth-Century Industry*, (1981), p. 209.

31. W.J. Shelton, *English Hunger and Industrial Disorders*, (1973), pp. 46–9, 108, 119–20.

32. Francis Place's treachery, once he became a successful master is well-known.

33. R.A.E. Wells, *Riot and Political Disaffection in Nottinghamshire in the Age of Revolutions 1776–1803*, (University of Nottingham, 1984), pp. 37–8. M.I. Thomis, 'Gravenor Henson: the man and the myth', *Transactions of the Thoroton Society of Nottingham*, LXXV, (1971), pp. 91–7.

34. R. Wells, 'Rural rebels in southern England in the 1830s', in C. Emsley and J. Walvin (eds), *Artisans, Peasants and Proletarians 1760–1860*, (1985), pp. 124–65.

35. C. Calhoun, *The Question of Class Struggle: Social Foundations of Popular Radicalism during the Industrial Revolution*, (Oxford, 1982), pp. 105–15.

36. For a judicious review of the opposing theses of Edward Thompson and Harold Perkin see R.J. Morris, *Class and Class Consciousness in the Industrial Revolution 1780–1850*, (1979), chs. 2 and 6.

37. R. Wells, 'Tolpuddle in the context of English agrarian labour history 1750–1850', in J.G. Rule (ed), *British Trade Unionism; the Formative Years 1700–1850*, (forthcoming).

38. Bohstedt, *op. cit.*, p. 220.

39. Wells, 'Rural rebels . . .', esp. pp. 132–47. *Idem.*, 'Resistance to the New Poor Law in the rural South', in M. Chase (ed), *The New Poor Law*, (University of Leeds, 1985), pp. 15–48. *Idem.*, 'Social conflict and protest in the English countryside in the early nineteenth century; a rejoinder', *Jnl. PS.*, 8, no. 4, (1981), pp. 514–30.

40. E.g. P. Dunkley, *The Crisis of the Old Poor Law in England 1795–1834*, (1982), pp. 117–8.
41. Holland to Caroline Fox, 19 Dec. 1800, BL. Add. Mss. 51735, ff. 226–7. However, the parliamentary Whigs were neither united, nor the leadership consistent in this view throughout their years in opposition during the early nineteenth century. E.A. Wasson, 'The great Whigs and parliamentary reform 1809–30', *Journal of British Studies*, 24, 4, (1985), p. 445.
42. Cited in *ibid.*, p. 459.
43. Sir Francis Burdett, the only other MP to vote against, was not a Whig at this juncture; indeed he was closely implicated in the revolutionary plottings associated with Colonel Despard. Wells, *Insurrection. . .*, esp. pp. 240–6.

APPENDICES

APPENDIX 1. WHEAT-BASED SUBSISTENCE DIET

'The Charge Per Week for Keeping a Poor Man, Wife and Two Children,
with Nothing Superior to Gaol Allowance'.

Item.	s.d.	Percentage
Subsistence for man, wife and two children.	7-9	64.5
Beer..	8	5.5
Clothing and shoes..........................	1-4	11.1
Washing, soap and candles..................	3	2.1
Fuel	6	4.1
Rent	1-6	12.5
	12.0	99.8

Subsistence breakdown

33½ lbs wheat bread.

1 lb 11 ozs meat.

1 lb 1 oz bacon.

4¼ lbs cheese.

6 lbs potatoes.

(Source: R.S. Neale. 'The standard of living, 1780-1844: a regional
and class study', in A.J. Taylor (ed.), The Standard of Living in
Britain in the Industrial Revolution, (1975), p. 165

APPENDIX 2.   CALCULATED SUBSISTENCE BUDGETS,   BARLEY

About 9½ gallons (cost equivalent of one sixth of a wholesale quarter).

4 lbs meat.

2 lbs butter.

2 lbs cheese.

12 lbs potatoes.

APPENDIX 3.   CALCULATED SUBSISTENCE BUDGETS,   OATS

About 27lbs oatmeal (cost equivalent of one fifth of a wholesale quarter).

2 lbs meat.

2 lbs bacon.

20 lbs potatoes.

6 quarts milk.

Both the above estimated for the weekly consumption of a family with two children.

Source Appendices 2 and 3:   D. Davies, The Case of the Labourers in Husbandry, (1795), pp. 138-41, 146-7

APPENDIX 4.   AVERAGE WEEKLY COSTS OF COMPLETE DIET PER QUARTER, AT
SELECTED MARKETS   (IN SHILLINGS)

Wheaten	1	2	3	4	5	6
6. 9.1794 to 29.11.1794	7.9	8.3	7.6	6.3	7.6	8.9
6.12.1794 to 28. 2.1795	8.7	9.3	8.1	7.2	8.8	8.7
7. 3.1795 to 30. 5.1795	9.8	10.3	9.4	7.8	10.6	10.1
6. 6.1795 to 29. 8.1795	13.0	14.2	14.1	11.2	13.0	12.3
Barley	1	2	3	4	5	6
6. 9.1794 to 29.11.1794	8.8	10.3	8.7	7.5	8.9	8.4
6.12.1794 to 28. 2.1795	10.9	11.7	9.6	8.9	10.2	10.0
7. 3.1795 to 30. 5.1795	12.3	12.8	11.4	9.6	10.9	11.1
6. 6.1795 to 29. 8.1795	12.7	13.7	12.3	10.8	11.2	11.3
Oaten	1	2	3	4	5	6
6. 9.1794 to 29.11.1794	8.6	9.3	7.6	6.7	8.4	9.2
6.12.1794 to 28. 2.1795	9.7	11.2	8.4	8.0	9.6	8.4
7. 3.1795 to 30. 5.1795	11.2	12.1	9.7	9.3	11.2	11.6
6. 6.1795 to 29. 8.1795	12.3	13.1	9.0	11.3	12.1	12.9
Wheaten	1	2	3	4	5	6
5. 9.1795 to 28.11.1795	12.1	12.1	12.0	9.9	11.5	10.4
5.12.1795 to 27. 2.1796	14.4	14.3	13.3	10.8	14.3	13.5
5. 3.1796 to 28. 5.1796	13.5	13.8	13.6	11.1	12.7	13.4
4. 6.1796 to 27. 8.1796	11.4	12.3	11.5	10.1	11.0	10.0
Barley	1	2	3	4	5	6
5. 9.1795 to 28.11.1795	11.2	11.2	12.1	9.1	10.3	11.2
5.12.1795 to 27. 2.1796	11.7	12.8	11.3	10.9	10.8	11.3
5. 3.1796 to 28. 5.1796	11.2	13.0	10.4	9.6	10.0	11.3
4. 6.1796 to 27. 8.1796	9.6	10.8	10.8	8.3	8.6	9.4
Oaten	1	2	3	4	5	6
5. 9.1795 to 28.11.1795	11.3	11.0	10.2	9.5	10.4	12.5
5.12.1795 to 27. 2.1796	11.9	12.2	11.2	10.8	11.4	14.1
5. 3.1796 to 28. 5.1796	11.4	13.1	11.3	10.5	11.0	13.5
4. 6.1796 to 27. 8.1796	9.0	10.1	8.7	8.3	8.5	10.3
Wheaten	1	2	3	4	5	6
7. 9.1799 to 30.11.1799	11.5	12.5	11.4	10.0	11.4	11.5
7.12.1799 to 1. 3.1800	14.5	15.3	13.7	12.2	14.6	14.7
8. 3.1800 to 31. 5.1800	18.0	18.9	15.9	14.5	17.6	18.1
7. 6.1800 to 30. 8.1800	17.9	18.7	16.4	15.5	18.1	18.3

Barley	1	2	3	4	5	6
7. 9.1799 to 30.11.1799	10.8	12.9	10.4	9.2	11.0	9.8
7.12.1799 to 1. 3.1800	13.5	15.3	12.4	11.5	13.0	13.4
8. 3.1800 to 31. 5.1800	14.6	17.5	14.1	15.7	15.8	16.5
7. 6.1800 to 30. 8.1800	17.3	17.1	16.0	17.1	16.4	18.1
Oaten	1	2	3	4	5	6
7. 9.1800 to 30.11.1799	13.1	12.8	11.3	9.8	11.7	11.4
7.12.1799 to 1. 3.1800	14.4	15.6	13.0	11.4	13.6	13.6
8. 3.1800 to 31. 5.1800	16.2	18.9	16.3	15.2	15.7	16.1
7. 6.1800 to 30. 8.1800	17.2	21.0	16.9	17.0	15.7	16.8
Wheaten	1	2	3	4	5	6
6. 9.1800 to 29.11.1800	17.5	17.7	15.5	14.6	17.4	17.7
6.12.1800 to 28. 2.1801	20.2	22.3	18.2	16.7	20.6	21.2
7. 3.1801 to 30. 5.1801	20.6	24.2	18.8	17.8	20.3	20.9
6. 6.1801 to 29. 8.1801	17.7	21.5	17.2	16.5	17.6	19.6
Barley	1	2	3	4	5	6
6. 9.1800 to 29.11.1800	16.6	18.8	17.4	14.5	16.9	19.1
6.12.1800 to 28. 2.1801	20.5	26.7	19.3	16.7	20.6	21.2
7. 3.1801 to 30. 5.1801	19.9	26.1	20.4	18.7	18.0	22.3
6. 6.1801 to 29. 8.1801	17.7	21.5	17.2	15.8	14.3	17.8
Oaten	1	2	3	4	5	6
6. 9.1800 to 29.11.1800	17.3	19.1	15.6	14.2	15.1	18.2
6.12.1800 to 28. 2.1801	19.5	22.4	17.4	16.6	16.6	20.4
7. 3.1801 to 30. 5.1801	18.1	21.1	16.8	16.0	15.7	19.5
6. 6.1801 to 29. 8.1801	16.0	19.2	14.5	13.0	13.7	15.4

Col. 1 London   Col. 2 Birmingham   Col. 3 Pontefract
Col. 4 Malton   Col. 5 Colchester   Col. 6 Chichester

Sources; cereal prices components derive from the official returns, MAF. 10/273-285. Non-cereal dietary elements have been calculated from evidence extracted from a considerable miscellany of sources. For details of calculations, and full statistical details, see R.A.E. Wells, 'The Grain Crises in England 1794-6, 1799-1801', (Unpublished DPhil. thesis, University of York, 1978), pp. 932-67.

APPENDIX 5   STANDARD OF LIVING CALCULATIONS.

Column 1.   Quarterly earnings.

Column 2.   Quarterly surplus/deficit after purchase of a wheat-based diet.

Column 3.   Quarterly surplus/deficit after purchase of a barley-based diet.

Column 4.   Quarterly surplus/deficit after purchase of an oat-based diet.

All figures are in shillings.

APPENDIX 5A.   SUSSEX AGRICULTURAL LABOURERS.

Quarter		1	2	3	4
6. 9.1794	to 29.11.1794	91	-25.3	-18.6	-28.4
6.12.1794	to 28. 2.1795	110.5	+ 2.1	-19.2	-32.8
7. 3.1795	to 30. 5.1795	117	-14.5	-26.7	-32.2
6. 6.1795	to 29. 8.1795	117	-42.8	-26.8	-50.0
TOTALS			-89.5	-91.3	-144.4
5. 9.1795	to 28.11.1795	143	+7.7	-2.3	-19.3
5.12.1795	to 27. 2.1796	143	-32.5	-9.5	-39.6
5. 3.1796	to 28. 5.1796	156	-4.8	+9.1	-19.2
4. 6.1796	to 27. 8.1796	143	+13.5	+20.5	+9.2
TOTALS			-16.1	+17.8	-68.9
7. 9.1799	to 30.11.1799	143	-6.6	+16.3	-4.7
7.12.1799	to 1. 3.1800	143	-45.0	-31.5	-33.6
8. 3.1800	to 30. 5.1800	156	-79.8	-57.9	-53.5
7. 6.1800	to 31. 8.1800	156	-72.1	-69.4	-62.2
TOTALS			-198.5	-142.5	-154.0
6. 9.1800	to 29.11.1800	169	-61.0	-88.7	-67.1
6.12.1800	to 28. 2.1801	169	-106.0	-106.0	-96.4
7. 3.1801	to 30. 5.1801	169	-102.9	-121.2	-84.0
6. 6.1801	to 29. 8.1801	169	-85.8	-62.2	-31.2
TOTALS			-355.7	-378.1	-288.7

APPENDIX 5B   NORFOLK AGRICULTURAL LABOURERS

Quarter			1	2	3	4
6. 9.1794	to	29.11.1794	97.5	+.4	-35.0	-10.1
6.12.1794	to	28. 2.1795	100.7	-8.1	-47.5	-22.5
7. 3.1795	to	30. 5.1795	100.7	-33.0	-63.6	-46.1
6. 6.1795	to	29. 8.1795	117	-40.7	-74.2	-58.0
TOTALS				-81.4	-200.3	-116.7
5. 9.1795	to	28.11.1795	117	-29.3	-13.4	-13.6
5.12.1795	to	27. 2.1796	130	-48.0	-6.9	-20.8
5. 3.1796	to	28. 5.1796	130	-34.4	+1.5	-14.0
4. 6.1796	to	27. 8.1796	130	+.9	+19.8	+16.9
TOTALS				-110.8	+1.0	-31.5
7. 9.1799	to	30.11.1799	130	-15.6	+7.6	-12.0
7.12.1799	to	1. 3.1800	130	-51.4	-30.6	-35.5
8. 3.1800	to	30. 5.1800	156	-63.7	-40.4	-57.4
7. 6.1800	to	31. 8.1800	156	-77.7	-58.0	-41.4
TOTALS				-207.4	-121.4	-146.3
6. 9.1800	to	29.11.1800	156	-60.3	-62.5	-43.0
6.12.1800	to	28. 2.1801	156	-99.0	-99.0	-83.0
7. 3.1801	to	30. 5.1801	156	-102.7	-69.5	-71.5
6. 6.1801	to	29. 8.1801	156	-69.3	-17.2	-23.1
TOTALS				-331.3	-248.2	-220.6

APPENDIX 5C   WEST RIDING AGRICULTURAL LABOURERS

Quarter			1	2	3	4
6. 9.1794	to	29.11.1794	92.8	-5.3	-20.4	-5.9
6.12.1794	to	28. 2.1795	91.9	-13.7	-32.4	-16.7
7. 3.1795	to	30. 5.1795	103.8	-18.3	-44.8	-22.6
6. 6.1795	to	29. 8.1795	114.5	-70.6	-44.0	-2.7
TOTALS				-101.9	-141.6	-47.7
5. 9.1795	to	28.11.1795	111.7	-44.8	-45.1	-21.0
5.12.1795	to	27. 2.1796	105.6	-66.8	-41.4	-39.9
5. 3.1796	to	28. 5.1796	109.4	-67.0	-26.0	-36.9
4. 6.1796	to	27. 8.1796	115.3	-34.0	-20.8	+2.6
TOTALS				-212.6	-133.3	-95.2
7. 9.1799	to	30.11.1799	117.8	-30.8	-17.7	-29.1
7.12.1799	to	1. 2.1800	110.9	-67.1	-50.7	-58.4
8. 3.1800	to	30. 5.1800	135.1	-71.3	-48.0	-76.8
7. 6.1800	to	31. 8.1800	138.8	-74.0	-68.8	-77.8
TOTALS				-243.2	-185.2	-240.1
6. 9.1800	to	29.11.1800	135.0	-66.5	-90.9	-67.3
6.12.1800	to	28. 2.1801	156.0	-81.1	-94.6	-69.9
7. 3.1801	to	30. 5.1801	175.5	-69.1	-89.5	-43.2
6. 6.1801	to	29. 8.1801	253.0	+29.5	+29.5	+65.2
TOTALS				-187.2	-243.5	-115.2

APPENDIX 5D   WEST RIDING SKILLED RURAL WORKERS

Quarter		1	2	3	4
6. 9.1794	to 29.11.1794	156.0	+57.9	+42.8	+57.3
6.12.1794	to 28. 2.1795	156.0	+50.4	+31.7	+47.4
7. 3.1795	to 30. 5.1795	156.0	+33.9	+7.4	+29.6
6. 6.1795	to 29. 8.1795	156.0	-29.1	-3.3	+38.8
TOTALS			+113.1	+78.6	+173.1
5. 9.1795	to 28.11.1795	169.0	+12.5	+12.2	+36.3
5.12.1795	to 27. 2.1796	169.0	-3.4	+22.0	+23.5
5. 3.1796	to 28. 5.1796	169.0	-7.4	+33.6	+22.7
4. 6.1796	to 27. 8.1796	169.0	+19.7	+32.9	+56.3
TOTALS			+21.4	+100.7	+138.8
7. 9.1799	to 30.11.1799	182.0	+33.4	+46.5	+35.1
7.12.1799	to 1. 3.1800	182.0	+4.0	+20.4	+12.7
8. 3.1800	to 30. 5.1800	182.0	-24.4	-1.1	-29.9
7. 6.1800	to 31. 8.1800	182.0	-30.8	-25.6	-37.6
TOTALS			-17.8	-20.2	-5.2
6. 9.1800	to 29.11.1800	195.0	-6.5	-30.9	-7.3
6.12.1800	to 28. 2.1801	195.0	-42.1	-55.6	-30.9
7. 3.1801	to 30. 5.1801	195.0	-49.6	-70.0	-23.7
6. 6.1801	to 29. 8.1801	234.0	+10.5	+10.5	+46.2
TOTALS			-87.7	-145.5	-15.7

APPENDIX 5E   GEORGE HAY, LABOURER, KIRKSTALL FORGE

Quarter		1	2	3	4
6. 9.1794	to 29.11.1794	111.8	+14.7	-1.4	+13.1
6.12.1794	to 28. 2.1795	110.6	+5.0	-13.7	+2.0
7. 3.1795	to 30. 5.1795	111.2	-10.9	-37.4	-15.2
6. 6.1796	to 29. 8.1795	136.5	-46.6	-22.8	+19.3
TOTALS			-37.8	-75.3	+19.2
5. 9.1795	to 28.11.1795	136.5	-20.0	-20.3	+3.8
5.12.1795	to 27. 2.1796	135.7	-36.7	-11.3	-9.8
5. 3.1796	to 28. 5.1796	133.9	-42.5	-1.5	-12.4
4. 6.1796	to 27. 8.1796	133.9	-15.4	-2.2	+21.2
TOTALS			-116.6	-35.3	+4.8
7. 9.1799	to 30.11.1799	184.6	+36.0	+49.1	+37.7
7.12.1799	to 1. 2.1800	158.8	-20.0	-2.8	-10.5
8. 3.1800	to 30. 5.1800	176.8	-29.6	-6.3	-27.3
7. 6.1800	to 31. 8.1800	192.3	-20.5	-15.3	-27.3
TOTALS			-33.9	+25.7	-27.4
6. 9.1800	to 29.11.1800	217.1	+15.6	-8.8	+14.8
6.12.1800	to 28. 2.1801	231.5	-5.6	-19.1	+5.6
7. 3.1801	to 30. 5.1801	237.9	-6.7	-27.1	+19.2
6. 6.1801	to 29. 8.1801	299.0	+75.5	+75.5	+111.2
TOTALS			+78.8	+20.0	+150.8

APPENDIX 5F   JOHN ATKINSON, TILTER, KIRKSTALL FORGE

Quarter		1	2	3	4
6. 9. 1794	to 29.11.1794	499.2	+401.1	+386.0	+400.5
6.12. 1794	to 28. 2.1795	454.2	+348.6	+329.9	+345.6
7. 3. 1795	to 30. 5.1795	434.2	+312.1	+285.6	+307.8
6. 6. 1795	to 29. 8.1795	408.0	+224.9	+248.7	+290.8
TOTALS			+1286.8	+1001.5	+1254.7
5. 9. 1795	to 28.11.1795	465.4	+308.9	+308.6	+332.7
5.12. 1795	to 27. 2.1796	465.4	+293.0	+318.4	+319.9
5. 3. 1796	to 28. 5.1796	466.7	+290.3	+331.3	+320.4
4. 6. 1796	to 27. 8.1796	469.0	+319.7	+332.9	+356.3
TOTALS			+1211.9	+1291.2	+1329.3
7. 9. 1799	to 30.11.1799	615.7	+467.1	+480.2	+468.8
7.12. 1799	to 1. 3.1800	533,7	+355.7	+372.1	+364.4
8. 3. 1800	to 30. 5.1800	499.2	+292.8	+316.1	+287.3
7. 6. 1800	to 31. 8.1800	499.2	+286.4	+291.6	+279.6
TOTALS			+1312.0	+1460.0	+1393.1
6. 9. 1800	to 29.11.1800	488.8	+287.3	+262.9	+286.5
6.12. 1800	to 28. 2.1801	532.9	+295.8	+282.3	+307.0
7. 3.1801	to 30. 5.1801	558.2	+313.6	+293.2	+339.5
6. 6.1801	to 29. 8.1801	577.2	+353.7	+353.7	+389.4
TOTALS			+1250.4	+1192.1	+1322.4

APPENDIX 5G   MATTHEW COOK, PATTERN-RING MAKER, KIRKSTALL FORGE

Quarter		1	2	3	4
6. 9.1794	to 29.11.1794	399.1	+301.0	+285.9	+300.4
6.12.1794	to 28. 2.1795	350.9	+245.3	+226.6	+242.3
7. 3.1795	to 30. 5.1795	300.3	+178.2	+151.7	+137.9
6. 6.1795	to 29. 8.1795	300.3	+115.2	+141.0	+183.1
TOTALS			-841.7	+805.2	+863.7
5. 9.1795	to 28.11.1795	311.4	+154.9	+154.6	+178.7
5.12.1795	to 27. 2.1796	319.8	+147.4	+172.8	+174.3
5. 3.1796	to 28. 5.1796	296.6	+120.2	+161.2	+150.3
4. 6.1796	to 27. 8.1796	282.1	+132.8	+146.0	+169.4
TOTALS			+555.3	+634.6	+672.7
7. 9.1799	to 30.11.1799	317.2	+168.6	+181.7	+170.3
7.12.1799	to 1. 2.1800	328.0	+150.0	+166.9	+158.7
8. 3.1800	to 30. 5.1800	371.9	+165.5	+188.8	+160.0
7. 6.1800	to 31. 8.1800	341.9	+129.1	+134.3	+122.3
TOTALS			+613.2	+671.7	+611.3
6. 9.1800	to 29.11.1800	357.5	+156.0	+131.6	+155.2
6.12 1800	to 23. 2.1801	306.3	+69.2	+55.7	+80.4
7. 3.1801	to 30. 5.1801	253.5	+8.9	-11.5	+34.8
6. 6.1801	to 29. 8.1801	256.2.	+32.7	+32.7	+68.4
TOTALS			+266.8	+208.5	+338.8

APPENDIX 5I   JOSHUA HAGUE, SKILLED EMPLOYEE, NOWILL'S SPRING-KNIFE WORKS, SHEFFIELD

Quarter	1	2	3	4
6. 9.1794 to 29.11.1794	378	+279.9	+264.8	+279.3
6.12.1794 to 28. 2.1795	226	+120.4	+101.7	+117.4
7. 3.1795 to 30. 5.1795	175	+52.9	+26.4	+48.6
6. 6.1795 to 29. 8.1795	231	+45.9	+71.7	+113.8
TOTALS		+499.1	+464.6	+559.1
5. 9.1795 to 28.11.1795	238	+81.5	+81.2	+105.3
5.12.1795 to 27. 2.1796	297	+124.6	+150.0	+151.5
5. 3.1796 to 28. 5.1796	361	+184.6	+225.6	+214.7
4. 6.1796 to 27. 8.1796	386	+236.7	+249.9	+273.3
TOTALS		+627.4	+706.7	+746.1
7. 9.1799 to 30.11.1799	524	+375.4	+388.5	+377.1
7.12.1799 to 1. 2.1800	610	+432.0	+448.4	+440.7
8. 3.1800 to 30. 5.1800	605	+398.6	+421.9	+393.1
7. 6.1800 to 31. 8.1800	549	+336.2	+341.4	+329.4
TOTALS		+1542.2	+1600.3	+1530.3
6. 9.1800 to 29.11.1800	533	+331.5	+307.1	+330.7
6.12.1800 to 28. 2.1801	425	+187.9	+174.4	+199.1
7. 3.1801 to 30. 5.1801	441	+196.4	+176.0	+222.3
6. 6.1801 to 29. 8.1801	334	+110.5	+110.5	+146.2
TOTALS		+826.3	+768.0	+898.3

APPENDIX 5H   BENJAMIN THOMPSON, LABOURER, NOWILL'S SPRING-KNIFE WORKS, SHEFFIELD

Quarter	1	2	3	4
6. 9.1794 to 29.11.1794	76	-22.1	-37.2	-22.7
6.12.1794 to 28. 2.1795	103	-2.6	-21.3	-5.6
7. 3.1795 to 30. 5.1795	98	-24.1	-50.6	-28.4
6. 6.1795 to 29. 8.1795	131	-54.1	-28.3	+13.8
TOTALS		-102.9	-137.4	-42.8
5. 9.1795 to 28.11.1795	170	+13.5	+13.2	+37.3
5.12.1795 to 27. 2.1796	128	-44.5	-19.0	-17.5
5. 3.1796 to 28. 5.1796	113	-63.4	-22.4	-33.3
4. 6.1796 to 27. 8.1796	90	-59.3	-46.1	-20.7
TOTALS		-153.7	-74.3	-34.2
7. 9.1799 to 30.11.1799	117	-31.6	-18.5	-29.9
7.12.1799 to 1. 3.1800	117	-61.0	-44.6	-52.3
8. 3.1800 to 30. 5.1800	108	-98.4	-75.1	-103.9
7. 6.1800 to 31. 8.1800	113	-99.8	-94.6	-106.6
TOTALS		-290.8	-232.8	-292.7
6. 9.1800 to 29.11.1800	108	-93.5	-117.9	-94.3
6.12.1800 to 28. 2.1801	108	-129.1	-142.6	-117.9
7. 3.1801 to 30. 5.1801	108	-136.6	-157.0	-110.7
6. 6.1801 to 29. 8.1801	122	-101.5	-101.5	-65.8
TOTALS		-460.7	-519.0	-358.7

APPENDIX 5J   JOHN WILKINSON, SKILLED EMPLOYEE, NOWILL'S SPRING-KNIFE WORKS
             SHEFFIELD

Quarter			1	2	3	4
6. 9.1794	to	29.11.1794	349	+250.9	+235.8	+250.3
6.12.1794	to	28. 2.1795	251	+145.4	+126.7	+142.8
7. 3.1795	to	30. 5.1795	132	+9.9	-16.6	+5.6
6. 6.1795	to	29. 8.1795	258	+72.9	+98.7	+140.8
TOTALS				+479.1	+444.6	+649.1
5. 9.1795	to	28.11.1795	195	+38.5	+38.2	+62.3
5.12.1795	to	27. 2.1796	314	+141.6	+167.0	+168.5
5. 3.1796	to	28. 5.1796	219	+42.6	+83.6	+72.7
4. 6.1796	to	27. 8.1796	233	+83.7	+96.9	+120.3
TOTALS				+306.4	+385.7	+423.8
7. 9.1799	to	30.11.1799	495	+346.4	+359.5	+348.1
7.12.1799	to	1. 3.1800	478	+300.0	+316.4	+308.7
8. 3.1800	to	30. 5.1800	478	+271.6	+294.9	+266.1
7. 6.1800	to	31. 8.1800	476	+263.2	+268.4	+256.4
TOTALS				+1181.2	+1239.2	+1179.3
6. 9.1800	to	29.11.1800	494	+292.5	+268.1	+291.7
6.12.1800	to	28. 2.1801	533	+295.9	+282.4	+307.1
7. 3.1801	to	30. 5.1801	589	+344.4	+324.0	+370.3
6. 6.1801	to	29. 8.1801	556	+332.5	+332.5	+368.2
TOTALS				+1265.3	+1207.0	+1537.3

Sources.: The calculations in appendices 5A to 5D are based on a considerable
           range of miscellaneous evidence. Appendices 5E to 5J are based on
           these workers' earnings as recorded in their firms' ledgers. But
           the entries for the skilled men may conceal their responsibility
           for the employment of unskilled mates. LCA., KF/S1, Kirkstall
           Forge wage book 1794-1802.   SCL. Nowill Deposit, MD. 204-5
           wage books, 1794-1802

APPENDIX 6.   VALUE OF CHARITABLE POOR RELIEF, NEWBOLD TOWNSHIP, NEAR
              CHESTERFIELD, FEBRUARY TO AUGUST, 1795

Column 1   Cost of oatmeal to be purchased on the open market.

Column 2   Cost of non-cereal component of diet.

Column 3   Total cost of diet, including the cost of subsidised meal sold
            by charity administrators.

Column 4   Weekly deficit/surplus after purchase of diet.
    4A   Thomas Fryer, collier, earning 12/- per week, with wife and
            two children.
    4B   John Silcock, steelworker, earning 9/- per week, with wife and
            two children.
    4C   James Spooner, agricultural labourer, earning 7/- per week,
            with wife and two children.

Week	1	2	3	4A	4B	4C
28/2	2.0	4.5	8.5	+3.5	+.5	-1.5
7/3	2.1	5.4	9.5	+2.5	-.5	-2.5
14/3	2.0	5.4	9.4	+2.6	-.4	-2.4
21/3	1.9	5.4	9.3	+2.7	-.3	-2.3
28/3	2.0	5.4	9.4	+2.6	-.4	-2.4
4/4	2.0	5.4	9.4	+2.6	-.4	-2.4
11/4	2.1	5.4	9.5	+2.5	-.5	-2.5
18/4	2.2	5.4	9.6	+2.4	-.6	-2.6
25/4	2.2	5.4	9.6	+2.4	-.6	-2.6
2/5	2.3	5.4	9.7	+2.3	-.7	-2.7
9/5	2.3	5.4	9.7	+2.3	-.7	-2.7
16/5	2.3	5.4	9.7	+2.3	-.7	-2.7
23/5	2.4	5.4	9.8	+2.2	-.8	-2.8
30/5	2.5	5.4	9.9	+2.1	-.9	-2.9
6/6	2.5	5.8	10.3	+1.7	-1.3	-3.3
13/6	2.5	5.8	10.3	+1.7	-1.3	-3.3
20/6	2.5	5.8	10.3	+1.7	-1.3	-3.3
27/6	2.5	5.8	10.3	+1.7	-1.3	-3.3
4/7	2.8	5.8	10.6	+1.4	-1.6	-3.6
11/7	2.9	5.8	10.7	+1.3	-1.7	-3.7
18/7	2.9	5.8	10.7	+1.3	-1.7	-3.7
25/7	3.5	5.8	11.3	+.7	-2.3	-4.3
1/8	3.8	5.8	11.6	+.4	-2.6	-4.6
8/8	4.4	5.8	12.2	-.2	-3.2	-5.2
15/8	4.4	5.8	12.2	-.2	-3.2	-5.2
22/8	3.3	5.8	11.1	+.9	-2.1	-4.1
29/8	3.2	5.8	11.0	+1.0	-2.0	-4.0

All figures in shillings: only part of cereal requirements were available at
low cost from the charity.

Source: Notts. CRO.   DD. CW. 8f/1, Newbold Charity Accounts, 1795

APPENDIX 7   EROSION OF THE VALUE OF STATIC FAMILY/WAGE SUPPLEMENTS, 1795-6

The figures (in shillings) relate to the surplus/deficit after a family with two children had purchased the cereal component of a wheat-based diet out of their income plus supplement from the parish.

Column A. Great Bardfield, Essex. Although the vestry minutes make no reference to any withdrawal of the supplement, it is possible that these were withdrawn during part of the autumn of 1795-

Column B. Great Sampford, Essex.

Column C. Terrington, St. Clement, Norfolk

Week	A	B	C
20. 6.1795	+2.3		
27. 6.1795	+2.5		
4. 7.1795	+2.2		
11. 7.1795	+2.2		
18. 7.1795	+.6	+1.6	
25. 7.1795	+.5	+1.5	
1. 8.1795	+.2	+1.0	
8. 8.1795	-.6	+.4	
15. 8.1795	-.9	+.3	
22. 8.1795	-1.5	-.5	
29. 8.1795	-.6	+.4	
5. 9.1795	+2.5	+3.5	
12. 9.1795	+3.7	+4.7	
19. 9.1795	+3.3		
26. 9.1795	+2.8		
3.10.1795	+2.6		
10.10.1795	+2.6		
17.10.1795	+2.2		
24.10.1795	+1.4		
31.10.1795	+.6		
7.11.1795	+.6		
14.11.1795	+1.8		
21.11.1795	+1.8		

Week	A	B	C
28.11.1795	+1.8		
5.12.1795	+1.2		
12.12.1795	+.9	+1.2	
19.12.1795	0	+.3	+1.1
26.12.1795	0	+.3	+1.0
2. 1.1796	-1.3	-1.0	+.3
9. 1.1796	-.8	-1.0	+.3
16. 1.1796	-.9	+.1	+.5
23. 1.1796	-.1	+.9	+.3
30. 1.1796	0	+1.0	+1.3
6. 2.1796	+.2	+1.2	+1.6
13. 2.1796	-.3	+.7	+1.6
20. 2.1796	-.7	+.3	+1.3
27. 2.1796	-1.4	-.4	+.3
5. 3.1796	-2.1	-1.1	-.7
12. 3.1796	-1.7	-.7	-.6
19. 3.1796	-1.8	-.8	-.6
26. 3.1796	-.5	-.7	-.9
2. 4.1796	+.5		+1.0
9.4. 1796	+2.0		+2.7
16.4.1796	+3.4		+3.9
23.4.1796	+4.0		+4.7

Sources: ECRO. DP. 67/8/2; 289/8/2

            NNRO. uncatalogued St. Clement town book, 1758-1823

APPENDIX 8 EROSION OF THE VALUE OF STATIC FAMILY/WAGE SUPPLEMENTS,1799-1801

The figures (in shillings) relate to the surplus/deficit after a family
with two children had purchased the cereal component of a wheat-based
diet out of their income, plus supplement from the parish.

Column 1   Wrabness, Essex.

Column 2   Wingfield, Suffolk.

Column 3   Stowmarket, Suffolk.

Week	1	2
16.11.1799		+1.5
23.11.1799		+.6
30.11.1799		+.5
7.12.1799		+.8
14.12.1799		+.6
21.12.1799		+1.7
28.12.1799		+1.2
4. 1.1800		+.5
11. 1.1800		+.5
18. 1.1800		+.3
25. 1.1800		+.5
1. 2.1800		+.8
8. 2.1800		-.2
15. 2.1800		-.5
22. 2.1800		-.8
1. 3.1800		+.8
8. 3.1800		-1.6
15. 3.1800	+1.2	-.7
22. 3.1800	+1.0	-.5
29. 3.1800	+.5	-.8
5. 4.1800	+.4	-1.0
12. 4.1800	+.2	-1.0
19. 4.1800	+.5	-.8
26. 4.1800	-.2	
3. 5.1800	-.6	
10. 5.1800	o	
17. 5.1800	-.4	

Week	1
24. 5.1800	-.1
31. 5.1800	+.6
7. 6.1800	-.2
14. 6.1800	-2.0
21. 6.1800	-2.2
28. 6.1800	-2.8
5. 7.1800	-2.8
12. 7.1800	-2.8
19. 7.1800	-1.6
26. 7.1800	-.6
2. 8.1800	+1.6
9. 8.1800	
16. 8.1800	
23. 8.1800	
30. 8.1800	
6. 9.1800	
13. 9.1800	-.4
20. 9.1800	-.6
27. 9.1800	
4.10.1800	
11.10.1800	
18.10.1800	

Week	2	3
25.10.1800	+.7	+1.0
1.11.1800	+.2	+.5
8.11.1800	-.2	+.1
15.11.1800	+.4	+.7
22.11.1800	o	+.3
29.11.1800	-.5	-.2
6.12.1800	-.7	-.4
13.12.1800	-1.0	-.7
20.12.1800	-1.6	-1.3
27.12.1800	-2.3	-2.0
3. 1.1801	-2.1	-1.8
10. 1.1801	-1.9	-1.6
17. 1.1801	-1.0	-1.7
24. 1.1801	-1.9	-2.6
31. 1.1801	-3.0	-3.7
7. 2.1801	-2.5	-3.2
14. 2.1801	-2.2	-2.9
21. 2.1801	-2.5	-3.2
28. 2.1801	-3.3	-4.0
7. 3.1801	-3.7	-4.4
14. 3.1801	-3.7	-4.4
21. 3.1801	-3.9	-4.6
28. 3.1801	-3.4	-4.1
4. 4.1801	-3.0	-3.7
11. 4.1801	-2.3	-3.0
18. 4.1801		-3.5
25. 4.1801		-2.1

Note: Blanks reflect the inadequacy of the record for analysis, not the
         non-payment of supplement. Wrabness and Stowmarket recorded no
         alterations in the supplements paid during the weeks to which the
         figures relate. Adjustments were made at Wingfield

Sources.   ECRO. DP.6, 8/1A. IESRO. FC.84, G16/3. R.J. Ince, 'The care of the
           poor in the parish of Stowmarket 1780-1830', (Unpublished BA
           dissertation, University of Oxford, n.d., copy in IESRO)

APPENDIX 9 POOR RELIEF COSTS, 1790–1806

Examples of rising poor relief costs. All figures in pounds.

Columns 1, 2 and 3	Rural parishes; St. Mabyn's,Cornwall; Kidlington, Oxfordshire; Rosedale, North Riding
Columns 4 and 5	Market towns; Wallingford (St. Peter's), Berkshire; Mells, Somerset
Columns 6, 7 and 8	Industrial parishes; Roach, Cornwall; Atherstone, Lancashire; and Houghton-le-Spring, Co. Durham.
Columns 9, 10 and 11	Industrial towns; Slimbridge, Gloucestershire; Halifax; and six Sheffield parishes.

Year	1	2	3	4	5	6	7	8	9	10	11
1791-2	81	223	35	294	368	170	695	46	314	1170	-
1792-3	72	265	41	253	371	143	608	61	257	1180	-
1793-4	53	280	36	253	465	147	765	89	288	1536	-
1794-5	67	236	23	280	461	271	976	83	358	1689	-
1795-6	60	337	28	281	475	356	829	133	384	1840	-
1796-7	77	369	19	337	691	342	817	142	561	1845	-
1797-8	77	262	40	-	544	253	688	122	483	2009	-
1798-9	72	235	71	448	546	304	739	116	435	2000	14755
1799-0	130	349	108	389	807	407	808	165	578	2640	14623
1800-1	136	551	122	768	980	543	1474	208	656	3384	22245
1801-2	184	756	76	543	1064	752	1213	133	925	4273	-
1802-3	82	388	80	354	848	434	553	133	576	-	-
1803-4	90	385	72	378	603	538	672	151	477	-	-
1804-5	119	491	60	444	-	426	506	140	625	-	-
1805-6	148	604	103	438	-	469	480	135	486		

Sources: Overseers' accounts, CCRO. DD. P.132, 12/19; DD. P.198, 12/2. SCRO. DP. mls, 13/2/3. BCRO. DP. 139, 12/2-4. OCRO. Kidlington overseers' accounts, unindexed. GCRO.P.298, OV. 2/6. Lancs.CRO. PR. 1738, 1681/14-5. NYRO. PR. ROS/3. Dur.CRO. EP.Ho, 45-7. HPL. HAS.164. SCL. WWM, F47/12, H. Parker to Fitzwilliam, 2 June 1801

APPENDIX 10 RELATIVE COSTS OF POOR RELIEF, 1791-1806

Costs of poor relief in parishes paying Speenhamland supplements based on
sliding scales, and parishes not adopting sliding scales to govern relief
payments.

Column 1 Frampton-in-Severn, Gloucestershire. Population 860. Speenhamland.
          (See note at and of table.)

Column 2 Brimpton, Berkshire. Population, 330. Speenhamland

Column 3 Charlton Kings, Gloucestershire. Population, 730, non-Speenhamland.

Column 4 Uffington, Berkshire. Population, 813, non-Speenhamland.

All figures in pounds. The total yearly expenditure under the poor law is
given in column A. Per capita expenditure is given in column B.

	1		2		3		4	
Year	A	B	A	B	A	B	A	B
1791-2	199	.23	246	75	202	.28	337	.41
1792-3	209	.24	190	.58	184	.25	277	.34
1793-4	214	.25	207	.63	206	.28	293	.36
1794-5	206	.24	233	.71	220	.3	255	.31
1795-6	258	.3	294	.89	207	.28	469	.58
1796-7	363	.42	617	1.87	261	.36	424	.52
1797-8	350	.41	544	1.65	254	.35	448	.55
1798-9	261	.3	422	1.28	216	.3	349	.43
1799-1800	431	.5	431	1.31	281	.38	499	.61
1800-1	652	.76	784	2.38	356	.49	707	.87
1801-2	693	.81	1142	3.46	441	.6	657	.81
1802-3	572	.67	864	2.38	347	.48	358	.44
1803-4	632	.73	508	1.54	274	.38	390	.48
1804-5	499	.58	436	1.32	258	.35	442	.54
1805-6	567	.66	645	1.96	285	.39	466	.57

The total expenditure is particularly interesting at Frampton-in-Severn. The
parish had a workhouse. In 1794-6 money payments appear to have been made on an
ad.hoc. basis when claimants applied. A few were given cereals on occasions.
In December 1799 the parish introduced a sliding scale, based on bread prices,
to regulate relief payments, although some cheap flour was also sold. The
massive increase in expenditure on the adoption of the sliding scale is apparent.
Relief costs st Brimpton increased much more than those at Uffington when the
former adopted the scale advocated by the Bench at the Pelican Inn meeting on 6 May
1795.

Sources: Overseers' accounts, GCRO. P.149, OV. 2/2; P.76,VE.2/1. BCRO.
          DP.26, 12/4-5; DP.134, 12/3

TABLES

Tables 1 to 12. Explanatory Notes

Columns 1 to 9; a cross denotes.

Col. 1. Evidence does not permit an assessment of crowd objective
Col. 2. Taxation populaire predominant objective
Col. 3. Stoppage of despatch of foodstuffs and retaining them for local
         consumption predominates
Col. 4. Crowd tours farms
Col. 5. Crowd opposed by the Volunteers
Col. 6. Crowd opposed by regular army
Col. 7. Arrests made during policing
Col. 8. Legal prosecutions follow crowd action
Col. 9   Courts (where known) impose custodial, transportation or capital
         sentences

Where more than one entry appears in Cols. 2-4 an asterisk denotes major
crowd objective.

Table 1. Disturbances in the "Early Phases" of the Famines. (December to May inclusive).

Midlands: comprising, Nottinghamshire, Leicestershire, Warwickshire, Worcestershire, Staffordshire, Shropshire and Derbyshire.

Date	Location	Target	Primary Participants	1	2	3	4	5	6	7	8	9
2. 4. 1795	Kibworth		Miners	X	X			X		X		
3. 4. 1795	Shackerstone		Miners, navvies		X			X				
17. 4. 1795	Coventry	Market retailers	Miners		X			X		X		
17. 4. 1795	Hinkley				X							
18. 4. 1795	Nottingham				X			X	X	X		
18. 4. 1795	Bedworth		Miners		X							
18. 4. 1795	Nuneaton		Miners		X							
18. 4. 1795	Coventry	Huxters			X			X				
20. 4. 1795	Coventry	Jail		X								
20. 4. 1795	Hinkley				X			X		X		X
21. 4. 1795	Coventry	Authorities		X				X				
22. 4. 1795	Burton-on-Trent	Warehouses				X		X				X
24. 4. 1795	Lichfield	Huxters		X								
25. 4. 1795	Nuneaton		Miners		X			X				
27. 4. 1795	Hinkley				X				X	X	X	
29. 4. 1795	Solihull	Fair		X*	X							
30. 4. 1795	Kidderminster				X				X			
1. 5. 1795	Bewdley				X							
3. 5. 1795	Wolverhampton	Troops		X	X*							
2. 6. 1795	Wolverhampton		Miners		X				X			X
2. 6. 1795	Dudley				X							
2. 6. 1795	Walsall				X							

Table 1 continued

Date	Location	Target	Primary Participants	1	2	3	4	5	6	7	8	9
2. 6. 1795	Tipton				X							
2. 6. 1795	Darlaston				X							
2. 6. 1795	Wednesbury				X							
5. 4. 1796	Nottingham	Baker,butchers		X	X*			X	X	X	X	
28. 4. 1796	Stone	Huxters			X			X	X	X	X	
30. 4. 1796	Stone	Huxters			X				X	X	X	
May 1796	Chesterfield	Salesmen	Peak miners		X							
Dec. 1799	Darlaston	Millers		X								
5. 2. 1800	Wolverhampton		Miners, nailers	X	X*			X	X	X	X	
5. 2. 1800	Leek		Miners		X			X				
13. 2. 1800	Birmingham	Potato sellers	Women and boys		X							
19. 2. 1800	Wolverhampton	Do.and butter rets.			X							X
19. 4. 1800	Nottingham	Butchers	Textile workers		X			X	X	X	X	
26. 4. 1800	Lane End		200 +		X	X	X		X	X	X	
28. 4. 1800	Newcastle/Lyne				X							
28. 4. 1800	Lane End		Women, nailers		X	X	X		X	X	X	
28. 4. 1800	Dudley		Miners. nailers	X	X*	X		X	X	X	X	X
28. 4. 1800	Leek				X							
29. 4. 1800	Sedgeley	Farmers	Miners, nailers, women				X	X	X	X	X	
29. 4. 1800	Penn	Farmers	Do. (600)				X	X	X	X	X	
1. 5. 1800	Claverley	Carter			X							
1. 5. 1800	Wrockwardine	Bakers,potato rets.				X						X
1. 5. 1800	Birmingham				X				X			
1. 5. 1800	Coseley		Miners		X							
1. 5. 1800	Kidderminster				X							

Table 1 continued

Date	Location	Target	Primary Participants	1	2	3	4	5	6	7	8	9
2. 5. 1800	Birmingham	Do. and farmers	Women initiators (150)	X	X		X	X	X	X	X	
3. 5. 1800	Belper				X							
6. 5. 1800	Grindon	Wharfs				X				X	X	
7. 5. 1800	Market Drayton	Huxters		X	X					X	X	
9. 5. 1800	Redditch			X	X*					X	X	
1O. 5. 1800	Birmingham	Potato sellers		X	X*							
May 1800	Breaston				X							
25.12. 1800	Nottingham	Soup shop		X					X			
29.12. 1800	Kingswinsford	Farmers					X					
12. 2. 1801	Darlaston			X						X	X	
23. 3. 1801	Ednall				X							
23. 3. 1801	Birmingham	Bakers, dealers		X	X*			X	X	X	X	
23. 3. 1801	Coventry				X				X			
28. 3. 1801	Worcester	Bakers		X	X*				X			
30. 3. 1801	Worcester	Bakers			X							
30. 3. 1801	Stratford				X			X		X	X	
30. 3. 1801	Birmingham	Huxters		X	X					X	X	
1. 6. 1801	Darlaston	Millers, bakers		X	X					X	X	

Table 2. Disturbances in the "Early Phases" of the Famines. (December to May inclusive).

North: comprising, Cheshire, Lancashire, Westmoreland, Cumberland, Northumberland, Co. Durham and Yorkshire.

Date	Location	Target	Primary Participants	1	2	3	4	5	6	7	8	9
18. 4. 1795	Thirsk				X					X		
22. 4. 1795	Stockton	Huxters		X								X
23. 4. 1795	Ripon	Potato retailers	Women		X							
25. 4. 1795	Durham		Miners		X							
27. 4. 1795	Darlington		Miners		X							
30. 4. 1795	Durham		Miners		X							
30. 4. 1795	Gateshead		Miners		X			X				
30. 4. 1795	Chester-le-Street		Miners		X			X				
4. 5. 1795	Stockport		Miners		X			X				
6. 5. 1795	Newcastle/Tyne		Miners		X							
12. 5. 1795	Ellesmere	Carters				X						
23. 5. 1795	Hull	Butchers (bad meat)		X		X						
11.12. 1795	Yarm	Carters				X						
21. 1. 1796	Kirby-in-Kendal	Bacon wholesaler				X				X	X	
23. 1. 1796	Burton (Lancs.)	Carters				X		X				
2. 2. 1796	Sheffield		Women	X								
13. 2. 1796	Kettlewell	Carters	300		X	X		X		X	X	
29. 3. 1796	Berwick-on-Tweed	Carters			X	X		X				
2. 5. 1796	Hull	Miller			X			X	X			
3. 5. 1796	Hull	Market retailers			X			X	X			
31.10. 1799	Oldham	Potato sellers	Weavers		X							
19.11. 1799	Huddersfield	Potato sellers	Women		X					X	X	
31. 1. 1800	Stockport	Wholesalers	Miners,navvies		X							

Table 2 continued.

Date	Location	Target	Primary Participants	1	2	3	4	5	6	7	8	9
Jan.1800	Lancaster				X							
Jan.1800	Manchester				X							
1. 2.1800	Stockport	Millers			X					X	X	
1. 2.1800	Macclesfield				X							
3. 2.1800	Ashton-under-Lyne	Bakers	Weavers		X					X	X	
Feb.1800	Oldham				X							
Feb.1800	Ashton-under-Lyne				X							
Feb.1800	Ulverston				X							
26. 4.1800	Sheffield	Butchers		X						X		
28. 4.1800	Sheffield	Authorities		X						X		
29. 4.1800	Sheffield				X			X	X	X	X	
29. 4.1800	Leeds				X			X				
2. 5.1800	Wakefield	Millers, dealers			X*	X						
3. 5.1800	Barnsley	Miller	Women		X*	X						
5. 5.1800	Bolton				X					X	X	
6. 5.1800	Leeds							X		X	X	
7. 5.1800	Barnsley				X				X		X	
May 1800	Oldham				X							
27.12.1800	Hull	Butchers			X	X						
13. 1.1801	Whitehaven					X						
Jan.1801	Chorley				X							
Jan.1801	Bury				X							
23. 3.1801	Ashton-under-Lyne			X						X	X	
27. 3.1801	Chorley				X							
27. 3.1801	Sunderland	Farmer in market			X*	X		X	X			
Mar.1801	Wigan				X				X			

Table 3. Disturbances in the "Early Phases" of the Famines (December to May inclusive).
South: comprising, Kent, Sussex, Surrey, Berkshire and Hampshire

Date	Location	Target	Primary Participants	1	2	3	4	5	6	7	8	9
15. 1. 1795	Harrietsham	Miller	40+	X								
22. 1. 1795	Lamberhurst	Miller		X								X
26. 1. 1795	Wadhurst	Miller		X								X
17. 2. 1795	Sedley Green	Miller	Women		X*	X						
2. 3. 1795	Worth			X	X*					X		
4. 3. 1795	Fordingbridge			X						X	X	
21. 3. 1795	Chatham	Butchers	Shipwrights		X							
28. 3. 1795	Canterbury		Militiamen		X				X			
11. 4. 1795	Portsmouth		Militiamen		X							
12. 4. 1795	Portsmouth		Townspeople		X							
13. 4. 1795	Chichester	Dealers, jail	Militia and people (3000)	X	X*					X		X
16. 4. 1795	Brighton	Market room	Women (200)	X								
16. 4. 1795	Petworth	Millers		X								X
16. 4. 1795	Seaford	Butchers	Militia mutiny		X*	X		X	X	X	X	
18. 4. 1795	Porchester		Militiamen		X							
18. 4. 1795	Petersfield		Militiamen		X							
23. 4. 1795	Guildford	Butchers	Militiamen		X							
4. 5. 1795	Brenchley	Retailers		X							X	
13. 5. 1795	Minster	Huxters		X							X	
19. 5. 1795	Fordingbridge	Butter dealer			X							X
23. 5. 1795	West Cowes				X							X
12. 4. 1796	Petworth	Miller		X				X	X			
3. 5. 1796	Portsmouth	Authorities		X				X	X			X

Table 3 continued

Date	Location	Target	Primary Participants	1	2	3	4	5	6	7	8	9
4. 5. 1796	Chichester	Millers		X				X				
7. 5. 1796	Chichester	Jail		X						X		
11. 5. 1796	Hastings	Bakers	Women and girls (300)	X	X*							X
17. 2. 1800	Petworth	Authorities	Labourers (50)	X								
22. 2. 1800	Lewes	Authorities		X								
1. 3. 1800	Westerham	Miller			X							
6. 3. 1800	Dorking	Authorities	Labourers	X					X			X
5. 4. 1800	Romsey	Miller's cart				X						X
18. 4. 1800	Ardingley	Authorities	Labourers	X								
5. 2. 1801	Lewes	Millers re. brown bread	Agricultural labourers	X								
6. 2. 1801	Eastbourne	Authorities	Fishermen, labourers	X								X
7. 2. 1801	Lingfield	Authorities,millers		X								X
10. 2. 1801	Hastings	Authorities		X								
14. 2. 1801	Lewes	Authorities		X								
15. 2. 1801	Chiddingfold				X							
19. 2. 1801	Haslemere	Authorities		X								

Table 4. Disturbances in the "Early Phases" of the Famines (December to May inclusive).

East Anglia: comprising, Essex, Hertfordshire, Huntingdonshire, Cambridgeshire, Suffolk, Norfolk and Lincolnshire

Date	Location	Target	Primary Participants	1	2	3	4	5	6	7	8	9
1.12. 1794	Kenninghall	Retailers, carters		X	X							
8.12. 1794	Kenninghall		Local villagers	X				X		X		
30. 1. 1795	Burlingham	Principal inhabitants		X								
16. 3. 1795	West Dudham	Principal inhabitants		X				X		X		
29. 4. 1795	Bury St.Edmunds				X							
2. 5. 1795	Norwich				X							
14. 5. 1795	Newmarket	Carters	Troops			X						
20. 4. 1796	Norwich	Millers	400	X	X			X				
25. 4. 1796	Norwich	Bakers	Women and boys	X						X		
25. 1. 1800	Brank Broughton	Shopkeeper		X								X
5. 2. 1800	Malden		Women and children	X								
6. 3. 1800	Romford				X							
3. 5. 1800	Norwich				X							
3. 5. 1800	Great Yarmouth				X							
25. 2. 1801	Frinkley		Drainage workers		X							
10. 3. 1801	King's Lynn	Farmers, millers			X	X				X		
11. 3. 1801	King's Lynn	Jail		X						X		

Table 5.   Disturbances in the "Early Phases" of the Famines (December to May inclusive) Western Counties: comprising, Wiltshire, Dorset, Devon, Cornwall, Somerset and Gloucester east of the Severn.

N.B.   Excludes disturbances in the South-west in December 1800 to May 1801

Date	Location	Target	Primary Participants	1	2	3	4	5	6	7	8	9
16. 1. 1795	Cullompton	Farmers	Miners	X								
23. 3. 1795	Kingswood	Tithe-owner					X					
24. 3. 1795	Bideford		Militiamen		X							
25. 3. 1795	Exeter		Women (50)		X							
27. 3. 1795	Stroud		Irish troops		X							
27. 3. 1795	Exeter		Women (300)		X							
28. 3. 1795	Exeter	Carters	Women		X	X				X		X
2. 4. 1795	Barnstaple		Troops		X					X		
2. 4. 1795	Plymouth		Troops		X					X		
2. 4. 1795	Devonport		Militiamen and dockyard workers		X							
4. 4. 1795	Plymouth				X							
4. 4. 1795	Devonport		Militiamen and dockyard workers (800)		X							
4. 4. 1795	Totnes				X							
4. 4. 1795	Dartmouth				X							
4. 4. 1795	Newton Abbot				X							
4. 4. 1795	Ashburton				X							
9. 4. 1795	Modbury		Women		X							
10. 4. 1795	South Molton				X							
10. 4. 1795	Tavistock		Tinners	X					X			
11. 4. 1795	Tiverton		Women		X					X		
13. 4. 1795	Kingsteighton	Miller				X					X	
16. 4. 1795	Modbury				X						X	

Table 5 continued

Date	Location	Target	Primary Participants	1	2	3	4	5	6	7	8	9
16. 4. 1795	Kingswood	Tithe-owner	Miners	x								
25. 4. 1795	Wells	Wholesalers, retailers	Irish troops		x	x						
2. 5. 1795	Bruton		Women		x						x	
7. 5. 1795	Kingswood		Miners	x	x	x						
14. 5. 1795	Trowbridge		500		x							
17. 3. 1800	East Cohen	Carters				x						
7. 5. 1800	Bath	Potato retailers	Women		x		x				x	
4. 4. 1801	Bristol				x			x	x	x	x	
6. 4. 1801	Kingswood	Authorities	Miners	x				x	x	x		x
8. 4. 1801	Weymouth		Women and children	x								x

Table 6.   The Stoppage of the Circulation of Grain, Summer 1795

Date	Location	Target	Primary Participants	1	2	3	4	5	6	7	8	9
East Anglia												
13. 7. 1795	Barham	Carters		X								
14. 7. 1795	Rainham								X			X
14. 7. 1795	Norwich	Carters				X						X
15. 7. 1795	Godmanchester	Barges				X						
16. 7. 1795	Tollesbury	Barges				X					X	
17. 7. 1795	Cambridge	Barges			X	X*						X
18. 7. 1795	Cambridge	Wholesale Butchers			X*	X						
21. 7. 1795	Tydd St.Mary	Millers	Drainage workers		X	X*						
21. 7. 1795	Windham			X				X				
21. 7. 1795	Houghton			X				X				
22. 7. 1795	Wells	Merchants				X						X
22. 7. 1795	Fakenham	Merchants				X						X
22. 7. 1795	Great Yarmouth	Merchants				X						X
22. 7. 1795	Lynewood Bridge	Merchants				X						X
22. 7. 1795	Tydd St. Mary	Farmers	Drainage workers (100+)	X	X*	X*	X					
24. 7. 1795	Chatteris	Authorities		X	X*	X*						
27. 7. 1795	Saffron Walden	Dealers,carters	300+	X	X	X*		X			X	X
27. 7. 1795	Ramsay			X				X				
27. 7. 1795	St. Ives					X						
29. 7. 1795	Great Chesterford	Itinerant baker	Women (100+)	X	X*	X*					X	
30. 7. 1795	Wisbech	Authorities,jail	Drainage Workers	X	X	X				X		X
31. 7. 1795	Halstead	Millers				X					X	X
2. 8. 1795	Bures St. Adams	Farmer			X	X	X*					
4. 8. 1795	Bishop's Stortford									X		
5. 8. 1795	Halstead					X		X				
8. 8. 1795	Boston		Drainage workers	X								

Table 6 continued

Date	Location	Target	Primary Participants	1	2	3	4	5	6	7	8	9
7. 9. 1795	Sudbury	Millers	Weavers		X	X*						
22. 9. 1795	Glemsford	Authorities	Weavers (300+)	X								X
18.10. 1795	Diss	Miller	300+			X						
19.10. 1795	Diss	Millers				X						
23.10. 1795	Barham	Bakers, farmers			X	X	X					
17.11. 1795	Hadstock	Itinerant baker	Women and children (40)		X							
5.12. 1795	Mildenhall	Barges			X	X*				X		
14.12. 1795	Wells	Wharfs				X		X				
17.12. 1795	Sharrington	Carters				X		X		X	X	
20.12. 1795	Sharrington	Carters				X						

N.B. The interruptions to the coastal shipments of grain from this area was much more extensive than the numbers of concrete examples imply.

Table 7. The Stoppage of the Circulation of Grain, Summer 1795.

South Midlands: comprising Northamptonshire, Buckinghamshire, Bedfordshire, Berkshire, Oxfordshire and Gloucestershire east of the Severn.

Date	Location	Target	Primary Participants	1	2	3	4	5	6	7	8	9
4. 6. 1795	Bristol	Fish wholesalers										
24. 6. 1795	Wellingborough	Farmer/dealer	200+	X		X*		X	X			
24. 6. 1795	Tewkesbury	Barges	Women			X				X	X	X
1. 7. 1795	Towcester	Dealers			X	X*		X				X
1. 7. 1795	Luton	Dealers				X						
10. 7. 1795	Oxford	Dealers				X						
15. 7. 1795	Oxford	Dealers	Women			X						
16. 7. 1795	Newbury		Navvies	X								
16. 7. 1795	Burford	Dealers' stocks				X						X
18. 7. 1795	Stroud	Barges				X						
20. 7. 1795	Standerwick	Carters			X	X*			X			
20. 7. 1795	Stroud	Barges			X	X*						
21. 7. 1795	Bedford	Millers' carts				X						X
21. 7. 1795	Westbury	Dealers, farmers	Weavers		X	X*	X					
21. 7. 1795	Warminster	Dealers, farmers	Weavers		X	X*						
22. 7. 1795	Frome	Millers						X				X
24. 7. 1795	Blaxham	Carters				X						X
25. 7. 1795	Northampton	Carters, barges	Women			X		X				X
27. 7. 1795	Peterborough					X						
28. 7. 1795	Northampton	Barges				X						
3. 8. 1795	Bath	Barges				X		X				
4. 8. 1795	Long Handborough	Carters	300+		X	X*					X	X
5. 8. 1795	Witney	Carters			X	X*						X

Table 7 continued

Date	Location	Target	Primary Participants	1	2	3	4	5	6	7	8	9
6. 8. 1795	Devizes	Dealers			X	X*		X				
21. 8. 1795	Hertfordbridge			X				X		X	X	
5. 9. 1795	Maidenhead	Baker		X								
18. 9. 1795	Bristol	Baker		X								
25. 9. 1795	Aylesbury	Dealers				X						

Table 8. Disturbances in the Midlands (as Table 1) during the Summer of 1795

Date	Location	Target	Primary Participants	1	2	3	4	5	6	7	8	9
8. 6. 1795	Newcastle/Lyme			X					X			
22. 6. 1795	Birmingham	Miller	Women and boys (1,000)	X	X*	X		X	X	X	X	
22. 6. 1795	Dudley	Farmers	Miners, nailers (2,000)		X	X	X*	X		X	X	
22. 6. 1795	Stourbridge	Miller		X	X							
23. 6. 1795	Birmingham	Soldier		X								
20. 7. 1795	Nottingham	Bakers		X	X			X	X			
21. 7. 1795	Ilkeston		Miners (60)	X								
22. 7. 1795	Newark	Barges		X	X	X*		X	X			X
24. 7. 1795	Stamford (Rutland)	Miller/dealer	Women	X		X						
26. 7. 1795	Shardlow Wharf	Warehouses				X						
27. 7. 1795	Coalbrookdale	Miller	Miners (500)	X	X			X		X		
29. 7. 1795	Wolverhampton	Carters			X	X*		X	X	X		
31. 7. 1795	Eastwood	Farmers	Miners		X	X*	X*	X	X	X	X	
4. 8. 1795	Shardlow Wharf	Warehouses		X		X		X	X			
4. 8. 1795	Stafford	Barge							X			
4. 8. 1795	Bromsgrove		1,000		X*	X*		X	X	X	X	
6. 8. 1795	Barrow on Soar	Escorted corn carts							X		X	X
6. 8. 1795	Sheephead	Baker			X			X				
10. 8. 1795	Swandlicote	Farmers	Miners		X		X*				X	X
29. 8. 1795	Coventry				X							

Table 9. Disturbances in the North (as in Table 2) during the Summer of 1795

Date	Location	Target	Primary Participants	1	2	3	4	5	6	7	8	9
2. 6. 1795	Sheffield			X								
17. 6. 1795	Bishop Auckland		Miners	X							X	
24. 6. 1795	Sheffield		Women	X								
14. 7. 1795	Bridforth	Carters				X					X	
16. 7. 1795	Berwick-on-Tweed		Women, miners	X	X*			X				
18. 7. 1795	Berwick-on-Tweed		Women, miners					X	X			
22. 7. 1795	Easton	Carters										
24. 7. 1795	Jarrow			X		X					X	
27. 7. 1795	Carlisle	Dealers	2,000+		X	X*				X		X
28. 7. 1795	Carlisle	Jail		X								X
28. 7. 1795	Delph	Itinerant baker	Weavers		X							
28. 7. 1795	Sheffield	Miller	50	X				X		X	X	
29. 7. 1795	Sheffield	Miller		X						X	X	
30. 7. 1795	Manchester	Dealers	100+	X				X	X	X	X	
31. 7. 1795	Manchester			X	X			X	X	X	X	
31. 7. 1795	Stockport	Dealers		X	X*				X			
1. 8. 1795	Stockport	Dealers		X	X*			X	X	X	X	
1. 8. 1795	Brough	Carters		X	X	X*						
3. 8. 1795	Rochdale	Authorities, dealers	Women	X	X*					X		
3. 8. 1795	Shipley	Dealer	Apprentices	X	X*						X	
3. 8. 1795	Macclesfield			X						X		
4. 8. 1795	Sheffield			X					X			
4. 8. 1795	Sheffield	Relief committee	Women, apprentices	X				X				

Table 9 continued

Date	Location	Target	Principal Participants								
			1	2	3	4	5	6	7	8	9
5. 8. 1795	Wormfield	Carter			X						
6. 8. 1795	Knottingly	Barges			X		X	X			
7. 8. 1795	Knottingly	Barges			X		X	X	X		
7. 8. 1795	Castleford	Barges			X		X	X	X	X	
7. 8. 1795	Methley	Barges			X		X	X	X	X	
8. 8. 1795	Almondbury	Dealers	X	X*							
8. 8. 1795	Lancaster	Retailer		X							
9. 8. 1795	Macclesfield			X							
17. 8. 1795	Halifax	Miller	X								

Table 10. Disturbances in the Autumn of 1795.

National survey, excluding East Anglia (see Table 7), West Gloucestershire (see Table 11), and Cornwall (see Table 12)

Date	Location	Target	Primary Participants	1	2	3	4	5	6	7	8	9
14. 9. 1795	Dudley	Warehouses	Miners		X			X		X	X	
18. 9. 1795	Bristol	Baker			X							
21. 9. 1795	Liverpool	Provision dealers			X							
29. 9. 1795	Handsworth	Magistrate		X							X	
30. 9. 1795	Chichester		Women		X							
7.10. 1795	Nantwich				X			X				
10.10. 1795	Darlington				X							
15.10. 1795	Holywell	Carters	Women			X						
19.10. 1795	Barnard Castle	Millers		X								X
27.10. 1795	Wolsingham	Farmers	Miners		X							X
10.11. 1795	Newcastle	Dealers	Miners,keelmen		X					X		
11. 11. 1795	Morpeth		Miners		X				X			
13. 11. 1795	Bristol		Miners	X								
17. 11. 1795	Westbury	Authorities		X	X*							
2. 12. 1795	Oswestry		Navvies (100+)		X			X				
11. 12. 1795	Yarm	Carters				X					X	

Table 11. Disturbances in West Gloucestershire and Monmouthshire 1794–6, 1799–1801.

Date	Location	Target	Primary Participants	1	2	3	4	5	6	7	8	9
9. 5. 1795	Monmouth		Miners		X							
20. 6. 1795	Wilton	Barges	Miners (130)			X						
23. 6. 1795	Mitcheldeane	Miller /dealers	Miners	X		X						
24. 6. 1795	Blakeney	Wharfs,barges	Miners			X						X
3. 8. 1795	Forest of Dean	Millers,farmers	Miners	X		X*	X					
31.10. 1795	Newnham	Carters	Miners		X	X*						
31.10. 1795	Ross-on-Wye	Carters	Miners		X	X*						
7.11. 1795	Ross-on-Wye	Carters	Miners		X	X*		X		X		
7.11. 1795	Newnham	Barges	Miners (350)			X						
30.11. 1795	Billitree	Carters	Miners			X					X	
22. 3. 1796	Ruardean	Barges				X						
7. 3. 1800	Mitcheldeane	Carters			X	X*		X				X
26. 3. 1800	Lidbrooke	Barges	Miners			X		X				
27. 3. 1800	Redbrooke	Barges	Miners			X			X			
29. 3. 1800	Redbrooke	Barges	Miners			X						
14. 3. 1801	Bigsweare	Barges	300		X	X*						
16. 3. 1801	Chepstow	Barges				X		X	X	X		
17. 3. 1801	Chepstow	Barges				X		X	X	X		
17. 3. 1801	Abby	Barges,farmers				X*	X					
17. 3. 1801	Woolaston	Barges				X		X				
17. 3. 1801	Nr. Chepstow	Farmers			X	X	X*					
23. 3. 1801	English Bicknor	Warehouses			X	X*					X	
25. 3. 1801	Westbury/Severn	Warehouses			X	X*					X	
27. 3. 1801	Oxenhall	Warehouses			X	X*					X	
27. 3. 1801	Dymcock	Farmers				X	X*					

Table 12. Disturbances in Cornwall 1794–6, 1799–1801

Date	Location	Target	Primary Participants	1	2	3	4	5	6	7	8	9
10. 3. 1795	Penzance	Coasters	Miners (600)		x	X*			x	x		
12. 3. 1795	Penzance		Miners (200)		x	X*			x			
14. 3. 1795	Helstone	Authorities	Miners	x								
19. 3. 1795	Port Isaac	Dealers,merchants	Miners		x	X*						
19. 3. 1795	Padstow	Merchants	Miners		x	X*						
26. 3. 1795	Penryn	Merchants	Miners			x						
27. 3. 1795	St. Austle	Farmers	Miners				x					
27. 3. 1795	Polgarth	Dealerw	Miners	x		x						
30. 3. 1795	Launceston				x							
30. 3. 1795	Callington				x							
11. 4. 1795	Callington		Miners		x				x			
18. 4. 1795	Fowey				x							
5.11. 1795	Callington	Retailers,farmers	Miners (80)	x	x		x					
5. 4. 1796	Redruth	Retailers,farmers	Miners		x		x	x		x	x	
6. 4. 1796	Truro	Authorities,jail	Miners (3,000)	x				x		x	x	
6. 4. 1796	Helstone		Miners		x							
6. 4. 1796	Penzance		Miners		x							
12. 4. 1800	Callington	Farmers	Miners				x					
26. 1. 1801	Grampound	Farmers	Miners				x		x			
27. 1. 1801	Grampound	Farmers	Miners				x		x			
31. 1. 1801	Tregony	Farmers	Miners				x					
9. 4. 1801	Falmouth		Miners		x							x
9. 4. 1801	St. Austle	Farmers	Miners				x					
9. 4. 1801	Penzance		Miners		x					x		x
9. 4. 1801	St. Mawes	Farmers	Miners				x	x		x		

Table 12 continued

Date	Location	Target	Primary Participants	1	2	3	4	5	6	7	8	9
10. 4. 1801	Redruth		Miners		X							
11. 4. 1801	Helstone				X			X	X			X
13. 4. 1801	Torpoint	Barges				X						
15. 4. 1801	St.Stephens	Farmers	Miners				X					
15. 4. 1801	St.Just	Farmers	Miners				X				X	
15. 4. 1801	Liskeard	Farmers	Miners				X				X	
15. 4. 1801	Pelynt	Farmers	Miners				X				X	
2. 5. 1801	St. Ives	Butchers			X							

Table 13.   The Incidence of Arson 1794-6, 1799-1801

a)   The South-east (Surrey, Sussex and Kent)

Date	Location	County	Target
6.12. 1794	Heyshot	Sussex	Barn
29. 4. 1795	Carshalton	Surrey	Barn
2. 6. 1795	Worth	Sussex	Barn
19. 1. 1796	Hastings	Sussex	Wheat rick
7.12. 1799	East Greenwich	Kent	Barn
Dec. 1799	Lancing	Sussex	Several corn stacks
7. 3. 1800	Friston	Sussex	Wheat stack
5. 4. 1800	East Dean	Sussex	Wheat rick
12. 4. 1800	Beeding	Sussex	Wheat rick
4. 5. 1800	Worthing	Sussex	Stack of faggots
5.12. 1800	Rochester	Kent	Wheat stack
26.12. 1800	Ninfield	Sussex	Wheat stack

b)   The West (Berkshire, Hampshire, Somerset, Wiltshire and Gloucestershire)

Date	Location	County	Target
30. 1. 1795	Peasemore	Berkshire	Barn
25. 2. 1795	Boxford	Berkshire	Farmhouse
9. 4. 1795	Wilton	Wiltshire	Barn
10. 7. 1795	Wokingham	Berkshire	Baker's store
11. 7. 1795	East Garston	Berkshire	Farmhouse and stable
8. 3. 1796	East Perrot	Somerset	Tithe barn
12. 2. 1800	Whiteparish	Wiltshire	Barn
28. 2. 1800	Odiham	Hampshire	Barn
7. 3. 1800	Bath	Somerset	Brewery store
13. 3. 1800	Kingsweaton	Somerset	Several hay stacks
10. 6. 1800	Wimborne	Dorset	Two barns
21. 6. 1800	Minehead	Somerset	Farmhouse and barns
24. 8. 1800	Coleford	Gloucestershire	Magistrate's barn
28. 8. 1800	Speen	Berkshire	Barn newly-housed wheat
15.11. 1800	Stoke Green	Berkshire	Wheat ricks and barns
17. 2. 1801	East Quanstockhead	Somerset	Wheat ricks
8. 3. 1801	Painswick	Gloucestershire	Hayrick

c)   The Midlands and the North

Date	Location	County	Target
5. 1. 1795	Liverpool	Lancashire	Merchant's house,warehouse
13. 2. 1796	Swinefleet	West Riding	Barn

Table 13 continued

Date	Location	County	Target
14. 2. 1796	Swinefleet	West Riding	Barn
17. 2. 1800	Longer	Shropshire	Oat stack
27. 4. 1800	Shrewsbury	Shropshire	Wheat stacks
27. 4. 1800	Sutton	Shropshire	Wheat stacks
12.10. 1800	Twyford	Derbyshire	Wheat stacks
19.10. 1800	Market Bosworth	Leicestershire	Wheat stacks
27.10. 1800	Sawley	Derbyshire	Mill owner's barn
1.11. 1800	Not given	Derbyshire	Rick
17.11. 1800	King's Nawton	Derbyshire	Farm buildings
18.11. 1800	Nr. Nottingham	Nottinghamshire	Hayrick
1.12. 1800	Keighley	West Riding	Corn mill
17. 4. 1801	Burford	Shropshire	Wheat rick
26.10. 1801	Elsdon	Northumberland	Seven corn and one hay stacks

d) East Anglia (Essex, Hertfordshire, Cambridgeshire, Huntingdonshire, Suffolk and Norfolk).

Date	Location	County	Target
10. 1. 1795	Eye	Suffolk	Straw sacks
11. 1. 1795	Eye	Suffolk	Barn
30.11. 1795	Blo' Norton	Norfolk	Barley stack
30.12. 1795	Diss area	Norfolk	Several fires, no detail
14. 1. 1796	Ware	Hertfordshire	Hay stacks
11. 2. 1800	Watford	Hertfordshire	Wheat stack
April 1800	Trinley	Suffolk	Barn
April 1800	Harleychurch	Suffolk	Barn
29. 4. 1800	Harlow	Essex	Barns
23. 6. 1800	Blackmore	Essex	Stables and piggery
15. 7. 1800	Essendon	Hertfordshire	Barn
5. 8. 1800	Bickham	Essex	Woodpiles
23. 9. 1800	Braintree	Essex	Barns
23. 9. 1800	Gissing	Norfolk	Mill
24. 9. 1800	Little Swaffham	Suffolk	Barn
16.10. 1800	Braintree	Essex	No detail but third fire
18.10. 1800	Clare	Suffolk	No detail but third fire
20.10. 1800	Dunstable	Bedfordshire	Barley rick
26.10. 1800	Clare	Suffolk	Overseer's corn stack
29.10. 1800	Linsell	Essex	Barn

Table 13 continued

Date	Location	County	Target
5.11. 1800	Chatteris	Cambridgeshire	Farmhouse and barn
22.11. 1800	Braintree	Essex	Malt office and store
22.11. 1800	Brocking	Essex	Straw ricks
22.11. 1800	Bracken	Essex	Stable
24.12. 1800	Southwold	Suffolk	Barn
25.12. 1800	Holt	Norfolk	Several corn ricks
July 1801	Walham	Hertfordshire	Barn

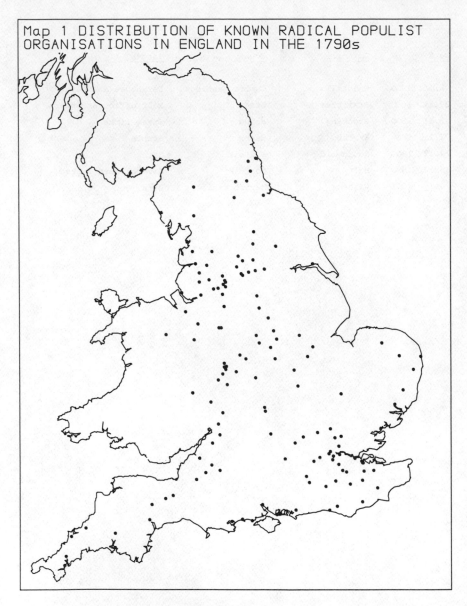

Map 1 DISTRIBUTION OF KNOWN RADICAL POPULIST
ORGANISATIONS IN ENGLAND IN THE 1790s

FIGURES

Grain prices in selected markets: London, Birmingham, Pontefract, Malton,
Colchester, Chichester.

Figure   1   Wheat   September 1794 - August 1795

Figure   2   Wheat   September 1795 - August 1796

Figure   3   Wheat   September 1799 - August 1800

Figure   4   Wheat   September 1800 - August 1801

Figure   5   Barley   September 1794 - August 1795

Figure   6   Barley   September 1795 - August 1796

Figure   7   Barley   September 1799 - August 1800

Figure   8   Barley   September 1800 - August 1801

Figure   9   Oats   September 1794 - August 1795

Figure 10   Oats   September 1795 - August 1796

Figure 11   Oats   September 1799 - August 1800

Figure 12   Oats   September 1800 - August 1801

The Figures are based on the official returns of the market inspectorate,
MAF. 10/273-85.

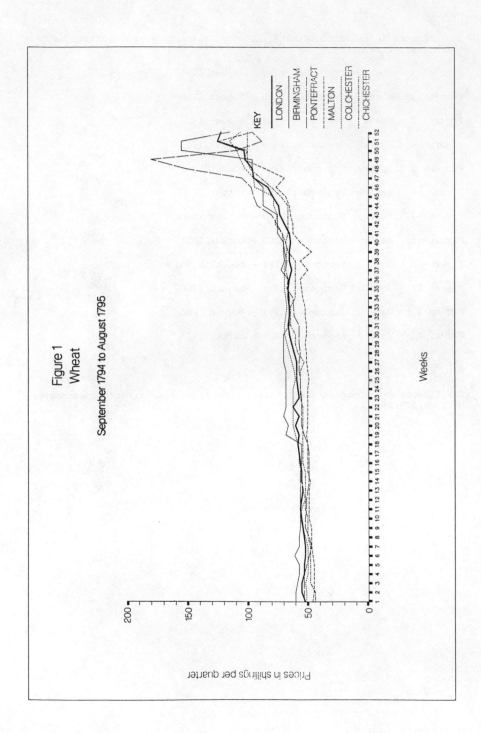

Figure 1
Wheat

September 1794 to August 1795

KEY

LONDON
BIRMINGHAM
PONTEFRACT
MALTON
COLCHESTER
CHICHESTER

Prices in shillings per quarter

Weeks

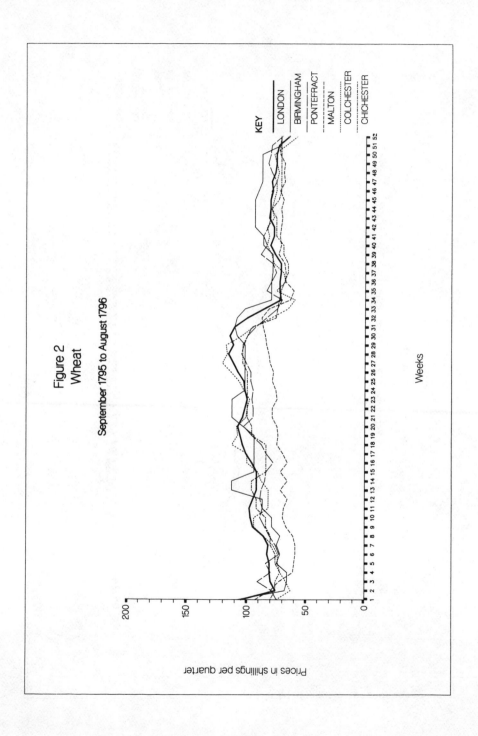

Figure 2
Wheat

September 1795 to August 1796

KEY

LONDON
BIRMINGHAM
PONTEFRACT
MALTON
COLCHESTER
CHICHESTER

Prices in shillings per quarter

Weeks

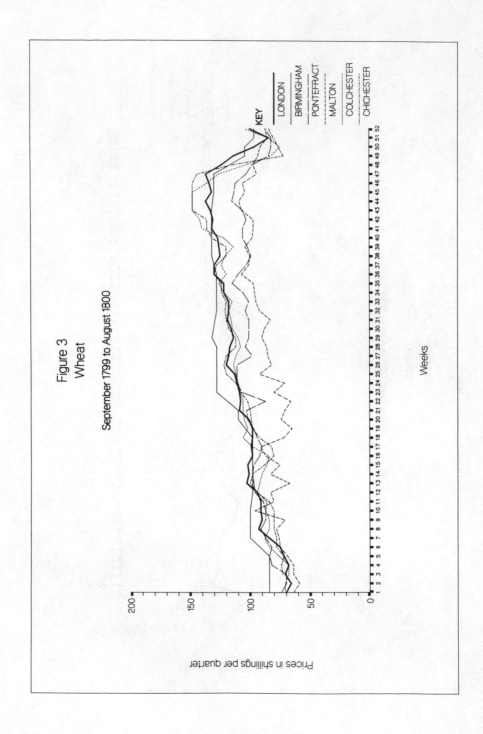

Figure 3
Wheat

September 1799 to August 1800

KEY

LONDON
BIRMINGHAM
PONTEFRACT
MALTON
COLCHESTER
CHICHESTER

Prices in shillings per quarter

Weeks

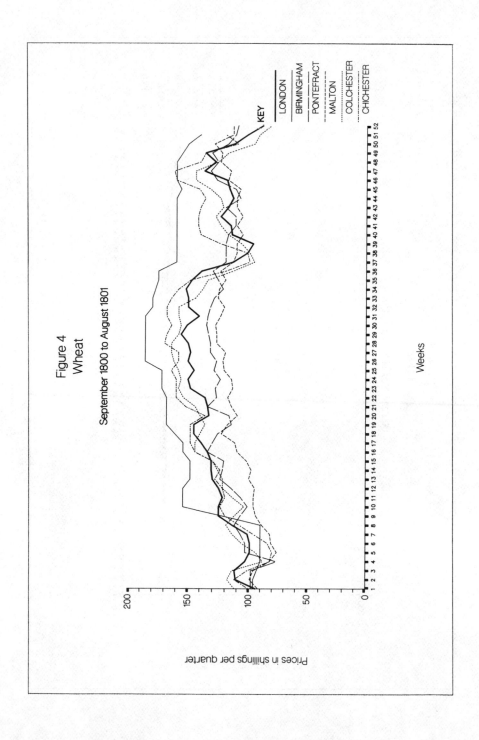

Figure 4
Wheat

September 1800 to August 1801

KEY

LONDON
BIRMINGHAM
PONTEFRACT
MALTON
COLCHESTER
CHICHESTER

Prices in shillings per quarter

Weeks

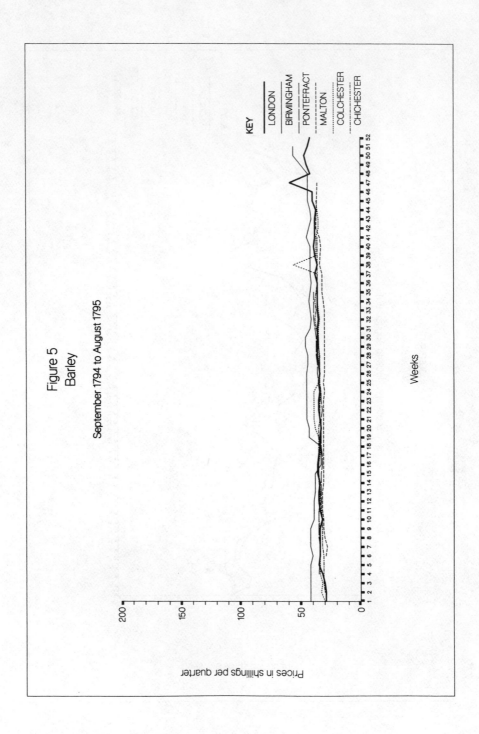

Figure 5
Barley

September 1794 to August 1795

KEY

LONDON
BIRMINGHAM
PONTEFRACT
MALTON
COLCHESTER
CHICHESTER

Weeks

Prices in shillings per quarter

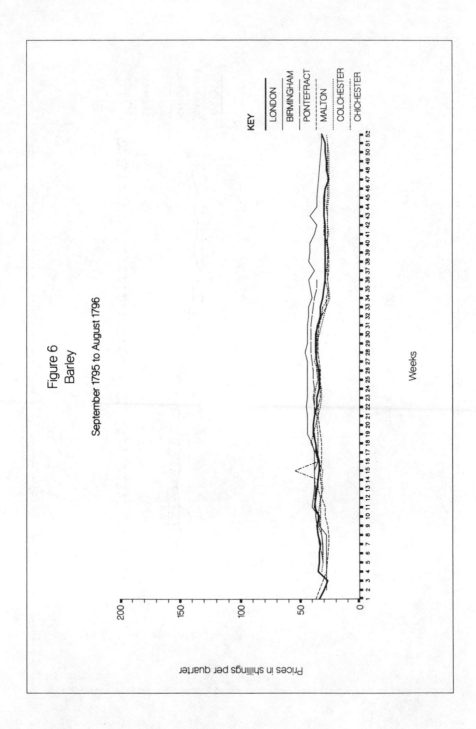

Figure 6
Barley

September 1795 to August 1796

KEY

LONDON
BIRMINGHAM
PONTEFRACT
MALTON
COLCHESTER
CHICHESTER

Prices in shillings per quarter

Weeks

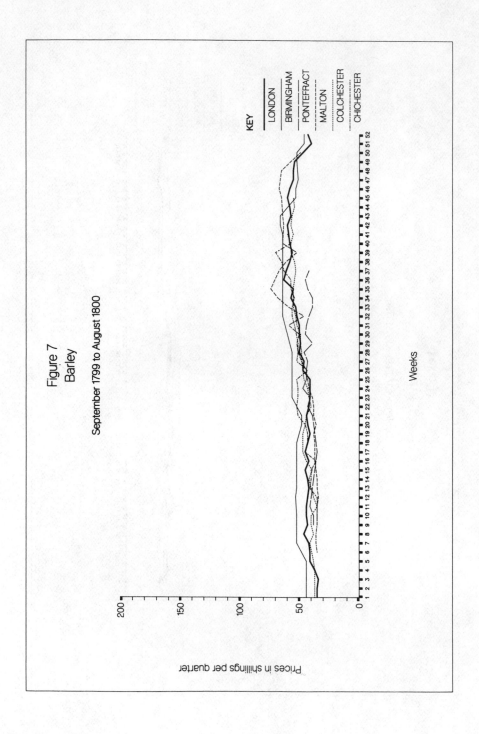

Figure 7
Barley

September 1799 to August 1800

Prices in shillings per quarter

Weeks

KEY

LONDON
BIRMINGHAM
PONTEFRACT
MALTON
COLCHESTER
CHICHESTER

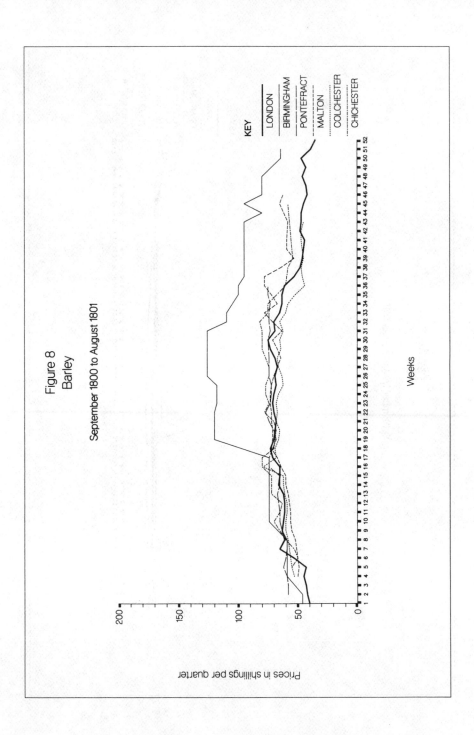

Figure 8
Barley

September 1800 to August 1801

KEY

LONDON
BIRMINGHAM
PONTEFRACT
MALTON
COLCHESTER
CHICHESTER

Prices in shillings per quarter

Weeks

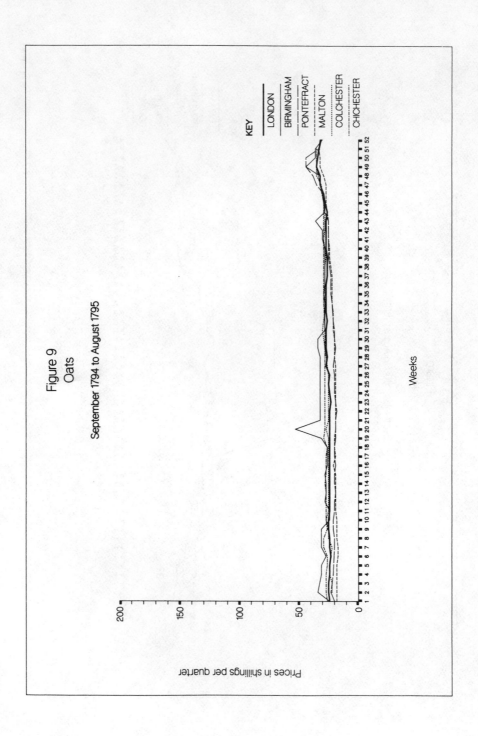

Figure 9
Oats

September 1794 to August 1795

Prices in shillings per quarter

Weeks

KEY

LONDON
BIRMINGHAM
PONTEFRACT
MALTON
COLCHESTER
CHICHESTER

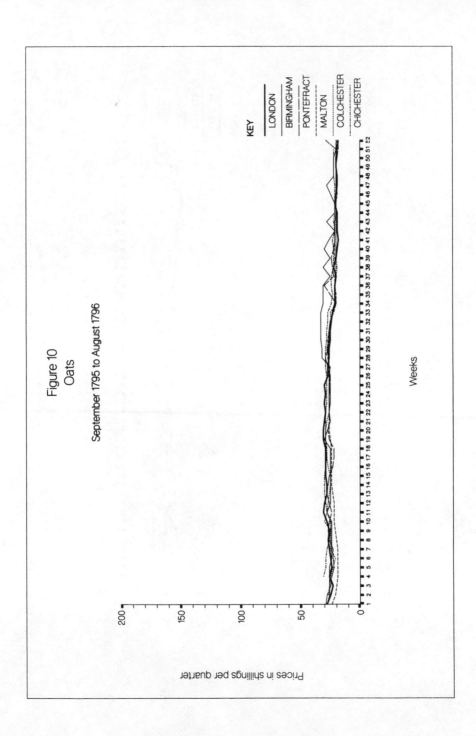

Figure 10
Oats

September 1795 to August 1796

KEY

LONDON
BIRMINGHAM
PONTEFRACT
MALTON
COLCHESTER
CHICHESTER

Prices in shillings per quarter

Weeks

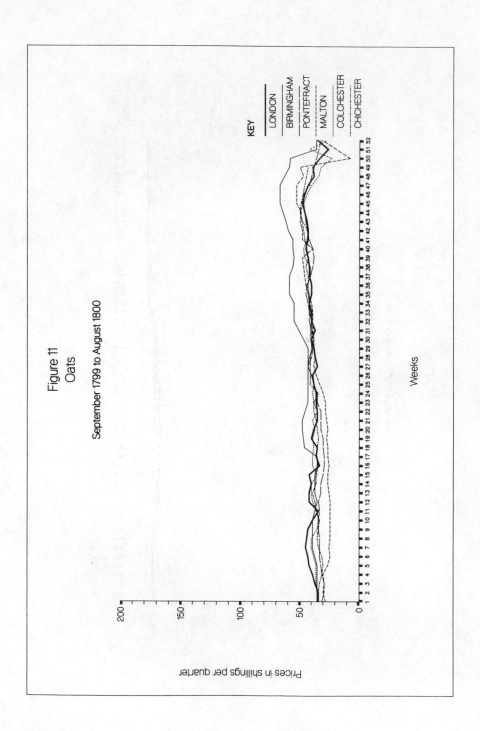

Figure 11
Oats

September 1799 to August 1800

KEY

LONDON
BIRMINGHAM
PONTEFRACT
MALTON
COLCHESTER
CHICHESTER

Prices in shillings per quarter

Weeks

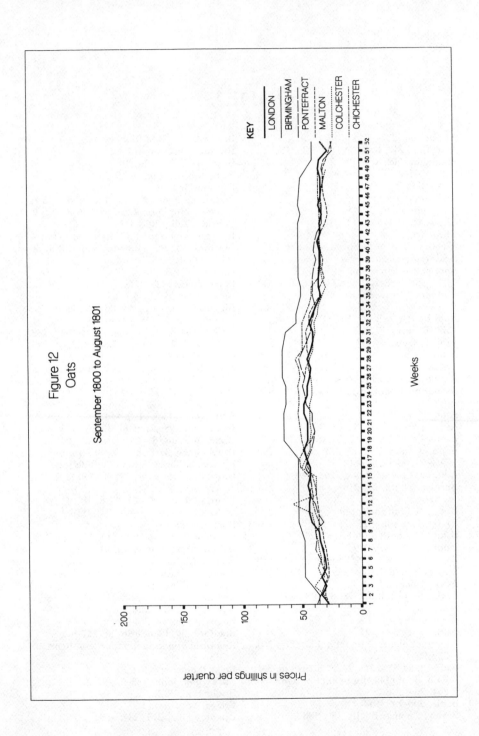

Figure 12
Oats

September 1800 to August 1801

KEY

LONDON
BIRMINGHAM
PONTEFRACT
MALTON
COLCHESTER
CHICHESTER

Weeks

Prices in shillings per quarter

INDEX

Abbotsham, 227
Abingdon, 247; Riots in, 101, 126, 180
Addington, Henry, 3, 199, 216, 218, 243, 247, 259, 313–4
Africa, 186–7
Ainsworth, Thomas, 66, 157
Aire and Calder, 23, 111
Albion Flour Mills, 214, 217
Alien Act, 285
American War of Independence, 159, 185
Anals of Agriculture, 36
Anonymous letters, 76, 90, 101, 123, 164–7, 175, 228–9, 241, 271, 277, 282, 300, 302
Anthony (Cornwall), 68
Anti-Jacobin Review, 240
Appleby, Dr A.B., 4, 53, 317
Aris, Thomas, 17
Armed Neutrality, 57
Army, Mutinies, 99–105, 134, 146–7
Arnold (Nottinghamshire), 121
Ashburnham, Earl of, 307
Ashburton, Charity in, 295; Riots in, 93, 100, 176
Ashley, Thomas, 137
Ashton, Professor T.S., 63, 333
Ashton-under-Lyne, 14; Riots in, 278–9
Assize of Bread, 21–2, 27–8, 33, 179, 190, 202, 204–6, 208–11, 214–18
Athorpe, Colonel, 114–5, 263, 269
Auckland, Lord, 35, 210

Baker, William, MP, 188
Bakers' Company, 28, 204, 217
Baltic, 57, 184–8, 191–2, 196, 200
Bamford, Samuel, 219
Banbury, 27, 239, 256; Radicals at, 141, 159; Riots in, 126–7, 180, 255, 264, 266, 271–2
Bank of England, 55
Banks, Sir Joseph, 35, 78, 88, 190, 207, 211, 327
Barming (Kent), 71
Barnsley, riots in, 97
Bastard, Colonel, MP, 119, 156, 257, 260, 289–90
Bath, 18, 81, 115, 213, 242; Charities in, 301; Radicals at, 145; Riots in, 109, 178, 180, 264, 266
Battle, 206–7
Bayley, Thomas B., JP, 150, 198

Bedford, 110, 208; Riots in, 108, 259
Bedford, Duke of, 167
Bedfordshire, 21, 36, 38
Bedworth, riots in, 94, 97, 124
Benson, Dr J., 18
Berkshire, 15–6, 38, 45, 107, 138, 165–6, 206–7, 216; Poor Relief in, 226–7, 291–9
Bernard, T.B., 303, 312
Berwick-on-Tweed, 213; Riots in, 113
Bideford, 50, 203; Poor Relief in, 228; Riots in, 100, 179
Bilston, 47, 83, 264
Binns, John, 142
Bird, W.W. MP, 245–6
Birdchanger (Essex), 44; Poor Relief in, 295
Birmingham, 17, 25, 28, 40, 43–5, 47–8, 51, 57–60, 64–5, 69, 71, 104, 107, 109–12, 188, 198, 207, 214, 217–8, 220–1, 231–2, 243, 256, 327–8; Charity in, 290, 302, 304; Flour and Bread Company, 327; Poor Relief in, 227; Radicalism in, 136–7, 142–5, 149–50; Riots in, 92, 95–8, 113, 124–5, 143, 178, 180, 263–8
Bishopp, Lt. Col., 102–4, 134
Blackburn, 198; Riots in, 132, 178
Blake, William, 56
Blatchington Barracks, 99, 102–5
Blything (Gilbert) Union (Suffolk), 289
Board of Agriculture, 37, 40, 190, 202, 206, 212, 245, 247, 334
Board of Trade, 47, 65, 87–8, 180–1, 184–5, 194–6, 199–202, 214–7, 243, 321–2
Bodmin, 188
Bohstedt, Professor John, 91, 95, 326, 328
Bolton, 65, 269; Riots in, 91, 278
Bonaparte, Napoleon, 146, 256
Booth, Dr Alan, 76
Boroughbridge, 24
Boulton, Matthew, 310, 327
Bovey Tracy (Devon), 281
Boyne, Lord, 27, 261–2
Bradford, 39; Radicalism in, 137–9
Bramfield (Berkshire), 225; Poor Relief in, 228
Brent (Somerset), 165
Brickwood, John, 185–6, 191–3
Bridlington, 327
Briggs, Lord Asa, 3
Brighton, 102, 215, 284, 309

Bristol, 26, 43, 45, 111, 116–7, 178, 181, 185, 194, 231, 309, 327; Radicalism in, 144; Riots in, 115, 132, 180
Brown Bread Act, 201, 223, 319–22
Buckingham, Marquis of, 148, 166
Buckinghamshire, 36, 66, 107; Poor Relief in, 291–2, 299
Buntingford, 63
Burdett, Sir Francis, MP, 246
Burford, 44–5, 110–2, 231
Burgh-le-Marsh (Lincolnshire), 169
Burke, Edmund, 245
Burnley, 243
Buxton, R.J. MP, 110, 134–5, 185
Byron, Lord, 74

Cadiz, 185
Calhoun, Dr C., 284, 286
Callington, charity in, 299; Riots in, 118
Cambridge, 45–6, 94, 213; Poor Relief in, 309; Riots in, 107–8, 162, 180
Cambridge Intelligencer, 143, 158, 307
Cambridgeshire, 29, 62, 110; Riots in, 162
Canada, 184–7, 190
Canning, George, 38
Canterbury, charity in, 301; Riots in, 101, 180
Capital sentences on rioters, 258–9
Cardington (Bedfordshire), 21
Carlisle, 24, 43, 113; Radicalism in, 139; Riots in, 95
Carnarvon, Lord, 207, 295
Catholic Emanicipation, 247
Catterick, 63
Catts, Dr, 68
Chalmers, George, 88–9
Chambers, Professor J.D., 3
Charities (see also under counties and larger towns) in: Aldermaston, 297; Barnstaple, 290; Barton (Cambridgeshire), 303; Ford (Northumberland), 290; Henley-on-Thames, 290; Hexham, 299; Hunstanton, 290; Lambeth, 300; Maidstone, 225; Taplow, 294; Wallingford, 294
Charles I, 141
Charlesworth, Andrew, 166
Chartism, 76, 326
Chatham, 135; Riots in, 101
Chatteris (Cambridgeshire), 108
Chepstow, 116; Riots in, 262
Cheshire, 13–4, 20, 30, 44, 62, 77, 81, 91, 198, 215, 243; Riots in, 43
Chester, 24, 27, 43, 111
Chesterfield, 16; Riots in, 124
Chichester, 52, 59, 197, 213; Charity in, 295; Radicalism in, 136, 139, 142; Riots in, 102, 135, 162
Chiltern Hills, 44
Christie, Professor I.R., 6, 9–10, 12, 75, 315, 318

Church and King Riots, 136, 142
Clarence, Duke of, 218
Cleveland, 25
Clifton, Sir Gervase, 122–3
Clinton, Colonel, 35
Coats, Professor A.W., 32–3
Cobb, Rev Dr, 261
Cobbett, William, 29
Colchester, 51
Cold Bath Fields Prison, 17
Coldham, George, 120, 123
Coleridge, Samuel Taylor, 312
Collins, Dr E.J.T., 13
Colquhoun, Patrick, JP, 28, 298, 310
Combe, Lord Mayor of London, 128–30, 256, 258, 263
Combination Acts, 75–6, 171–3, 325, 339
Condorcet, 7
Co-operation, 3, 7, 326–8
Corn Bounties, 192–201
Corn Laws, 10, 34, 328, 337
Cornwall, 13, 15–16, 23, 38, 65, 216, 299; Charity in, 306–7, 324; Radicalism in, 133–4, 153–5; Riots in, 91, 99–100, 116–8, 180, 274, 279, 285, 294
Cotswolds, 44
Coventry, 42, 58, 109–10, 245; Radicalism in, 137; Riots in, 41, 94, 97, 124, 180
Cumberland, 15, 81
Curren, John Christian, MP, 189
Cusworth (West Riding), 17–8

Dagenham, 206
Dalrymple, Sir Hugh, 101
Danzig, 181, 185
Dartmouth, riots in, 100, 272; Volunteers, 154
Davies, Rev David, 15, 21, 281–2
Dawson, William, JP, 92
Dean, Forest of, 83; Poor Relief in, 313–4; Riots in, 96, 116–8, 180, 235, 258
De Dunstanville, Lord, 281
Defenders, 142
De la Pole, Reginald, 262, 281
Delaval, Lord, 178
Democratic Movement, 2, 75–6, 133–60, 335–9
Demographic Disturbance, 1–6, 68–71, 315–8
Derby, 198; Riots in, 124, 180, 326
Derbyshire, 15, 18, 64, 66, 166; Riots in, 113, 120, 124–5
Derwent, river, 25, 27, 198
Despard, Colonel Edward Marcus, 149, 153, 284
Devaynes, William, MP, 169
Devizes, 41, 47; Riots in, 132
Devon, 13, 23, 30, 57–8, 60, 63, 69–70, 83, 203, 206–8, 212, 216, 220, 244, 270; Poor Relief in, 255–6, 312; Riots in, 91, 99–100, 153–8

Devonport, 23; Radicalism in, 336; Riots in, 100

Dewsbury, Poor Relief in, 311–3; Radicalism in, 142; Riots in, 92, 94, 97

Distillaries, stoppage of, 195

Doncaster, 43, 221

Dorset, 13, 58, 62, 91; Riots in, 128, 162, 180

Dover, 44

Driffield, 27

Dublin, 142, 147

Dudley, 198; Riots in, 99, 112

Dudley, Rev Henry Bate, 164, 260

Dundas, Charles, MP, 292

Dundas, Henry, 202, 244, 330

Durham, 83, 85, 206; Charity in, 303; Riots in, 97, 279

East Anglia, (see also under component counties) 23–4, 26, 28, 44–5, 66, 106–7, 165–6, 303, 333; Poor Relief in, 294, 300; Radicalism in, 140; Riots in, 116, 128, 232, 235, 296

Eastbourne, 165

East Brent (Somerset), 63

Eccleshall (Staffordshire), 63

Eden, Sir Frederick Morton, 281, 310, 317–8

Edenbridge (Kent), 163

Edinburgh, 86

Egypt, 186

Elbing, 185

Ely, 107

Emmerton, J.W., 122–3

Emsley, Clive, 6, 284

Enclosure, General Act, 247

Epsom, 28

Erskine, Thomas, MP, 88, 148

Essay on Population, 7–8

Essex, 16, 26, 29, 34, 36, 44–5, 90, 108, 165–6, 168, 175, 220; Poor Relief in, 300, 313; Riots in, 162

Eversley, Professor, D.C.E., 8

Executions, of food rioters, 275, 278–9, 286

Exeter, 31, 45, 67, 104, 169, 227, 267, 272, 281; Poor Relief in, 302; Radicalism in, 136, 153; Riots in, 100, 153, 155–6

Fakenham, 110

Faldingworth (Sussex), 248

Farington, Joseph R.A., 330

Fawcett, William, 332–3, 339

Fawkener, William, 243

Ferrybridge, 43

Fillongley (Warwickshire), 295

Fittleworth (Sussex), 168

Fitzwilliam, Earl, 24, 58, 95, 114, 151, 170, 211, 215, 220–1, 227–8, 262–3, 265–6, 270, 312, 320

Flinn, Professor M.W., 54

Flower, Benjamin, 143, 158–9

Foley, Rev J., 281

Ford, Richard JP, 131, 256

Fortescue, Earl, 83, 215, 259–60, 271, 275–6, 279, 286, 290

Fox, Charles James, 6–7, 141, 159, 191, 195, 210–1, 223, 234–5, 303, 329–30

France, 2–4, 6, 11–2, 16, 107, 109, 135, 196; Invasion by, 55; Revolution in, 7, 75, 134, 159

Friendly Societies, 317–8, 326–8

Friends of Liberty, 138

Friends of the People, 339

Funtingdon (Sussex), 163

Gagging Act, 141–3, 233, 336

Garbett, Samuel, 188

Genovese, E.F., 32

Gentleman's Magazine, 78

George III, 105, 140–1, 149, 190, 204, 211, 220–2, 273, 283, 320

George, Dr M.D., 71

Giddy, Rev E., 117, 185, 266

Gilboy, Dr E.W., 18, 296–7

Glamorganshire, 62, 299; Riots in, 279–80

Gloucester, 40, 43, 81–3, 117, 188, 212, 267; Riots in, 95–6

Gloucestershire, 38, 43, 67, 102, 179, 215, 254; Poor Relief in, 294, 297, 299; Radicalism in, 135; Riots in, 91, 109, 132, 177, 180, 281

Godmanchester (Huntingdonshire), 110

Godwin, William, 7

Golby, J. 120–2, 145

Gordon Riots, 120, 130, 263

Gosport, 187

Gould, Professor J.D., 39

Grafton, Duke of, 231–2

Graham, Aaron, J.P., 285

Grand National Consolidated Trades Union, 338

Gravesend, 213; Poor Relief in, 309; Radicalism in, 142

Great Yarmouth, 40, 45, 110, 187–8

Green Dragon, London, 142, 146

Grenville, Lord, 88, 168, 199–200, 243–4, 246, 248

Grey, Charles, MP, 245–7, 338

Guisborough (North Riding), 30

Gulval (Cornwall), 67

Habeas Corpus, Suspension Acts, 138, 285

Haden, Rev A.B. 70, 83, 85, 216, 230, 235, 237, 241, 264, 266, 275, 277

Hadfield, James, 147–9, 330

Hadstock (Essex), 29; Riots in, 162

Hair-powder tax, 6, 138, 185, 204

Halifax, 43, 58, 224; Charity in, 303

Halevy, Elie, 10

Hampshire, 23–4, 26, 44, 48, 62, 81–2, 164, 166, 207, 271; Poor Relief in, 291–7, 306; Riots in, 101, 128, 162, 180

Hampton Court, 138
Handsworth, Poor relief in, 308, 310; Riots in, 125, 310
Hanley, 327
Harben, Thomas, JP, 102–3
Hardinge, Mr Justice, 279–80
Hardwicke, Lord, 107
Hardy, Thomas, 152, 169, 182
Harrison, Professor J.F.C., 148
Harvest, 1794, 36, 84, 184, 232–3; 1795, 36–7, 44, 84, 186, 189–90, 192, 199, 209, 232–4; 1796, 37, 48, 89; 1797, 37; 1798, 37; 1799, 37–8, 62, 84–5, 195; 1800, 38, 47, 87–9, 218–9, 237, 240–8; 1801, 38–9, 48, 64, 69, 89; Press coverage, 77–9
Hastings, 100, 104–5, 197
Hawkesbury, Lord, President Board of Trade, 1, 41, 65, 87–8, 164, 188–202, 204, 208, 210, 214–8, 232–3, 236
Hay, Dr Douglas, 259
Hayes (Kent), poor relief in, 289; Charity in, 289
Hayter, Dr Tony, 52, 263
Heacham (Norfolk), 163
Helston, 118; Radicalism in, 133; Riots in, 118
Henson, Gravenor, 337
Hereford, 117
Herefordshire, 24; Militia, 24, 100–2; Riots in, 124
Hertford, 197
Hertfordshire, 21, 36, 44, 163, 166, 189, 212, 224, 316; Poor Relief in, 292, 304, 312
Hobart, Henry, MP, 188
Hobhouse, Henry, MP, 339
Hobsbawm, Professor E.J., 76
Hoddesdon (Hertfordshire), 163
Holborn, 67
Holderness, 20
Holland, invasion of, 155
Holland, Lord, 215, 245, 330, 338
Holland, Rev William, 67, 82, 87
Honiton, Charity in, 295; Riots in, 272
Horner, Francis, 338–9
Horner, James, 86
Horsham, 282–4
Horton-in-Ribblesdale, 39
Hove, 283
Howard, Lord, 45
Huddersfield, 58
Hull, 16, 26, 40, 42–3, 46, 169, 173, 187–8, 194, 198, 223, 227; Charity in, 290, 295, 301, 312; Poor Relief in, 308; Riots in, 115, 131
Huntingdonshire, 135

Incendiarism, 76, 161, 164–7, 175, 302
Income Tax, 55
Ipswich, 234, 242; Radicalism in, 142; Riots in, 94

Ireland, 2, 24, 99, 147, 187, 285, 322; Rebellion (1798), 71, 145–6
Iris, The, 59, 115, 143, 172

James II, 141
Jedburgh, 168
Jenkinson, Charles, 2nd., 192, 218
Jones, John Gale, 141, 265, 268
Jones, Theophilus, MP, 245

Kenilworth, 296
Kennet, river, 106
Kent, 36, 38–9, 78, 101, 164, 216; Hoymen, 26; Poor Relief in, 224; Radicalism in, 151–2; Riots in, 105, 224
Kenyan, Lord Chief Justice, 84–8, 148, 164, 240–5, 245, 247, 257, 322
Kidderminster, 242; Radicalism in, 151; Riots in, 97, 125
King, John, 187, 237, 253, 256
King's Lynn, 110; Poor Relief in, 304, 308
Kingston-upon-Thames, 138
Kingswood, 170, 242
Kirkham, (Lancashire), 85
Kirkstall Forge, 16–8, 61–2
Knaresborough, 23–4, 29
Knightsbridge, 29
Knollis, Rev, 111–2, 231–2
Konisberg, 185

Lancashire, 14, 22, 24, 30, 42–3, 57, 66, 70, 111, 169–72, 198, 208, 212, 331; Charity in, 311–2, 321; Light Dragoons, 102–4; Poor Relief in, 301; Radicalism in, 152, 278, 336; Riots in, 91, 97–8
Lancaster, 29, 171; Riots in, 132
Landaff, Lord, 101
Langton, Lt.Col., 102–3
Lansdowne, Lord, 167
Lea, river, 197
Lechmore, Edward, MP, 234–5
Leeds, 16, 23, 27, 31, 43, 57, 60–1, 66–7, 169–70, 173, 207, 333; Charity in, 225, 301–2; Radicalism in, 151; Riots in, 94, 131, 261
Legge, Heneage, 65, 69, 92, 95, 113, 188
Leicester, 42, 45, 65, 112, 123, 171, 198, 232, 241; Riots in, 97, 120, 124, 180
Leicestershire, 14; Riots in, 92
Lennox, Lord George, 100–1
Lewes, 83, 103–4, 163, 215, 282; Radicalism in, 136; Riots in, 101
Lincoln, 45
Lincolnshire, 23, 36, 62, 111, 167, 198
Lindert, Professor J.H., 5, 316
Liverpool, 23, 26, 31, 34, 43–4, 70, 83, 88, 95, 185, 188, 194, 198, 227; Radicalism in, 136, 144
Loes and Wilford Gilbert Union, 300

London, 6, 14, 17–34, 37, 40–8, 51, 59–60, 64–5, 69–70, 75, 84–8, 111, 169, 172, 214–5, 242–4; Charity in, 298, 310–3; Common Council, 150; Corresponding Society, 136–8, 140–4, 150–4, 265, 271, 325, 329–30, 337; Flour Company, 217–8, 299, 319–22; Light Horse Volunteers, 270–1, 323–5; Poor Relief in, 310; Radicalism in, 128, 137–8, 140–3, 146, 150–3, 336–7; Riots in, 91, 94, 115–6, 120, 128–32, 137–8, 180, 256
Lonsdale, Earl of, 43, 189
Loughborough, Earl of, 243, 246
Lowery, Robert, 316
Luddism, 57, 228, 335–7
Luton, 150
Lynwade Bride, 110

McCahill, Dr M.W., 6
McKendrick, Dr N., 18

Machine-breaking, 169–74
Maidenhead, 46
Makesy, Dr P., 3
Malden, 220; Radicalism in, 144
Malmesbury, 213
Malthus, T.R., 5–10, 30, 318, 323, 325, 330, 338
Malton, 27, 51, 59, 198, 215, 220–1; Charity in, 306; Poor Relief in, 227
Mansfield, 122–3, 326; Riots in, 120–180
Manchester, 30–1, 64, 69–70, 98, 173, 188, 198, 214, 225, 326–7; Charity in, 289, 301–4, 310–2; Radicalism in, 146, 150; Riots in, 115, 178, 180, 264, 266
Manchester Gazette, 143
Maresfield (Sussex), 163
Mark Lane (London Corn Exchange), 24–6, 30, 33–4, 39–40, 44–8, 85–6, 88, 187, 190, 193, 196–201, 203, 212, 218, 247; Riots in, 128–30
Marlborough, Duke of, 127, 239–41, 245
Martin, Dr J., 7
Mediterranean, 186
Middle Bockhampton (Hampshire), 166
Middlesex, 216, 330
Middleton, Lord, 122, 167–70
Midhurst, Poor relief in, 308; Riots in, 131
Mills, Dr D., 20
Mitchison, Professor R., 53
Modbury, Poor relief in, 302; Riots in, 156, 160, 176
Mokyr, Professor J., 316
Monmouthshire, 43
Montgomery, James, 115, 143
Moral and Political Magazine, 142–3; 'Moral Economy', 79–89; and democratic politics, 132, 143, 153–60; and food riots, 90–1, 105–8, 118–9; and markets, 178–81
Moreton (Essex), 225, 305

Morning Chronicle, 35, 64, 89, 140, 216, 218, 271
Mortality crises, 69–71

Naval mutinies (1797), 159
Navy Board, 154
Neale, Professor, R.S., 19
Neuman, Dr M., 3, 292, 308
Newbold (Derbyshire), 16; Charity in, 295, 298, 310–1
Newcastle-upon-Tyne, 26, 29, 40–3, 169, 172–3, 206, 212–4; Poor Relief in, 227, 305; Riots in, 97, 279
Newgate, 138
Night Poaching Act (1800), 167
Norfolk, 38, 44, 60–1, 78, 81, 163–6, 212, 215; Agricultural Society, 303; Duke of, 312; Militia, 101; Poor Relief in, 226–7, 309; Radicalism in, 134, 139; Riots in, 110
Northam, 23
Northampton, 47
Northamptonshire, 14, 20, 24, 45, 58, 82, 112, 207, 231; Militia, 100; Radicalism in, 159; Riots in, 109
Northumberland, 168, 269; Riots in, 279
Norwich, 28–9, 46, 64, 110, 188, 316, 327; Poor Relief in, 227, 308–9; Radicalism in, 136, 139, 142; Riots in, 91, 108–9, 262–5, 326
Nottingham, 28, 30–1, 42–3, 47, 70, 110, 188, 206, 241–2; Charity in, 295, 312; Radicalism in, 142, 151–2, 159, 337; Riots in, 91, 96–8, 115, 120–4, 126, 145, 179–80, 238, 255–6, 263, 265, 268, 271, 274–5, 280, 312, 326
Nottinghamshire, 21, 28, 36, 167, 169–70, 221; Riots in, 113, 120–4, 174, 177, 274–5, 277

O'Connor, Arthur, MP, 284
Oddy, Dr J., 54, 316
Odiham, 165
Oldham, 58–9, 63, 65, 70, 102, 318, 334; Riots in, 94–5, 98, 115, 268
Ongar, 188
Over Stowey (Somerset), 63, 82, 168; Riots in, 157
Oxford, 13, 24, 86, 241–3; Castle, 126–7; Charity in, 225, 301; Poor Relief in, 306; Riots in, 92–3, 96, 108–9, 126–8, 176, 179–80, 238–9, 259; University, 1, 126, 238–9
Oxfordshire, 24, 81–2, 84, 107, 111, 167–8, 179, 207, 232, 241; Militia, 99–105, 135–6, 258, 280–4; Poor Relief in, 226–7, 291–4, 297, 299, 303; Riots in, 120, 126–8, 231, 238–9, 256, 259, 261

Padstow, 23; Riots in, 118
Paine, Tom, 135, 292
Palmer, Professor R.R., 3

Paret, river, 153
Parochial Relief Act (1800), 48, 223–7, 302, 307–8, 319
Paul, Sir G.O., 109, 135, 177, 303
Peel, Sir Robert, 66
Pembroke, 235
Penrith, 43
Penryn, 134
Pentrich Rising, 337
Penzance, 49, 188; Riots in, 117–8, 266
Perceval, Spencer, MP, 218
Perkin, Professor H.J., 333
Perry, James, 35, 89
Peterborough, 110
Peterloo, 337
Petworth, 101, 168; Poor Relief in, 226
Pickering, 17, 198
Pitt, William, the younger, 3, 6, 11–2, 35, 37, 55, 57, 64, 88, 99, 104–6, 133, 136, 138–40, 143, 146, 150, 158–9, 172, 181, 185, 189, 191–2, 195–6, 199–204, 210–4, 220–5, 228–30, 233–6, 242–7, 253, 258–9, 272, 284–5, 289, 313, 315, 319–22, 329–31, 334–5
Plymouth, 23, 49–50, 156, 178, 187–8, 267, 277, 281; Radicalism in, 153–4; Riots in, 100–2, 176–9, 260–3, 276
Plympton, 66
Pole-Carew, Reginald, MP, 68
Pontefract, 23, 40, 268; Riots in, 97
Poole, 65, 271; Riots in, 128, 178–80
Poole, Tom, 206, 313
Poor Law Amendment Act, 338–9; Commission, 291
Poor Relief (see also under counties and larger towns) in: Bardfield (Berkshire), 295; Barton (Cambridgeshire), 309; Bingfield (Berkshire), 303; Brede (Sussex), 299; Brewood (Staffordshire), 308; Brimpton (Berkshire), 294; Burtonwood (Staffordshire), 305; Burwash (Sussex), 309; Cartmel (Cornwall), 289; Charlton Adam (Somerset), 289; Chelmsford, 297–8; Chiddingly (Sussex), 163; Chigwell (Essex), 306; Clitheroe, 227–8; Conisbrough (West Riding), 309–10; Copford (Essex), 295; East Hoathly (Sussex), 163; Faringdon (Berkshire), 225; Framfield (Sussex), 163; Gnosall (Staffordshire), 302; Great Bardfield (Essex), 298; Great Parndon (Essex), 295, 304; Great Sampford (Essex), 298; Greenford (Middlesex), 304; Hatfield, 308; Henfield (Sussex), 309; Hethersett (Norfolk), 299, 304; Hurstpierpoint (Sussex), 163; Icklesham (Sussex), 224; Kingston-Lisle (Berkshire), 300–1; Lower Bramber (Sussex), 227; Ludgran (Cornwall), 289, 305–6, 308–9; Melling (Kent), 309; Moreton (Essex), 305; Old Windsor, 297, 303–4; Queen Camel (Somerset), 300; Romford,

295; Saxtead (Suffolk), 299; Scruton (North Yorkshire), 310; Shinfield (Berkshire), 302; Sledmere (East Yorkshire), 306; South Weald (Essex), 304–5; Terling (Essex), 301, 305; Thurgarton, 226; Tilehurst, 294; Tolleshunt Darcy (Essex), 298; Uffington, 294; Wentworth Woodhouse, 227; Werlingworth, 299; West Pennard (Somerset), 302; Williton (Somerset), 216, 218; Wingfield (Suffolk), 300; Wrabness (Essex), 300
Portchester, 104
Portland, Duke of, 7, 35, 87, 93, 111, 127–8, 137, 148–50, 153, 157, 185–91, 197, 202, 218, 221–2, 225, 230, 232, 235–48, 253–9, 263, 269, 285–6, 322, 329
Portsmouth, 65, 131; Radicalism in, 137, 142–3, 149; Riots in, 102, 128, 180
Portugal, 3
Post, Professor J.D., 5, 317
Potteries, 18, 198, 270; Riots in, 98, 125, 277
Poughill (Devon), 164
Poulter, Rev Edmund, 296
Pownall, Governor, 85
Poynter, Dr J.R., 3
Preston, Miller, of Birmingham, 113, 124–5
Privy Council, 109–10, 148, 184, 187–91, 202–6, 209, 211, 231, 233, 236
Probus (Cornwall), 212
Pulteney, Sir William, MP, 245

Quakers, 129
Quebec, 186
Queen Caroline, 337

Radicalism (see also under counties and larger towns) in: Bingley, 139; Bourne (Lincolnshire), 142; Hitchin, 144; Leominster, 137; Melbourne (Derbyshire), 142; North Shields, 149; Saxlingham, 139; Saxmundham, 139; Selby, 142; Spilsby, 139; Stratton, 154; Uley, 139; Whitchurch (Shropshire), 139
Rashleigh, Charles, 178, 241, 269
Reading, 27, 104, 169, 179, 212, 216; Charity in, 295, 301; Radicalism in, 136
Redruth, 118
Reed, Mick, 20
Reform Bill (1832), 337–8
Reigate, 213
Rhuddlan, 27
Richmond, Duke of, 102–5, 108, 282–4
Richmond (Yorkshire), 43, 113
Rickman, John, 330
Riot Act, 93–4, 113–4, 121–4, 128, 130, 255–7, 260, 266; And journalism, 93–4; And regular army, 265–8
Riots (see also under counties and larger towns) in: Arundel, 102; Ashby-de la-Zouch, 97, 124; Atherstone, 99; Barham

(Norfolk), 110; Barrow-on-Soar (Leicestershire), 112; Bewdley, 97; Bishop Auckland, 113; Blandford, 128, 180; Brank Broughton (Lincolnshire), 162; Bridforth (North Riding), 110; Brixham, 260, 272, 276; Bunbury, 132; Burton-on-Trent, 97; Buxted (Sussex), 163; Calverton (Nottinghamshire), 122; Chard, 176; Charlbury, 261; Chester-le-Street, 97; Chilworth (Hampshire), 162; Chorley, 278; Cirencester, 180; Cocking (Sussex); 162–3; Colyton (Devon), 262; Crediton, 100, 176; Cullompton, 156; Darlaston, 96, 112; Darlington, 97, 131–2; Deal, 131, 180; Eastbourne (Sussex), 131; Eccles, 278; Edgebaston, 98, 125; Exmouth, 156; Fordingbridge, 101; Gateshead, 97; Glasgow, 326; Great Chesterford (Essex), 108; Guildford, 104; Halstead (Essex), 268; High Wycombe, 178; Hinkley (Leicestershire), 94, 97; Hinton Ampner (Hampshire), 131, 178; Ide (Devon), 100; Kingsbridge, 179; Kingsteighton, 100, 181; Kingswood, 101; Lamberhurst, 101; Lane End, 98–9; Leek, 97, 177; Lichfield, 97; Lifton (Devon), 162; Long Hanborough (Oxon), 109; Margate, 131, 180, 271; Milbourne Port, 132; Monmouth, 147; Montacute (Somerset), 132, 162; New Alresford, 162, 266, 274; Newark-on-Trent, 109, 267; Newhaven, 103–4; Newton Abbot, 100, 156; Nuneaton, 94, 97, 124; Overton, 128, 274; Penn, 98; Petersfield, 104; Port Isaac, 118; Portsea, 102; Ruardean, 117; St. Agnes, 118; Sandwich, 180; Scotland, 326; Seaford, 102–3; Shackerstone, 97; Sheepwash, 156; Sheerness, 131, 178, 180; Sidmouth, 272; Solihull, 97; Southwark, 129; Stockton-on-Tees, 87; Sudbury (Suffolk), 174; Tipton, 112; Uffculm, 156; Wednesbury, 112; Wellington (Somerset), 156; Whitechapel, 129; Wisbech, 253; Worth, 101; Yarpole (Herefordshire), 109
Ripon, 14, 24; Riots in, 92
Ritson, Joseph, 134
Robson, R.B., MP, 245
Rochdale, 173, 269; Riots in, 113
Rochester, 131, 187; Riots in, 131, 180, 267
Rolle, Lord, 257
Romilly, Sir Samuel, MP, 265
Romsey, 220; Riots in, 128, 162, 180, 274
Rose, George, MP, 85, 88, 199, 215, 218, 243, 313
Rose, Professor, R.B., 325
Ross-on-Wye, 116
Rostow, Professor W.W., 56
Rowbottom, William, 58, 63–5, 70, 98, 104, 268, 318, 334
Rudé, Professor George, 76
Rule, Dr John, 75, 168, 335

Rumford, Count, 214–5, 301, 322
Rusby, cornfactor, 86–7, 129
Russell, Lord John, 296
Rutland, 91, 167
Ryder, Dudley, MP, 192
Rye, 197; Radicalism in, 152
Ryedale, 23

Saddleworth, 64, 94; Poor Relief in, 228
Saffron Walden, 45–6, 129; Poor Relief in, 310; Riots in, 107–8, 162, 310
St. Albans, 213
St. Austell, 62; Riots in, 118
St. Columb, 118
St. Stephen-in-Branwell (Cornwall), 225
Salford, 31, 98; Poor Relief in, 306
Salisbury, 81, 213
Salisbury, Marquis of, 308
Sampford (Essex), 108
Sandford Gilbert Union, 303
Scandanavia, 8
Scarborough, 43, 189
Schofield, Dr R.S., 4
Schrimshaw, Professor, 68
Scott, Claude, 24, 26, 88, 180–1, 184–8, 190–6, 199–200, 203, 322
Seer, Isaac, 163
Settlement Laws, 289, 308–10
Severn, river, 43, 106, 111, 116
Shaw, Dennis, 138–9
Sheepscombe, 38
Sheffield, 16, 25, 30–1, 38, 42, 47, 56–8, 60–1, 67, 70, 173, 175, 188, 207–8, 221, 242, 269–70, 326; Charity in, 301, 304, 311–2; Constitutional Society, 138, 150; Radicalism in, 114–5, 136–7, 143; Riots in, 94–8, 114–5, 120, 124, 178–80, 261–9, 274, 326
Sheffield, Lord, 87, 101–3, 189–92, 203–9, 212, 215–21, 224–8, 301, 335
Shepton Mallett, 171
Sherborne, 81; Charity in, 290
Sheridan, Richard Brinsley, MP, 245
Shoreditch, 66; Riots in, 129
Shoreham, 197
Shrewsbury, 43
Shropshire, 43, 166, 299, 302, 307; Riots in, 99, 111–2, 177
Simcoe, General, 153–5, 251, 259, 267–8, 271–2
Sinclair, Sir John, 40
Six Acts (1820), 337
Skipton, 23
Smith, Adam, 35, 46, 86–8, 234, 236, 244, 292, 315
Smithfield, 29–30, 41, 86
Smollett, Henry, 14
Smout, Professor J.C., 53
Snell, Dr K.D.M., 5
Society for Bettering the Condition of the

Poor, 214, 303

Somerset, 23, 26, 38–9, 44, 67, 85–6, 166, 170–1, 206, 224, 316; Poor Relief in, 300, 312; Radicalism in, 154–5; Riots in, 145, 153–8, 162, 180, 258, 275–6

Soup Kitchens, 66–7, 206, 214–5, 218–22, 289–90, 299–302, 310–2, 322–4

Southampton, 128, 131; Riots in, 180

South Molton, 215; Charity in, 290; Poor Relief in, 305

South Shields, 188

South-west, 23–4, 41–3, 48–50, 52, 55, 296; Poor Relief in, 300; Riots in, 50, 99–101, 132, 153–8, 175–7, 179–80, 225, 248, 251, 256–62, 267–76, 279, 286–7, 324–6

Spain, 3, 185

Speenhamland, 3, 6, 219, 290–7, 299–301

Spence, Thomas, 151–3, 155–9

Spencer-Stanhope, William, MP, 268, 272

Spitalfields, 70, 169

Stafford, 277; Poor Relief in, 227; Riots in, 113, 125

Staffordshire, 64, 83, 85, 270; Poor Relief in, 227; Riots in, 98, 275–9

Stale Bread Act (1800), 217–20, 223

Stamford, 24; Charity in, 290

Stamford, Earl of, 188

Stapleton, Barry, 7

Statute of Articifers (1563), 292

Steeple (Essex), 164

Stevenage, 197

Stevenson, Dr John, 6, 53, 76–7, 90

Stewart, Dugald, 86

Stockland (Devon), 167

Stockport, 207; Charity in, 227; Riots in, 264, 278, 280

Storrington (Sussex), 163

Stourbridge, 42–3; Riots in, 99

Stourport, 198

Stowmarket, 212

Strikes, 97, 101, 113, 132, 144, 163–4, 169–73

Stroud, poor relief in, 304; Riots in, 180

Stuart, E.J., 189

Stuart, Sir James, 10

Suffolk, 17, 165–6; Poor Relief in, 306; Riots in, 94, 110, 212

Surrey, 7, 206, 213, 216; Poor Relief in, 224; Riots in, 224, 279

Sussex, 20, 44, 48, 60–1, 78, 81, 144, 165, 189, 197–8, 203, 207, 212, 215, 224, 231, 282–3; Militia, 136; Poor Relief in, 219, 224, 226, 335; Riots in, 161, 224

Swanbourne (Buckinghamshire), 131

Swindon, 21

Swing, Captain, 167, 175, 228, 338

Sykes, Sir C., 292, 306, 320

Tann, Dr J., 3

Taunton, 281

Taunton, W.E., 238–9

Teign, river, 153

Tewkesbury, 198, 311; Radicalism in, 137, 139; Riots in, 108–9

Thames, river, 44, 87, 106, 197–8, 201

Thatcham, 164; Poor Relief in, 305

Theft, 167–8, 174–5

Thirsk, 37, 94; Poor Relief in, 309; Riots in, 97

Thomis, Professor M.I., 76

Thompson, E.P., 3, 7, 78–9, 90, 133–4, 178, 236, 315

Threshing machines, 337

Tilly, Professor C., 10, 95

Times The, 77–8, 84, 121, 147–8, 164, 172, 210, 240, 266

Tithe, 66, 82, 162, 165, 218

Tiverton, 67; Riots in, 156

Tolpuddle Martyrs, 338

Totnes, 259; Riots in, 100, 156, 176, 179, 276, 286

Towcester, 107; Riots in, 109

Trade Unionism, 75–8, 163–4, 173–5, 260, 278, 325–8, 332–3, 336–8; And food riots, 153–7, 173–4; And royal dockyards, 172–3; In rural regions, 163–4; In urban districts, 168–74

Treason Trials (1794), 134, 148

Treasury Solicitor, 105, 257, 260, 276, 279

Trent, river, 44, 107, 113, 123; Vale, 70

Truck, 294, 297–9

Truelock, Bannister, 148

Truro, 49, 118; Radicalism in, 139; Riots in, 118, 176–7; 266–8

Tunbridge Wells, 27; Riots in, 131, 180, 261–2

Turkey Company, 186

Turnbull-Forbes, 190

Turton, Sir Thomas, MP, 224

United Britons, 12

United Englishmen, 143–52, 272

United Irishmen, 12, 142, 146

United Scotsmen, 12

United States of America, 184–5, 187

Van de Walle, Dr 68

Volunteers, 92–3, 95–7, 102, 112–5, 118, 121–32, 134, 144, 153, 175, 254–6, 260–73, 281, 285–7, 322–5, 329

Waddington, hop-dealer, 86–7

Wakefield, 23, 30, 66, 173, 228, 268

Wales, 55, 65; Riots in, 239

Wales, Prince of, 148, 185

Wallace, Robert, 7

Walsall, 264; Riots in, 112, 125

Walter, Dr J., 90

Walvin, Dr J., 76

Wanstead, 308, 327

Ware, 197

Warrington, 88
Warwick, 113
Warwick, Earl of, 112, 245–7
Warwickshire, 20, 23, 44, 65; Militia, 104–5;
  Poor Relief in, 227, 300, 305; Riots in, 97,
  124, 180
Webb, Sidney and Beatrice, 75
Wellington (Shropshire), 113
Wells (Norfolk), 45, 110; Poor Relief in, 307,
  Riots in, 95
Wells (Somerset), 171; Riots in, 101
Wendren, 118
West Bromwich, 270
Weston, Professor, J.R., 329
West Middlesex Militia, 139
Wetherby, 43
Weymouth, 242; Riots in, 93
Wharfedale, 14
Whitbread, Samuel, MP, 163, 233–4, 292,
  296, 299
Whitby, 327
Whitehaven, 42, 189
White Waltham (Berkshire), 79
White, Colonel Richard, 93
Wigan, Charity in, 290; Riot in, 132
Wight, Isle of, 82–3, 193
Wilberforce, William, MP, 66, 88, 216, 218,
  245–7, 313
Wilkinson, John, 307
Wilkinson, Rev James, 114, 242, 262
Williams, Dr D.E., 91, 328
Williams, Professor G.A., 285
Williamson, Professor J.G., 5, 316
Willoughby, Sir Charles, 81–2, 167–8, 291
Wilton, 67
Wiltshire, 166, 170–1, 208, 316; Poor Relief in,
  313, 332; Radicalism in, 144; Riots in, 171–2
Wincanton, 81, 171
Winchester, 24, 213; Riots in, 277
Windham, William, MP, 243
Windle, 21, 44
Windsor, 138; Radicalism in, 151; Riots in,

131
Winkleigh, 164
Winterslow (Wiltshire), 62
Wirkworth, 17
Witney, 110; Riots in, 92, 109, 127, 180, 239
Woburn, 167
Wolverhampton, 47, 64, 83–4, 198, 264, 275;
  Radicalism in, 285; Riots in, 97, 112, 125,
  267
Woodstock, 232
Woolwich, 43; Riots in, 131
Wootton Bassett, 213
Worksop, 254
Worcester, 40, 43, 221, 242; Radicalism in,
  142
Worcestershire, 13, 83, 86; Militia, 266; Riots
  in, 124
Workington, 42, 189
Wrightson, Dr K., 90
Wrigley, Professor E.A., 4
Wrottesley, Sir John, 242, 275, 277
Wycombe, Lord, 215
Wye, river, 43, 116

Yarlington (Somerset), 81
York, 17, 21, 24, 27, 30, 41, 67, 173, 327, 333;
  Charity in, 295, 311
York, Duke of, 146–8, 256, 267, 281
Yorkshire, 37–8, 41, 47, 58, 60–1, 69–70, 170,
  187, 212, 299; Charity in, 225; Poor Relief
  in, 300, 321, 332; Radicalism in, 138–9, 151;
  Riots in, 111, 262
Yorkshire, East Riding, 23, 30, 36, 59–60, 62,
  111
Yorkshire, North Riding, 18, 59–60; Riots in,
  110
Yorkshire, West Riding, 16–9, 23–4, 39, 46,
  57–60, 66, 111, 166, 198, 215, 334, 336;
  Poor Relief in, 311; Radicalism in, 134,
  151–2, 336; Riots in, 94–7, 268
Young, Arthur, 20, 25, 36, 40, 77, 152, 186,
  195–6, 240, 245, 288, 307